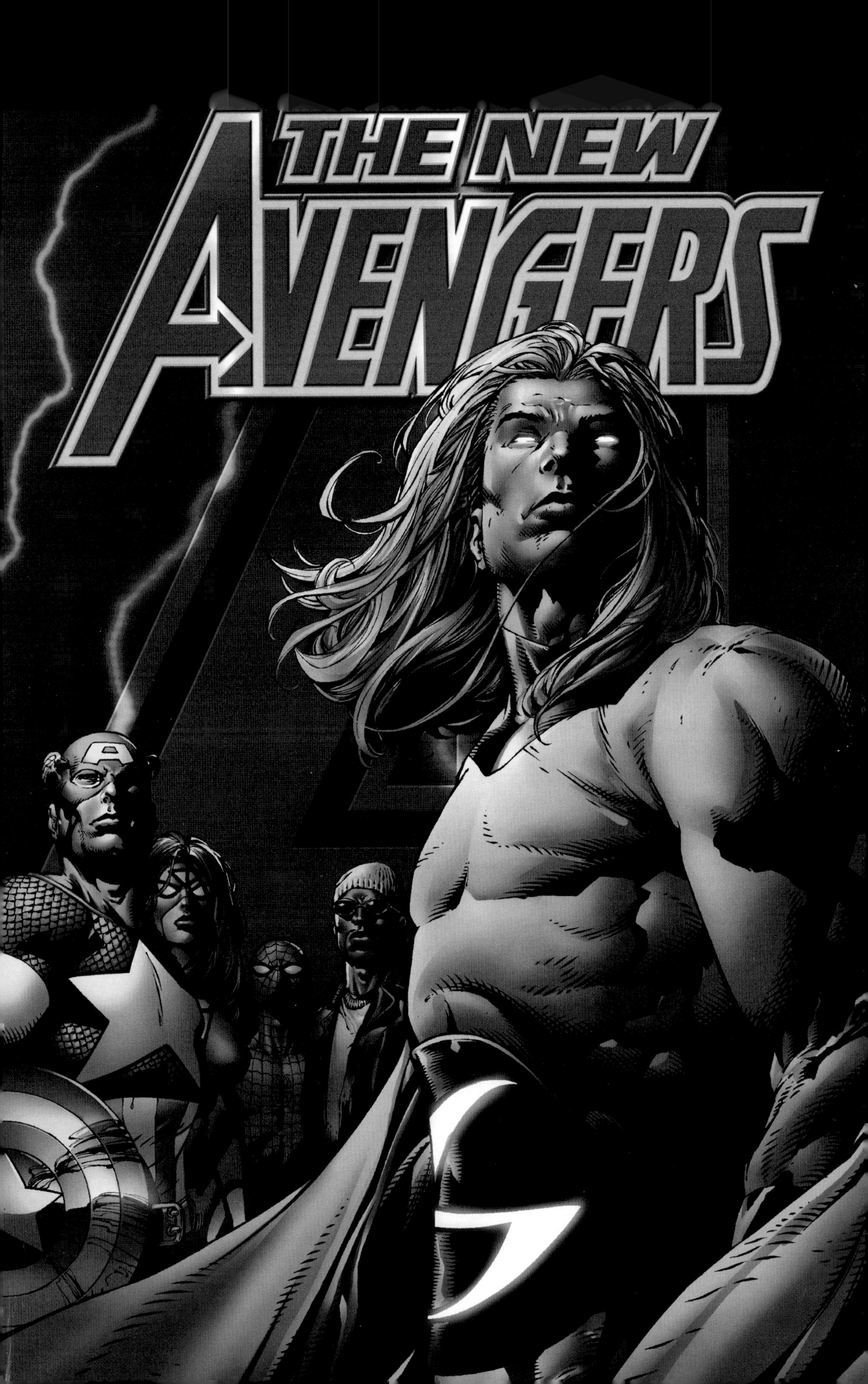
THE NEW
AVENGERS

THE NEW AVENGER

WRITER: *Brian Michael Bendis*

"BREAKOUT"

PENCILER: *David Finch*

INKER: *Danny Miki with Mark Morales, Allen Martinez & Victor Olazaba*

COLORIST: *Frank D'Armata*

"SENTRY"

PENCILER: *Steve McNiven*

INKER: *Mark Morales with John Dell*

COLORIST: *Morry Hollowell with Laura Martin*

ORIGINAL SENTRY ART: *Jae Lee & Jose Villarrubia*

VINTAGE SENTRY PHOTO: *Jose Villarrubia*

VARIANT COVERS: *Neal Adams, John Romita Sr., Herb Trimpe & Sal Buscema*

LETTERER: *Richard Starkings & Comicraft's Albert Deschesne*
COVER ARTIST: *David Finch*
ASSISTANT EDITORS: *Nicole Boose, Molly Lazer, Stephanie Moore & Aubrey Sitterson*
ASSOCIATE EDITOR: *Andy Schmidt*

EDITOR: *Tom Brevoort*

"SPECIAL GUESTS"

BREAKDOWNS: *Dan Jurgens*

FINISHES: *Sandu Florea*

COLORIST: *Frank D'Armata*

LETTERER: *Richard Starkings & Comicraft's Albert Deschesne*

ASSISTANT EDITOR: *John Barber*

EDITOR: *Ralph Macchio*

NEW AVENGERS VOL. 1. Contains material originally published in magazine form as NEW AVENGERS #1-10, NEW AVENGERS MOST WANTED FILES and NEW AVENGERS FEATURING THE FANTASTIC FOUR. First printing 2007. ISBN# 978-0-7851-2464-1. Published by MARVEL PUBLISHING, INC., a subsidiary of MARVEL ENTERTAINMENT, INC. OFFICE OF PUBLICATION: 417 5th Avenue, New York, NY 10016. Copyright © 2005 and 2007 Marvel Characters, Inc. All rights reserved. $29.99 per copy in the U.S. and $48.00 in Canada (GST #R127032852); Canadian Agreement #40668537. All characters featured in this issue and the distinctive names and likenesses thereof, and all related indicia are trademarks of Marvel Characters, Inc. No similarity between any of the names, characters, persons, and/or institutions in this magazine with those of any living or dead person or institution is intended, and any such similarity which may exist is purely coincidental. **Printed in the U.S.A.** ALAN FINE, CEO Marvel Toys & Publishing Divisions and CMO Marvel Entertainment, Inc.; DAVID GABRIEL, Senior VP of Publishing Sales & Circulation; DAVID BOGART, VP of Business Affairs & Editorial Operations; MICHAEL PASCIULLO, VP Merchandising & Communications; JIM BOYLE, VP of Publishing Operations; DAN CARR, Executive Director of Publishing Technology; JUSTIN F. GABRIE, Managing Editor; SUSAN CRESPI, Production Manager; STAN LEE, Chairman Emeritus. For information regarding advertising in Marvel Comics or on Marvel.com, please

NEW AVENGERS: MOST WANTED FILES

HEAD WRITER/COORDINATOR: *Jeff Christiansen*

WRITERS: *Sean McQuaid, Michael Hoskin, Mark O'English, Ronald Byrd, Stuart Vandal, Eric J. Moreels, Anthony Flamini & Barry Reese*

COVER ARTIST: *David Finch*

DESIGNER: *Jeof Vita*

EDITOR: *Jeff Youngquist*

Captain America created by Joe Simon & Jack Kirby

COLLECTION EDITOR: *Mark D. Beazley*

ASSISTANT EDITORS: *John Denning & Cory Levine*

ASSOCIATE EDITOR: *Jennifer Grünwald*

SENIOR EDITOR, SPECIAL PROJECTS: *Jeff Youngquist*

SENIOR VICE PRESIDENT OF SALES: *David Gabriel*

PRODUCTION: *Jerry Kalinowski*

DESIGNER: *Patrick McGrath*

VICE PRESIDENT OF CREATIVE: *Tom Marvelli*

EDITOR IN CHIEF: *Joe Quesada*

PUBLISHER: *Dan Buckley*

*Special Thanks to Spencer Beck of www.theartistschoice.com,
TJ Dietsch of Wizard Entertainment, Michael Young & AAFES and
the US Department of Defense*

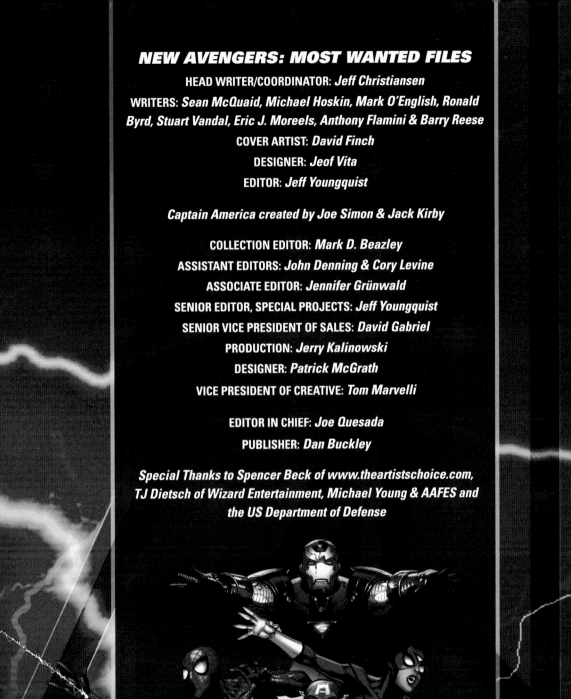

Whoo boy!

OK, here we go. This is going to hurt a little.

I lied!

Matt Murdock WAS supposed to be Ronin.

OK, I said it!! It's out there!! I can't take it back now!! I lied! I'm a lying liar from lyingville.

Oh, uh, if this is the first time reading this material then what I just said means absolutely nothing to you because you have no idea who Ronin is or what the hell I am talking about.

You just turn the page and enjoy the comic—oh, I mean GRAPHIC NOVEL—and you and I will speak another time.

This intro is really for those of you, and God bless each and every one of you, who are buying this in hardback because you have read these issues before, or you have read all the mishegas this book causes online on a monthly basis and you want it on your bookshelf.

That's cool. I do that too. If they put out *Nextwave* as a sticker book, I'll buy it again.

So here we are. I've confessed and you're giving me that look with arms folded and a toe tapping in patient disgust waiting for me to explain myself. OK…

Yes. A few years ago you may have read reports that Matt Murdock was supposed to take the role of this new mystery character who debuted on a *New Avengers* cover group shot with a kind of revamped bubbleheaded design by Joe Quesada, months before this book saw the light of day.

And yes, at the time, bubblehead, as it/he/she was referred to online made its debut, Matt Murdock was the boy in the bubble. But, sweet Jesus, before you go on my message board at jinxworld.com (PLUG INCOMING!) or any of the other bazillion boards on the Web, to curse my family name, hear me out.

I have a reason I lied.

I have two reasons really, Jessica Drew and Jessica Jones.

See, years before I got my mitts on Earth's Mightiest Heroes, Marvel offered me a shot at a noir Marvel book. And man, I wanted to do a Jessica Drew series. I pitched a Jessica Drew series and I got a 'go' on the book for a Jessica Drew series. A private eye in the Marvel Universe who had glory days and had fallen on hard times.

And as much as I loved Jessica Drew, obviously, I mean, hey, look who's on the cover of this thingamabob, the concepts behind what was to become *Alias* and who Jessica Drew actually was as a character were veering very far apart from each other. The Jessica in my pitch,

So much so, that it occurred to me that it didn't HAVE to be Jessica Drew. Well, it occurred to me after then Marvel President Bill Jemas, flat out said to me that I should make it a new character, because no one gives a flying %&@* about Jessica Drew but me anyway. His exact quote: "It's not like the world's clamoring for a Jessica Drew series. Just make her Jessica Moskowitz and let's go!"

So I did; and Jessica Jones was born, had her own series, launched Marvel's first adult-themed mainstream comic book, got knocked up by Luke Cage, got married, had a short-lived TV deal, mentored the Young Avengers, and life was good.

Except that I decided at some point to tell anyone who would listen that at one point Jessica Jones was going to be Jessica Drew.

Everyone who writes for a living got it. They understood the development process and the hard to define magic that can happen in it. They understand happy and not so happy accidents that can smack you in the face as you strive to create something from where there was once nothing. But sadly, that was only 000.2214 percent of the people who heard me say this. Everyone else was confused and some think that the two Jessicas are the same person. Even though Jessica Drew actually appeared in *Alias* as Jessica Drew for a Jessica Drew/Jessica Jones team-up. Nope. Didn't clear the air.

I was besieged with those who didn't get it. And frankly nor did they need to or have to; it's not their job to. All they have to do is read the comic and enjoy, I'm the one who has to be mister open and share every thought I've ever had about everything. It's my fault for opening my mouth.

And this was all going on when it became clear, based on what was happening in the Daredevil monthly comic, which I was writing at the time, that there was no way, as cool as it sounded, for Matt Murdock to put on this new identity and join the coolest Avengers team ever. Biased? Yes.

We had taken Matt Murdock down a very dark road, outing him. Ruining him. And on top of that, with Ed Brubaker's run coming up, we knew that there was no room for Matt Murdock on this team. Of course, the very next day a reporter, who shall remain nameless, broke a confidence and blabbed it. I know, boo-hoo. But hey, that's what happened.

So on top of me not wanting to confuse the situation I really didn't want to let this weasel dude get away with his weasel behavior. I just wanted to tell my story. I wanted it pure. I wanted Ronin, as she/he was to become, to have her/his moment in the sun with no baggage.

Like before the days of the Internet. When you read a comic and you didn't know all the crazy @*#$ that went

Like I didn't know the fact that Marvel had a huge plan in the '90s to re-brand and recycle a bunch of books that were slowly dying off. The only one that actually happened was *Avengers West Coast* becoming *Force Works*, but there was a whole orchestrated plan for this—*Silver Sable* was going to become *Wild Pack*, *Quasar* was going to become *Star Masters*, *New Warriors* would become *The Warriors*, *Silver Surfer* was to become *Sky-Rider*, and so forth.

No, I didn't know this. Why? No one blabbed on the Internet.

Or the fact that Jim Shooter's New Universe "Big Bang" originally was going to kill off all of the classic Marvel characters and replace them with his own new guys in the costumes of those who would become the New Universe books. But he was faced with a full-scale editorial revolt and had to contain his ideas to the New Universe itself.

Didn't know this!! Why? No one blabbed on the Internet!

Or over at DC, when the true identity of their secret villain for the *Armageddon 2001* crossover leaked so they quickly and haphazardly changed around the entire ending to their story to make him somebody else, and pretty much killed the story doing it.

OK, that sounds like it was the Internet's fault, but my change happened because I wanted to change it. The story we were telling changed it. Not because I was trying to outrun anyone.

But, man, I hated lying about it. This feels good to get this out there. I like sharing. I like to pull the curtain and give everyone an honest peek behind the scenes. I like BSing with comic readers online and being an open book, so this little lie wore heavy on my heart. It's the only time I've ever flat out looked my message board right in the eye and lied.

Unless, I'm lying now, and I just said all this to fill an intro.

But the truth is—and this is the truth—that by the time Ronin was really born, not just a bubbleheaded placeholder, she was Echo, Maya Lopez, the co-creation of Joe Quesada and David Mack, who along with the Sentry and the Hood, ranked as one of the truly amazing new Marvel creations of the last decade. All of whom I feared might slip away into the footnote history of comics because no one outside their creators was using them for anything.

I loved re-introducing her. I loved introducing her in this book. In fact, now if I may be more traditional in my intro, I loved everything there was to love about writing this comic. I loved the people I was working with and the amazing job every single person who worked on this comic did.

But David Finch and Steve McNiven and Danny Miki and everyone else did the work of their careers in this book and have gotten the credit they deserve. The man who hasn't is Tom Brevoort. This book was as out

of his safety zone as the *Avengers* had ever been, and he never let that get in his way of helping us make the book as excellent as it needed to be. Now I know he loves the book, and he never despised it, but during the birthing process he was worried about it. But—and here's the thing—instead of attacking the book as some who shared his worries have done, he embraced it. He trusted me and everyone who ever worked on it, coaxing the best work out of all of us.

I know a lot of people don't exactly know what an editor does, and sometimes it's hard to define, because it's hardly sexy. The best way to say it is they get the book out. But that is such an understatement when describing what an excellent editor does. He even gave me all that dirt I just spilled earlier in the intro.

So to everyone who worked on this book, everyone who supported this book, everyone who praised and damned this book, everyone who second-guessed and played along, I thank you on levels it's so hard to describe in words.

I recently found an *Avengers* comic that was probably the first *Avengers* comic I ever owned—*Avengers* #149. I looked at it, awash with all those awesome childhood comic nerd memories that hit you when you find an oldy and goody, but then I was struck with the realization that… I actually write the *Avengers* now.

Thank you for allowing me that honor.

I won't lie to you ever again.

(There's a Skrull in the first issue. See, now I can't stop telling the truth.)

BENDIS!
October 2007

P.S. Also included in this collection is a oneshot we did as a gift for the armed services. It was a giveaway at all military outpost stores all over the world. Nothing preachy, just good old-fashioned Marvel Comics fun, as a present to those who have chosen to serve. It's basically the comic book version of a USO show. It's never been published for the general public before, so it's great to finally present it to you here. Yay!

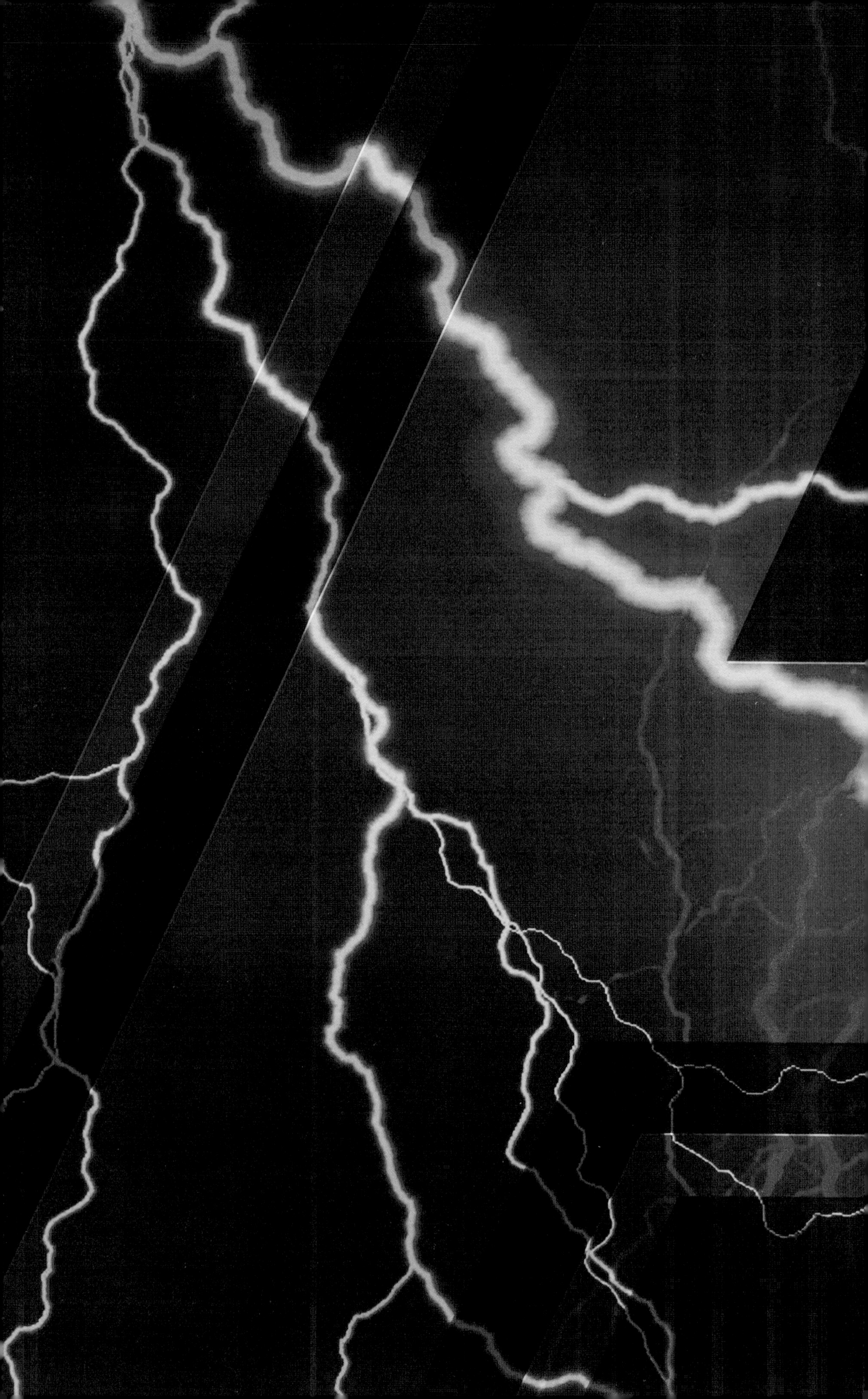

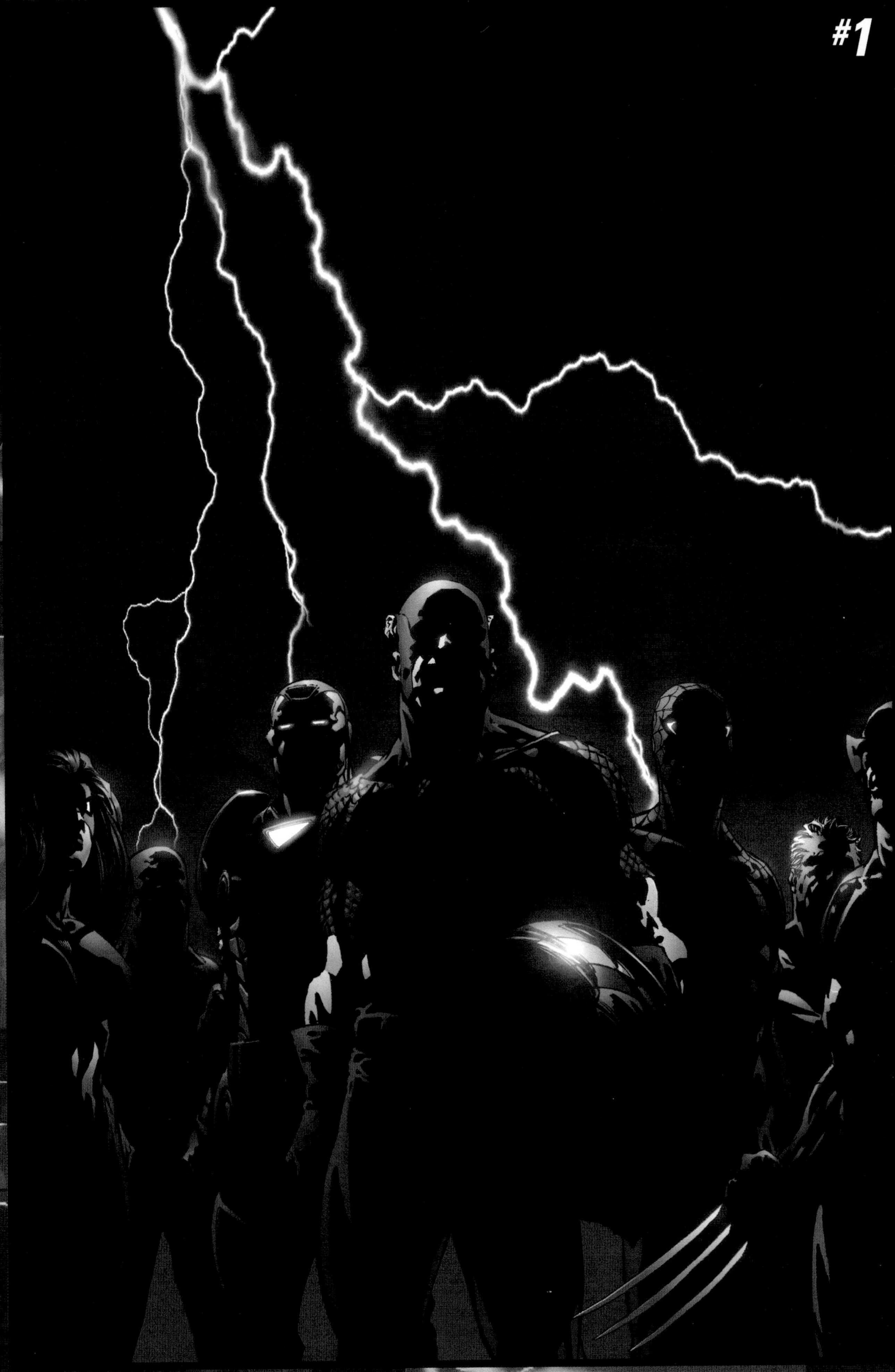
#1

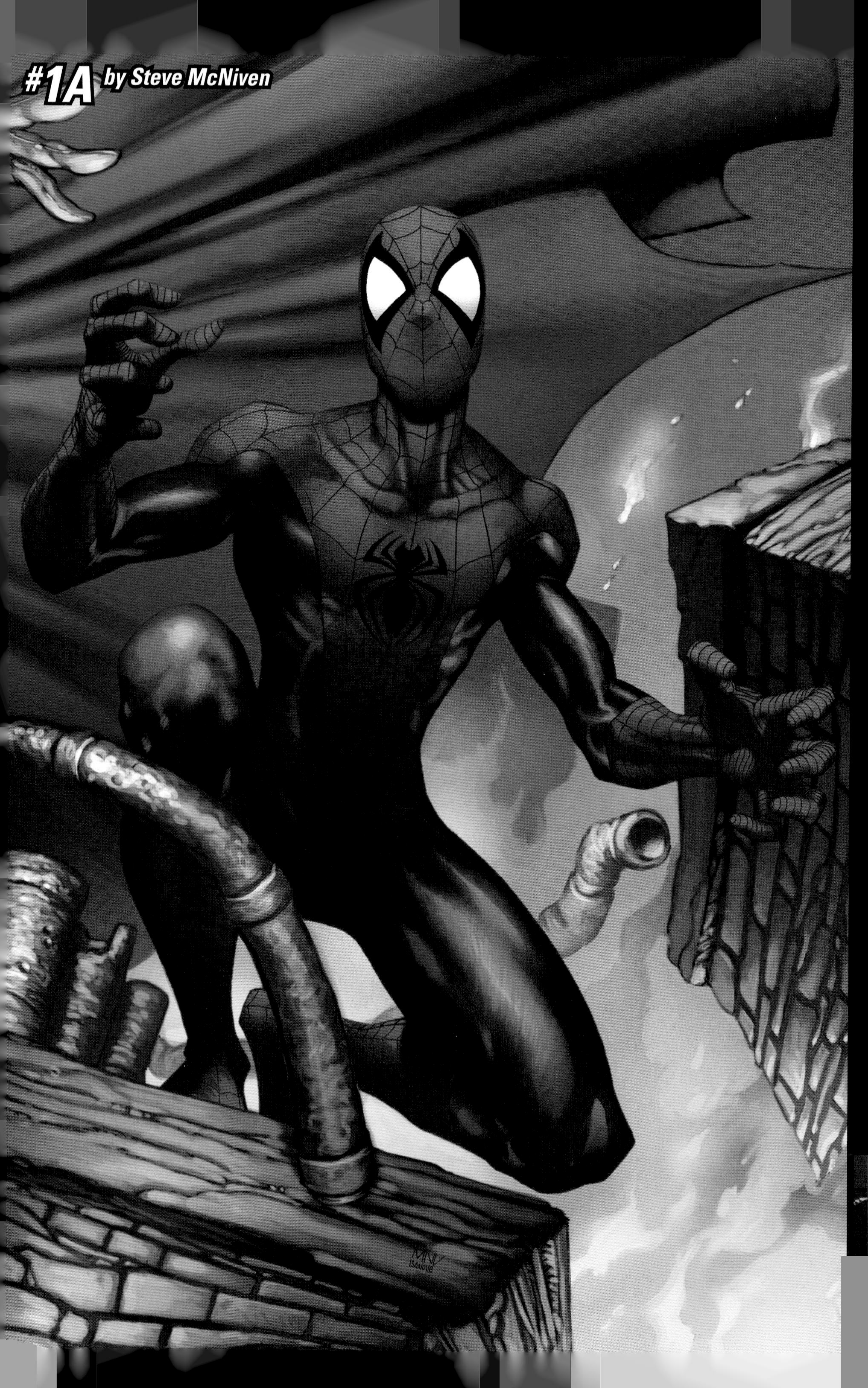
#1A by Steve McNiven

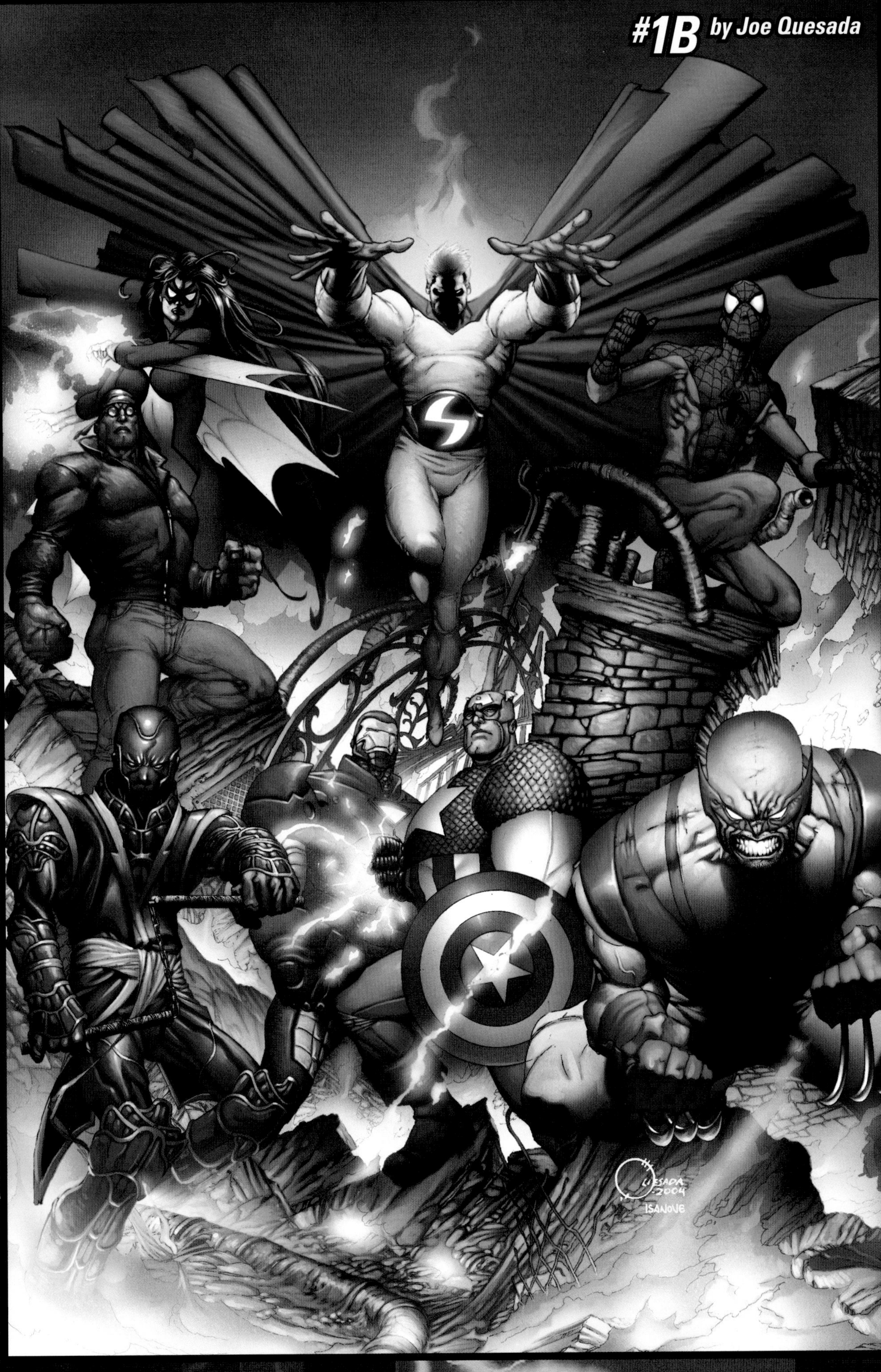
#1B by Joe Quesada
QUESADA 2004
ISANOVE

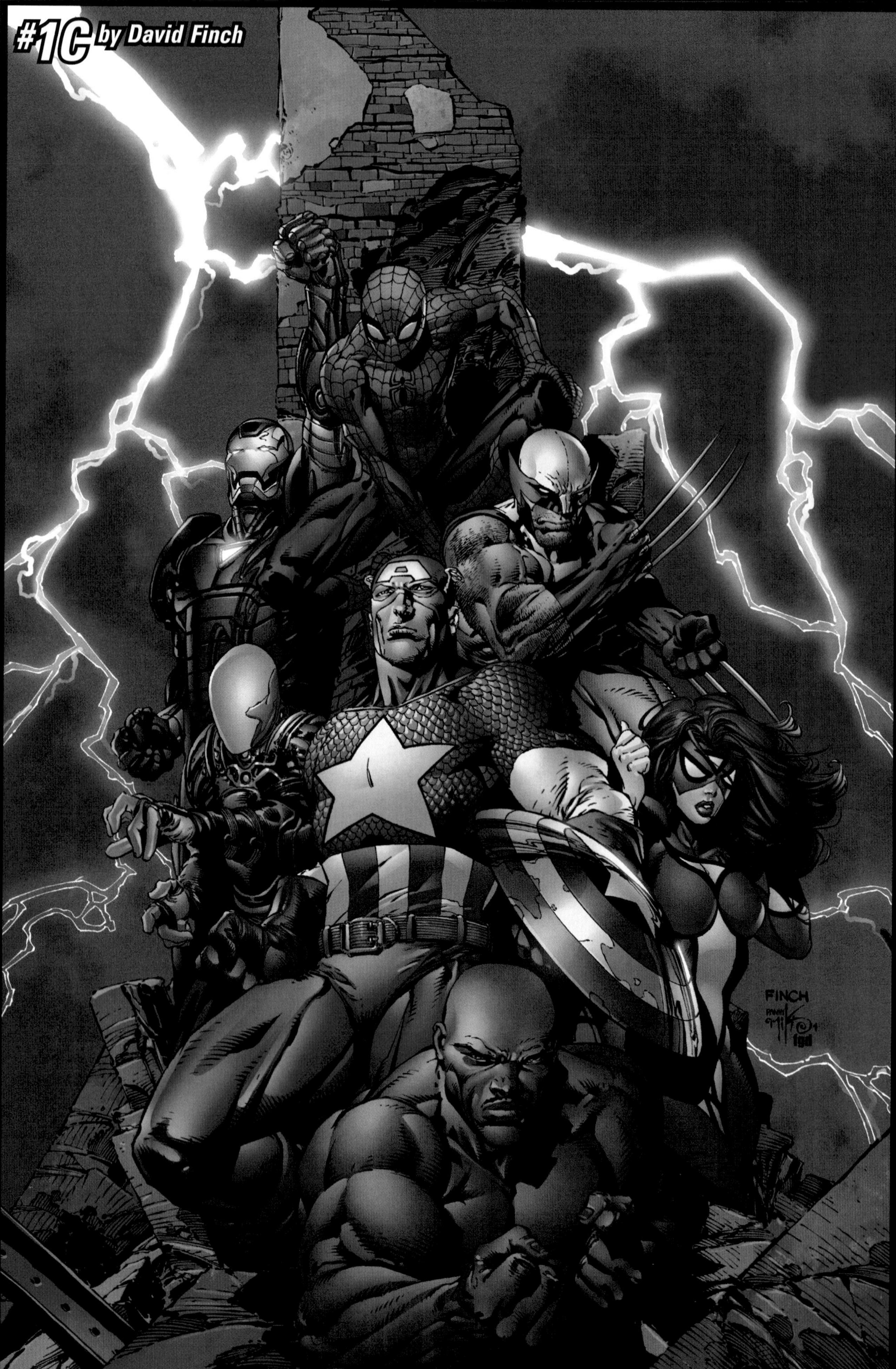
#1C by David Finch
FINCH

It was the worst day in Avengers history.

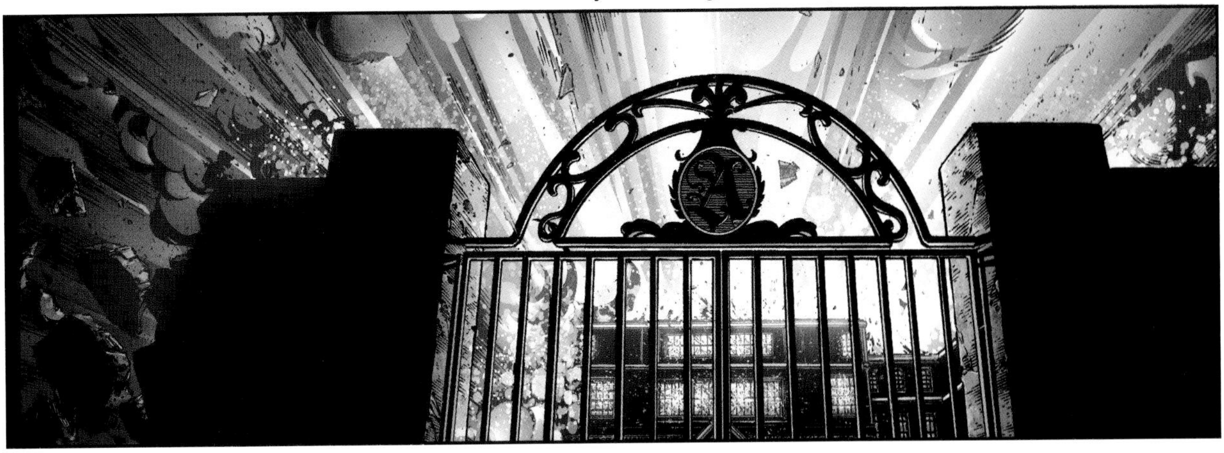

The Scarlet Witch suffered a total nervous breakdown after losing control of her reality-altering powers.

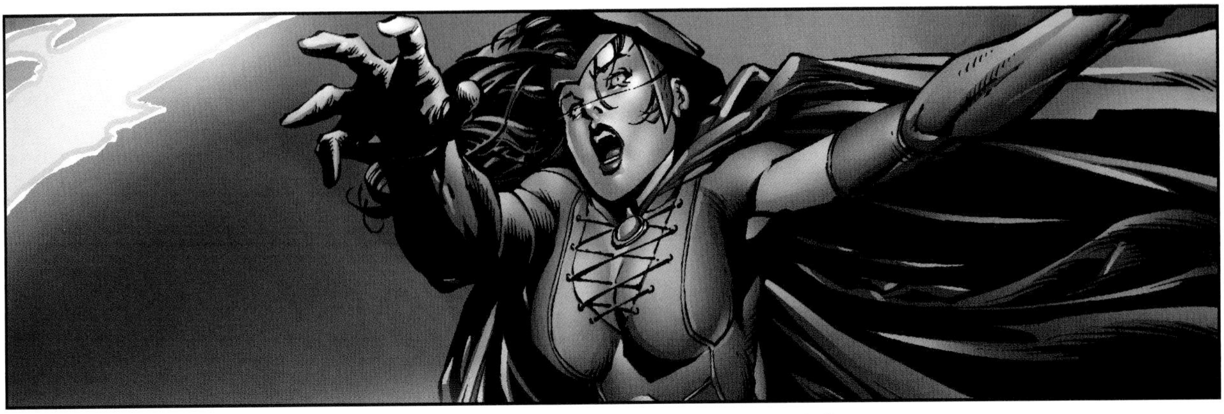

In the chaos created around the breakdown,
beloved Avengers Hawkeye, Ant-Man and the Vision lost their lives.

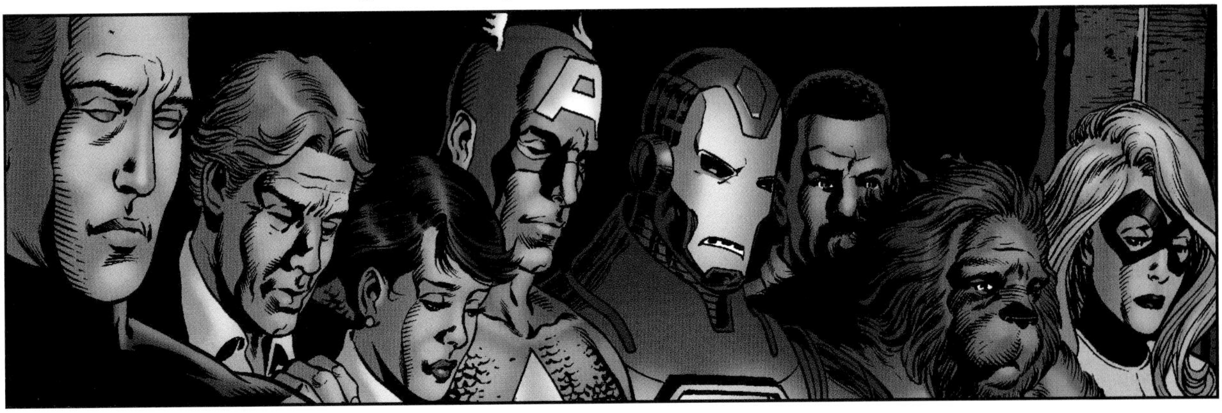

Many of the other Avengers were hurt, both emotionally and physically.
Without funding to keep going, the rest of the team quietly disbanded.

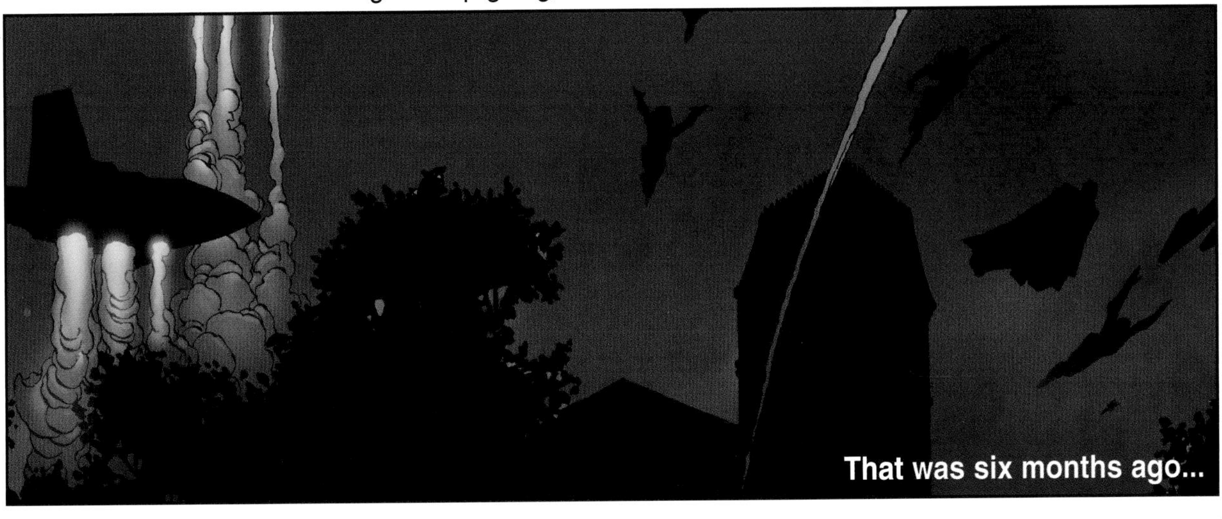
That was six months ago...

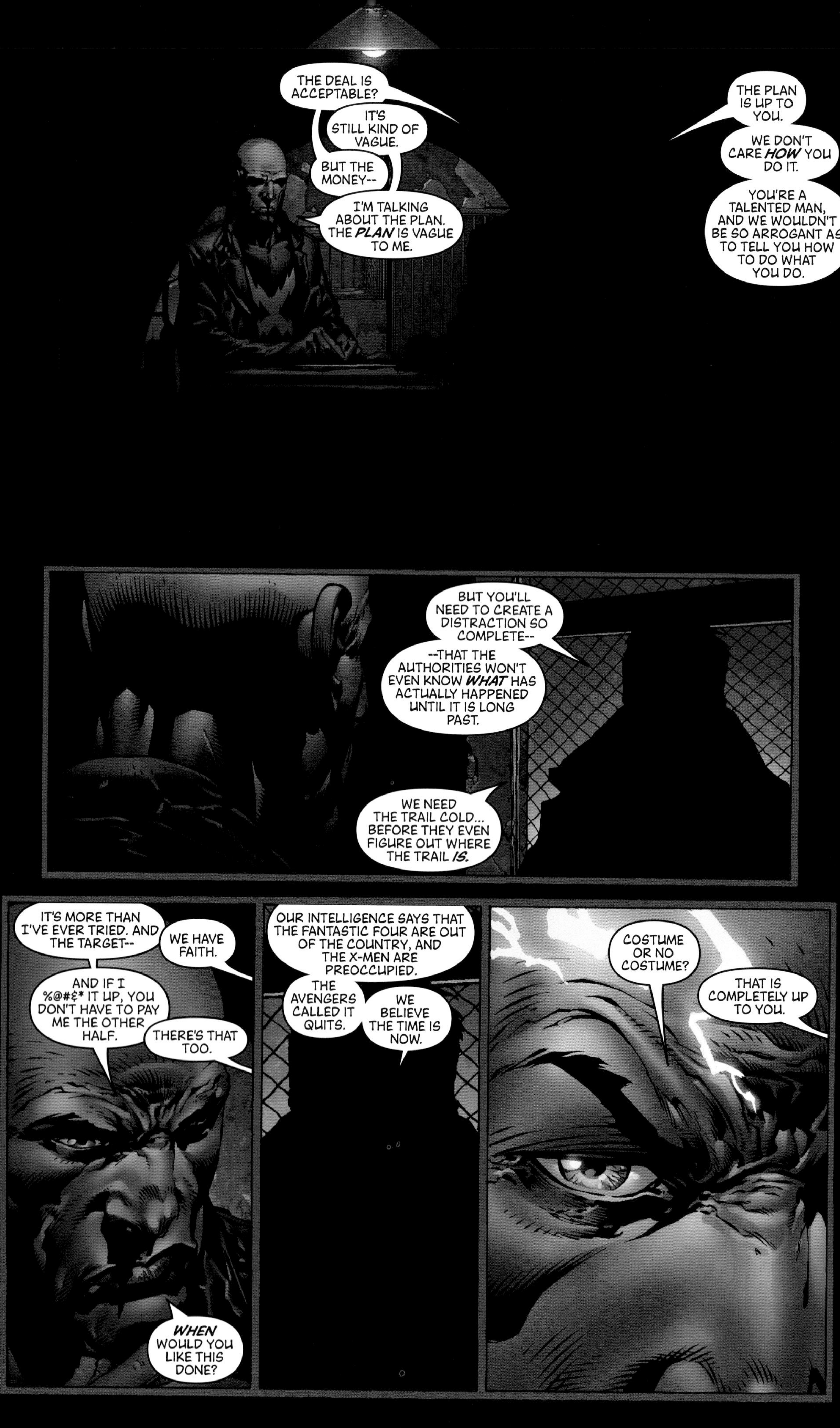
THE DEAL IS ACCEPTABLE?
IT'S STILL KIND OF VAGUE.
BUT THE MONEY--
I'M TALKING ABOUT THE PLAN. THE *PLAN* IS VAGUE TO ME.
THE PLAN IS UP TO YOU.
WE DON'T CARE *HOW* YOU DO IT.
YOU'RE A TALENTED MAN, AND WE WOULDN'T BE SO ARROGANT AS TO TELL YOU HOW TO DO WHAT YOU DO.
BUT YOU'LL NEED TO CREATE A DISTRACTION SO COMPLETE--
--THAT THE AUTHORITIES WON'T EVEN KNOW *WHAT* HAS ACTUALLY HAPPENED UNTIL IT IS LONG PAST.
WE NEED THE TRAIL COLD... BEFORE THEY EVEN FIGURE OUT WHERE THE TRAIL *IS.*
IT'S MORE THAN I'VE EVER TRIED. AND THE TARGET--
WE HAVE FAITH.
AND IF I %@#&* IT UP, YOU DON'T HAVE TO PAY ME THE OTHER HALF.
THERE'S THAT TOO.
WHEN WOULD YOU LIKE THIS DONE?
OUR INTELLIGENCE SAYS THAT THE FANTASTIC FOUR ARE OUT OF THE COUNTRY, AND THE X-MEN ARE PREOCCUPIED.
THE AVENGERS CALLED IT QUITS.
WE BELIEVE THE TIME IS NOW.
COSTUME OR NO COSTUME?
THAT IS COMPLETELY UP TO YOU.

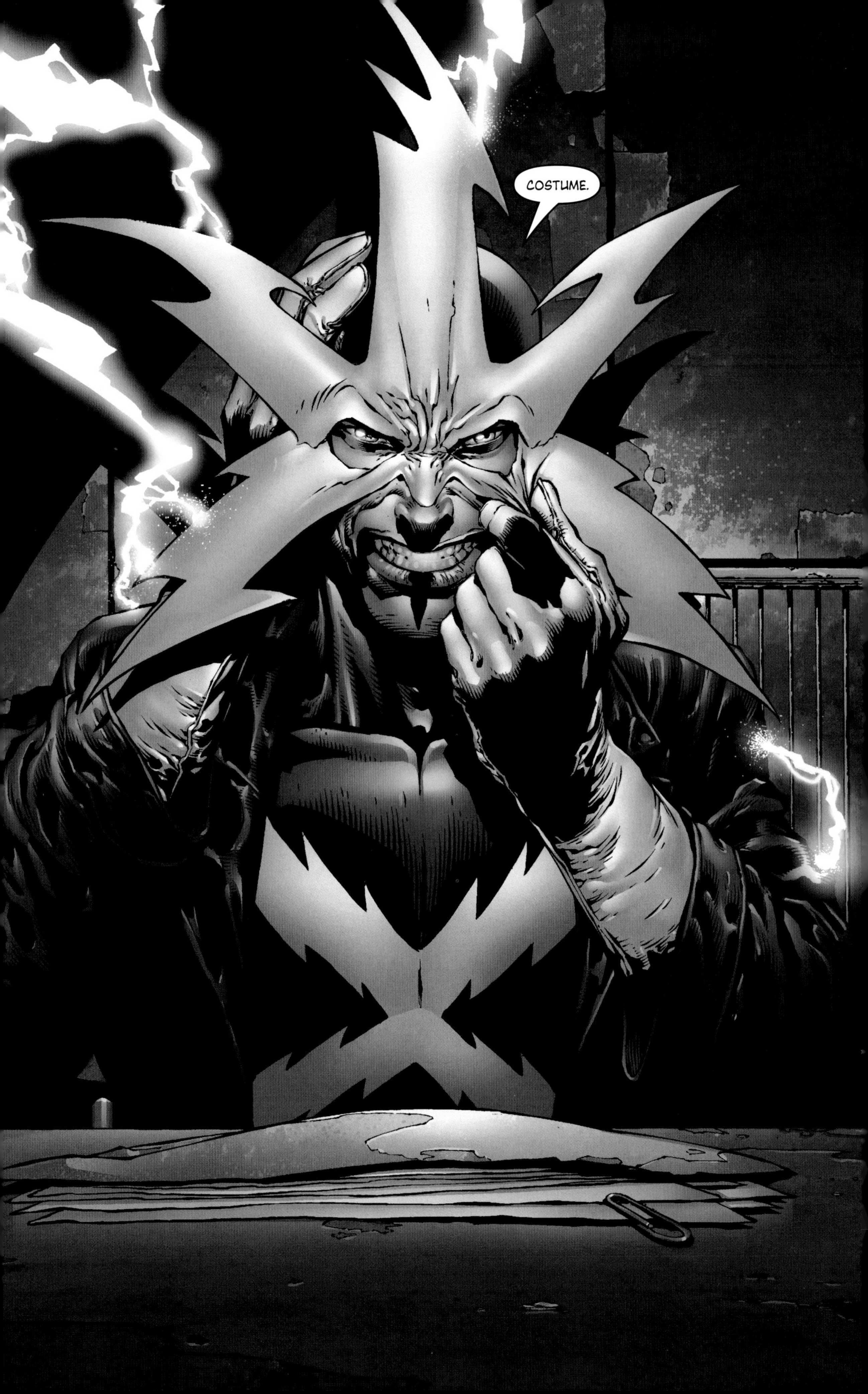
COSTUME.

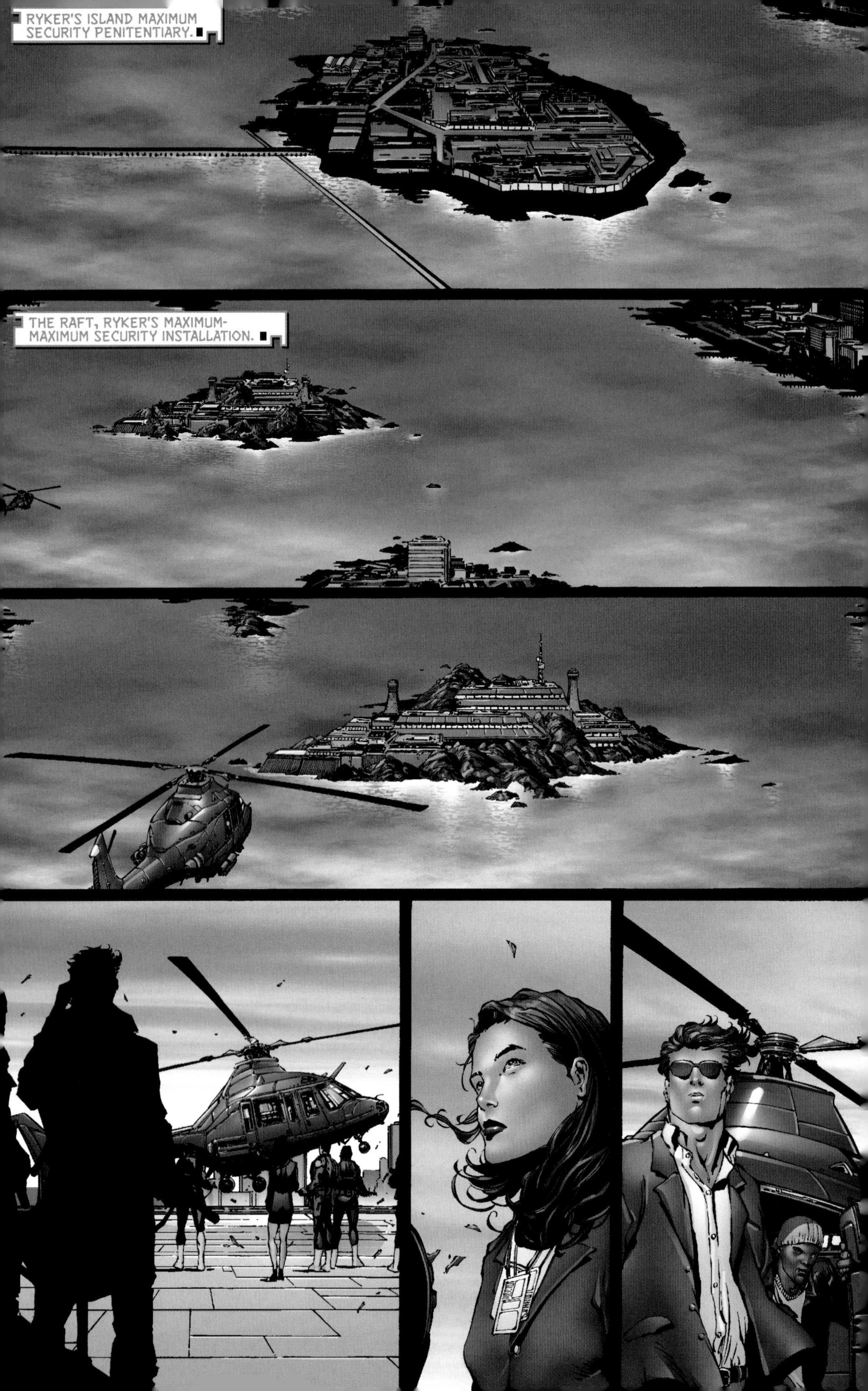
RYKER'S ISLAND MAXIMUM SECURITY PENITENTIARY.
THE RAFT, RYKER'S MAXIMUM-MAXIMUM SECURITY INSTALLATION.

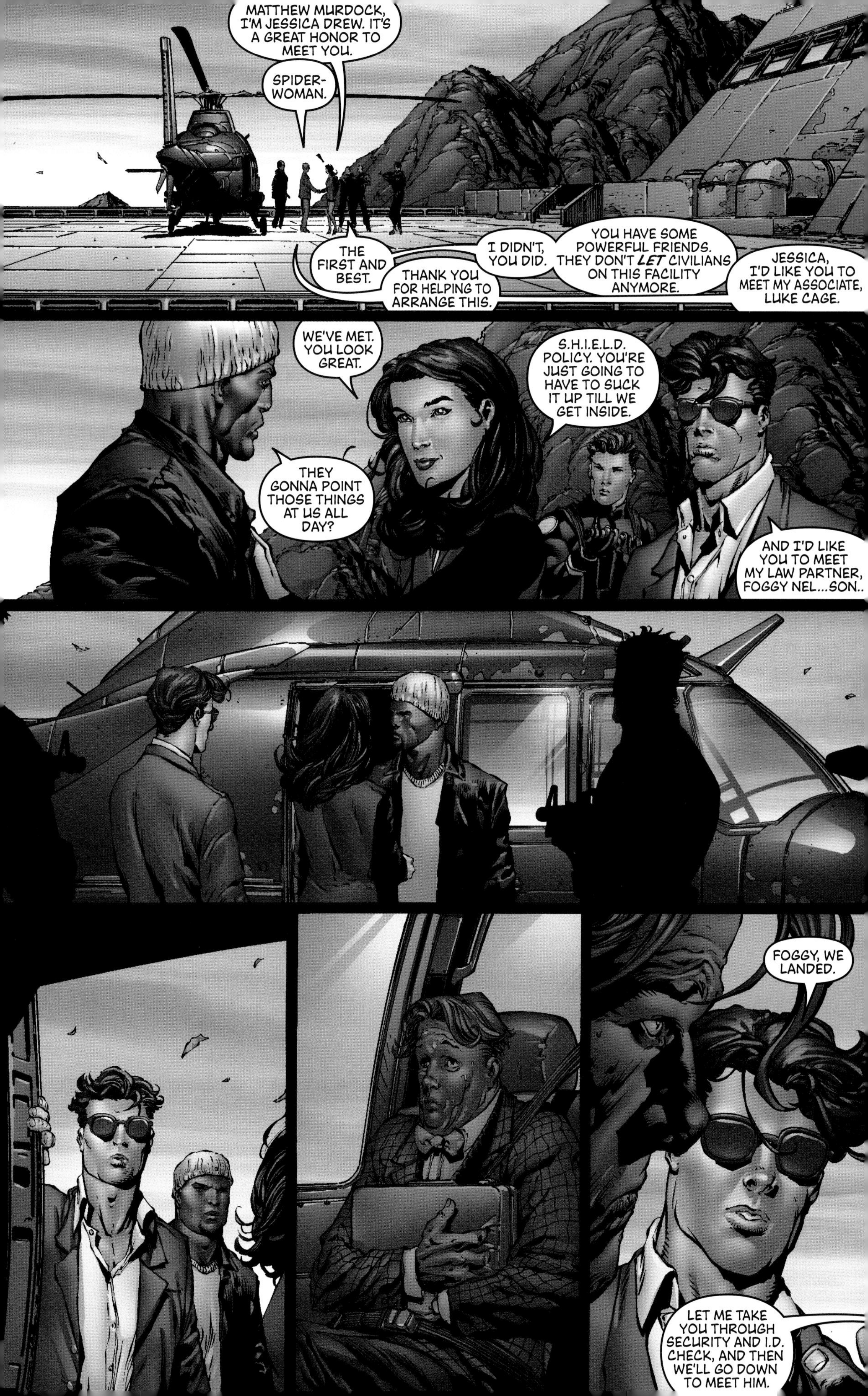
MATTHEW MURDOCK, I'M JESSICA DREW. IT'S A GREAT HONOR TO MEET YOU.
SPIDER-WOMAN.
THE FIRST AND BEST.
THANK YOU FOR HELPING TO ARRANGE THIS.
I DIDN'T, YOU DID.
YOU HAVE SOME POWERFUL FRIENDS. THEY DON'T LET CIVILIANS ON THIS FACILITY ANYMORE.
JESSICA, I'D LIKE YOU TO MEET MY ASSOCIATE, LUKE CAGE.
WE'VE MET. YOU LOOK GREAT.
THEY GONNA POINT THOSE THINGS AT US ALL DAY?
S.H.I.E.L.D. POLICY. YOU'RE JUST GOING TO HAVE TO SUCK IT UP TILL WE GET INSIDE.
AND I'D LIKE YOU TO MEET MY LAW PARTNER, FOGGY NEL...SON..
FOGGY, WE LANDED.
LET ME TAKE YOU THROUGH SECURITY AND I.D. CHECK, AND THEN WE'LL GO DOWN TO MEET HIM.

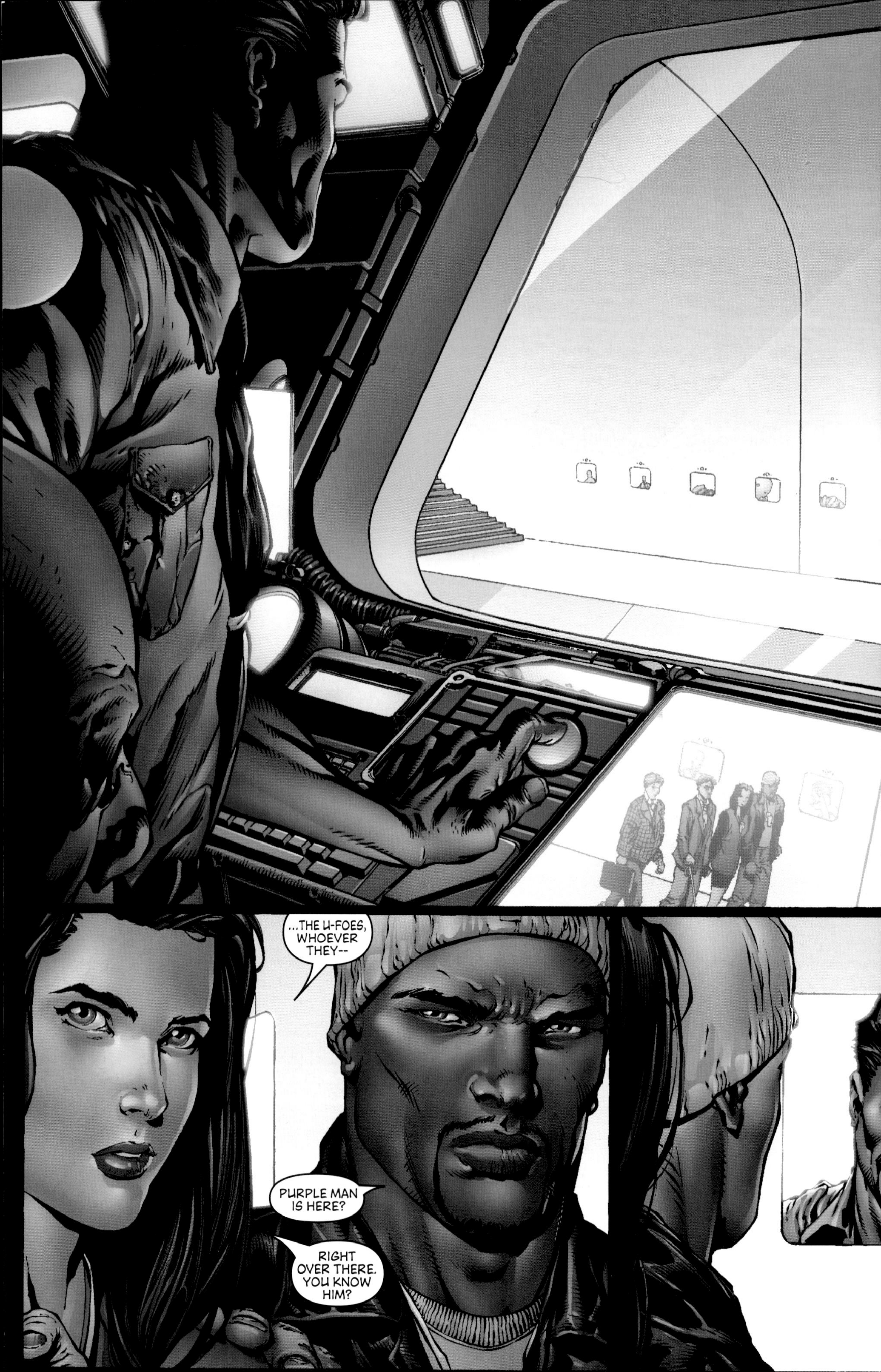
...THE U-FOES, WHOEVER THEY--
PURPLE MAN IS HERE?
RIGHT OVER THERE. YOU KNOW HIM?

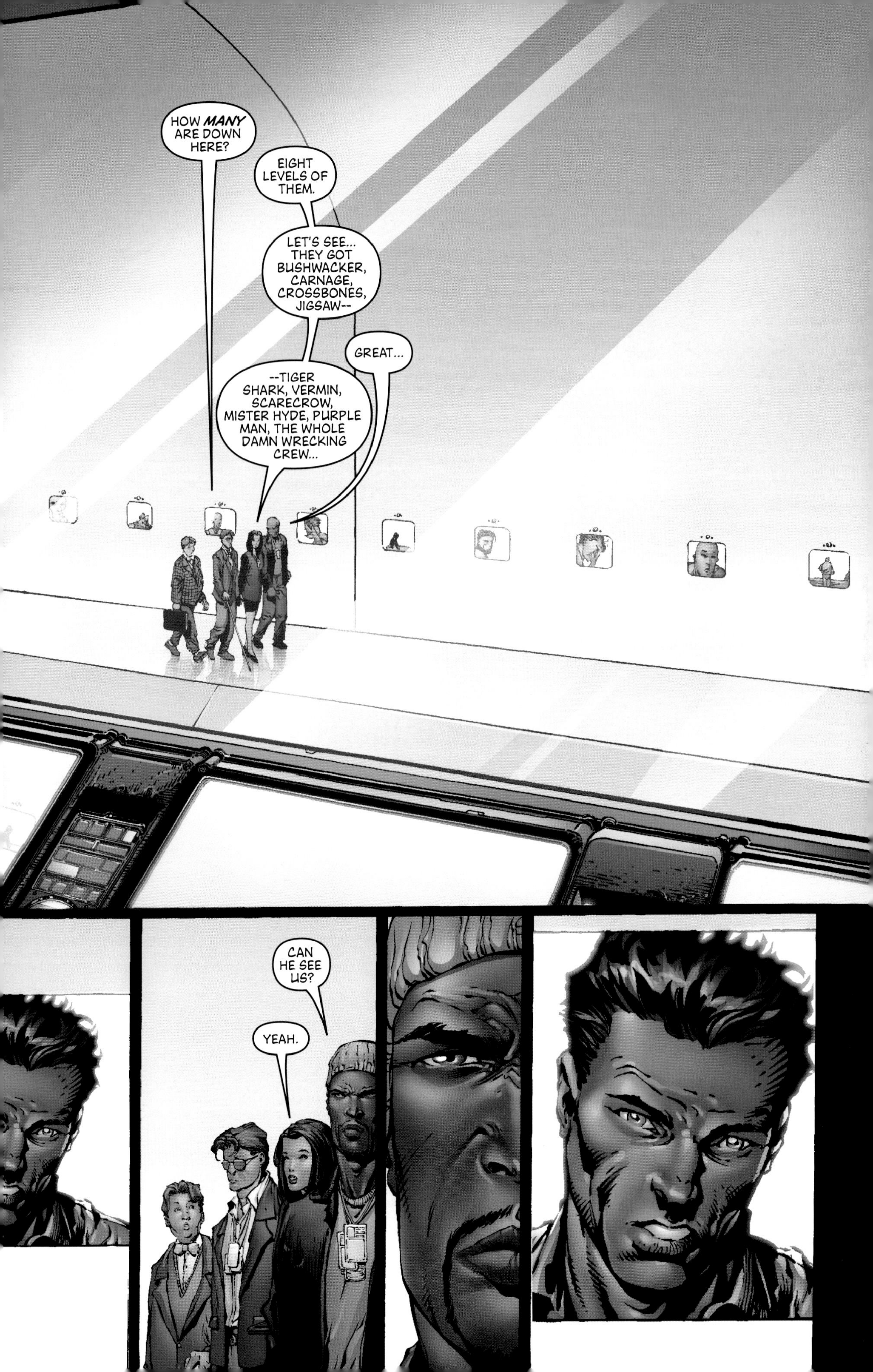
HOW *MANY* ARE DOWN HERE?
EIGHT LEVELS OF THEM.
LET'S SEE... THEY GOT BUSHWACKER, CARNAGE, CROSSBONES, JIGSAW--
--TIGER SHARK, VERMIN, SCARECROW, MISTER HYDE, PURPLE MAN, THE WHOLE DAMN WRECKING CREW...
GREAT...
CAN HE SEE US?
YEAH.

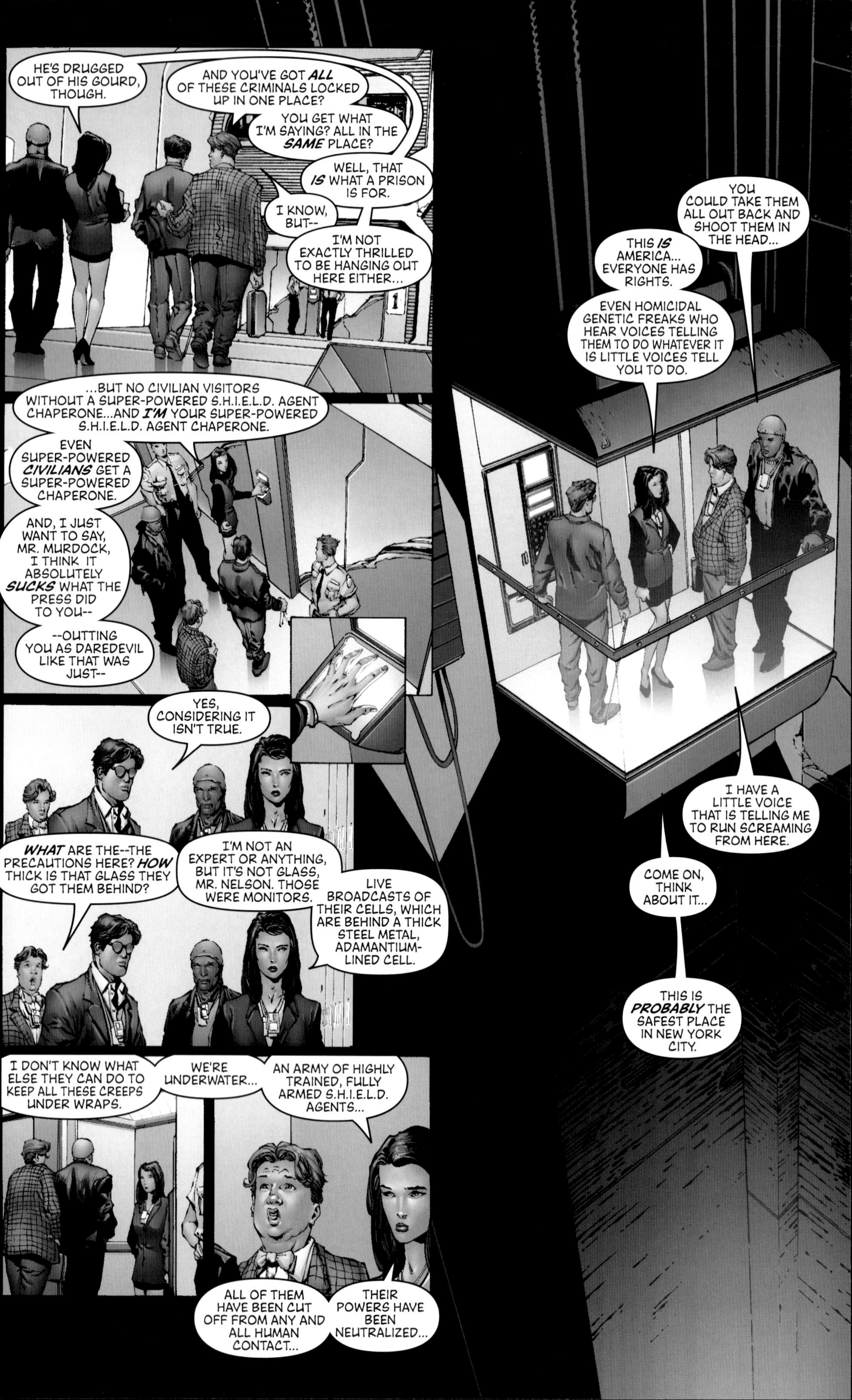
HE'S DRUGGED OUT OF HIS GOURD, THOUGH.
AND YOU'VE GOT ALL OF THESE CRIMINALS LOCKED UP IN ONE PLACE?
YOU GET WHAT I'M SAYING? ALL IN THE SAME PLACE?
WELL, THAT IS WHAT A PRISON IS FOR.
I KNOW, BUT--
I'M NOT EXACTLY THRILLED TO BE HANGING OUT HERE EITHER...
...BUT NO CIVILIAN VISITORS WITHOUT A SUPER-POWERED S.H.I.E.L.D. AGENT CHAPERONE...AND I'M YOUR SUPER-POWERED S.H.I.E.L.D. AGENT CHAPERONE.
EVEN SUPER-POWERED CIVILIANS GET A SUPER-POWERED CHAPERONE.
AND, I JUST WANT TO SAY, MR. MURDOCK, I THINK IT ABSOLUTELY SUCKS WHAT THE PRESS DID TO YOU--
--OUTTING YOU AS DAREDEVIL LIKE THAT WAS JUST--
YES, CONSIDERING IT ISN'T TRUE.
WHAT ARE THE--THE PRECAUTIONS HERE? HOW THICK IS THAT GLASS THEY GOT THEM BEHIND?
I'M NOT AN EXPERT OR ANYTHING, BUT IT'S NOT GLASS, MR. NELSON. THOSE WERE MONITORS.
LIVE BROADCASTS OF THEIR CELLS, WHICH ARE BEHIND A THICK STEEL METAL, ADAMANTIUM-LINED CELL.
I DON'T KNOW WHAT ELSE THEY CAN DO TO KEEP ALL THESE CREEPS UNDER WRAPS.
WE'RE UNDERWATER...
AN ARMY OF HIGHLY TRAINED, FULLY ARMED S.H.I.E.L.D. AGENTS...
ALL OF THEM HAVE BEEN CUT OFF FROM ANY AND ALL HUMAN CONTACT...
THEIR POWERS HAVE BEEN NEUTRALIZED...
YOU COULD TAKE THEM ALL OUT BACK AND SHOOT THEM IN THE HEAD...
THIS IS AMERICA... EVERYONE HAS RIGHTS.
EVEN HOMICIDAL GENETIC FREAKS WHO HEAR VOICES TELLING THEM TO DO WHATEVER IT IS LITTLE VOICES TELL YOU TO DO.
I HAVE A LITTLE VOICE THAT IS TELLING ME TO RUN SCREAMING FROM HERE.
COME ON, THINK ABOUT IT...
THIS IS PROBABLY THE SAFEST PLACE IN NEW YORK CITY.

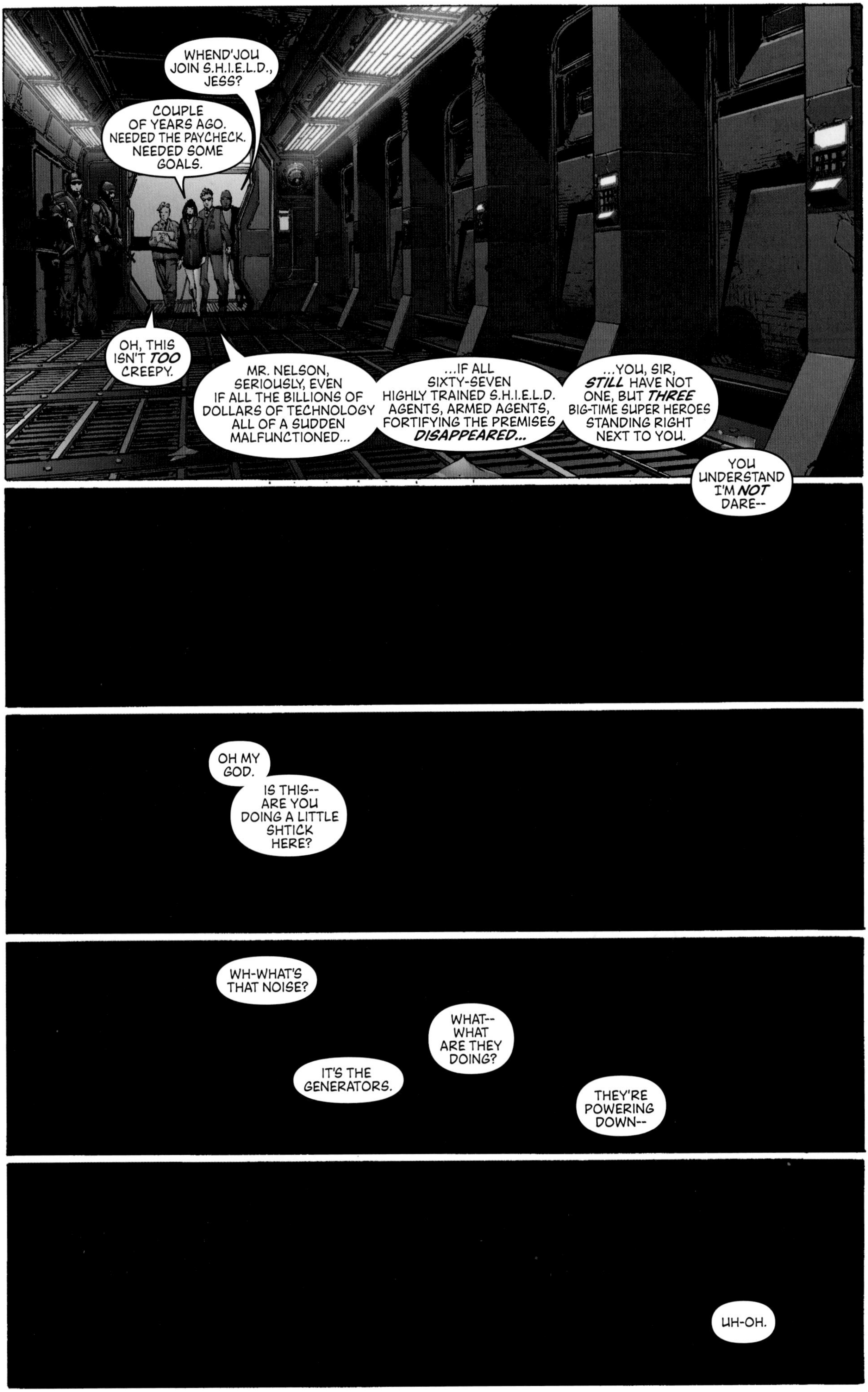
WHEND'JOU JOIN S.H.I.E.L.D., JESS?
COUPLE OF YEARS AGO. NEEDED THE PAYCHECK. NEEDED SOME GOALS.
OH, THIS ISN'T *TOO* CREEPY.
MR. NELSON, SERIOUSLY, EVEN IF ALL THE BILLIONS OF DOLLARS OF TECHNOLOGY ALL OF A SUDDEN MALFUNCTIONED...
...IF ALL SIXTY-SEVEN HIGHLY TRAINED S.H.I.E.L.D. AGENTS, ARMED AGENTS, FORTIFYING THE PREMISES *DISAPPEARED...*
...YOU, SIR, *STILL* HAVE NOT ONE, BUT *THREE* BIG-TIME SUPER HEROES STANDING RIGHT NEXT TO YOU.
YOU UNDERSTAND I'M *NOT* DARE--
OH MY GOD.
IS THIS-- ARE YOU DOING A LITTLE SHTICK HERE?
WH-WHAT'S THAT NOISE?
WHAT-- WHAT ARE THEY DOING?
IT'S THE GENERATORS.
THEY'RE POWERING DOWN--
UH-OH.

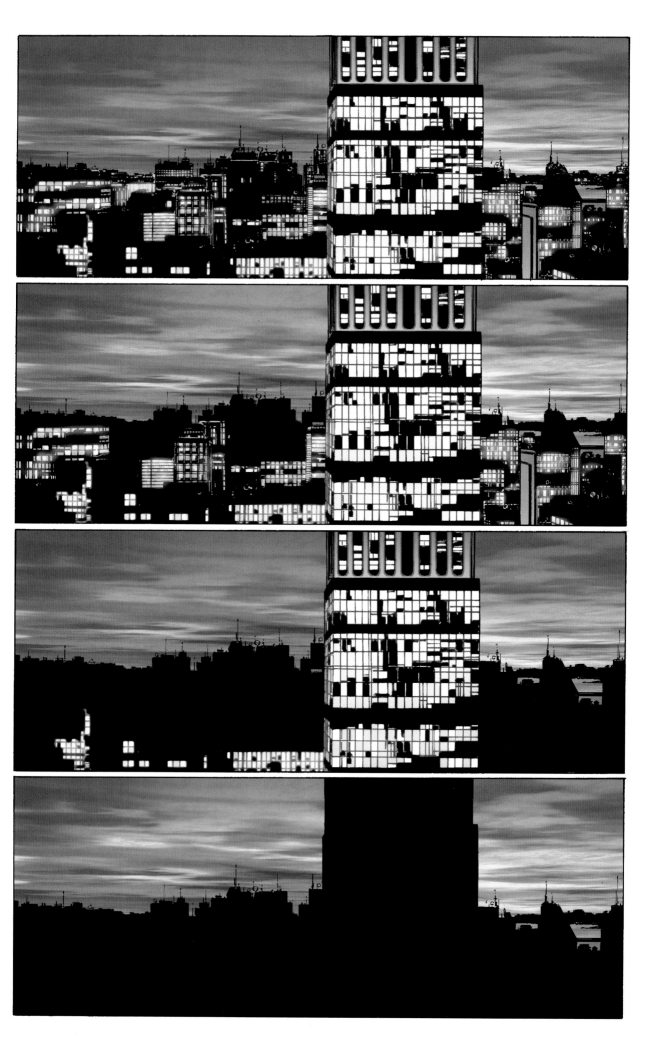

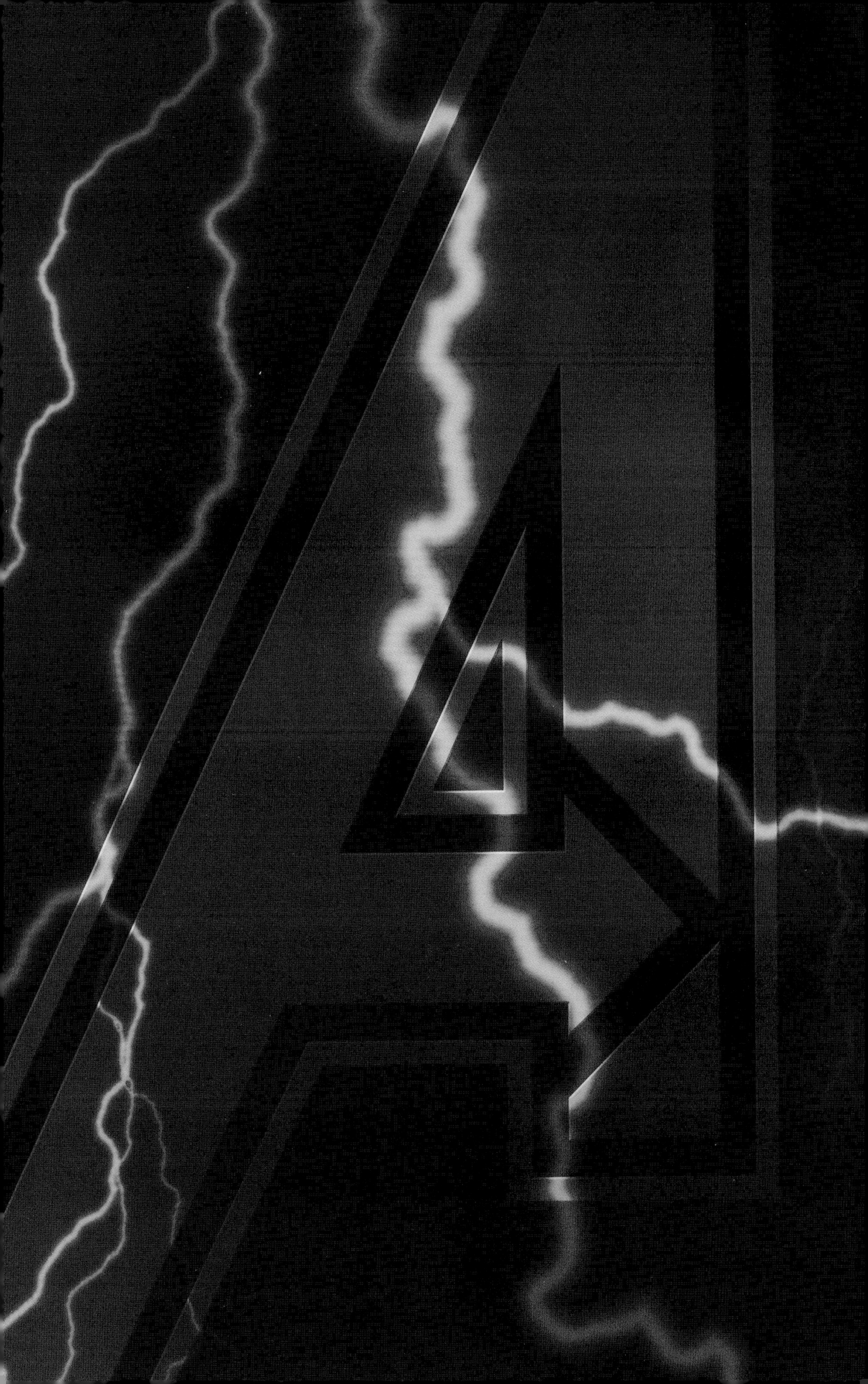

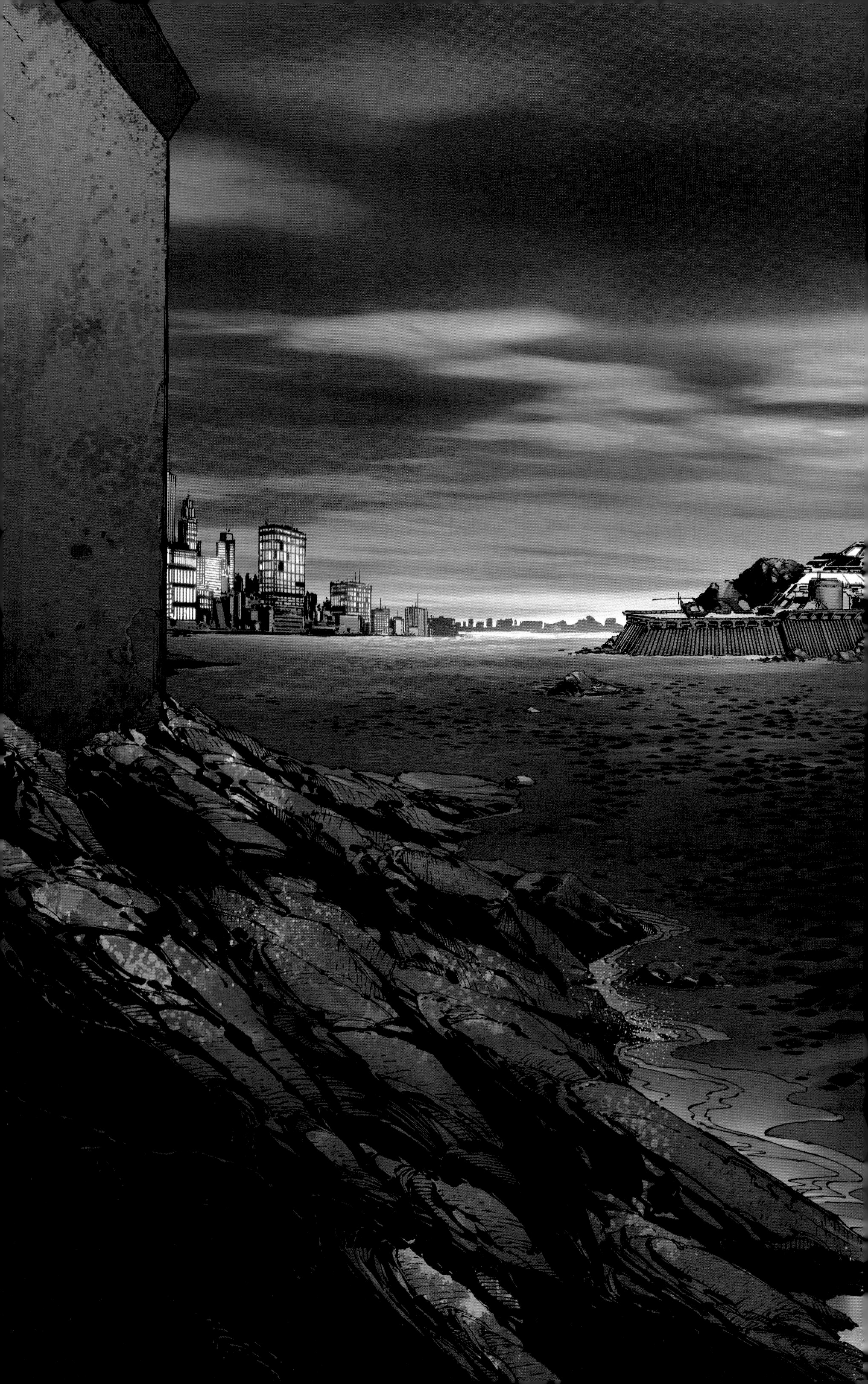

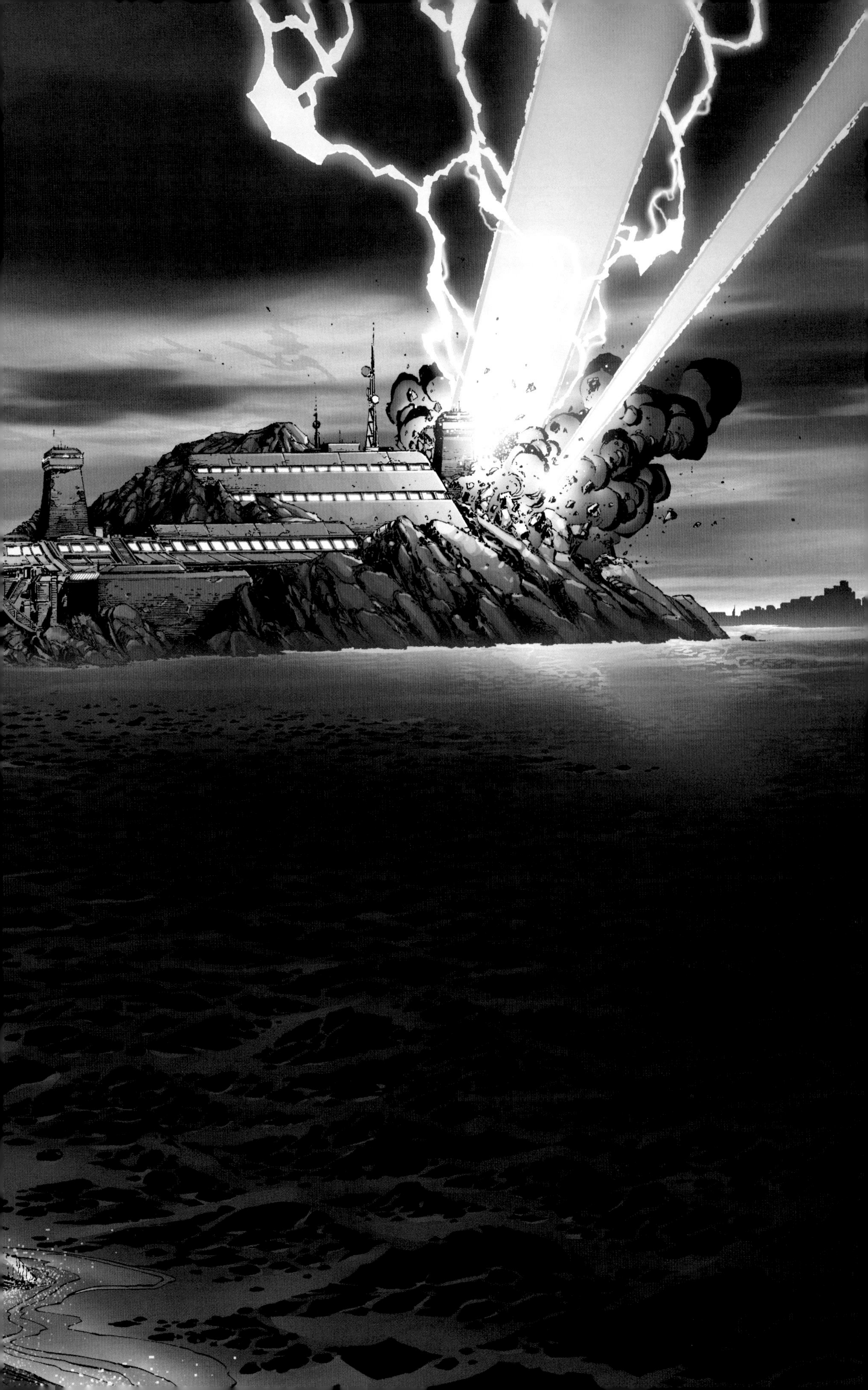

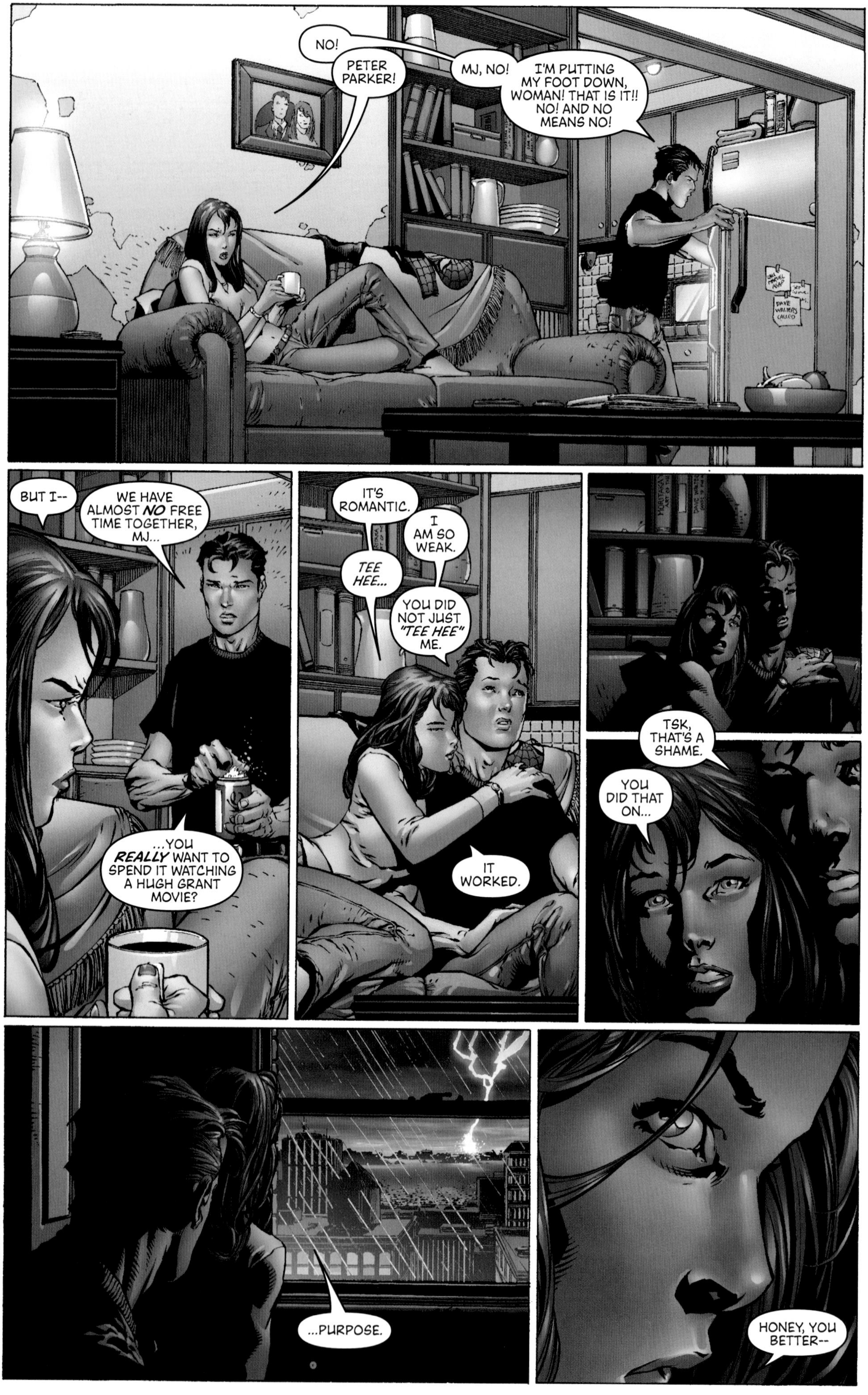

NO!
PETER PARKER!
MJ, NO!
I'M PUTTING MY FOOT DOWN, WOMAN! THAT IS IT!! NO! AND NO MEANS NO!
BUT I--
WE HAVE ALMOST ***NO*** FREE TIME TOGETHER, MJ...
...YOU ***REALLY*** WANT TO SPEND IT WATCHING A HUGH GRANT MOVIE?
IT'S ROMANTIC.
TEE HEE...
I AM SO WEAK.
YOU DID NOT JUST *"TEE HEE"* ME.
IT WORKED.
TSK, THAT'S A SHAME.
YOU DID THAT ON...
...PURPOSE.
HONEY, YOU BETTER--

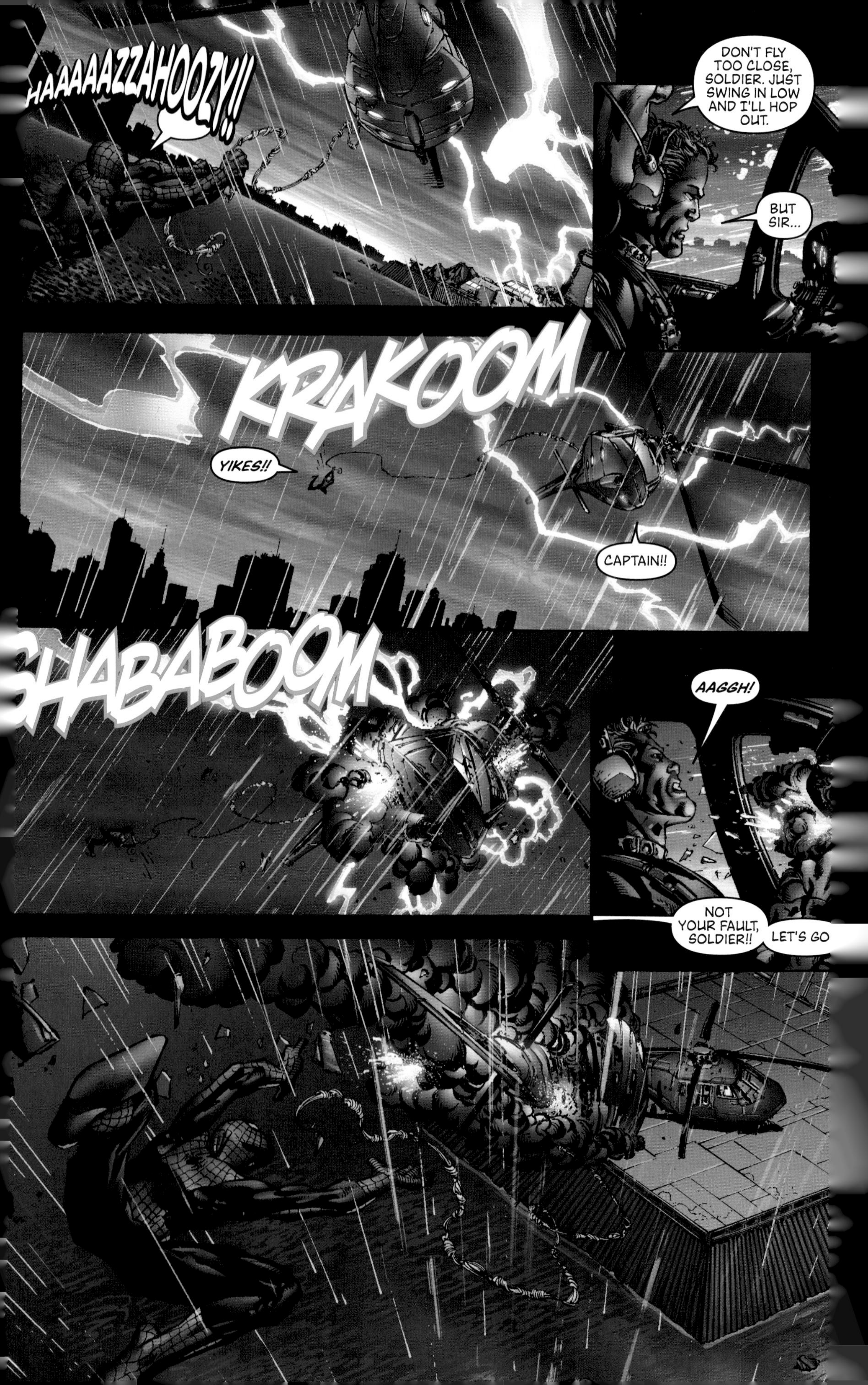
HAAAAAZZAHOOZY!!
DON'T FLY TOO CLOSE, SOLDIER. JUST SWING IN LOW AND I'LL HOP OUT.
BUT SIR...
KRAKOOM
YIKES!!
CAPTAIN!!
SHABABOOM
AAGGH!
NOT YOUR FAULT, SOLDIER!!
LET'S GO

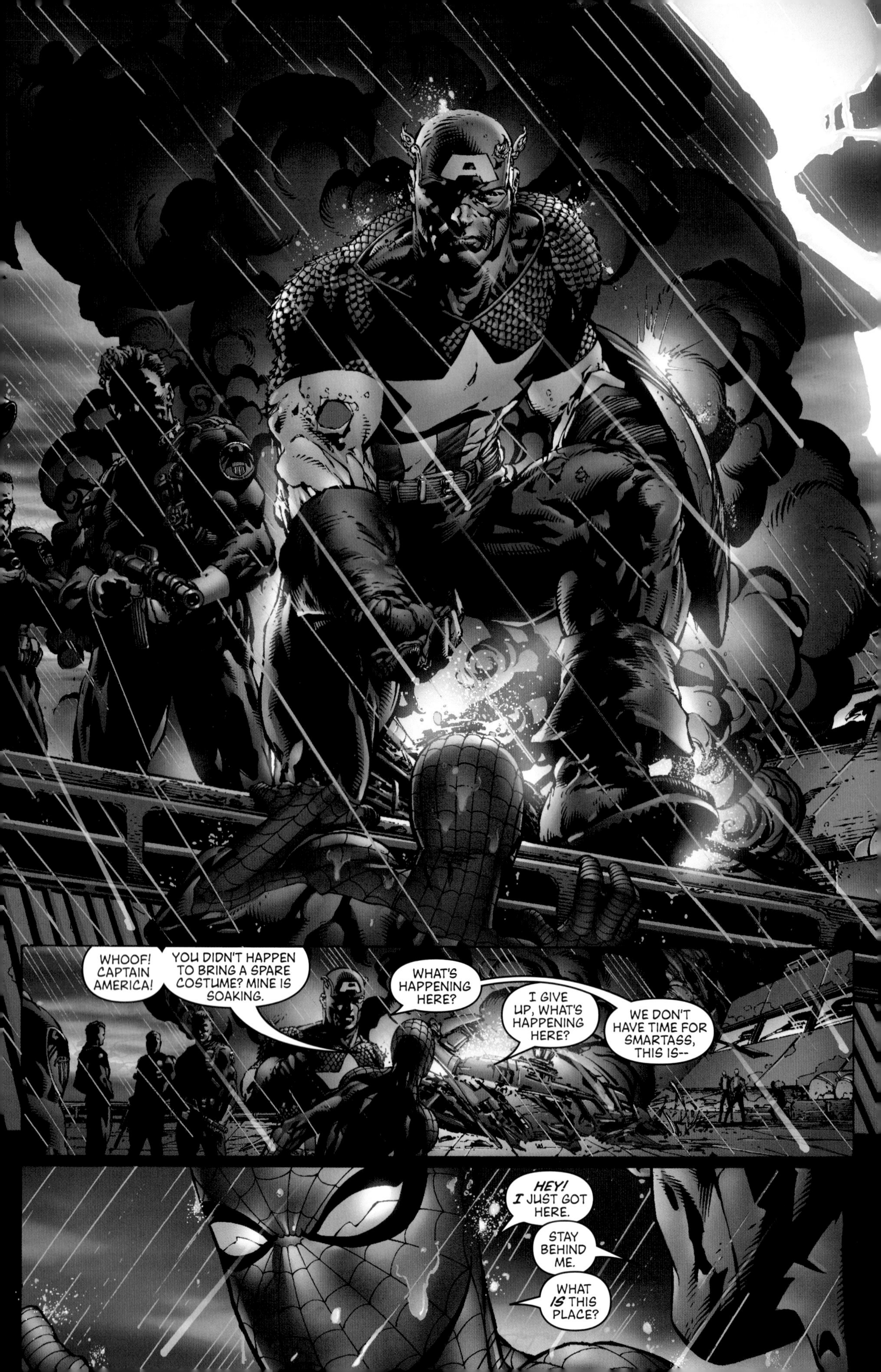
WHOOF! CAPTAIN AMERICA!
YOU DIDN'T HAPPEN TO BRING A SPARE COSTUME? MINE IS SOAKING.
WHAT'S HAPPENING HERE?
I GIVE UP, WHAT'S HAPPENING HERE?
WE DON'T HAVE TIME FOR SMARTASS, THIS IS--
HEY! I JUST GOT HERE.
STAY BEHIND ME.
WHAT IS THIS PLACE?

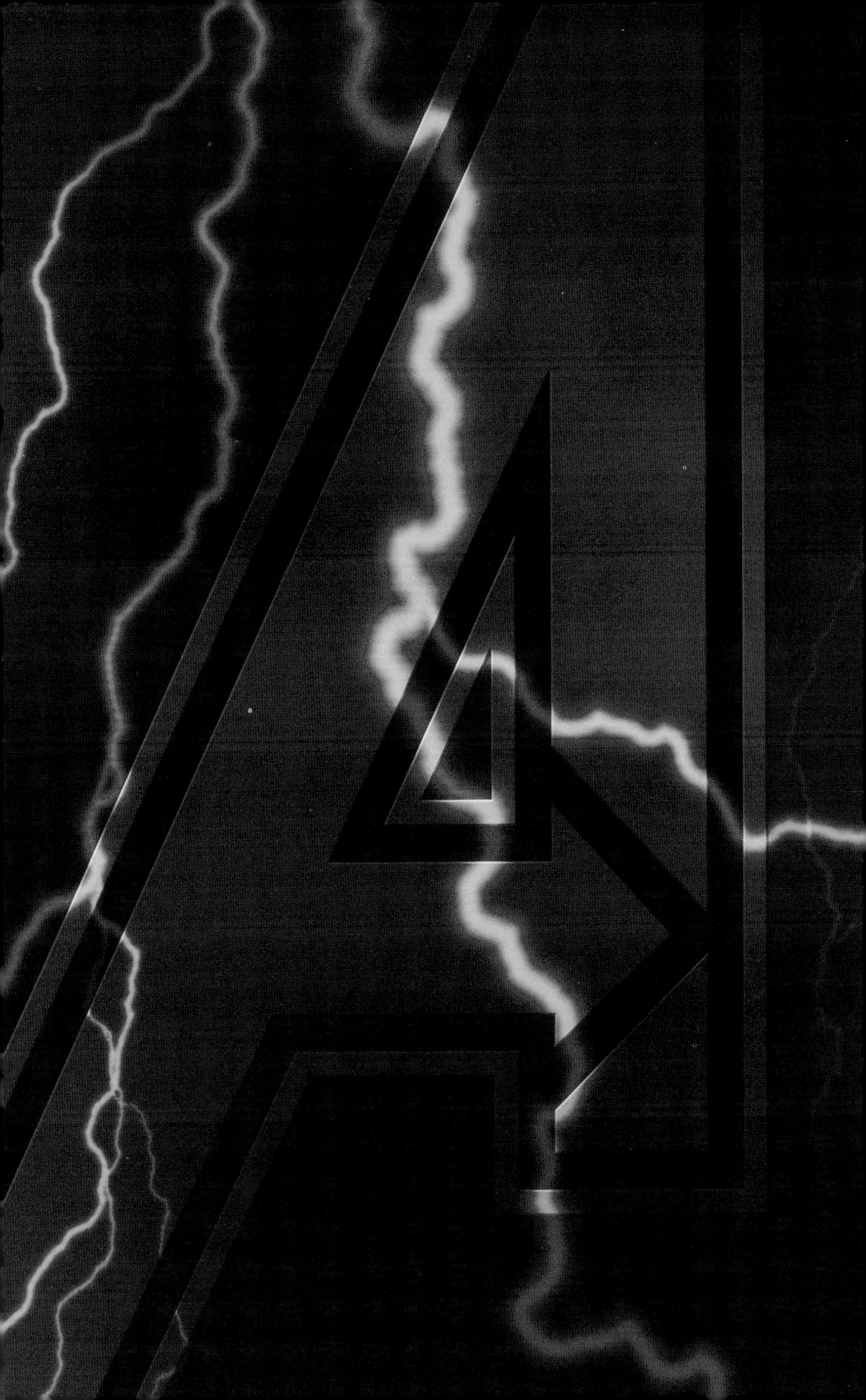

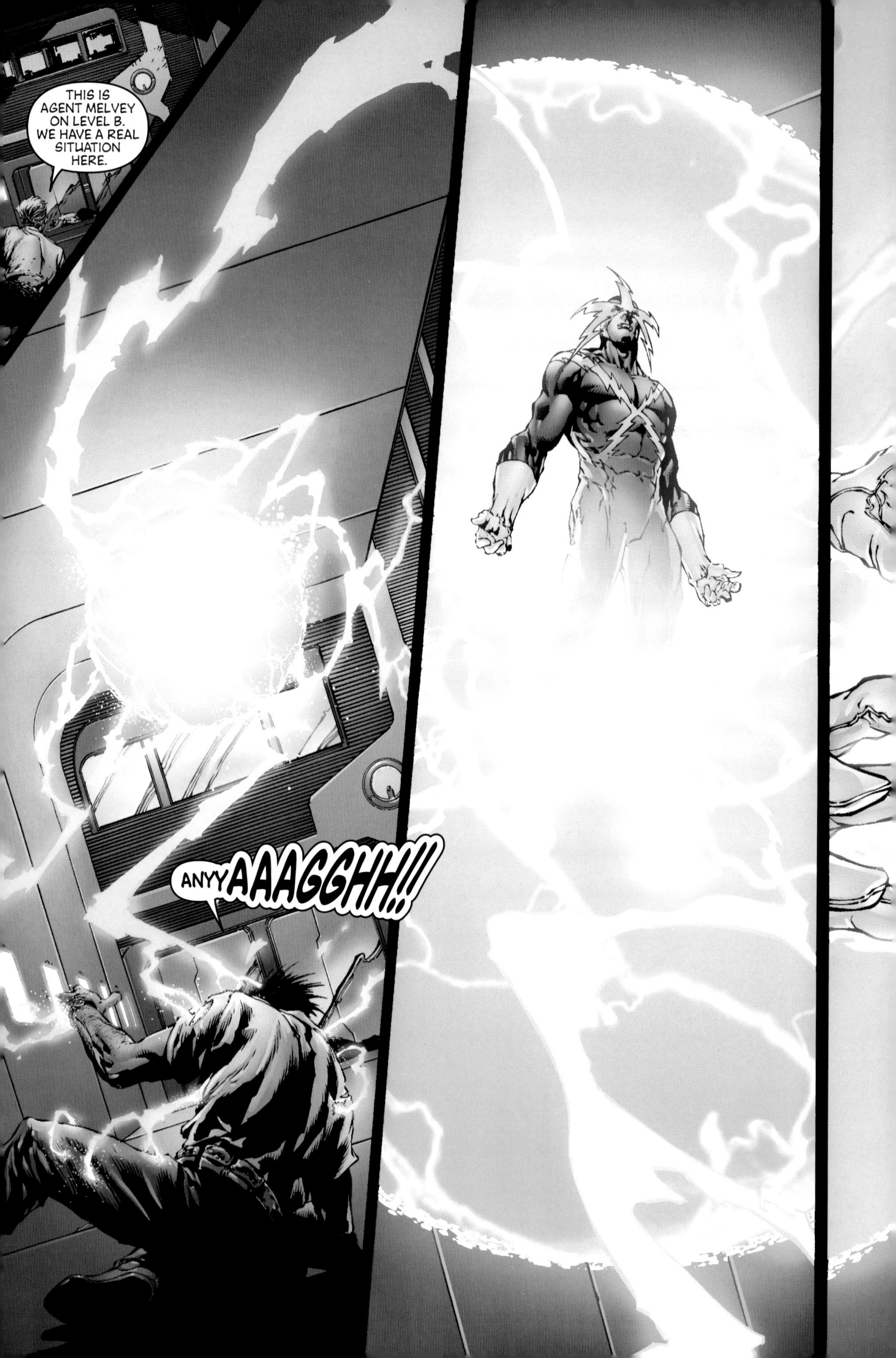
THIS IS AGENT MELVEY ON LEVEL B. WE HAVE A REAL SITUATION HERE.
ANYYAAAGGHH!!

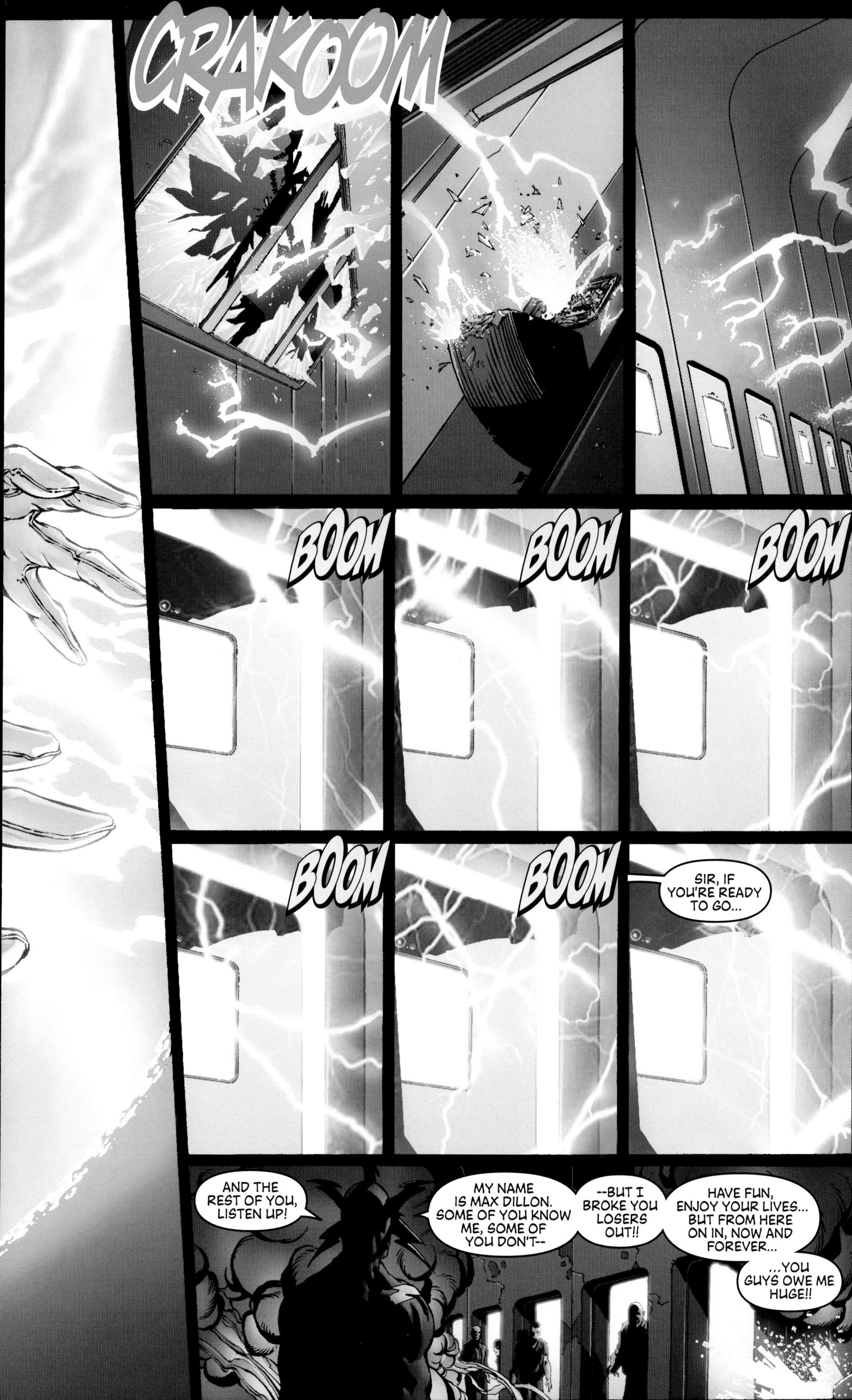
CRAKOOM
BOOM
BOOM
BOOM
BOOM
BOOM
SIR, IF YOU'RE READY TO GO...
AND THE REST OF YOU, LISTEN UP!
MY NAME IS MAX DILLON. SOME OF YOU KNOW ME, SOME OF YOU DON'T--
--BUT I BROKE YOU LOSERS OUT!!
HAVE FUN, ENJOY YOUR LIVES... BUT FROM HERE ON IN, NOW AND FOREVER...
...YOU GUYS OWE ME HUGE!!

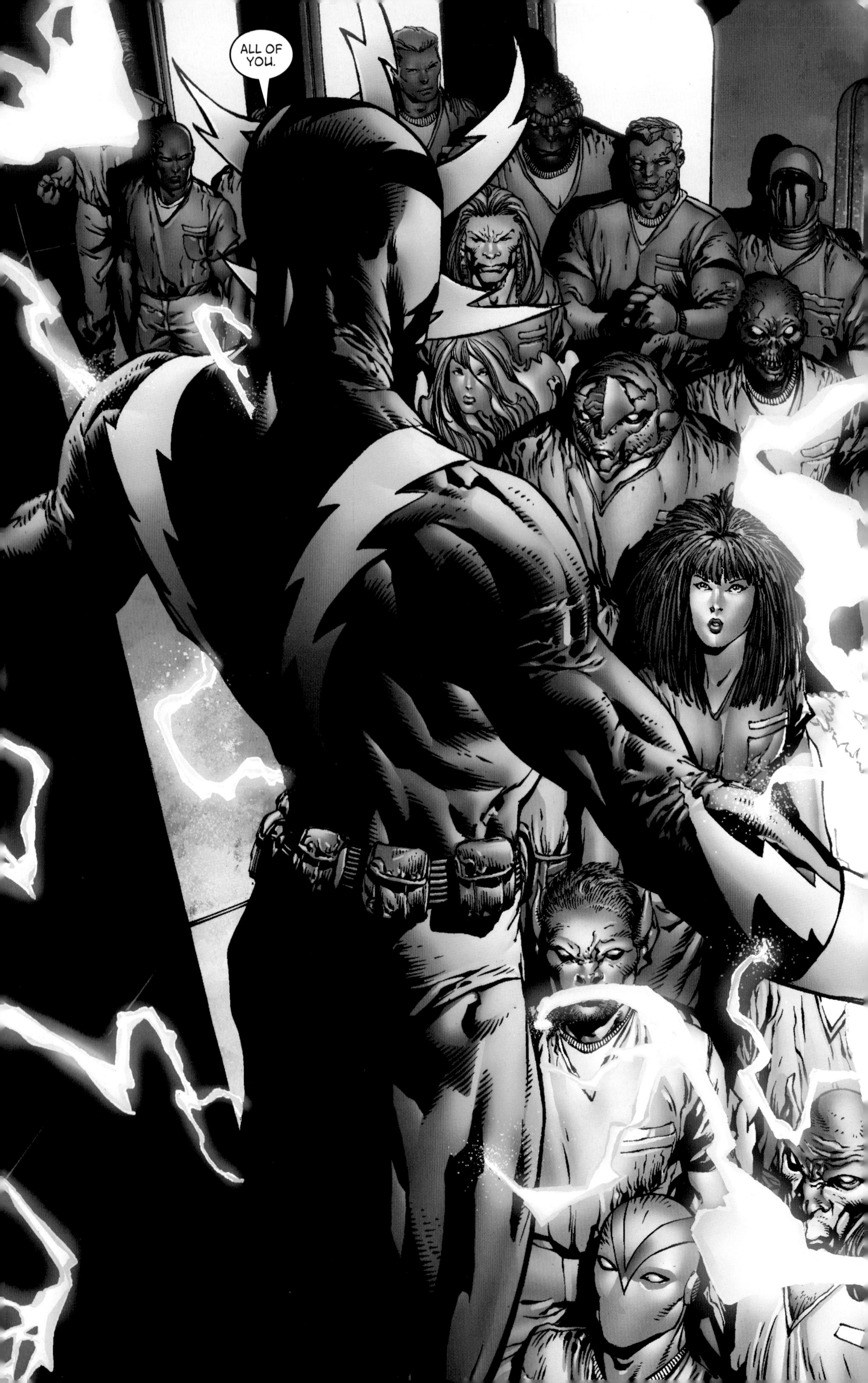
ALL OF YOU.

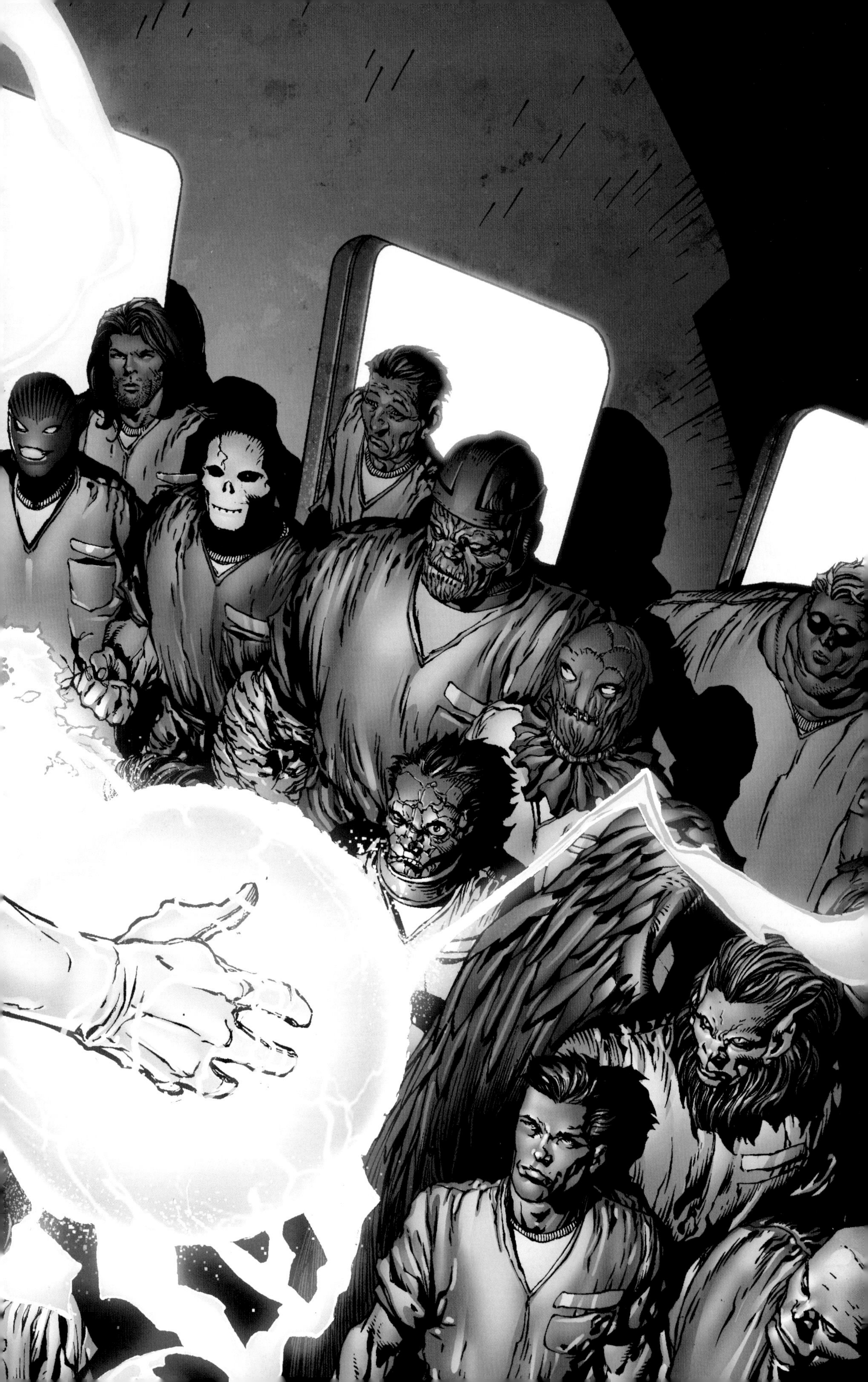

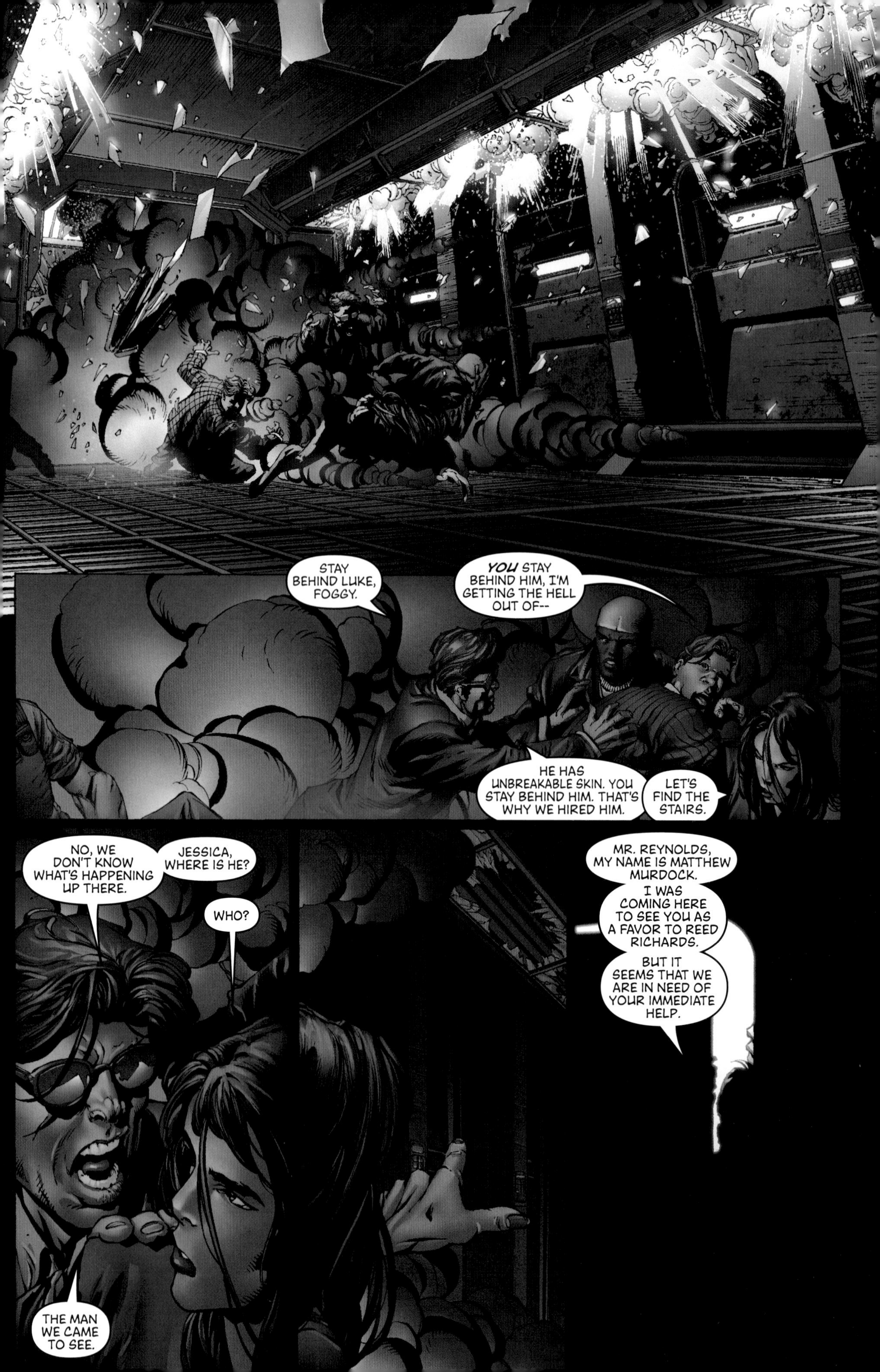
STAY BEHIND LUKE, FOGGY.
YOU STAY BEHIND HIM, I'M GETTING THE HELL OUT OF--
HE HAS UNBREAKABLE SKIN. YOU STAY BEHIND HIM. THAT'S WHY WE HIRED HIM.
LET'S FIND THE STAIRS.
NO, WE DON'T KNOW WHAT'S HAPPENING UP THERE.
JESSICA, WHERE IS HE?
WHO?
THE MAN WE CAME TO SEE.
MR. REYNOLDS, MY NAME IS MATTHEW MURDOCK.
I WAS COMING HERE TO SEE YOU AS A FAVOR TO REED RICHARDS.
BUT IT SEEMS THAT WE ARE IN NEED OF YOUR IMMEDIATE HELP.

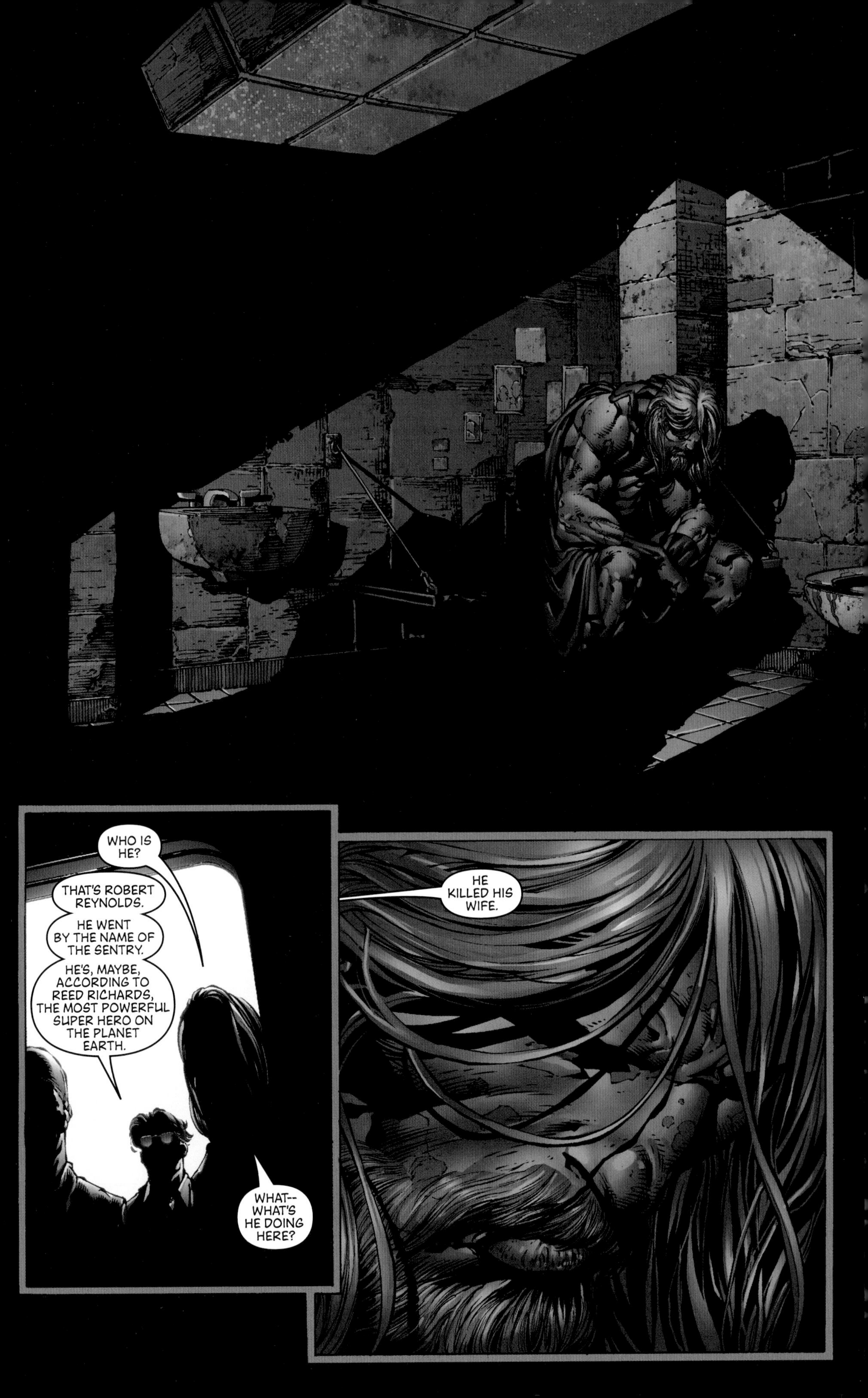
WHO IS HE?
THAT'S ROBERT REYNOLDS.
HE WENT BY THE NAME OF THE SENTRY.
HE'S, MAYBE, ACCORDING TO REED RICHARDS, THE MOST POWERFUL SUPER HERO ON THE PLANET EARTH.
WHAT-- WHAT'S HE DOING HERE?
HE KILLED HIS WIFE.

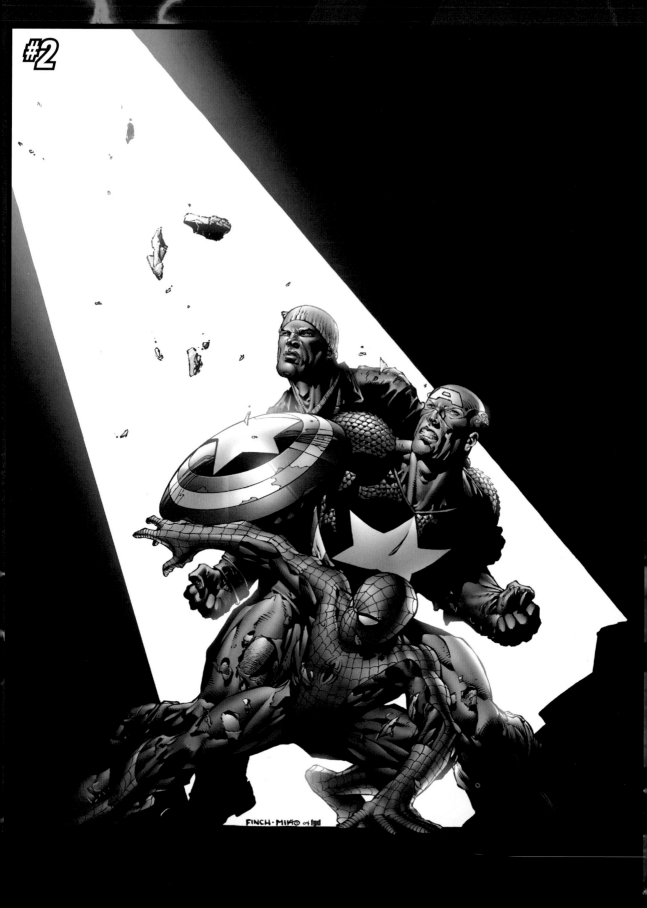

FINCH · MIKO oi fgd

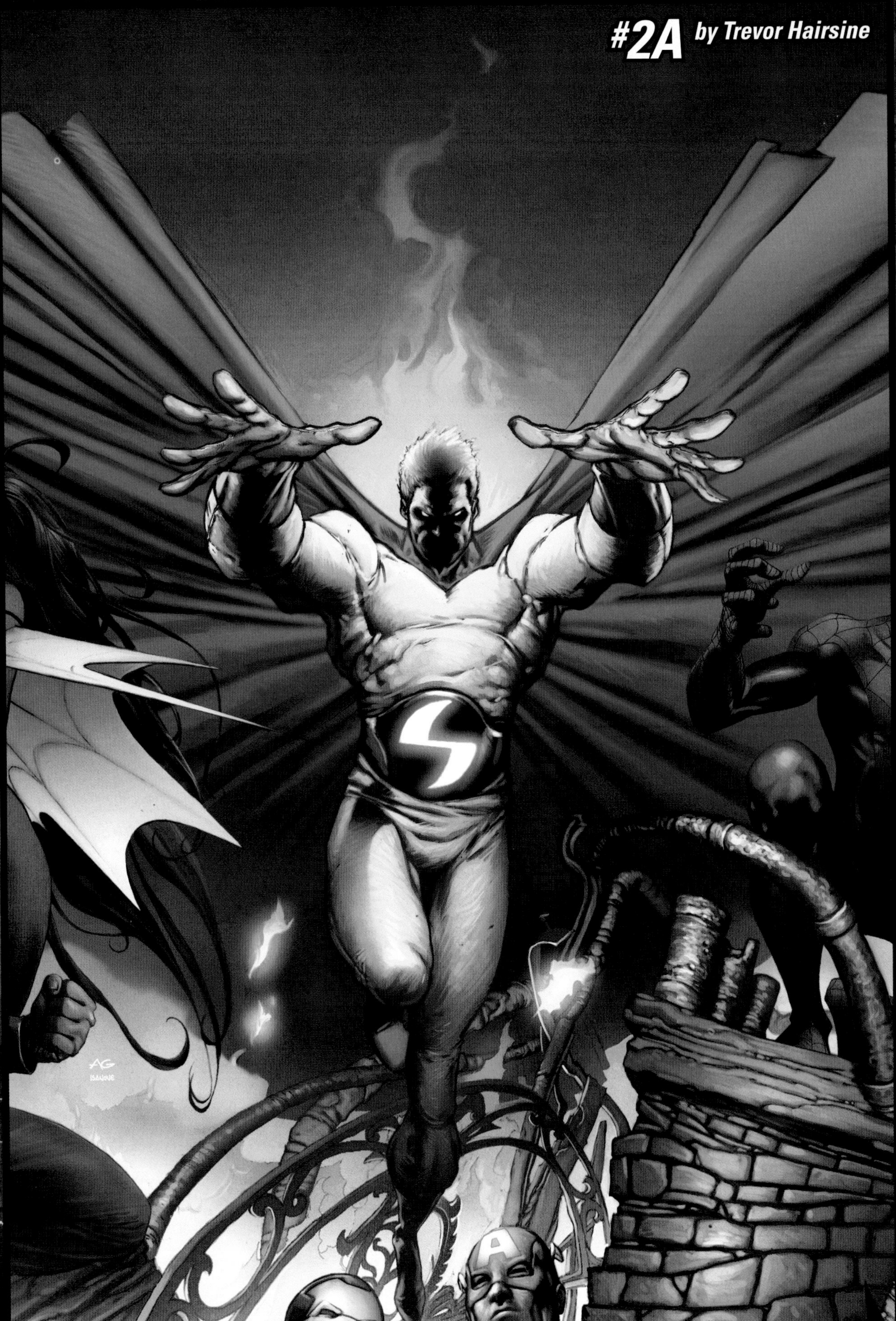

#2A by Trevor Hairsine

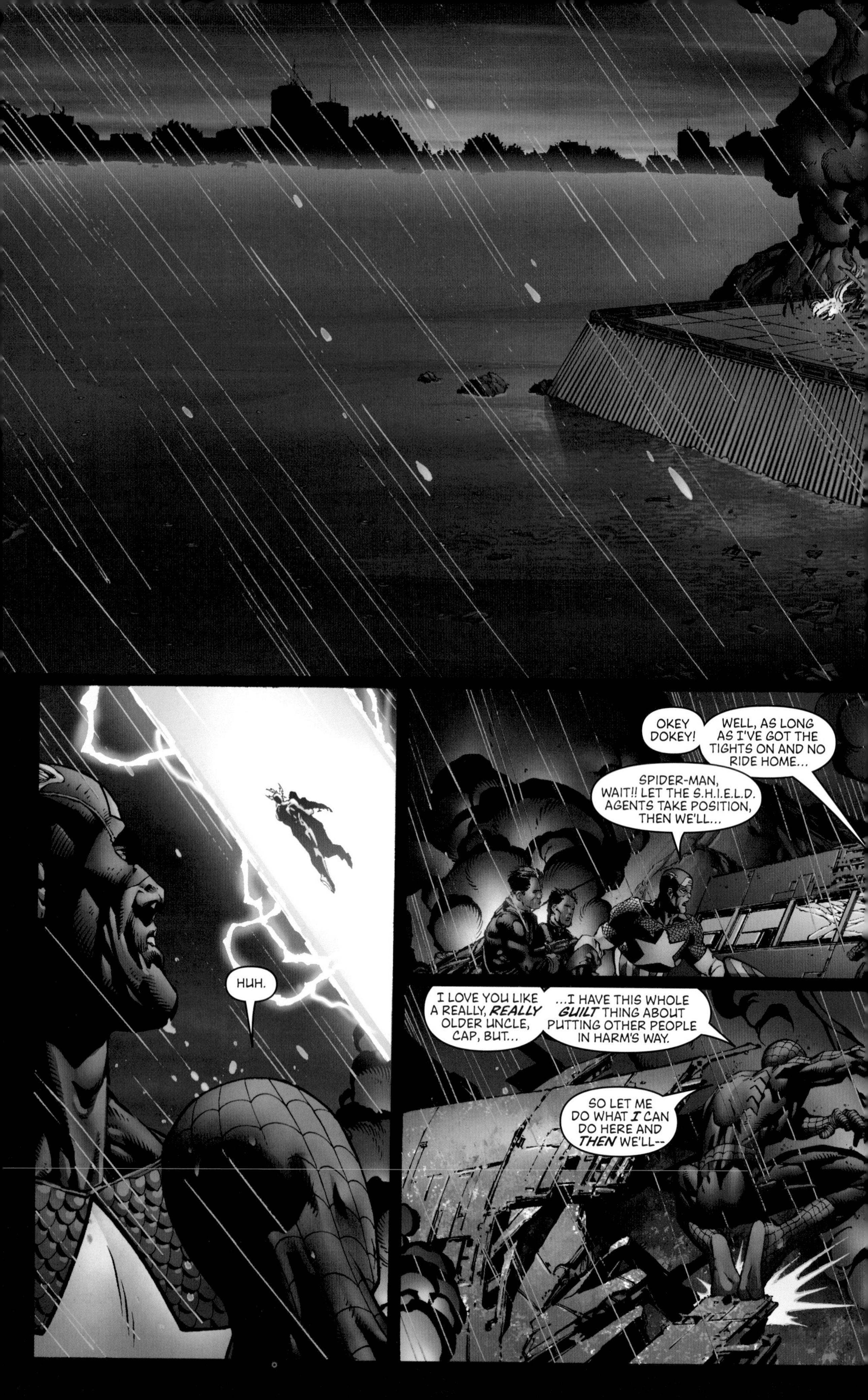
HUH.
OKEY DOKEY!
WELL, AS LONG AS I'VE GOT THE TIGHTS ON AND NO RIDE HOME...
SPIDER-MAN, WAIT!! LET THE S.H.I.E.L.D. AGENTS TAKE POSITION, THEN WE'LL...
I LOVE YOU LIKE A REALLY, REALLY OLDER UNCLE, CAP, BUT...
...I HAVE THIS WHOLE GUILT THING ABOUT PUTTING OTHER PEOPLE IN HARM'S WAY.
SO LET ME DO WHAT I CAN DO HERE AND THEN WE'LL--

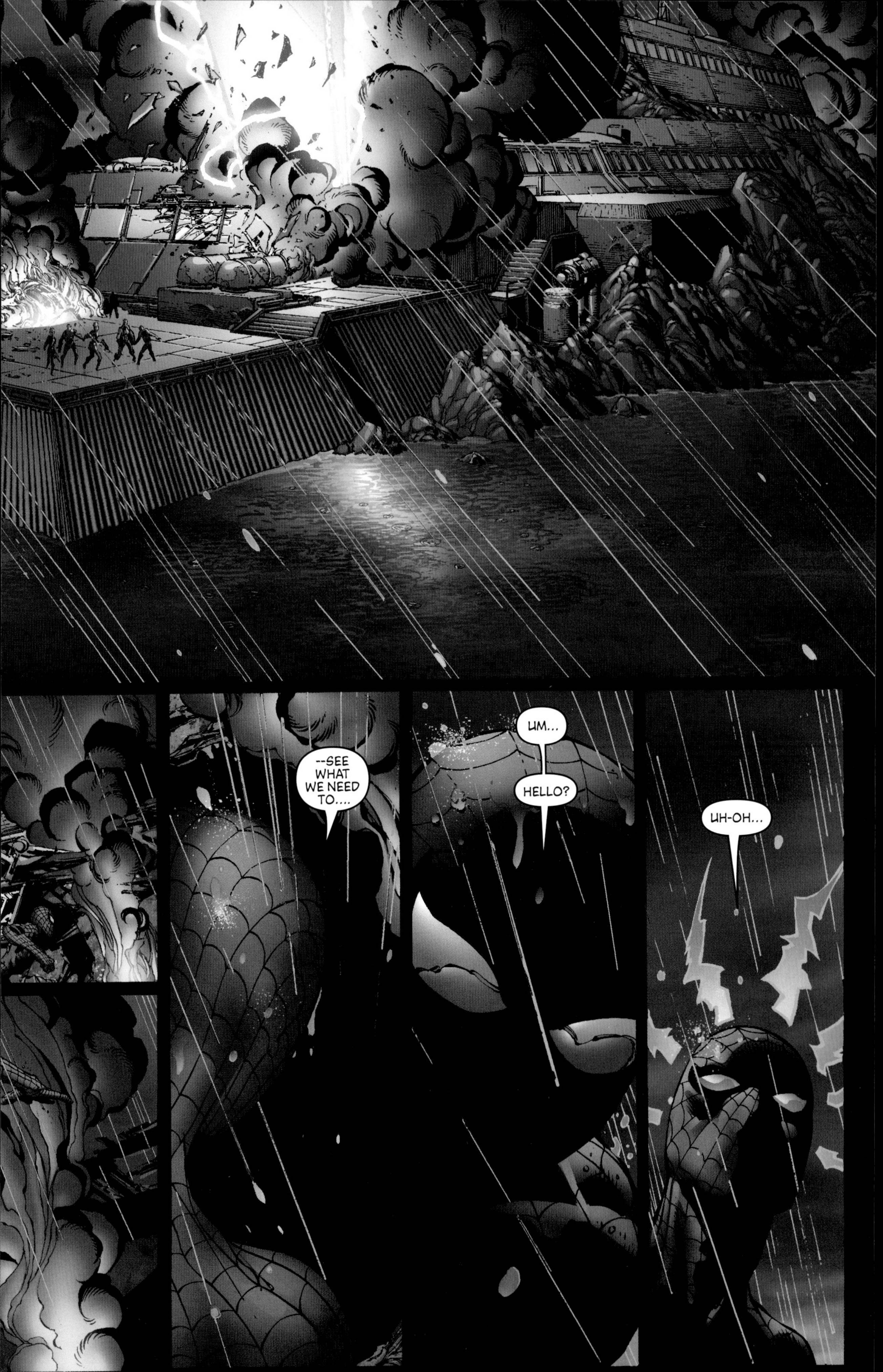
--SEE WHAT WE NEED TO....
UM...
HELLO?
UH-OH...

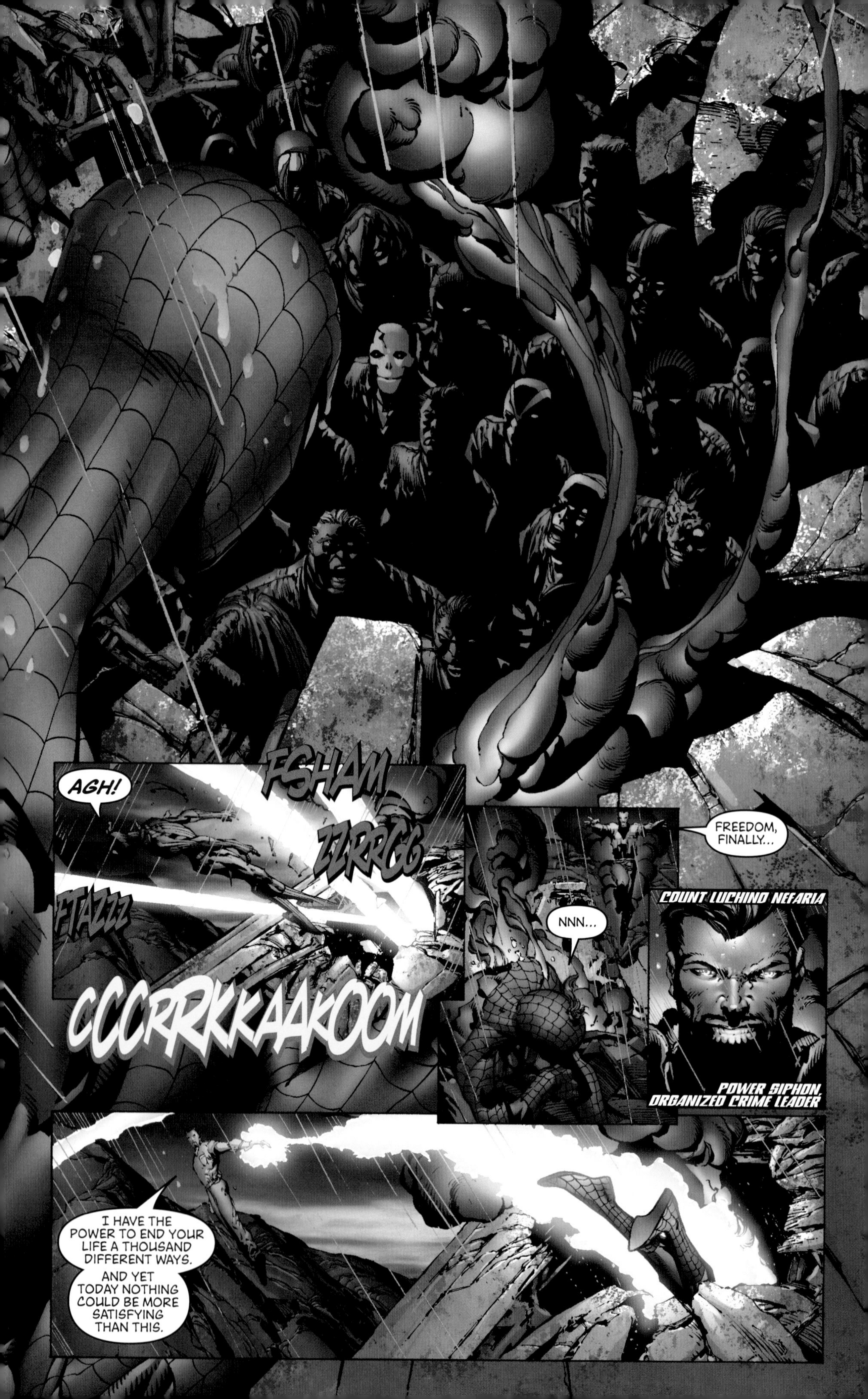

AGH!
FSHAM
ZZRRGG
FTAZZZ
CCCRRKKAAKOOM
FREEDOM, FINALLY...
NNN...
COUNT LUCHINO NEFARIA
POWER SIPHON, ORGANIZED CRIME LEADER
I HAVE THE POWER TO END YOUR LIFE A THOUSAND DIFFERENT WAYS.
AND YET TODAY NOTHING COULD BE MORE SATISFYING THAN THIS.

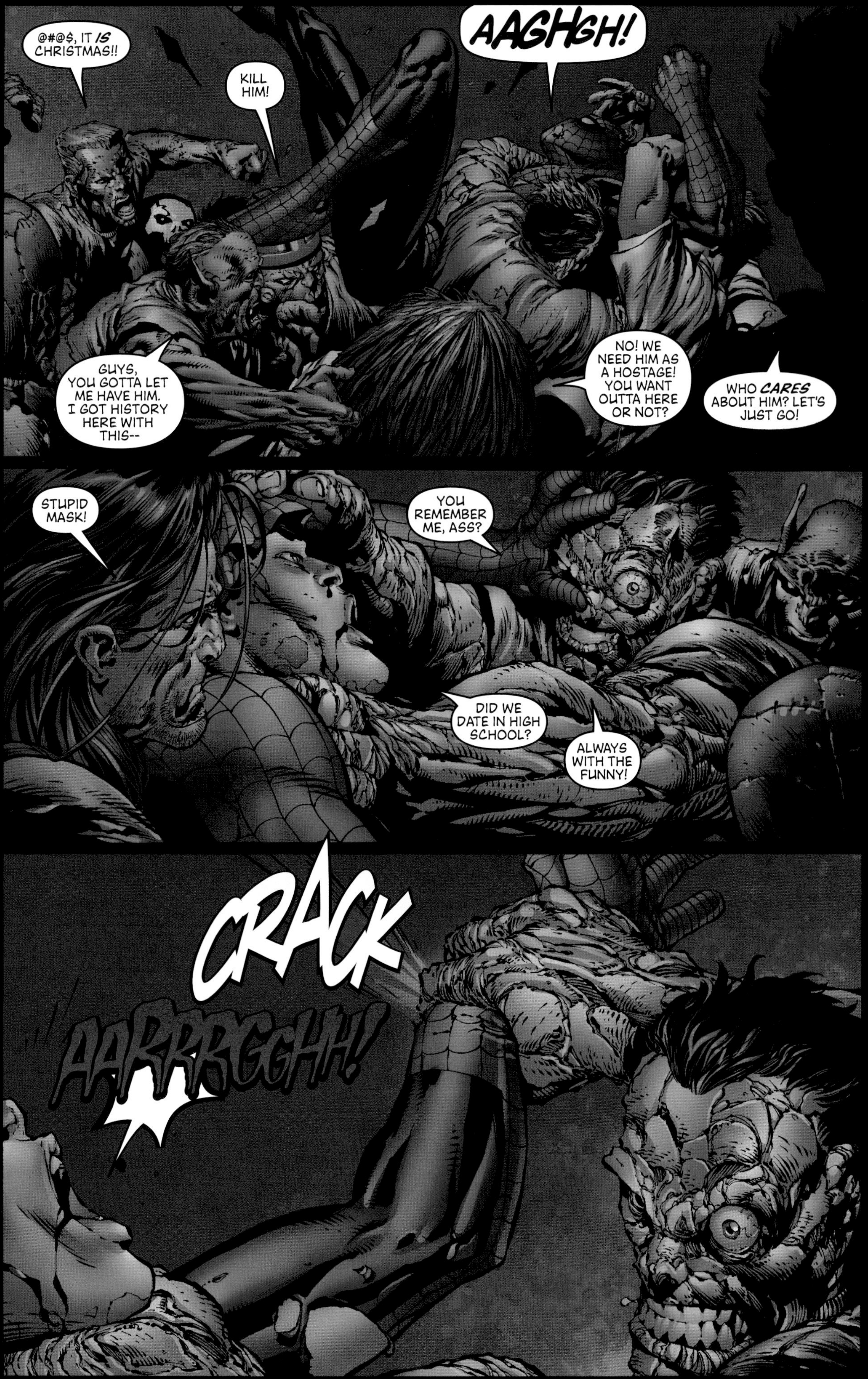
@#@$, IT IS CHRISTMAS!!
KILL HIM!
AAGHGH!
GUYS, YOU GOTTA LET ME HAVE HIM. I GOT HISTORY HERE WITH THIS--
NO! WE NEED HIM AS A HOSTAGE! YOU WANT OUTTA HERE OR NOT?
WHO CARES ABOUT HIM? LET'S JUST GO!
STUPID MASK!
YOU REMEMBER ME, ASS?
DID WE DATE IN HIGH SCHOOL?
ALWAYS WITH THE FUNNY!
CRACK
AARRRGGHH!

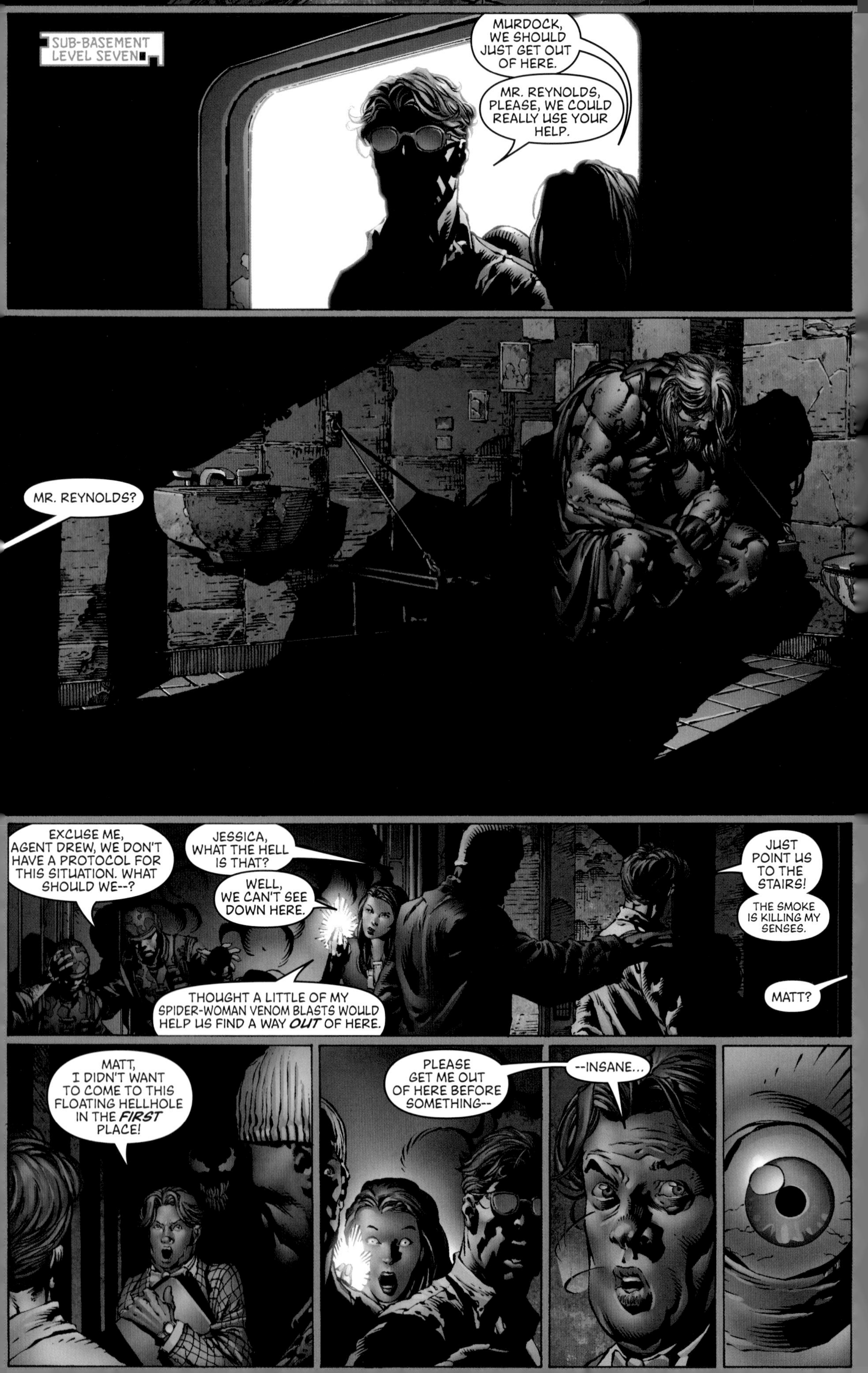
SUB-BASEMENT LEVEL SEVEN
MURDOCK, WE SHOULD JUST GET OUT OF HERE.
MR. REYNOLDS, PLEASE, WE COULD REALLY USE YOUR HELP.
MR. REYNOLDS?
EXCUSE ME, AGENT DREW, WE DON'T HAVE A PROTOCOL FOR THIS SITUATION. WHAT SHOULD WE--?
JESSICA, WHAT THE HELL IS THAT?
WELL, WE CAN'T SEE DOWN HERE.
THOUGHT A LITTLE OF MY SPIDER-WOMAN VENOM BLASTS WOULD HELP US FIND A WAY *OUT* OF HERE.
JUST POINT US TO THE STAIRS!
THE SMOKE IS KILLING MY SENSES.
MATT?
MATT, I DIDN'T WANT TO COME TO THIS FLOATING HELLHOLE IN THE *FIRST* PLACE!
PLEASE GET ME OUT OF HERE BEFORE SOMETHING--
--INSANE...

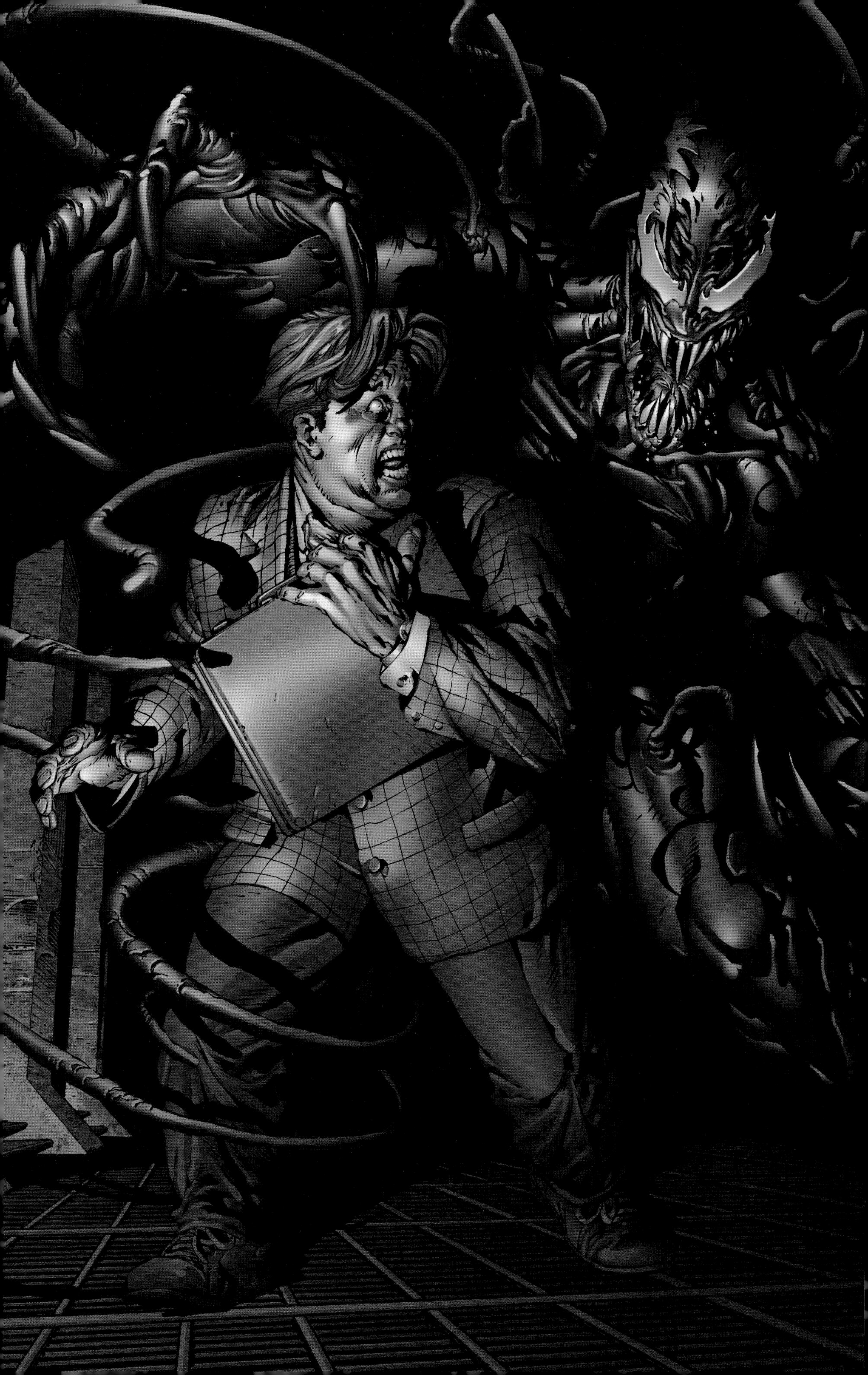

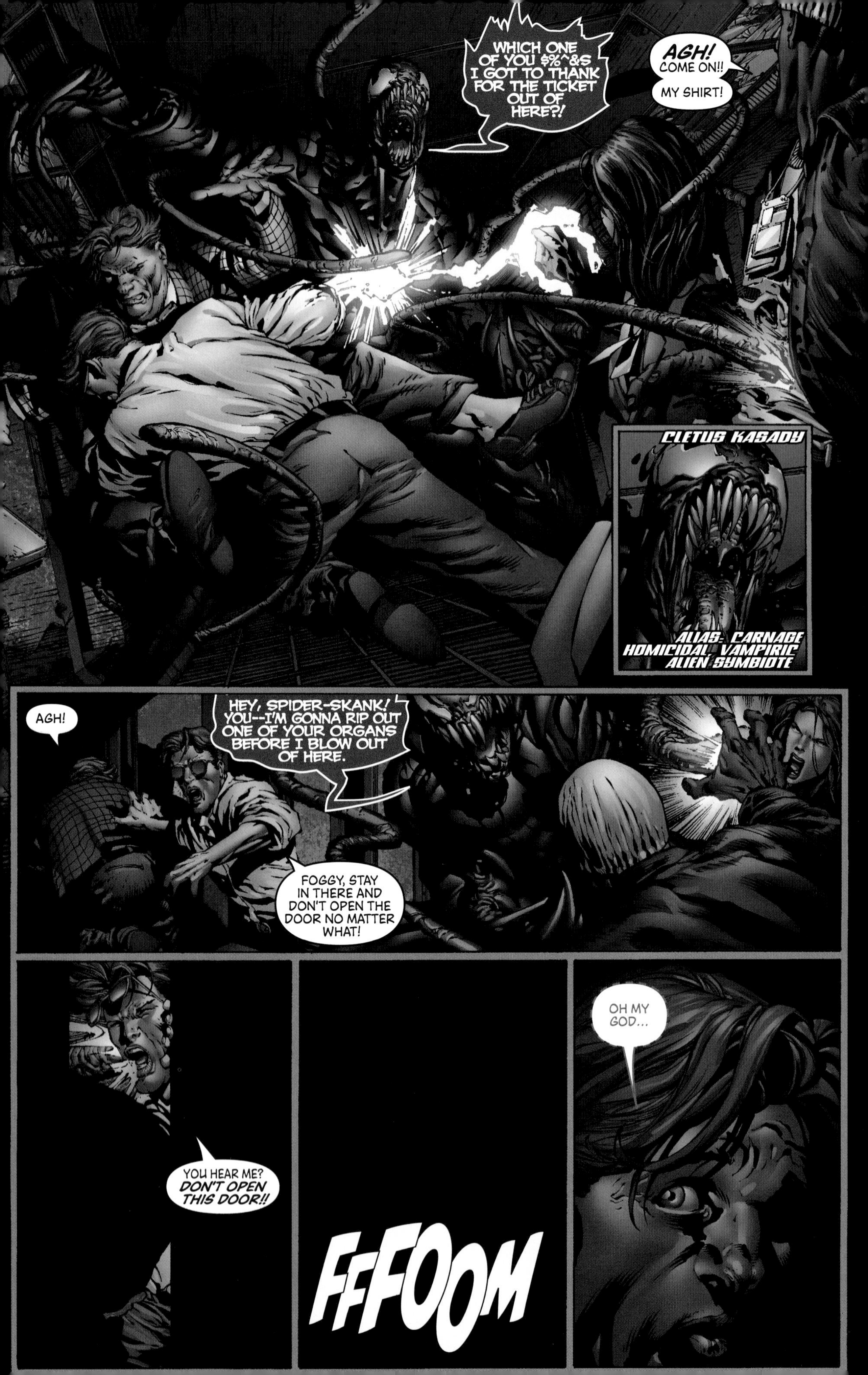
WHICH ONE OF YOU $%^&S I GOT TO THANK FOR THE TICKET OUT OF HERE?!
AGH! COME ON!!
MY SHIRT!
CLETUS KASADY
ALIAS: CARNAGE
HOMICIDAL, VAMPIRIC ALIEN SYMBIOTE
AGH!
HEY, SPIDER-SKANK! YOU--I'M GONNA RIP OUT ONE OF YOUR ORGANS BEFORE I BLOW OUT OF HERE.
FOGGY, STAY IN THERE AND DON'T OPEN THE DOOR NO MATTER WHAT!
YOU HEAR ME? DON'T OPEN THIS DOOR!!
FFFOOM
OH MY GOD...

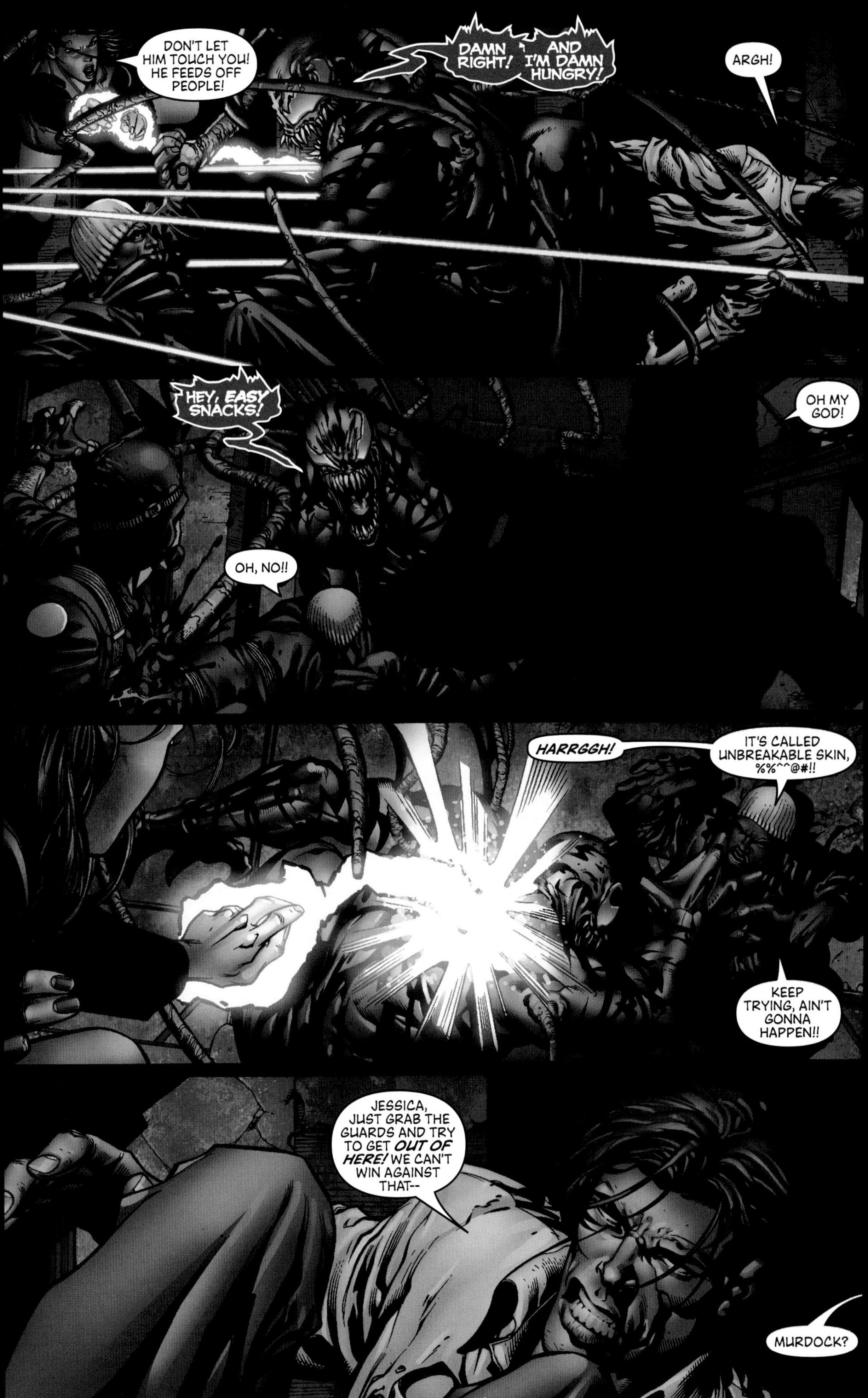
DON'T LET HIM TOUCH YOU! HE FEEDS OFF PEOPLE!
DAMN RIGHT!
AND I'M DAMN HUNGRY!
ARGH!
HEY, EASY SNACKS!
OH MY GOD!
OH, NO!!
HARRGGH!
IT'S CALLED UNBREAKABLE SKIN, %%^^@#!!
KEEP TRYING, AIN'T GONNA HAPPEN!!
JESSICA, JUST GRAB THE GUARDS AND TRY TO GET OUT OF HERE! WE CAN'T WIN AGAINST THAT--
MURDOCK?

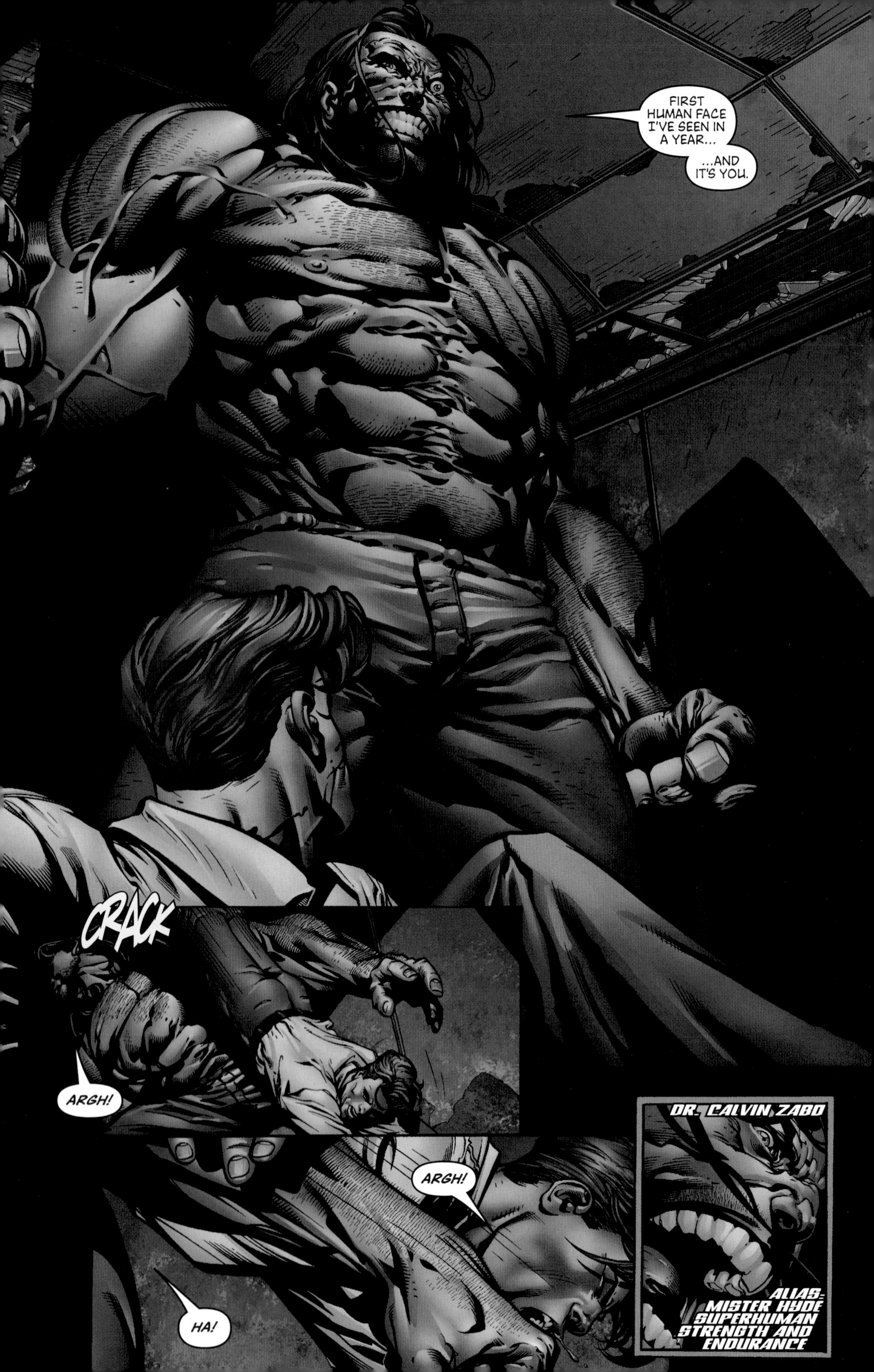
FIRST HUMAN FACE I'VE SEEN IN A YEAR...
...AND IT'S YOU.
CRACK
ARGH!
DR. CALVIN ZABO
ARGH!
HA!
ALIAS: MISTER HYDE
SUPERHUMAN STRENGTH AND ENDURANCE

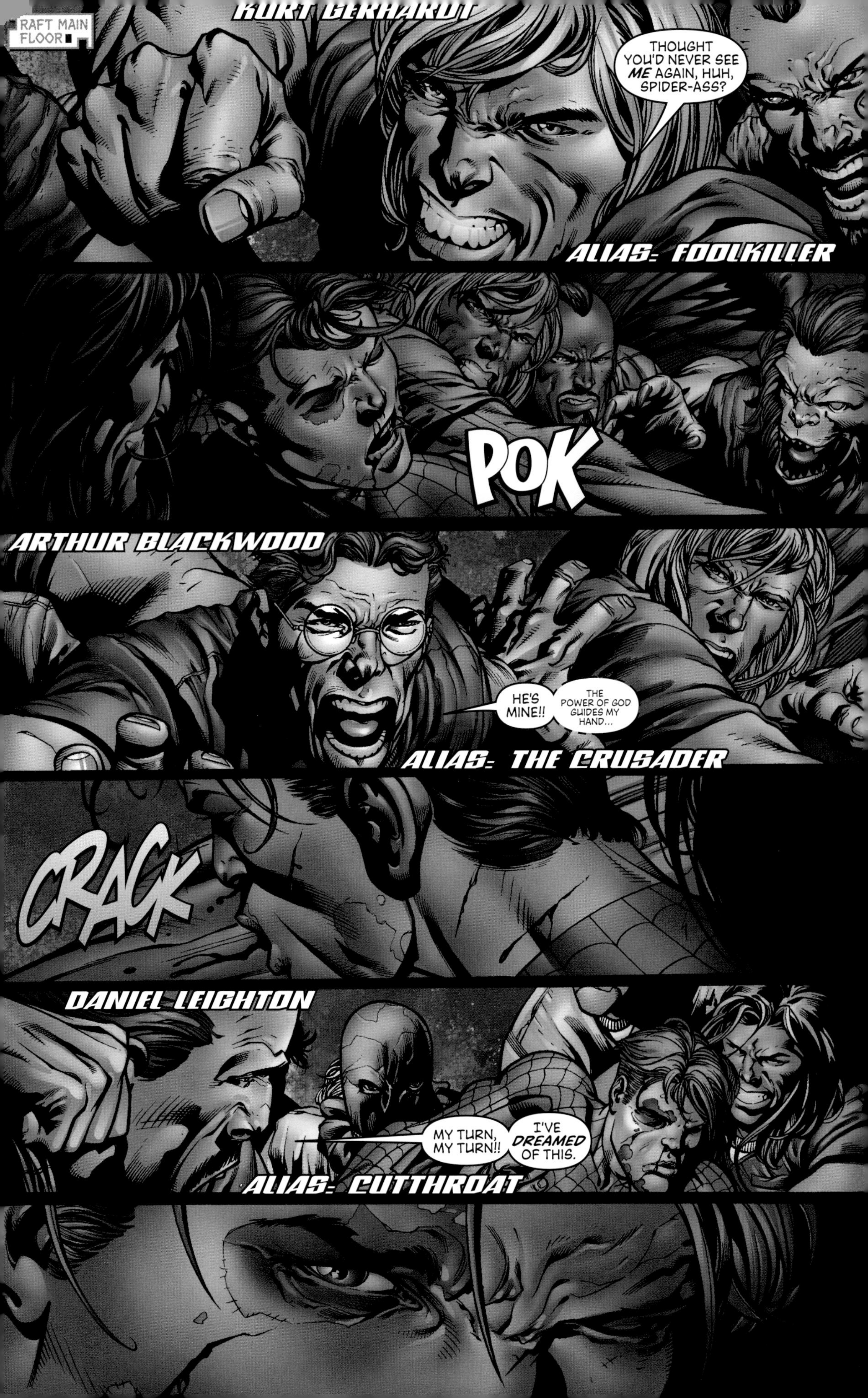
KURT GERHARDT
RAFT MAIN FLOOR
THOUGHT YOU'D NEVER SEE *ME* AGAIN, HUH, SPIDER-ASS?
ALIAS: FOOLKILLER
POK
ARTHUR BLACKWOOD
HE'S MINE!!
THE POWER OF GOD GUIDES MY HAND...
ALIAS: THE CRUSADER
CRACK
DANIEL LEIGHTON
MY TURN, MY TURN!!
I'VE *DREAMED* OF THIS.
ALIAS: CUTTHROAT

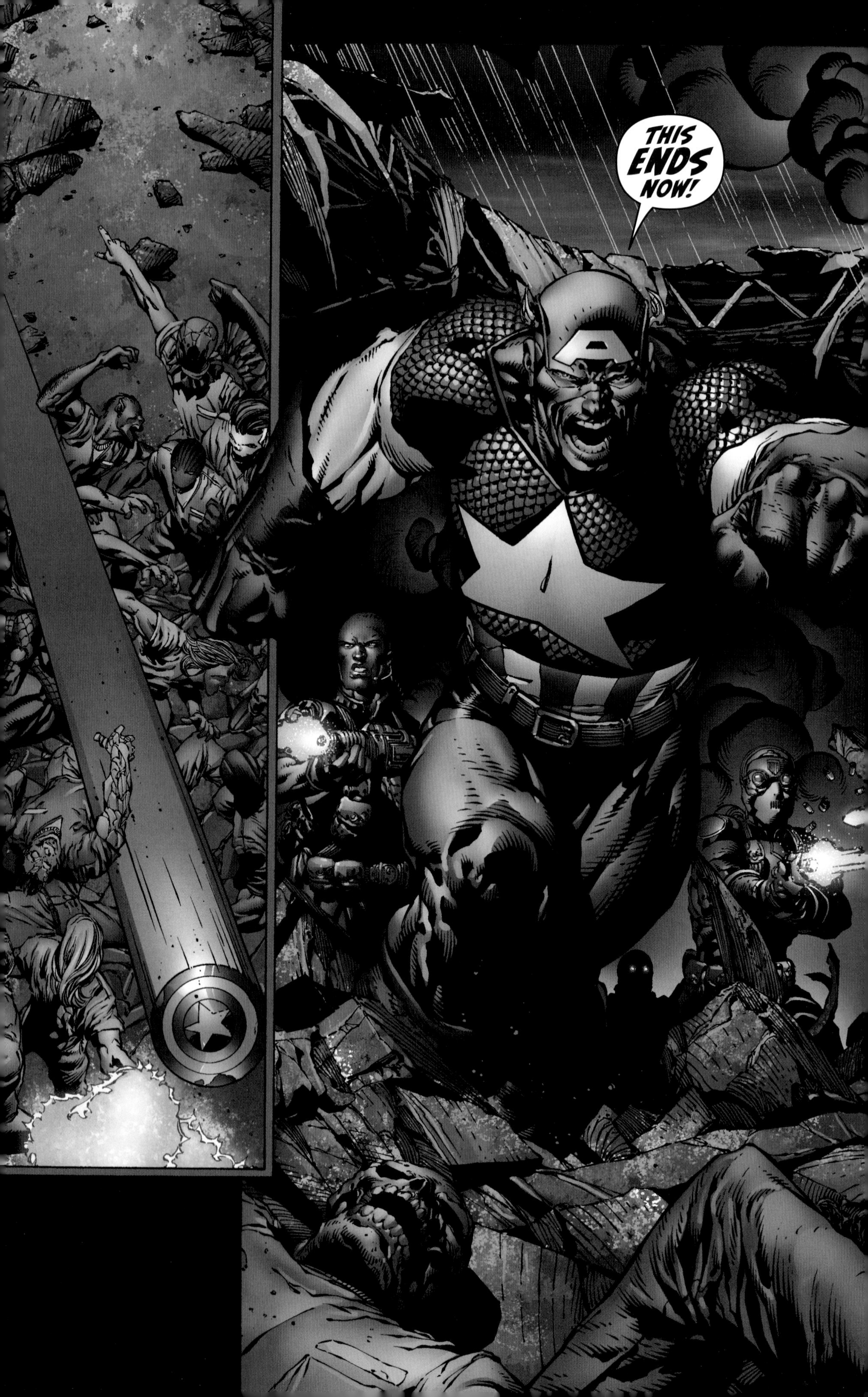
THIS ENDS NOW!

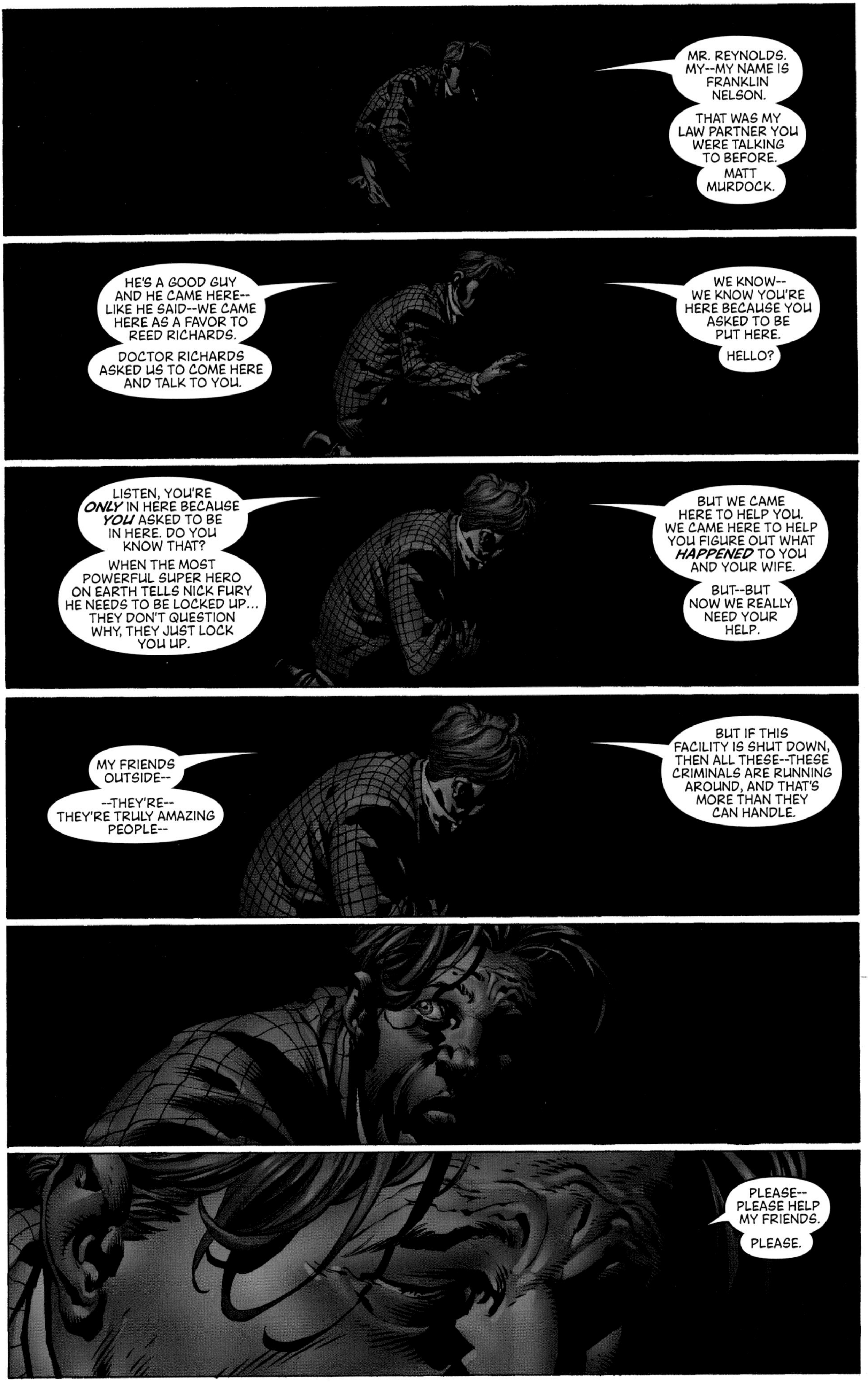
MR. REYNOLDS. MY--MY NAME IS FRANKLIN NELSON.
THAT WAS MY LAW PARTNER YOU WERE TALKING TO BEFORE. MATT MURDOCK.
HE'S A GOOD GUY AND HE CAME HERE-- LIKE HE SAID--WE CAME HERE AS A FAVOR TO REED RICHARDS.
DOCTOR RICHARDS ASKED US TO COME HERE AND TALK TO YOU.
WE KNOW-- WE KNOW YOU'RE HERE BECAUSE YOU ASKED TO BE PUT HERE.
HELLO?
LISTEN, YOU'RE *ONLY* IN HERE BECAUSE *YOU* ASKED TO BE IN HERE. DO YOU KNOW THAT?
WHEN THE MOST POWERFUL SUPER HERO ON EARTH TELLS NICK FURY HE NEEDS TO BE LOCKED UP... THEY DON'T QUESTION WHY, THEY JUST LOCK YOU UP.
BUT WE CAME HERE TO HELP YOU. WE CAME HERE TO HELP YOU FIGURE OUT WHAT *HAPPENED* TO YOU AND YOUR WIFE.
BUT--BUT NOW WE REALLY NEED YOUR HELP.
MY FRIENDS OUTSIDE--
--THEY'RE-- THEY'RE TRULY AMAZING PEOPLE--
BUT IF THIS FACILITY IS SHUT DOWN, THEN ALL THESE--THESE CRIMINALS ARE RUNNING AROUND, AND THAT'S MORE THAN THEY CAN HANDLE.
PLEASE-- PLEASE HELP MY FRIENDS.
PLEASE.

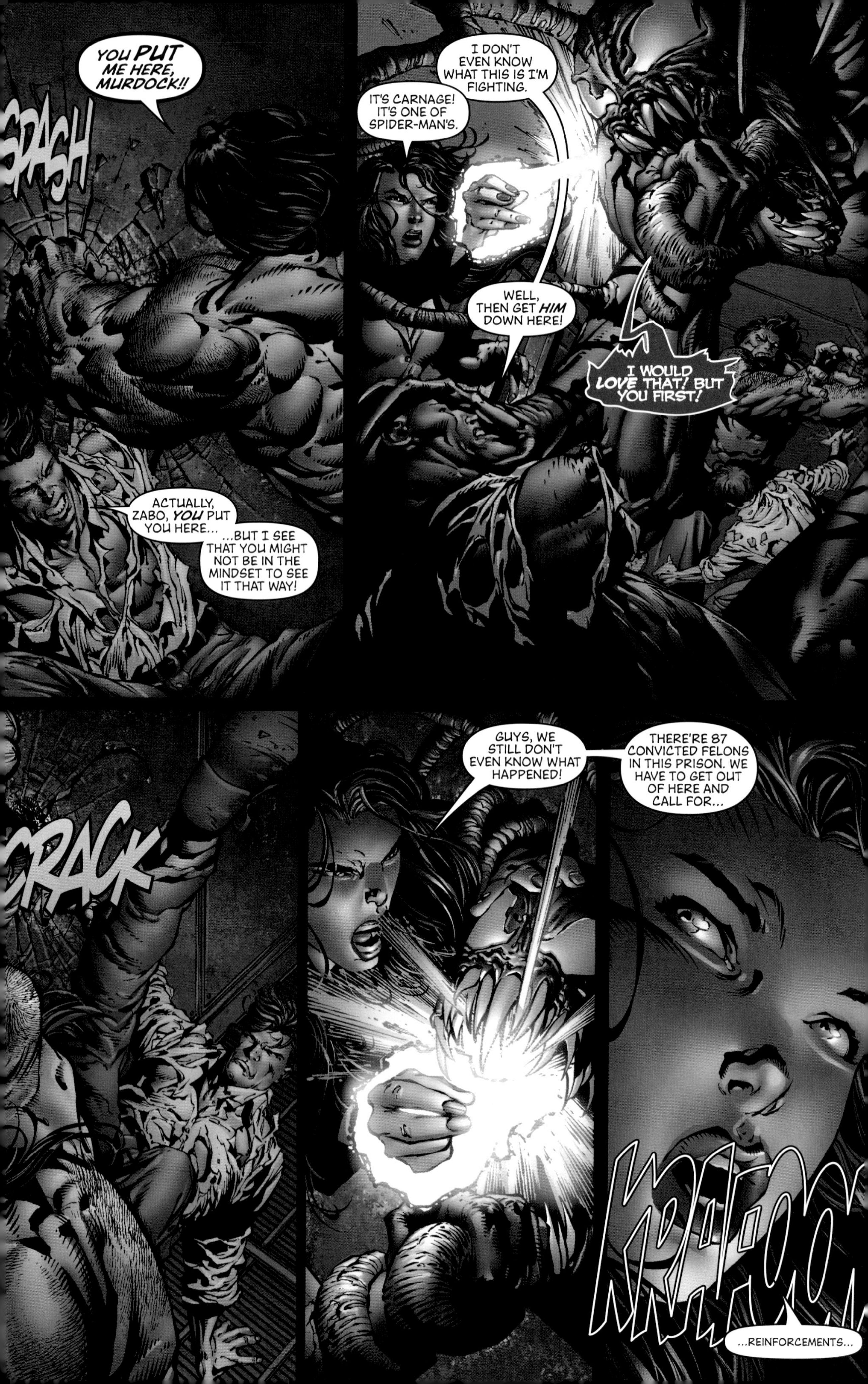
YOU PUT ME HERE, MURDOCK!!
SPASH
ACTUALLY, ZABO, YOU PUT YOU HERE...
...BUT I SEE THAT YOU MIGHT NOT BE IN THE MINDSET TO SEE IT THAT WAY!
I DON'T EVEN KNOW WHAT THIS IS I'M FIGHTING.
IT'S CARNAGE! IT'S ONE OF SPIDER-MAN'S.
WELL, THEN GET HIM DOWN HERE!
I WOULD LOVE THAT! BUT YOU FIRST!
CRACK
GUYS, WE STILL DON'T EVEN KNOW WHAT HAPPENED!
THERE'RE 87 CONVICTED FELONS IN THIS PRISON. WE HAVE TO GET OUT OF HERE AND CALL FOR...
...REINFORCEMENTS...

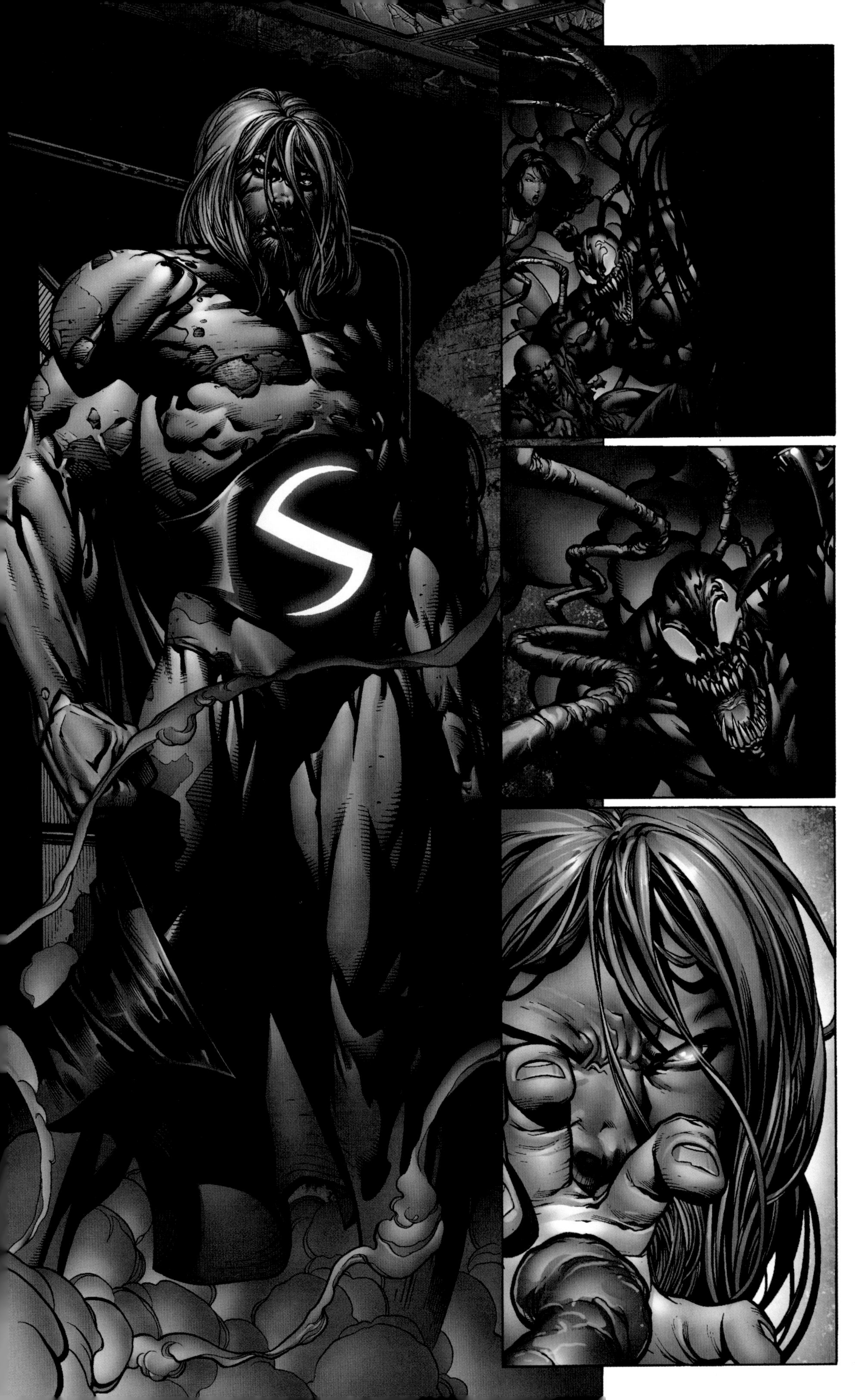

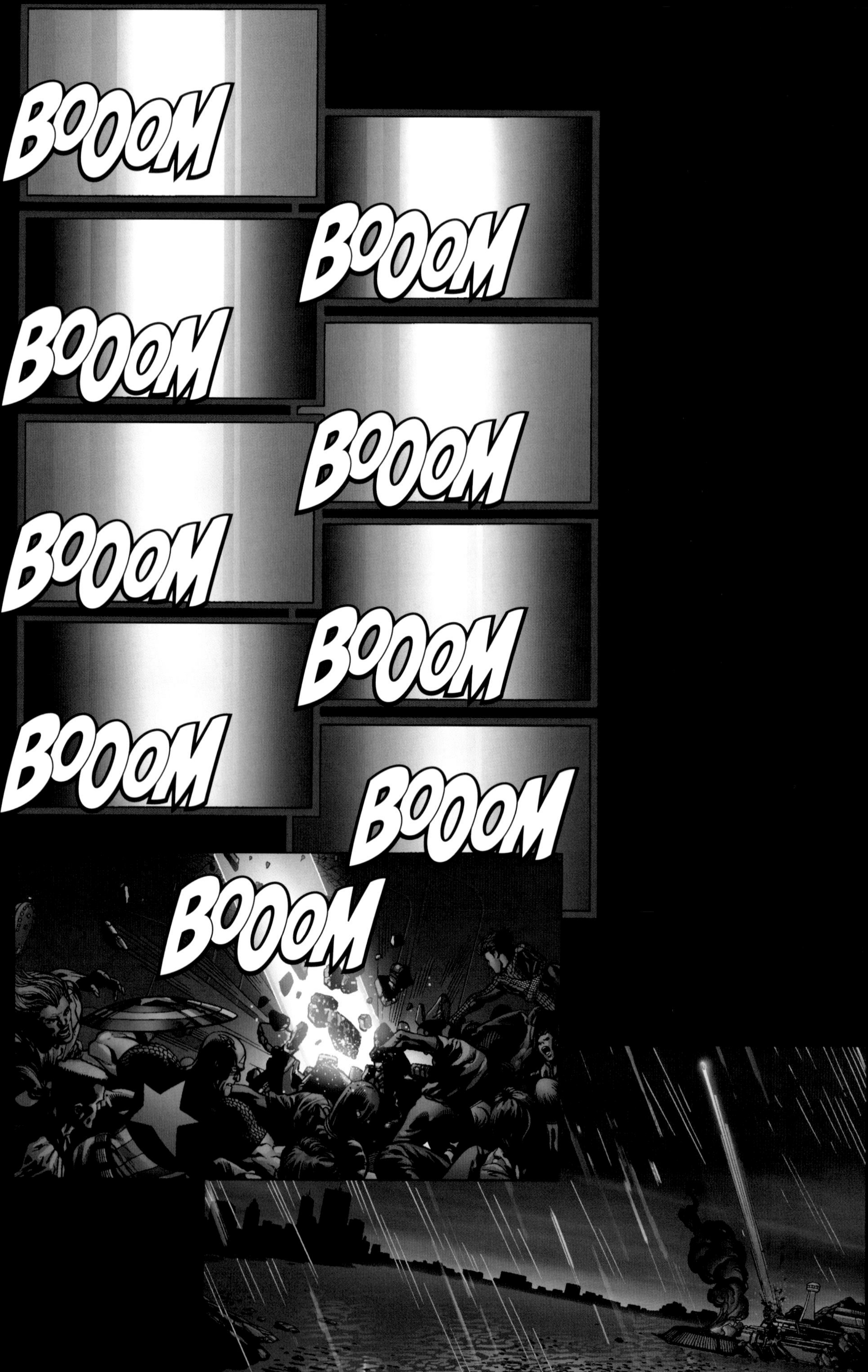

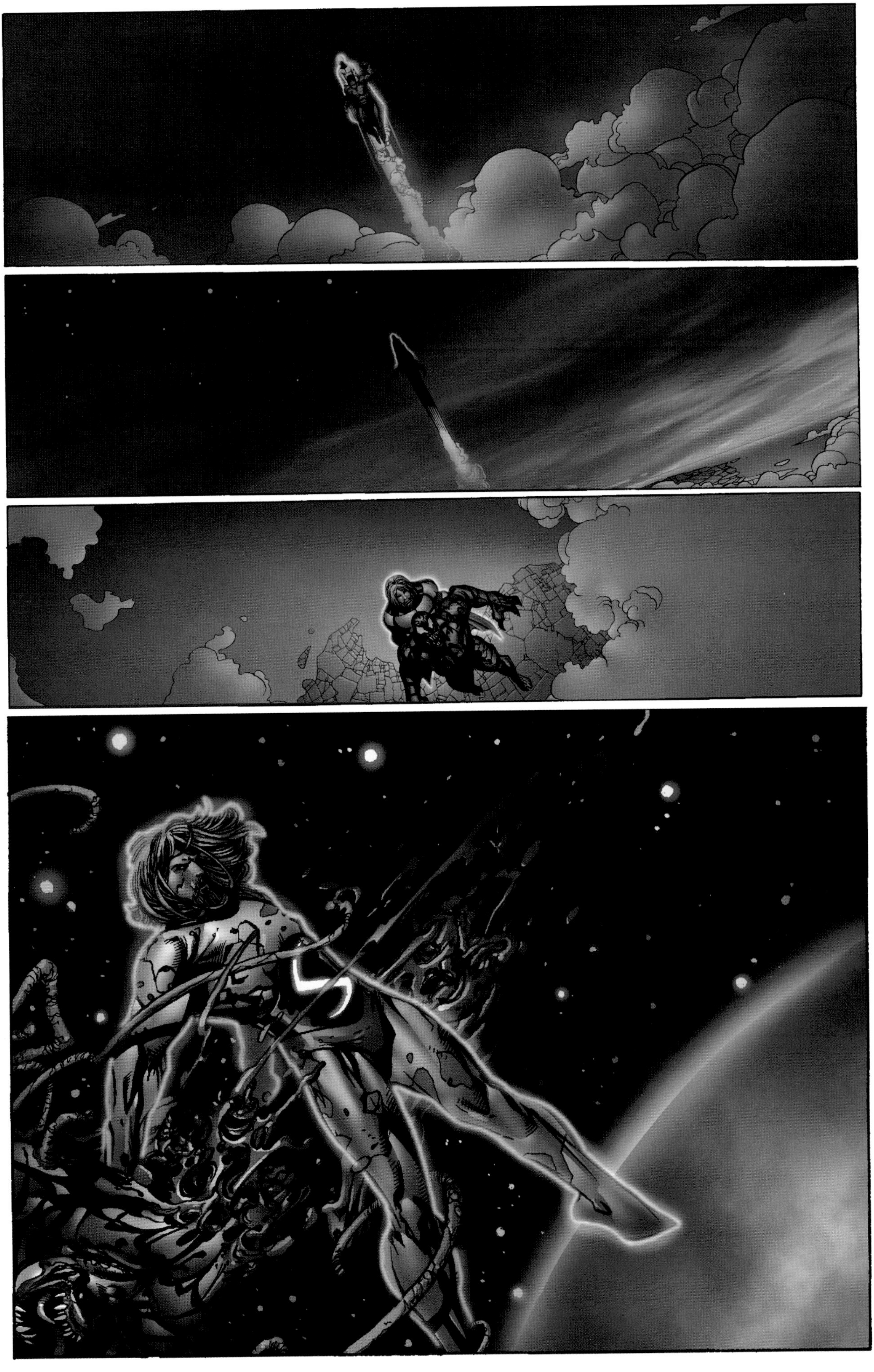

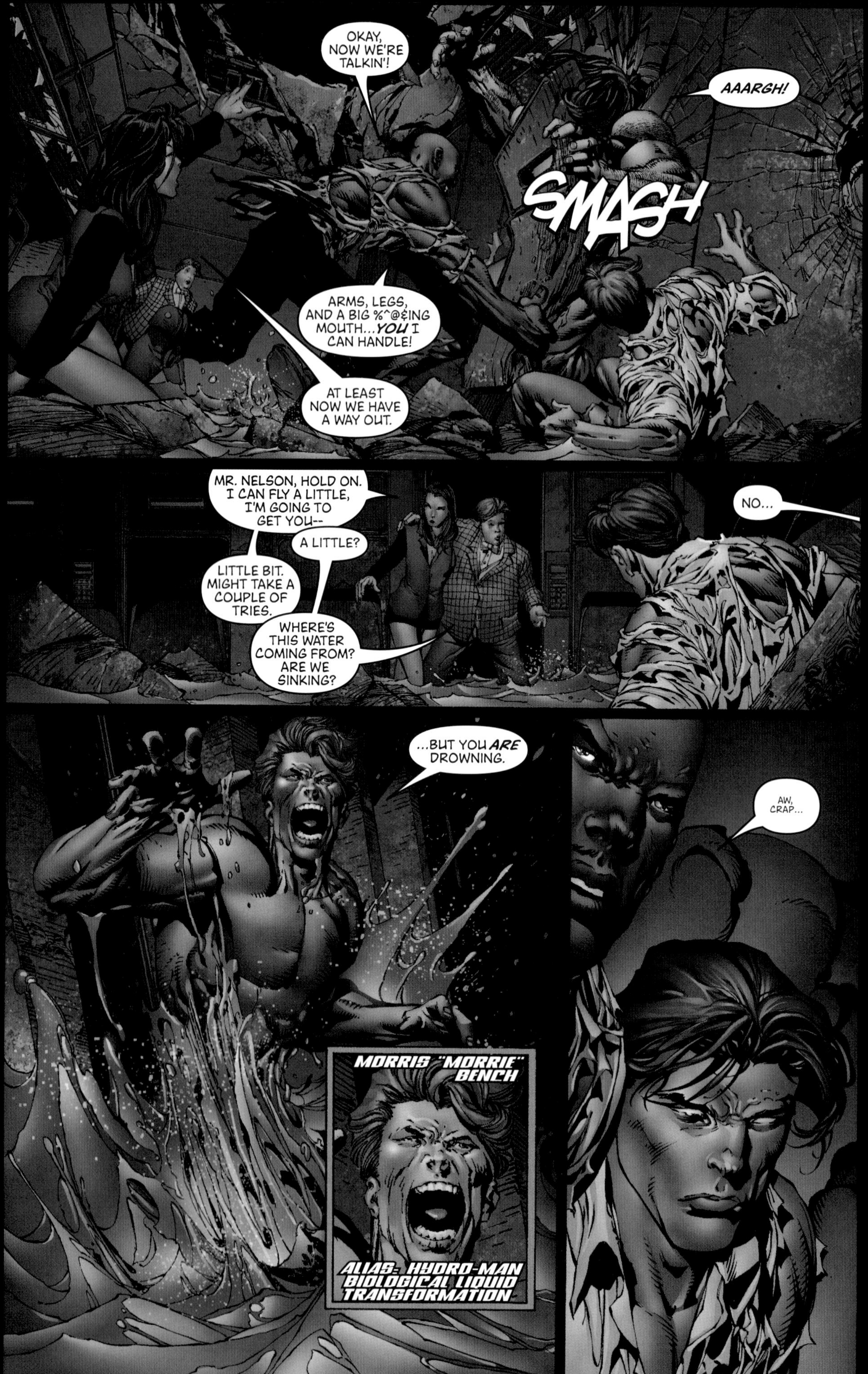
OKAY, NOW WE'RE TALKIN'!
AAARGH!
SMASH
ARMS, LEGS, AND A BIG %^@&ING MOUTH...YOU I CAN HANDLE!
AT LEAST NOW WE HAVE A WAY OUT.
MR. NELSON, HOLD ON. I CAN FLY A LITTLE, I'M GOING TO GET YOU--
A LITTLE?
LITTLE BIT. MIGHT TAKE A COUPLE OF TRIES.
WHERE'S THIS WATER COMING FROM? ARE WE SINKING?
NO...
...BUT YOU ARE DROWNING.
AW, CRAP...
MORRIS "MORRIE" BENCH
ALIAS: HYDRO-MAN
BIOLOGICAL LIQUID TRANSFORMATION

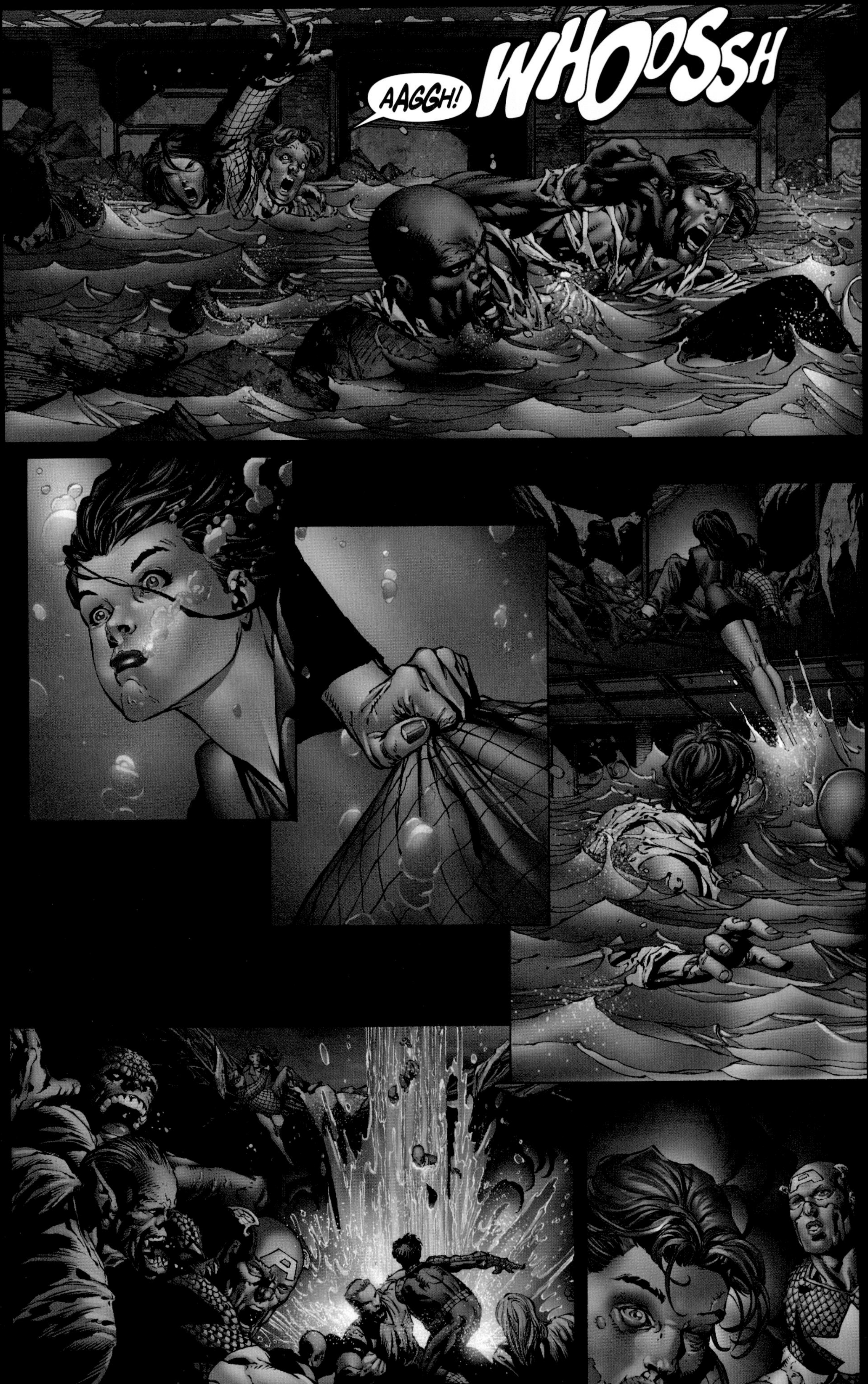
AAGGH!
WHOOSSH

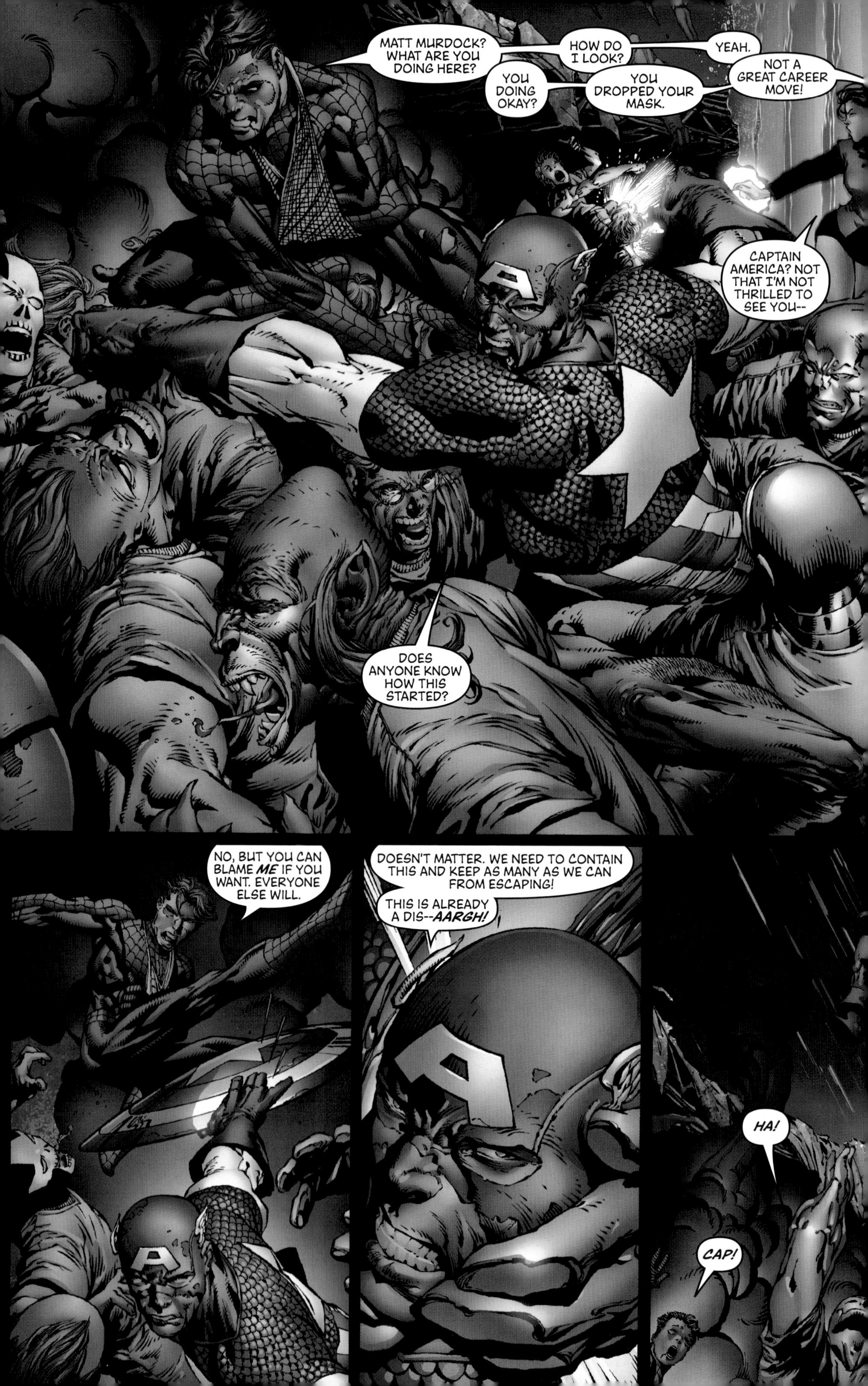
MATT MURDOCK? WHAT ARE YOU DOING HERE?
HOW DO I LOOK?
YEAH.
YOU DOING OKAY?
YOU DROPPED YOUR MASK.
NOT A GREAT CAREER MOVE!
CAPTAIN AMERICA? NOT THAT I'M NOT THRILLED TO SEE YOU--
DOES ANYONE KNOW HOW THIS STARTED?
NO, BUT YOU CAN BLAME *ME* IF YOU WANT. EVERYONE ELSE WILL.
DOESN'T MATTER. WE NEED TO CONTAIN THIS AND KEEP AS MANY AS WE CAN FROM ESCAPING!
THIS IS ALREADY A DIS--*AARGH!*
HA!
CAP!

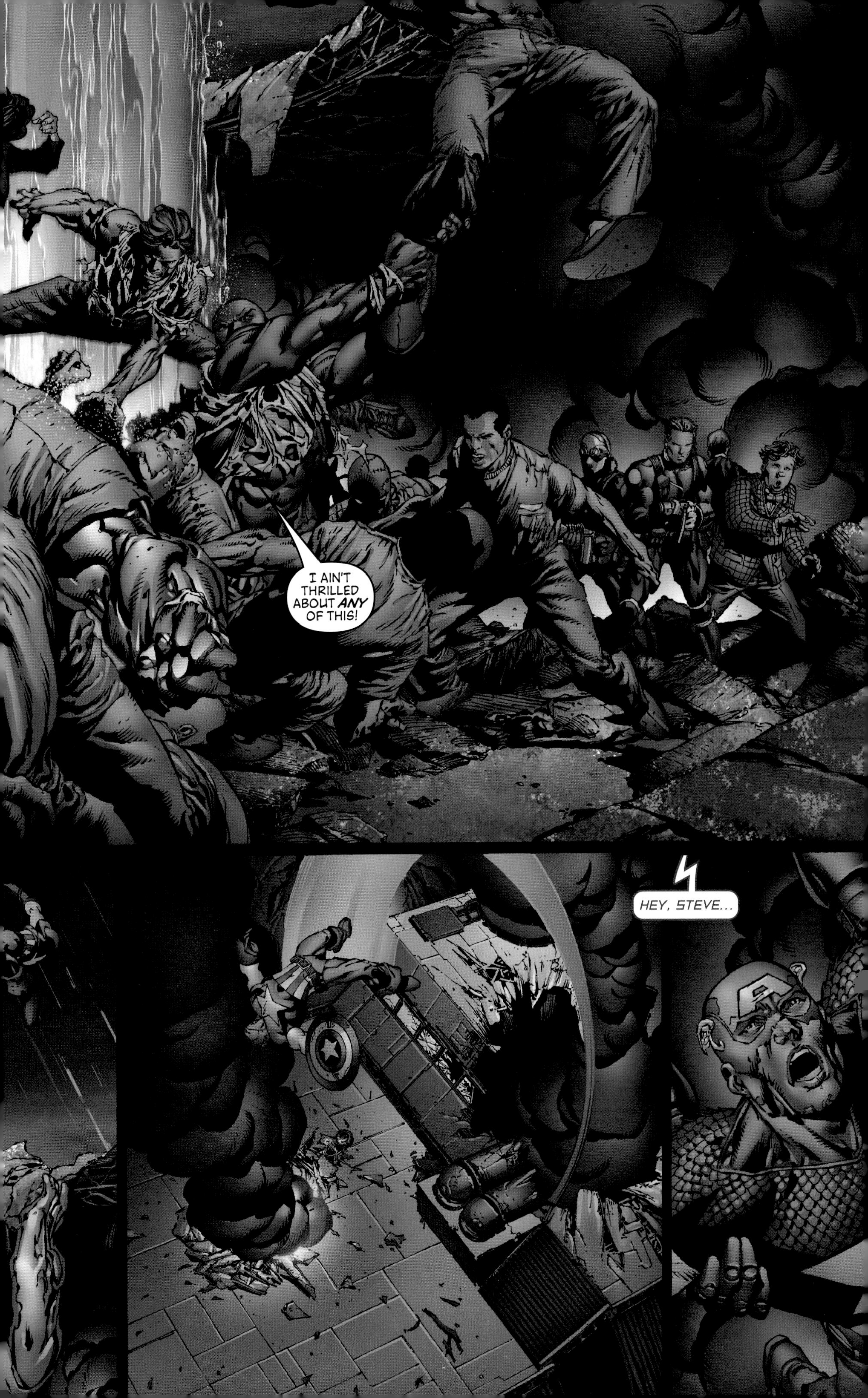
I AIN'T THRILLED ABOUT ANY OF THIS!
HEY, STEVE...

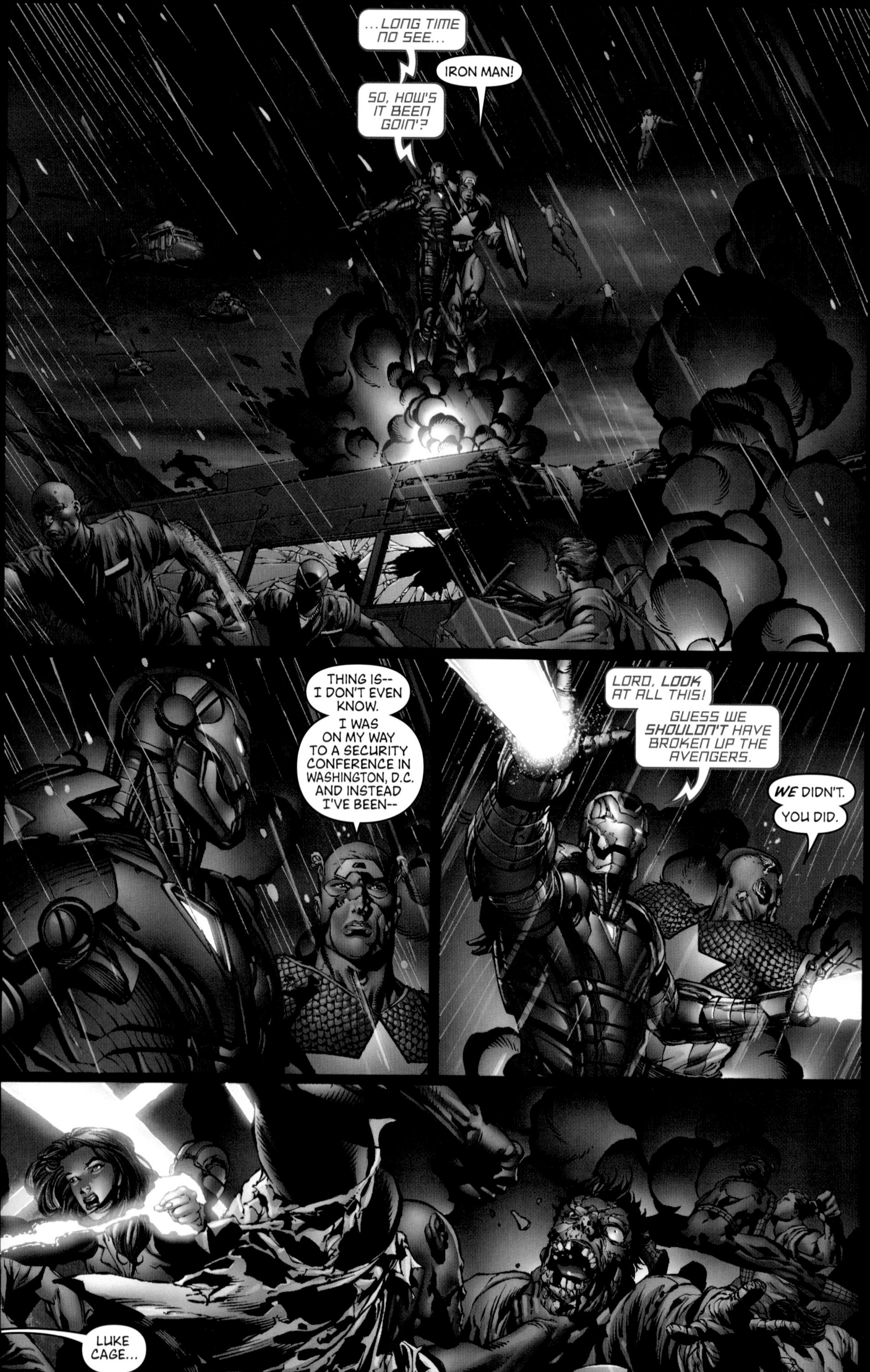
...LONG TIME NO SEE...
IRON MAN!
SO, HOW'S IT BEEN GOIN'?
THING IS-- I DON'T EVEN KNOW.
I WAS ON MY WAY TO A SECURITY CONFERENCE IN WASHINGTON, D.C. AND INSTEAD I'VE BEEN--
LORD, LOOK AT ALL THIS!
GUESS WE SHOULDN'T HAVE BROKEN UP THE AVENGERS.
WE DIDN'T.
YOU DID.
LUKE CAGE...

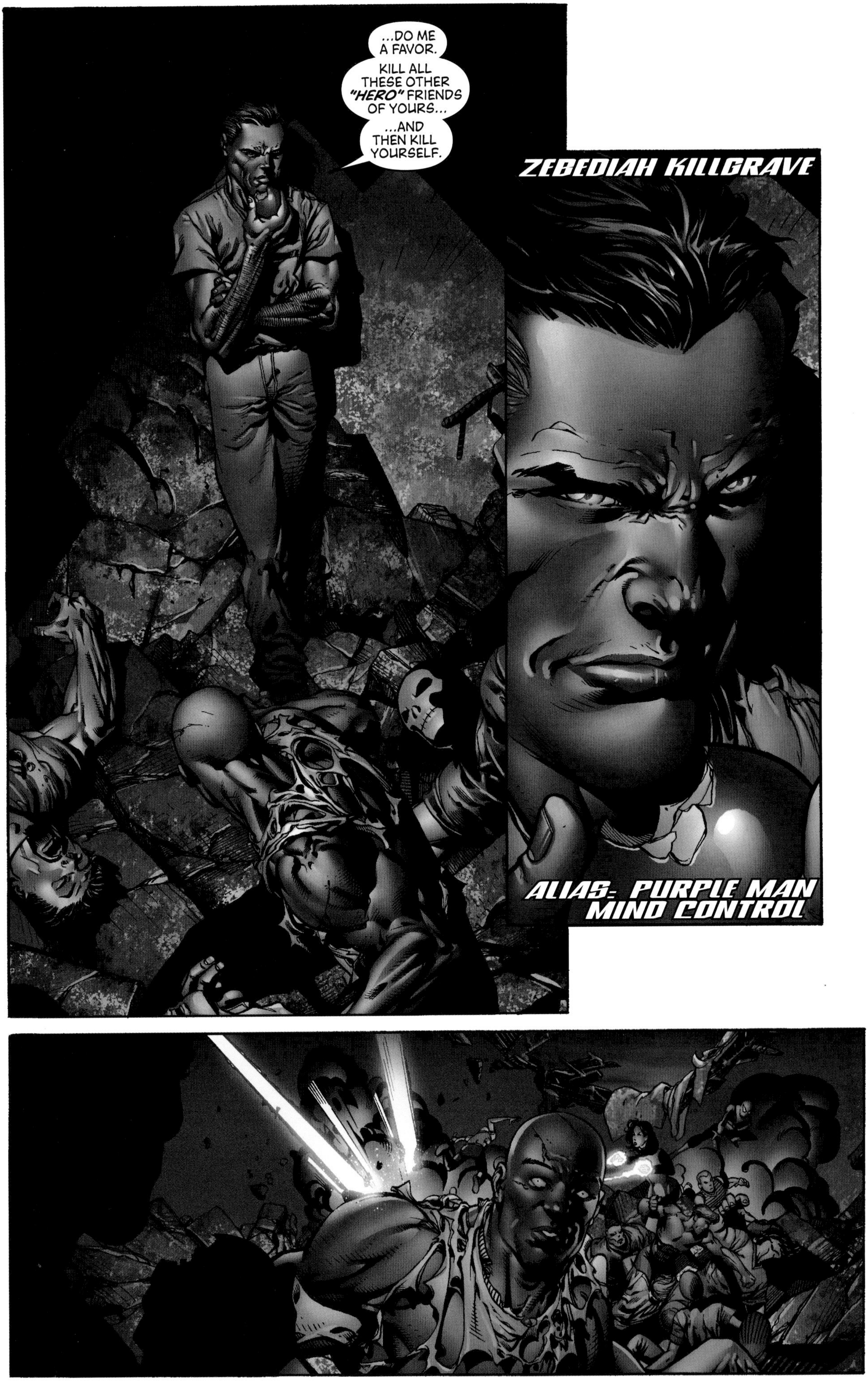
...DO ME A FAVOR.
KILL ALL THESE OTHER "HERO" FRIENDS OF YOURS...
...AND THEN KILL YOURSELF.
ZEBEDIAH KILLGRAVE
ALIAS: PURPLE MAN
MIND CONTROL

FINCH
DANNY MIKI

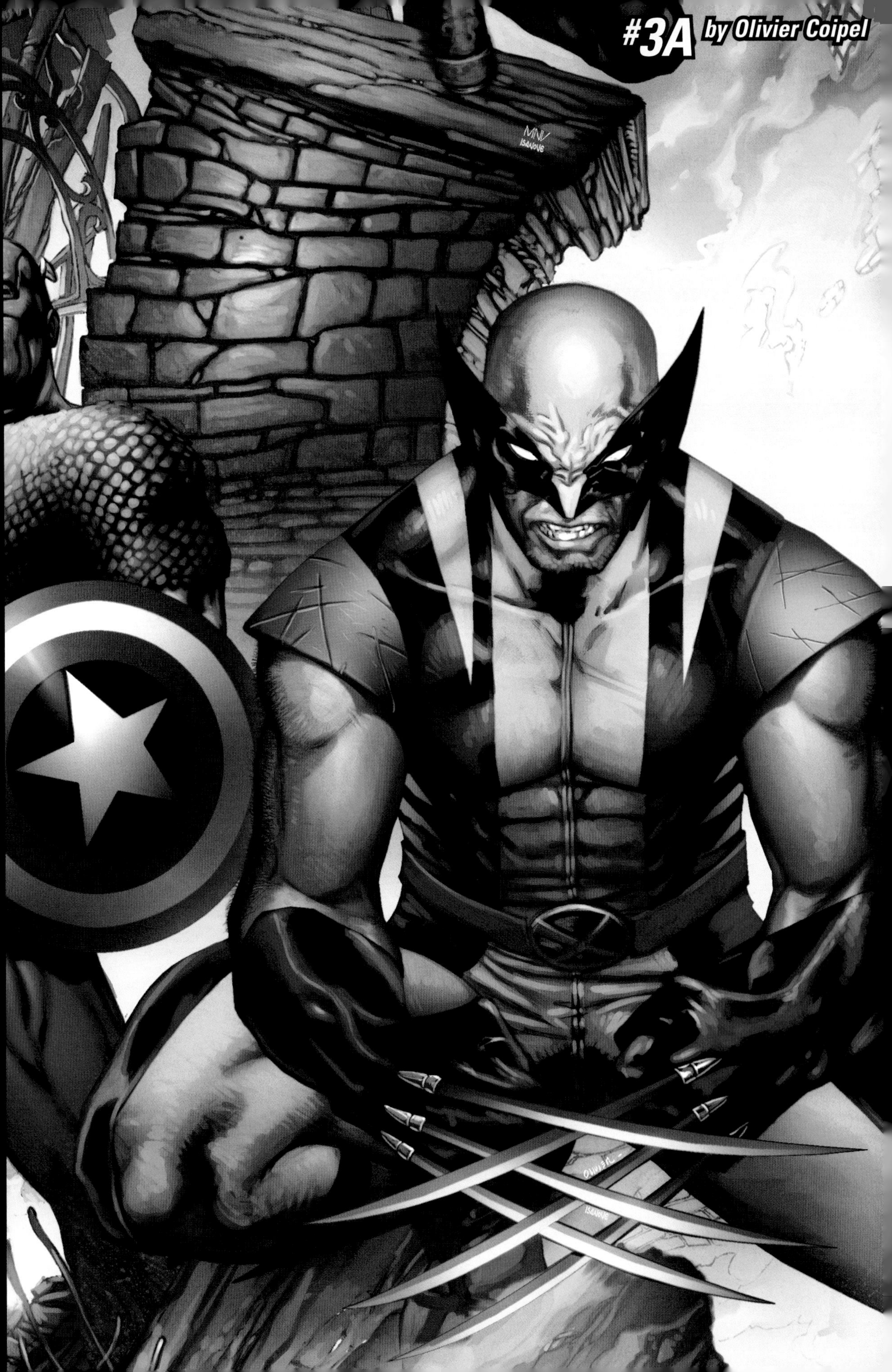
#3A by Olivier Coipel

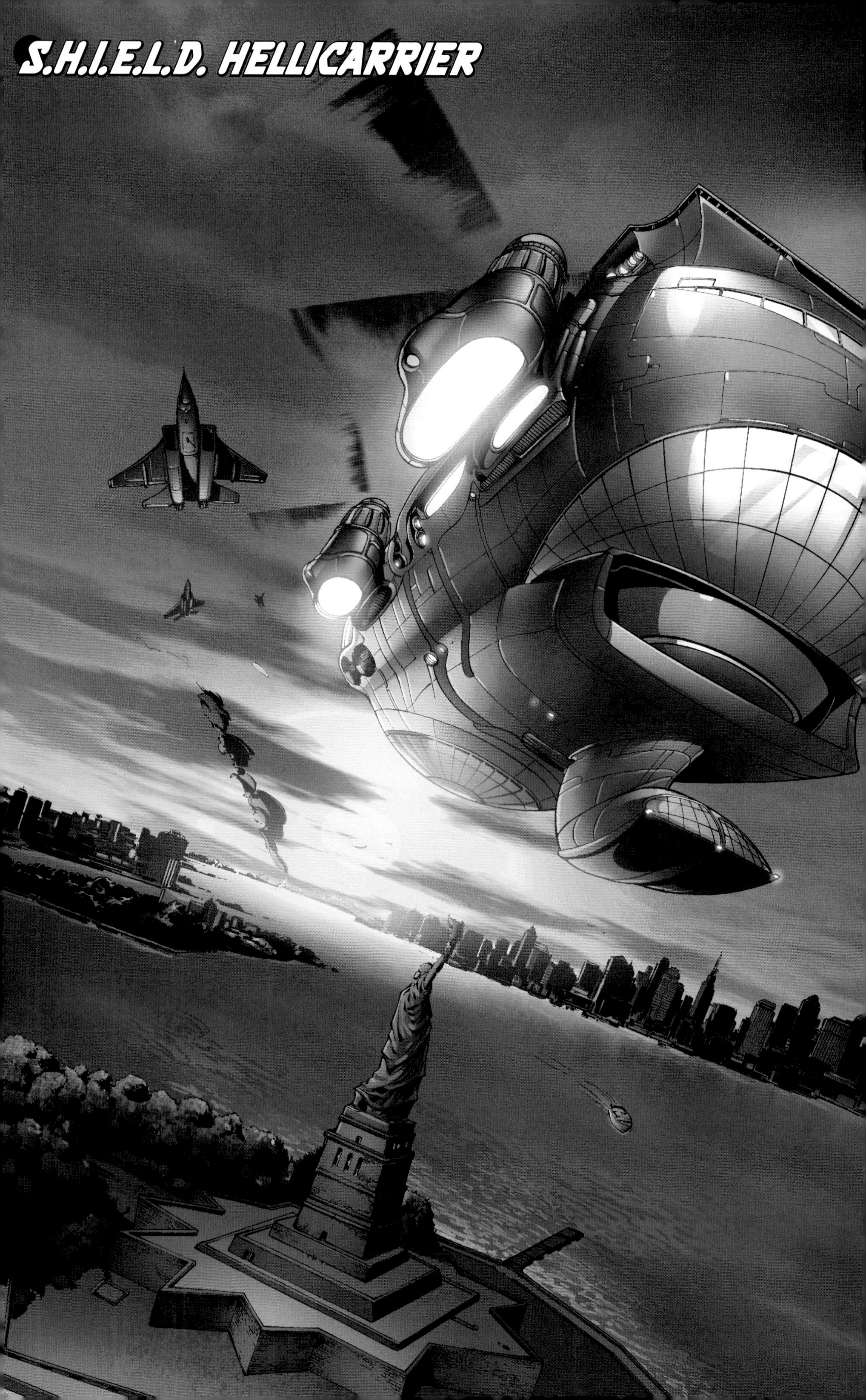
S.H.I.E.L.D. HELLICARRIER

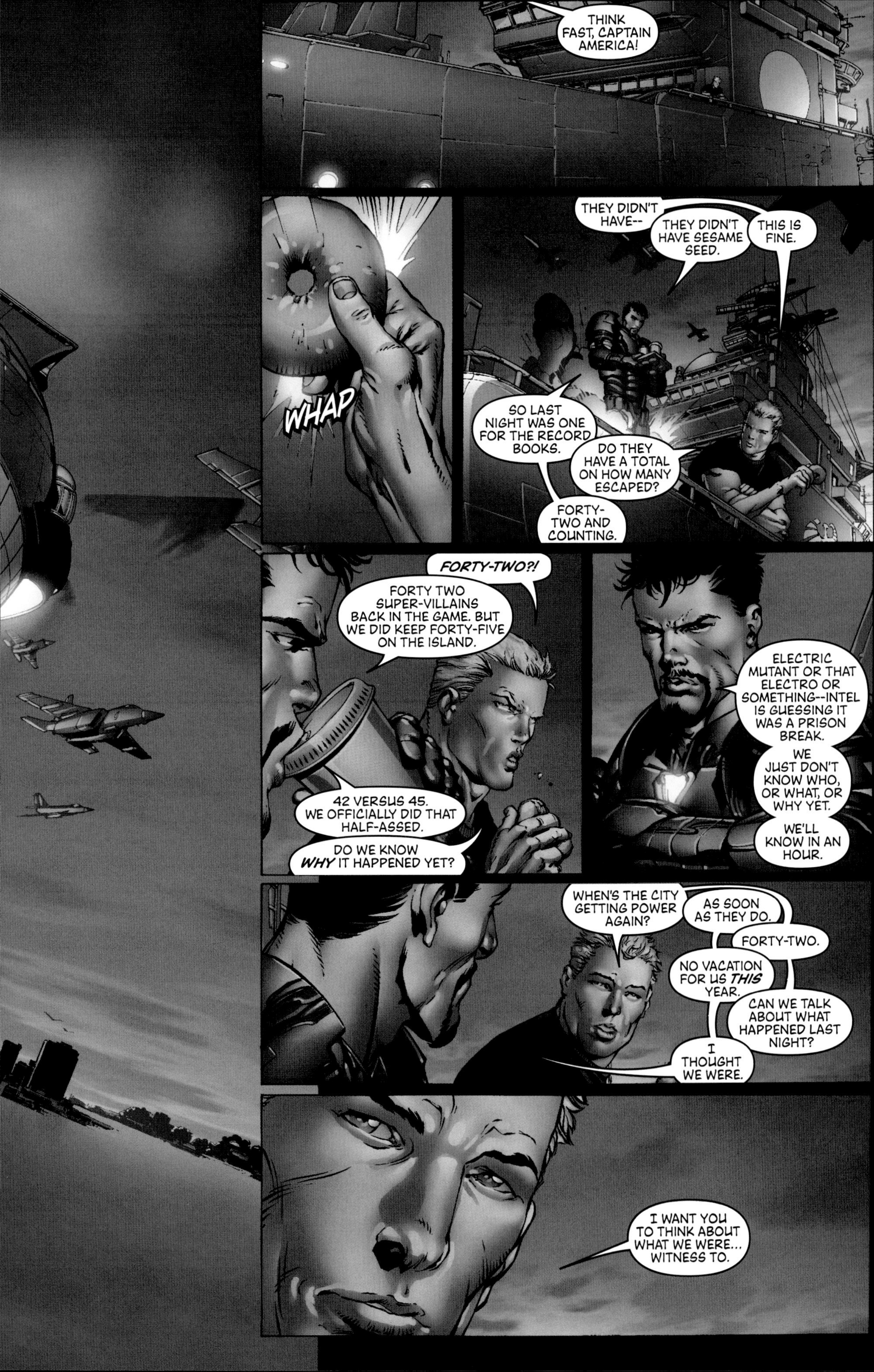

THINK FAST, CAPTAIN AMERICA!
WHAP
THEY DIDN'T HAVE--
THEY DIDN'T HAVE SESAME SEED.
THIS IS FINE.
SO LAST NIGHT WAS ONE FOR THE RECORD BOOKS.
DO THEY HAVE A TOTAL ON HOW MANY ESCAPED?
FORTY-TWO AND COUNTING.
FORTY-TWO?!
FORTY TWO SUPER-VILLAINS BACK IN THE GAME. BUT WE DID KEEP FORTY-FIVE ON THE ISLAND.
42 VERSUS 45. WE OFFICIALLY DID THAT HALF-ASSED.
DO WE KNOW WHY IT HAPPENED YET?
ELECTRIC MUTANT OR THAT ELECTRO OR SOMETHING--INTEL IS GUESSING IT WAS A PRISON BREAK.
WE JUST DON'T KNOW WHO, OR WHAT, OR WHY YET.
WE'LL KNOW IN AN HOUR.
WHEN'S THE CITY GETTING POWER AGAIN?
AS SOON AS THEY DO.
FORTY-TWO.
NO VACATION FOR US THIS YEAR.
CAN WE TALK ABOUT WHAT HAPPENED LAST NIGHT?
I THOUGHT WE WERE.
I WANT YOU TO THINK ABOUT WHAT WE WERE... WITNESS TO.

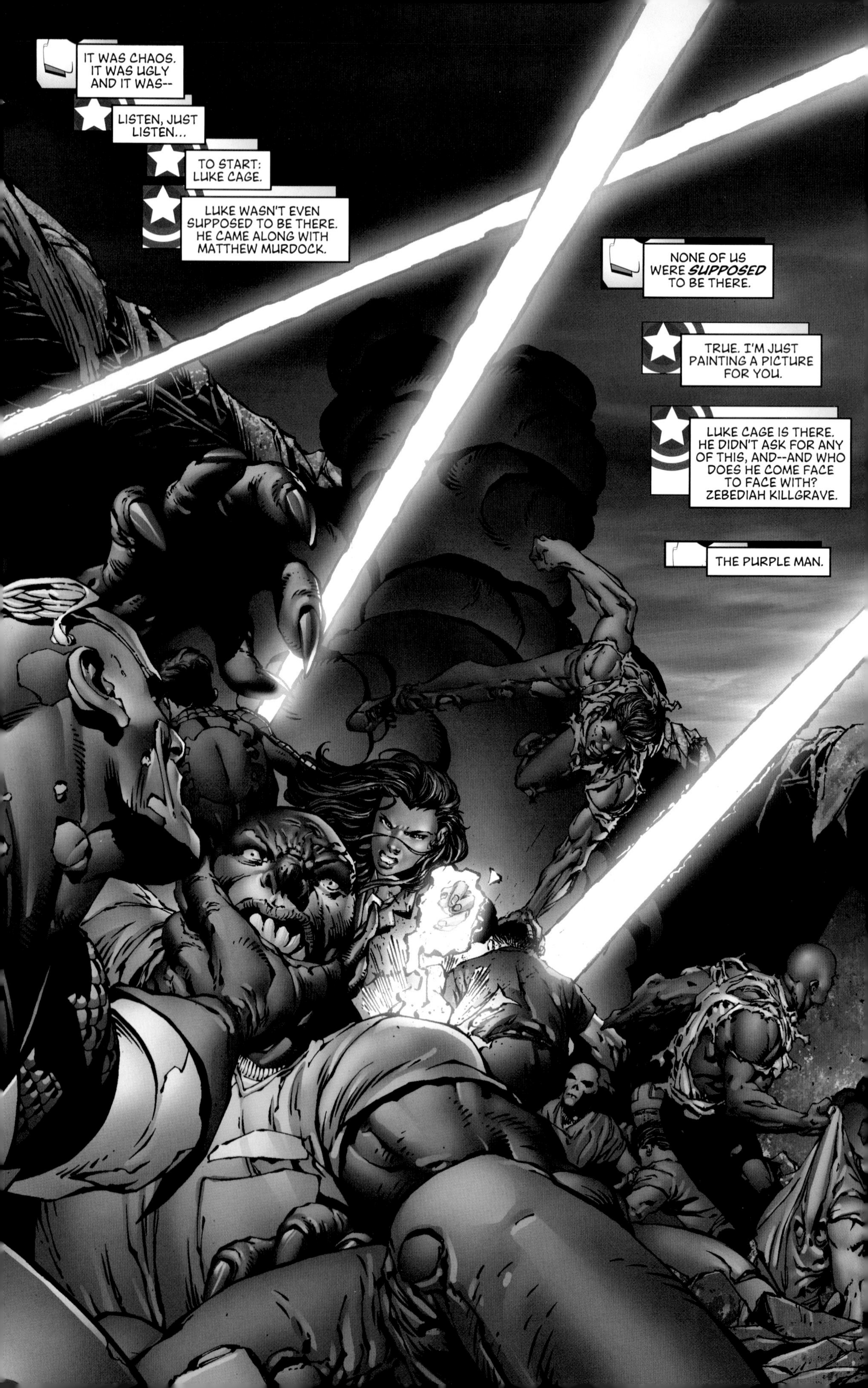
IT WAS CHAOS. IT WAS UGLY AND IT WAS--
LISTEN, JUST LISTEN...
TO START: LUKE CAGE.
LUKE WASN'T EVEN SUPPOSED TO BE THERE. HE CAME ALONG WITH MATTHEW MURDOCK.
NONE OF US WERE ***SUPPOSED*** TO BE THERE.
TRUE. I'M JUST PAINTING A PICTURE FOR YOU.
LUKE CAGE IS THERE. HE DIDN'T ASK FOR ANY OF THIS, AND--AND WHO DOES HE COME FACE TO FACE WITH? ZEBEDIAH KILLGRAVE.
THE PURPLE MAN.

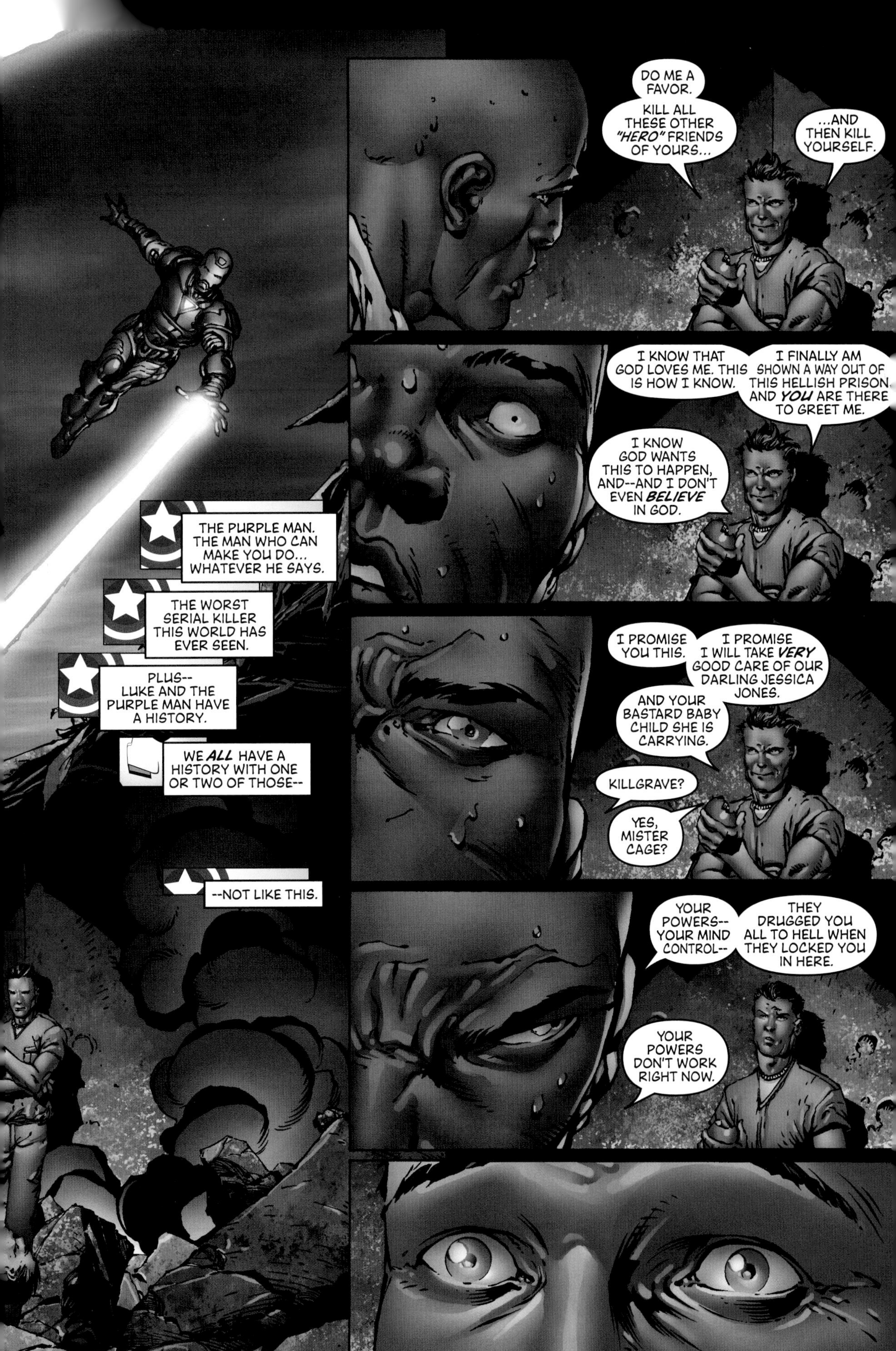
THE PURPLE MAN. THE MAN WHO CAN MAKE YOU DO... WHATEVER HE SAYS.
THE WORST SERIAL KILLER THIS WORLD HAS EVER SEEN.
PLUS-- LUKE AND THE PURPLE MAN HAVE A HISTORY.
WE ALL HAVE A HISTORY WITH ONE OR TWO OF THOSE--
--NOT LIKE THIS.
DO ME A FAVOR.
KILL ALL THESE OTHER "HERO" FRIENDS OF YOURS...
...AND THEN KILL YOURSELF.
I KNOW THAT GOD LOVES ME. THIS IS HOW I KNOW.
I FINALLY AM SHOWN A WAY OUT OF THIS HELLISH PRISON AND YOU ARE THERE TO GREET ME.
I KNOW GOD WANTS THIS TO HAPPEN, AND--AND I DON'T EVEN BELIEVE IN GOD.
I PROMISE YOU THIS.
I PROMISE I WILL TAKE VERY GOOD CARE OF OUR DARLING JESSICA JONES.
AND YOUR BASTARD BABY CHILD SHE IS CARRYING.
KILLGRAVE?
YES, MISTER CAGE?
YOUR POWERS-- YOUR MIND CONTROL--
THEY DRUGGED YOU ALL TO HELL WHEN THEY LOCKED YOU IN HERE.
YOUR POWERS DON'T WORK RIGHT NOW.

WHAT YOU'VE DONE TO ME AND MY LIFE!

YOU THREATEN MY KID?

YOU SAY THAT TO MY FACE?!

ARRGGH!

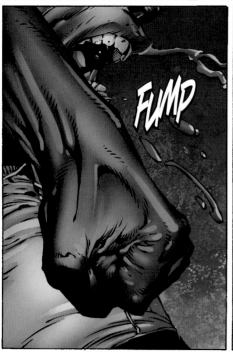

FUMP

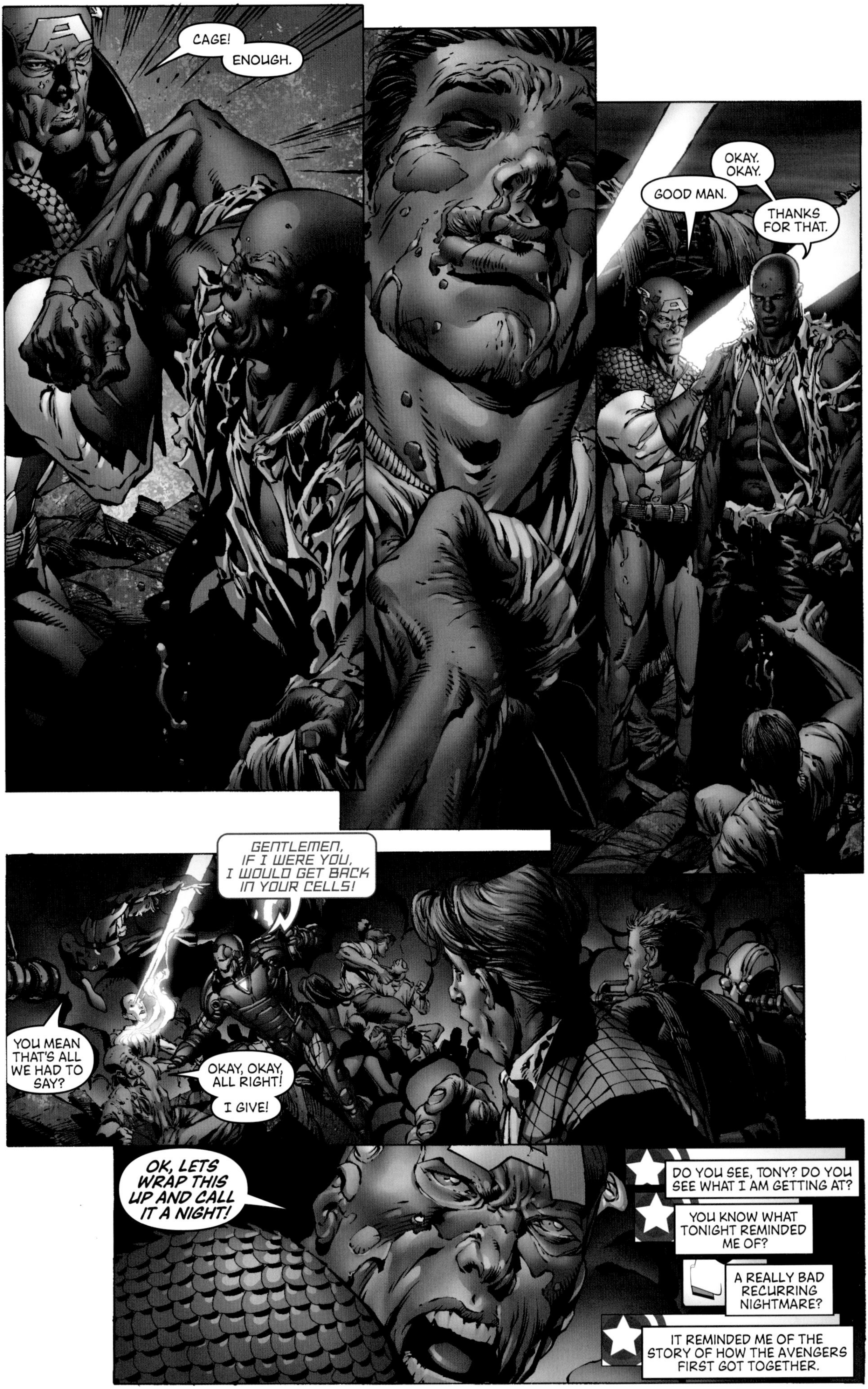
CAGE!
ENOUGH.
OKAY. OKAY.
GOOD MAN.
THANKS FOR THAT.
GENTLEMEN, IF I WERE YOU, I WOULD GET BACK IN YOUR CELLS!
YOU MEAN THAT'S ALL WE HAD TO SAY?
OKAY, OKAY, ALL RIGHT!
I GIVE!
OK, LETS WRAP THIS UP AND CALL IT A NIGHT!
DO YOU SEE, TONY? DO YOU SEE WHAT I AM GETTING AT?
YOU KNOW WHAT TONIGHT REMINDED ME OF?
A REALLY BAD RECURRING NIGHTMARE?
IT REMINDED ME OF THE STORY OF HOW THE AVENGERS FIRST GOT TOGETHER.

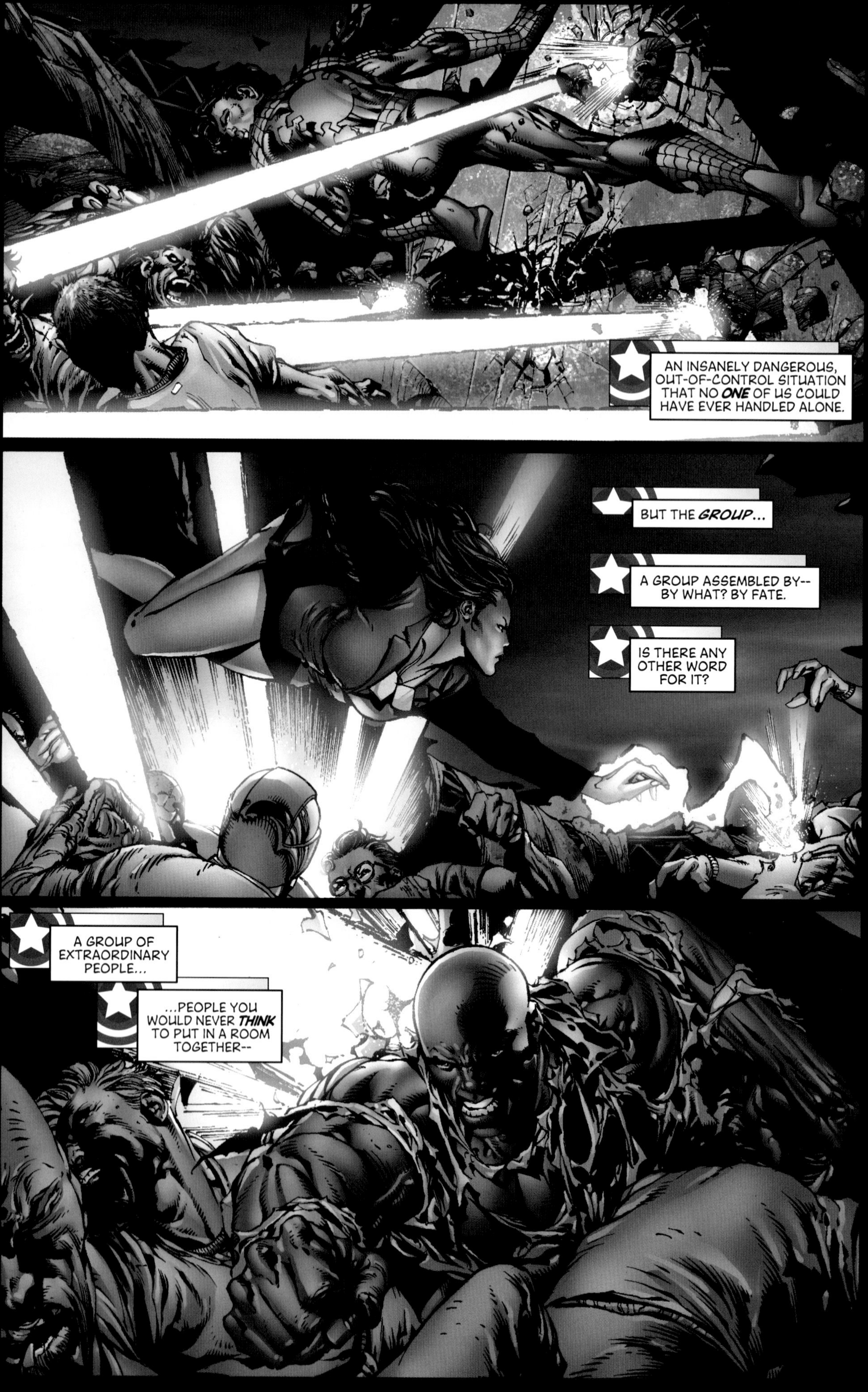
AN INSANELY DANGEROUS, OUT-OF-CONTROL SITUATION THAT NO ONE OF US COULD HAVE EVER HANDLED ALONE.
BUT THE GROUP...
A GROUP ASSEMBLED BY-- BY WHAT? BY FATE.
IS THERE ANY OTHER WORD FOR IT?
A GROUP OF EXTRAORDINARY PEOPLE...
...PEOPLE YOU WOULD NEVER THINK TO PUT IN A ROOM TOGETHER--

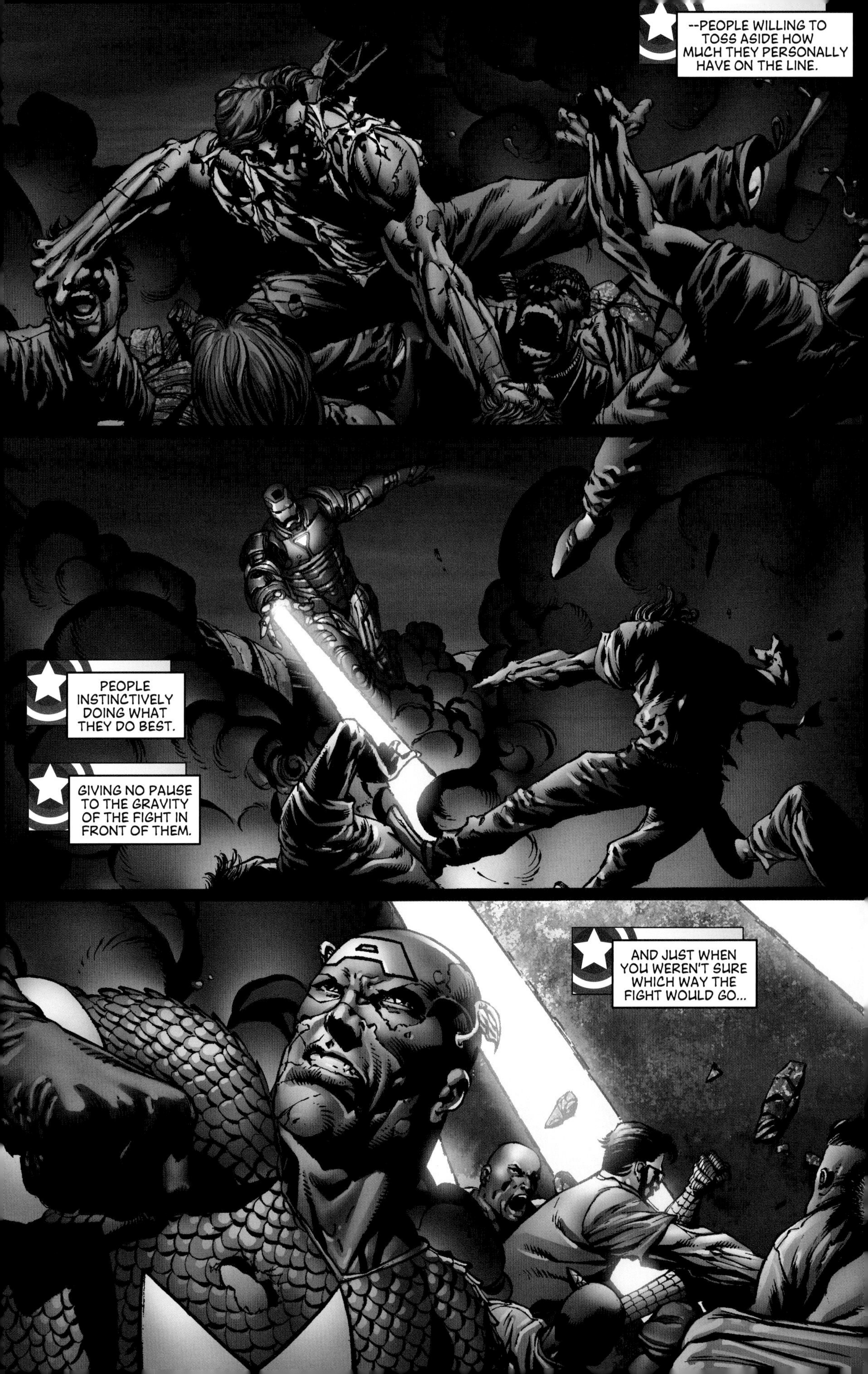
--PEOPLE WILLING TO TOSS ASIDE HOW MUCH THEY PERSONALLY HAVE ON THE LINE.
PEOPLE INSTINCTIVELY DOING WHAT THEY DO BEST.
GIVING NO PAUSE TO THE GRAVITY OF THE FIGHT IN FRONT OF THEM.
AND JUST WHEN YOU WEREN'T SURE WHICH WAY THE FIGHT WOULD GO...

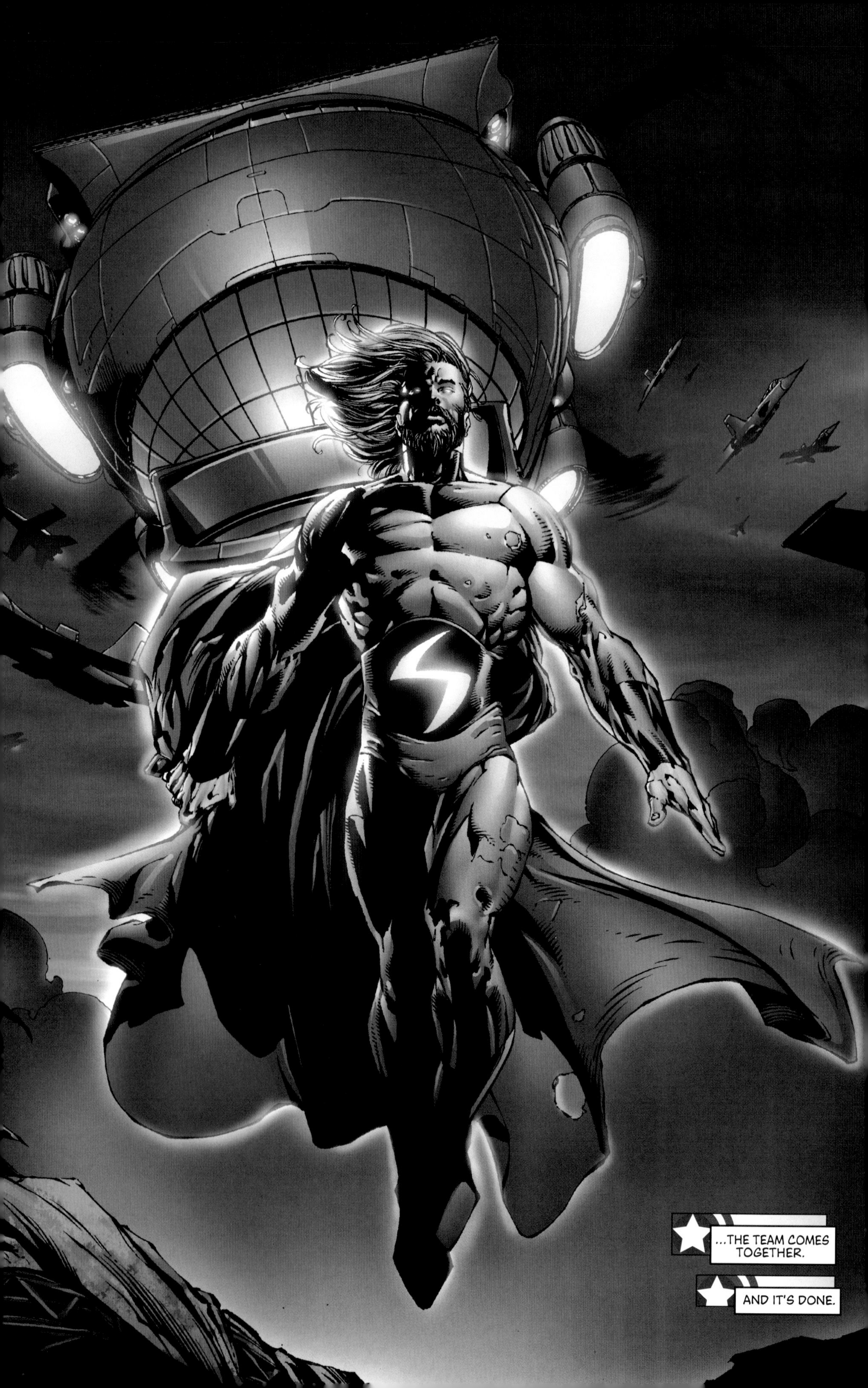
...THE TEAM COMES TOGETHER.
AND IT'S DONE.

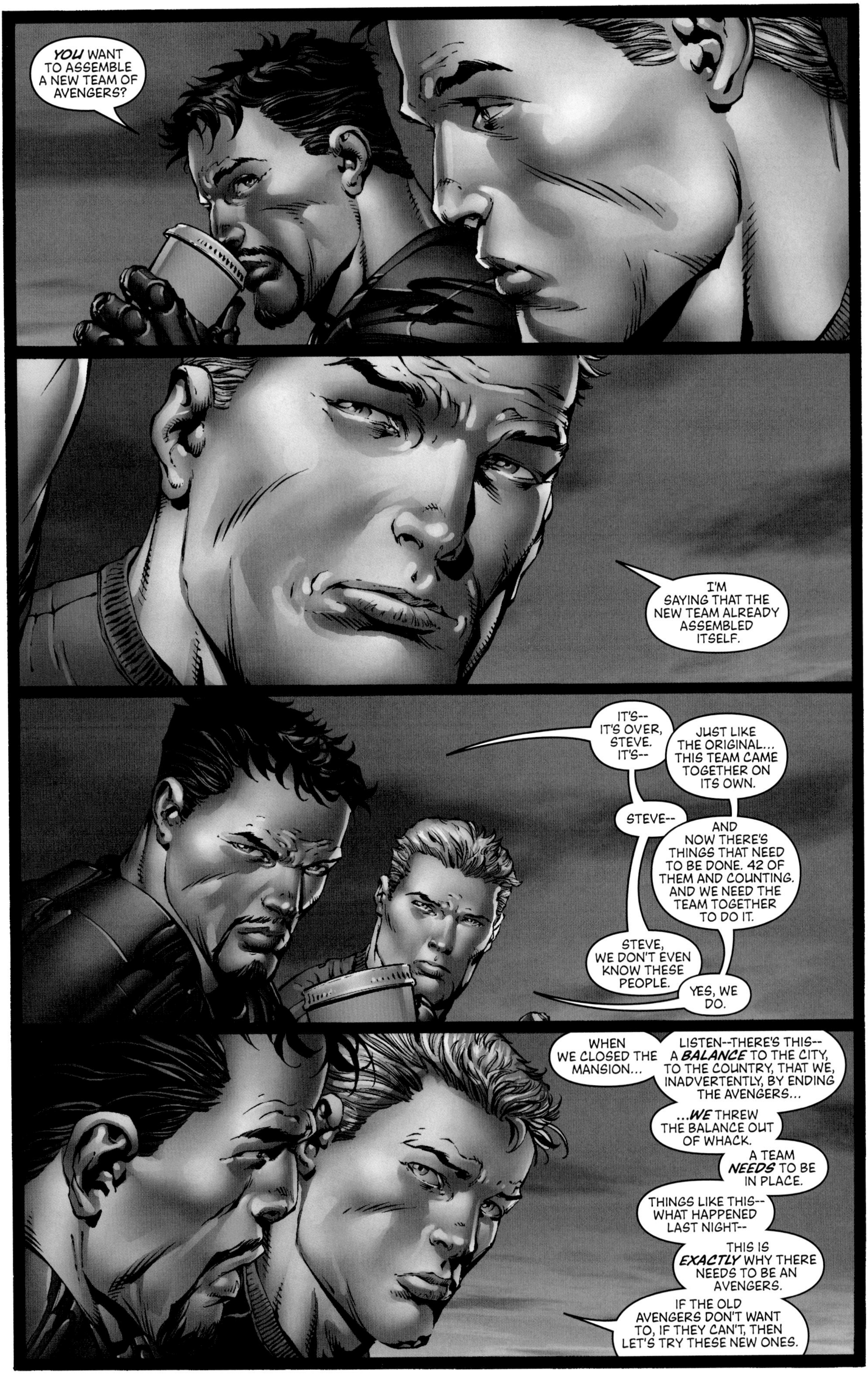
YOU WANT TO ASSEMBLE A NEW TEAM OF AVENGERS?
I'M SAYING THAT THE NEW TEAM ALREADY ASSEMBLED ITSELF.
IT'S-- IT'S OVER, STEVE. IT'S--
JUST LIKE THE ORIGINAL... THIS TEAM CAME TOGETHER ON ITS OWN.
STEVE--
AND NOW THERE'S THINGS THAT NEED TO BE DONE. 42 OF THEM AND COUNTING. AND WE NEED THE TEAM TOGETHER TO DO IT.
STEVE, WE DON'T EVEN KNOW THESE PEOPLE.
YES, WE DO.
WHEN WE CLOSED THE MANSION...
LISTEN--THERE'S THIS-- A BALANCE TO THE CITY, TO THE COUNTRY, THAT WE, INADVERTENTLY, BY ENDING THE AVENGERS...
...WE THREW THE BALANCE OUT OF WHACK.
A TEAM NEEDS TO BE IN PLACE.
THINGS LIKE THIS-- WHAT HAPPENED LAST NIGHT--
THIS IS EXACTLY WHY THERE NEEDS TO BE AN AVENGERS.
IF THE OLD AVENGERS DON'T WANT TO, IF THEY CAN'T, THEN LET'S TRY THESE NEW ONES.

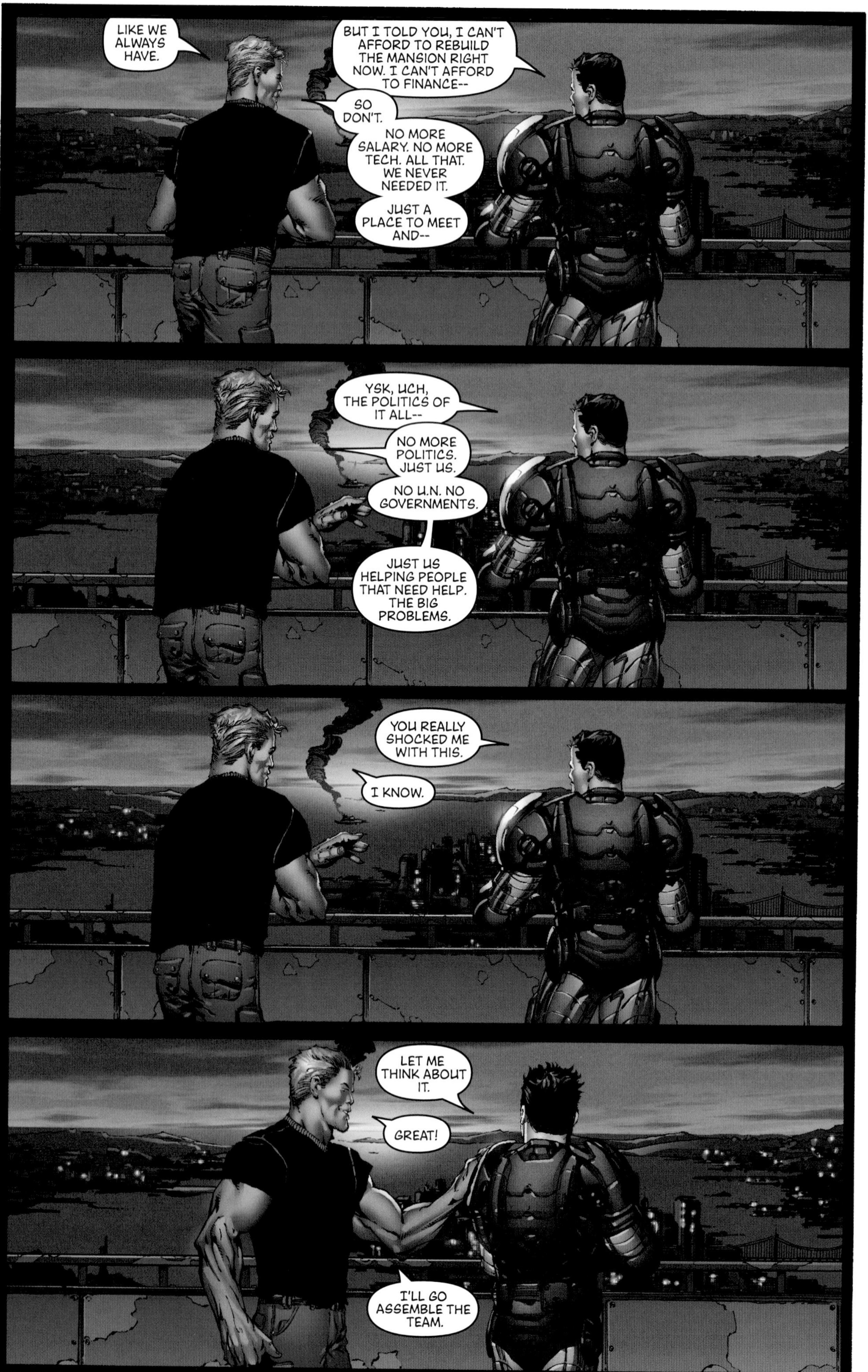
LIKE WE ALWAYS HAVE.
BUT I TOLD YOU, I CAN'T AFFORD TO REBUILD THE MANSION RIGHT NOW. I CAN'T AFFORD TO FINANCE--
SO DON'T.
NO MORE SALARY. NO MORE TECH. ALL THAT. WE NEVER NEEDED IT.
JUST A PLACE TO MEET AND--
YSK, UCH, THE POLITICS OF IT ALL--
NO MORE POLITICS. JUST US.
NO U.N. NO GOVERNMENTS.
JUST US HELPING PEOPLE THAT NEED HELP. THE BIG PROBLEMS.
YOU REALLY SHOCKED ME WITH THIS.
I KNOW.
LET ME THINK ABOUT IT.
GREAT!
I'LL GO ASSEMBLE THE TEAM.

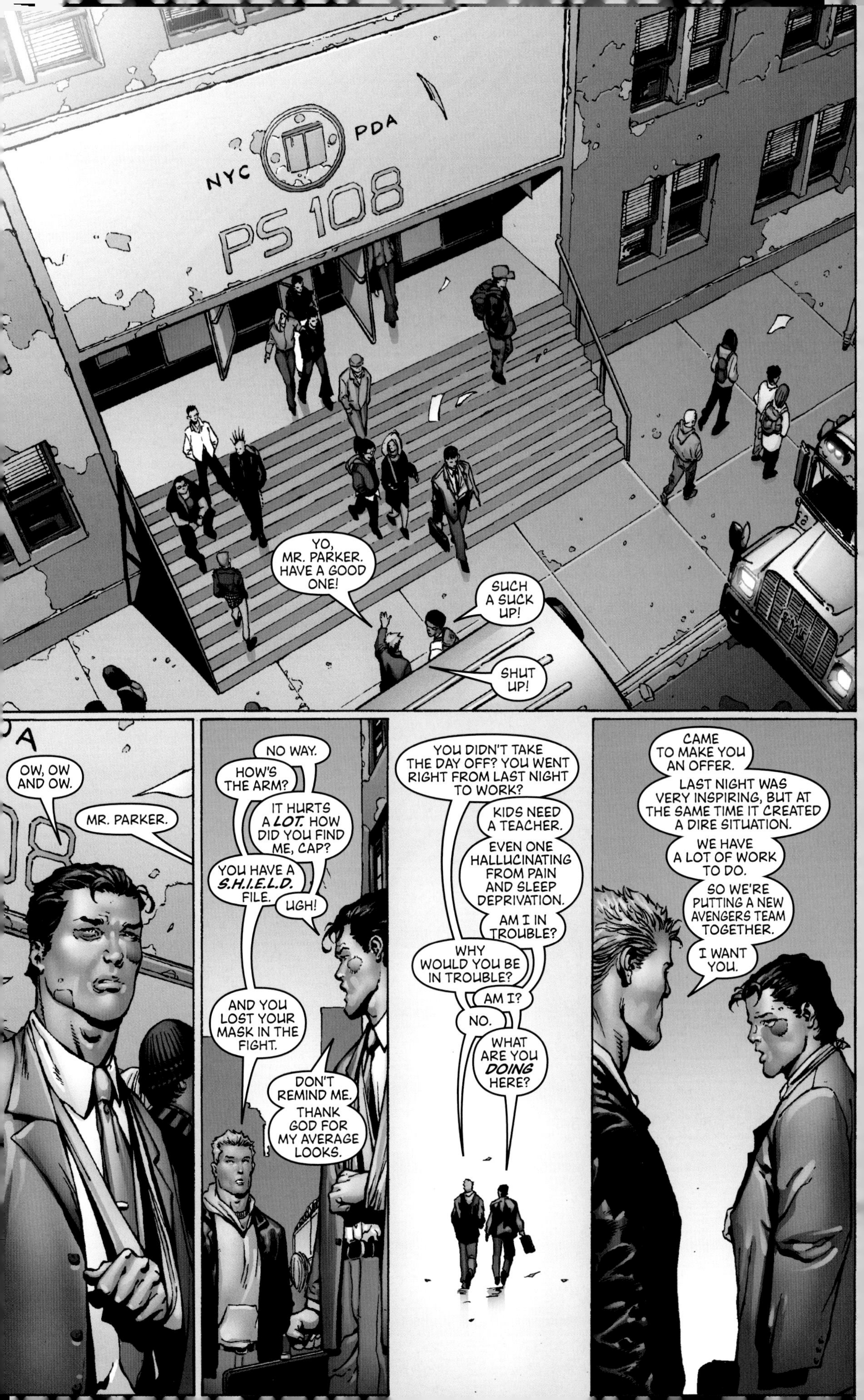
NYC
PDA
PS 108
YO, MR. PARKER. HAVE A GOOD ONE!
SUCH A SUCK UP!
SHUT UP!
OW, OW AND OW.
MR. PARKER.
NO WAY.
HOW'S THE ARM?
IT HURTS A *LOT.* HOW DID YOU FIND ME, CAP?
YOU HAVE A *S.H.I.E.L.D.* FILE.
UGH!
AND YOU LOST YOUR MASK IN THE FIGHT.
DON'T REMIND ME.
THANK GOD FOR MY AVERAGE LOOKS.
YOU DIDN'T TAKE THE DAY OFF? YOU WENT RIGHT FROM LAST NIGHT TO WORK?
KIDS NEED A TEACHER.
EVEN ONE HALLUCINATING FROM PAIN AND SLEEP DEPRIVATION.
AM I IN TROUBLE?
WHY WOULD YOU BE IN TROUBLE?
AM I?
NO.
WHAT ARE YOU *DOING* HERE?
CAME TO MAKE YOU AN OFFER.
LAST NIGHT WAS VERY INSPIRING, BUT AT THE SAME TIME IT CREATED A DIRE SITUATION.
WE HAVE A LOT OF WORK TO DO.
SO WE'RE PUTTING A NEW AVENGERS TEAM TOGETHER.
I WANT YOU.

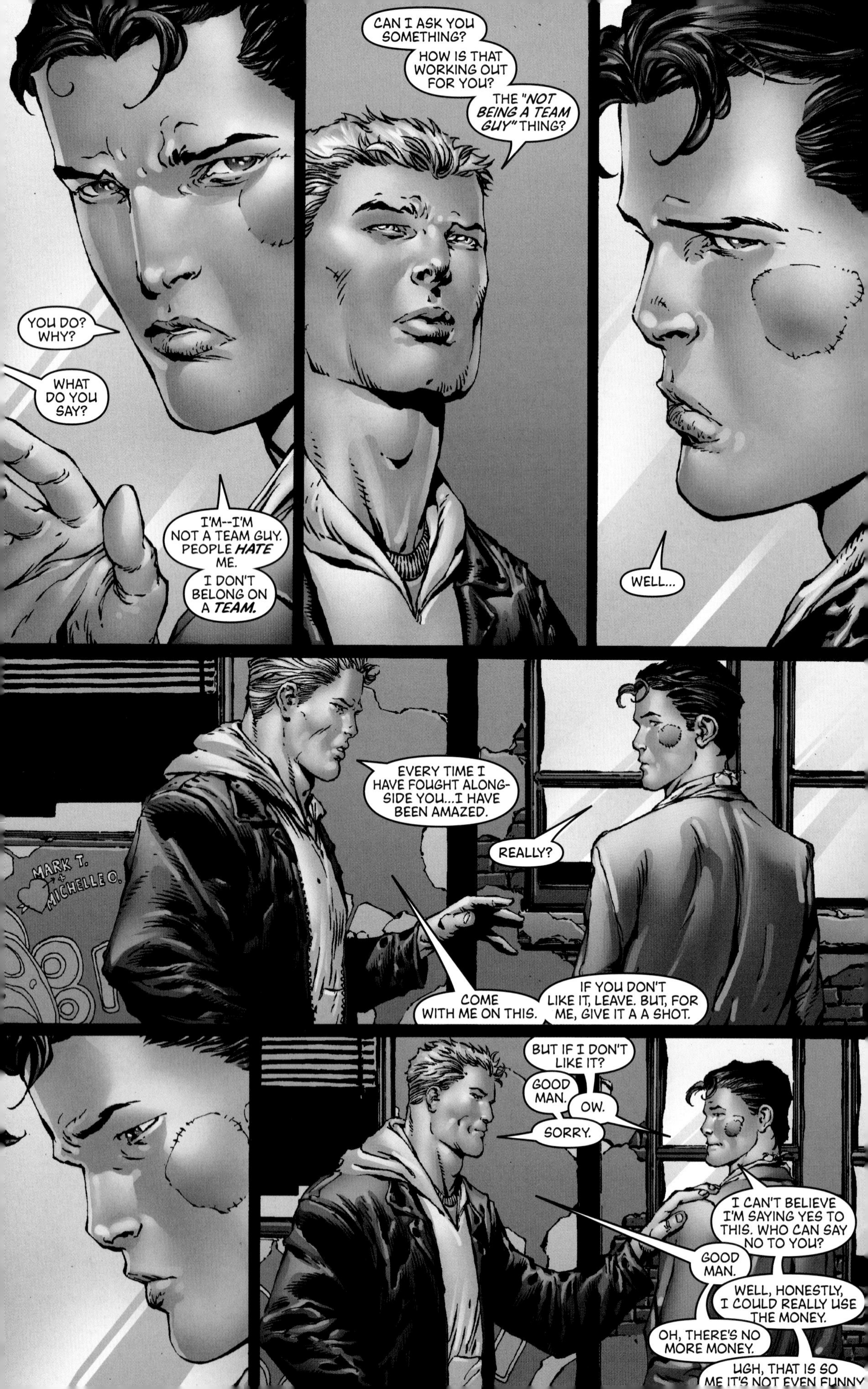
YOU DO? WHY?
WHAT DO YOU SAY?
I'M--I'M NOT A TEAM GUY. PEOPLE HATE ME.
I DON'T BELONG ON A TEAM.
CAN I ASK YOU SOMETHING?
HOW IS THAT WORKING OUT FOR YOU?
THE "NOT BEING A TEAM GUY" THING?
WELL...
EVERY TIME I HAVE FOUGHT ALONG-SIDE YOU...I HAVE BEEN AMAZED.
REALLY?
MARK T. + MICHELLE O.
COME WITH ME ON THIS.
IF YOU DON'T LIKE IT, LEAVE. BUT, FOR ME, GIVE IT A A SHOT.
BUT IF I DON'T LIKE IT?
GOOD MAN.
OW.
SORRY.
I CAN'T BELIEVE I'M SAYING YES TO THIS. WHO CAN SAY NO TO YOU?
GOOD MAN.
WELL, HONESTLY, I COULD REALLY USE THE MONEY.
OH, THERE'S NO MORE MONEY.
UGH, THAT IS SO ME IT'S NOT EVEN FUNNY

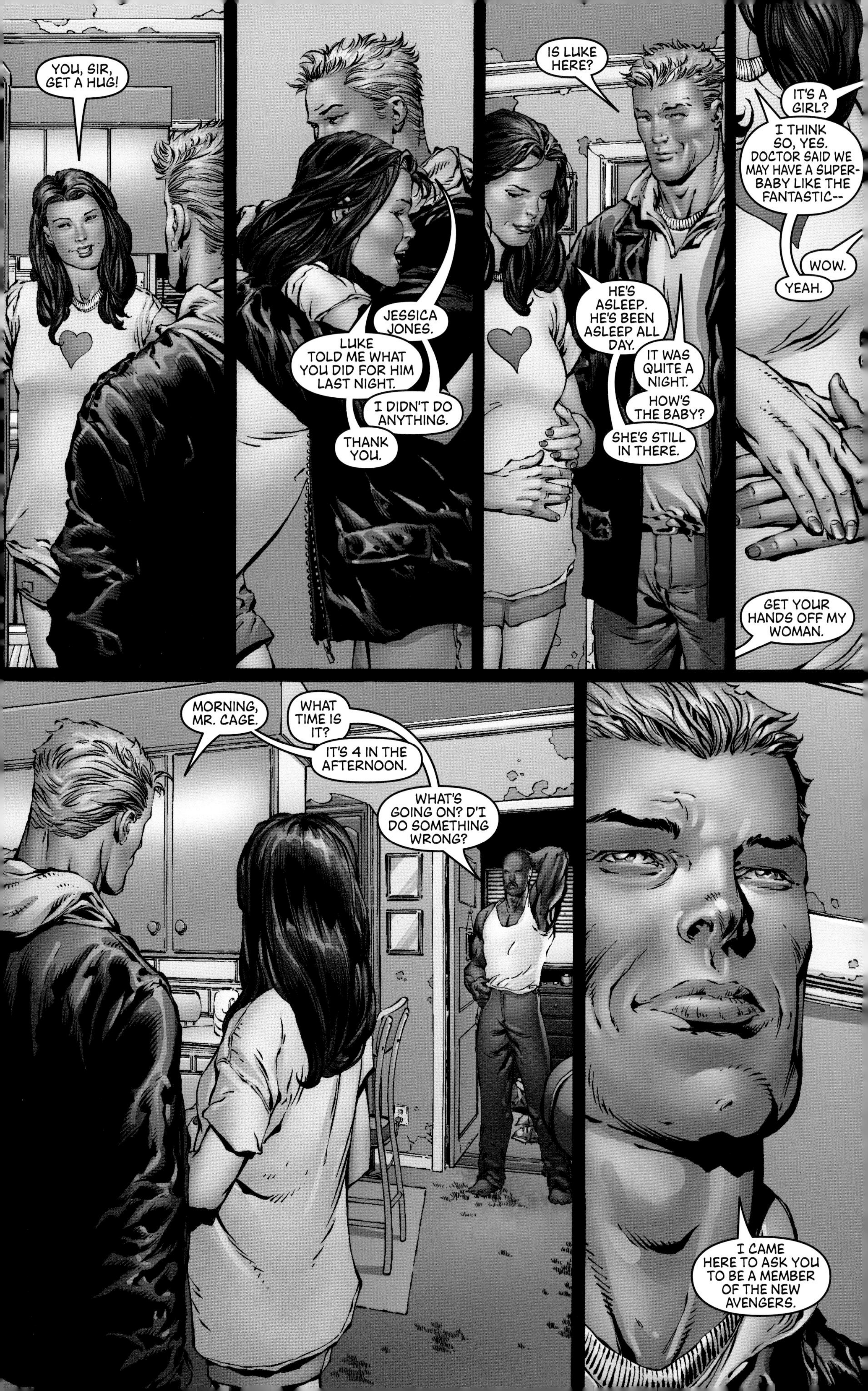
YOU, SIR, GET A HUG!
JESSICA JONES.
LUKE TOLD ME WHAT YOU DID FOR HIM LAST NIGHT.
I DIDN'T DO ANYTHING.
THANK YOU.
IS LUKE HERE?
HE'S ASLEEP. HE'S BEEN ASLEEP ALL DAY.
IT WAS QUITE A NIGHT.
HOW'S THE BABY?
SHE'S STILL IN THERE.
IT'S A GIRL?
I THINK SO, YES. DOCTOR SAID WE MAY HAVE A SUPER-BABY LIKE THE FANTASTIC--
WOW.
YEAH.
GET YOUR HANDS OFF MY WOMAN.
MORNING, MR. CAGE.
WHAT TIME IS IT?
IT'S 4 IN THE AFTERNOON.
WHAT'S GOING ON? D'I DO SOMETHING WRONG?
I CAME HERE TO ASK YOU TO BE A MEMBER OF THE NEW AVENGERS.

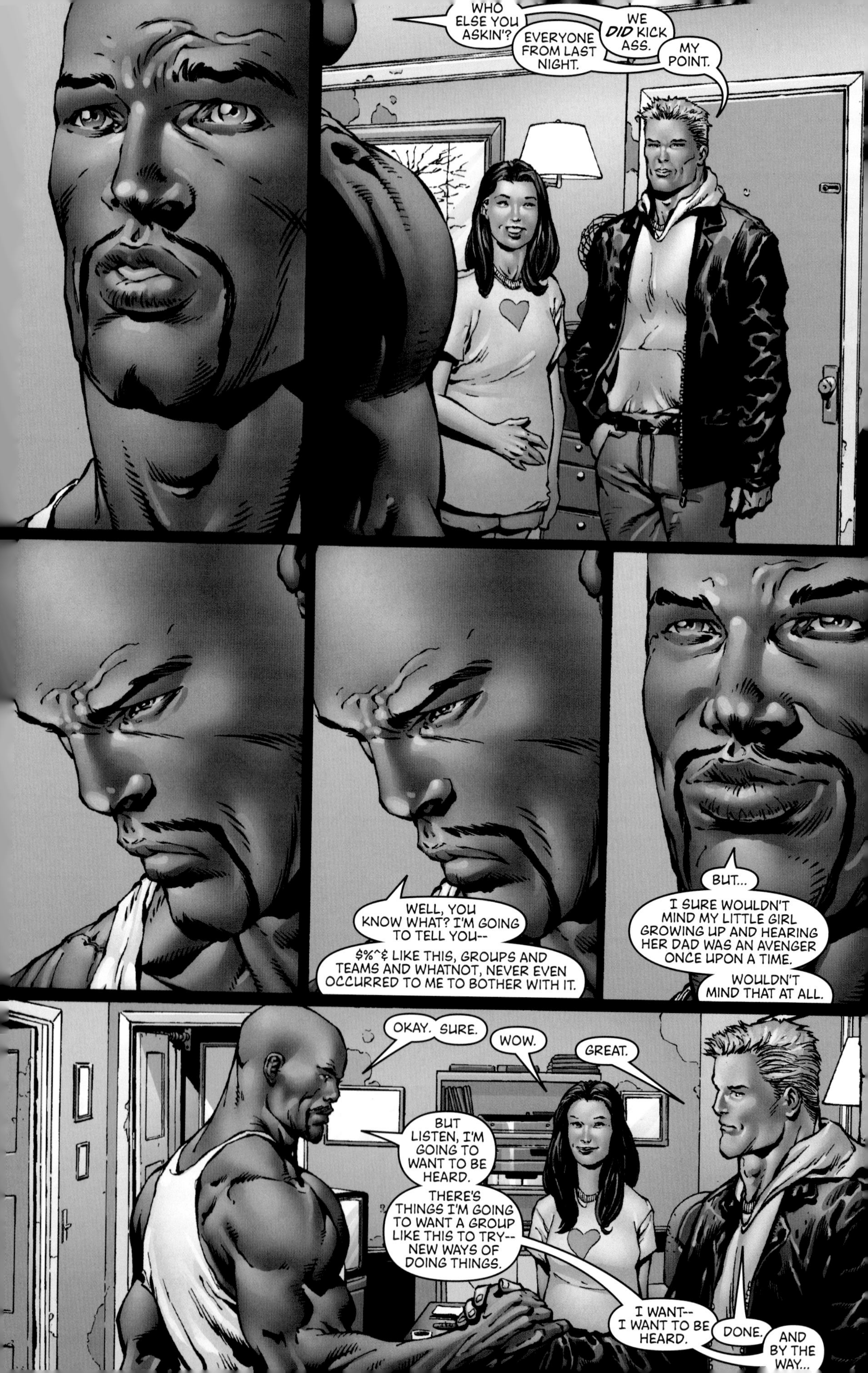
WHO ELSE YOU ASKIN'?
EVERYONE FROM LAST NIGHT.
WE DID KICK ASS.
MY POINT.
WELL, YOU KNOW WHAT? I'M GOING TO TELL YOU--
$%^& LIKE THIS, GROUPS AND TEAMS AND WHATNOT, NEVER EVEN OCCURRED TO ME TO BOTHER WITH IT.
BUT...
I SURE WOULDN'T MIND MY LITTLE GIRL GROWING UP AND HEARING HER DAD WAS AN AVENGER ONCE UPON A TIME.
WOULDN'T MIND THAT AT ALL.
OKAY. SURE.
WOW.
GREAT.
BUT LISTEN, I'M GOING TO WANT TO BE HEARD.
THERE'S THINGS I'M GOING TO WANT A GROUP LIKE THIS TO TRY-- NEW WAYS OF DOING THINGS.
I WANT-- I WANT TO BE HEARD.
DONE.
AND BY THE WAY...

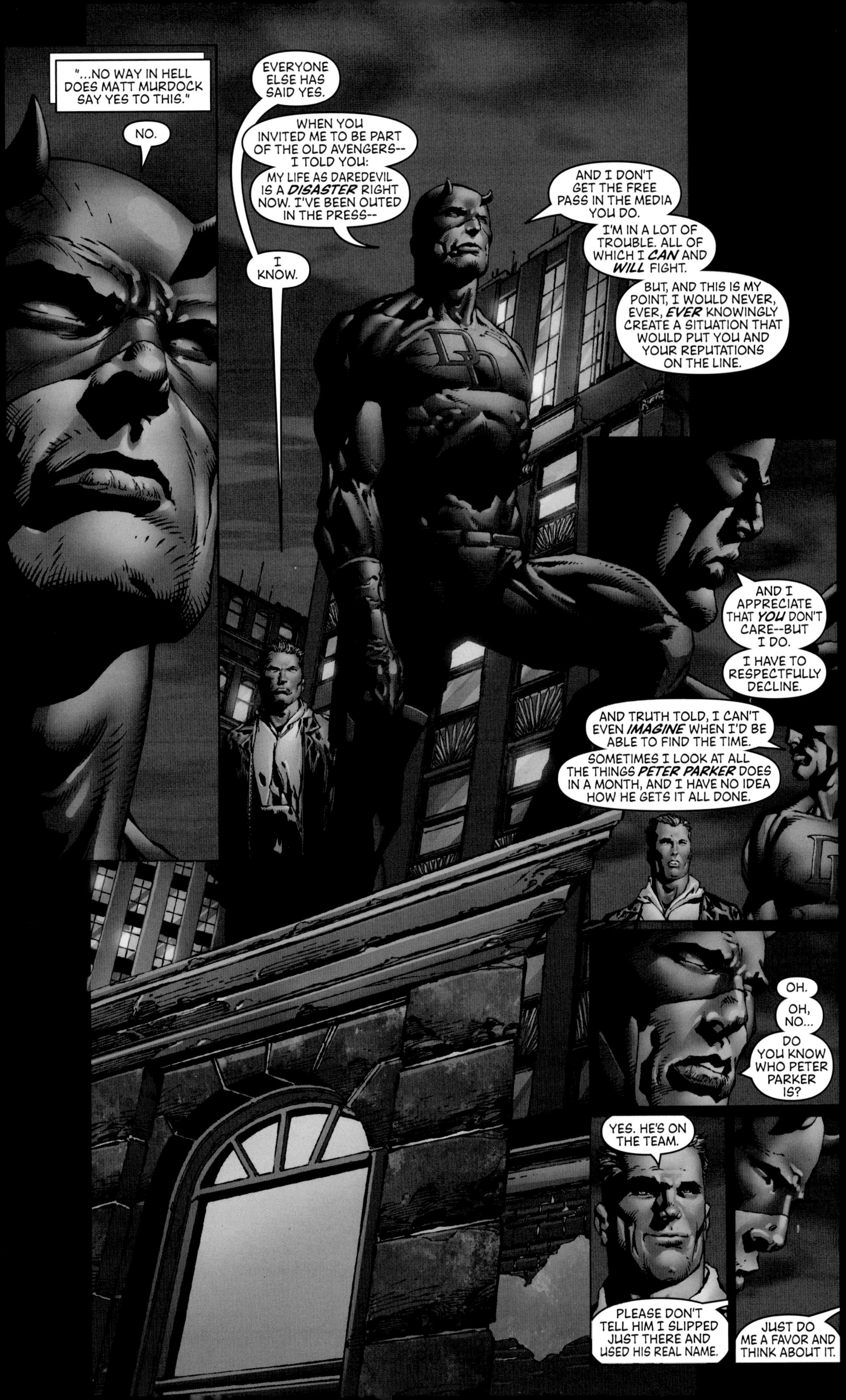
"...NO WAY IN HELL DOES MATT MURDOCK SAY YES TO THIS."
NO.
EVERYONE ELSE HAS SAID YES.
WHEN YOU INVITED ME TO BE PART OF THE OLD AVENGERS-- I TOLD YOU:
MY LIFE AS DAREDEVIL IS A DISASTER RIGHT NOW. I'VE BEEN OUTED IN THE PRESS--
I KNOW.
AND I DON'T GET THE FREE PASS IN THE MEDIA YOU DO.
I'M IN A LOT OF TROUBLE. ALL OF WHICH I CAN AND WILL FIGHT.
BUT, AND THIS IS MY POINT, I WOULD NEVER, EVER, EVER KNOWINGLY CREATE A SITUATION THAT WOULD PUT YOU AND YOUR REPUTATIONS ON THE LINE.
AND I APPRECIATE THAT YOU DON'T CARE--BUT I DO.
I HAVE TO RESPECTFULLY DECLINE.
AND TRUTH TOLD, I CAN'T EVEN IMAGINE WHEN I'D BE ABLE TO FIND THE TIME.
SOMETIMES I LOOK AT ALL THE THINGS PETER PARKER DOES IN A MONTH, AND I HAVE NO IDEA HOW HE GETS IT ALL DONE.
OH.
OH, NO...
DO YOU KNOW WHO PETER PARKER IS?
YES. HE'S ON THE TEAM.
PLEASE DON'T TELL HIM I SLIPPED JUST THERE AND USED HIS REAL NAME.
JUST DO ME A FAVOR AND THINK ABOUT IT.

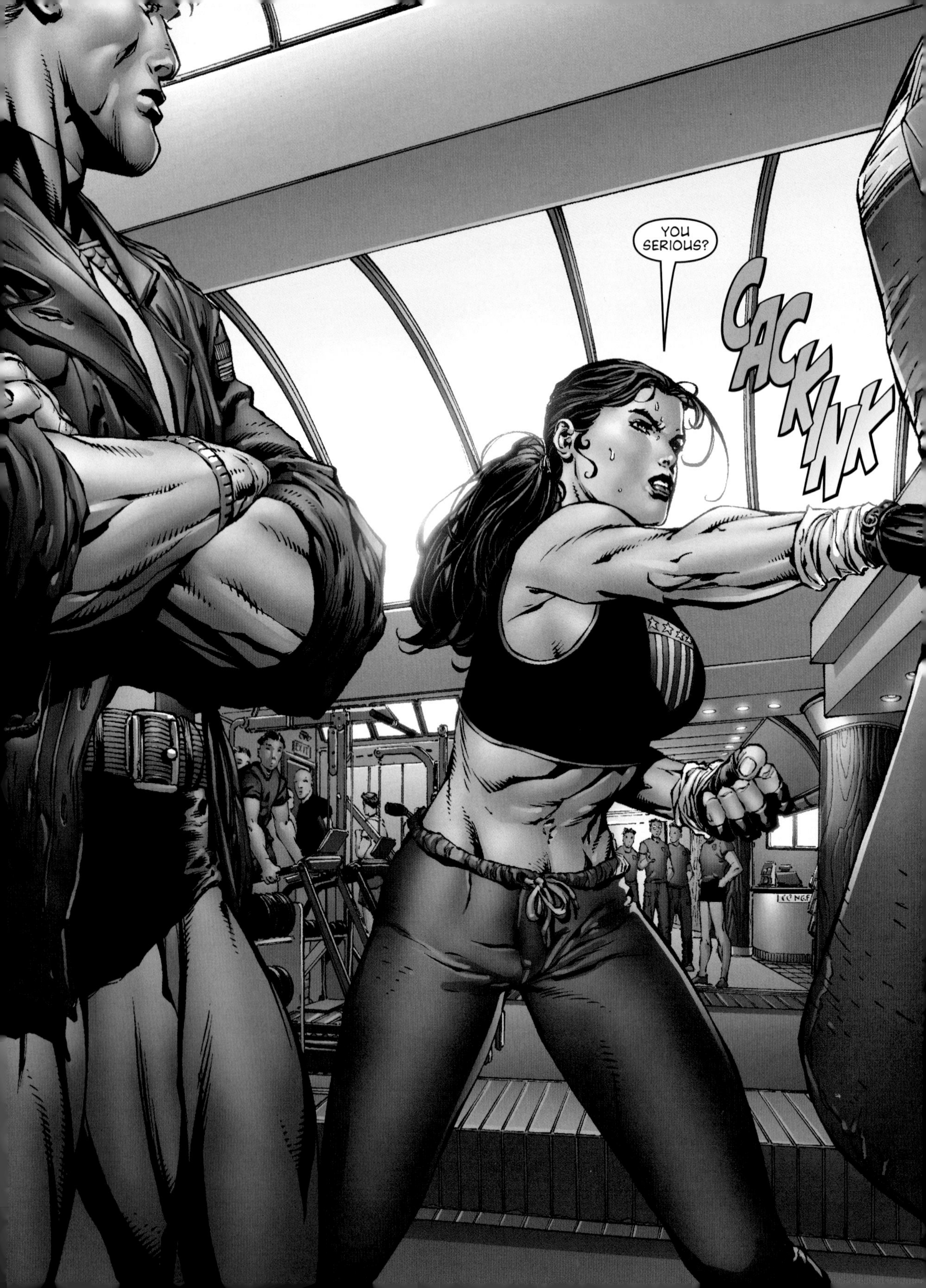

YOU SERIOUS?
CACKINK

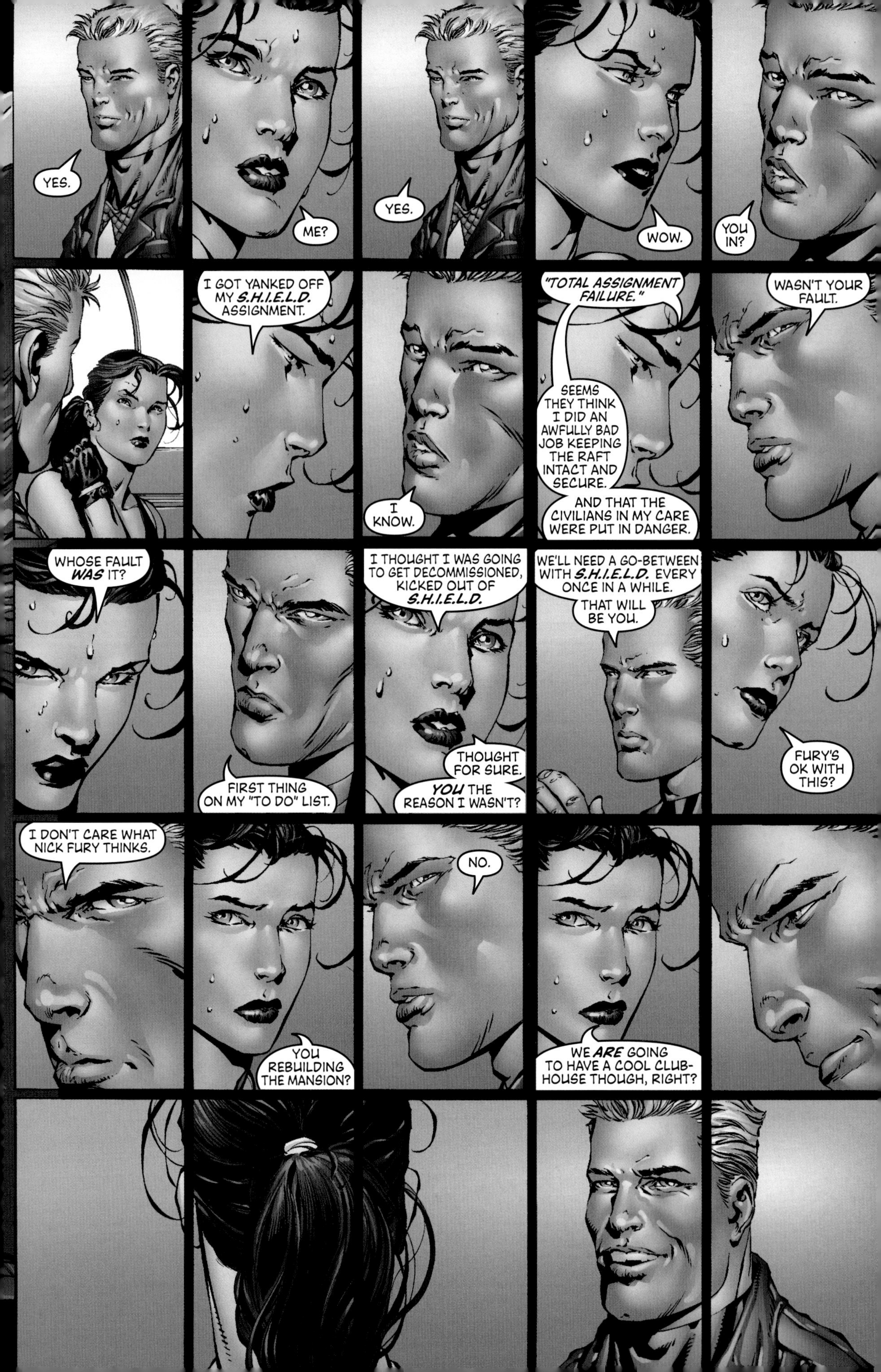

YES.
ME?
YES.
WOW.
YOU IN?
I GOT YANKED OFF MY S.H.I.E.L.D. ASSIGNMENT.
I KNOW.
"TOTAL ASSIGNMENT FAILURE."
SEEMS THEY THINK I DID AN AWFULLY BAD JOB KEEPING THE RAFT INTACT AND SECURE.
AND THAT THE CIVILIANS IN MY CARE WERE PUT IN DANGER.
WASN'T YOUR FAULT.
WHOSE FAULT WAS IT?
FIRST THING ON MY "TO DO" LIST.
I THOUGHT I WAS GOING TO GET DECOMMISSIONED, KICKED OUT OF S.H.I.E.L.D.
THOUGHT FOR SURE.
YOU THE REASON I WASN'T?
WE'LL NEED A GO-BETWEEN WITH S.H.I.E.L.D. EVERY ONCE IN A WHILE.
THAT WILL BE YOU.
FURY'S OK WITH THIS?
I DON'T CARE WHAT NICK FURY THINKS.
YOU REBUILDING THE MANSION?
NO.
WE ARE GOING TO HAVE A COOL CLUB-HOUSE THOUGH, RIGHT?

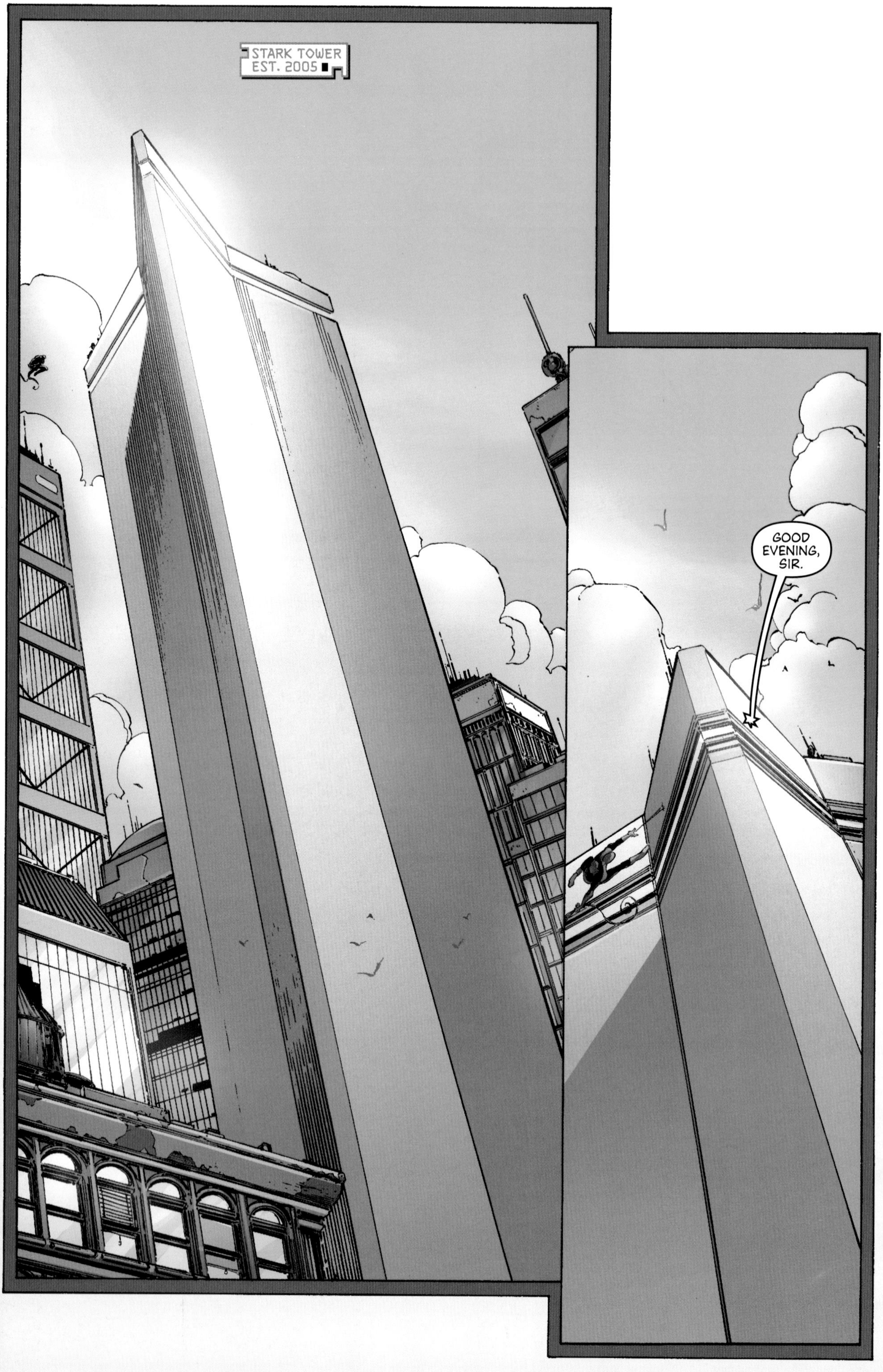
STARK TOWER
EST. 2005
GOOD EVENING, SIR.

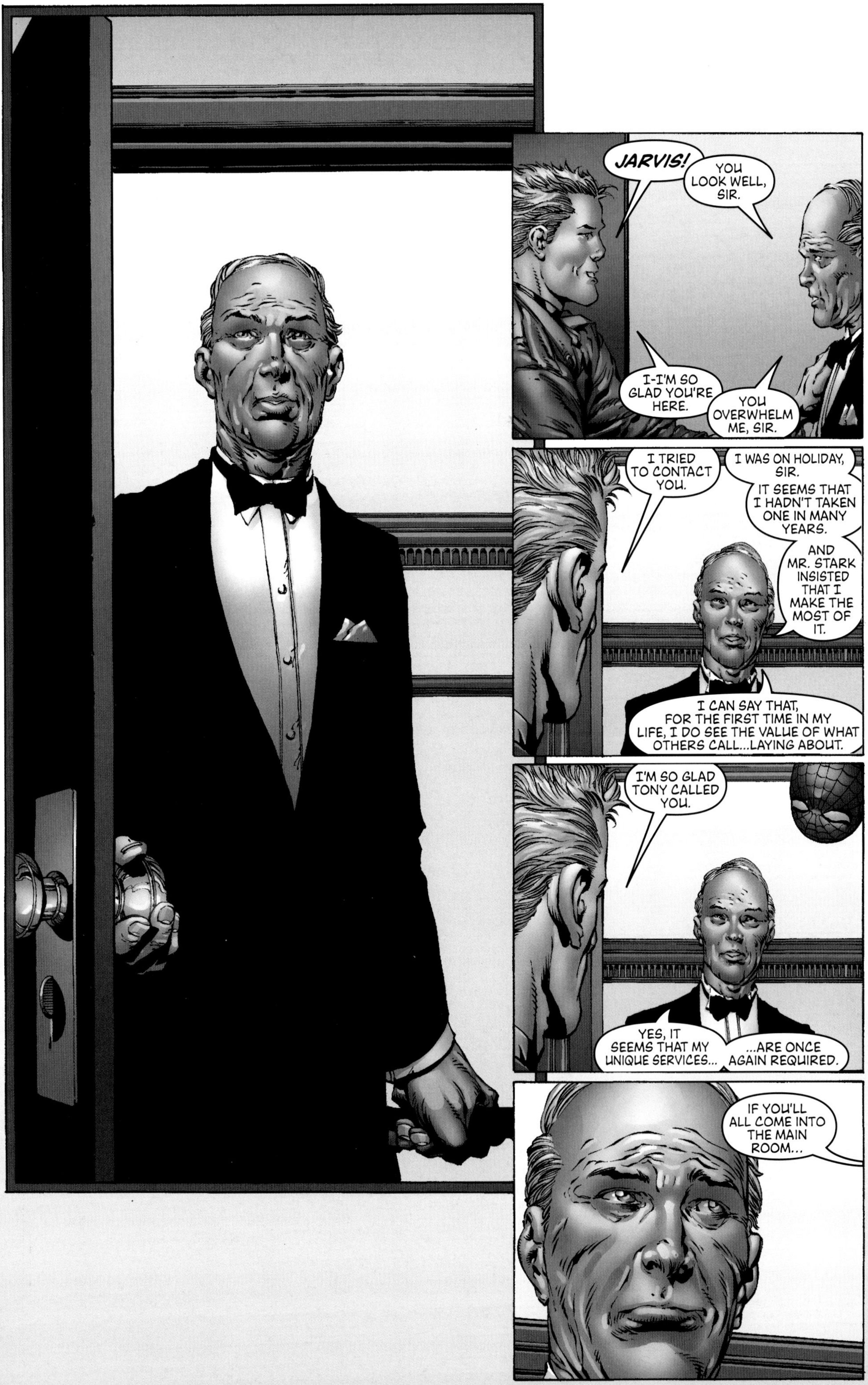
JARVIS!
YOU LOOK WELL, SIR.
I-I'M SO GLAD YOU'RE HERE.
YOU OVERWHELM ME, SIR.
I TRIED TO CONTACT YOU.
I WAS ON HOLIDAY, SIR.
IT SEEMS THAT I HADN'T TAKEN ONE IN MANY YEARS.
AND MR. STARK INSISTED THAT I MAKE THE MOST OF IT.
I CAN SAY THAT, FOR THE FIRST TIME IN MY LIFE, I DO SEE THE VALUE OF WHAT OTHERS CALL...LAYING ABOUT.
I'M SO GLAD TONY CALLED YOU.
YES, IT SEEMS THAT MY UNIQUE SERVICES...
...ARE ONCE AGAIN REQUIRED.
IF YOU'LL ALL COME INTO THE MAIN ROOM...

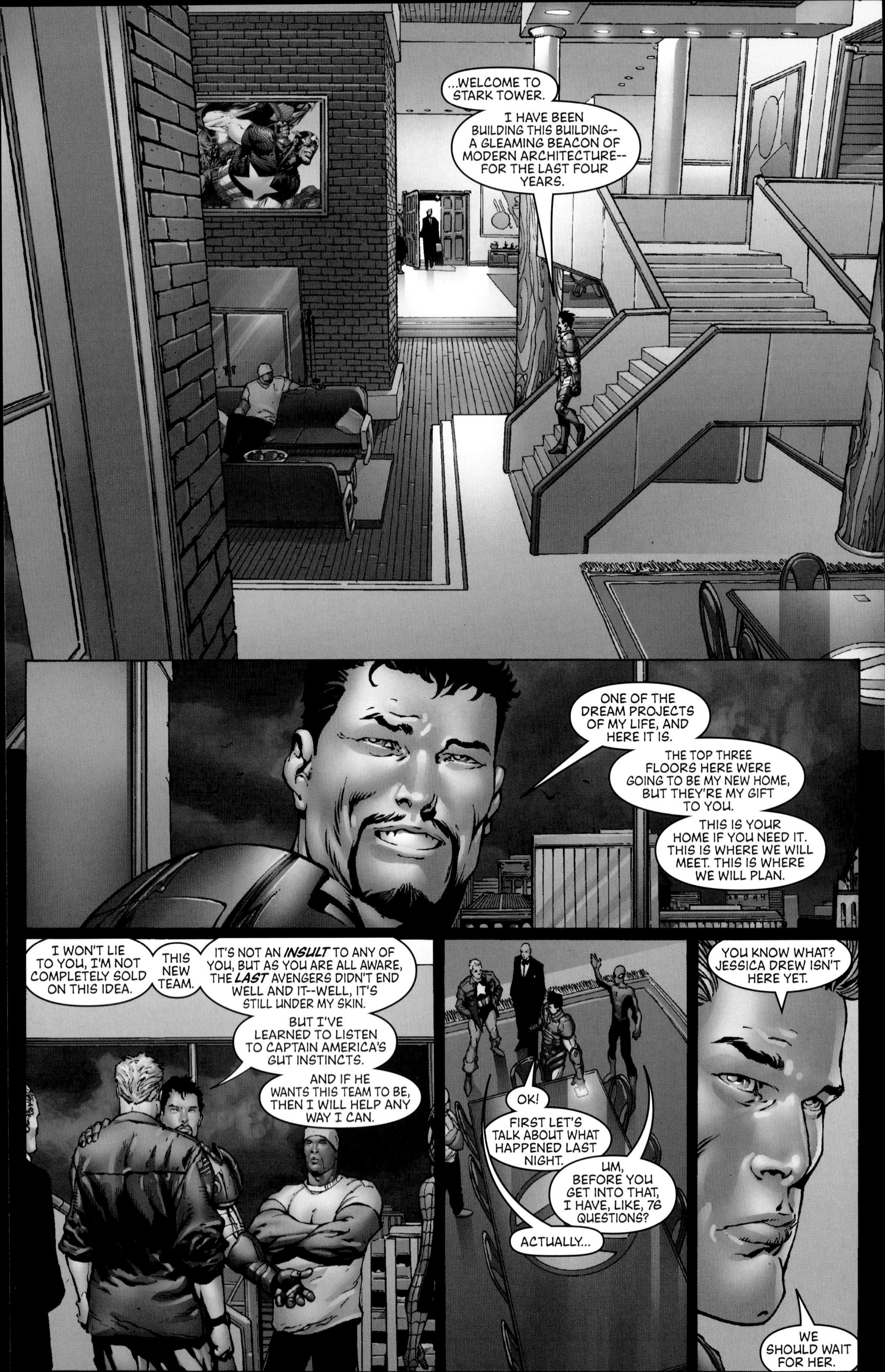
...WELCOME TO STARK TOWER.
I HAVE BEEN BUILDING THIS BUILDING-- A GLEAMING BEACON OF MODERN ARCHITECTURE-- FOR THE LAST FOUR YEARS.
ONE OF THE DREAM PROJECTS OF MY LIFE, AND HERE IT IS.
THE TOP THREE FLOORS HERE WERE GOING TO BE MY NEW HOME, BUT THEY'RE MY GIFT TO YOU.
THIS IS YOUR HOME IF YOU NEED IT. THIS IS WHERE WE WILL MEET. THIS IS WHERE WE WILL PLAN.
I WON'T LIE TO YOU, I'M NOT COMPLETELY SOLD ON THIS IDEA.
THIS NEW TEAM.
IT'S NOT AN INSULT TO ANY OF YOU, BUT AS YOU ARE ALL AWARE, THE LAST AVENGERS DIDN'T END WELL AND IT--WELL, IT'S STILL UNDER MY SKIN.
BUT I'VE LEARNED TO LISTEN TO CAPTAIN AMERICA'S GUT INSTINCTS.
AND IF HE WANTS THIS TEAM TO BE, THEN I WILL HELP ANY WAY I CAN.
OK!
FIRST LET'S TALK ABOUT WHAT HAPPENED LAST NIGHT.
UM, BEFORE YOU GET INTO THAT, I HAVE, LIKE, 76 QUESTIONS?
ACTUALLY...
YOU KNOW WHAT? JESSICA DREW ISN'T HERE YET.
WE SHOULD WAIT FOR HER.

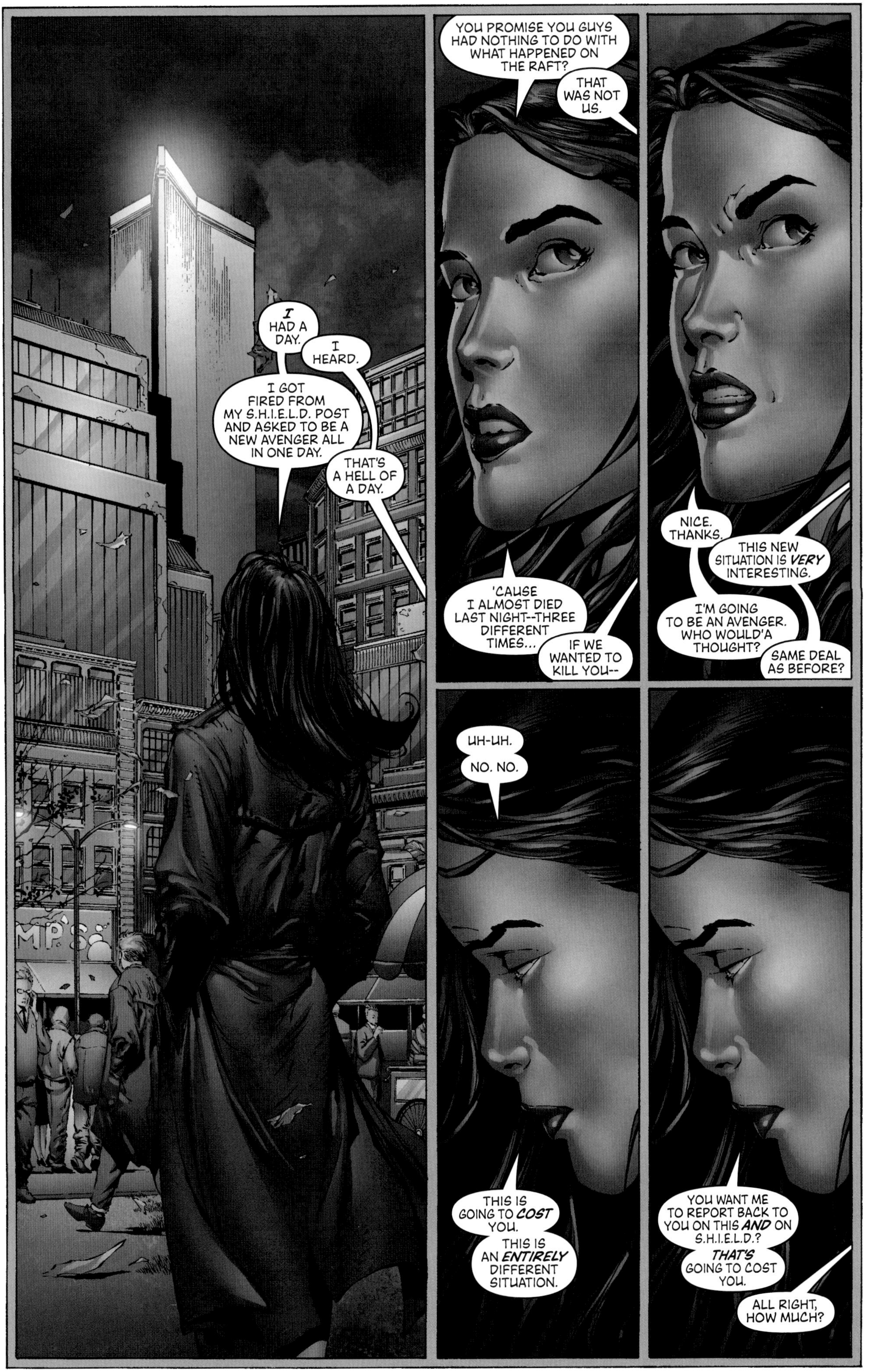

I HAD A DAY.
I HEARD.
I GOT FIRED FROM MY S.H.I.E.L.D. POST AND ASKED TO BE A NEW AVENGER ALL IN ONE DAY.
THAT'S A HELL OF A DAY.
YOU PROMISE YOU GUYS HAD NOTHING TO DO WITH WHAT HAPPENED ON THE RAFT?
THAT WAS NOT US.
'CAUSE I ALMOST DIED LAST NIGHT--THREE DIFFERENT TIMES...
IF WE WANTED TO KILL YOU--
NICE. THANKS.
THIS NEW SITUATION IS VERY INTERESTING.
I'M GOING TO BE AN AVENGER. WHO WOULD'A THOUGHT?
SAME DEAL AS BEFORE?
UH-UH.
NO. NO.
THIS IS GOING TO COST YOU.
THIS IS AN ENTIRELY DIFFERENT SITUATION.
YOU WANT ME TO REPORT BACK TO YOU ON THIS AND ON S.H.I.E.L.D.?
THAT'S GOING TO COST YOU.
ALL RIGHT, HOW MUCH?

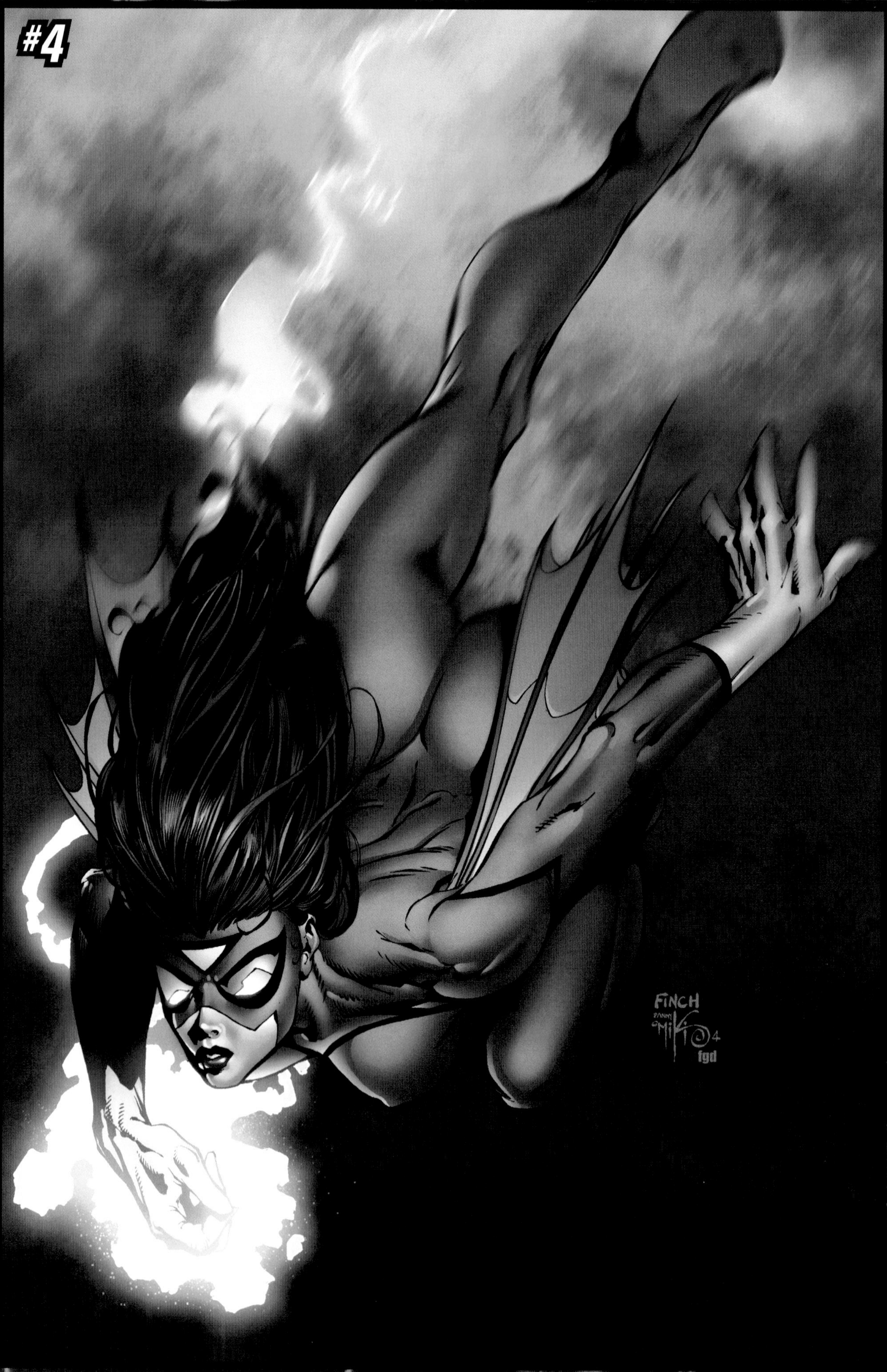
#4
FINCH

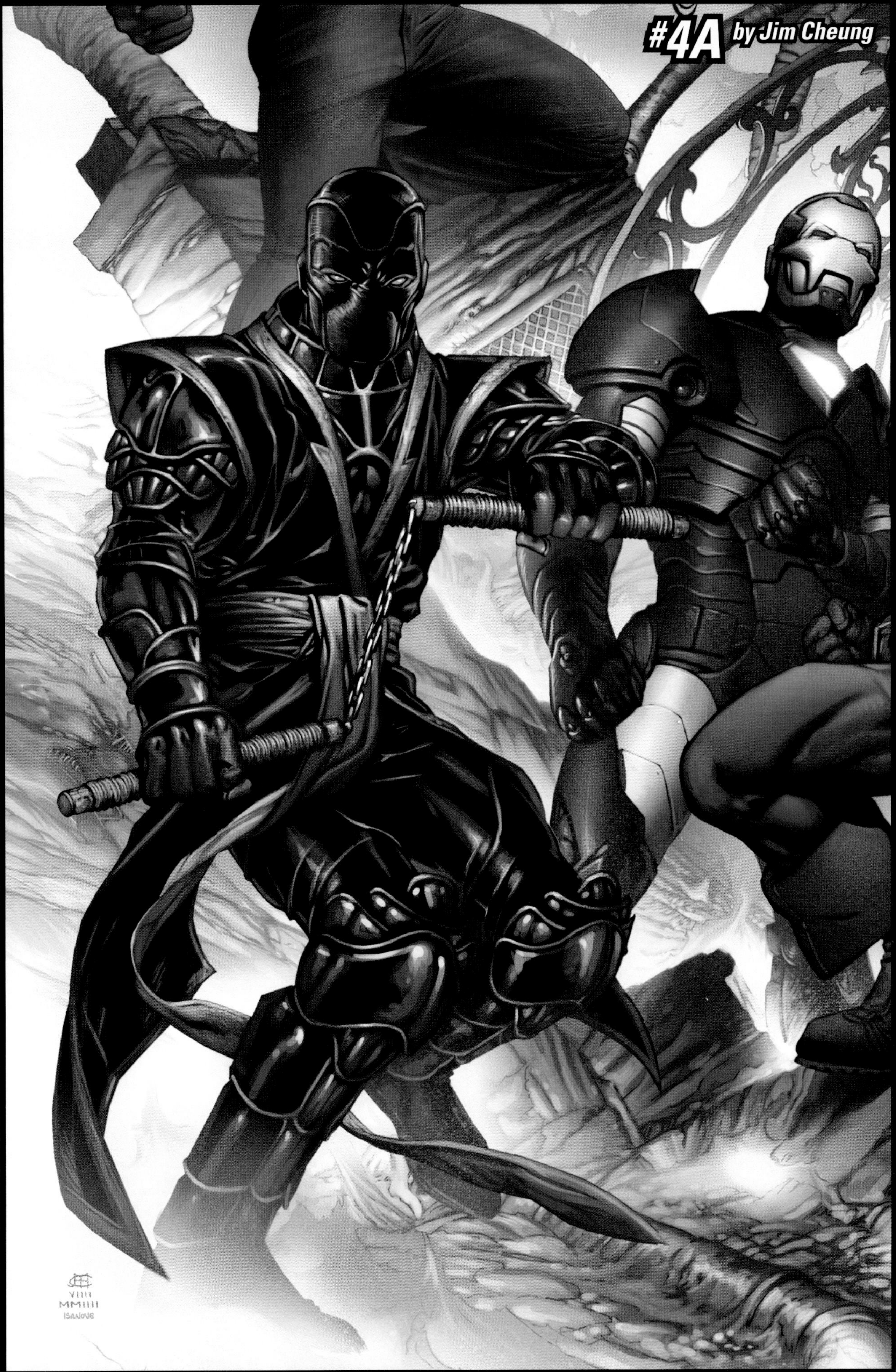

#4A by Jim Cheung

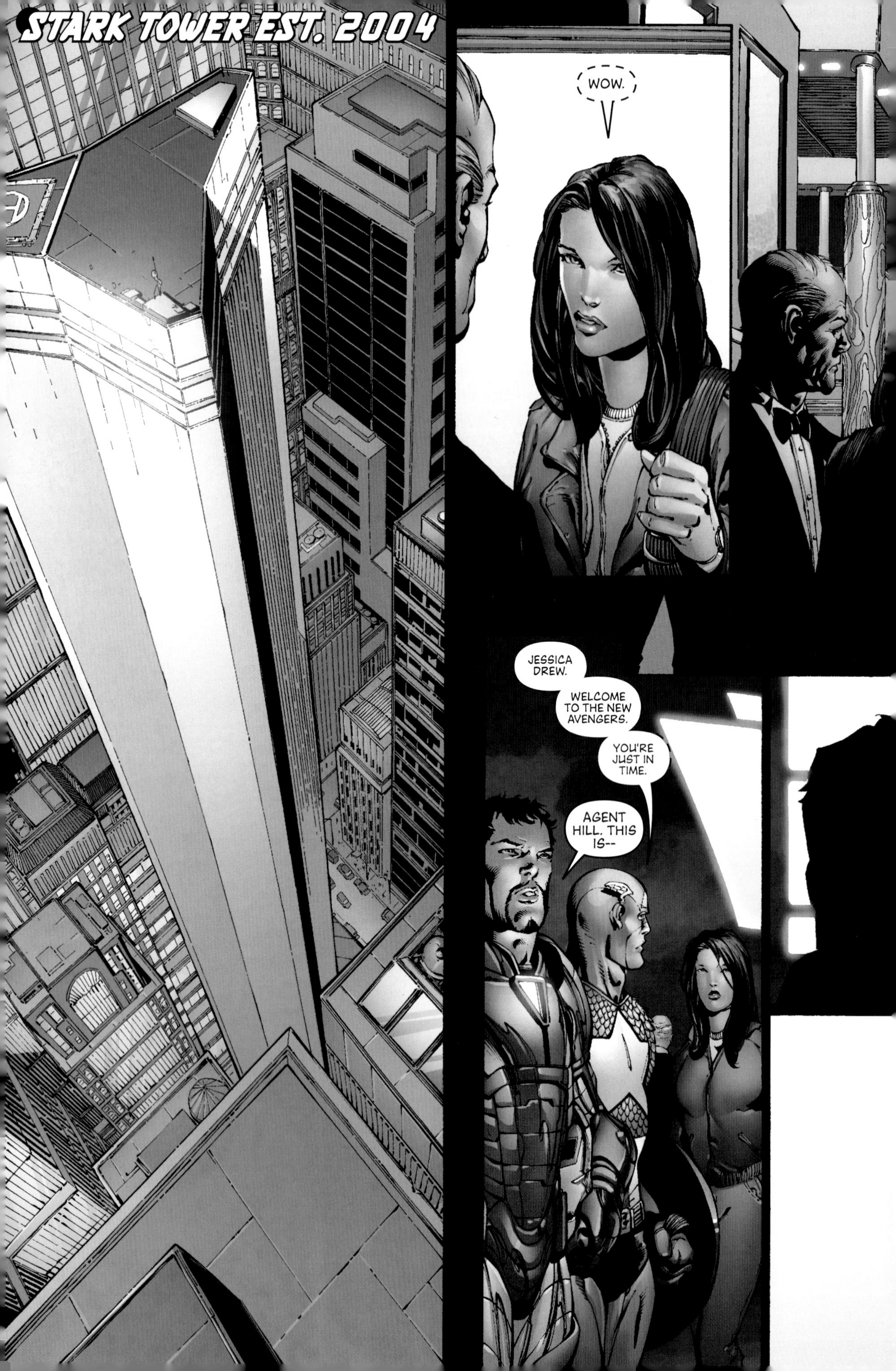
STARK TOWER EST. 2004
WOW.
JESSICA DREW.
WELCOME TO THE NEW AVENGERS.
YOU'RE JUST IN TIME.
AGENT HILL. THIS IS--

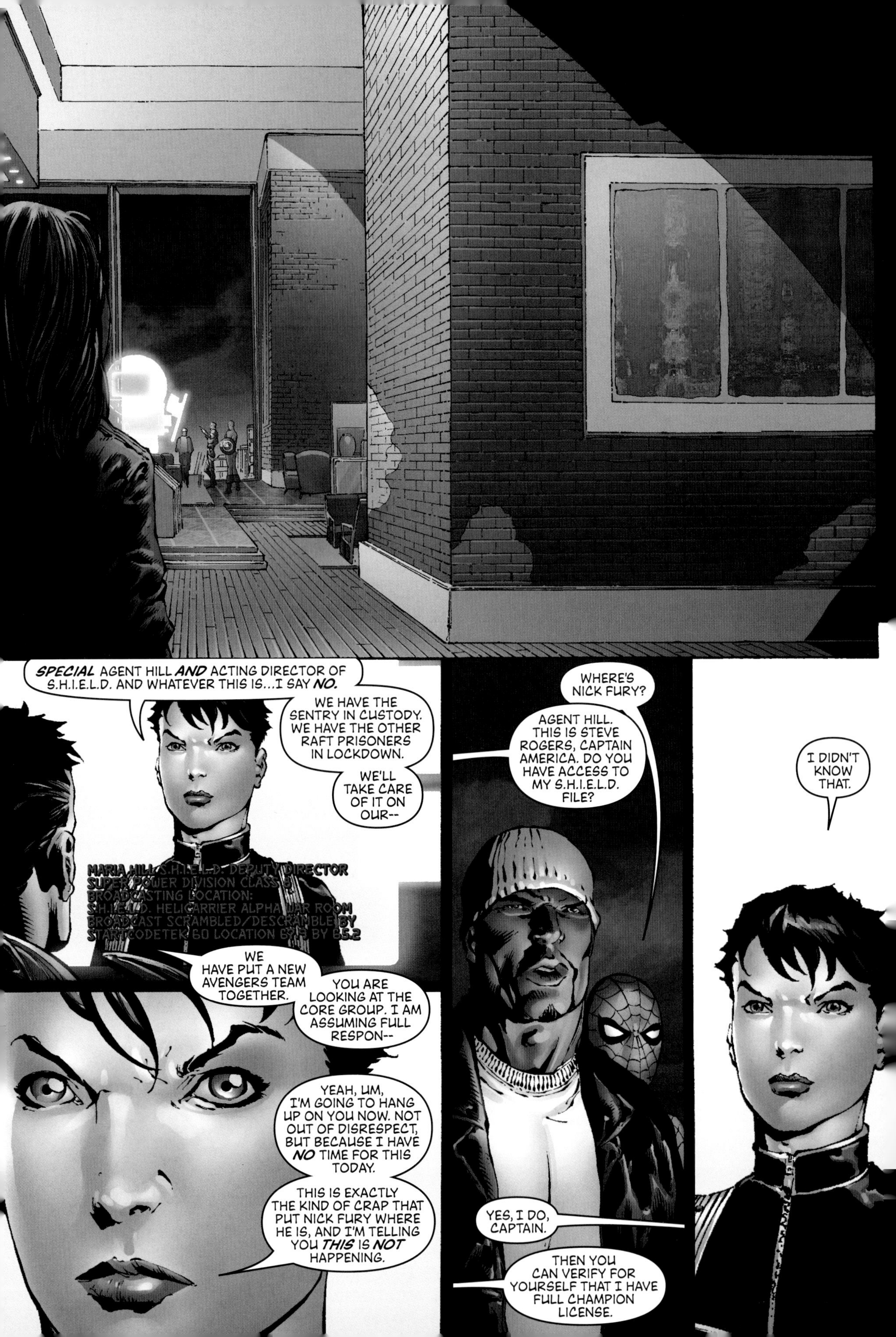

SPECIAL AGENT HILL AND ACTING DIRECTOR OF S.H.I.E.L.D. AND WHATEVER THIS IS...I SAY NO.
WE HAVE THE SENTRY IN CUSTODY. WE HAVE THE OTHER RAFT PRISONERS IN LOCKDOWN.
WE'LL TAKE CARE OF IT ON OUR--
MARIA HILL S.H.I.E.L.D. DEPUTY DIRECTOR SUPER POWER DIVISION CLASS 8 BROADCASTING LOCATION: S.H.I.E.L.D. HELICARRIER ALPHA WAR ROOM BROADCAST SCRAMBLED/DESCRAMBLE BY STARTCODETEK 60 LOCATION 67.9 BY 65.2
WE HAVE PUT A NEW AVENGERS TEAM TOGETHER.
YOU ARE LOOKING AT THE CORE GROUP. I AM ASSUMING FULL RESPON--
YEAH, UM, I'M GOING TO HANG UP ON YOU NOW. NOT OUT OF DISRESPECT, BUT BECAUSE I HAVE NO TIME FOR THIS TODAY.
THIS IS EXACTLY THE KIND OF CRAP THAT PUT NICK FURY WHERE HE IS, AND I'M TELLING YOU THIS IS NOT HAPPENING.
WHERE'S NICK FURY?
AGENT HILL. THIS IS STEVE ROGERS, CAPTAIN AMERICA. DO YOU HAVE ACCESS TO MY S.H.I.E.L.D. FILE?
I DIDN'T KNOW THAT.
YES, I DO, CAPTAIN.
THEN YOU CAN VERIFY FOR YOURSELF THAT I HAVE FULL CHAMPION LICENSE.

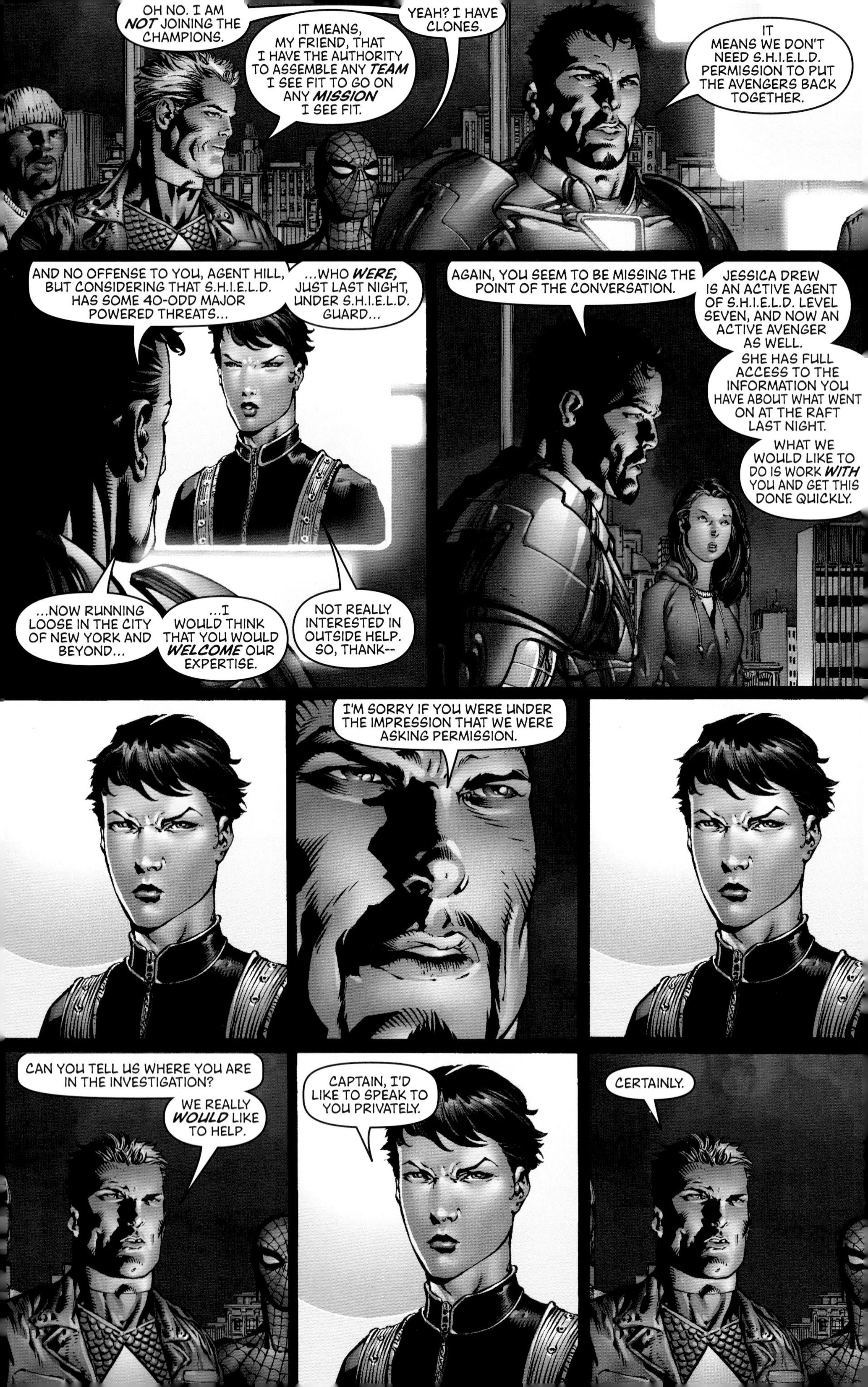
OH NO. I AM NOT JOINING THE CHAMPIONS.
IT MEANS, MY FRIEND, THAT I HAVE THE AUTHORITY TO ASSEMBLE ANY TEAM I SEE FIT TO GO ON ANY MISSION I SEE FIT.
YEAH? I HAVE CLONES.
IT MEANS WE DON'T NEED S.H.I.E.L.D. PERMISSION TO PUT THE AVENGERS BACK TOGETHER.
AND NO OFFENSE TO YOU, AGENT HILL, BUT CONSIDERING THAT S.H.I.E.L.D. HAS SOME 40-ODD MAJOR POWERED THREATS...
...WHO WERE, JUST LAST NIGHT, UNDER S.H.I.E.L.D. GUARD...
...NOW RUNNING LOOSE IN THE CITY OF NEW YORK AND BEYOND...
...I WOULD THINK THAT YOU WOULD WELCOME OUR EXPERTISE.
NOT REALLY INTERESTED IN OUTSIDE HELP. SO, THANK--
AGAIN, YOU SEEM TO BE MISSING THE POINT OF THE CONVERSATION.
JESSICA DREW IS AN ACTIVE AGENT OF S.H.I.E.L.D. LEVEL SEVEN, AND NOW AN ACTIVE AVENGER AS WELL.
SHE HAS FULL ACCESS TO THE INFORMATION YOU HAVE ABOUT WHAT WENT ON AT THE RAFT LAST NIGHT.
WHAT WE WOULD LIKE TO DO IS WORK WITH YOU AND GET THIS DONE QUICKLY.
I'M SORRY IF YOU WERE UNDER THE IMPRESSION THAT WE WERE ASKING PERMISSION.
CAN YOU TELL US WHERE YOU ARE IN THE INVESTIGATION?
WE REALLY WOULD LIKE TO HELP.
CAPTAIN, I'D LIKE TO SPEAK TO YOU PRIVATELY.
CERTAINLY.

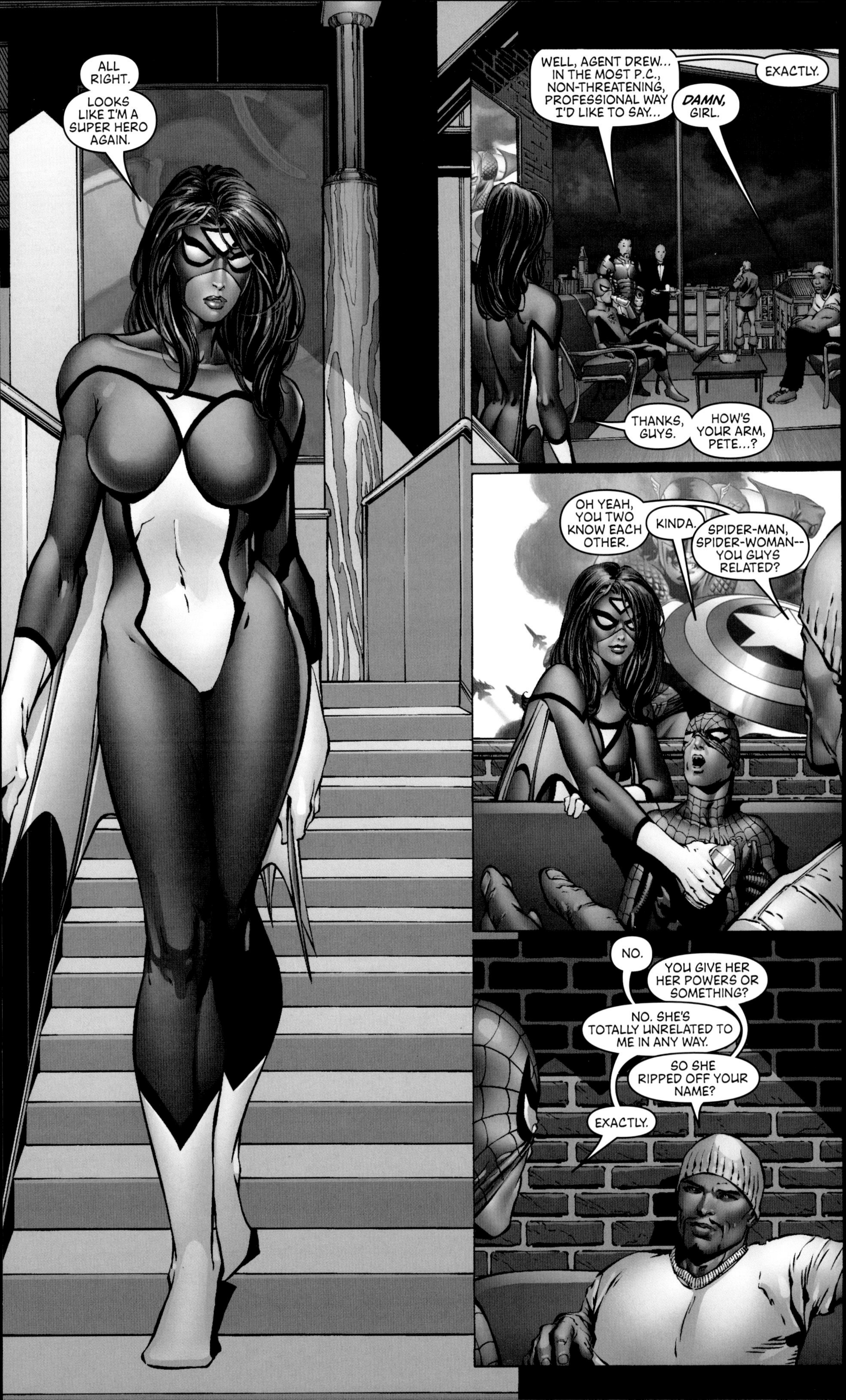
ALL RIGHT.
LOOKS LIKE I'M A SUPER HERO AGAIN.
WELL, AGENT DREW... IN THE MOST P.C., NON-THREATENING, PROFESSIONAL WAY I'D LIKE TO SAY...
DAMN, GIRL.
EXACTLY.
THANKS, GUYS.
HOW'S YOUR ARM, PETE...?
OH YEAH, YOU TWO KNOW EACH OTHER.
KINDA.
SPIDER-MAN, SPIDER-WOMAN-- YOU GUYS RELATED?
NO.
YOU GIVE HER HER POWERS OR SOMETHING?
NO. SHE'S TOTALLY UNRELATED TO ME IN ANY WAY.
SO SHE RIPPED OFF YOUR NAME?
EXACTLY.

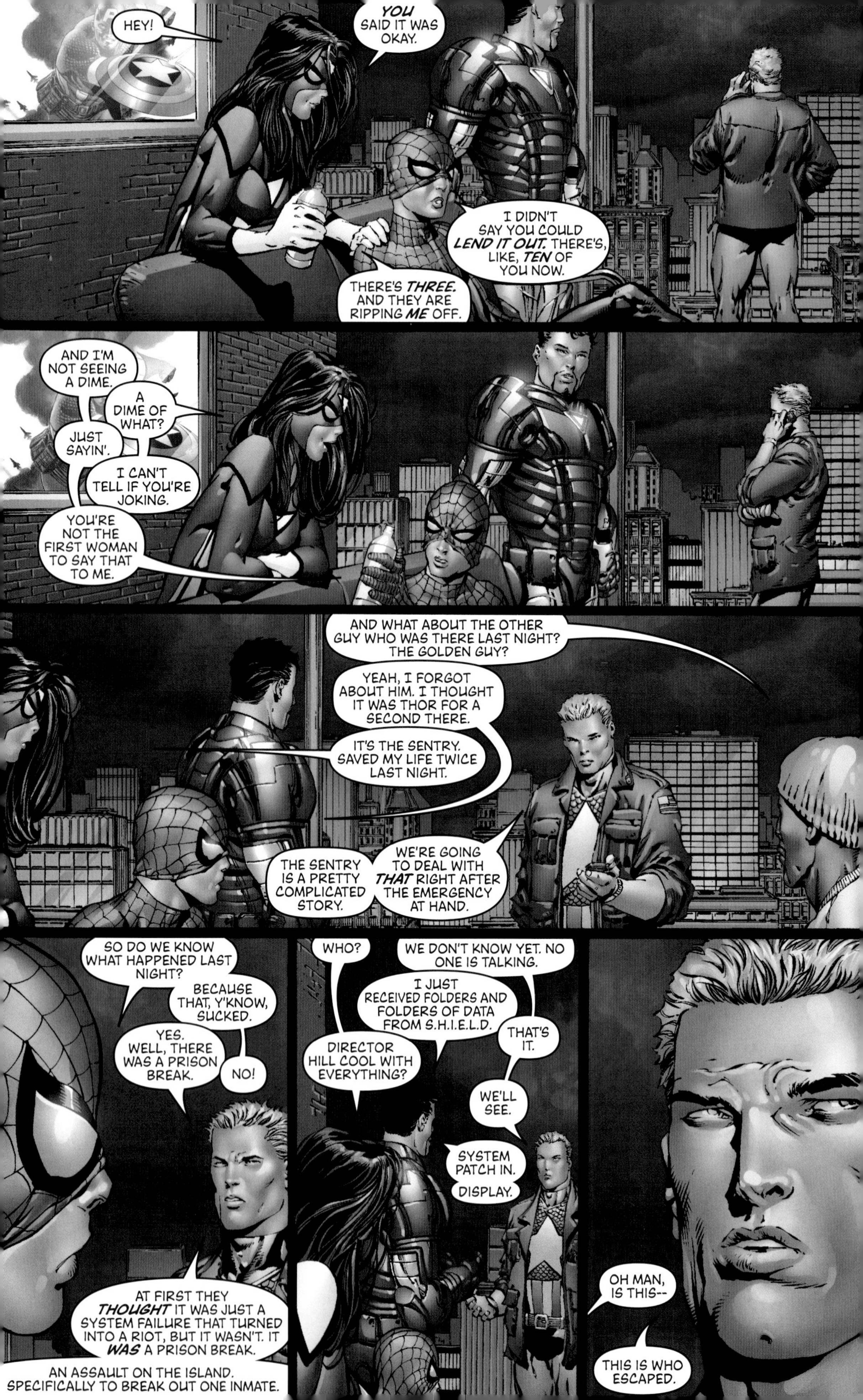

HEY!
YOU SAID IT WAS OKAY.
I DIDN'T SAY YOU COULD LEND IT OUT. THERE'S, LIKE, TEN OF YOU NOW.
THERE'S THREE. AND THEY ARE RIPPING ME OFF.
AND I'M NOT SEEING A DIME.
A DIME OF WHAT?
JUST SAYIN'.
I CAN'T TELL IF YOU'RE JOKING.
YOU'RE NOT THE FIRST WOMAN TO SAY THAT TO ME.
AND WHAT ABOUT THE OTHER GUY WHO WAS THERE LAST NIGHT? THE GOLDEN GUY?
YEAH, I FORGOT ABOUT HIM. I THOUGHT IT WAS THOR FOR A SECOND THERE.
IT'S THE SENTRY. SAVED MY LIFE TWICE LAST NIGHT.
THE SENTRY IS A PRETTY COMPLICATED STORY.
WE'RE GOING TO DEAL WITH THAT RIGHT AFTER THE EMERGENCY AT HAND.
SO DO WE KNOW WHAT HAPPENED LAST NIGHT?
BECAUSE THAT, Y'KNOW, SUCKED.
YES. WELL, THERE WAS A PRISON BREAK.
NO!
AT FIRST THEY THOUGHT IT WAS JUST A SYSTEM FAILURE THAT TURNED INTO A RIOT, BUT IT WASN'T. IT WAS A PRISON BREAK.
AN ASSAULT ON THE ISLAND. SPECIFICALLY TO BREAK OUT ONE INMATE.
WHO?
WE DON'T KNOW YET. NO ONE IS TALKING.
I JUST RECEIVED FOLDERS AND FOLDERS OF DATA FROM S.H.I.E.L.D.
DIRECTOR HILL COOL WITH EVERYTHING?
THAT'S IT.
WE'LL SEE.
SYSTEM PATCH IN.
DISPLAY.
OH MAN, IS THIS--
THIS IS WHO ESCAPED.

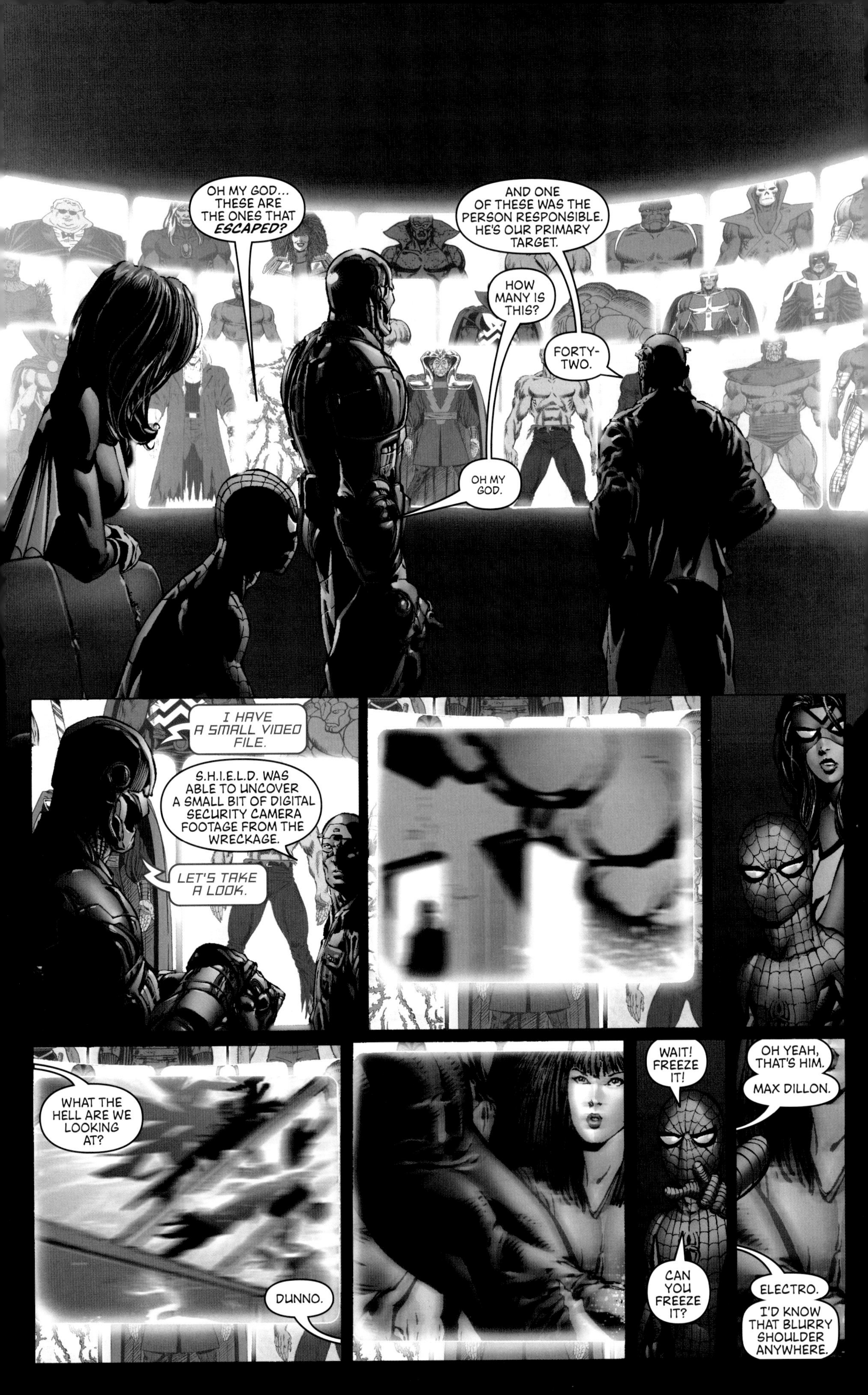

OH MY GOD... THESE ARE THE ONES THAT ESCAPED?
AND ONE OF THESE WAS THE PERSON RESPONSIBLE. HE'S OUR PRIMARY TARGET.
HOW MANY IS THIS?
FORTY-TWO.
OH MY GOD.
I HAVE A SMALL VIDEO FILE.
S.H.I.E.L.D. WAS ABLE TO UNCOVER A SMALL BIT OF DIGITAL SECURITY CAMERA FOOTAGE FROM THE WRECKAGE.
LET'S TAKE A LOOK.
WHAT THE HELL ARE WE LOOKING AT?
DUNNO.
WAIT! FREEZE IT!
CAN YOU FREEZE IT?
OH YEAH, THAT'S HIM.
MAX DILLON.
ELECTRO.
I'D KNOW THAT BLURRY SHOULDER ANYWHERE.

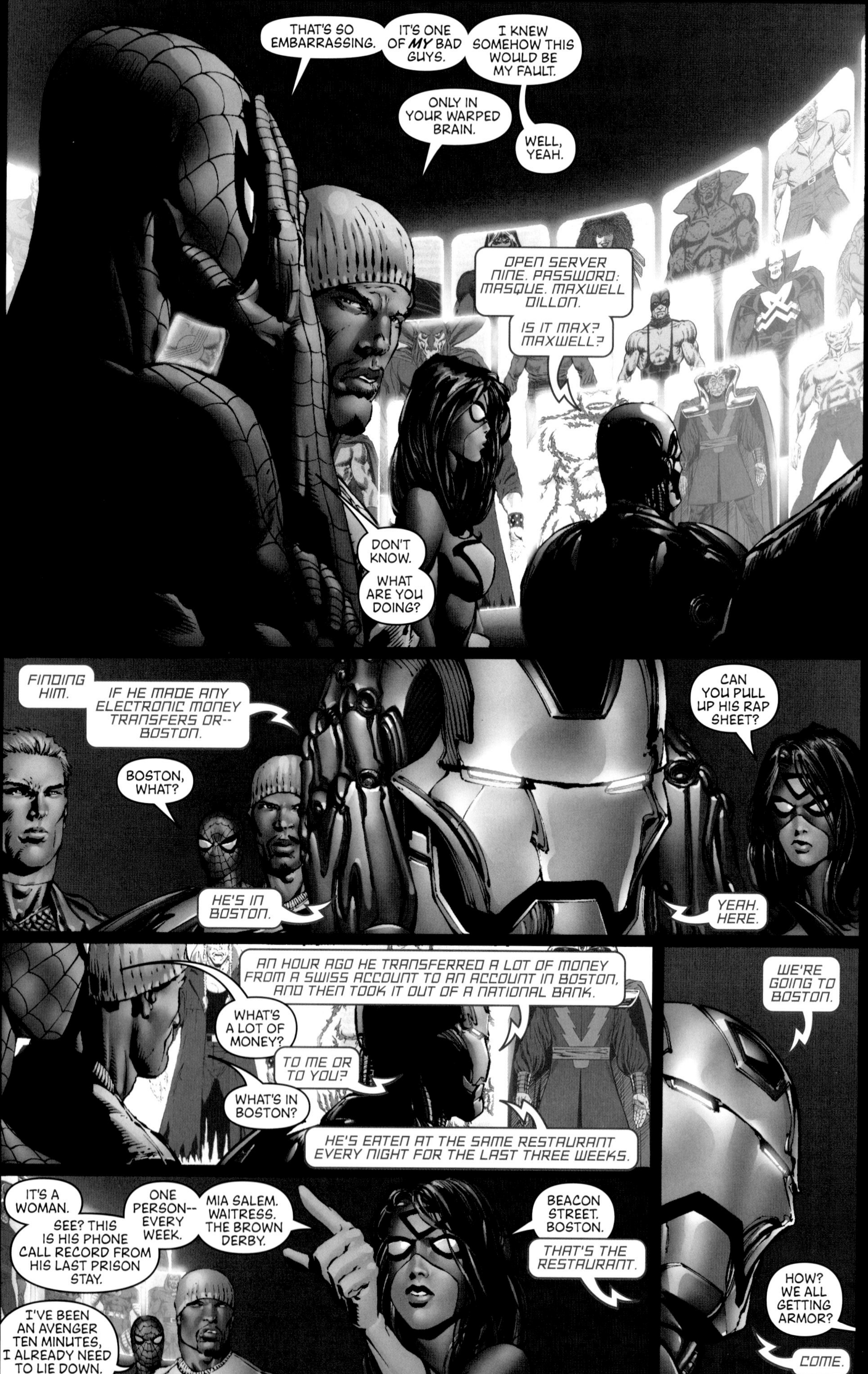
THAT'S SO EMBARRASSING.
IT'S ONE OF MY BAD GUYS.
I KNEW SOMEHOW THIS WOULD BE MY FAULT.
ONLY IN YOUR WARPED BRAIN.
WELL, YEAH.
OPEN SERVER NINE. PASSWORD: MASQUE. MAXWELL DILLON.
IS IT MAX? MAXWELL?
DON'T KNOW.
WHAT ARE YOU DOING?
FINDING HIM.
IF HE MADE ANY ELECTRONIC MONEY TRANSFERS OR-- BOSTON.
BOSTON, WHAT?
CAN YOU PULL UP HIS RAP SHEET?
HE'S IN BOSTON.
YEAH. HERE.
AN HOUR AGO HE TRANSFERRED A LOT OF MONEY FROM A SWISS ACCOUNT TO AN ACCOUNT IN BOSTON, AND THEN TOOK IT OUT OF A NATIONAL BANK.
WHAT'S A LOT OF MONEY?
TO ME OR TO YOU?
WHAT'S IN BOSTON?
HE'S EATEN AT THE SAME RESTAURANT EVERY NIGHT FOR THE LAST THREE WEEKS.
WE'RE GOING TO BOSTON.
IT'S A WOMAN.
SEE? THIS IS HIS PHONE CALL RECORD FROM HIS LAST PRISON STAY.
ONE PERSON-- EVERY WEEK.
MIA SALEM. WAITRESS. THE BROWN DERBY.
BEACON STREET. BOSTON.
THAT'S THE RESTAURANT.
I'VE BEEN AN AVENGER TEN MINUTES, I ALREADY NEED TO LIE DOWN.
HOW? WE ALL GETTING ARMOR?
COME.

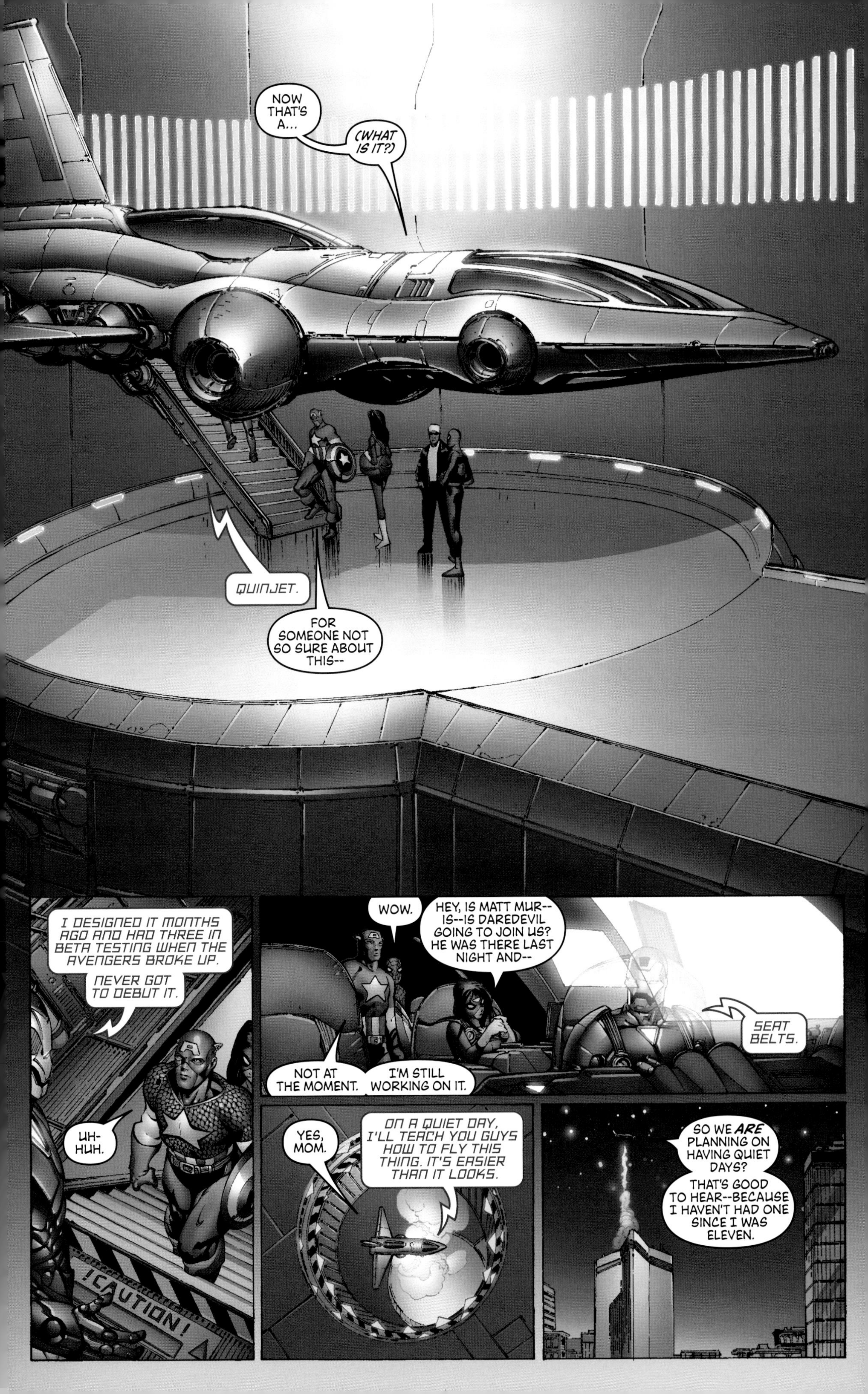
NOW THAT'S A...
(WHAT IS IT?)
QUINJET.
FOR SOMEONE NOT SO SURE ABOUT THIS--
I DESIGNED IT MONTHS AGO AND HAD THREE IN BETA TESTING WHEN THE AVENGERS BROKE UP.
NEVER GOT TO DEBUT IT.
UH-HUH.
!CAUTION!
WOW.
HEY, IS MATT MUR-- IS--IS DAREDEVIL GOING TO JOIN US? HE WAS THERE LAST NIGHT AND--
SEAT BELTS.
NOT AT THE MOMENT.
I'M STILL WORKING ON IT.
YES, MOM.
ON A QUIET DAY, I'LL TEACH YOU GUYS HOW TO FLY THIS THING. IT'S EASIER THAN IT LOOKS.
SO WE ARE PLANNING ON HAVING QUIET DAYS?
THAT'S GOOD TO HEAR--BECAUSE I HAVEN'T HAD ONE SINCE I WAS ELEVEN.

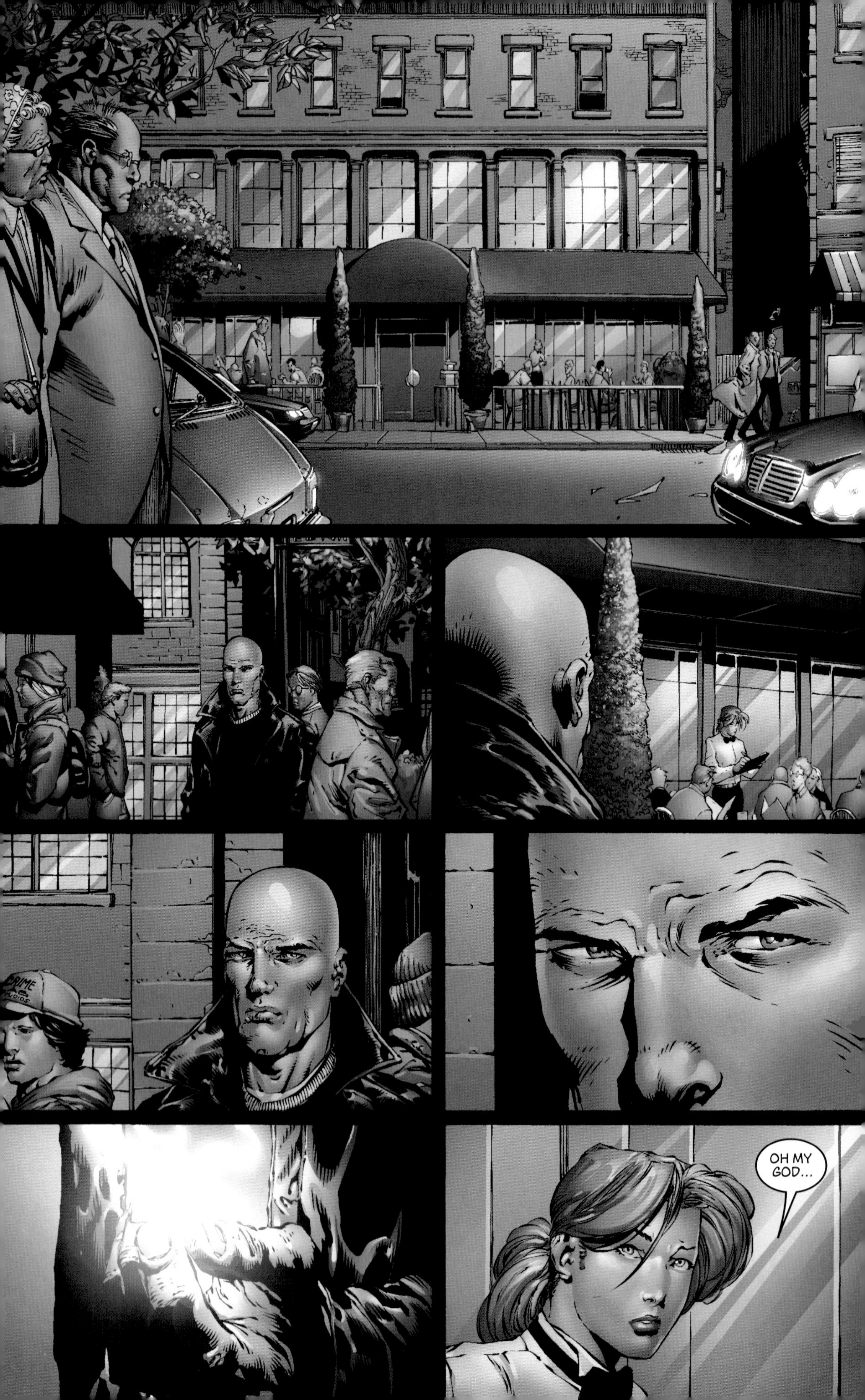
OH MY GOD...

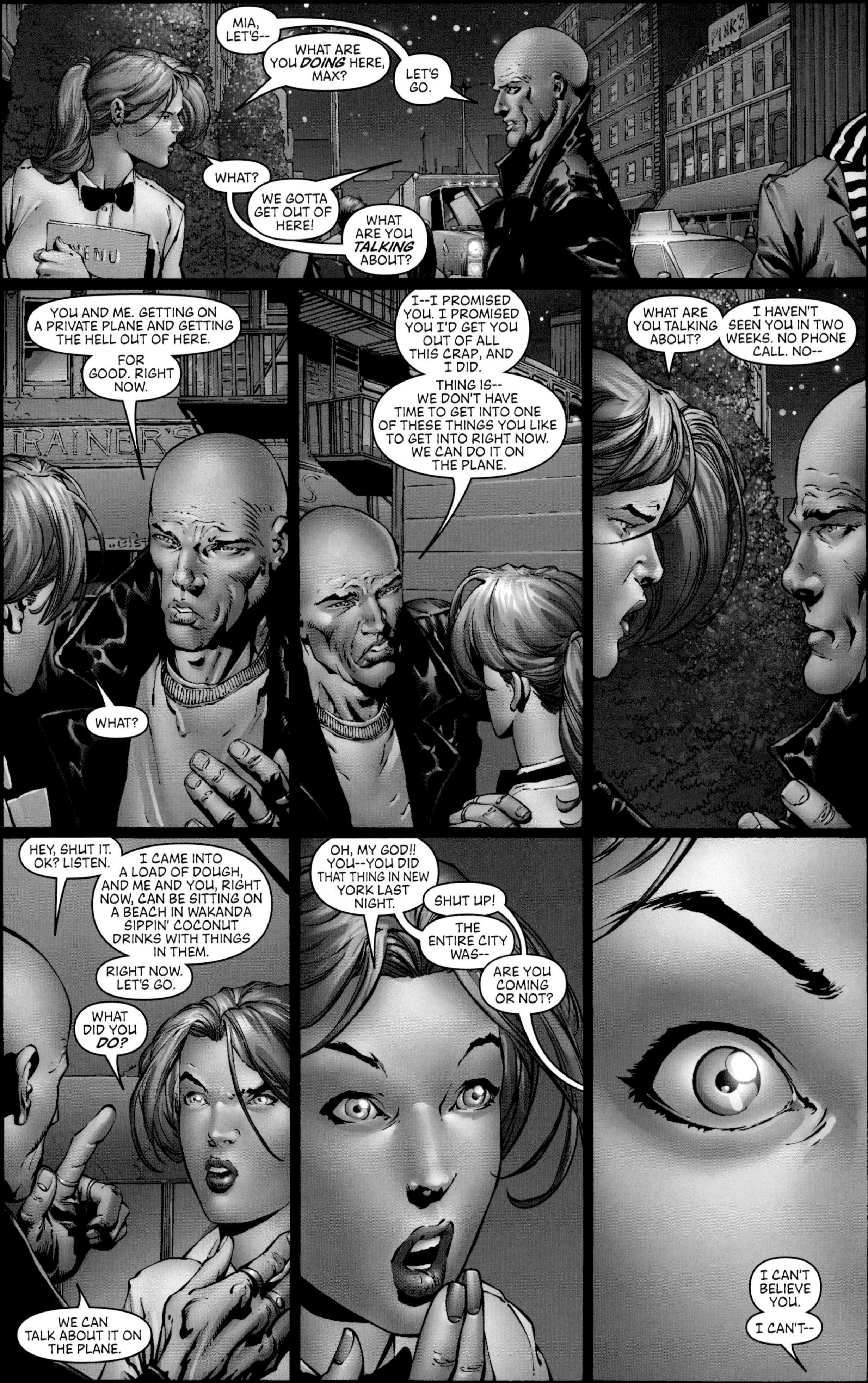
MIA, LET'S--
WHAT ARE YOU *DOING* HERE, MAX?
LET'S GO.
WHAT?
WE GOTTA GET OUT OF HERE!
WHAT ARE YOU *TALKING* ABOUT?
PINK'S
MENU
YOU AND ME. GETTING ON A PRIVATE PLANE AND GETTING THE HELL OUT OF HERE.
FOR GOOD. RIGHT NOW.
WHAT?
TRAINER'S
I--I PROMISED YOU. I PROMISED YOU I'D GET YOU OUT OF ALL THIS CRAP, AND I DID.
THING IS-- WE DON'T HAVE TIME TO GET INTO ONE OF THESE THINGS YOU LIKE TO GET INTO RIGHT NOW. WE CAN DO IT ON THE PLANE.
WHAT ARE YOU TALKING ABOUT?
I HAVEN'T SEEN YOU IN TWO WEEKS. NO PHONE CALL. NO--
HEY, SHUT IT. OK? LISTEN.
I CAME INTO A LOAD OF DOUGH, AND ME AND YOU, RIGHT NOW, CAN BE SITTING ON A BEACH IN WAKANDA SIPPIN' COCONUT DRINKS WITH THINGS IN THEM.
RIGHT NOW. LET'S GO.
WHAT DID YOU *DO?*
WE CAN TALK ABOUT IT ON THE PLANE.
OH, MY GOD!! YOU--YOU DID THAT THING IN NEW YORK LAST NIGHT.
SHUT UP!
THE ENTIRE CITY WAS--
ARE YOU COMING OR NOT?
I CAN'T BELIEVE YOU.
I CAN'T--

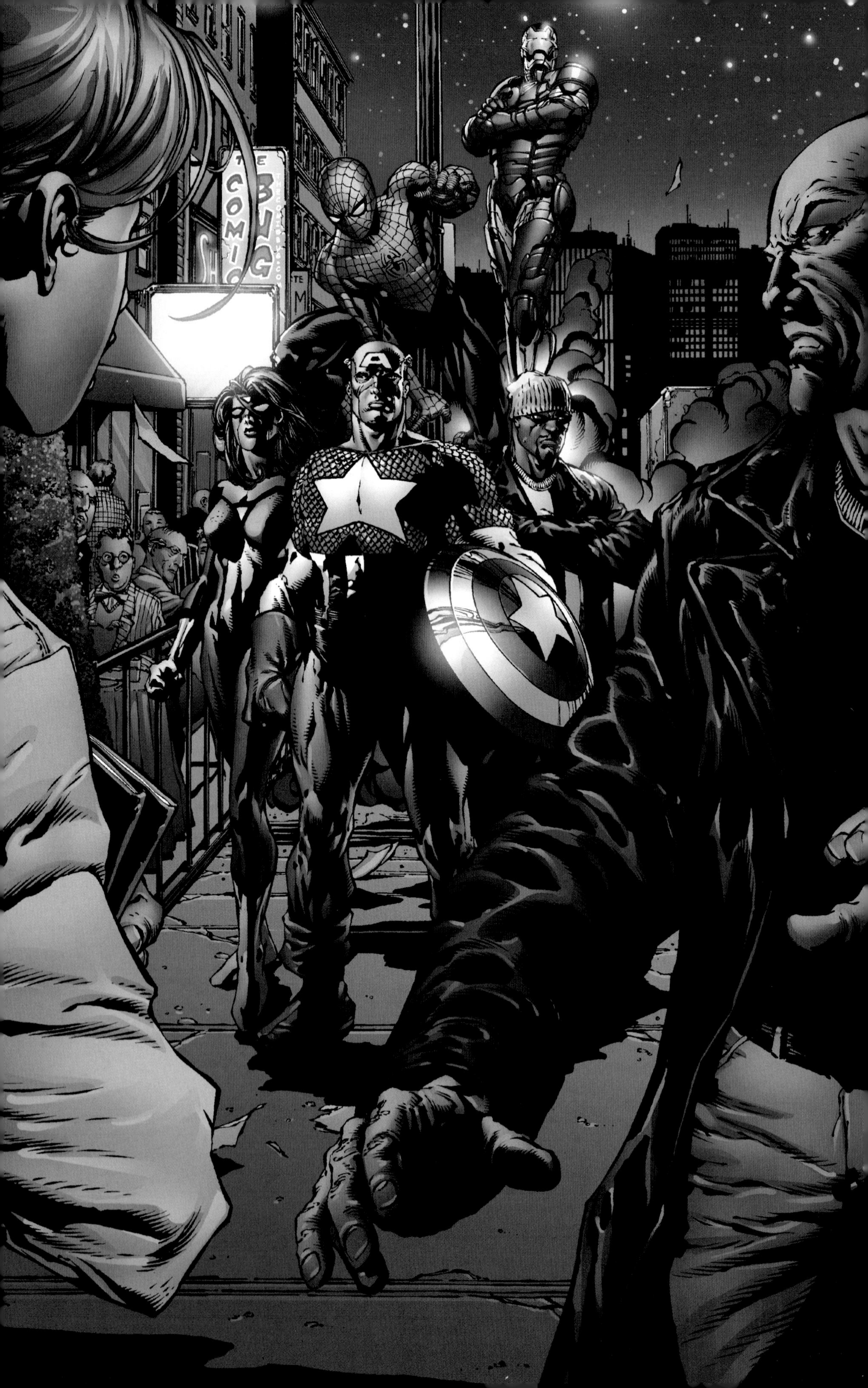
BUG
THECOMICBUG.COM

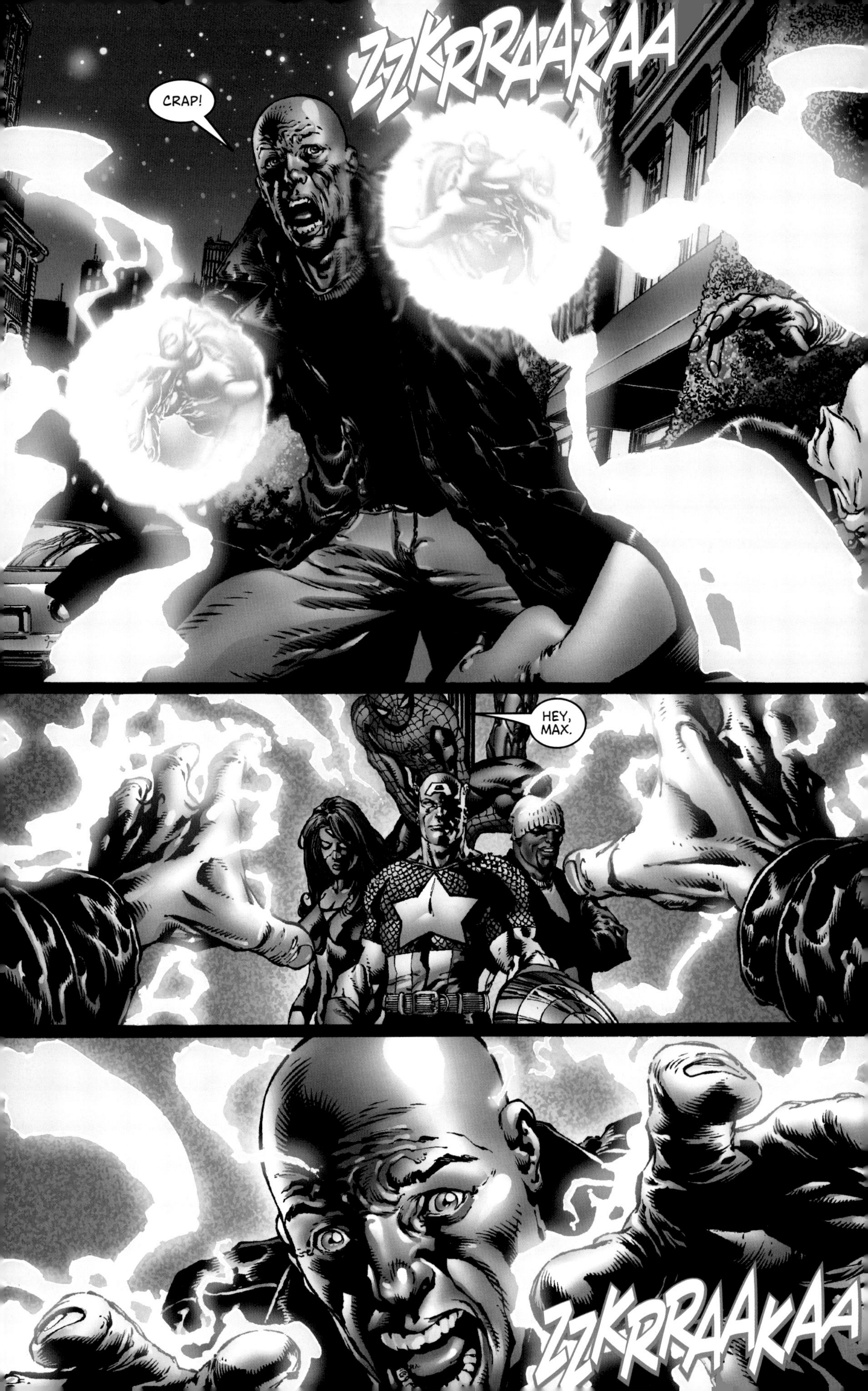
ZZKRRAAKAA
CRAP!
HEY, MAX.
ZZKRRAAKAA

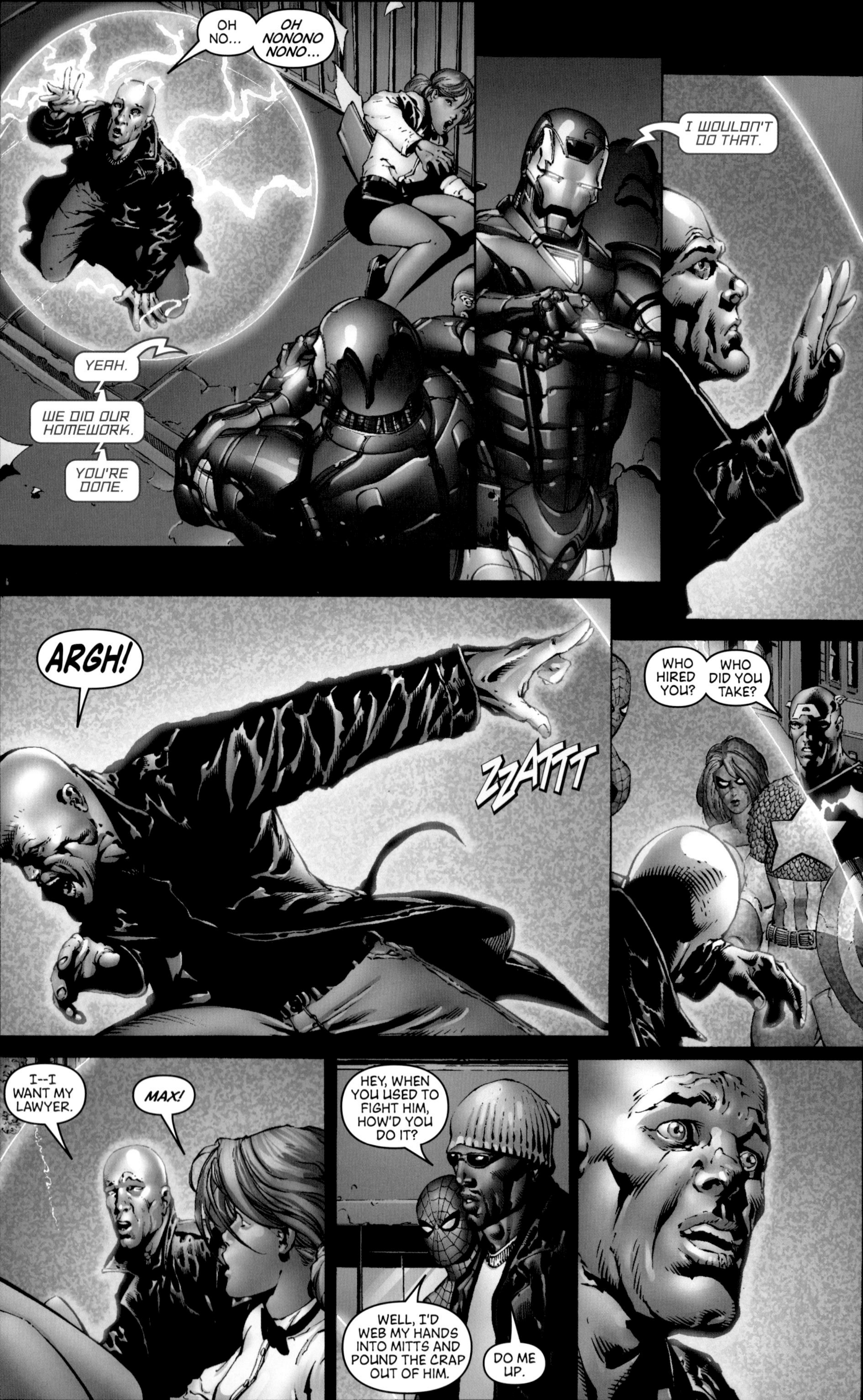

OH NO...
OH NONONO NONO...
I WOULDN'T DO THAT.
YEAH.
WE DID OUR HOMEWORK.
YOU'RE DONE.
ARGH!
ZZATTT
WHO HIRED YOU?
WHO DID YOU TAKE?
I--I WANT MY LAWYER.
MAX!
HEY, WHEN YOU USED TO FIGHT HIM, HOW'D YOU DO IT?
WELL, I'D WEB MY HANDS INTO MITTS AND POUND THE CRAP OUT OF HIM.
DO ME UP.

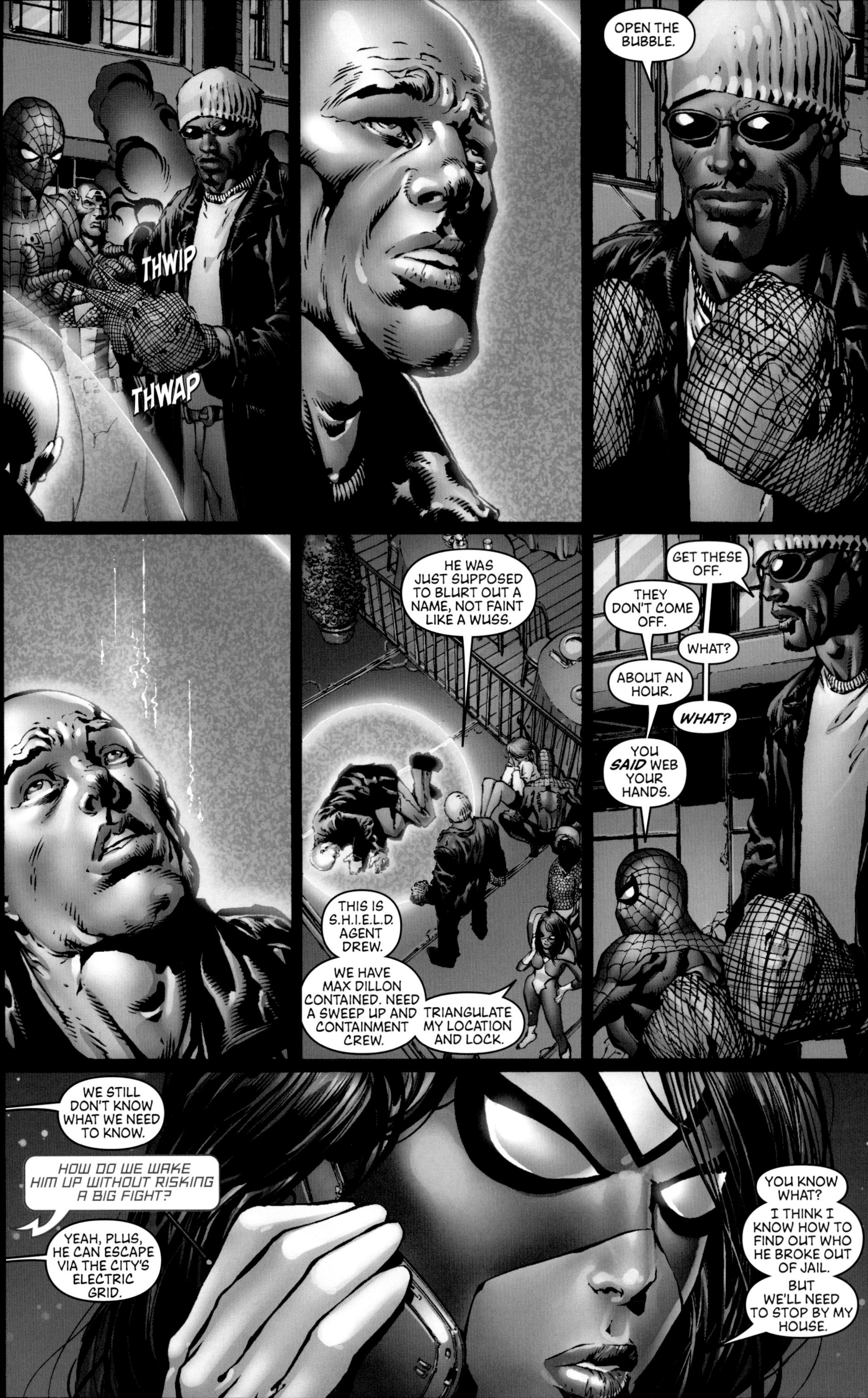
THWIP
THWAP
OPEN THE BUBBLE.
HE WAS JUST SUPPOSED TO BLURT OUT A NAME, NOT FAINT LIKE A WUSS.
THIS IS S.H.I.E.L.D. AGENT DREW.
WE HAVE MAX DILLON CONTAINED. NEED A SWEEP UP AND CONTAINMENT CREW.
TRIANGULATE MY LOCATION AND LOCK.
GET THESE OFF.
THEY DON'T COME OFF.
WHAT?
ABOUT AN HOUR.
WHAT?
YOU SAID WEB YOUR HANDS.
WE STILL DON'T KNOW WHAT WE NEED TO KNOW.
HOW DO WE WAKE HIM UP WITHOUT RISKING A BIG FIGHT?
YEAH, PLUS, HE CAN ESCAPE VIA THE CITY'S ELECTRIC GRID.
YOU KNOW WHAT?
I THINK I KNOW HOW TO FIND OUT WHO HE BROKE OUT OF JAIL.
BUT WE'LL NEED TO STOP BY MY HOUSE.

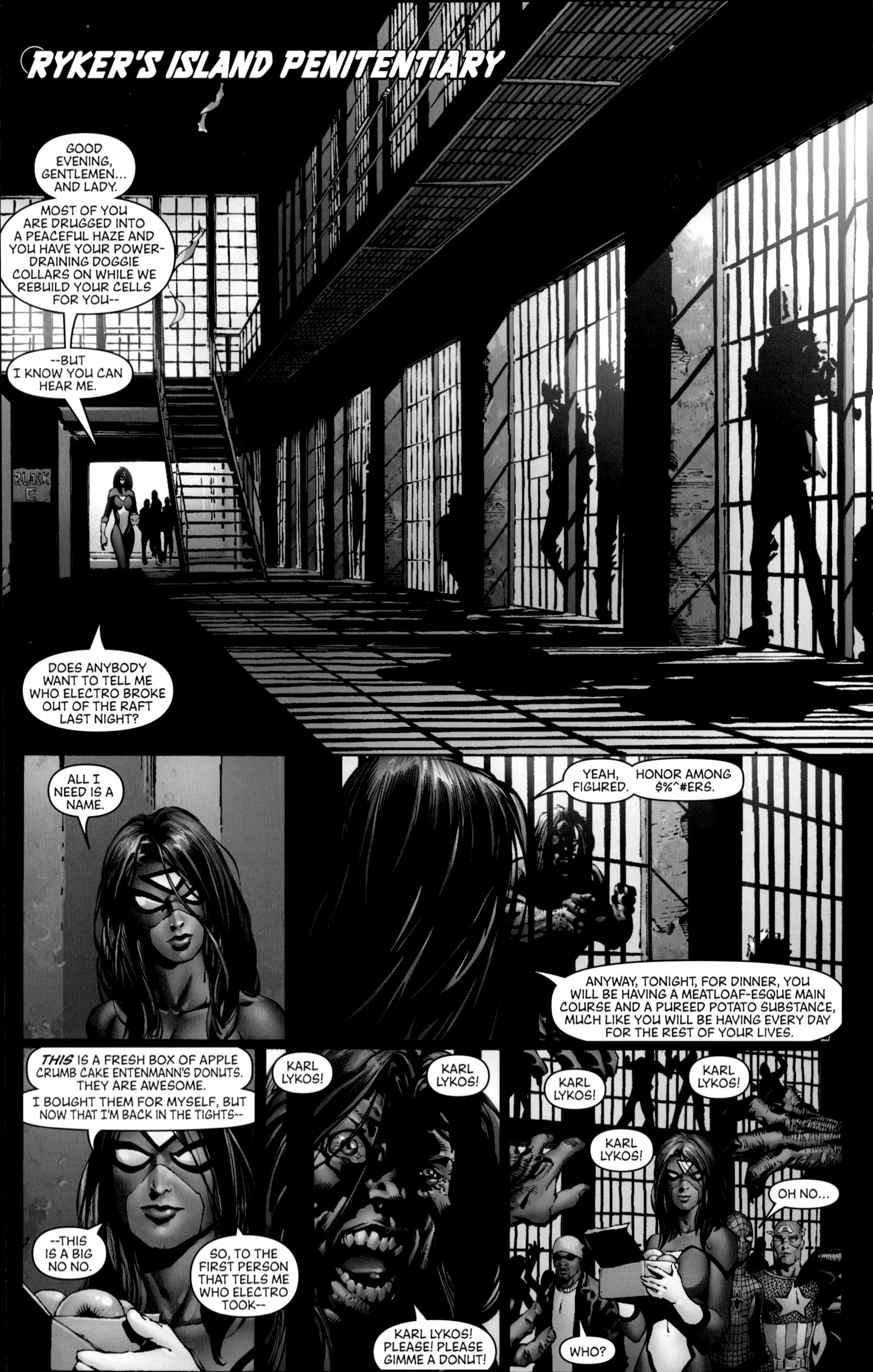
RYKER'S ISLAND PENITENTIARY
GOOD EVENING, GENTLEMEN... AND LADY.
MOST OF YOU ARE DRUGGED INTO A PEACEFUL HAZE AND YOU HAVE YOUR POWER-DRAINING DOGGIE COLLARS ON WHILE WE REBUILD YOUR CELLS FOR YOU--
--BUT I KNOW YOU CAN HEAR ME.
BLOCK C
DOES ANYBODY WANT TO TELL ME WHO ELECTRO BROKE OUT OF THE RAFT LAST NIGHT?
ALL I NEED IS A NAME.
YEAH, FIGURED.
HONOR AMONG $%^#ERS.
ANYWAY, TONIGHT, FOR DINNER, YOU WILL BE HAVING A MEATLOAF-ESQUE MAIN COURSE AND A PUREED POTATO SUBSTANCE, MUCH LIKE YOU WILL BE HAVING EVERY DAY FOR THE REST OF YOUR LIVES.
THIS IS A FRESH BOX OF APPLE CRUMB CAKE ENTENMANN'S DONUTS. THEY ARE AWESOME.
I BOUGHT THEM FOR MYSELF, BUT NOW THAT I'M BACK IN THE TIGHTS--
--THIS IS A BIG NO NO.
SO, TO THE FIRST PERSON THAT TELLS ME WHO ELECTRO TOOK--
KARL LYKOS!
KARL LYKOS!
KARL LYKOS! PLEASE! PLEASE GIMME A DONUT!
KARL LYKOS!
KARL LYKOS!
KARL LYKOS!
OH NO...
WHO?

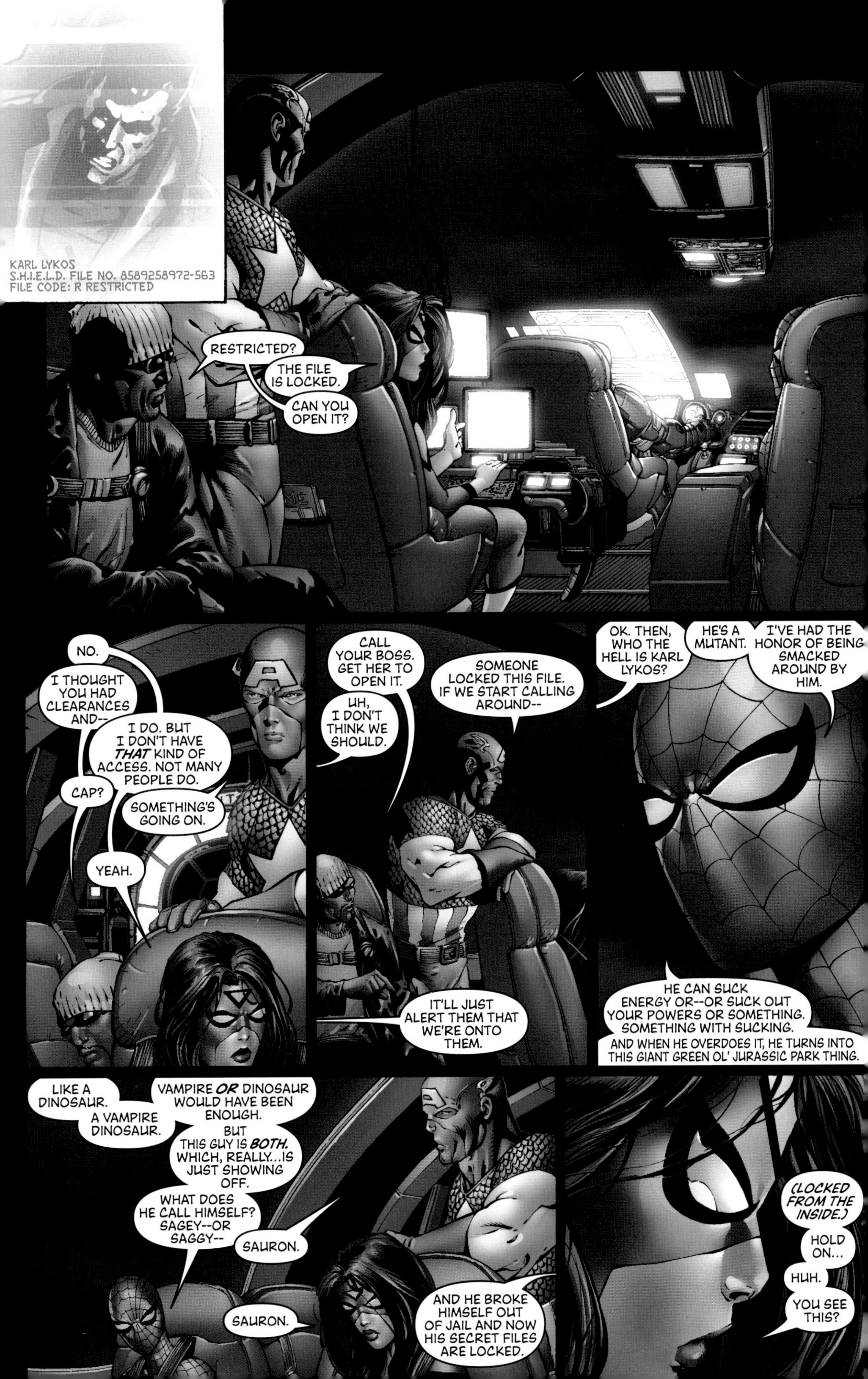
KARL LYKOS
S.H.I.E.L.D. FILE NO. 8589258972-563
FILE CODE: R RESTRICTED
RESTRICTED?
THE FILE IS LOCKED.
CAN YOU OPEN IT?
NO.
I THOUGHT YOU HAD CLEARANCES AND--
I DO. BUT I DON'T HAVE *THAT* KIND OF ACCESS. NOT MANY PEOPLE DO.
CAP?
SOMETHING'S GOING ON.
YEAH.
CALL YOUR BOSS. GET HER TO OPEN IT.
UH, I DON'T THINK WE SHOULD.
SOMEONE LOCKED THIS FILE. IF WE START CALLING AROUND--
IT'LL JUST ALERT THEM THAT WE'RE ONTO THEM.
OK. THEN, WHO THE HELL IS KARL LYKOS?
HE'S A MUTANT.
I'VE HAD THE HONOR OF BEING SMACKED AROUND BY HIM.
HE CAN SUCK ENERGY OR--OR SUCK OUT YOUR POWERS OR SOMETHING. SOMETHING WITH SUCKING.
AND WHEN HE OVERDOES IT, HE TURNS INTO THIS GIANT GREEN OL' JURASSIC PARK THING.
LIKE A DINOSAUR.
A VAMPIRE DINOSAUR.
VAMPIRE *OR* DINOSAUR WOULD HAVE BEEN ENOUGH.
BUT THIS GUY IS *BOTH.* WHICH, REALLY...IS JUST SHOWING OFF.
WHAT DOES HE CALL HIMSELF? SAGEY--OR SAGGY--
SAURON.
SAURON.
AND HE BROKE HIMSELF OUT OF JAIL AND NOW HIS SECRET FILES ARE LOCKED.
(LOCKED FROM THE INSIDE.)
HOLD ON...
HUH.
YOU SEE THIS?

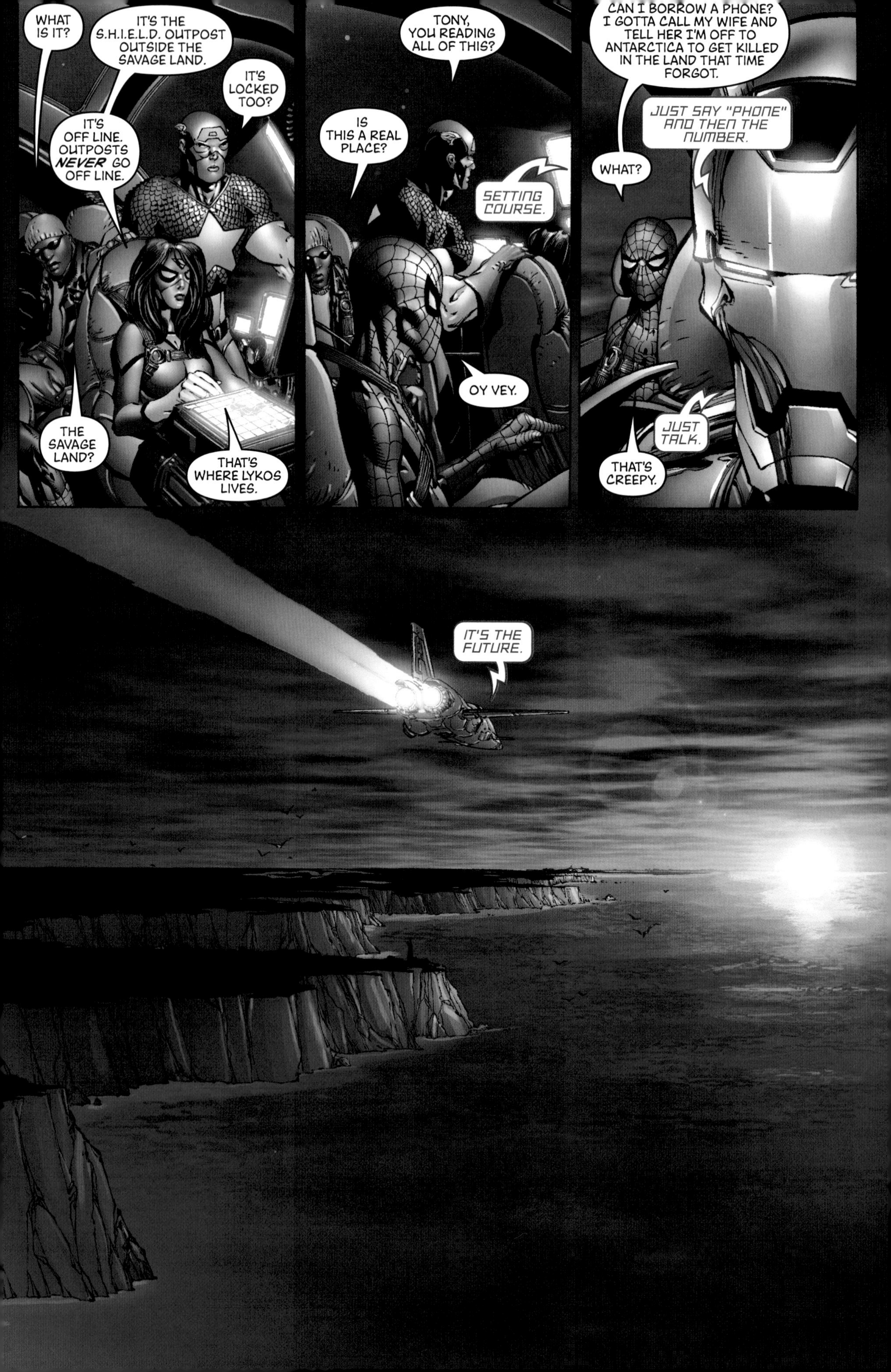

WHAT IS IT?
IT'S THE S.H.I.E.L.D. OUTPOST OUTSIDE THE SAVAGE LAND.
IT'S LOCKED TOO?
IT'S OFF LINE. OUTPOSTS NEVER GO OFF LINE.
THE SAVAGE LAND?
THAT'S WHERE LYKOS LIVES.
TONY, YOU READING ALL OF THIS?
IS THIS A REAL PLACE?
SETTING COURSE.
OY VEY.
CAN I BORROW A PHONE? I GOTTA CALL MY WIFE AND TELL HER I'M OFF TO ANTARCTICA TO GET KILLED IN THE LAND THAT TIME FORGOT.
JUST SAY "PHONE" AND THEN THE NUMBER.
WHAT?
JUST TALK.
THAT'S CREEPY.
IT'S THE FUTURE.

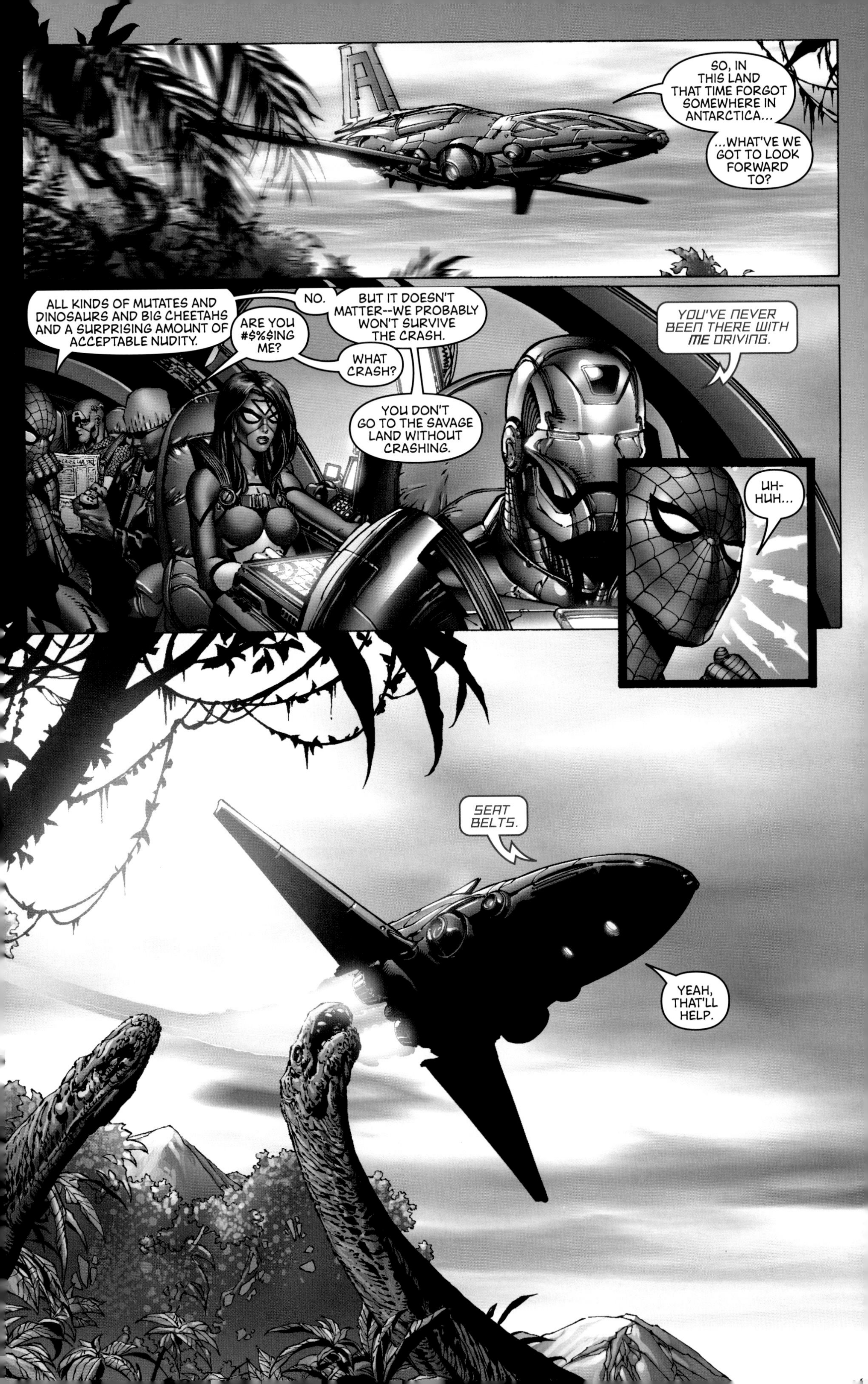
SO, IN THIS LAND THAT TIME FORGOT SOMEWHERE IN ANTARCTICA...
...WHAT'VE WE GOT TO LOOK FORWARD TO?
ALL KINDS OF MUTATES AND DINOSAURS AND BIG CHEETAHS AND A SURPRISING AMOUNT OF ACCEPTABLE NUDITY.
ARE YOU #$%$ING ME?
NO.
BUT IT DOESN'T MATTER--WE PROBABLY WON'T SURVIVE THE CRASH.
WHAT CRASH?
YOU DON'T GO TO THE SAVAGE LAND WITHOUT CRASHING.
YOU'VE NEVER BEEN THERE WITH ME DRIVING.
UH-HUH...
SEAT BELTS.
YEAH, THAT'LL HELP.

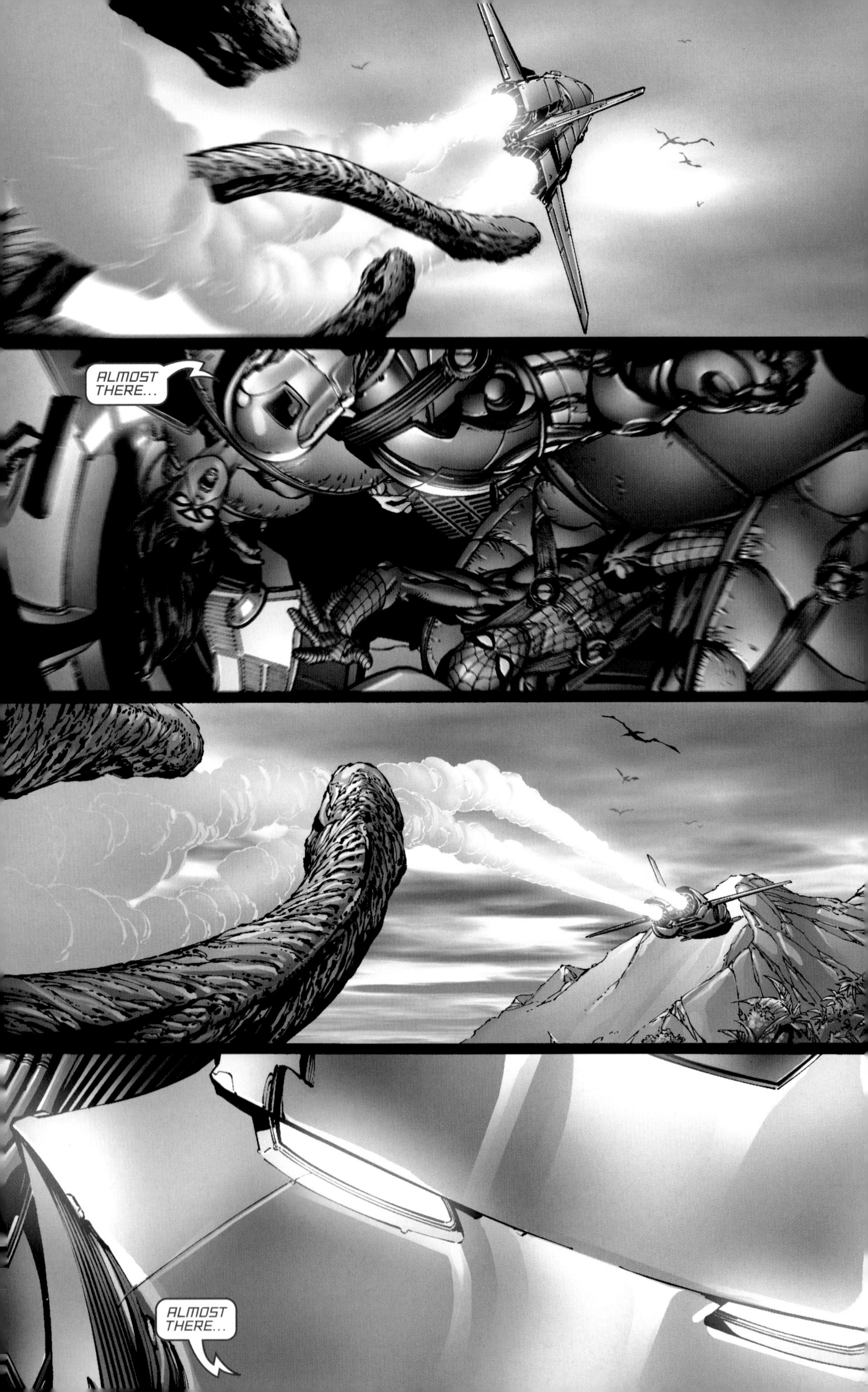
ALMOST THERE...
ALMOST THERE...

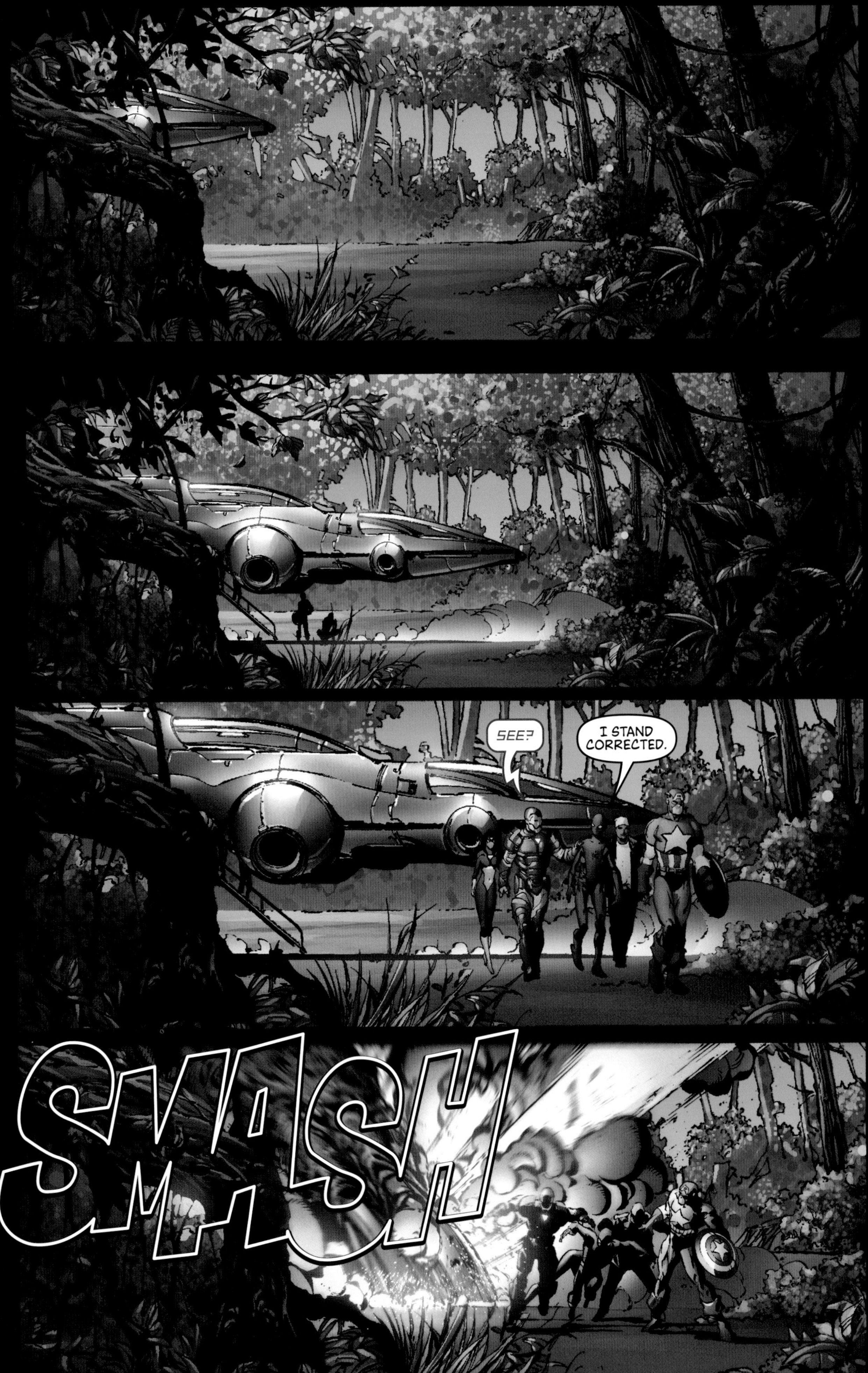
SEE?
I STAND CORRECTED.
SMASH

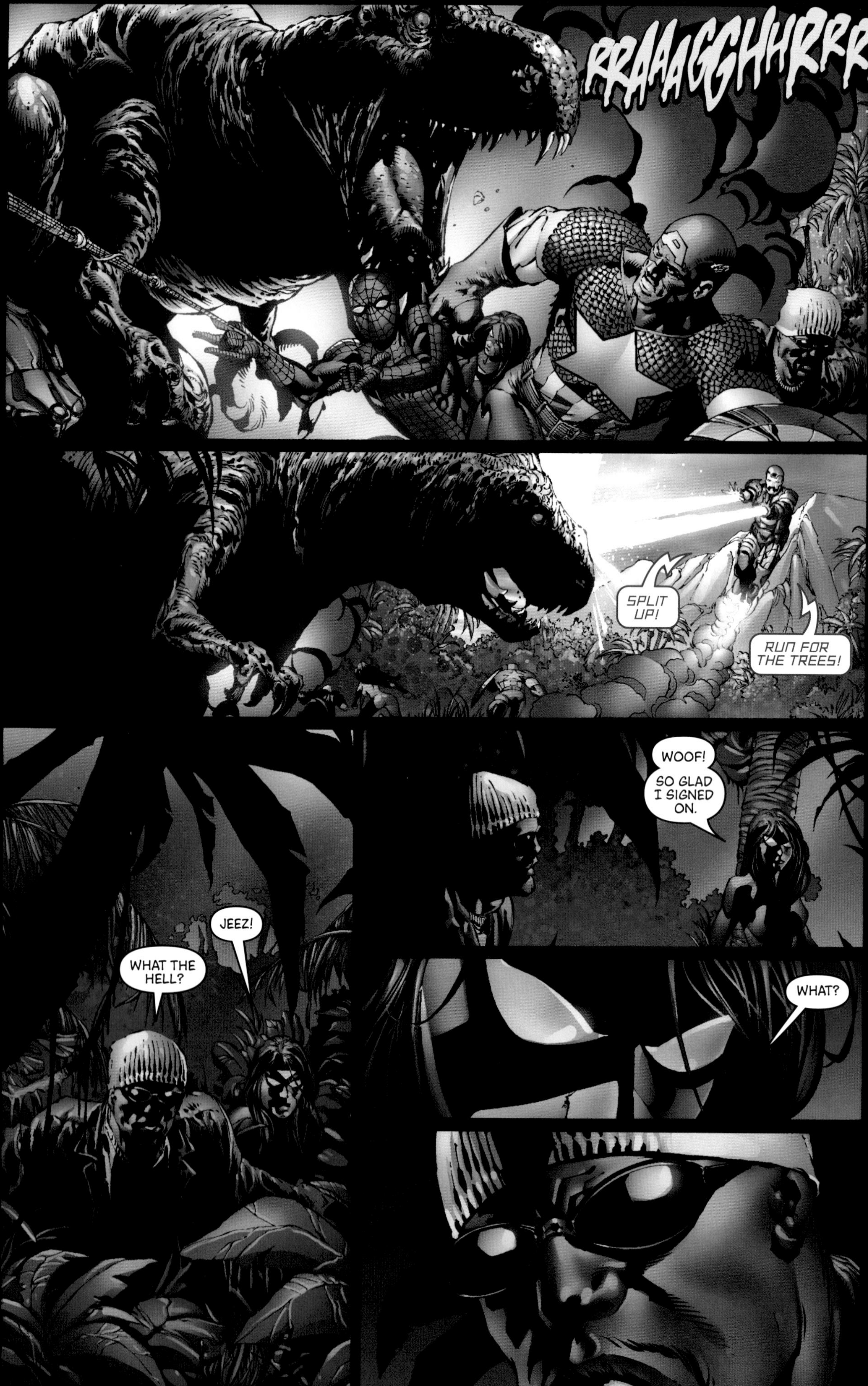
RRAAAGGHHRRR!
SPLIT UP!
RUN FOR THE TREES!
WHAT THE HELL?
JEEZ!
WOOF! SO GLAD I SIGNED ON.
WHAT?

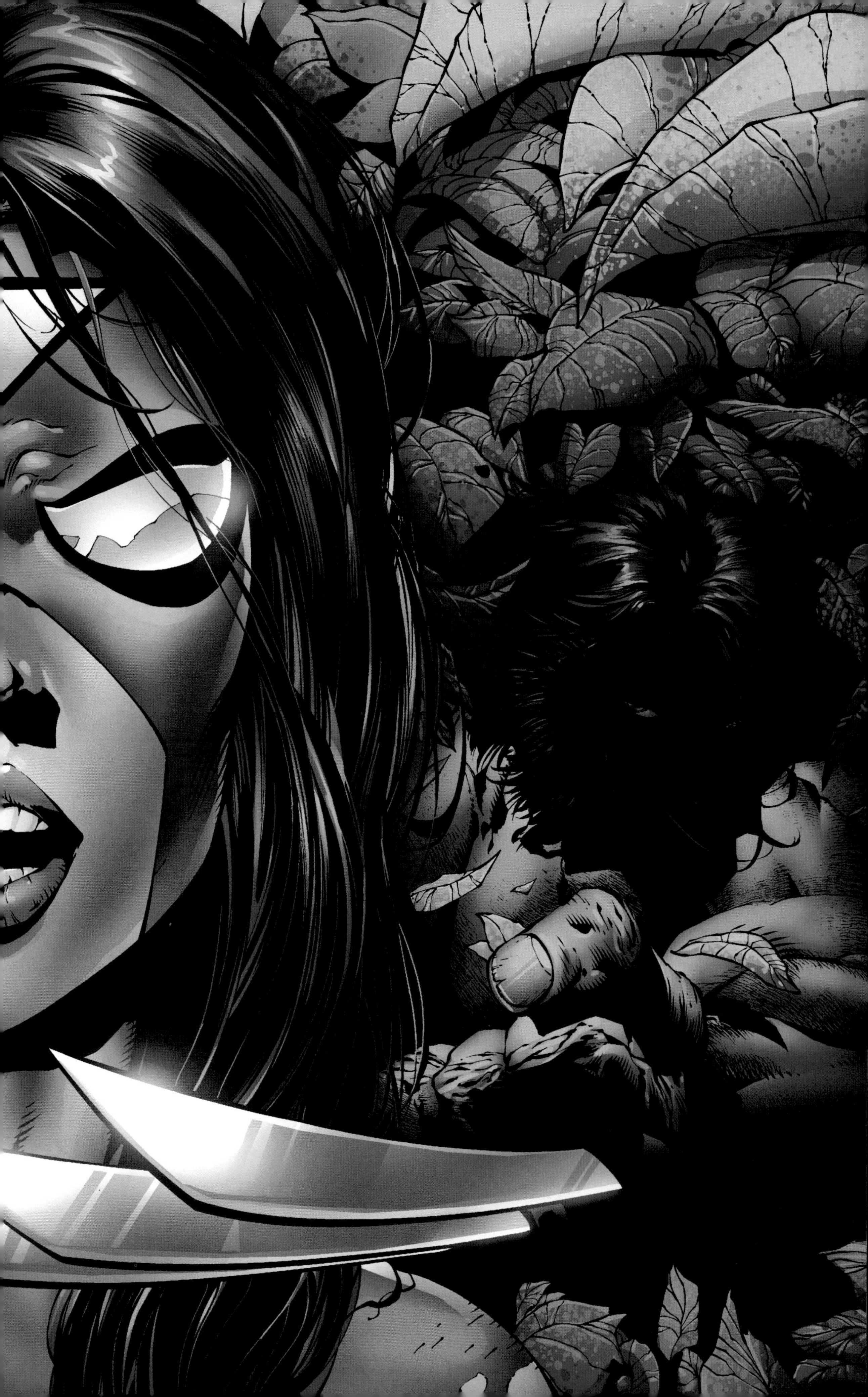

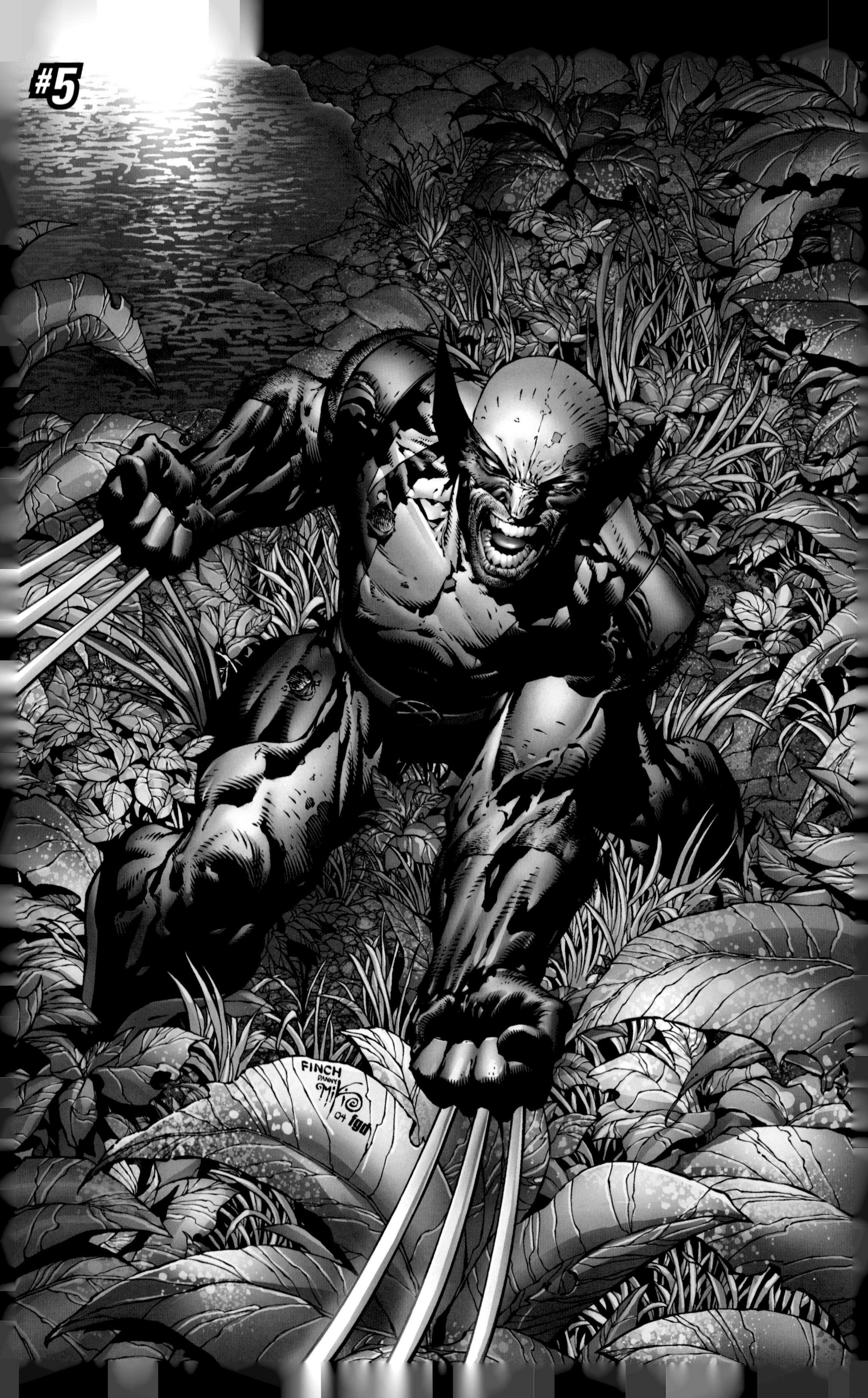
#5
FINCH

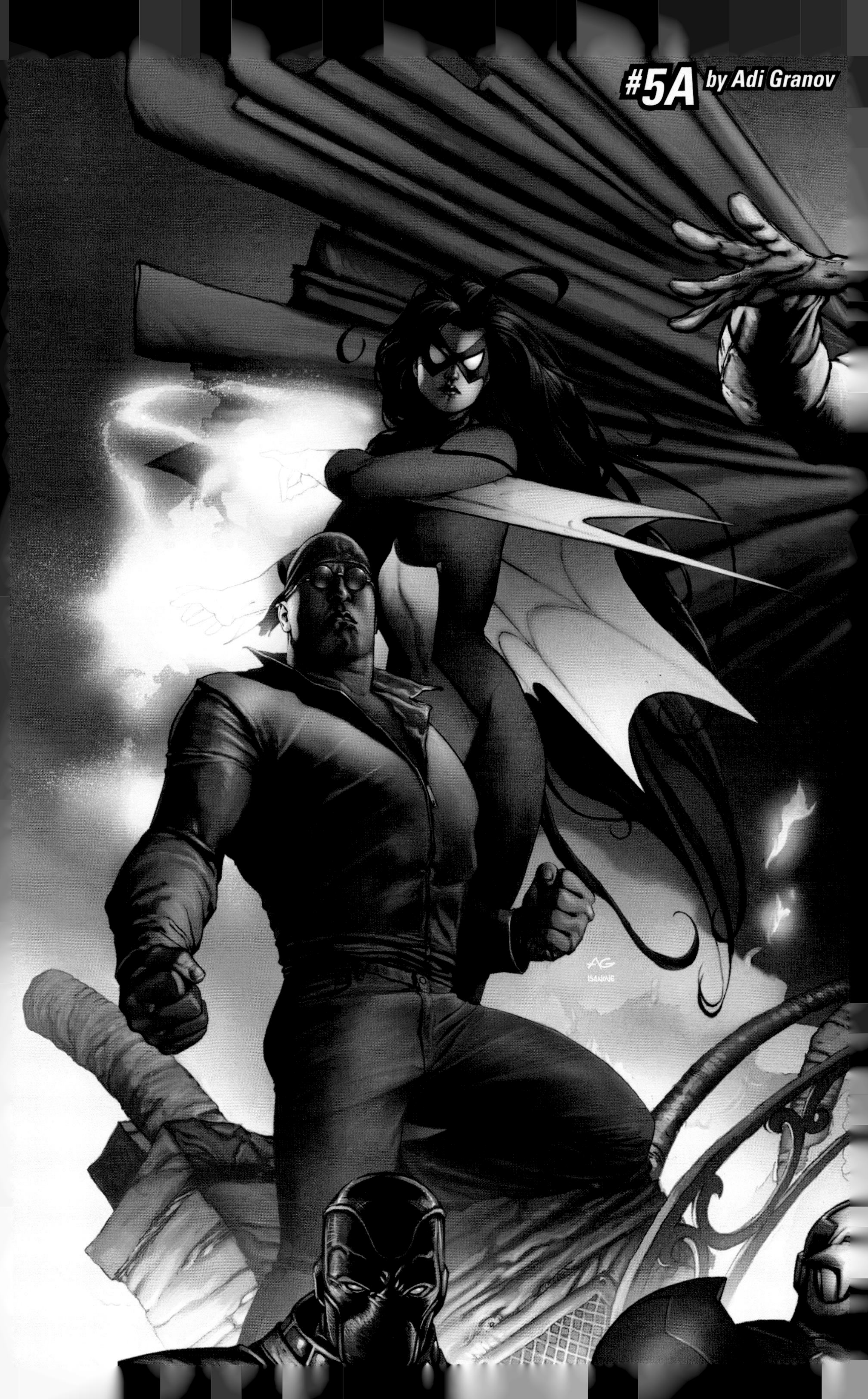

#5A by Adi Granov

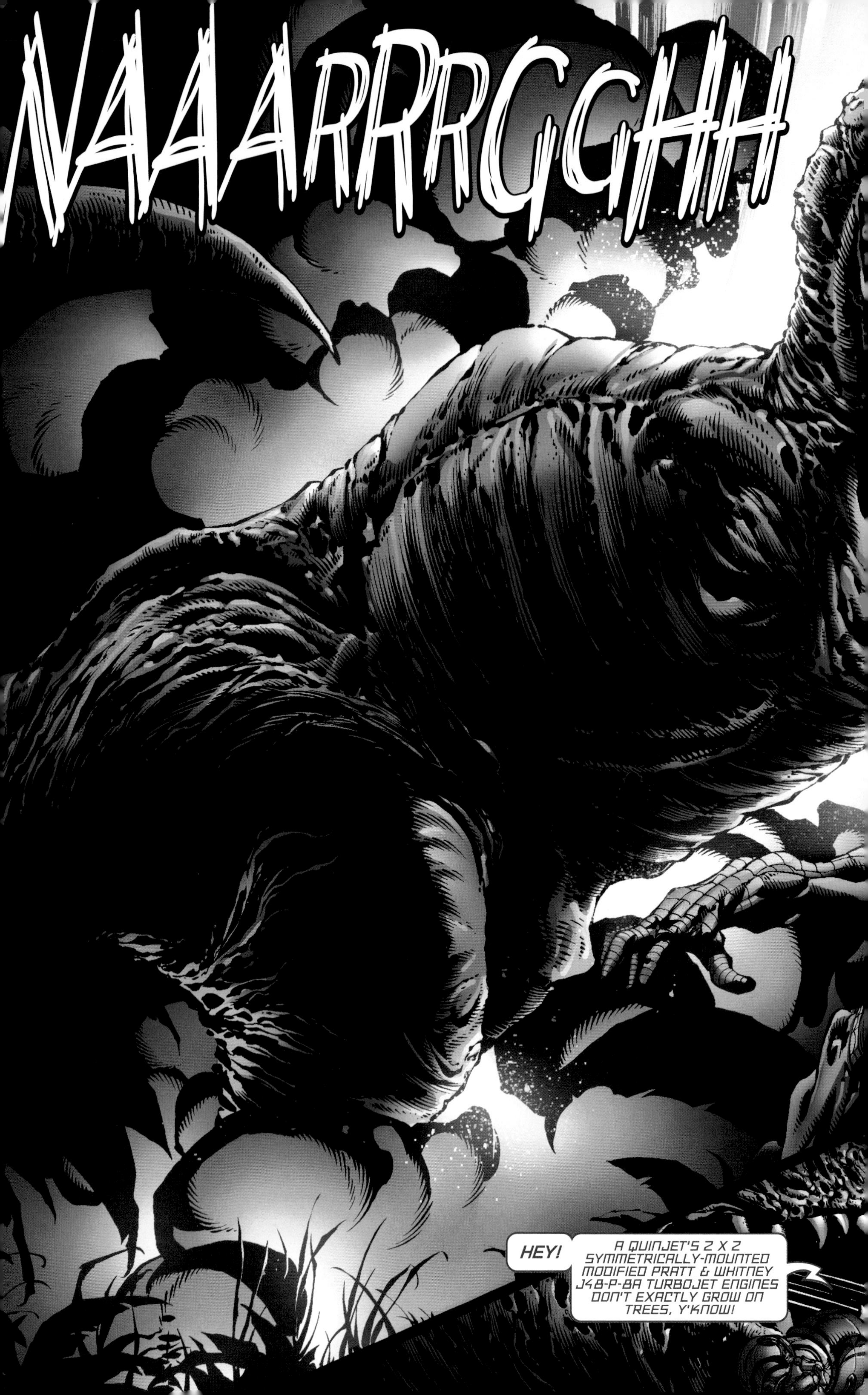
NAAARRRRGGHH
HEY!
A QUINJET'S 2 X 2 SYMMETRICALLY-MOUNTED MODIFIED PRATT & WHITNEY J48-P-8A TURBOJET ENGINES DON'T EXACTLY GROW ON TREES, Y'KNOW!

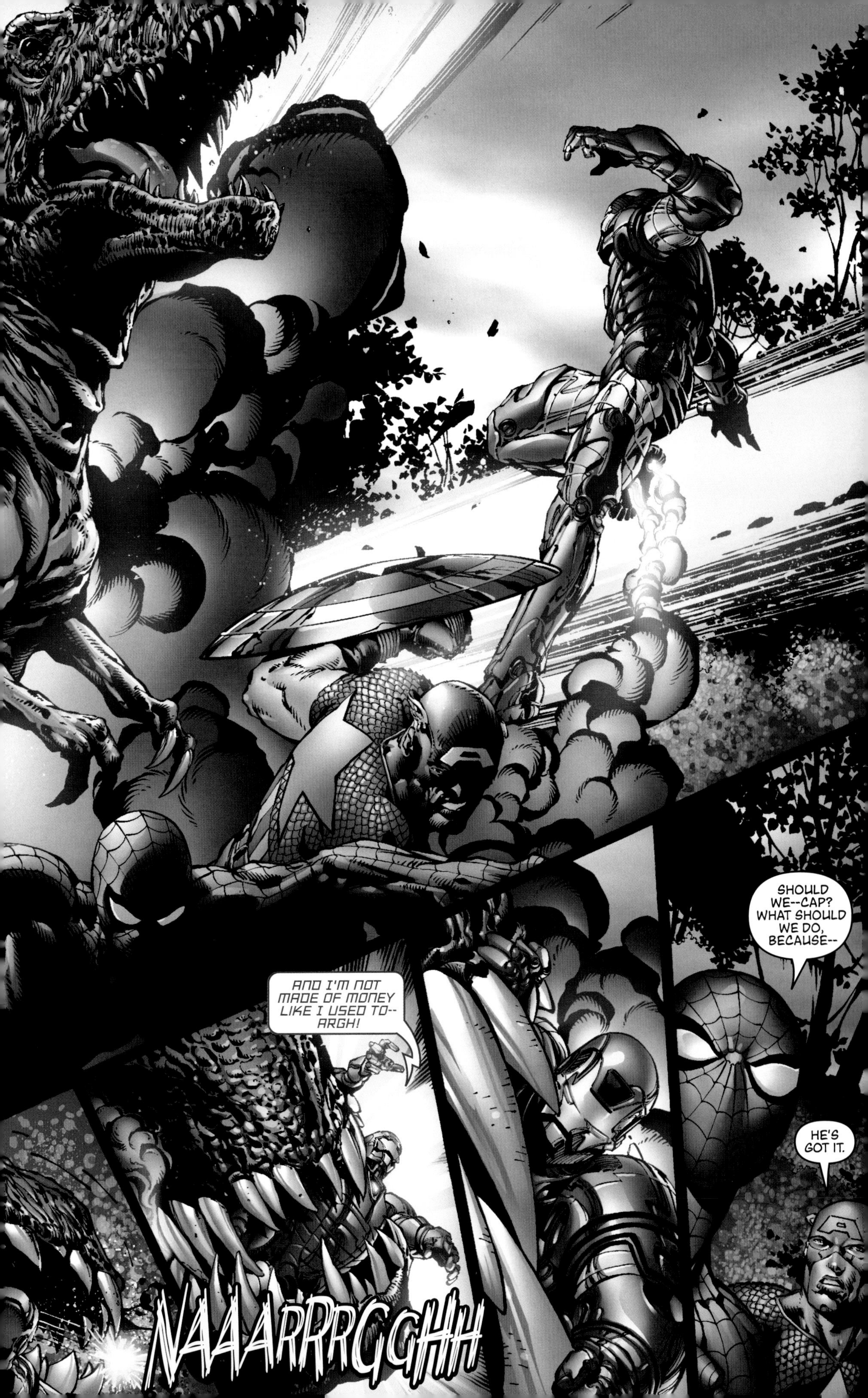
AND I'M NOT MADE OF MONEY LIKE I USED TO-- ARGH!
SHOULD WE--CAP? WHAT SHOULD WE DO, BECAUSE--
HE'S GOT IT.
NAAARRRGGHH

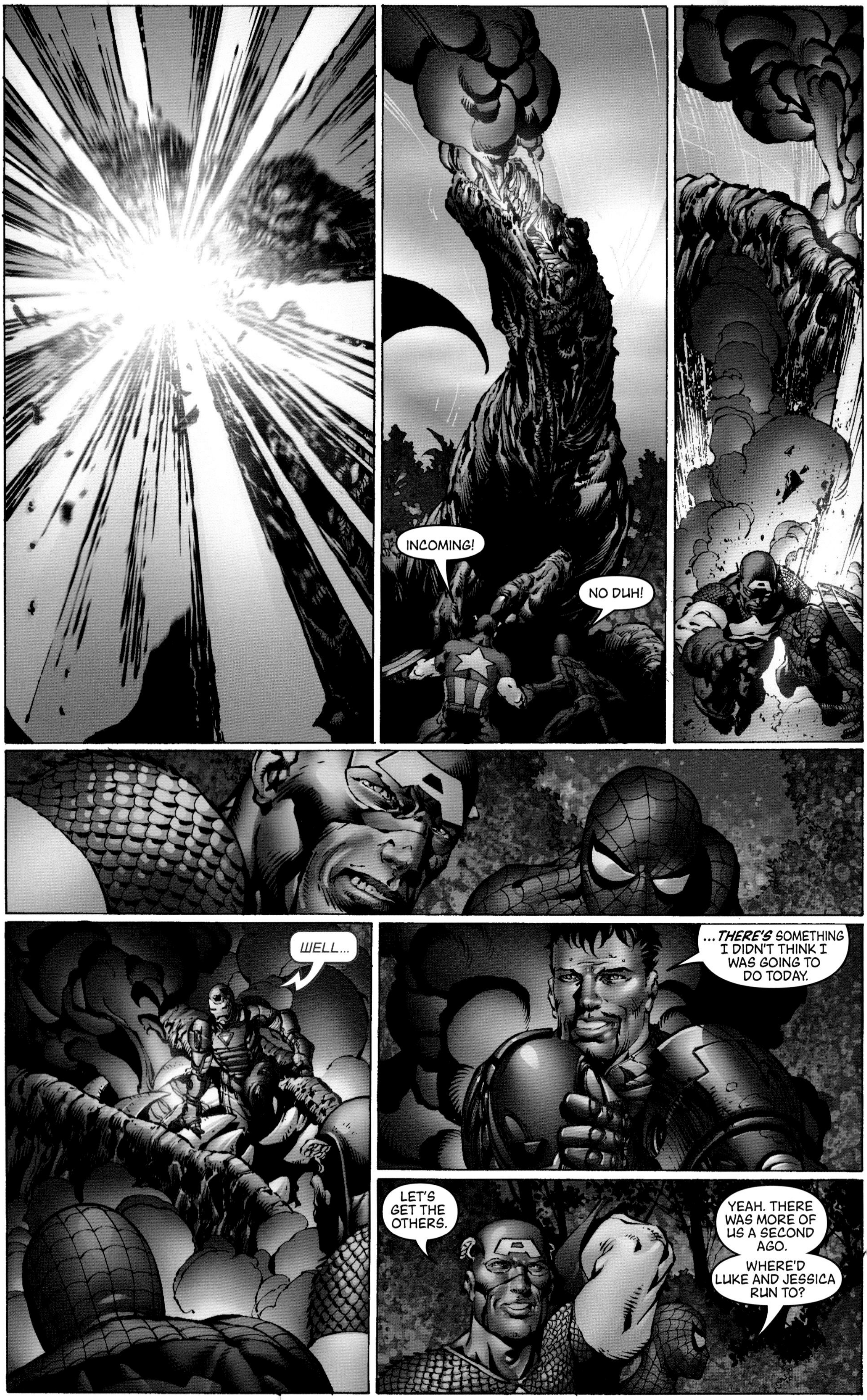
INCOMING!
NO DUH!
WELL...
...THERE'S SOMETHING I DIDN'T THINK I WAS GOING TO DO TODAY.
LET'S GET THE OTHERS.
YEAH. THERE WAS MORE OF US A SECOND AGO.
WHERE'D LUKE AND JESSICA RUN TO?

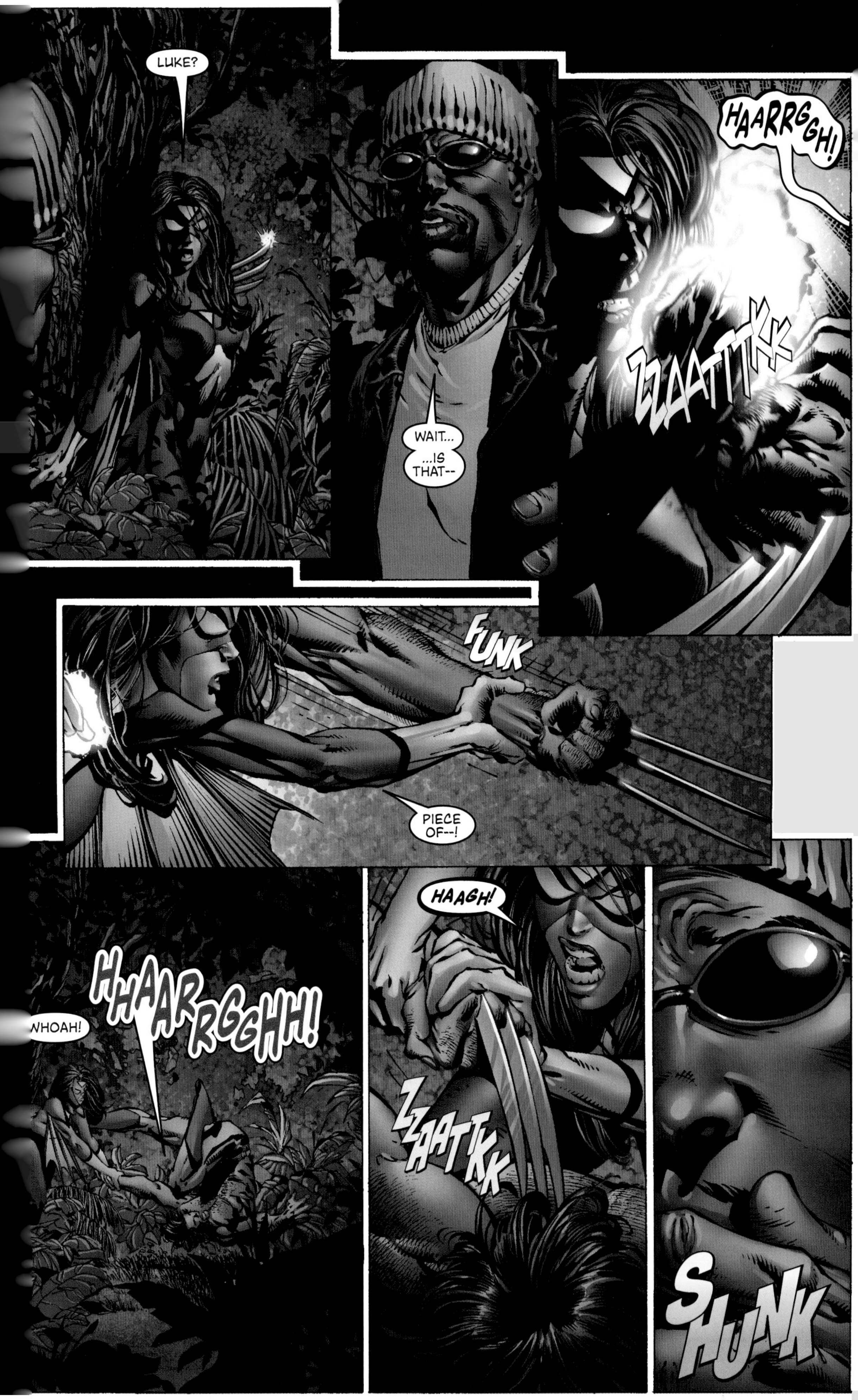
LUKE?
WAIT...
...IS THAT--
HAARRGGH!
ZZAATTTKK
FUNK
PIECE OF--!
HHAARRGGHH!
WHOAH!
HAAGH!
ZZAATTKK
SHUNK

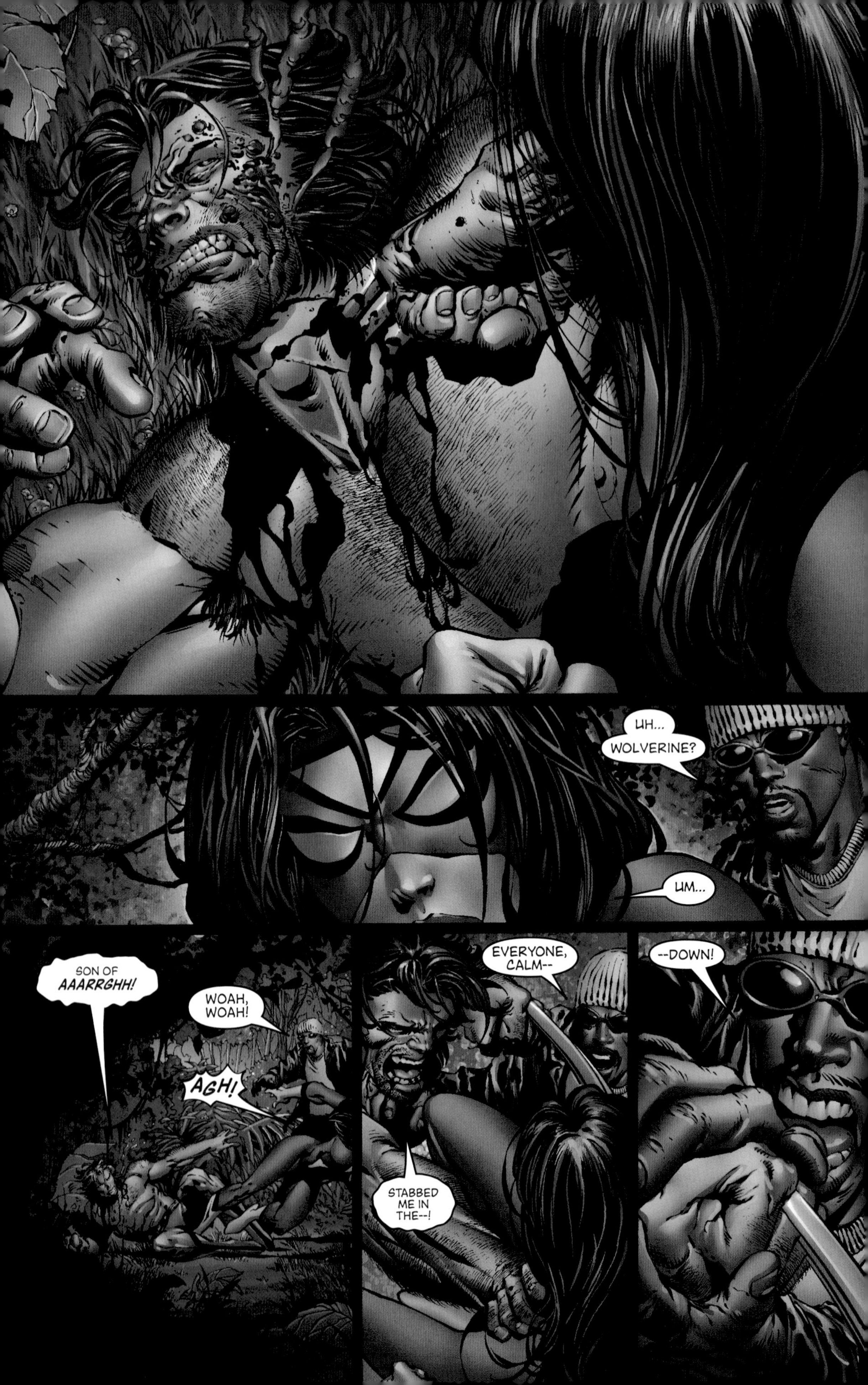
UH...
WOLVERINE?
UM...
SON OF AAAARRGHH!
WOAH, WOAH!
AGH!
EVERYONE, CALM--
STABBED ME IN THE--!
--DOWN!

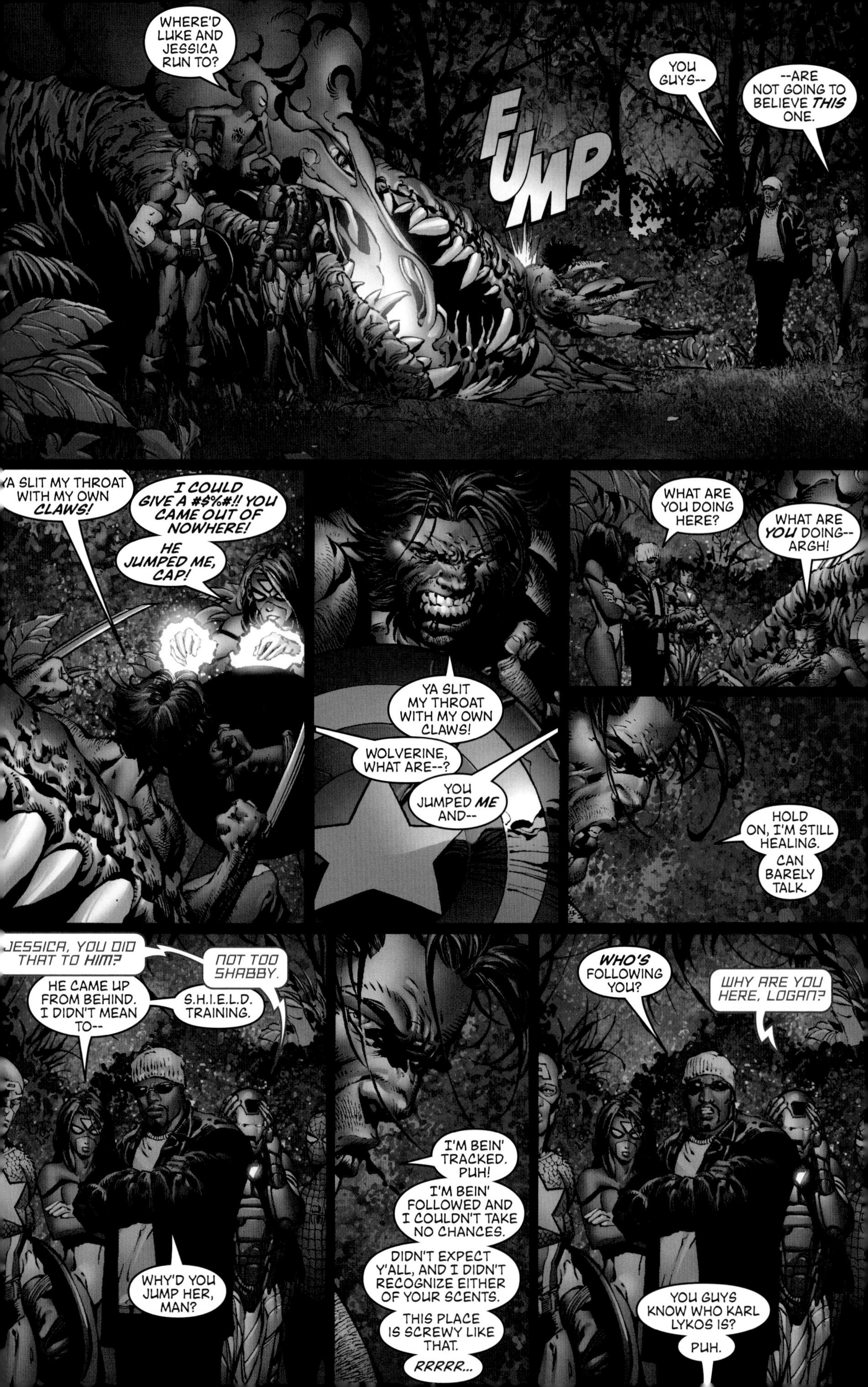
WHERE'D LUKE AND JESSICA RUN TO?
FUMP
YOU GUYS--
--ARE NOT GOING TO BELIEVE THIS ONE.
YA SLIT MY THROAT WITH MY OWN CLAWS!
I COULD GIVE A #$%#!! YOU CAME OUT OF NOWHERE!
HE JUMPED ME, CAP!
YA SLIT MY THROAT WITH MY OWN CLAWS!
WOLVERINE, WHAT ARE--?
YOU JUMPED ME AND--
WHAT ARE YOU DOING HERE?
WHAT ARE YOU DOING-- ARGH!
HOLD ON, I'M STILL HEALING.
CAN BARELY TALK.
JESSICA, YOU DID THAT TO HIM?
NOT TOO SHABBY.
HE CAME UP FROM BEHIND. I DIDN'T MEAN TO--
S.H.I.E.L.D. TRAINING.
WHY'D YOU JUMP HER, MAN?
I'M BEIN' TRACKED. PUH!
I'M BEIN' FOLLOWED AND I COULDN'T TAKE NO CHANCES.
DIDN'T EXPECT Y'ALL, AND I DIDN'T RECOGNIZE EITHER OF YOUR SCENTS.
THIS PLACE IS SCREWY LIKE THAT.
RRRRR...
WHO'S FOLLOWING YOU?
WHY ARE YOU HERE, LOGAN?
YOU GUYS KNOW WHO KARL LYKOS IS?
PUH.

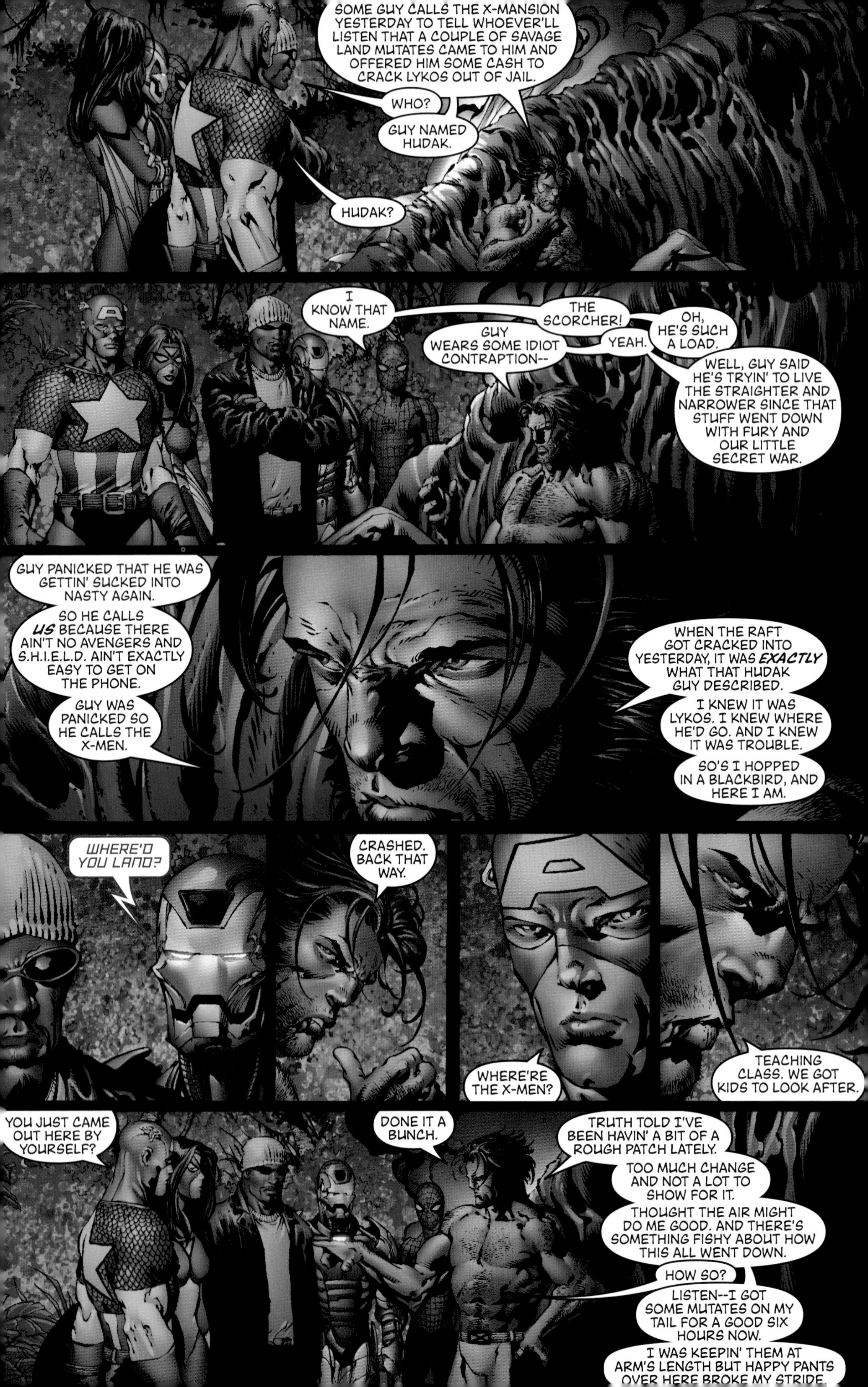
SOME GUY CALLS THE X-MANSION YESTERDAY TO TELL WHOEVER'LL LISTEN THAT A COUPLE OF SAVAGE LAND MUTATES CAME TO HIM AND OFFERED HIM SOME CASH TO CRACK LYKOS OUT OF JAIL.
WHO?
GUY NAMED HUDAK.
HUDAK?
I KNOW THAT NAME.
THE SCORCHER!
GUY WEARS SOME IDIOT CONTRAPTION--
YEAH.
OH, HE'S SUCH A LOAD.
WELL, GUY SAID HE'S TRYIN' TO LIVE THE STRAIGHTER AND NARROWER SINCE THAT STUFF WENT DOWN WITH FURY AND OUR LITTLE SECRET WAR.
GUY PANICKED THAT HE WAS GETTIN' SUCKED INTO NASTY AGAIN.
SO HE CALLS *US* BECAUSE THERE AIN'T NO AVENGERS AND S.H.I.E.L.D. AIN'T EXACTLY EASY TO GET ON THE PHONE.
GUY WAS PANICKED SO HE CALLS THE X-MEN.
WHEN THE RAFT GOT CRACKED INTO YESTERDAY, IT WAS *EXACTLY* WHAT THAT HUDAK GUY DESCRIBED.
I KNEW IT WAS LYKOS. I KNEW WHERE HE'D GO. AND I KNEW IT WAS TROUBLE.
SO'S I HOPPED IN A BLACKBIRD, AND HERE I AM.
WHERE'D YOU LAND?
CRASHED. BACK THAT WAY.
WHERE'RE THE X-MEN?
TEACHING CLASS. WE GOT KIDS TO LOOK AFTER.
YOU JUST CAME OUT HERE BY YOURSELF?
DONE IT A BUNCH.
TRUTH TOLD I'VE BEEN HAVIN' A BIT OF A ROUGH PATCH LATELY.
TOO MUCH CHANGE AND NOT A LOT TO SHOW FOR IT.
THOUGHT THE AIR MIGHT DO ME GOOD. AND THERE'S SOMETHING FISHY ABOUT HOW THIS ALL WENT DOWN.
HOW SO?
LISTEN--I GOT SOME MUTATES ON MY TAIL FOR A GOOD SIX HOURS NOW.
I WAS KEEPIN' THEM AT ARM'S LENGTH BUT HAPPY PANTS OVER HERE BROKE MY STRIDE.

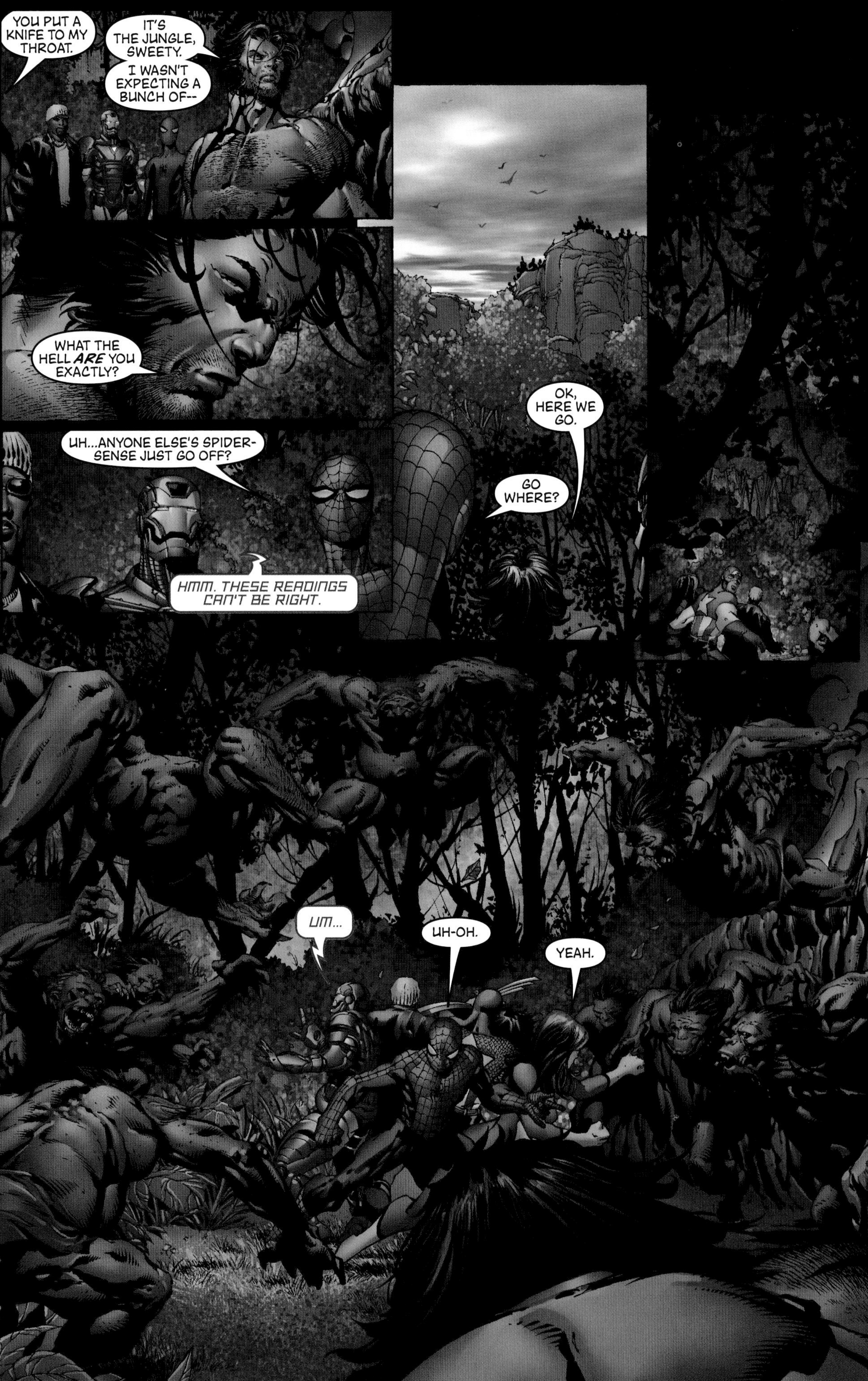
YOU PUT A KNIFE TO MY THROAT.
IT'S THE JUNGLE, SWEETY.
I WASN'T EXPECTING A BUNCH OF--
WHAT THE HELL *ARE* YOU EXACTLY?
UH...ANYONE ELSE'S SPIDER-SENSE JUST GO OFF?
HMM. THESE READINGS CAN'T BE RIGHT.
OK, HERE WE GO.
GO WHERE?
UM...
UH-OH.
YEAH.

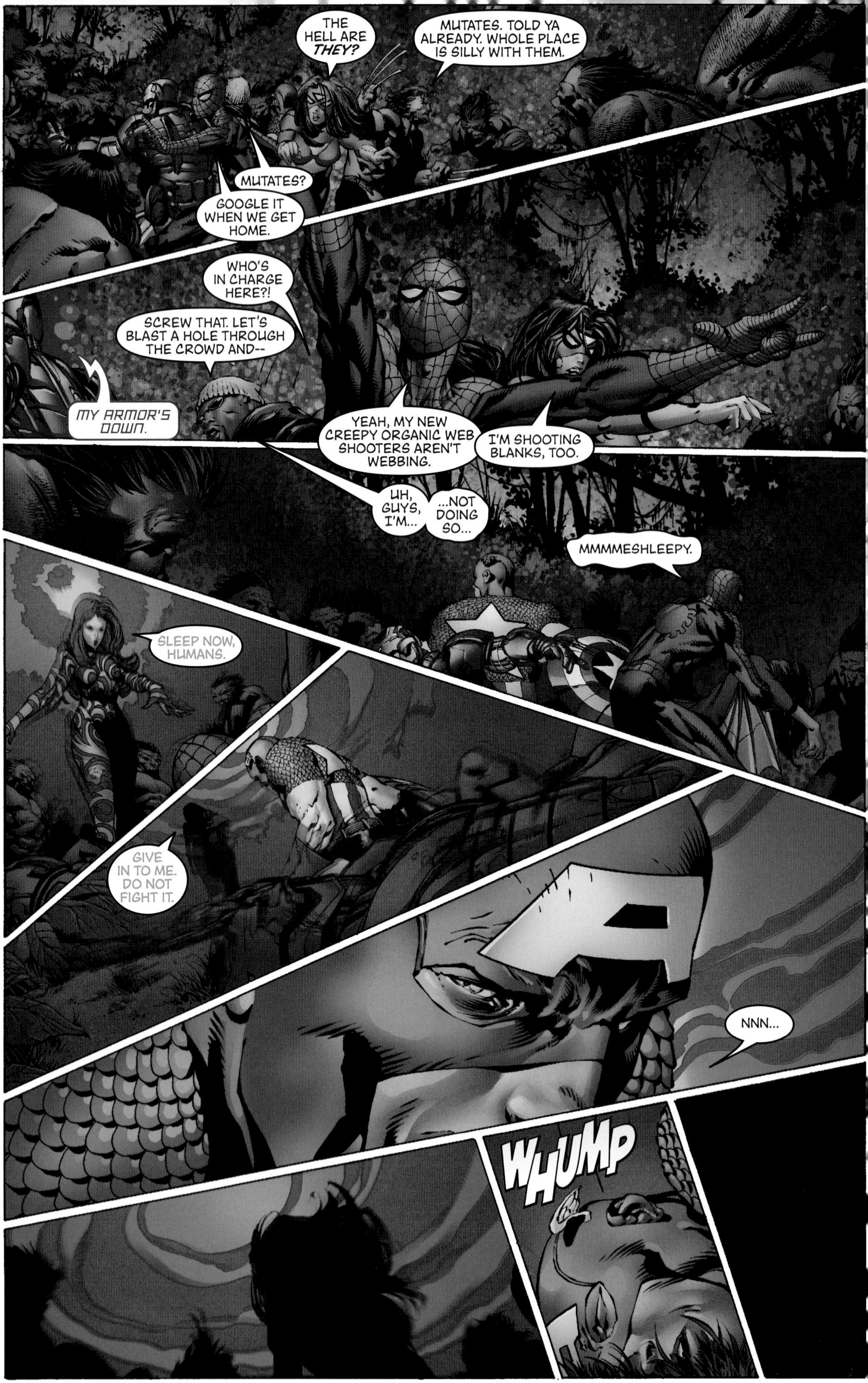
THE HELL ARE THEY?
MUTATES. TOLD YA ALREADY. WHOLE PLACE IS SILLY WITH THEM.
MUTATES?
GOOGLE IT WHEN WE GET HOME.
WHO'S IN CHARGE HERE?!
SCREW THAT. LET'S BLAST A HOLE THROUGH THE CROWD AND--
MY ARMOR'S DOWN.
YEAH, MY NEW CREEPY ORGANIC WEB SHOOTERS AREN'T WEBBING.
I'M SHOOTING BLANKS, TOO.
UH, GUYS, I'M...
...NOT DOING SO...
MMMMESHLEEPY.
SLEEP NOW, HUMANS.
GIVE IN TO ME. DO NOT FIGHT IT.
NNN...
WHUMP

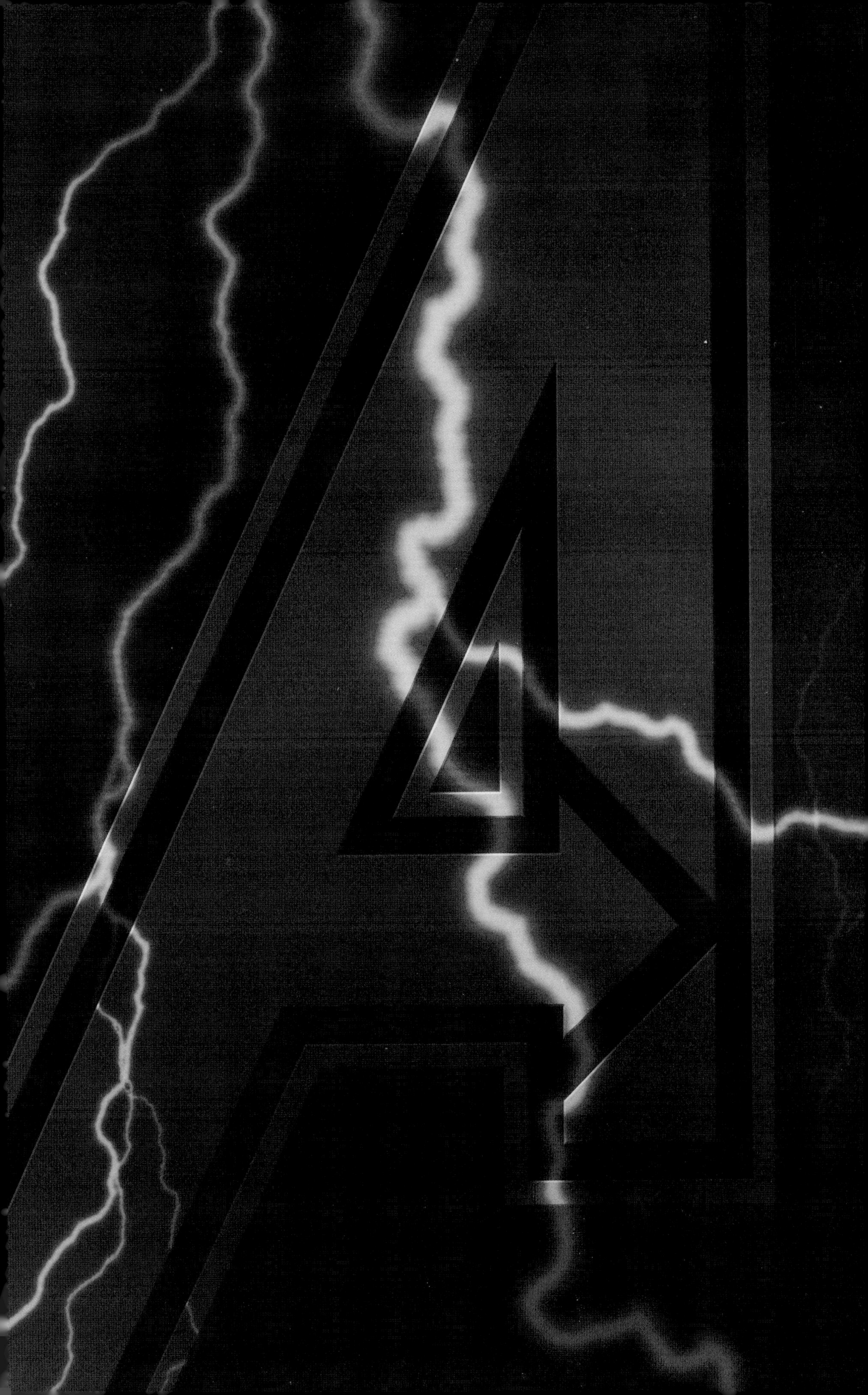

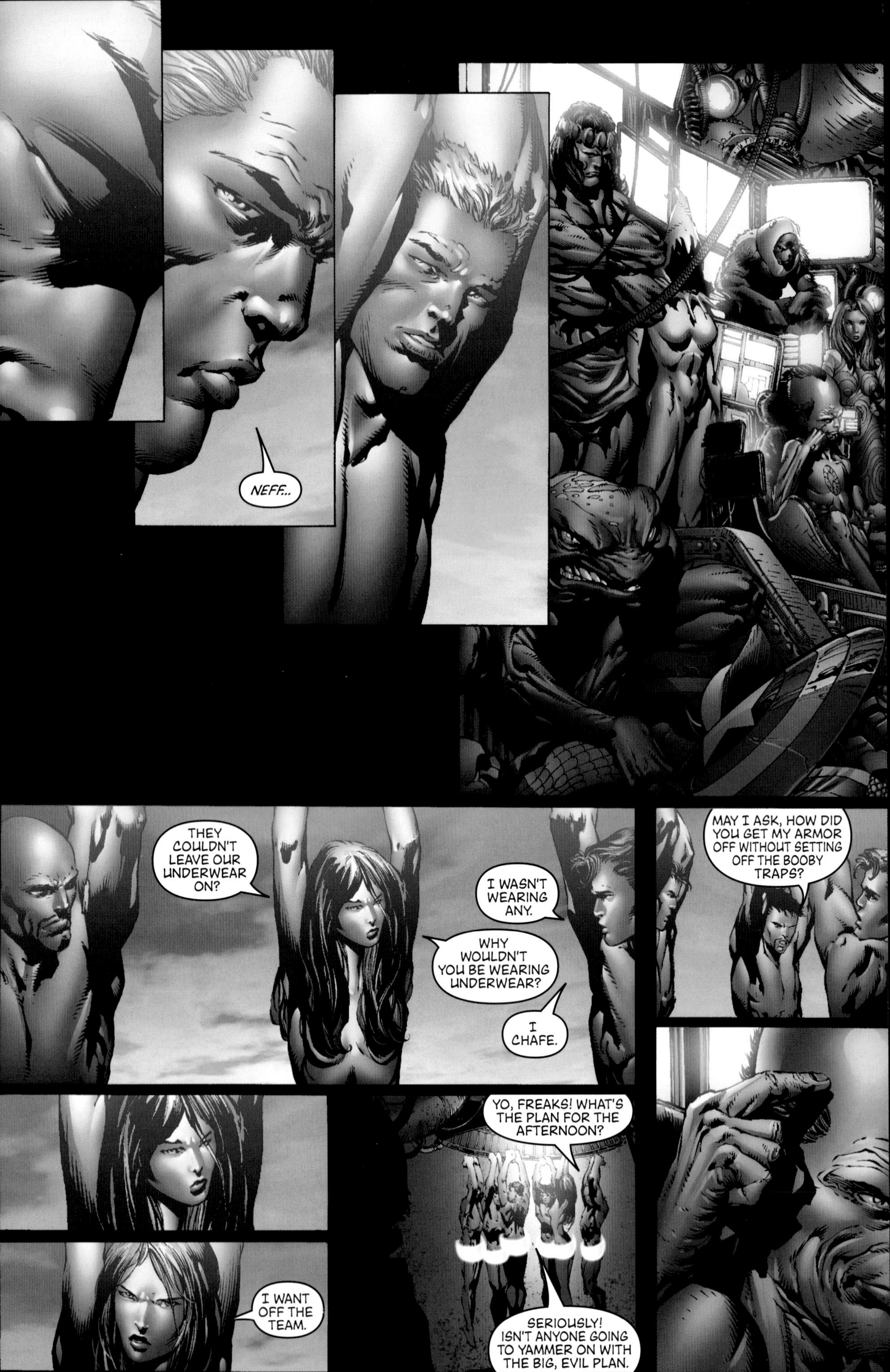
NEFF...
THEY COULDN'T LEAVE OUR UNDERWEAR ON?
I WASN'T WEARING ANY.
WHY WOULDN'T YOU BE WEARING UNDERWEAR?
I CHAFE.
MAY I ASK, HOW DID YOU GET MY ARMOR OFF WITHOUT SETTING OFF THE BOOBY TRAPS?
I WANT OFF THE TEAM.
YO, FREAKS! WHAT'S THE PLAN FOR THE AFTERNOON?
SERIOUSLY! ISN'T ANYONE GOING TO YAMMER ON WITH THE BIG, EVIL PLAN.

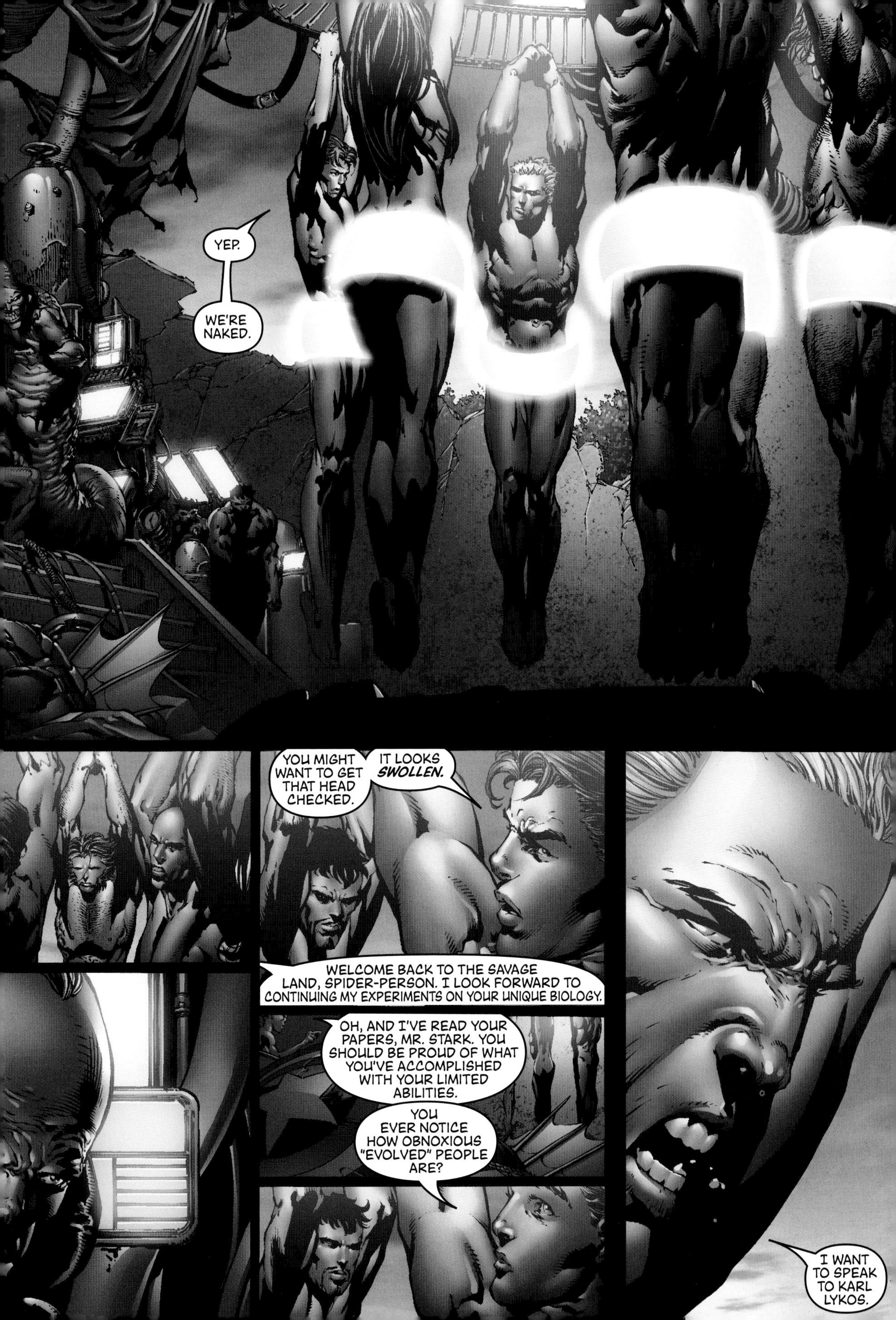
YEP.
WE'RE NAKED.
YOU MIGHT WANT TO GET THAT HEAD CHECKED.
IT LOOKS *SWOLLEN.*
WELCOME BACK TO THE SAVAGE LAND, SPIDER-PERSON. I LOOK FORWARD TO CONTINUING MY EXPERIMENTS ON YOUR UNIQUE BIOLOGY.
OH, AND I'VE READ YOUR PAPERS, MR. STARK. YOU SHOULD BE PROUD OF WHAT YOU'VE ACCOMPLISHED WITH YOUR LIMITED ABILITIES.
YOU EVER NOTICE HOW OBNOXIOUS "EVOLVED" PEOPLE ARE?
I WANT TO SPEAK TO KARL LYKOS.

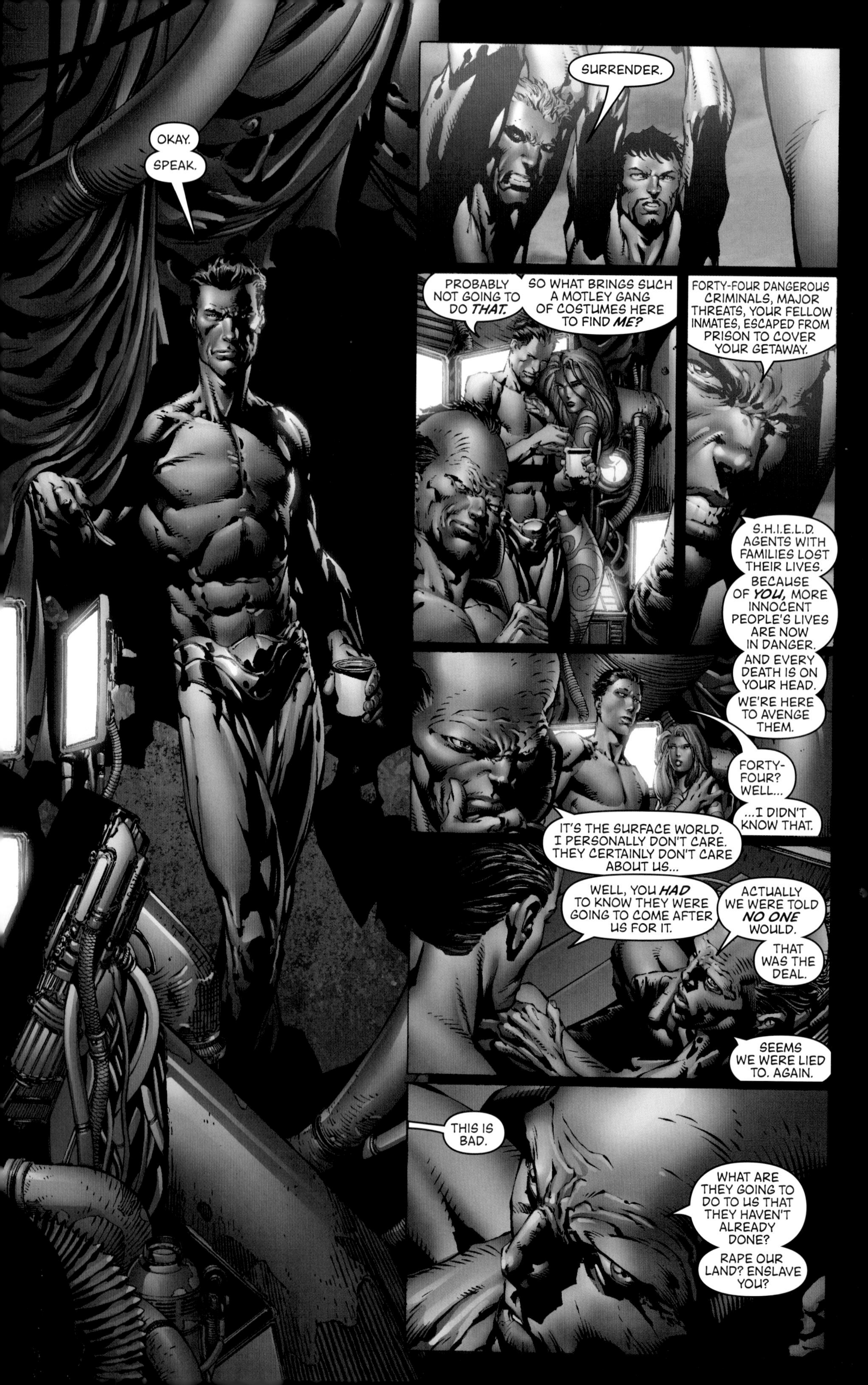
OKAY.
SPEAK.
SURRENDER.
PROBABLY NOT GOING TO DO THAT.
SO WHAT BRINGS SUCH A MOTLEY GANG OF COSTUMES HERE TO FIND ME?
FORTY-FOUR DANGEROUS CRIMINALS, MAJOR THREATS, YOUR FELLOW INMATES, ESCAPED FROM PRISON TO COVER YOUR GETAWAY.
S.H.I.E.L.D. AGENTS WITH FAMILIES LOST THEIR LIVES.
BECAUSE OF YOU, MORE INNOCENT PEOPLE'S LIVES ARE NOW IN DANGER.
AND EVERY DEATH IS ON YOUR HEAD.
WE'RE HERE TO AVENGE THEM.
FORTY-FOUR? WELL...
...I DIDN'T KNOW THAT.
IT'S THE SURFACE WORLD. I PERSONALLY DON'T CARE. THEY CERTAINLY DON'T CARE ABOUT US...
WELL, YOU HAD TO KNOW THEY WERE GOING TO COME AFTER US FOR IT.
ACTUALLY WE WERE TOLD NO ONE WOULD.
THAT WAS THE DEAL.
SEEMS WE WERE LIED TO. AGAIN.
THIS IS BAD.
WHAT ARE THEY GOING TO DO TO US THAT THEY HAVEN'T ALREADY DONE?
RAPE OUR LAND? ENSLAVE YOU?

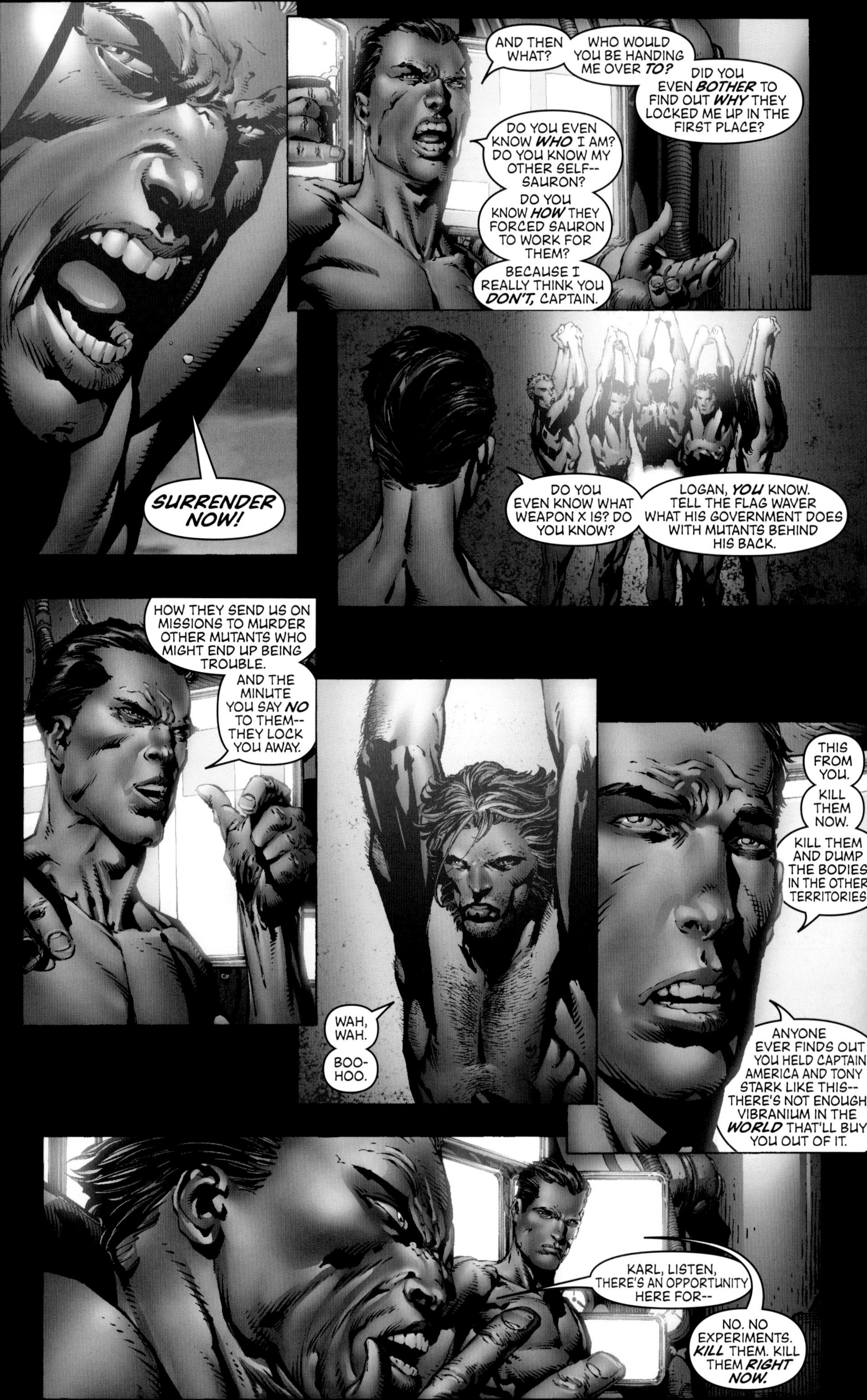
SURRENDER NOW!
AND THEN WHAT?
WHO WOULD YOU BE HANDING ME OVER TO?
DID YOU EVEN BOTHER TO FIND OUT WHY THEY LOCKED ME UP IN THE FIRST PLACE?
DO YOU EVEN KNOW WHO I AM? DO YOU KNOW MY OTHER SELF-- SAURON?
DO YOU KNOW HOW THEY FORCED SAURON TO WORK FOR THEM?
BECAUSE I REALLY THINK YOU DON'T, CAPTAIN.
DO YOU EVEN KNOW WHAT WEAPON X IS? DO YOU KNOW?
LOGAN, YOU KNOW. TELL THE FLAG WAVER WHAT HIS GOVERNMENT DOES WITH MUTANTS BEHIND HIS BACK.
HOW THEY SEND US ON MISSIONS TO MURDER OTHER MUTANTS WHO MIGHT END UP BEING TROUBLE.
AND THE MINUTE YOU SAY NO TO THEM-- THEY LOCK YOU AWAY.
WAH, WAH.
BOO-HOO.
THIS FROM YOU.
KILL THEM NOW.
KILL THEM AND DUMP THE BODIES IN THE OTHER TERRITORIES.
ANYONE EVER FINDS OUT YOU HELD CAPTAIN AMERICA AND TONY STARK LIKE THIS-- THERE'S NOT ENOUGH VIBRANIUM IN THE WORLD THAT'LL BUY YOU OUT OF IT.
KARL, LISTEN, THERE'S AN OPPORTUNITY HERE FOR--
NO. NO EXPERIMENTS. KILL THEM. KILL THEM RIGHT NOW.

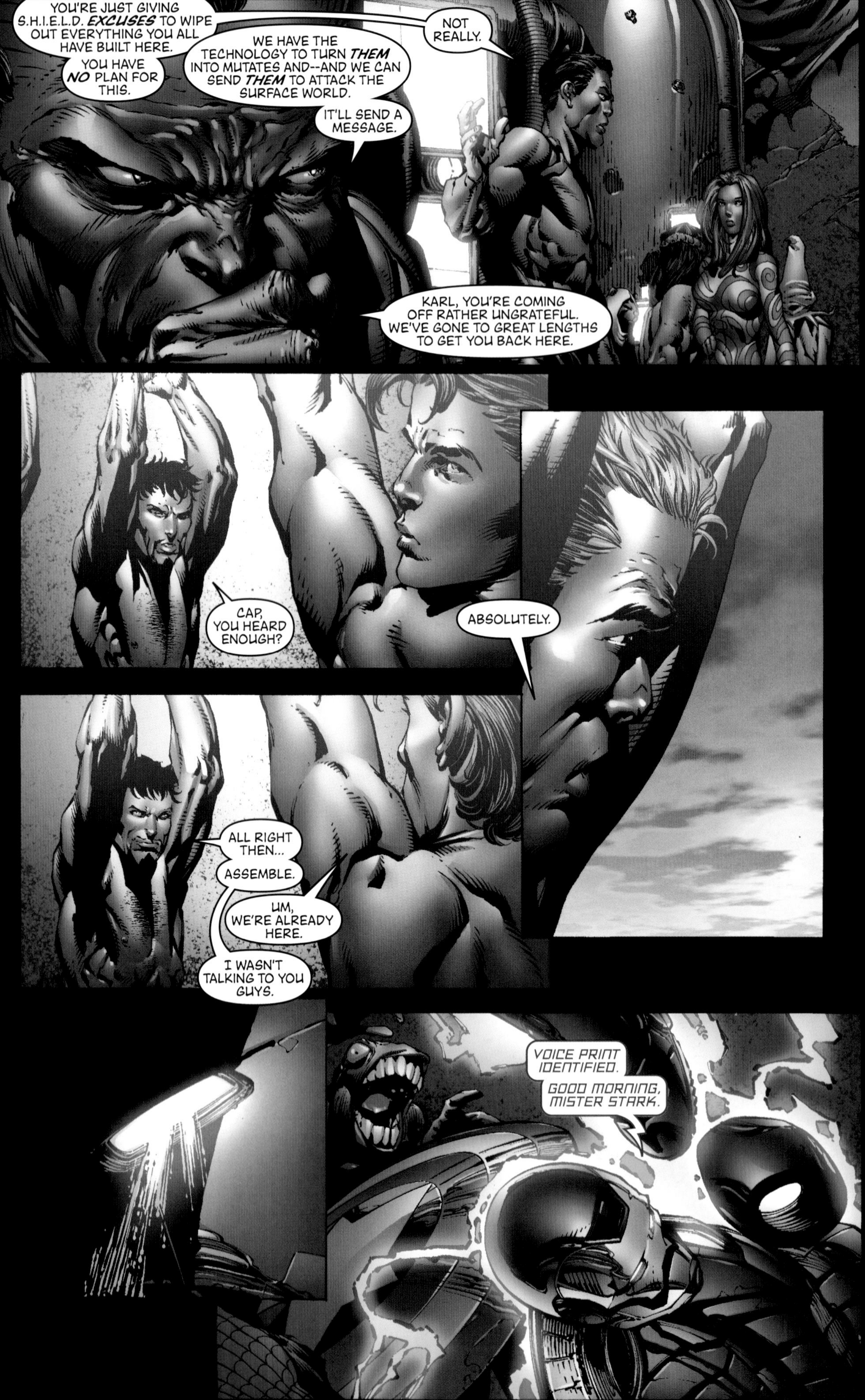
YOU'RE JUST GIVING S.H.I.E.L.D. EXCUSES TO WIPE OUT EVERYTHING YOU ALL HAVE BUILT HERE.
YOU HAVE NO PLAN FOR THIS.
NOT REALLY.
WE HAVE THE TECHNOLOGY TO TURN THEM INTO MUTATES AND--AND WE CAN SEND THEM TO ATTACK THE SURFACE WORLD.
IT'LL SEND A MESSAGE.
KARL, YOU'RE COMING OFF RATHER UNGRATEFUL. WE'VE GONE TO GREAT LENGTHS TO GET YOU BACK HERE.
CAP, YOU HEARD ENOUGH?
ABSOLUTELY.
ALL RIGHT THEN...
ASSEMBLE.
UM, WE'RE ALREADY HERE.
I WASN'T TALKING TO YOU GUYS.
VOICE PRINT IDENTIFIED.
GOOD MORNING, MISTER STARK.

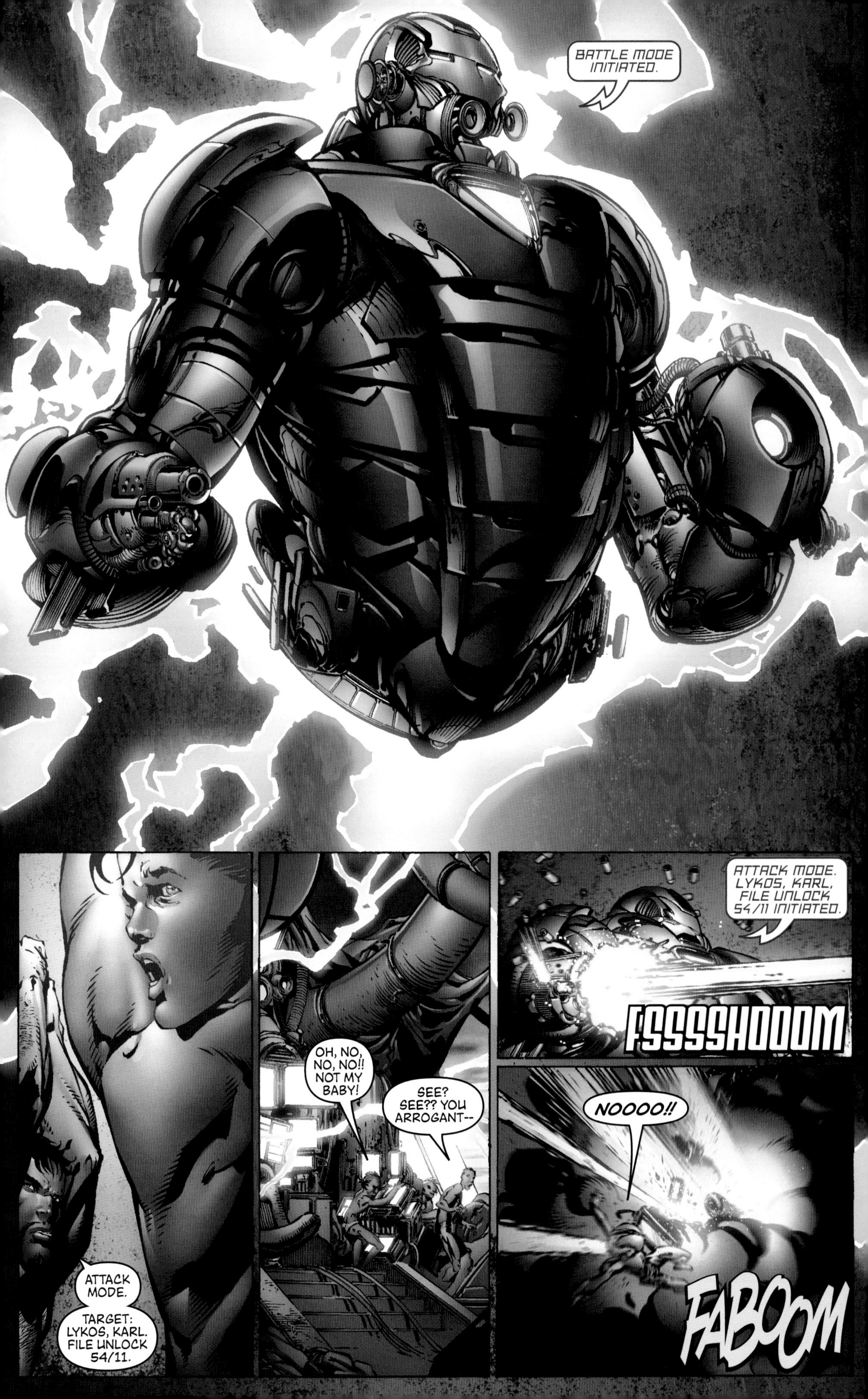
BATTLE MODE INITIATED.
ATTACK MODE.
TARGET: LYKOS, KARL. FILE UNLOCK 54/11.
OH, NO, NO, NO!! NOT MY BABY!
SEE? SEE?? YOU ARROGANT--
ATTACK MODE. LYKOS, KARL, FILE UNLOCK 54/11 INITIATED.
FSSSSHOOOM
NOOOO!!
FABOOM

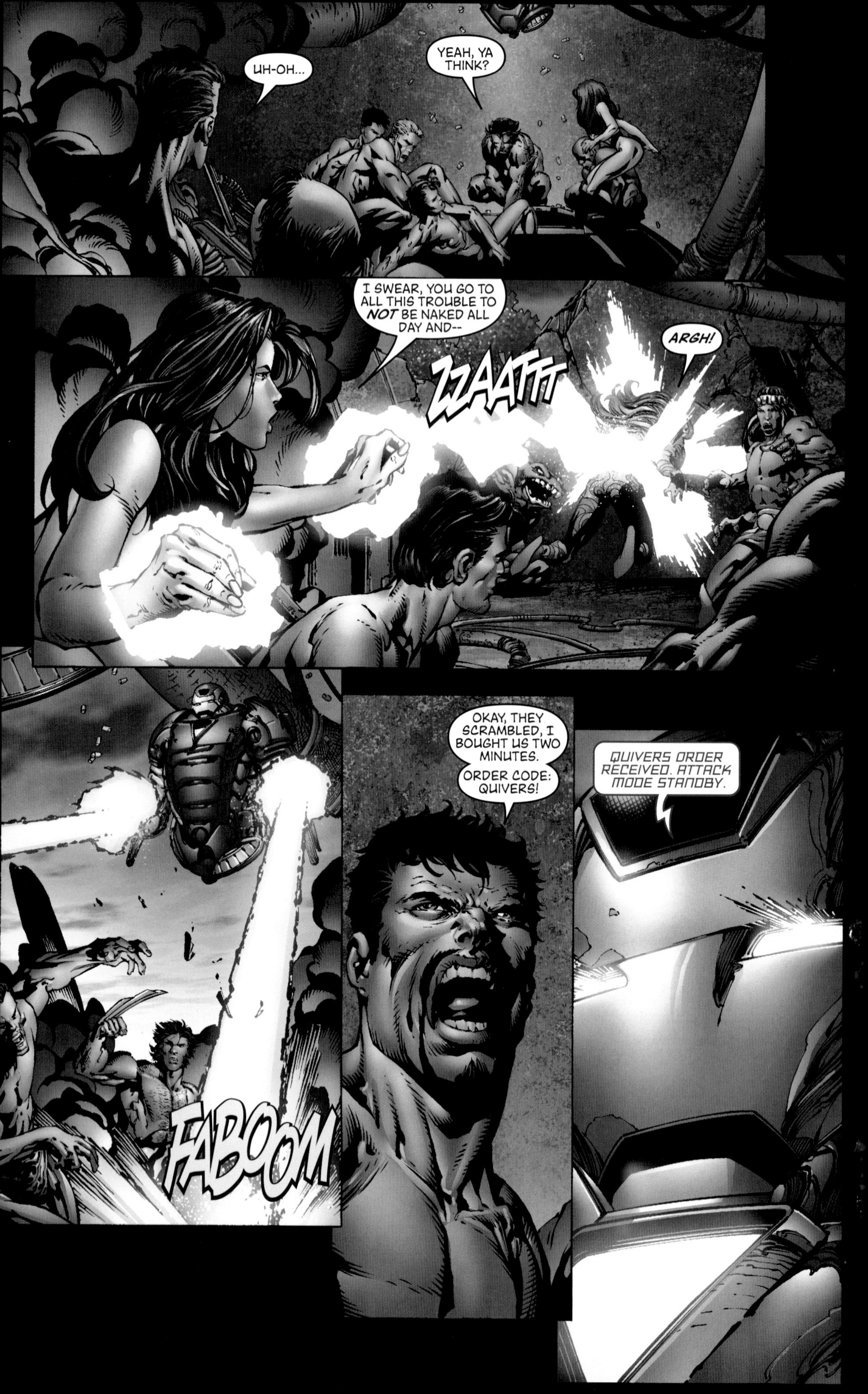
UH-OH...
YEAH, YA THINK?
I SWEAR, YOU GO TO ALL THIS TROUBLE TO **NOT** BE NAKED ALL DAY AND--
ZZAATTT
ARGH!
FABOOM
OKAY, THEY SCRAMBLED, I BOUGHT US TWO MINUTES.
ORDER CODE: QUIVERS!
QUIVERS ORDER RECEIVED. ATTACK MODE STANDBY.

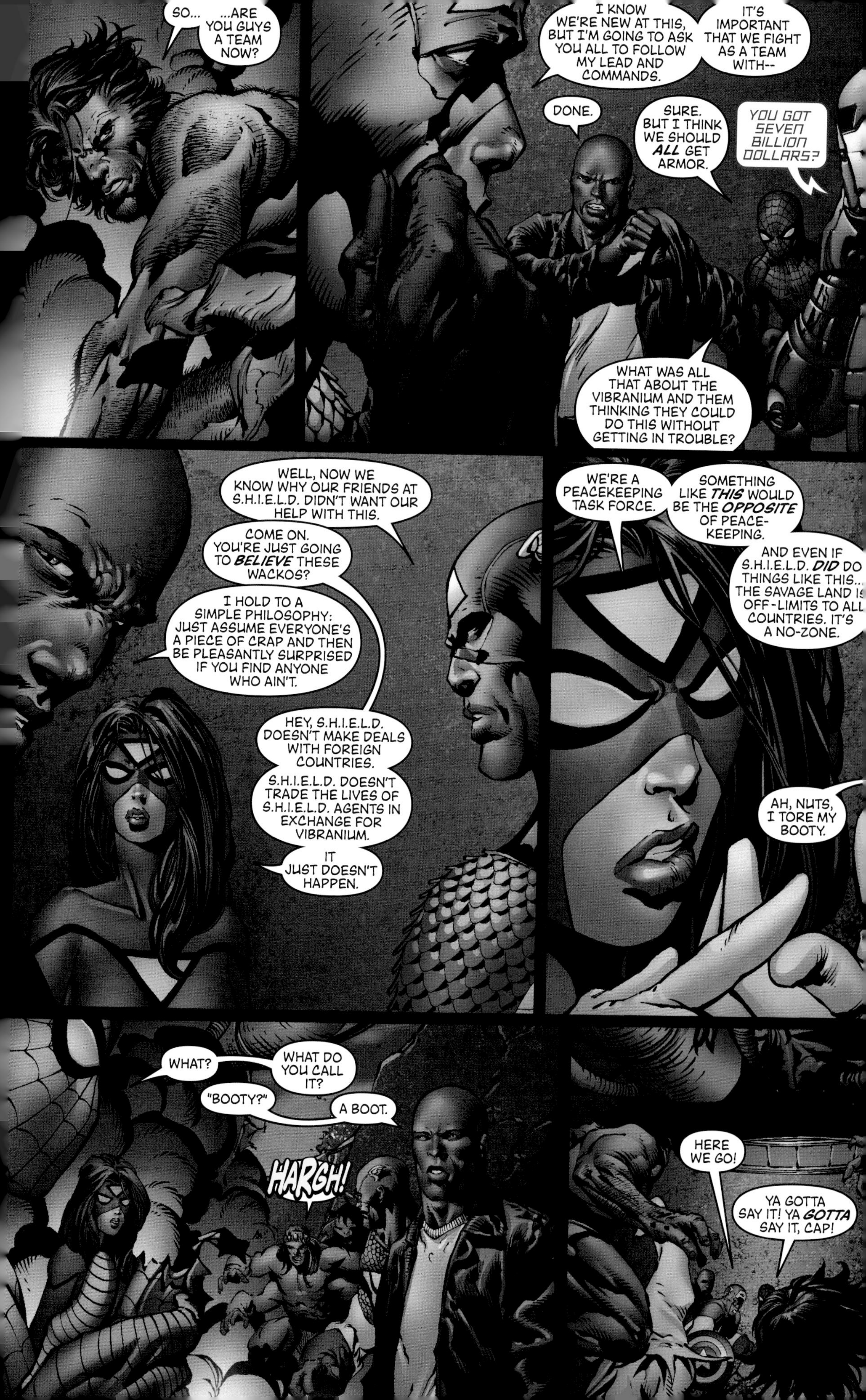
SO... ...ARE YOU GUYS A TEAM NOW?
I KNOW WE'RE NEW AT THIS, BUT I'M GOING TO ASK YOU ALL TO FOLLOW MY LEAD AND COMMANDS.
IT'S IMPORTANT THAT WE FIGHT AS A TEAM WITH--
DONE.
SURE. BUT I THINK WE SHOULD ALL GET ARMOR.
YOU GOT SEVEN BILLION DOLLARS?
WHAT WAS ALL THAT ABOUT THE VIBRANIUM AND THEM THINKING THEY COULD DO THIS WITHOUT GETTING IN TROUBLE?
WELL, NOW WE KNOW WHY OUR FRIENDS AT S.H.I.E.L.D. DIDN'T WANT OUR HELP WITH THIS.
COME ON. YOU'RE JUST GOING TO BELIEVE THESE WACKOS?
I HOLD TO A SIMPLE PHILOSOPHY: JUST ASSUME EVERYONE'S A PIECE OF CRAP AND THEN BE PLEASANTLY SURPRISED IF YOU FIND ANYONE WHO AIN'T.
HEY, S.H.I.E.L.D. DOESN'T MAKE DEALS WITH FOREIGN COUNTRIES.
S.H.I.E.L.D. DOESN'T TRADE THE LIVES OF S.H.I.E.L.D. AGENTS IN EXCHANGE FOR VIBRANIUM.
IT JUST DOESN'T HAPPEN.
WE'RE A PEACEKEEPING TASK FORCE.
SOMETHING LIKE THIS WOULD BE THE OPPOSITE OF PEACE-KEEPING.
AND EVEN IF S.H.I.E.L.D. DID DO THINGS LIKE THIS... THE SAVAGE LAND IS OFF-LIMITS TO ALL COUNTRIES. IT'S A NO-ZONE.
AH, NUTS, I TORE MY BOOTY.
WHAT?
WHAT DO YOU CALL IT?
"BOOTY?"
A BOOT.
HARGH!
HERE WE GO!
YA GOTTA SAY IT! YA GOTTA SAY IT, CAP!

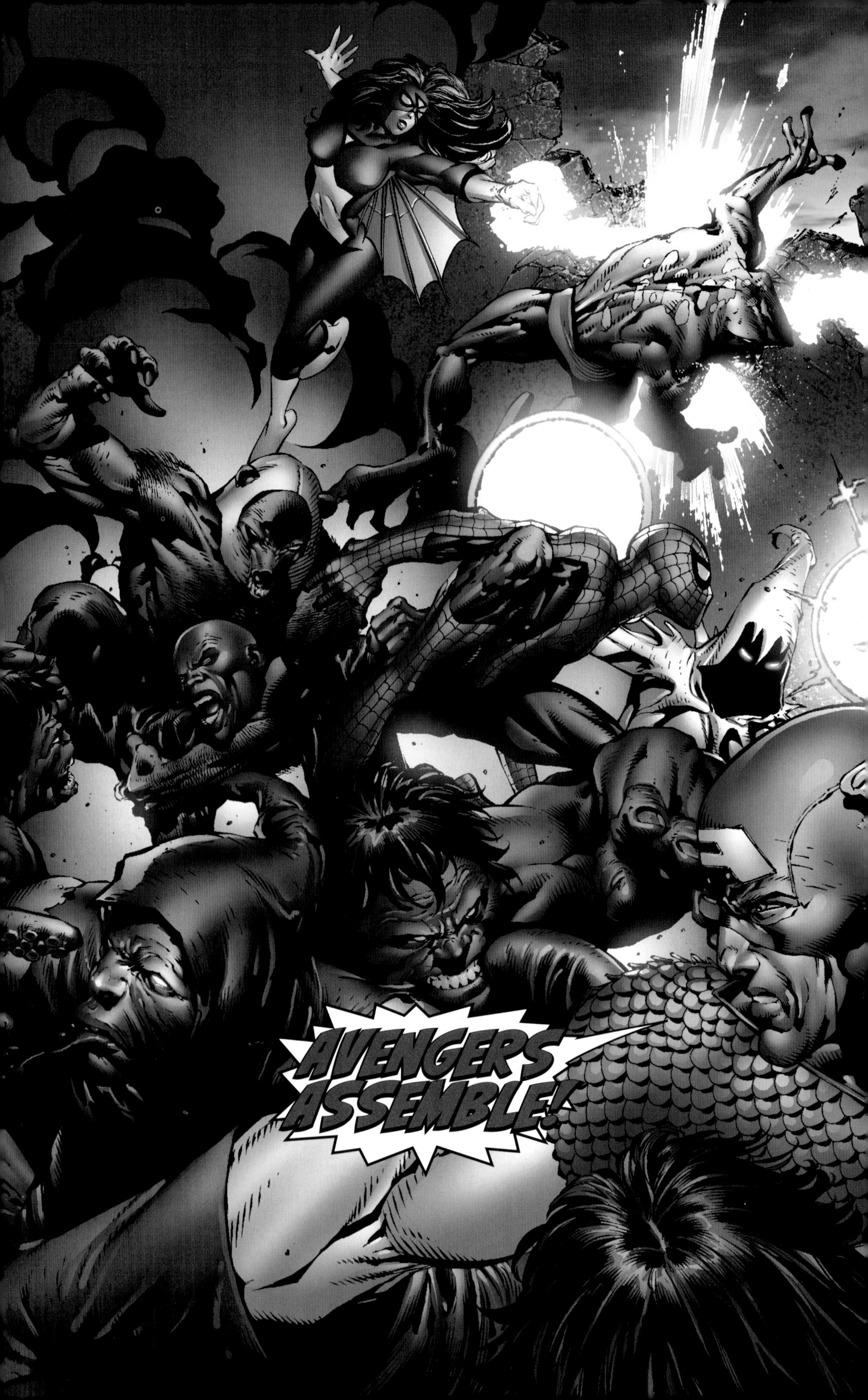
AVENGERS
ASSEMBLE!

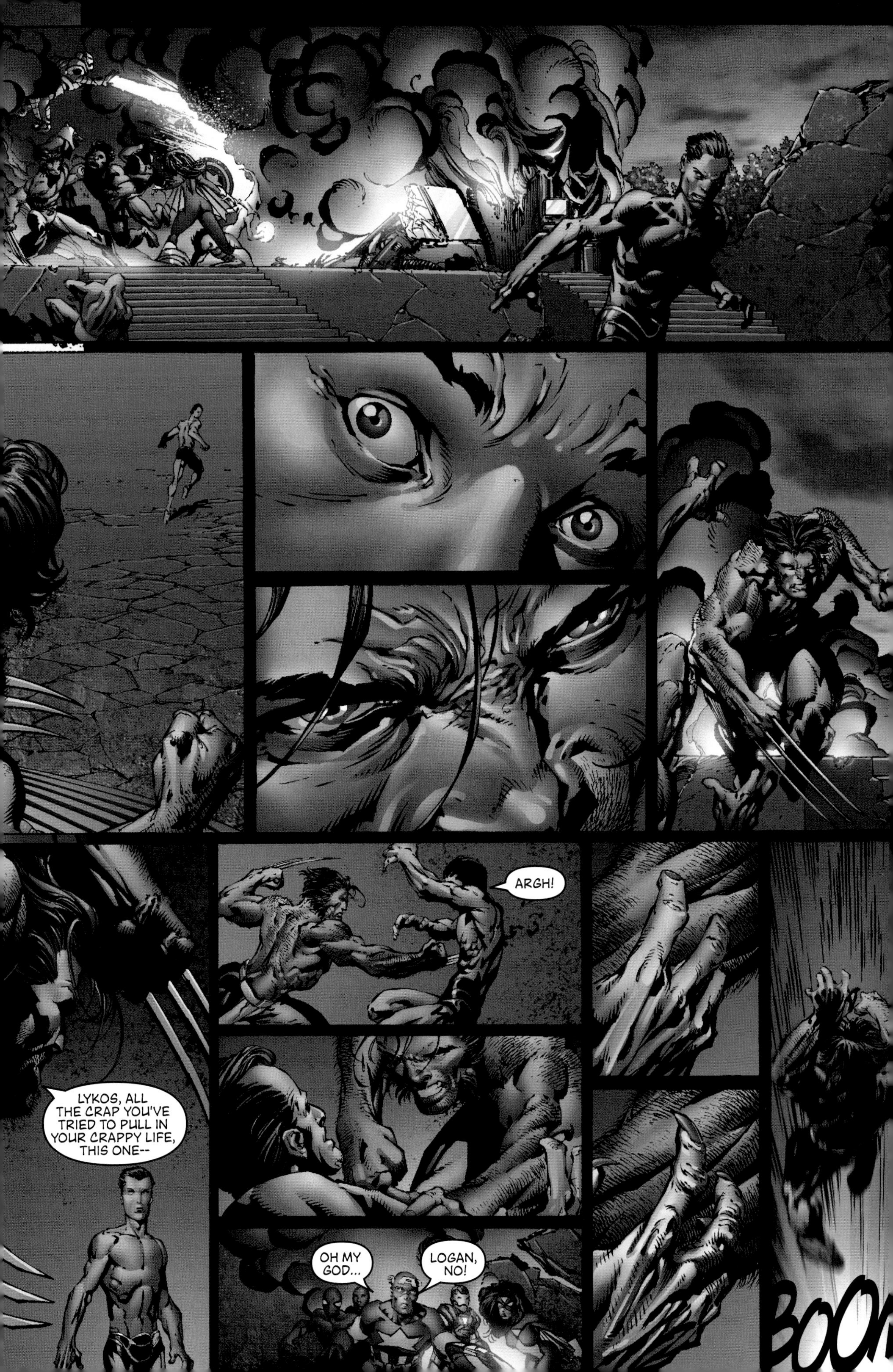
ARGH!
LYKOS, ALL THE CRAP YOU'VE TRIED TO PULL IN YOUR CRAPPY LIFE, THIS ONE--
OH MY GOD...
LOGAN, NO!
BOOM

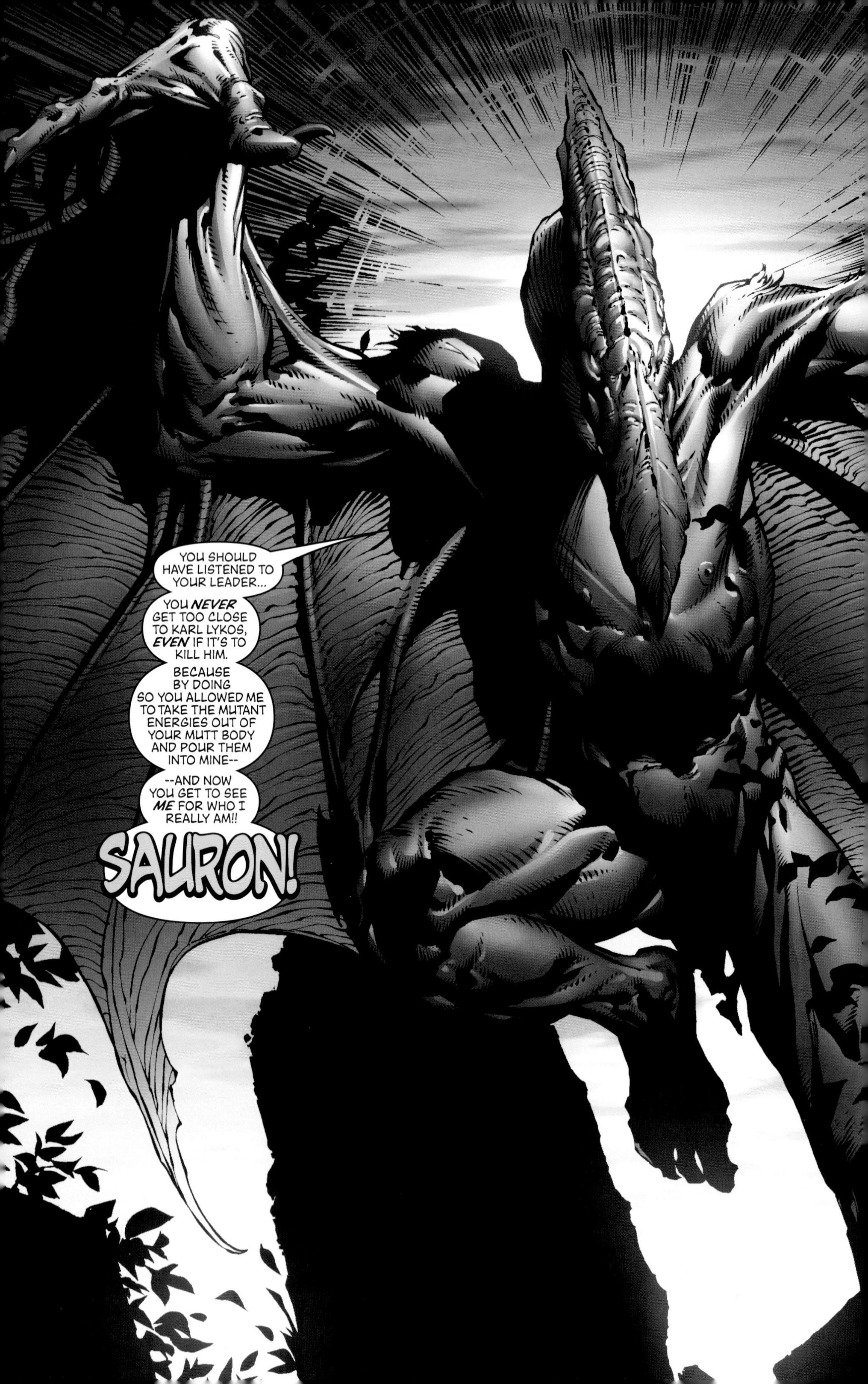
YOU SHOULD HAVE LISTENED TO YOUR LEADER...
YOU NEVER GET TOO CLOSE TO KARL LYKOS, EVEN IF IT'S TO KILL HIM.
BECAUSE BY DOING SO YOU ALLOWED ME TO TAKE THE MUTANT ENERGIES OUT OF YOUR MUTT BODY AND POUR THEM INTO MINE--
--AND NOW YOU GET TO SEE ME FOR WHO I REALLY AM!!
SAURON!

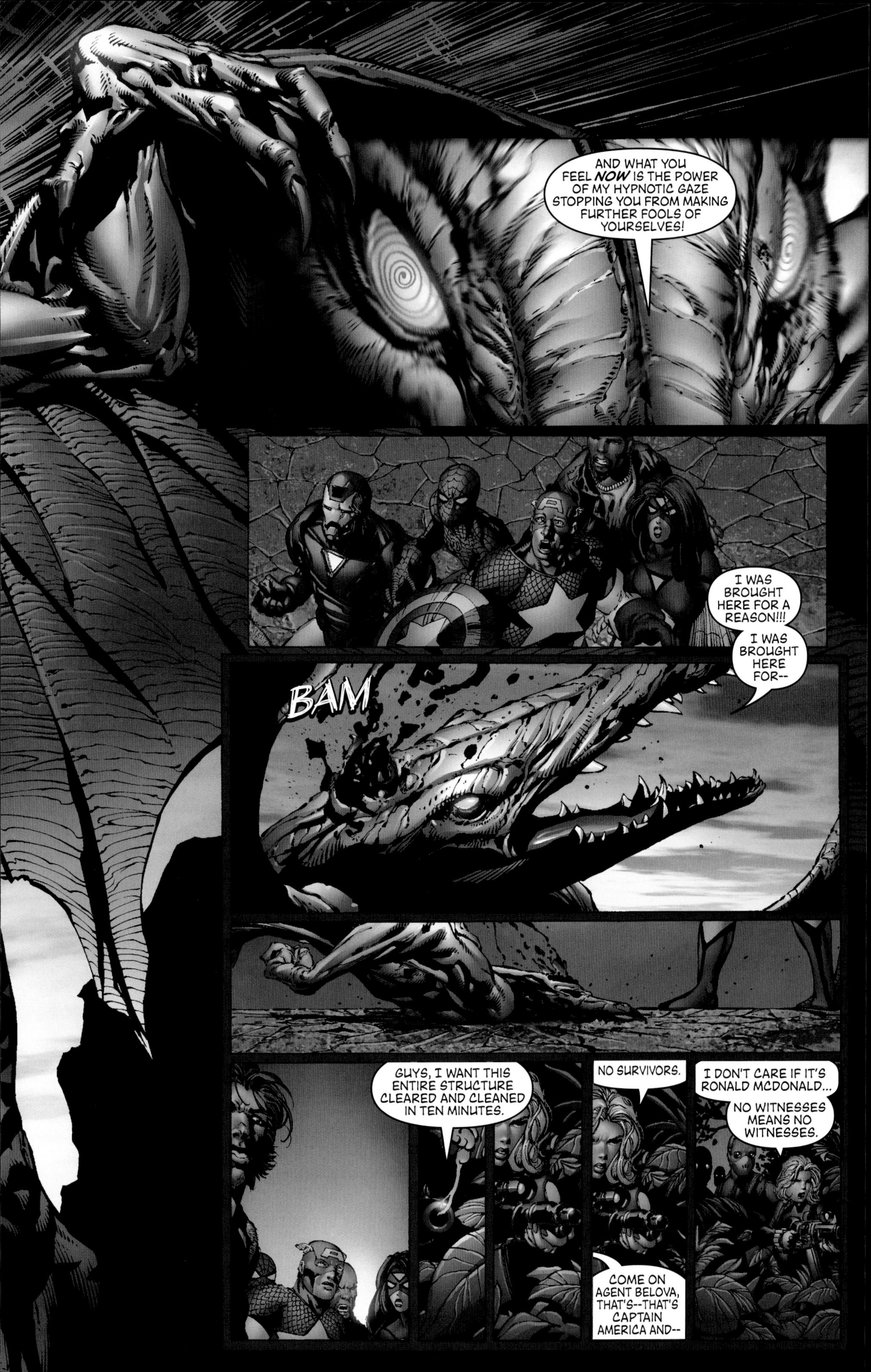
AND WHAT YOU FEEL NOW IS THE POWER OF MY HYPNOTIC GAZE STOPPING YOU FROM MAKING FURTHER FOOLS OF YOURSELVES!
I WAS BROUGHT HERE FOR A REASON!!!
I WAS BROUGHT HERE FOR--
BAM
GUYS, I WANT THIS ENTIRE STRUCTURE CLEARED AND CLEANED IN TEN MINUTES.
NO SURVIVORS.
COME ON AGENT BELOVA, THAT'S--THAT'S CAPTAIN AMERICA AND--
I DON'T CARE IF IT'S RONALD MCDONALD...
NO WITNESSES MEANS NO WITNESSES.

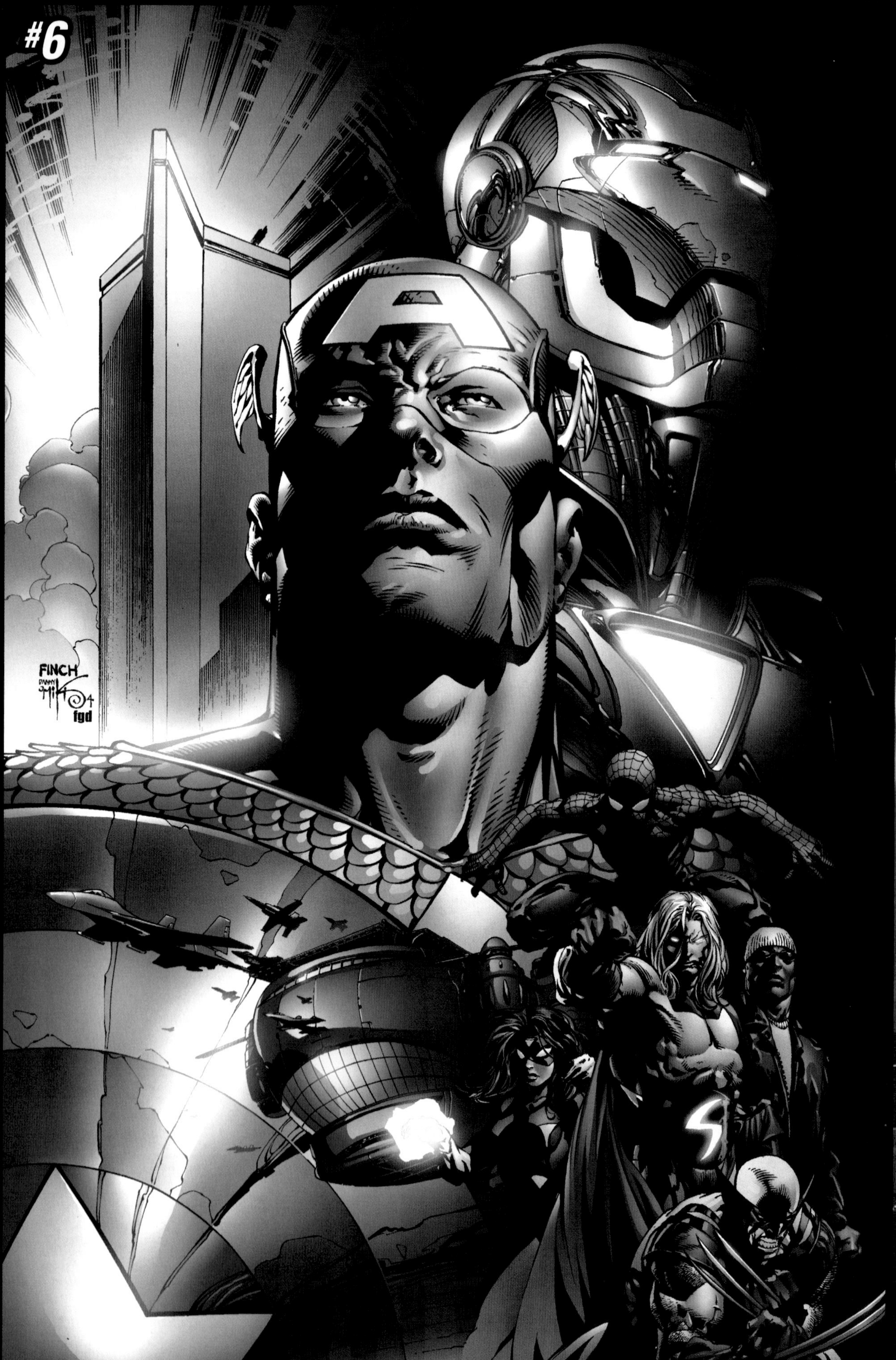
#6
FINCH
fgd

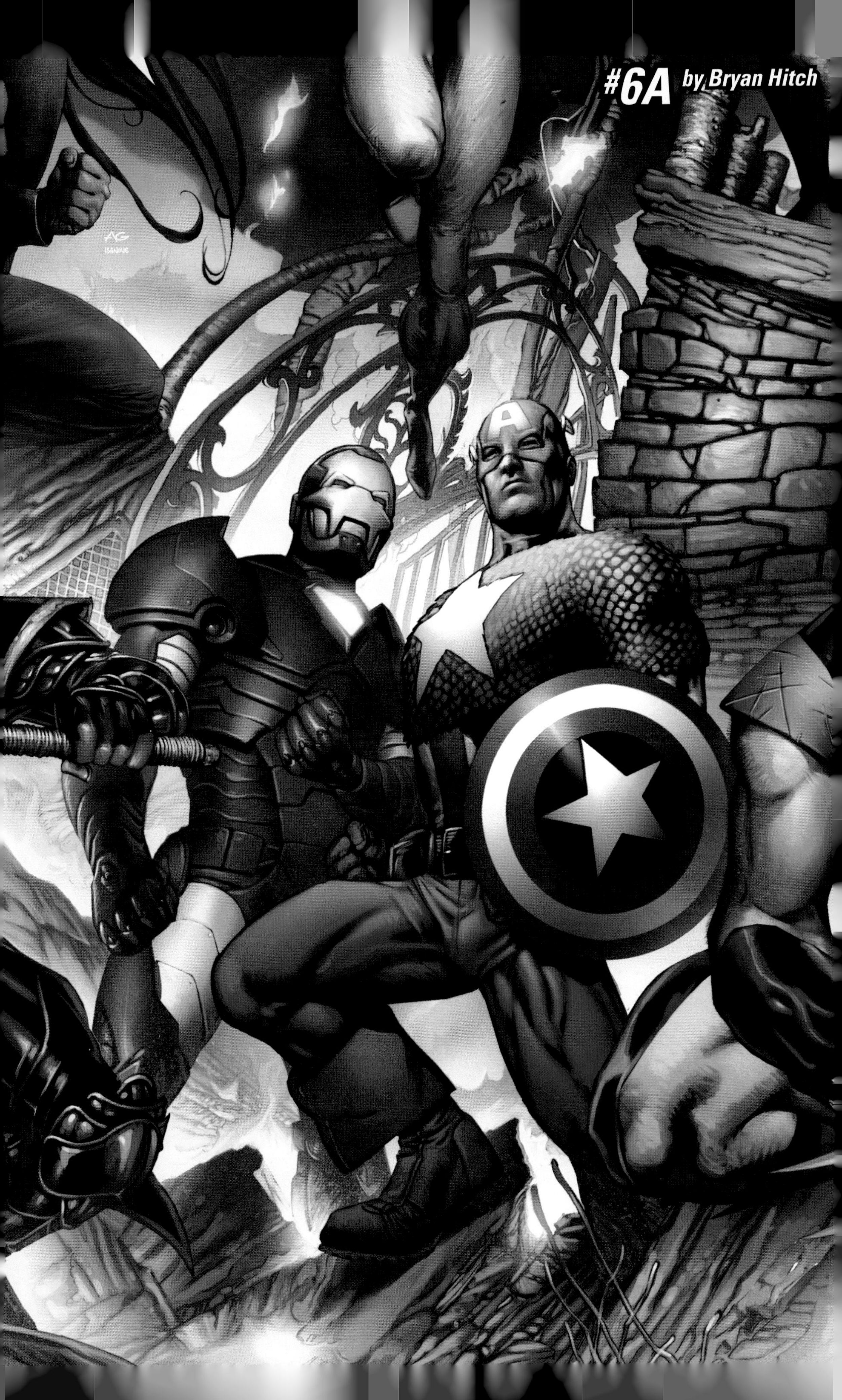
#6A by Bryan Hitch

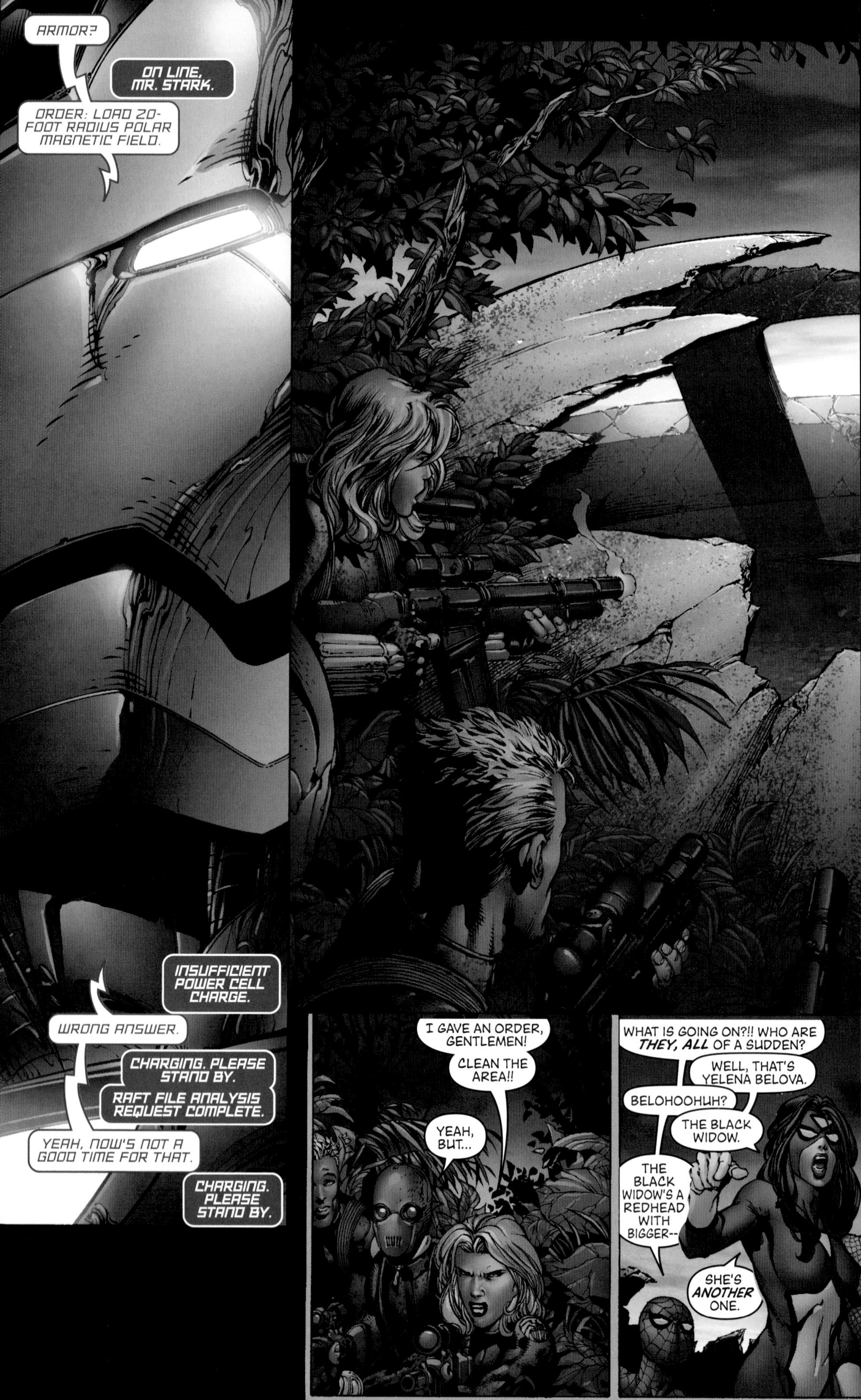
ARMOR?
ON LINE, MR. STARK.
ORDER: LOAD 20-FOOT RADIUS POLAR MAGNETIC FIELD.
INSUFFICIENT POWER CELL CHARGE.
WRONG ANSWER.
CHARGING. PLEASE STAND BY.
RAFT FILE ANALYSIS REQUEST COMPLETE.
YEAH, NOW'S NOT A GOOD TIME FOR THAT.
CHARGING. PLEASE STAND BY.
I GAVE AN ORDER, GENTLEMEN!
CLEAN THE AREA!!
YEAH, BUT...
WHAT IS GOING ON?!! WHO ARE *THEY, ALL* OF A SUDDEN?
WELL, THAT'S YELENA BELOVA.
BELOHOOHUH?
THE BLACK WIDOW.
THE BLACK WIDOW'S A REDHEAD WITH BIGGER--
SHE'S *ANOTHER* ONE.

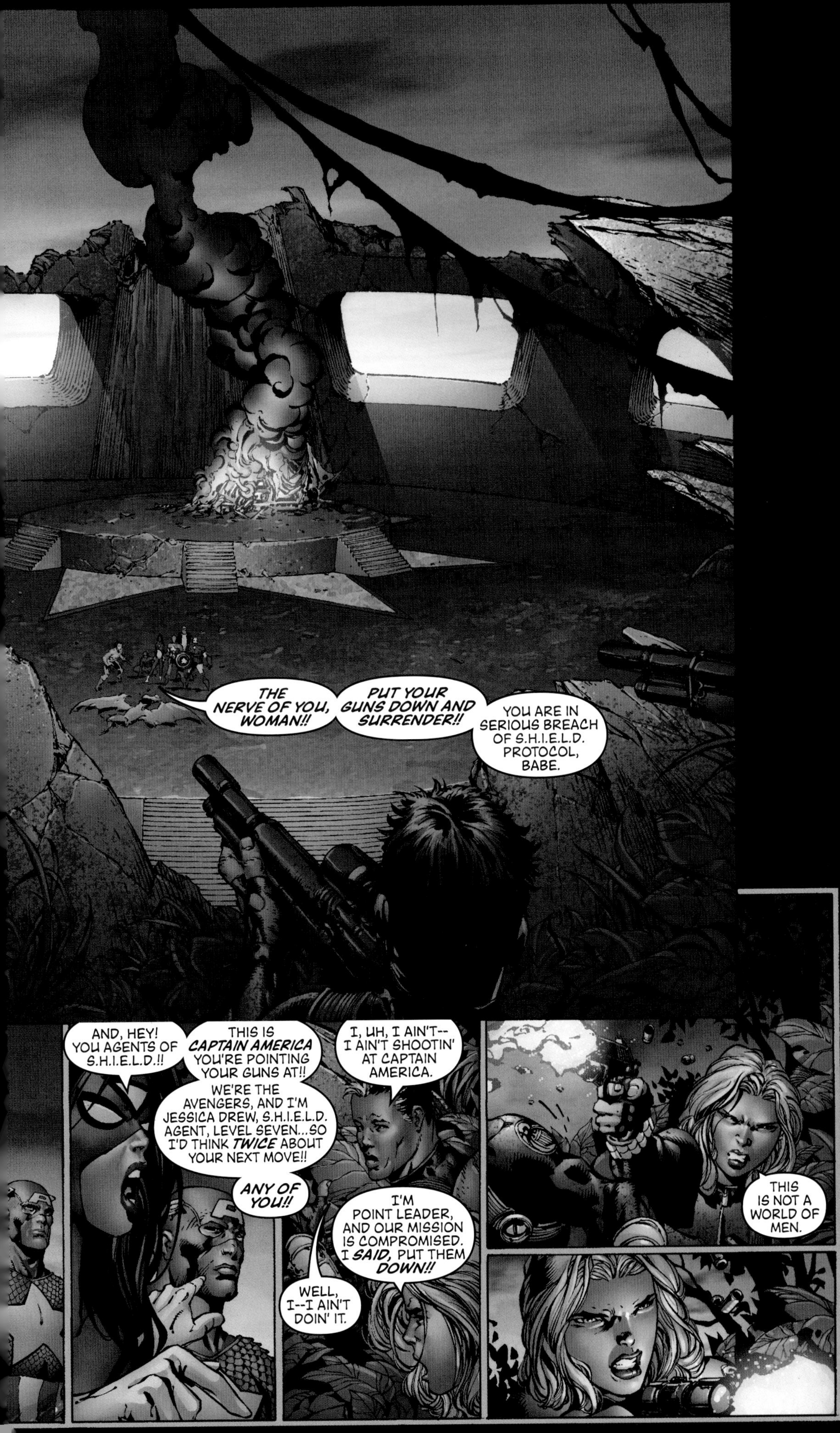
THE NERVE OF YOU, WOMAN!!
PUT YOUR GUNS DOWN AND SURRENDER!!
YOU ARE IN SERIOUS BREACH OF S.H.I.E.L.D. PROTOCOL, BABE.
AND, HEY! YOU AGENTS OF S.H.I.E.L.D.!!
THIS IS CAPTAIN AMERICA YOU'RE POINTING YOUR GUNS AT!!
WE'RE THE AVENGERS, AND I'M JESSICA DREW, S.H.I.E.L.D. AGENT, LEVEL SEVEN...SO I'D THINK TWICE ABOUT YOUR NEXT MOVE!!
ANY OF YOU!!
I, UH, I AIN'T-- I AIN'T SHOOTIN' AT CAPTAIN AMERICA.
I'M POINT LEADER, AND OUR MISSION IS COMPROMISED. I SAID, PUT THEM DOWN!!
WELL, I--I AIN'T DOIN' IT.
THIS IS NOT A WORLD OF MEN.

POWER CELLS
AT SIX PERCENT.

I'LL TAKE IT!

AGH!!

I CAN'T
BELIEVE THIS!!
S.H.I.E.L.D.
AGENTS!!

NO
CASUALTIES,
LOGAN! I
MEAN IT!

TELL
THEM!

AND I *STILL*
HAVE NO IDEA WHAT
IS *GOING ON*, EVEN
MORE SO THAN
USUAL!

DABUDDABUDDABUDDABU   ABUDDABUDDABUDDABU

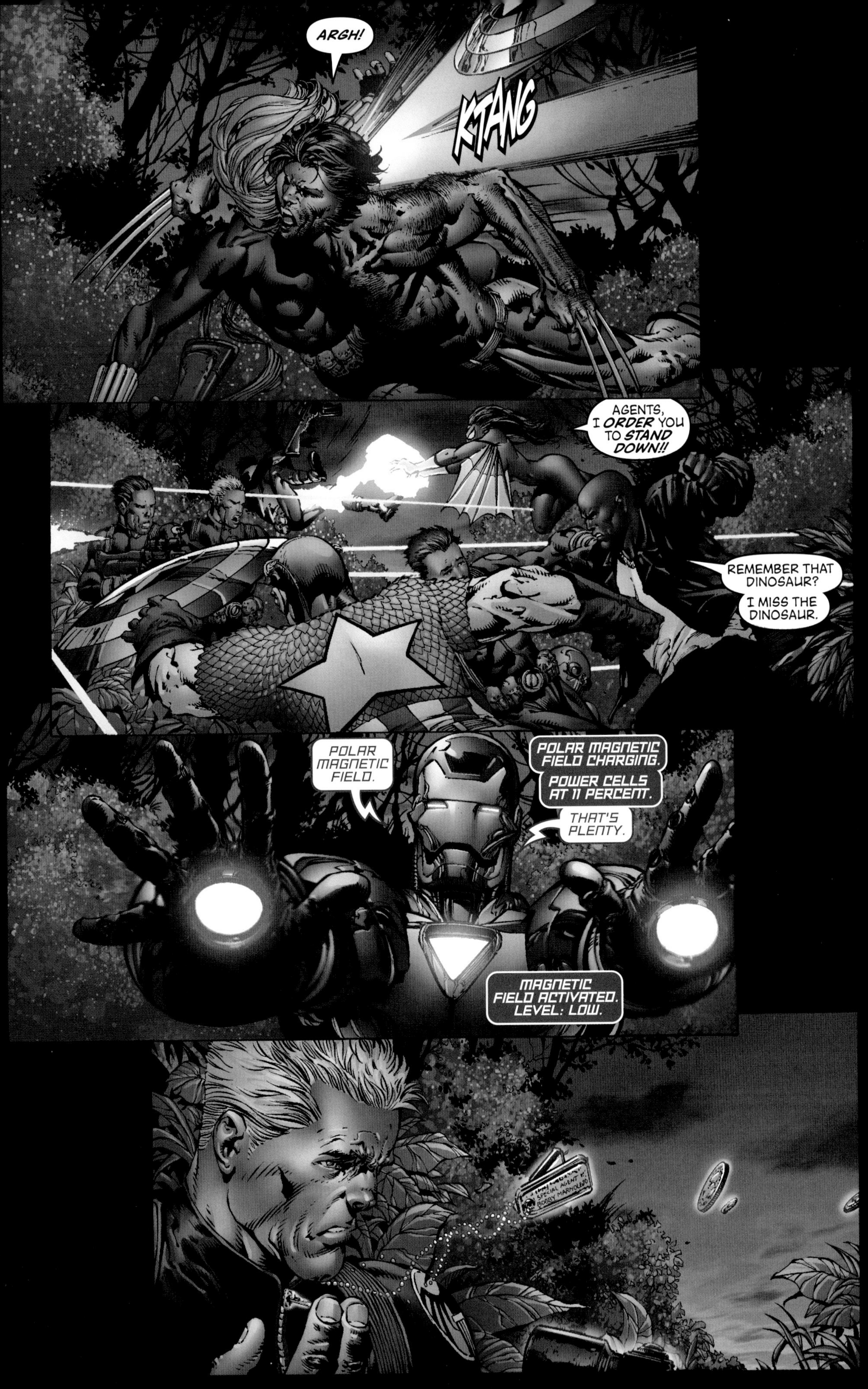
ARGH!
KTANG
AGENTS, I ORDER YOU TO STAND DOWN!!
REMEMBER THAT DINOSAUR?
I MISS THE DINOSAUR.
POLAR MAGNETIC FIELD.
POLAR MAGNETIC FIELD CHARGING.
POWER CELLS AT 11 PERCENT.
THAT'S PLENTY.
MAGNETIC FIELD ACTIVATED. LEVEL: LOW.

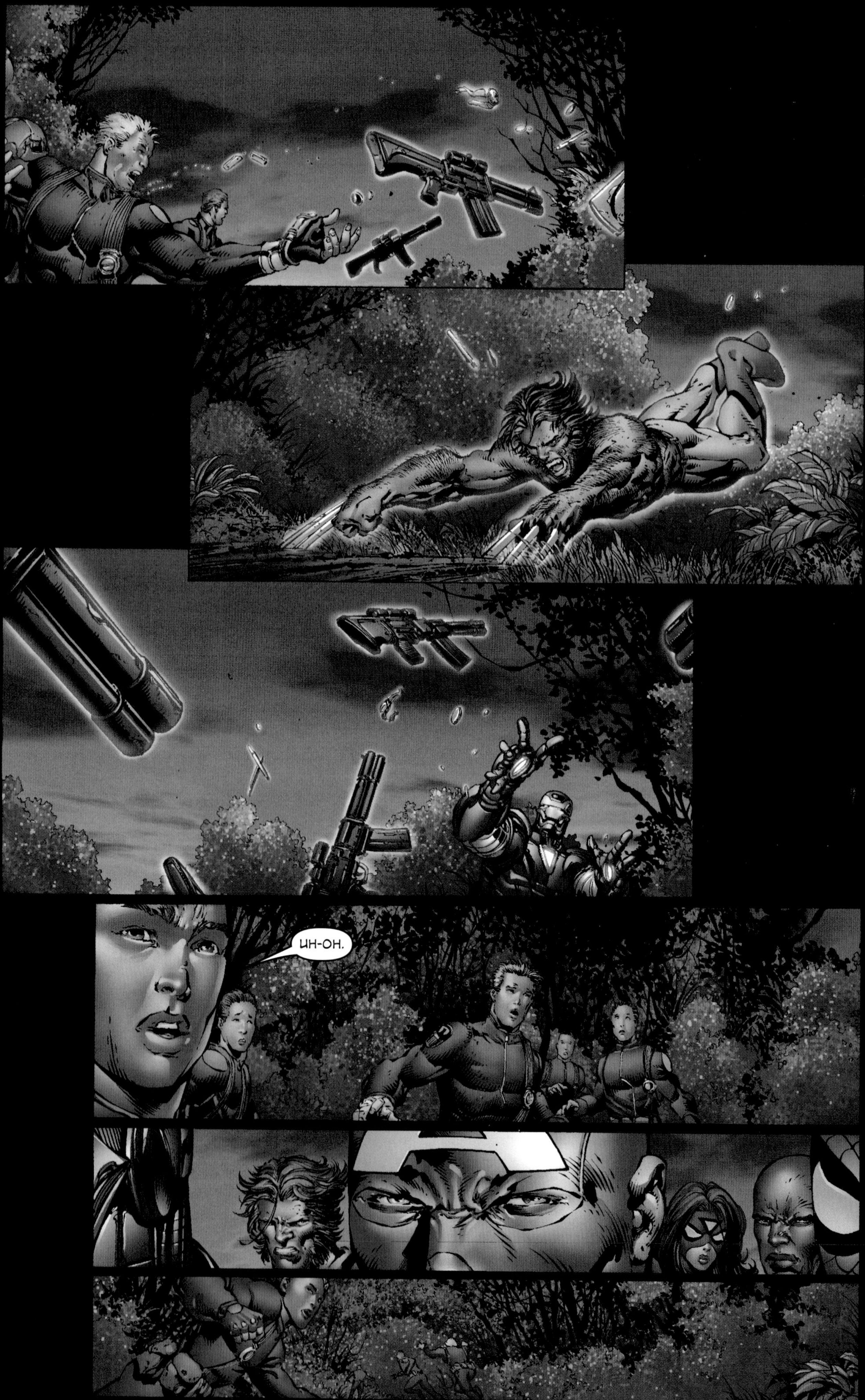
UH-OH.

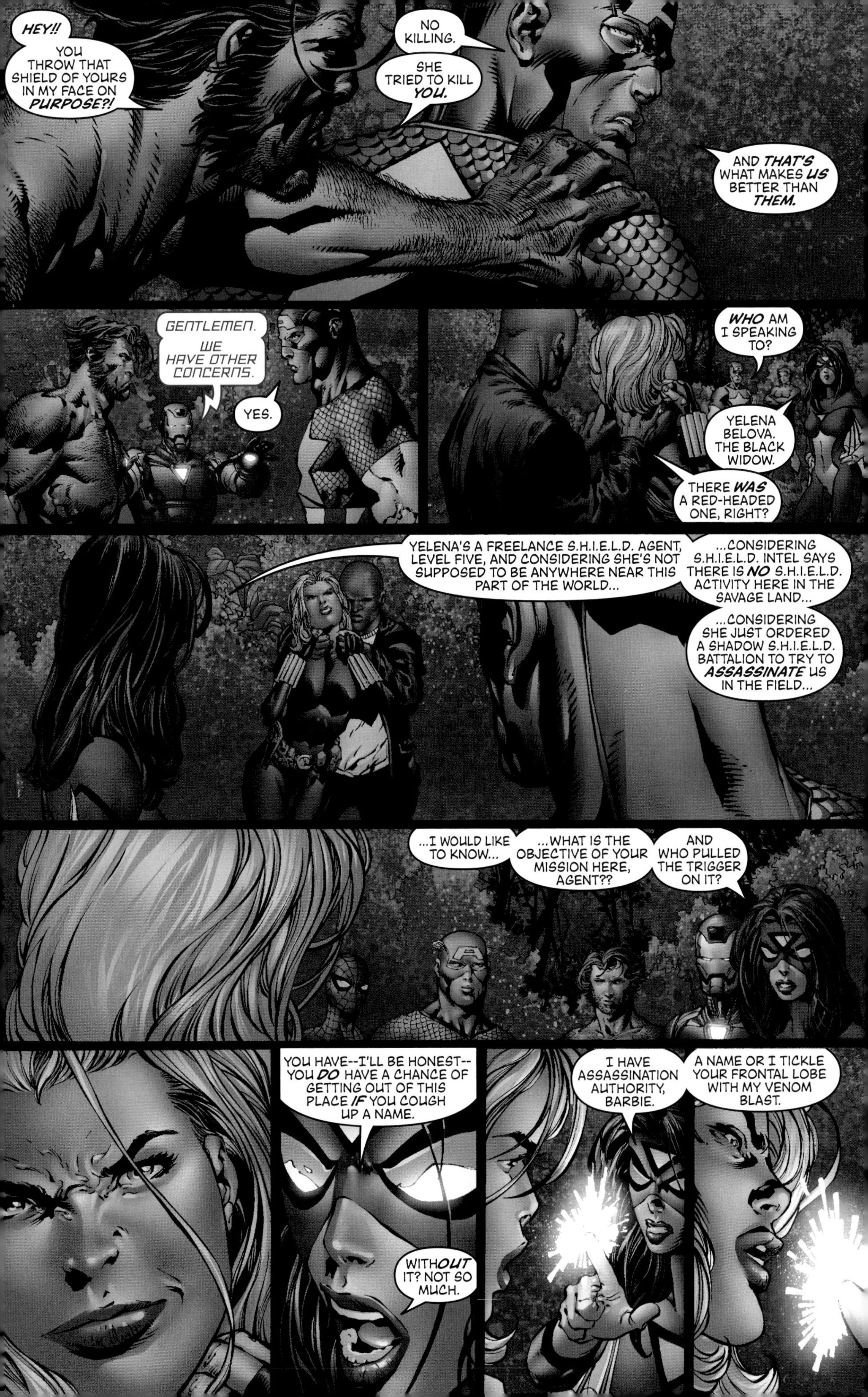
HEY!! YOU THROW THAT SHIELD OF YOURS IN MY FACE ON PURPOSE?!
NO KILLING.
SHE TRIED TO KILL YOU.
AND THAT'S WHAT MAKES US BETTER THAN THEM.
GENTLEMEN. WE HAVE OTHER CONCERNS.
YES.
WHO AM I SPEAKING TO?
YELENA BELOVA. THE BLACK WIDOW.
THERE WAS A RED-HEADED ONE, RIGHT?
YELENA'S A FREELANCE S.H.I.E.L.D. AGENT, LEVEL FIVE, AND CONSIDERING SHE'S NOT SUPPOSED TO BE ANYWHERE NEAR THIS PART OF THE WORLD...
...CONSIDERING S.H.I.E.L.D. INTEL SAYS THERE IS NO S.H.I.E.L.D. ACTIVITY HERE IN THE SAVAGE LAND...
...CONSIDERING SHE JUST ORDERED A SHADOW S.H.I.E.L.D. BATTALION TO TRY TO ASSASSINATE US IN THE FIELD...
...I WOULD LIKE TO KNOW...
...WHAT IS THE OBJECTIVE OF YOUR MISSION HERE, AGENT??
AND WHO PULLED THE TRIGGER ON IT?
YOU HAVE--I'LL BE HONEST--YOU DO HAVE A CHANCE OF GETTING OUT OF THIS PLACE IF YOU COUGH UP A NAME.
WITHOUT IT? NOT SO MUCH.
I HAVE ASSASSINATION AUTHORITY, BARBIE.
A NAME OR I TICKLE YOUR FRONTAL LOBE WITH MY VENOM BLAST.

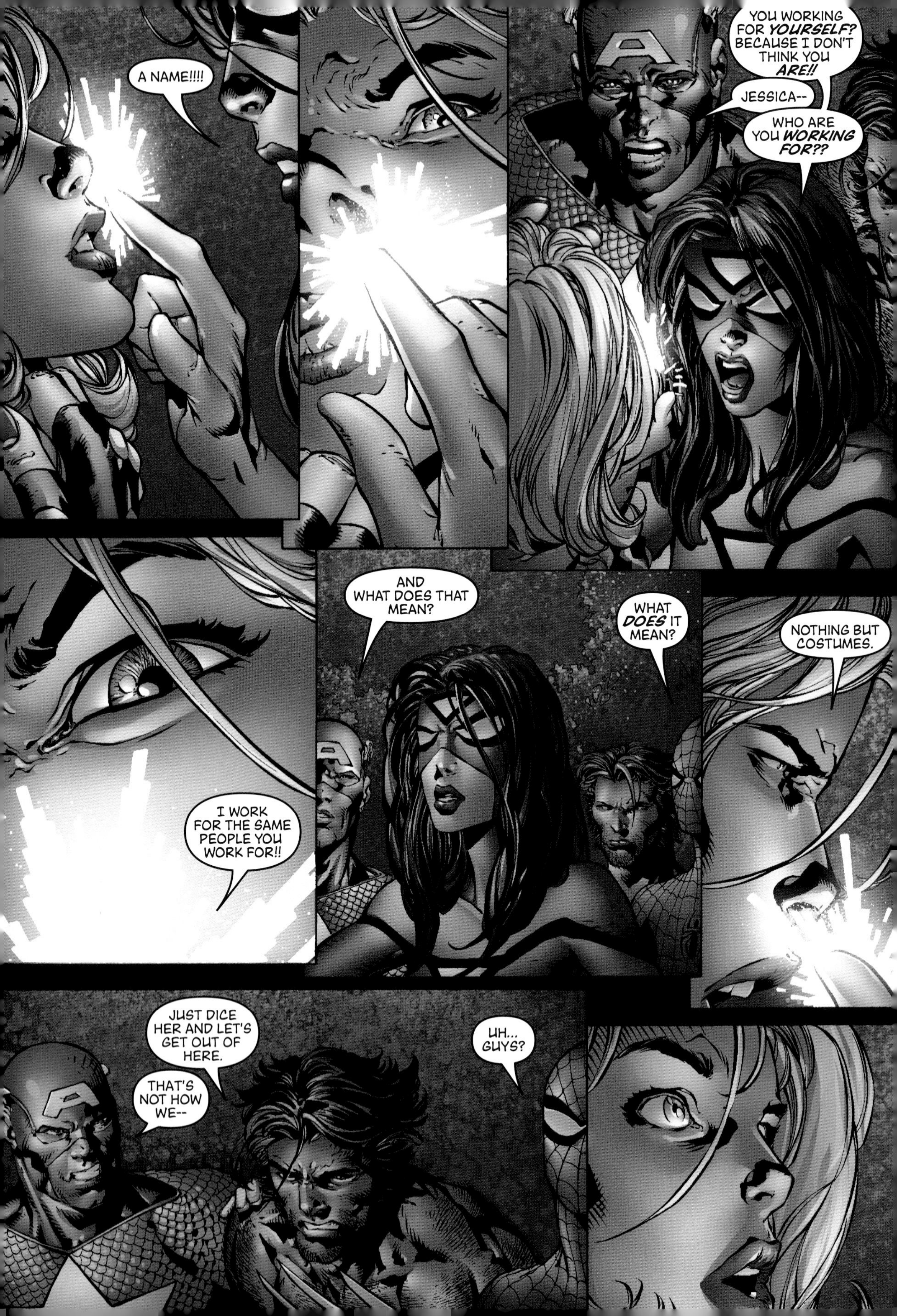

A NAME!!!!
YOU WORKING FOR YOURSELF? BECAUSE I DON'T THINK YOU ARE!!
JESSICA--
WHO ARE YOU WORKING FOR??
I WORK FOR THE SAME PEOPLE YOU WORK FOR!!
AND WHAT DOES THAT MEAN?
WHAT DOES IT MEAN?
NOTHING BUT COSTUMES.
JUST DICE HER AND LET'S GET OUT OF HERE.
THAT'S NOT HOW WE--
UH... GUYS?

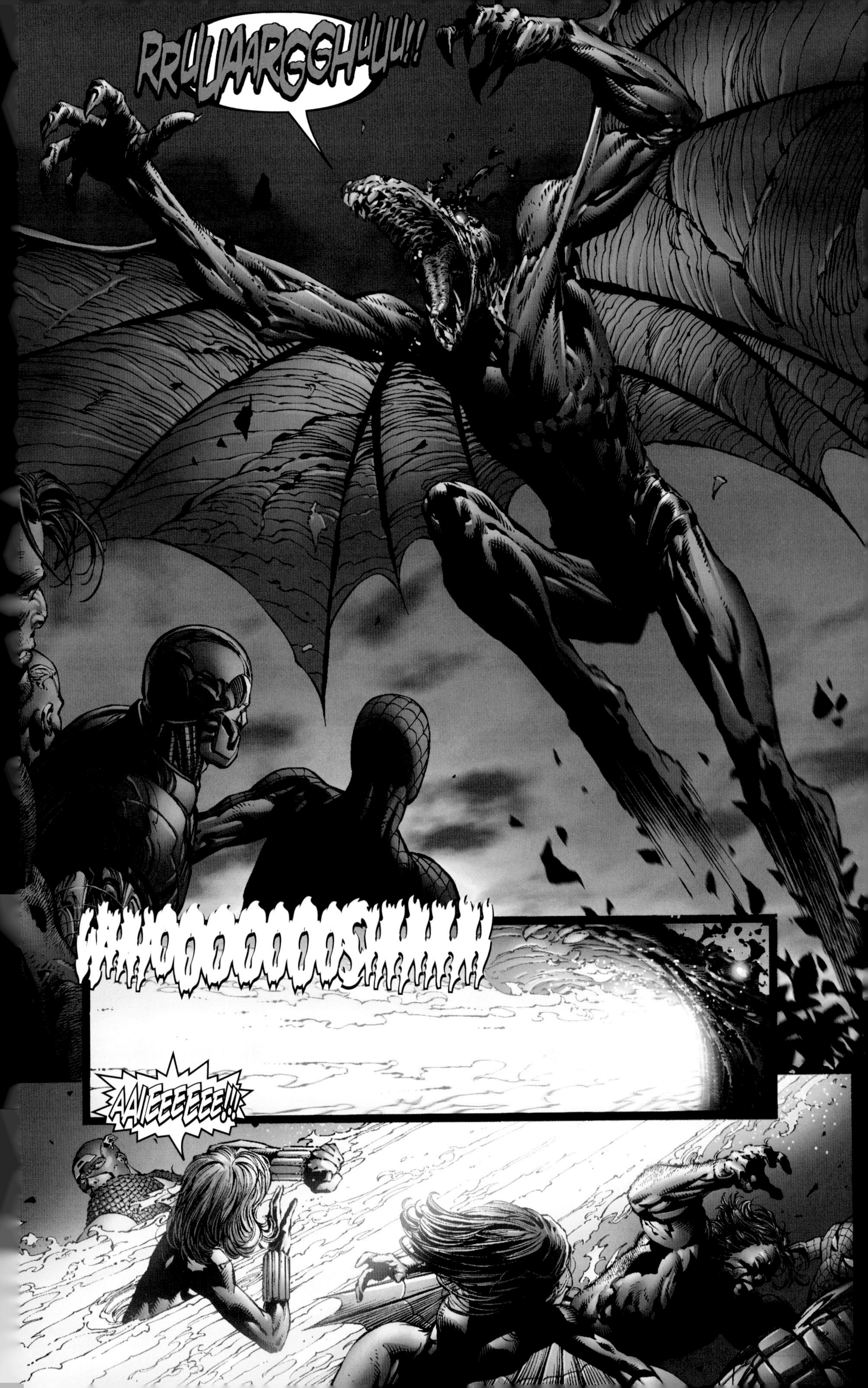
RRUUAARGGHUUU!!
WHOOOOOOOOSHHHHH
AAIEEEEEE!!!

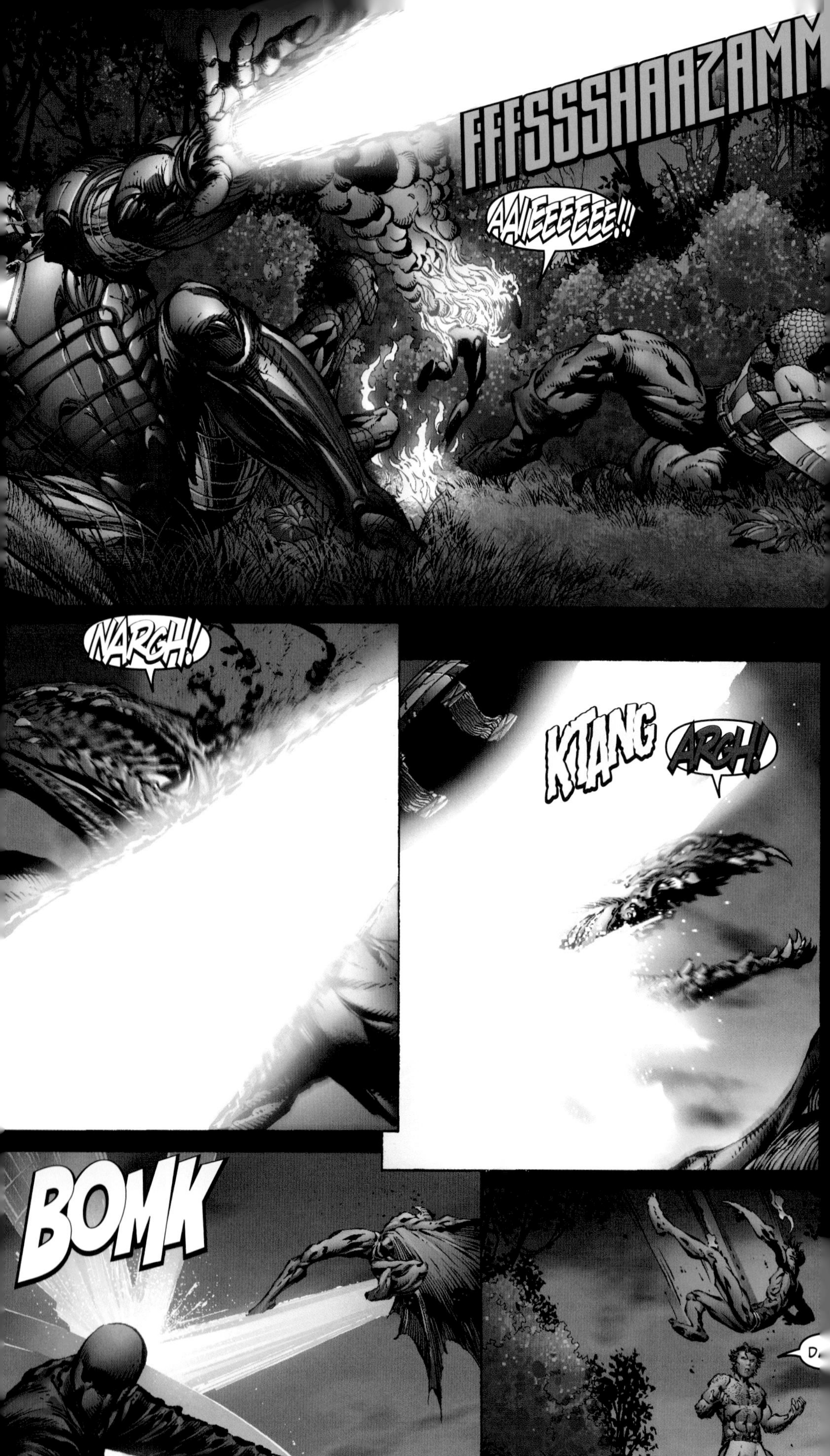
FFFSSSHAAZAMM
AAIIEEEEEE!!
NARGH!
KTANG
ARGH!
BOMK

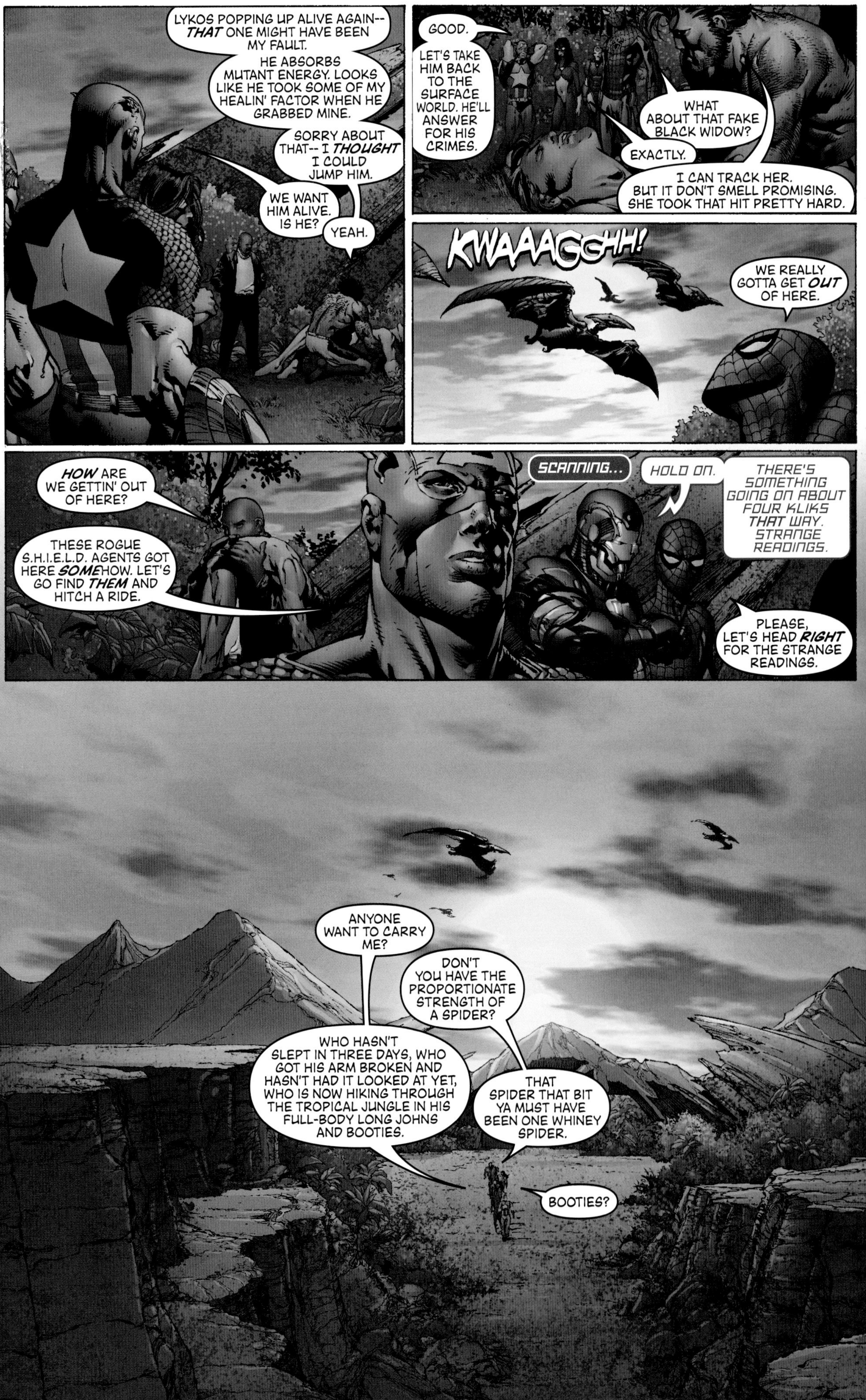

LYKOS POPPING UP ALIVE AGAIN-- THAT ONE MIGHT HAVE BEEN MY FAULT.
HE ABSORBS MUTANT ENERGY. LOOKS LIKE HE TOOK SOME OF MY HEALIN' FACTOR WHEN HE GRABBED MINE.
SORRY ABOUT THAT-- I THOUGHT I COULD JUMP HIM.
WE WANT HIM ALIVE. IS HE?
YEAH.
GOOD.
LET'S TAKE HIM BACK TO THE SURFACE WORLD. HE'LL ANSWER FOR HIS CRIMES.
WHAT ABOUT THAT FAKE BLACK WIDOW?
EXACTLY.
I CAN TRACK HER. BUT IT DON'T SMELL PROMISING. SHE TOOK THAT HIT PRETTY HARD.
KWAAAGGHH!
WE REALLY GOTTA GET OUT OF HERE.
HOW ARE WE GETTIN' OUT OF HERE?
THESE ROGUE S.H.I.E.L.D. AGENTS GOT HERE SOMEHOW. LET'S GO FIND THEM AND HITCH A RIDE.
SCANNING...
HOLD ON.
THERE'S SOMETHING GOING ON ABOUT FOUR KLIKS THAT WAY. STRANGE READINGS.
PLEASE, LET'S HEAD RIGHT FOR THE STRANGE READINGS.
ANYONE WANT TO CARRY ME?
DON'T YOU HAVE THE PROPORTIONATE STRENGTH OF A SPIDER?
WHO HASN'T SLEPT IN THREE DAYS, WHO GOT HIS ARM BROKEN AND HASN'T HAD IT LOOKED AT YET, WHO IS NOW HIKING THROUGH THE TROPICAL JUNGLE IN HIS FULL-BODY LONG JOHNS AND BOOTIES.
THAT SPIDER THAT BIT YA MUST HAVE BEEN ONE WHINEY SPIDER.
BOOTIES?

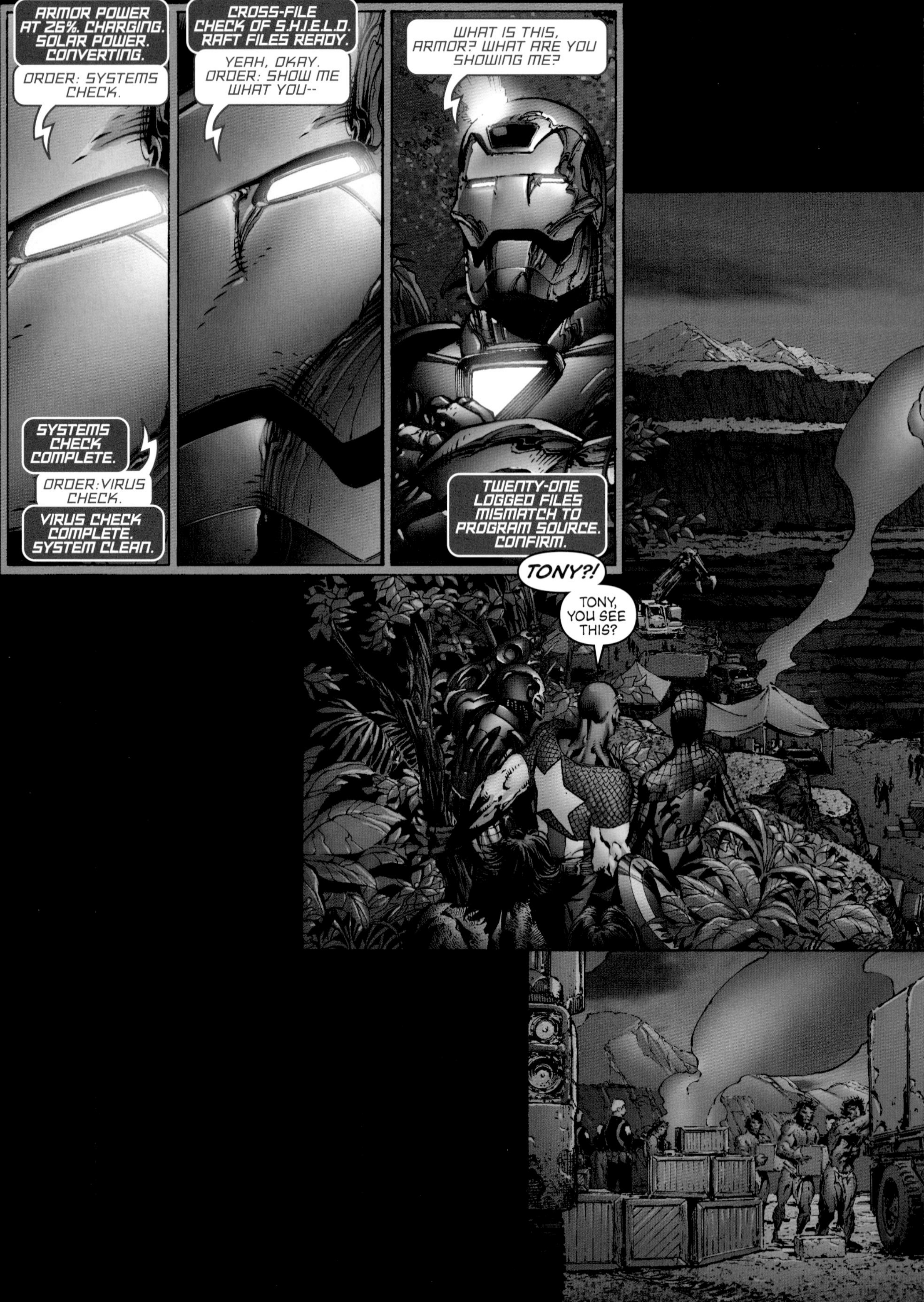
ARMOR POWER AT 26%. CHARGING. SOLAR POWER. CONVERTING.
ORDER: SYSTEMS CHECK.
SYSTEMS CHECK COMPLETE.
ORDER: VIRUS CHECK.
VIRUS CHECK COMPLETE. SYSTEM CLEAN.
CROSS-FILE CHECK OF S.H.I.E.L.D. RAFT FILES READY.
YEAH, OKAY. ORDER: SHOW ME WHAT YOU--
WHAT IS THIS, ARMOR? WHAT ARE YOU SHOWING ME?
TWENTY-ONE LOGGED FILES MISMATCH TO PROGRAM SOURCE. CONFIRM.
TONY?!
TONY, YOU SEE THIS?

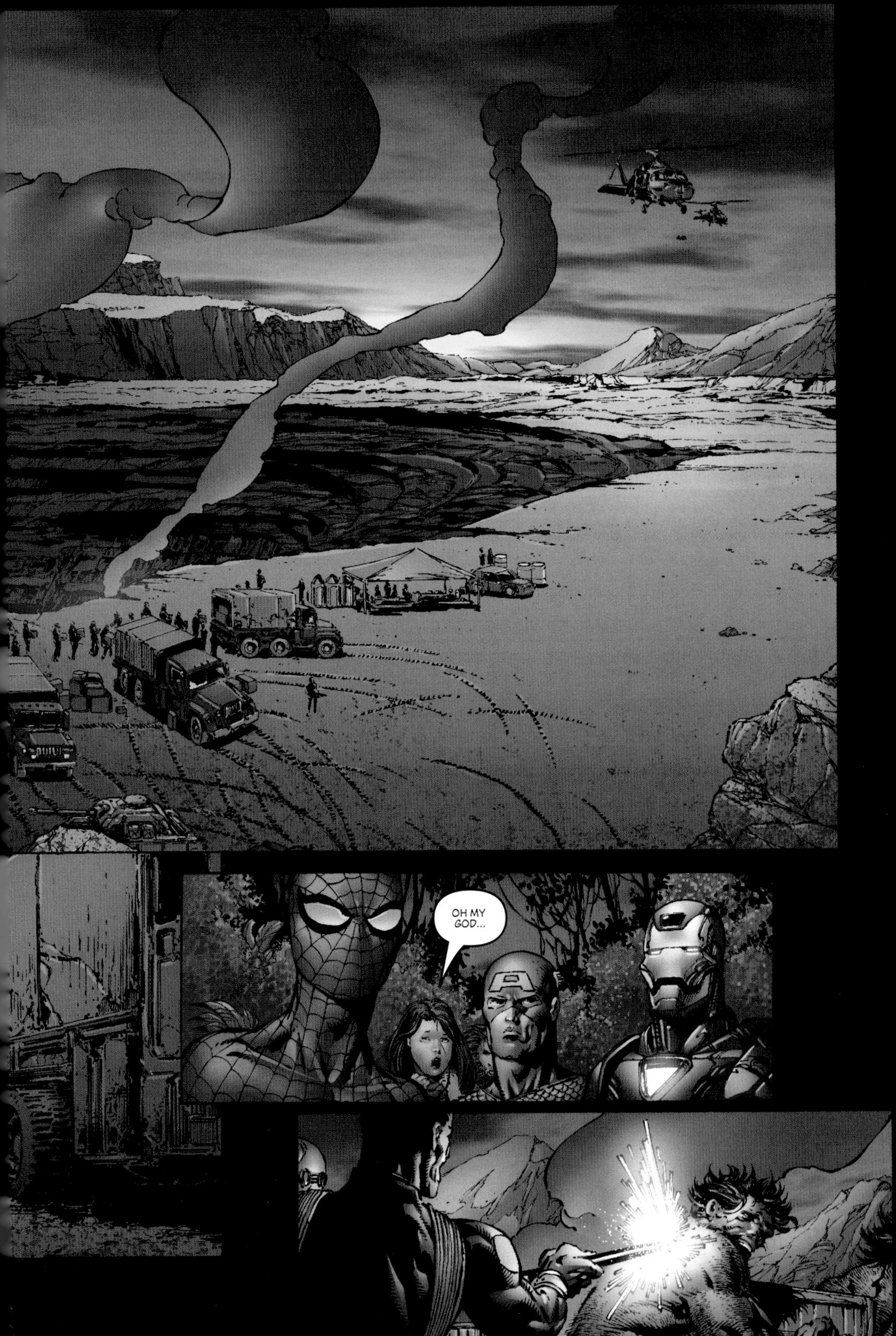
OH MY GOD...

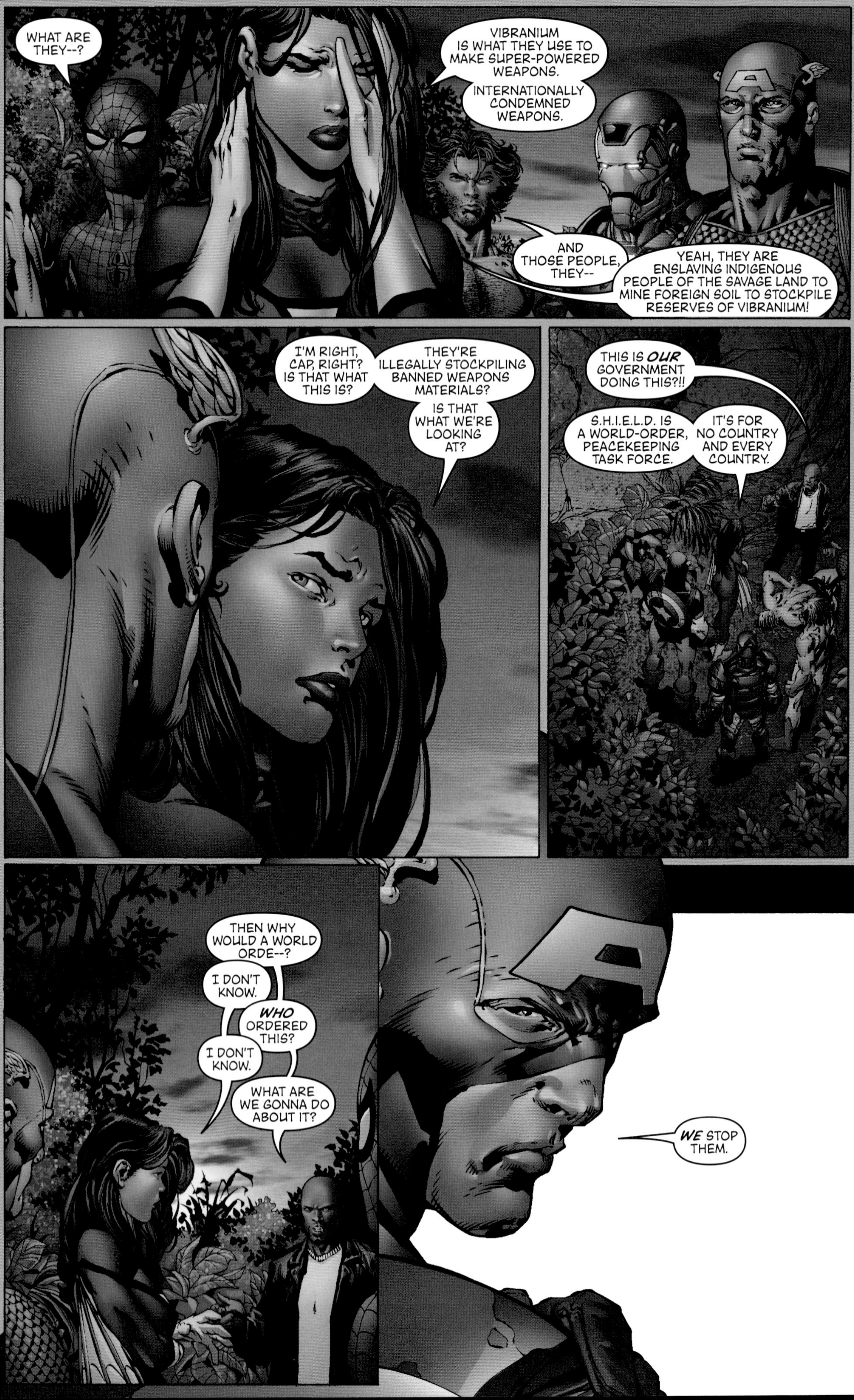
WHAT ARE THEY--?
VIBRANIUM IS WHAT THEY USE TO MAKE SUPER-POWERED WEAPONS.
INTERNATIONALLY CONDEMNED WEAPONS.
AND THOSE PEOPLE, THEY--
YEAH, THEY ARE ENSLAVING INDIGENOUS PEOPLE OF THE SAVAGE LAND TO MINE FOREIGN SOIL TO STOCKPILE RESERVES OF VIBRANIUM!
I'M RIGHT, CAP, RIGHT? IS THAT WHAT THIS IS?
THEY'RE ILLEGALLY STOCKPILING BANNED WEAPONS MATERIALS?
IS THAT WHAT WE'RE LOOKING AT?
THIS IS OUR GOVERNMENT DOING THIS?!!
S.H.I.E.L.D. IS A WORLD-ORDER, PEACEKEEPING TASK FORCE.
IT'S FOR NO COUNTRY AND EVERY COUNTRY.
THEN WHY WOULD A WORLD ORDE--?
I DON'T KNOW.
WHO ORDERED THIS?
I DON'T KNOW.
WHAT ARE WE GONNA DO ABOUT IT?
WE STOP THEM.

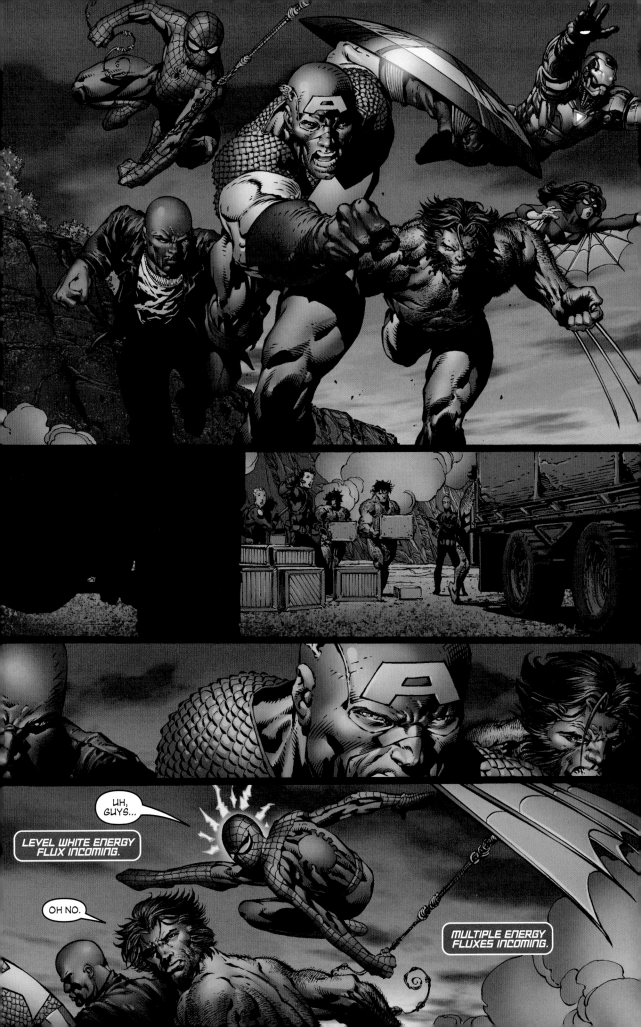

UH, GUYS...

LEVEL WHITE ENERGY FLUX INCOMING.

OH NO.

MULTIPLE ENERGY FLUXES INCOMING.

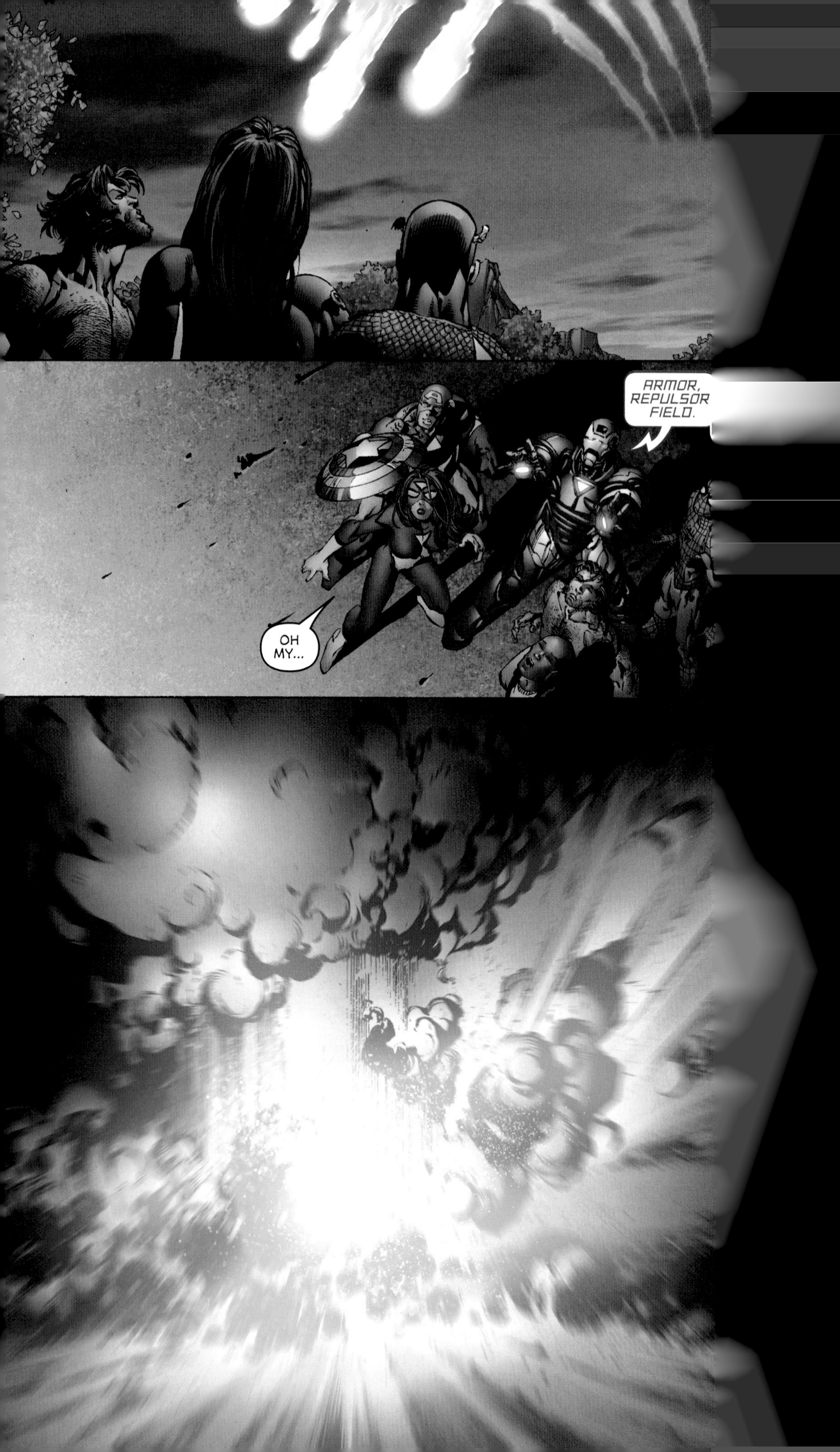
ARMOR, REPULSOR FIELD.
OH MY...

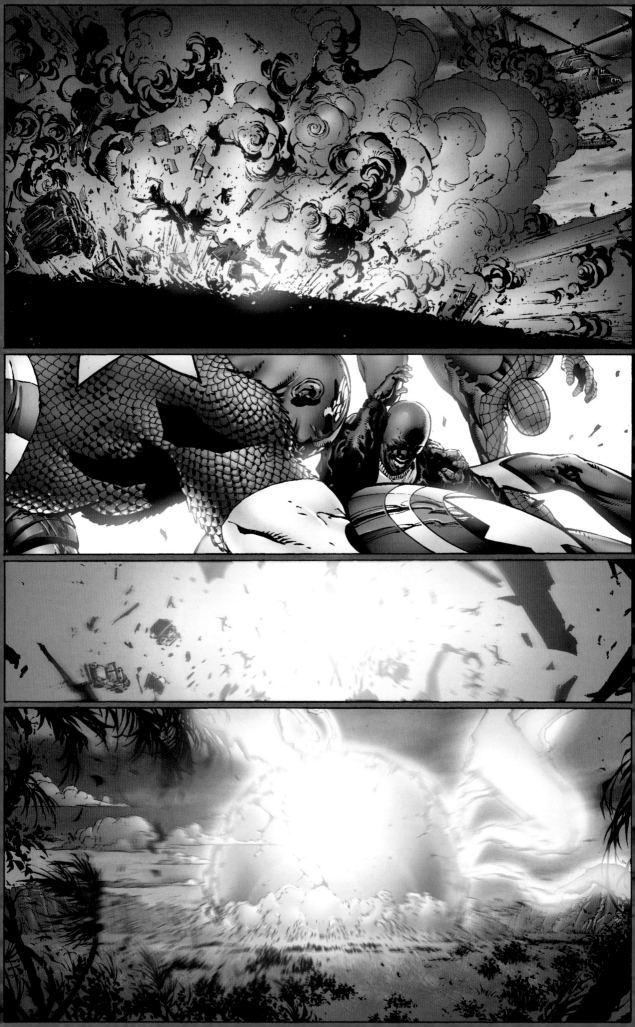

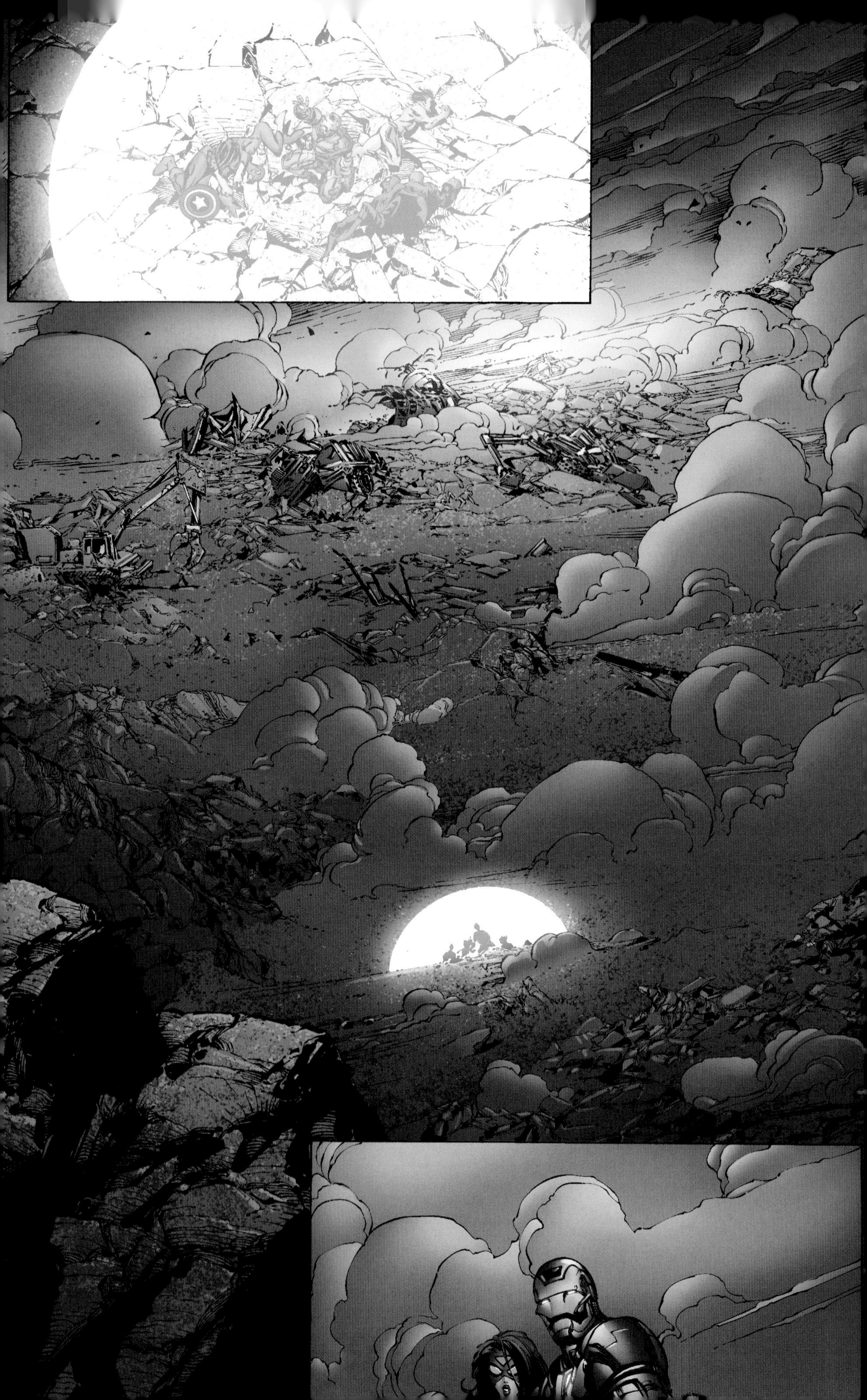

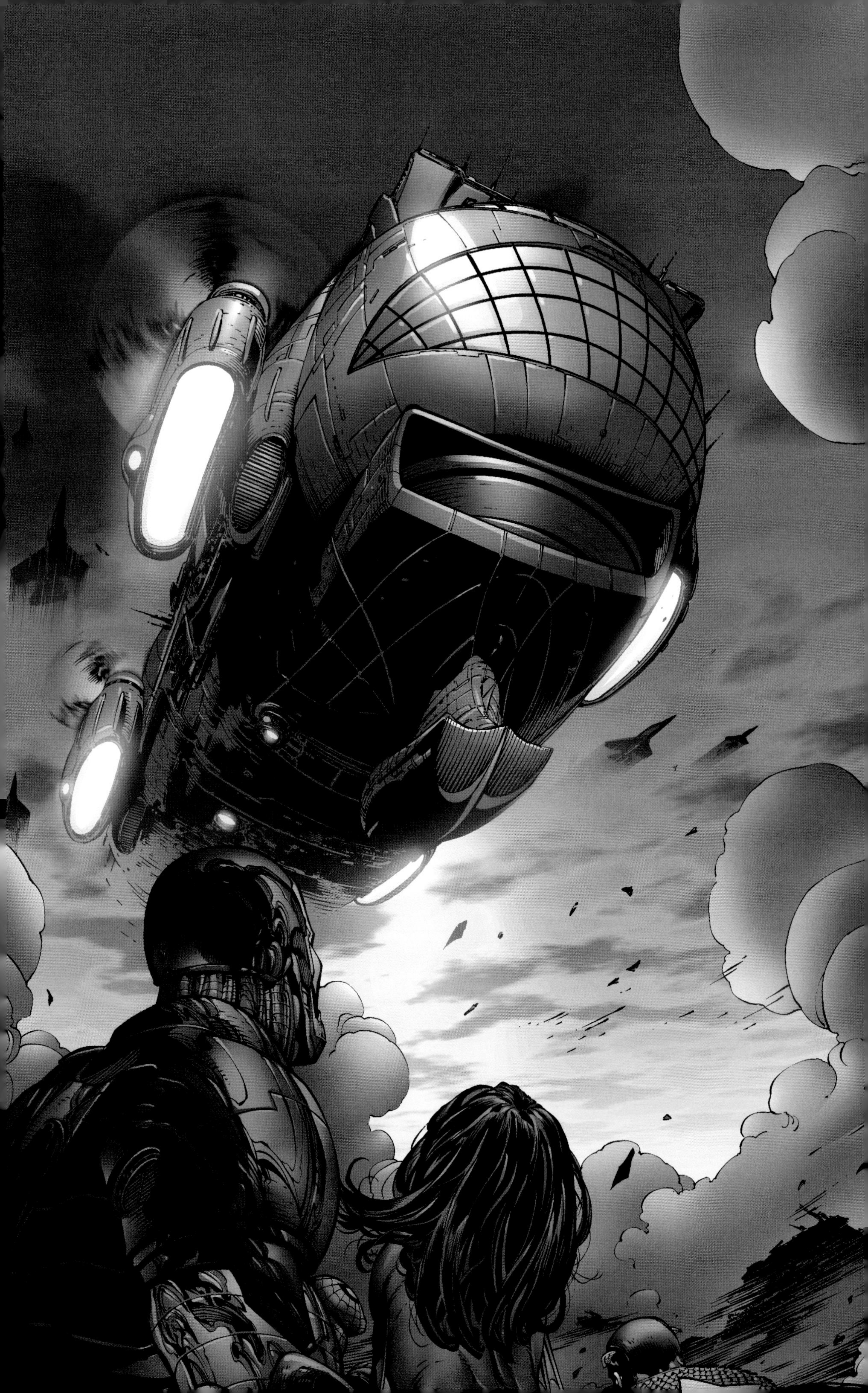

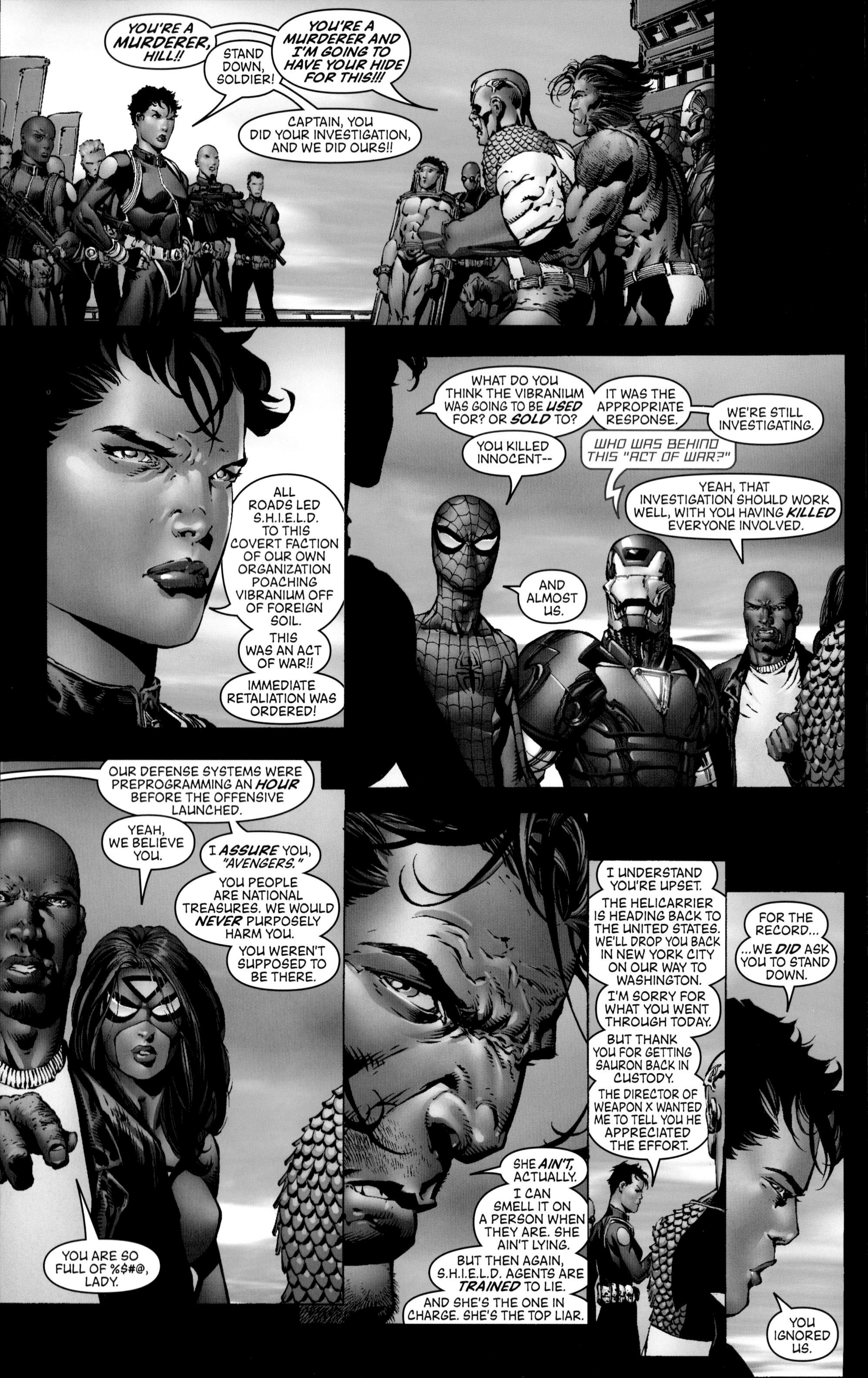
YOU'RE A MURDERER, HILL!!
YOU'RE A MURDERER AND I'M GOING TO HAVE YOUR HIDE FOR THIS!!!
STAND DOWN, SOLDIER!
CAPTAIN, YOU DID YOUR INVESTIGATION, AND WE DID OURS!!
ALL ROADS LED S.H.I.E.L.D. TO THIS COVERT FACTION OF OUR OWN ORGANIZATION POACHING VIBRANIUM OFF OF FOREIGN SOIL.
THIS WAS AN ACT OF WAR!!
IMMEDIATE RETALIATION WAS ORDERED!
WHAT DO YOU THINK THE VIBRANIUM WAS GOING TO BE USED FOR? OR SOLD TO?
IT WAS THE APPROPRIATE RESPONSE.
WE'RE STILL INVESTIGATING.
YOU KILLED INNOCENT--
WHO WAS BEHIND THIS "ACT OF WAR?"
YEAH, THAT INVESTIGATION SHOULD WORK WELL, WITH YOU HAVING KILLED EVERYONE INVOLVED.
AND ALMOST US.
OUR DEFENSE SYSTEMS WERE PREPROGRAMMING AN HOUR BEFORE THE OFFENSIVE LAUNCHED.
YEAH, WE BELIEVE YOU.
I ASSURE YOU, "AVENGERS."
YOU PEOPLE ARE NATIONAL TREASURES. WE WOULD NEVER PURPOSELY HARM YOU.
YOU WEREN'T SUPPOSED TO BE THERE.
YOU ARE SO FULL OF %$#@, LADY.
SHE AIN'T, ACTUALLY.
I CAN SMELL IT ON A PERSON WHEN THEY ARE. SHE AIN'T LYING.
BUT THEN AGAIN, S.H.I.E.L.D. AGENTS ARE TRAINED TO LIE.
AND SHE'S THE ONE IN CHARGE. SHE'S THE TOP LIAR.
I UNDERSTAND YOU'RE UPSET.
THE HELICARRIER IS HEADING BACK TO THE UNITED STATES. WE'LL DROP YOU BACK IN NEW YORK CITY ON OUR WAY TO WASHINGTON.
I'M SORRY FOR WHAT YOU WENT THROUGH TODAY.
BUT THANK YOU FOR GETTING SAURON BACK IN CUSTODY.
THE DIRECTOR OF WEAPON X WANTED ME TO TELL YOU HE APPRECIATED THE EFFORT.
FOR THE RECORD...
...WE DID ASK YOU TO STAND DOWN.
YOU IGNORED US.

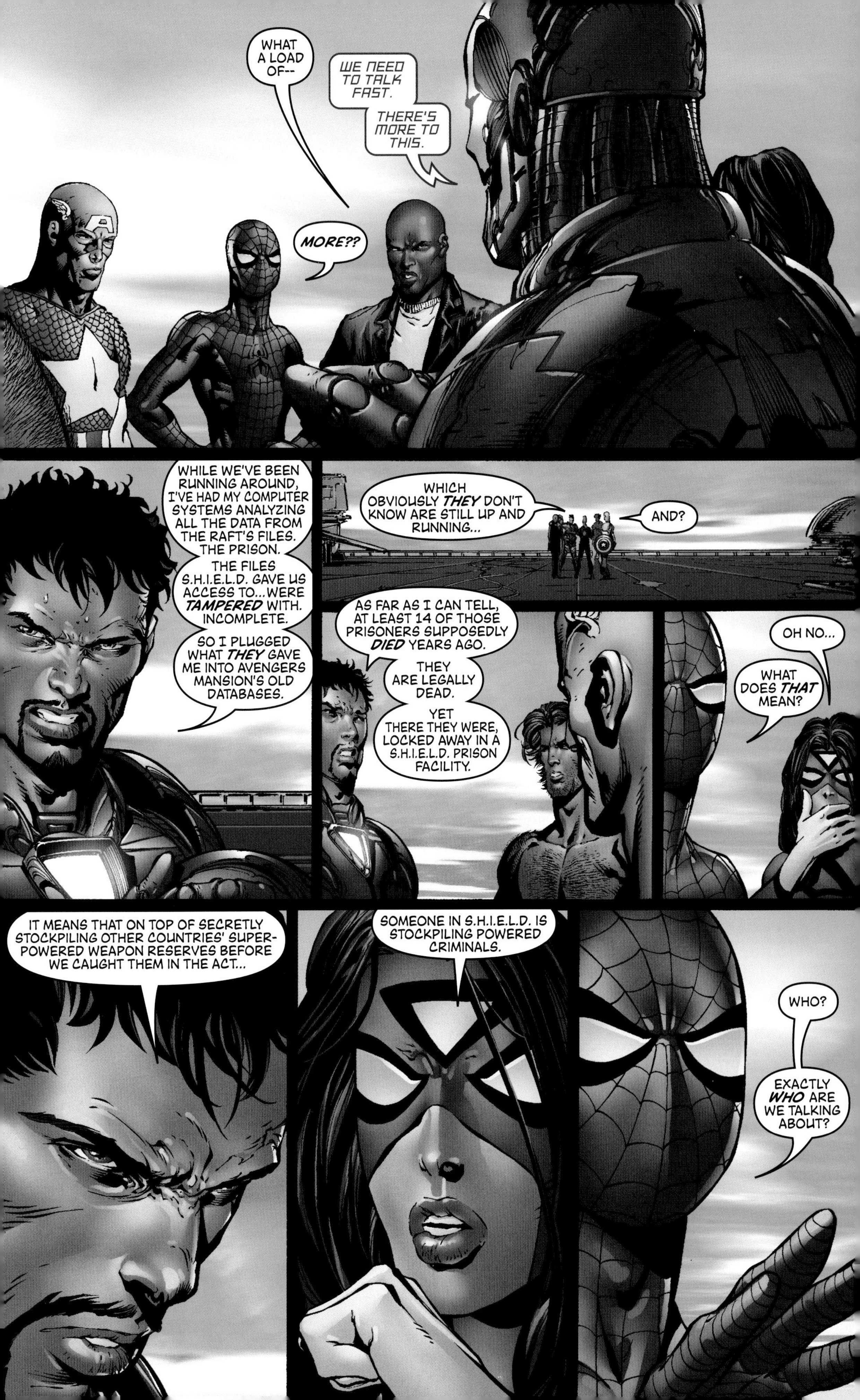
WHAT A LOAD OF--
WE NEED TO TALK FAST.
THERE'S MORE TO THIS.
MORE??
WHILE WE'VE BEEN RUNNING AROUND, I'VE HAD MY COMPUTER SYSTEMS ANALYZING ALL THE DATA FROM THE RAFT'S FILES. THE PRISON.
THE FILES S.H.I.E.L.D. GAVE US ACCESS TO...WERE TAMPERED WITH. INCOMPLETE.
SO I PLUGGED WHAT THEY GAVE ME INTO AVENGERS MANSION'S OLD DATABASES.
WHICH OBVIOUSLY THEY DON'T KNOW ARE STILL UP AND RUNNING...
AND?
AS FAR AS I CAN TELL, AT LEAST 14 OF THOSE PRISONERS SUPPOSEDLY DIED YEARS AGO.
THEY ARE LEGALLY DEAD.
YET THERE THEY WERE, LOCKED AWAY IN A S.H.I.E.L.D. PRISON FACILITY.
OH NO...
WHAT DOES THAT MEAN?
IT MEANS THAT ON TOP OF SECRETLY STOCKPILING OTHER COUNTRIES' SUPER-POWERED WEAPON RESERVES BEFORE WE CAUGHT THEM IN THE ACT...
SOMEONE IN S.H.I.E.L.D. IS STOCKPILING POWERED CRIMINALS.
WHO?
EXACTLY WHO ARE WE TALKING ABOUT?

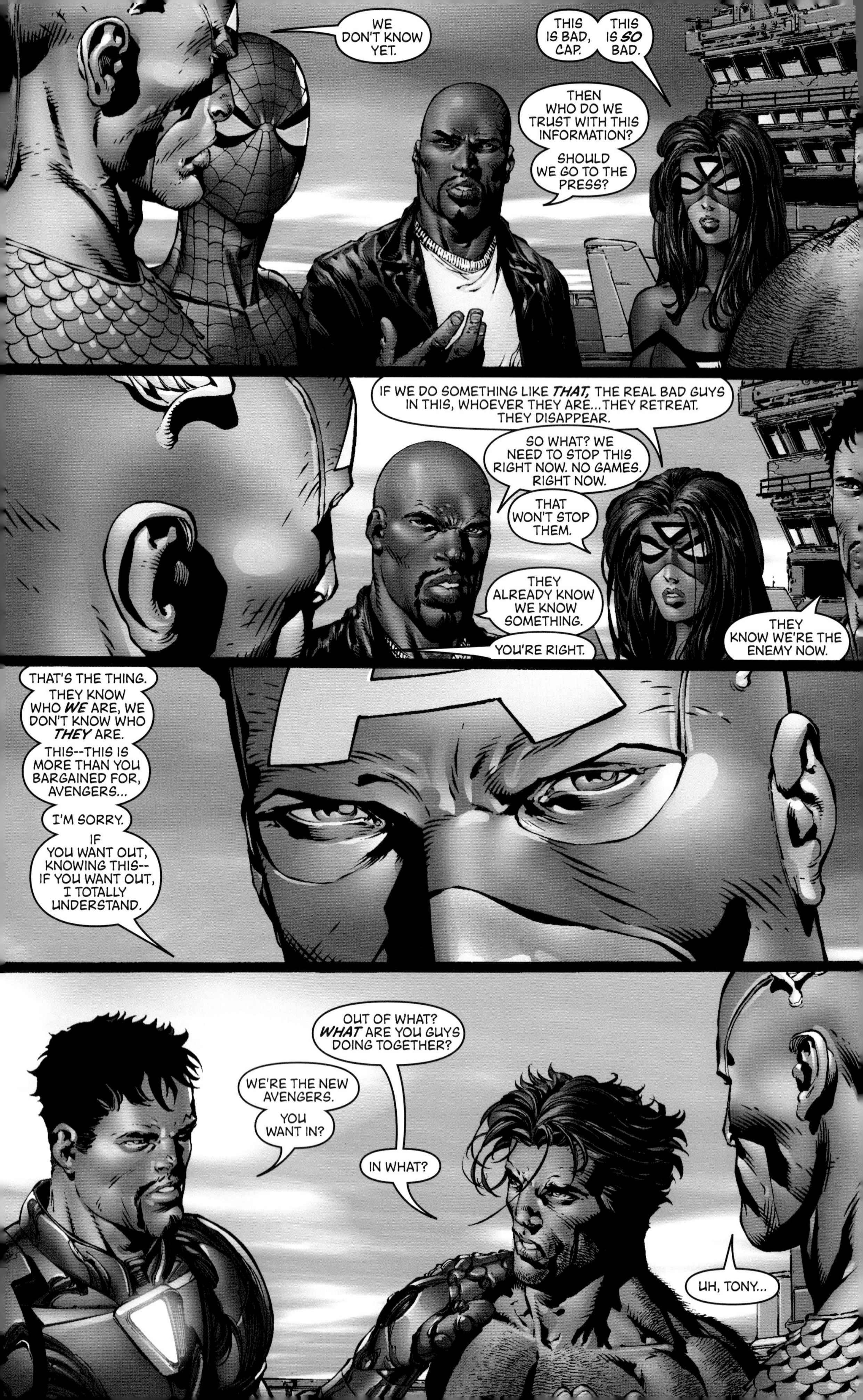

WE DON'T KNOW YET.
THIS IS BAD, CAP.
THIS IS *SO* BAD.
THEN WHO DO WE TRUST WITH THIS INFORMATION?
SHOULD WE GO TO THE PRESS?
IF WE DO SOMETHING LIKE *THAT,* THE REAL BAD GUYS IN THIS, WHOEVER THEY ARE...THEY RETREAT. THEY DISAPPEAR.
SO WHAT? WE NEED TO STOP THIS RIGHT NOW. NO GAMES. RIGHT NOW.
THAT WON'T STOP THEM.
THEY ALREADY KNOW WE KNOW SOMETHING.
YOU'RE RIGHT.
THEY KNOW WE'RE THE ENEMY NOW.
THAT'S THE THING.
THEY KNOW WHO *WE* ARE, WE DON'T KNOW WHO *THEY* ARE.
THIS--THIS IS MORE THAN YOU BARGAINED FOR, AVENGERS...
I'M SORRY.
IF YOU WANT OUT, KNOWING THIS-- IF YOU WANT OUT, I TOTALLY UNDERSTAND.
OUT OF WHAT? *WHAT* ARE YOU GUYS DOING TOGETHER?
WE'RE THE NEW AVENGERS.
YOU WANT IN?
IN WHAT?
UH, TONY...

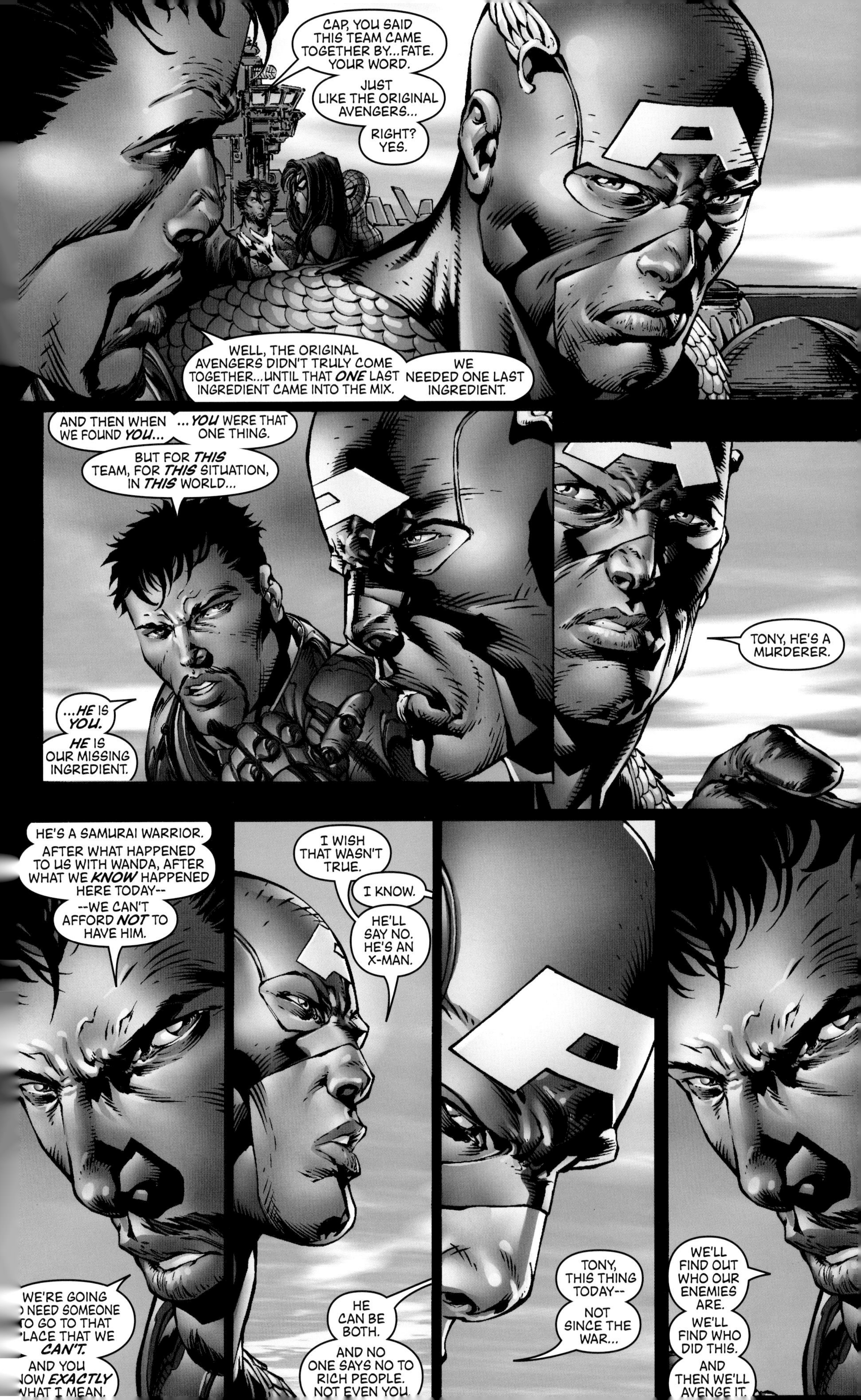
CAP, YOU SAID THIS TEAM CAME TOGETHER BY...FATE. YOUR WORD.
JUST LIKE THE ORIGINAL AVENGERS...
RIGHT? YES.
WELL, THE ORIGINAL AVENGERS DIDN'T TRULY COME TOGETHER...UNTIL THAT ONE LAST INGREDIENT CAME INTO THE MIX.
WE NEEDED ONE LAST INGREDIENT.
AND THEN WHEN WE FOUND YOU...
...YOU WERE THAT ONE THING.
BUT FOR THIS TEAM, FOR THIS SITUATION, IN THIS WORLD...
...HE IS YOU.
HE IS OUR MISSING INGREDIENT.
TONY, HE'S A MURDERER.
HE'S A SAMURAI WARRIOR.
AFTER WHAT HAPPENED TO US WITH WANDA, AFTER WHAT WE KNOW HAPPENED HERE TODAY--
--WE CAN'T AFFORD NOT TO HAVE HIM.
WE'RE GOING NEED SOMEONE GO TO THAT LACE THAT WE CAN'T.
AND YOU NOW EXACTLY WHAT I MEAN.
I WISH THAT WASN'T TRUE.
I KNOW.
HE'LL SAY NO. HE'S AN X-MAN.
HE CAN BE BOTH.
AND NO ONE SAYS NO TO RICH PEOPLE. NOT EVEN YOU.
TONY, THIS THING TODAY--
NOT SINCE THE WAR...
WE'LL FIND OUT WHO OUR ENEMIES ARE.
WE'LL FIND WHO DID THIS.
AND THEN WE'LL AVENGE IT.

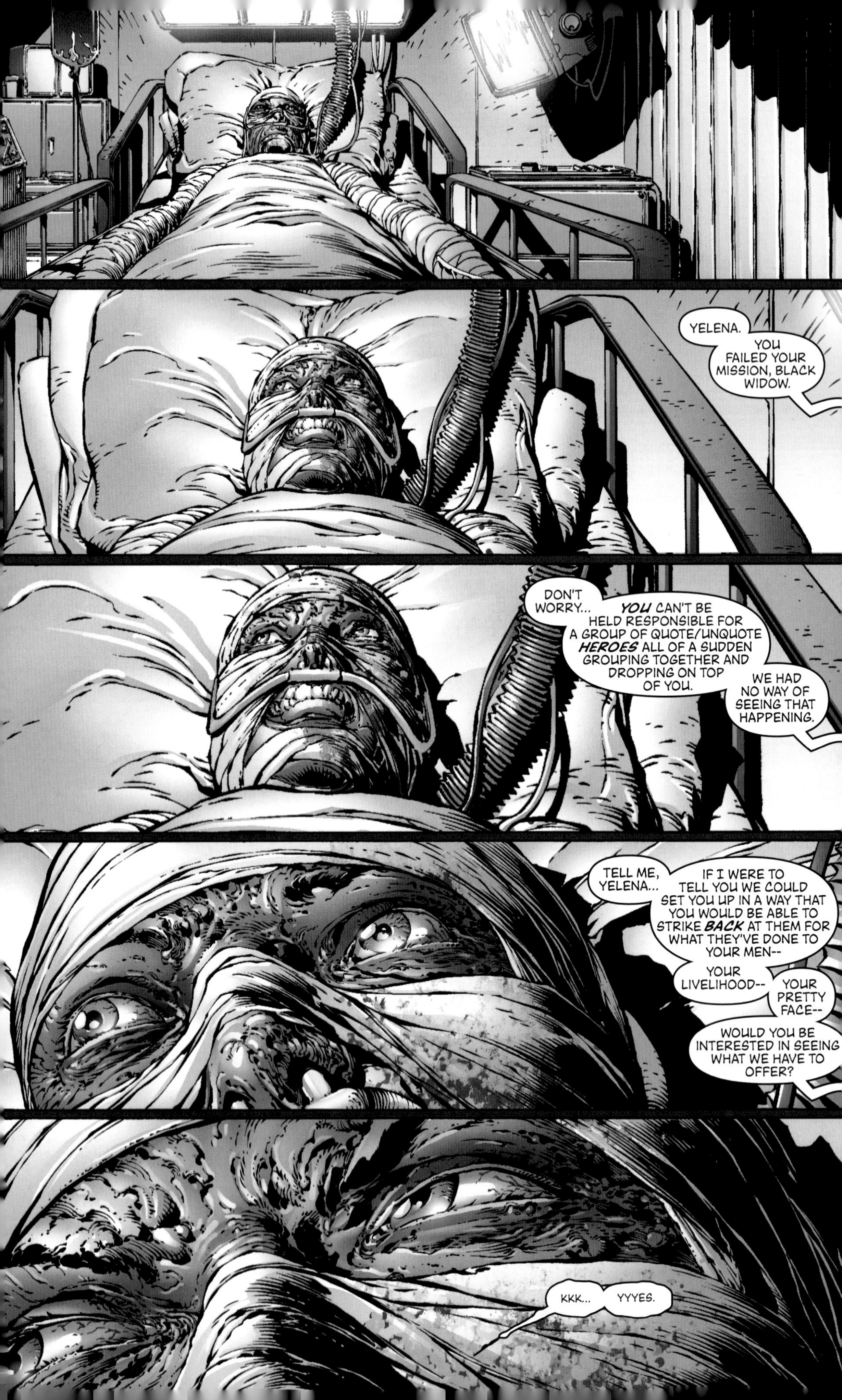
YELENA.
YOU FAILED YOUR MISSION, BLACK WIDOW.
DON'T WORRY...
YOU CAN'T BE HELD RESPONSIBLE FOR A GROUP OF QUOTE/UNQUOTE HEROES ALL OF A SUDDEN GROUPING TOGETHER AND DROPPING ON TOP OF YOU.
WE HAD NO WAY OF SEEING THAT HAPPENING.
TELL ME, YELENA...
IF I WERE TO TELL YOU WE COULD SET YOU UP IN A WAY THAT YOU WOULD BE ABLE TO STRIKE BACK AT THEM FOR WHAT THEY'VE DONE TO YOUR MEN--
YOUR LIVELIHOOD--
YOUR PRETTY FACE--
WOULD YOU BE INTERESTED IN SEEING WHAT WE HAVE TO OFFER?
KKK...
YYYES.

Combined Variants Colored by Richard Isanove

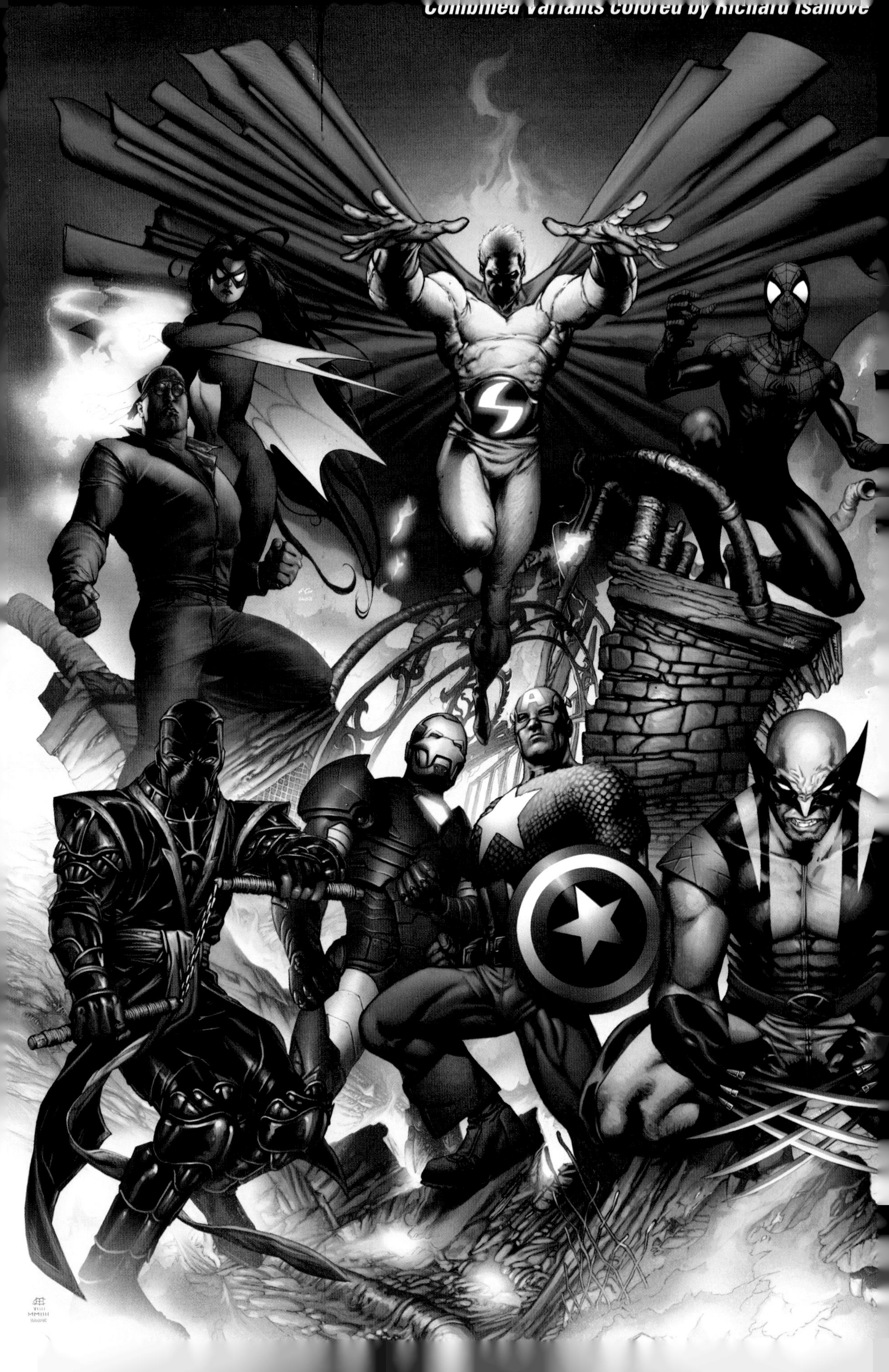

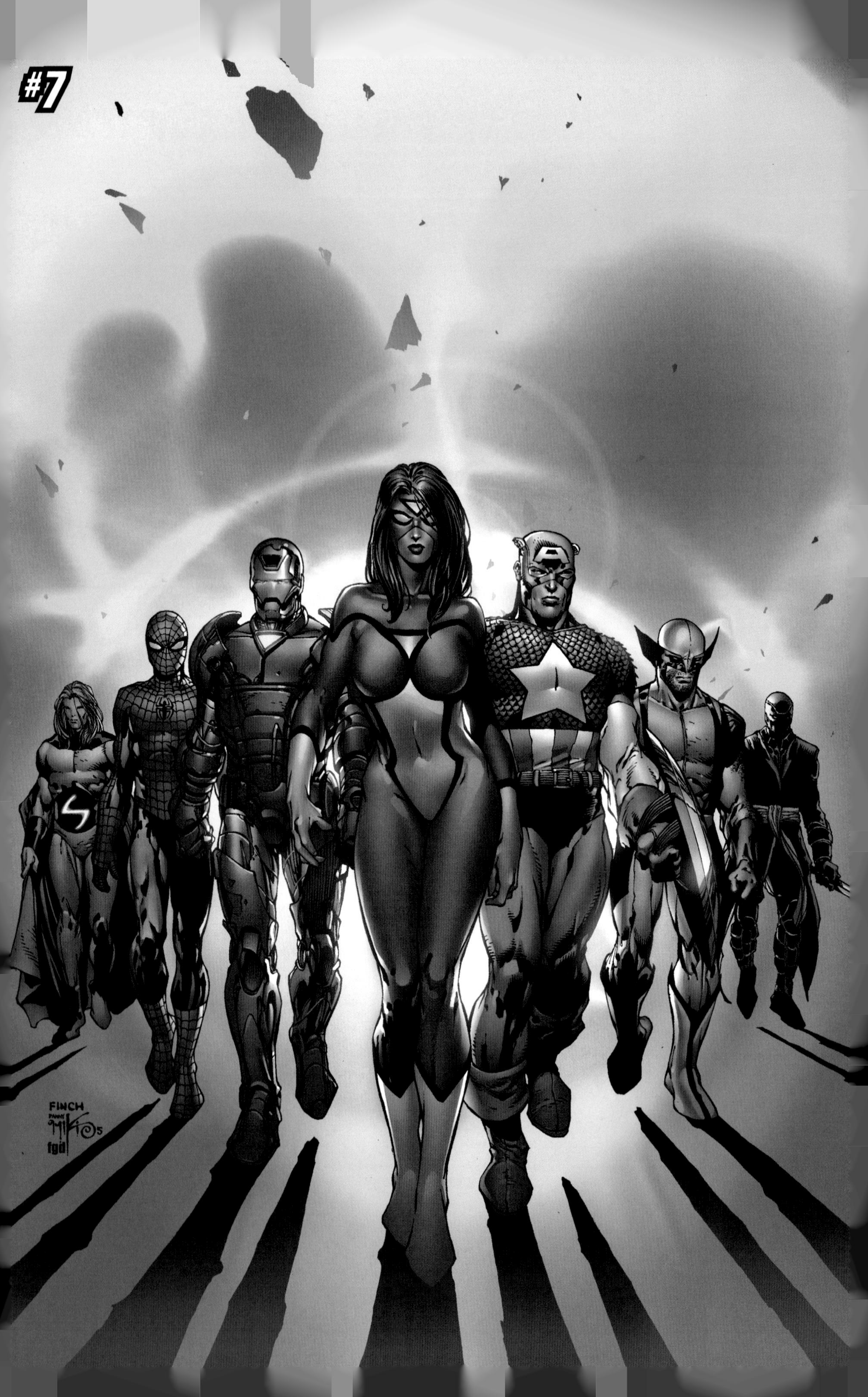
#7
FINCH
fgd

NEW AVENGERS
MARVEL® COMICS GROUP
NEW AVENGERS #7 VARIANT EDITION
$2.25
7 JUN
STARTLING STORIES Featuring
THE SENTRY!™
TM
YOU CAN'T FIGHT...
...WHAT YOU DON'T KNOW, SENTRY!

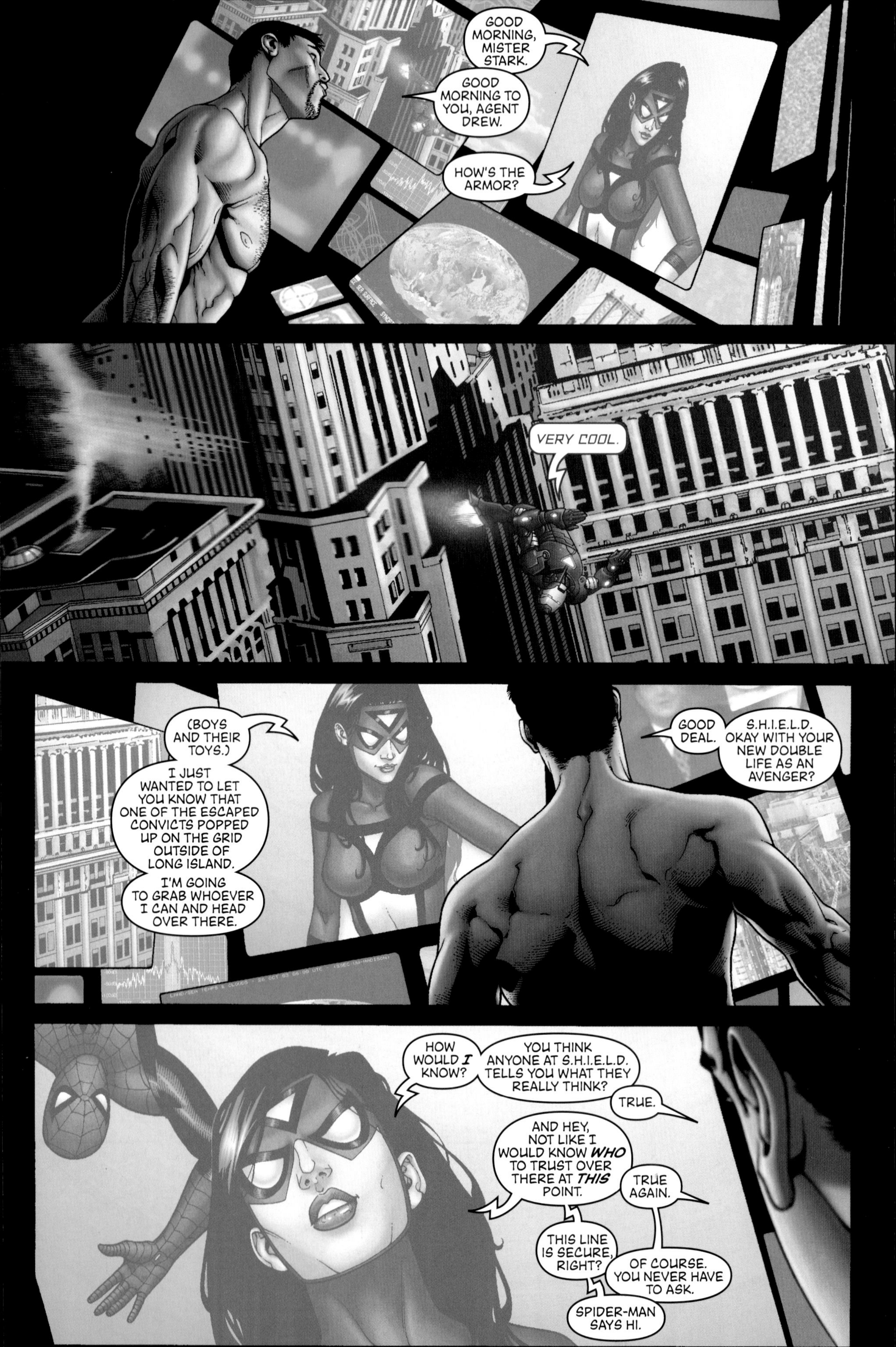
GOOD MORNING, MISTER STARK.
GOOD MORNING TO YOU, AGENT DREW.
HOW'S THE ARMOR?
VERY COOL.
(BOYS AND THEIR TOYS.)
I JUST WANTED TO LET YOU KNOW THAT ONE OF THE ESCAPED CONVICTS POPPED UP ON THE GRID OUTSIDE OF LONG ISLAND.
I'M GOING TO GRAB WHOEVER I CAN AND HEAD OVER THERE.
GOOD DEAL.
S.H.I.E.L.D. OKAY WITH YOUR NEW DOUBLE LIFE AS AN AVENGER?
HOW WOULD I KNOW?
YOU THINK ANYONE AT S.H.I.E.L.D. TELLS YOU WHAT THEY REALLY THINK?
TRUE.
AND HEY, NOT LIKE I WOULD KNOW WHO TO TRUST OVER THERE AT THIS POINT.
TRUE AGAIN.
THIS LINE IS SECURE, RIGHT?
OF COURSE. YOU NEVER HAVE TO ASK.
SPIDER-MAN SAYS HI.

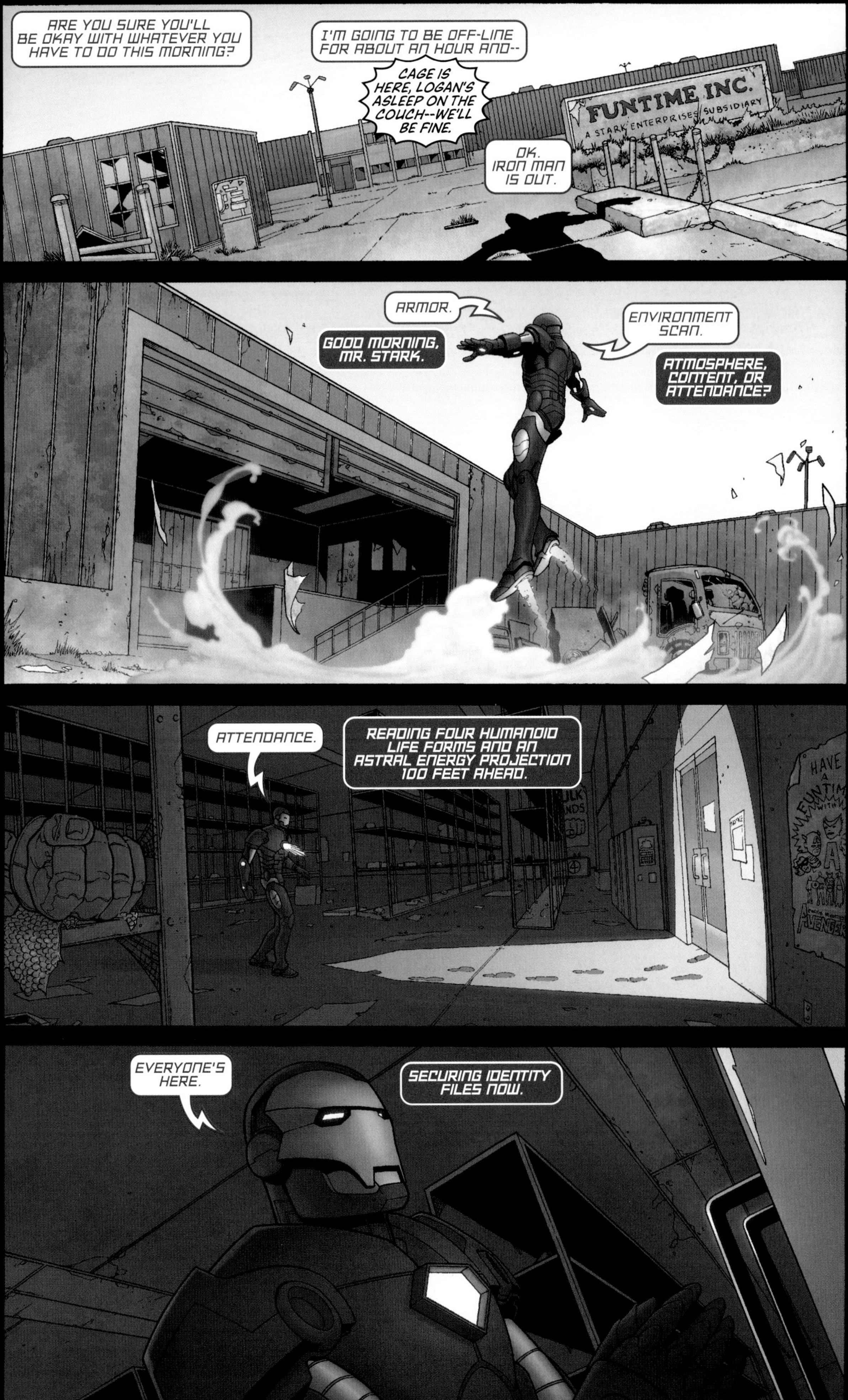
ARE YOU SURE YOU'LL BE OKAY WITH WHATEVER YOU HAVE TO DO THIS MORNING?
I'M GOING TO BE OFF-LINE FOR ABOUT AN HOUR AND--
CAGE IS HERE, LOGAN'S ASLEEP ON THE COUCH--WE'LL BE FINE.
OK. IRON MAN IS OUT.
FUNTIME INC.
A STARK ENTERPRISES SUBSIDIARY
ARMOR.
GOOD MORNING, MR. STARK.
ENVIRONMENT SCAN.
ATMOSPHERE, CONTENT, OR ATTENDANCE?
ATTENDANCE.
READING FOUR HUMANOID LIFE FORMS AND AN ASTRAL ENERGY PROJECTION 100 FEET AHEAD.
EVERYONE'S HERE.
SECURING IDENTITY FILES NOW.

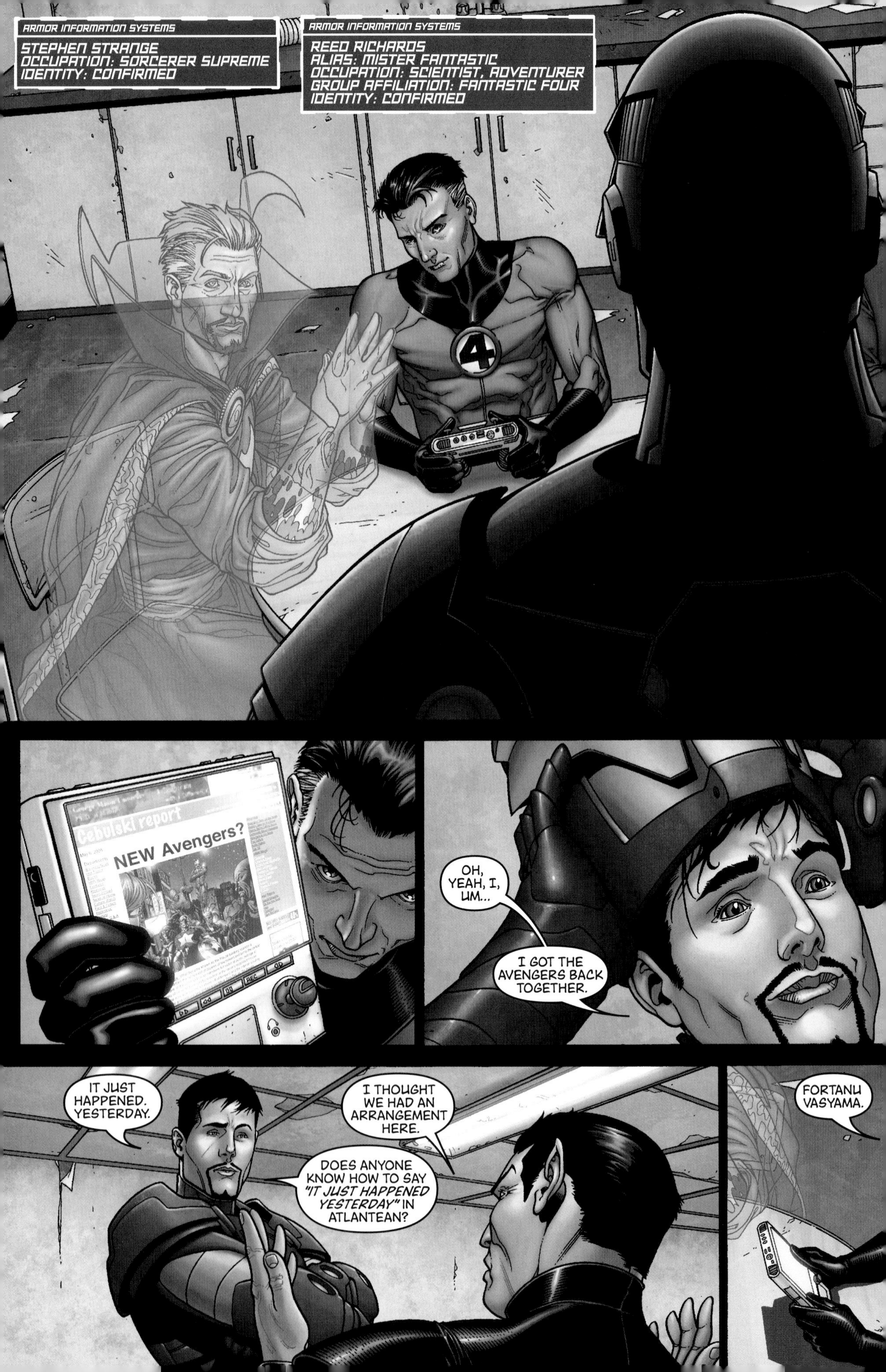
ARMOR INFORMATION SYSTEMS
STEPHEN STRANGE
OCCUPATION: SORCERER SUPREME
IDENTITY: CONFIRMED
ARMOR INFORMATION SYSTEMS
REED RICHARDS
ALIAS: MISTER FANTASTIC
OCCUPATION: SCIENTIST, ADVENTURER
GROUP AFFILIATION: FANTASTIC FOUR
IDENTITY: CONFIRMED
Cebulski report
NEW Avengers?
OH, YEAH, I, UM...
I GOT THE AVENGERS BACK TOGETHER.
IT JUST HAPPENED. YESTERDAY.
I THOUGHT WE HAD AN ARRANGEMENT HERE.
DOES ANYONE KNOW HOW TO SAY *"IT JUST HAPPENED YESTERDAY"* IN ATLANTEAN?
FORTANU VASYAMA.

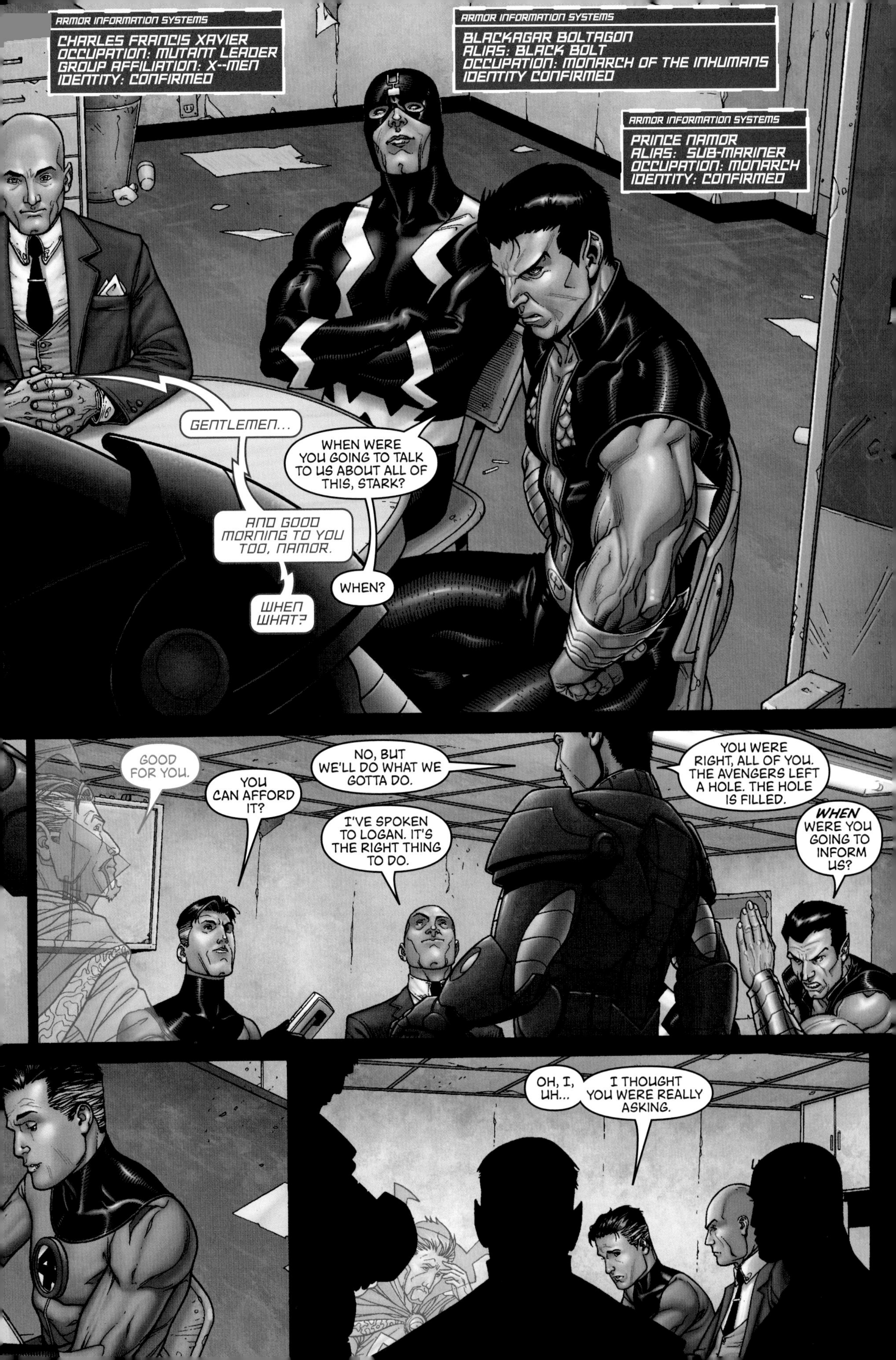
ARMOR INFORMATION SYSTEMS
CHARLES FRANCIS XAVIER
OCCUPATION: MUTANT LEADER
GROUP AFFILIATION: X--MEN
IDENTITY: CONFIRMED
ARMOR INFORMATION SYSTEMS
BLACKAGAR BOLTAGON
ALIAS: BLACK BOLT
OCCUPATION: MONARCH OF THE INHUMANS
IDENTITY CONFIRMED
ARMOR INFORMATION SYSTEMS
PRINCE NAMOR
ALIAS: SUB-MARINER
OCCUPATION: MONARCH
IDENTITY: CONFIRMED
GENTLEMEN...
WHEN WERE YOU GOING TO TALK TO US ABOUT ALL OF THIS, STARK?
AND GOOD MORNING TO YOU TOO, NAMOR.
WHEN?
WHEN WHAT?
GOOD FOR YOU.
YOU CAN AFFORD IT?
NO, BUT WE'LL DO WHAT WE GOTTA DO.
I'VE SPOKEN TO LOGAN. IT'S THE RIGHT THING TO DO.
YOU WERE RIGHT, ALL OF YOU. THE AVENGERS LEFT A HOLE. THE HOLE IS FILLED.
WHEN WERE YOU GOING TO INFORM US?
OH, I, UH...
I THOUGHT YOU WERE REALLY ASKING.

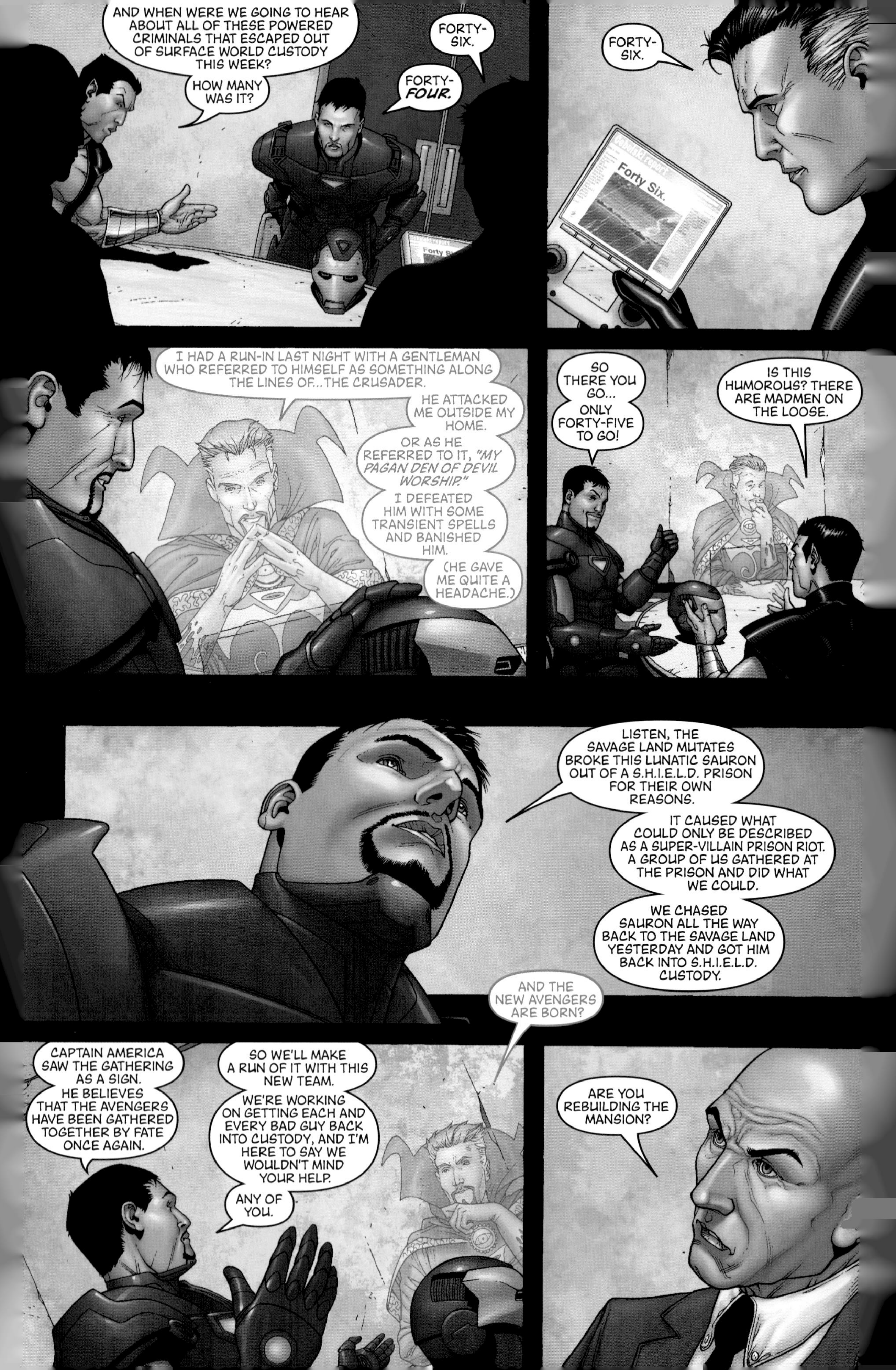
AND WHEN WERE WE GOING TO HEAR ABOUT ALL OF THESE POWERED CRIMINALS THAT ESCAPED OUT OF SURFACE WORLD CUSTODY THIS WEEK?
HOW MANY WAS IT?
FORTY-SIX.
FORTY-FOUR.
FORTY-SIX.
Forty Six.
I HAD A RUN-IN LAST NIGHT WITH A GENTLEMAN WHO REFERRED TO HIMSELF AS SOMETHING ALONG THE LINES OF...THE CRUSADER.
HE ATTACKED ME OUTSIDE MY HOME.
OR AS HE REFERRED TO IT, "MY PAGAN DEN OF DEVIL WORSHIP."
I DEFEATED HIM WITH SOME TRANSIENT SPELLS AND BANISHED HIM.
(HE GAVE ME QUITE A HEADACHE.)
SO THERE YOU GO... ONLY FORTY-FIVE TO GO!
IS THIS HUMOROUS? THERE ARE MADMEN ON THE LOOSE.
LISTEN, THE SAVAGE LAND MUTATES BROKE THIS LUNATIC SAURON OUT OF A S.H.I.E.L.D. PRISON FOR THEIR OWN REASONS.
IT CAUSED WHAT COULD ONLY BE DESCRIBED AS A SUPER-VILLAIN PRISON RIOT. A GROUP OF US GATHERED AT THE PRISON AND DID WHAT WE COULD.
WE CHASED SAURON ALL THE WAY BACK TO THE SAVAGE LAND YESTERDAY AND GOT HIM BACK INTO S.H.I.E.L.D. CUSTODY.
AND THE NEW AVENGERS ARE BORN?
CAPTAIN AMERICA SAW THE GATHERING AS A SIGN.
HE BELIEVES THAT THE AVENGERS HAVE BEEN GATHERED TOGETHER BY FATE ONCE AGAIN.
SO WE'LL MAKE A RUN OF IT WITH THIS NEW TEAM.
WE'RE WORKING ON GETTING EACH AND EVERY BAD GUY BACK INTO CUSTODY, AND I'M HERE TO SAY WE WOULDN'T MIND YOUR HELP.
ANY OF YOU.
ARE YOU REBUILDING THE MANSION?

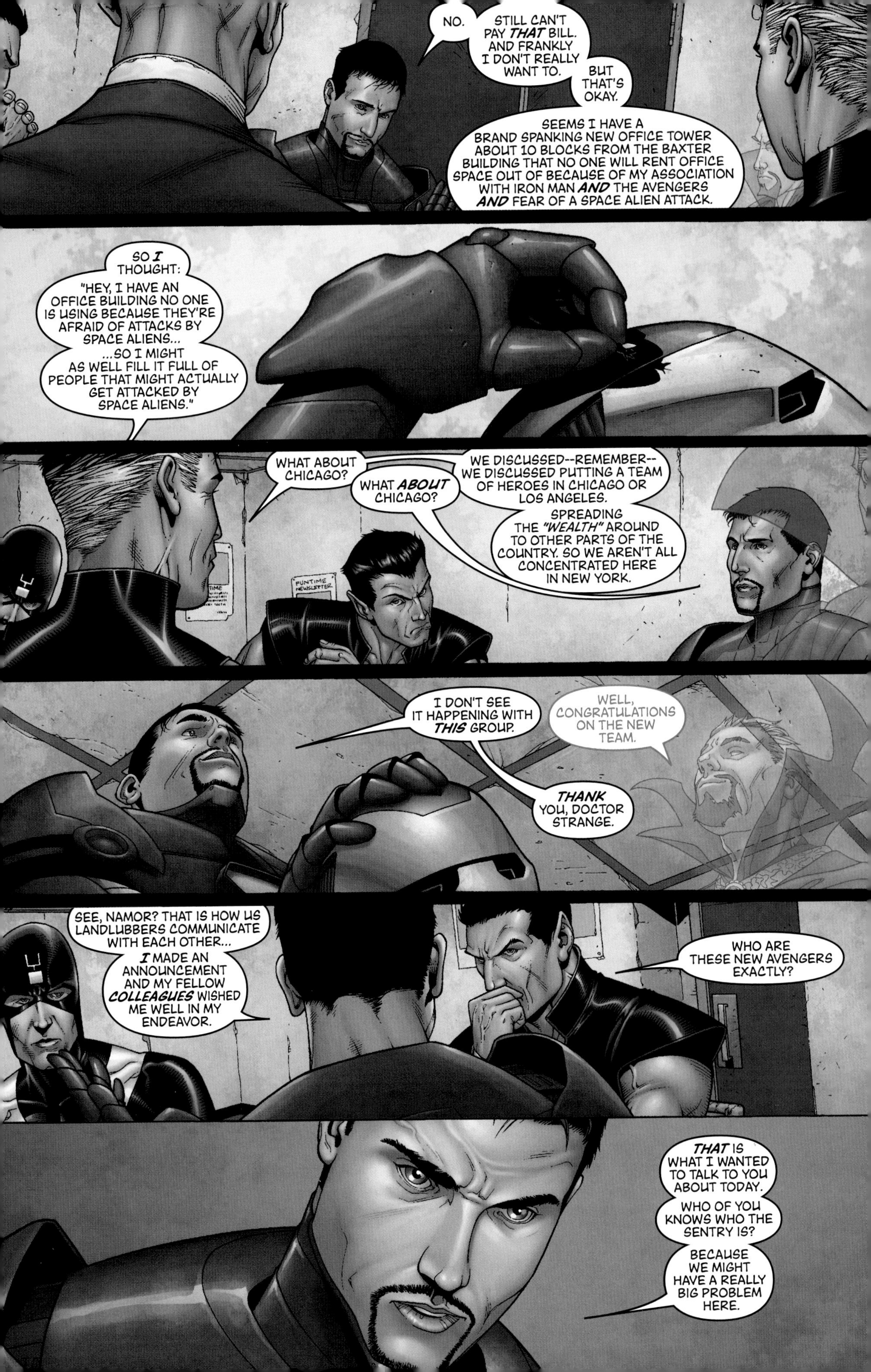

NO.
STILL CAN'T PAY THAT BILL. AND FRANKLY I DON'T REALLY WANT TO.
BUT THAT'S OKAY.
SEEMS I HAVE A BRAND SPANKING NEW OFFICE TOWER ABOUT 10 BLOCKS FROM THE BAXTER BUILDING THAT NO ONE WILL RENT OFFICE SPACE OUT OF BECAUSE OF MY ASSOCIATION WITH IRON MAN AND THE AVENGERS AND FEAR OF A SPACE ALIEN ATTACK.
SO I THOUGHT:
"HEY, I HAVE AN OFFICE BUILDING NO ONE IS USING BECAUSE THEY'RE AFRAID OF ATTACKS BY SPACE ALIENS...
...SO I MIGHT AS WELL FILL IT FULL OF PEOPLE THAT MIGHT ACTUALLY GET ATTACKED BY SPACE ALIENS."
WHAT ABOUT CHICAGO?
WHAT ABOUT CHICAGO?
WE DISCUSSED--REMEMBER--WE DISCUSSED PUTTING A TEAM OF HEROES IN CHICAGO OR LOS ANGELES.
SPREADING THE "WEALTH" AROUND TO OTHER PARTS OF THE COUNTRY. SO WE AREN'T ALL CONCENTRATED HERE IN NEW YORK.
I DON'T SEE IT HAPPENING WITH THIS GROUP.
WELL, CONGRATULATIONS ON THE NEW TEAM.
THANK YOU, DOCTOR STRANGE.
SEE, NAMOR? THAT IS HOW US LANDLUBBERS COMMUNICATE WITH EACH OTHER...
I MADE AN ANNOUNCEMENT AND MY FELLOW COLLEAGUES WISHED ME WELL IN MY ENDEAVOR.
WHO ARE THESE NEW AVENGERS EXACTLY?
THAT IS WHAT I WANTED TO TALK TO YOU ABOUT TODAY.
WHO OF YOU KNOWS WHO THE SENTRY IS?
BECAUSE WE MIGHT HAVE A REALLY BIG PROBLEM HERE.

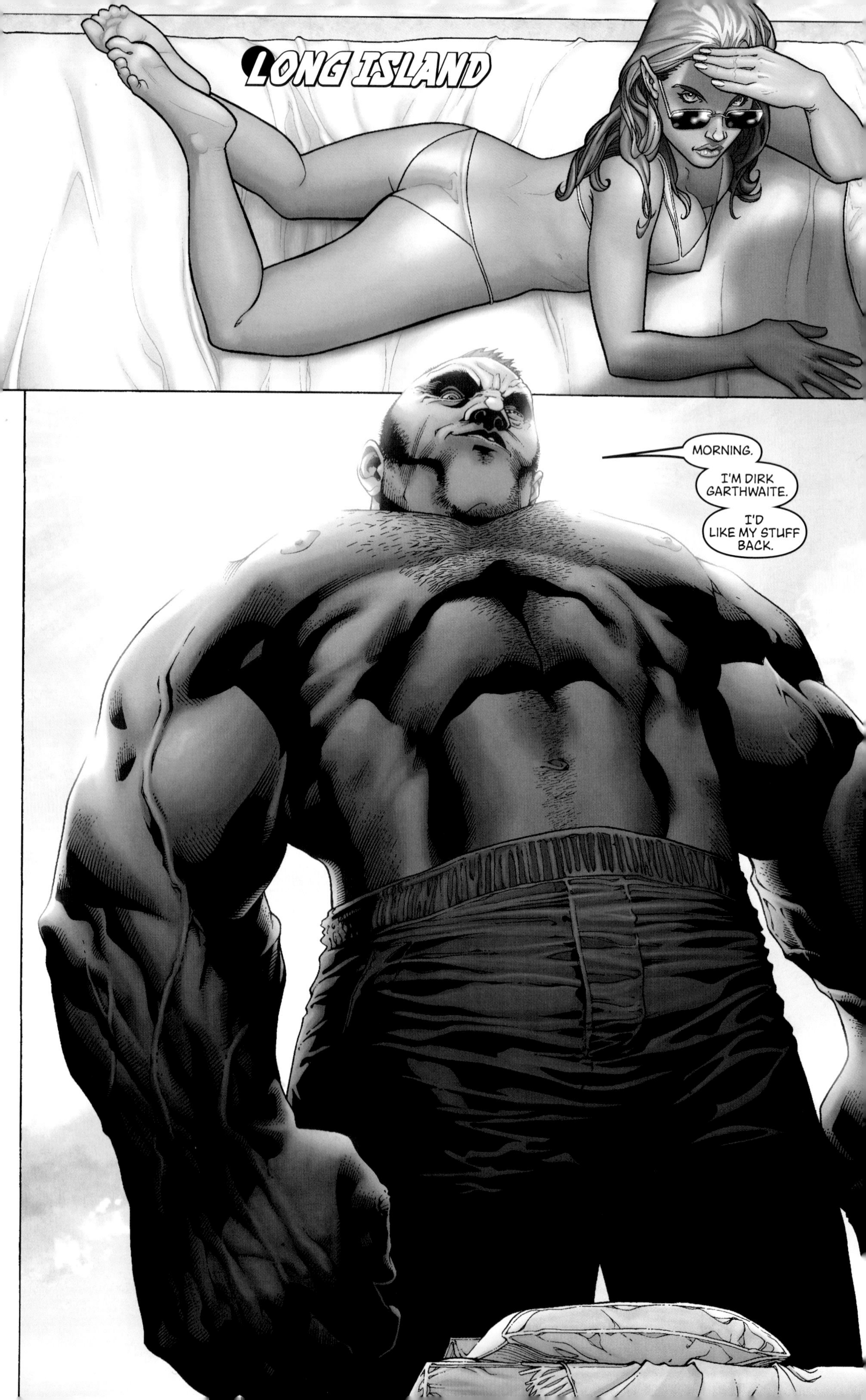
LONG ISLAND
MORNING.
I'M DIRK GARTHWAITE.
I'D LIKE MY STUFF BACK.

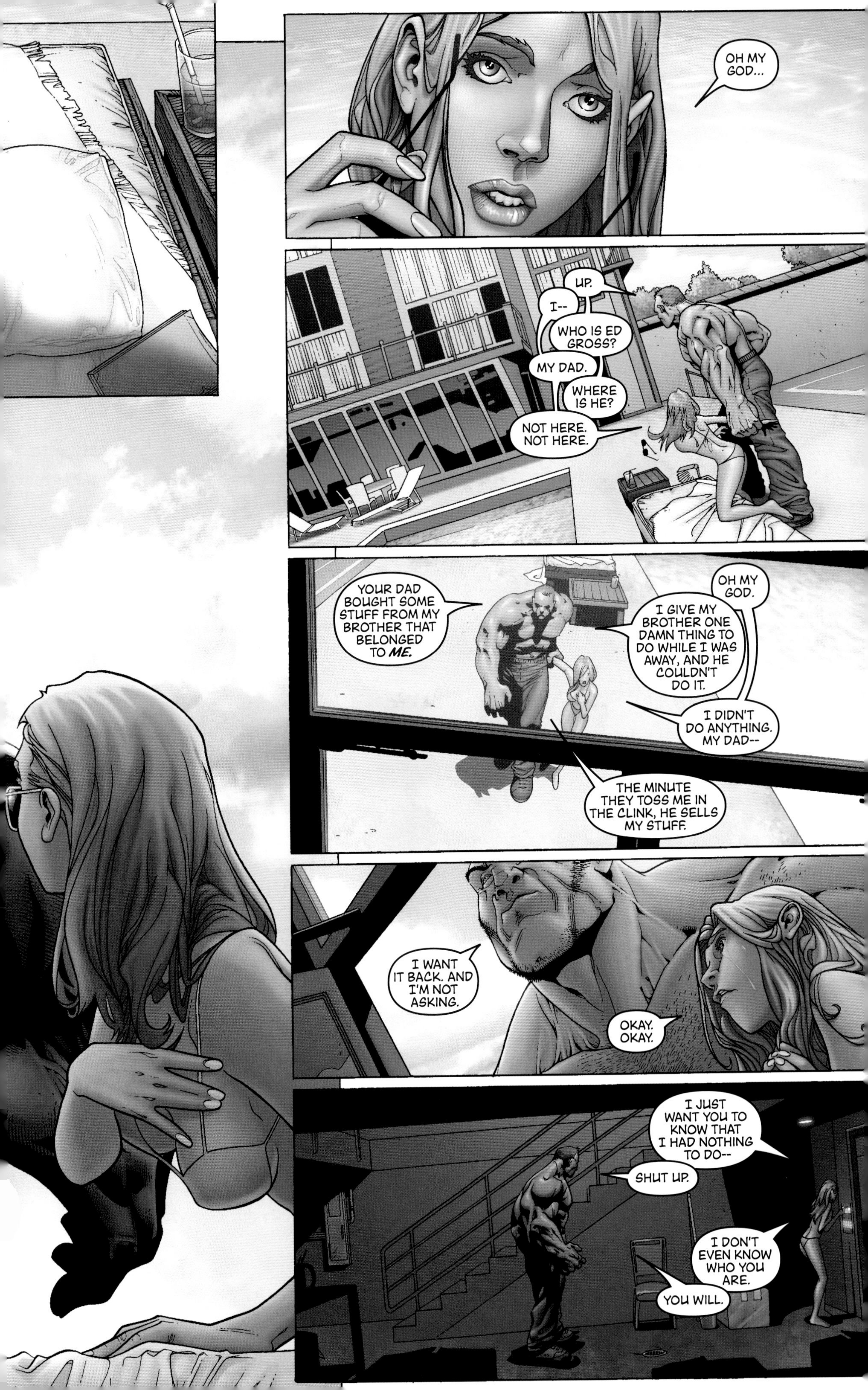
OH MY GOD...
UP.
I--
WHO IS ED GROSS?
MY DAD.
WHERE IS HE?
NOT HERE. NOT HERE.
YOUR DAD BOUGHT SOME STUFF FROM MY BROTHER THAT BELONGED TO *ME.*
OH MY GOD.
I GIVE MY BROTHER ONE DAMN THING TO DO WHILE I WAS AWAY, AND HE COULDN'T DO IT.
I DIDN'T DO ANYTHING. MY DAD--
THE MINUTE THEY TOSS ME IN THE CLINK, HE SELLS MY STUFF.
I WANT IT BACK. AND I'M NOT ASKING.
OKAY. OKAY.
I JUST WANT YOU TO KNOW THAT I HAD NOTHING TO DO--
SHUT UP.
I DON'T EVEN KNOW WHO YOU ARE.
YOU WILL.

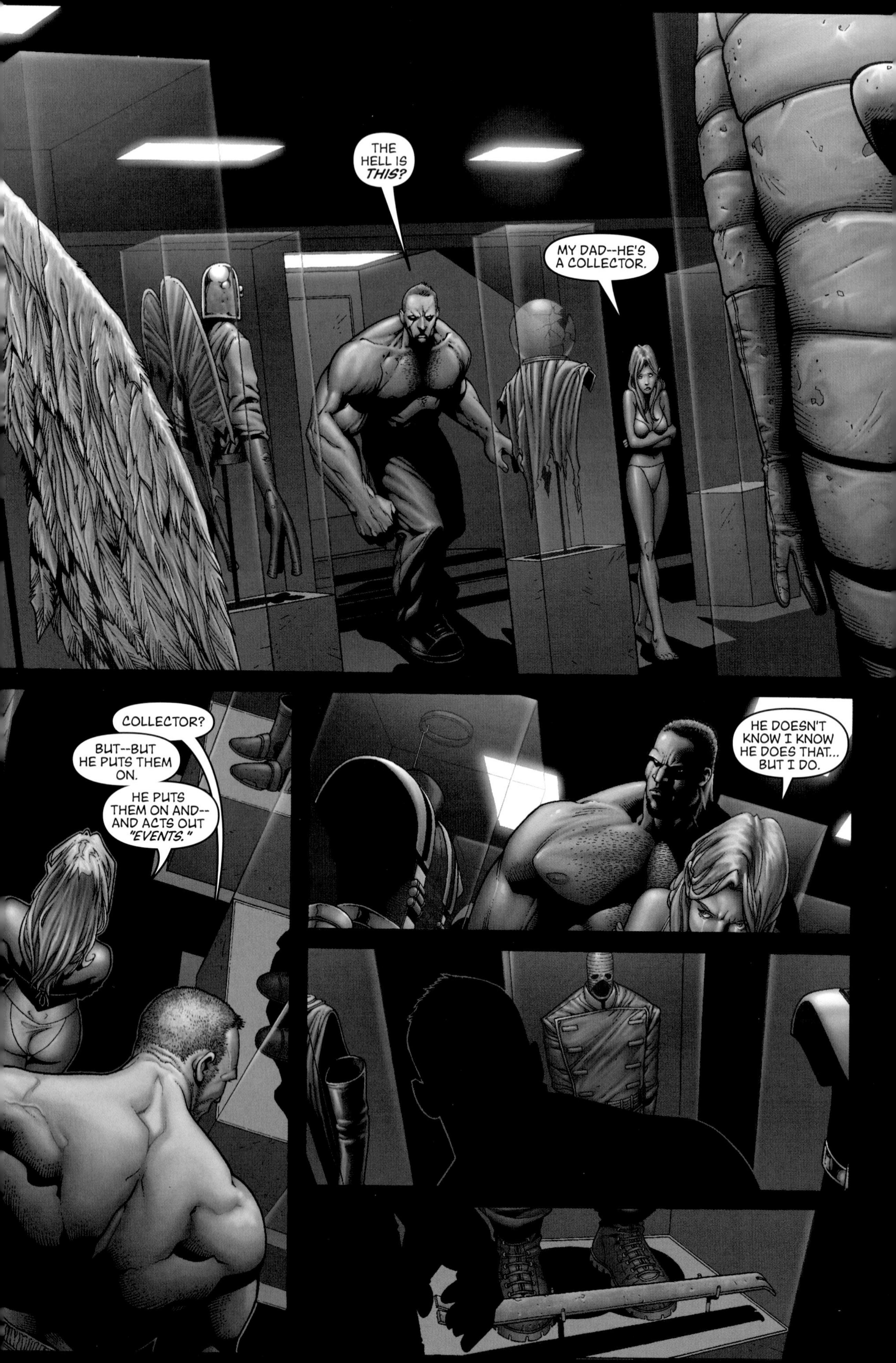
THE HELL IS THIS?
MY DAD--HE'S A COLLECTOR.
COLLECTOR?
BUT--BUT HE PUTS THEM ON.
HE PUTS THEM ON AND--AND ACTS OUT "EVENTS."
HE DOESN'T KNOW I KNOW HE DOES THAT... BUT I DO.

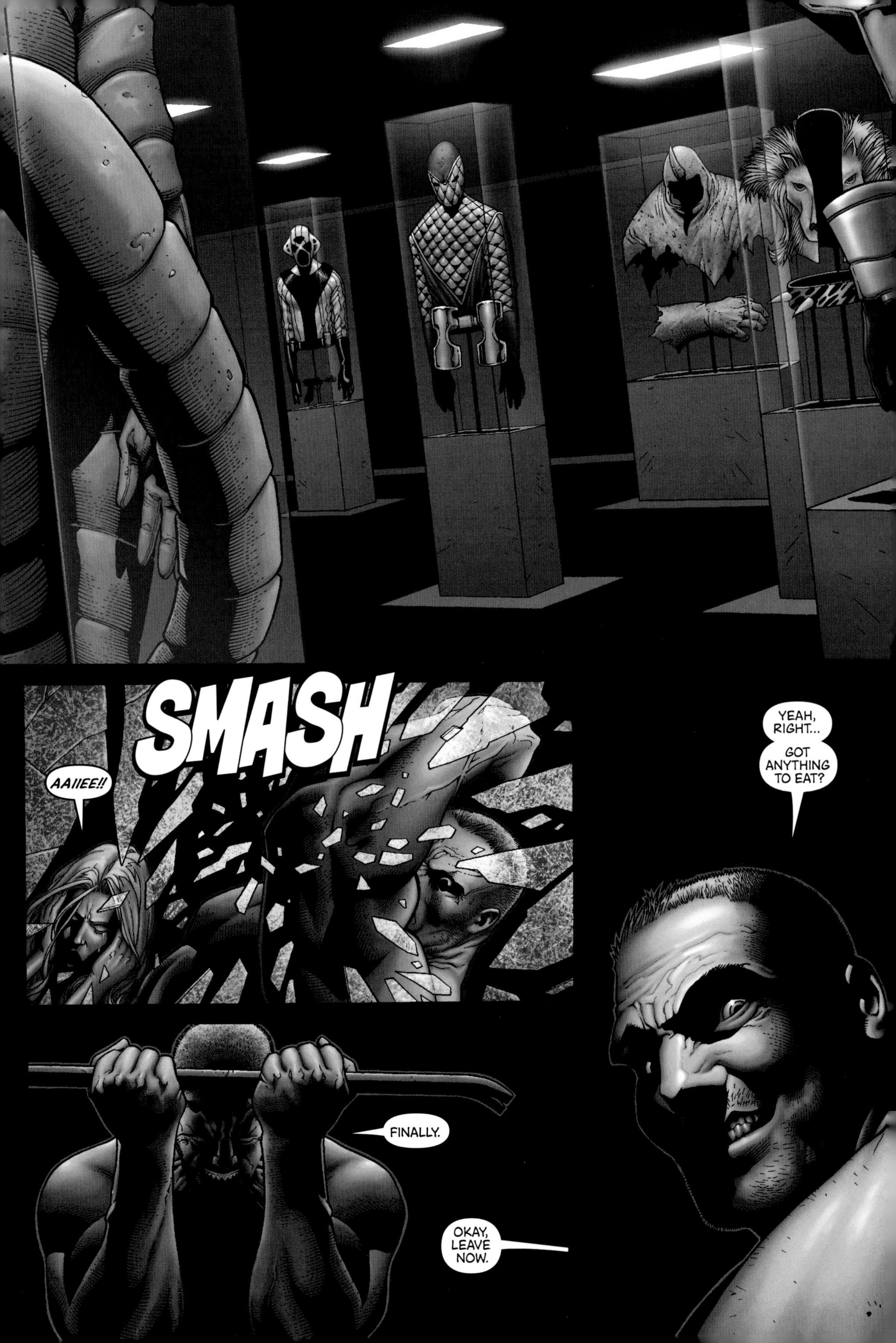
SMASH
AAIIEE!!
YEAH, RIGHT...
GOT ANYTHING TO EAT?
FINALLY.
OKAY, LEAVE NOW.

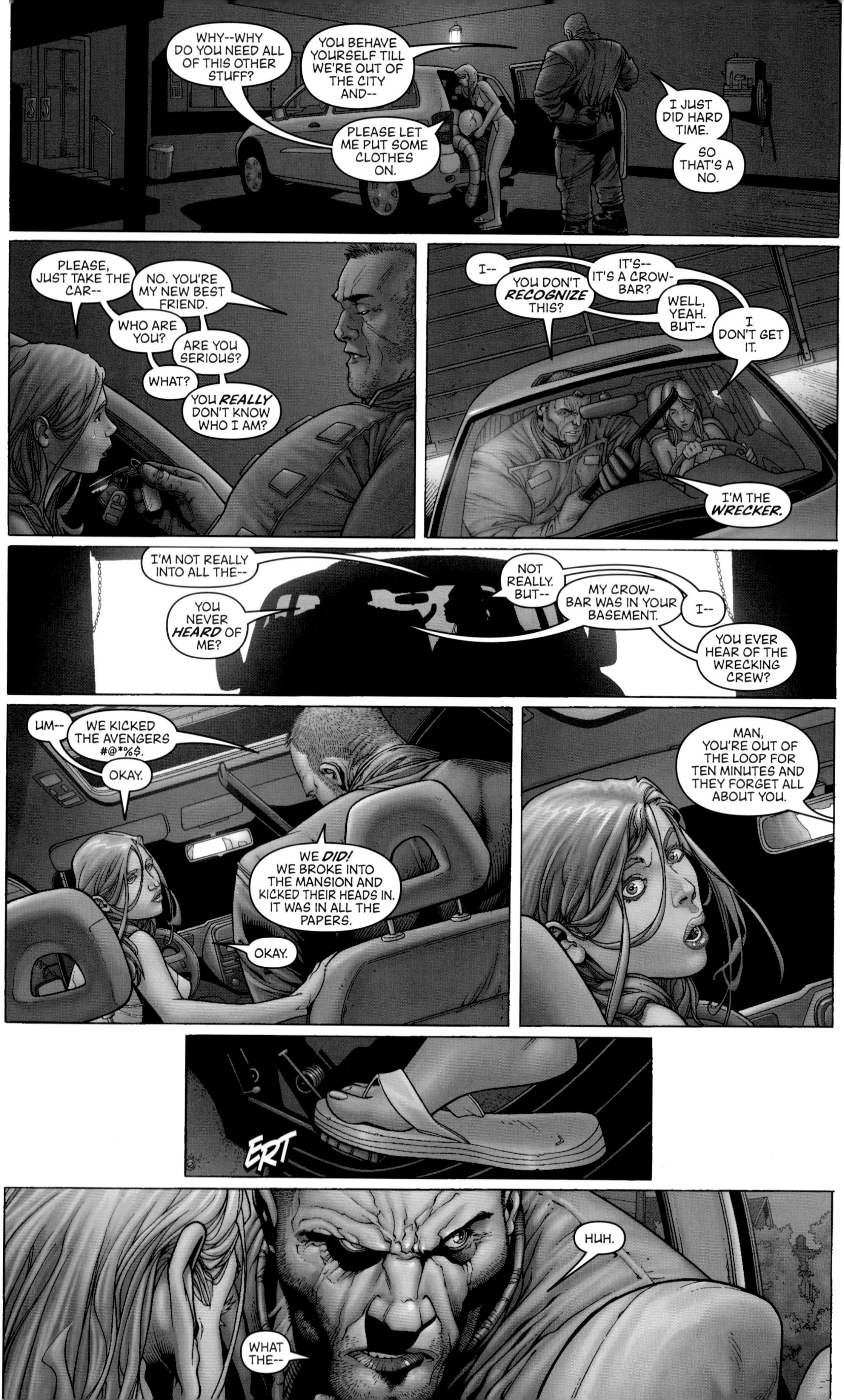
WHY--WHY DO YOU NEED ALL OF THIS OTHER STUFF?
YOU BEHAVE YOURSELF TILL WE'RE OUT OF THE CITY AND--
PLEASE LET ME PUT SOME CLOTHES ON.
I JUST DID HARD TIME.
SO THAT'S A NO.
PLEASE, JUST TAKE THE CAR--
NO. YOU'RE MY NEW BEST FRIEND.
WHO ARE YOU?
ARE YOU SERIOUS?
WHAT?
YOU REALLY DON'T KNOW WHO I AM?
I--
YOU DON'T RECOGNIZE THIS?
IT'S-- IT'S A CROW-BAR?
WELL, YEAH. BUT--
I DON'T GET IT.
I'M THE WRECKER.
I'M NOT REALLY INTO ALL THE--
YOU NEVER HEARD OF ME?
NOT REALLY. BUT--
MY CROW-BAR WAS IN YOUR BASEMENT.
I--
YOU EVER HEAR OF THE WRECKING CREW?
UM--
WE KICKED THE AVENGERS #@*%$.
OKAY.
WE DID! WE BROKE INTO THE MANSION AND KICKED THEIR HEADS IN. IT WAS IN ALL THE PAPERS.
OKAY.
MAN, YOU'RE OUT OF THE LOOP FOR TEN MINUTES AND THEY FORGET ALL ABOUT YOU.
ERT
HUH.
WHAT THE--

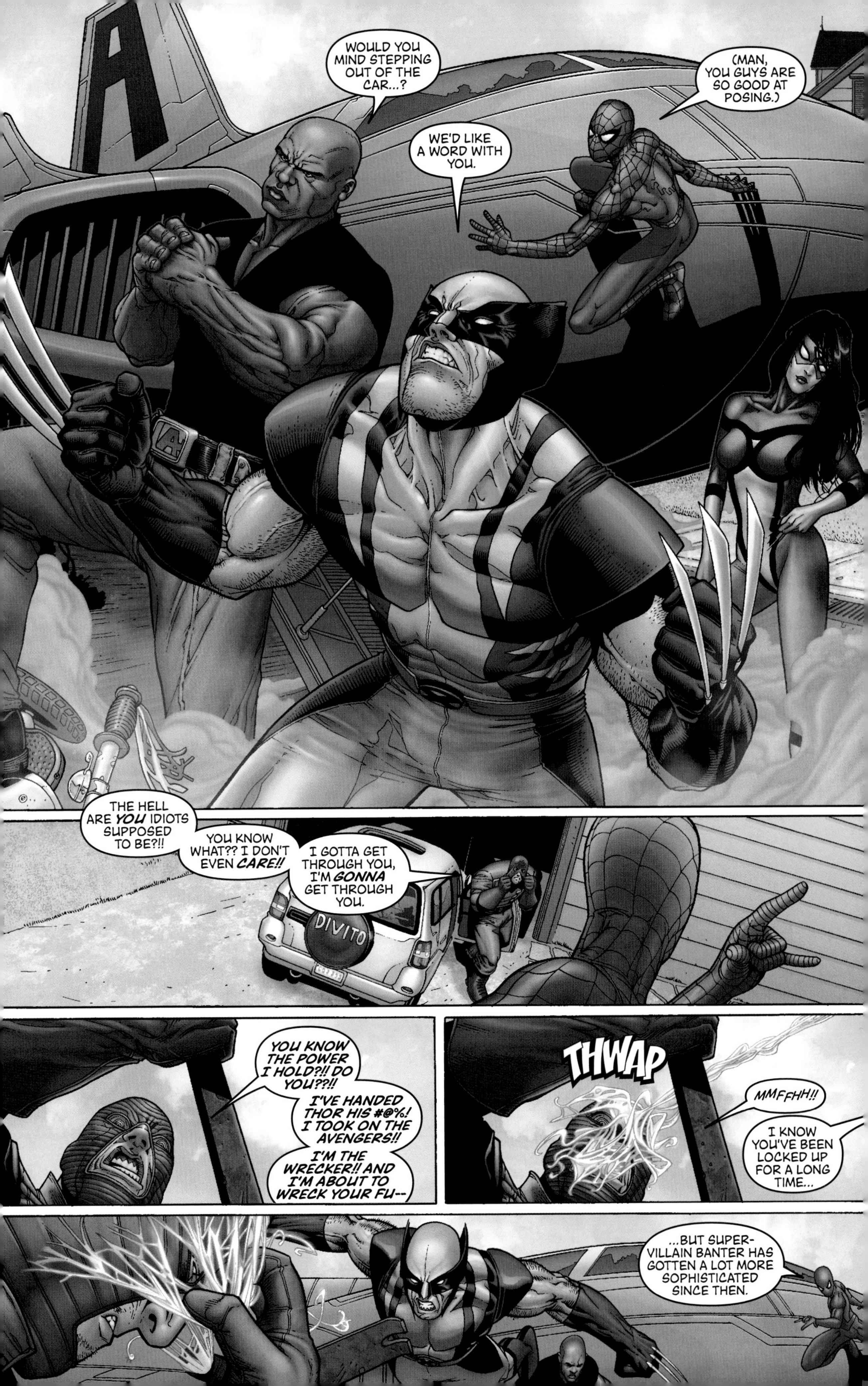

WOULD YOU MIND STEPPING OUT OF THE CAR...?
WE'D LIKE A WORD WITH YOU.
(MAN, YOU GUYS ARE SO GOOD AT POSING.)
THE HELL ARE YOU IDIOTS SUPPOSED TO BE?!!
YOU KNOW WHAT?? I DON'T EVEN CARE!!
I GOTTA GET THROUGH YOU, I'M GONNA GET THROUGH YOU.
DIVITO
YOU KNOW THE POWER I HOLD?!! DO YOU??!!
I'VE HANDED THOR HIS #@%! I TOOK ON THE AVENGERS!!
I'M THE WRECKER!! AND I'M ABOUT TO WRECK YOUR FU--
THWAP
MMFFHH!!
I KNOW YOU'VE BEEN LOCKED UP FOR A LONG TIME...
...BUT SUPER-VILLAIN BANTER HAS GOTTEN A LOT MORE SOPHISTICATED SINCE THEN.

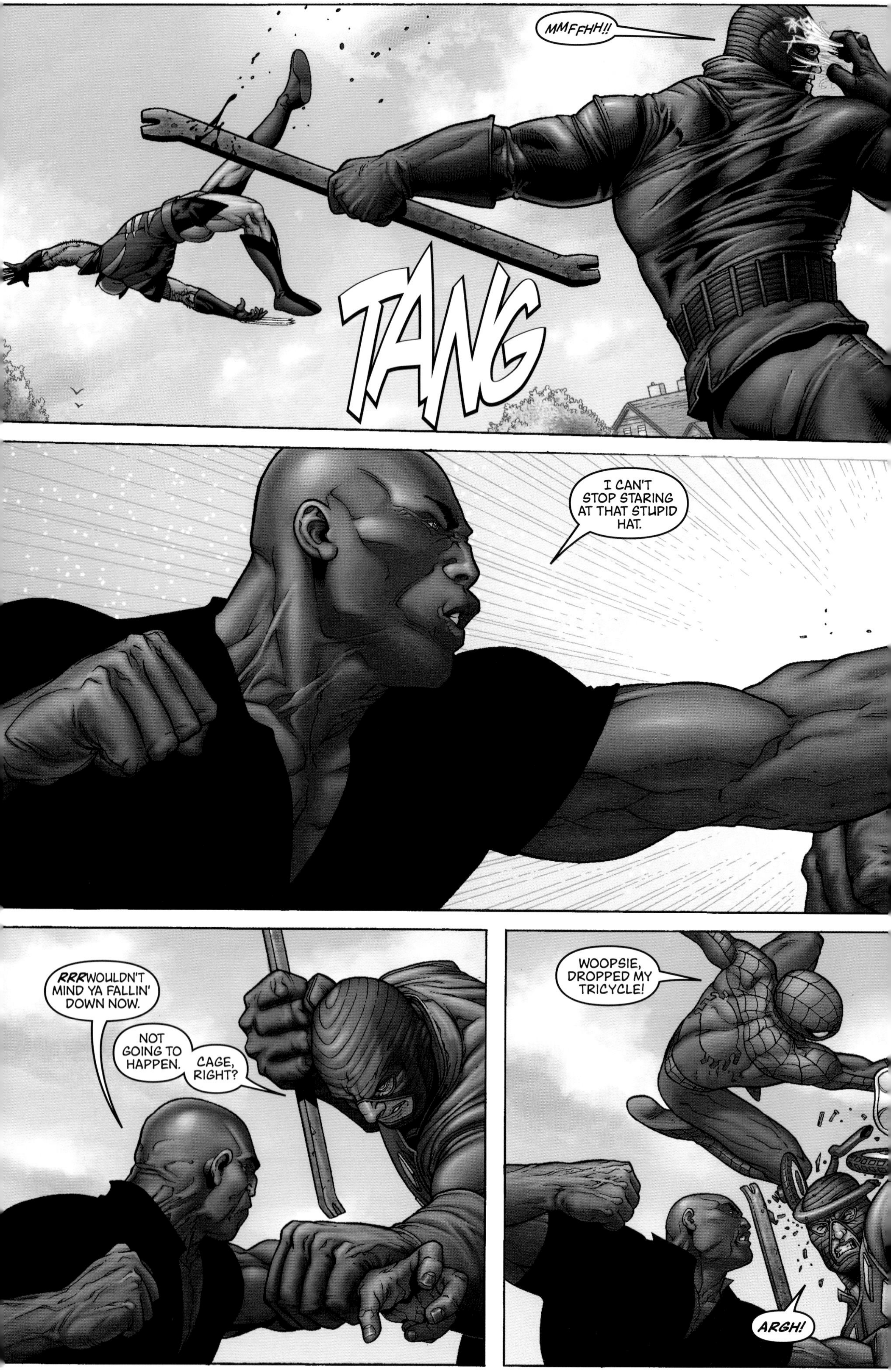
MMFFHH!!
TANG
I CAN'T STOP STARING AT THAT STUPID HAT.
RRRWOULDN'T MIND YA FALLIN' DOWN NOW.
NOT GOING TO HAPPEN.
CAGE, RIGHT?
WOOPSIE, DROPPED MY TRICYCLE!
ARGH!

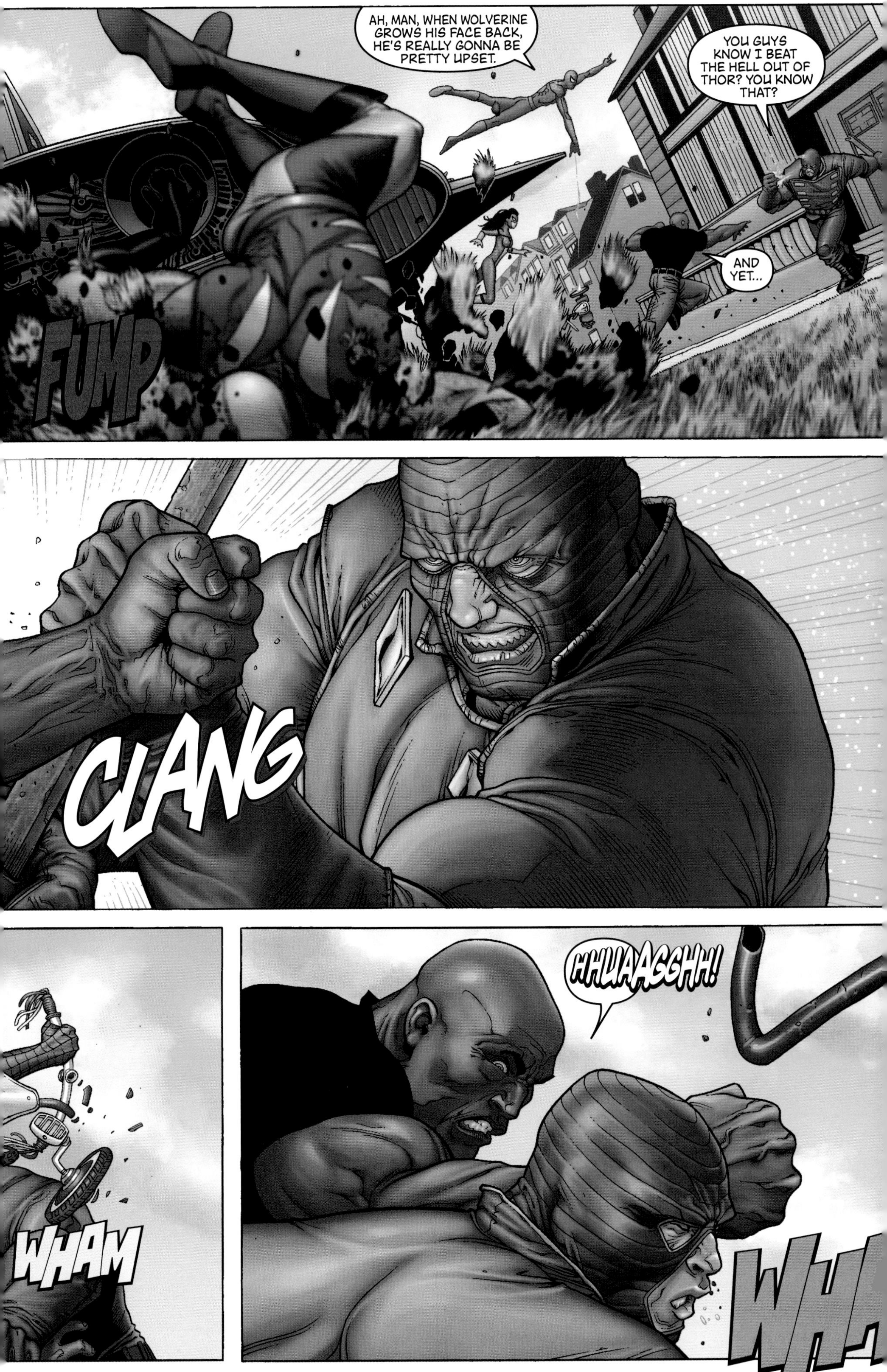

AH, MAN, WHEN WOLVERINE GROWS HIS FACE BACK, HE'S REALLY GONNA BE PRETTY UPSET.
YOU GUYS KNOW I BEAT THE HELL OUT OF THOR? YOU KNOW THAT?
AND YET...
FUMP
CLANG
WHAM
HHUAAGGHH!
WH

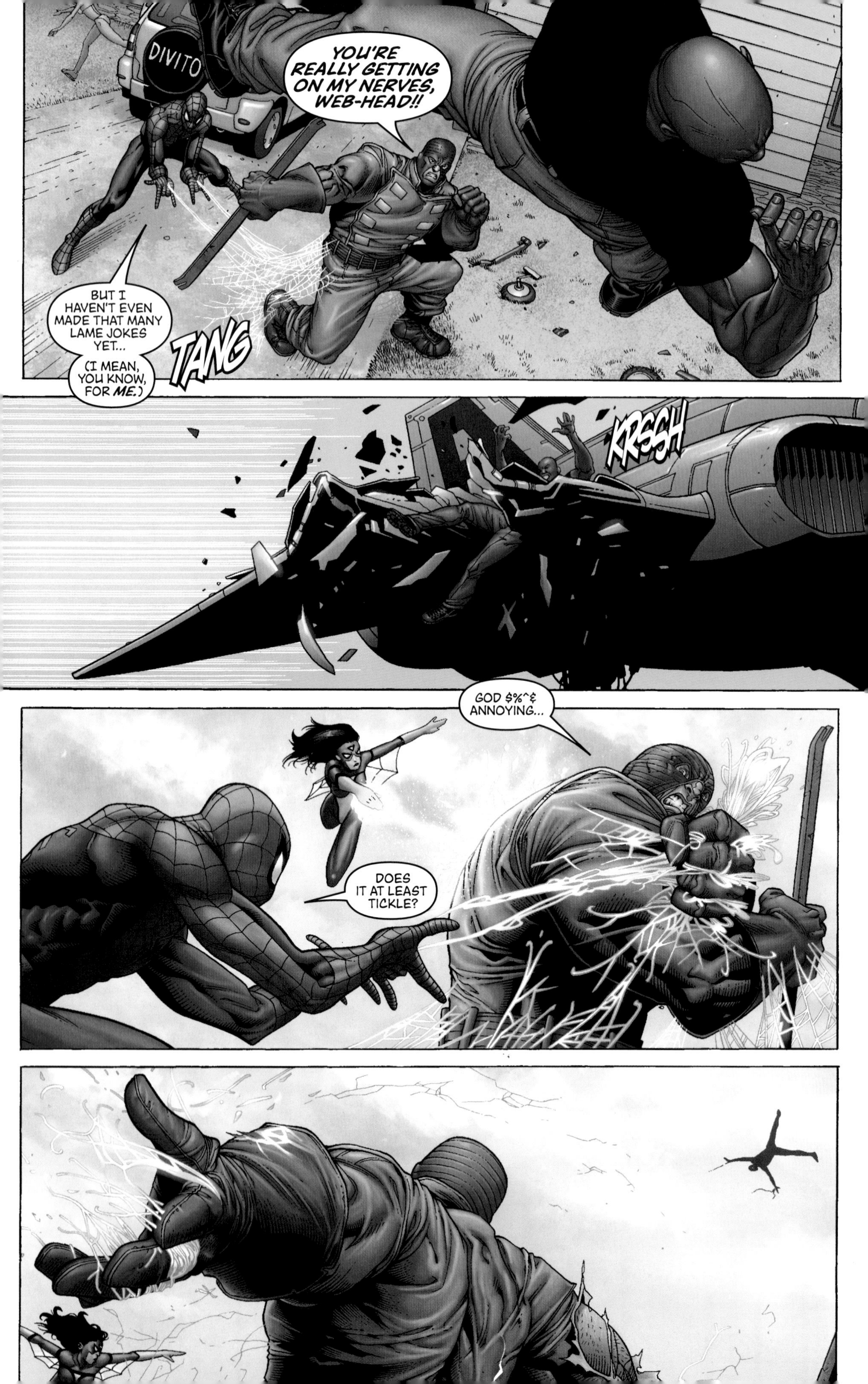
DIVITO
YOU'RE REALLY GETTING ON MY NERVES, WEB-HEAD!!
BUT I HAVEN'T EVEN MADE THAT MANY LAME JOKES YET...
(I MEAN, YOU KNOW, FOR ME.)
TANG
KRSSH
GOD $%^& ANNOYING...
DOES IT AT LEAST TICKLE?

SLICE

ARGH!!

DAMN, THAT *HURTS!*

GET USED TO IT.

SHUT UP!

WHAM

CRASH

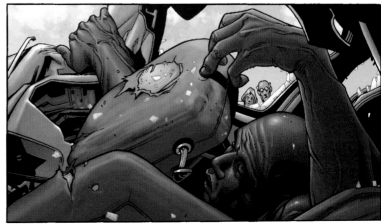

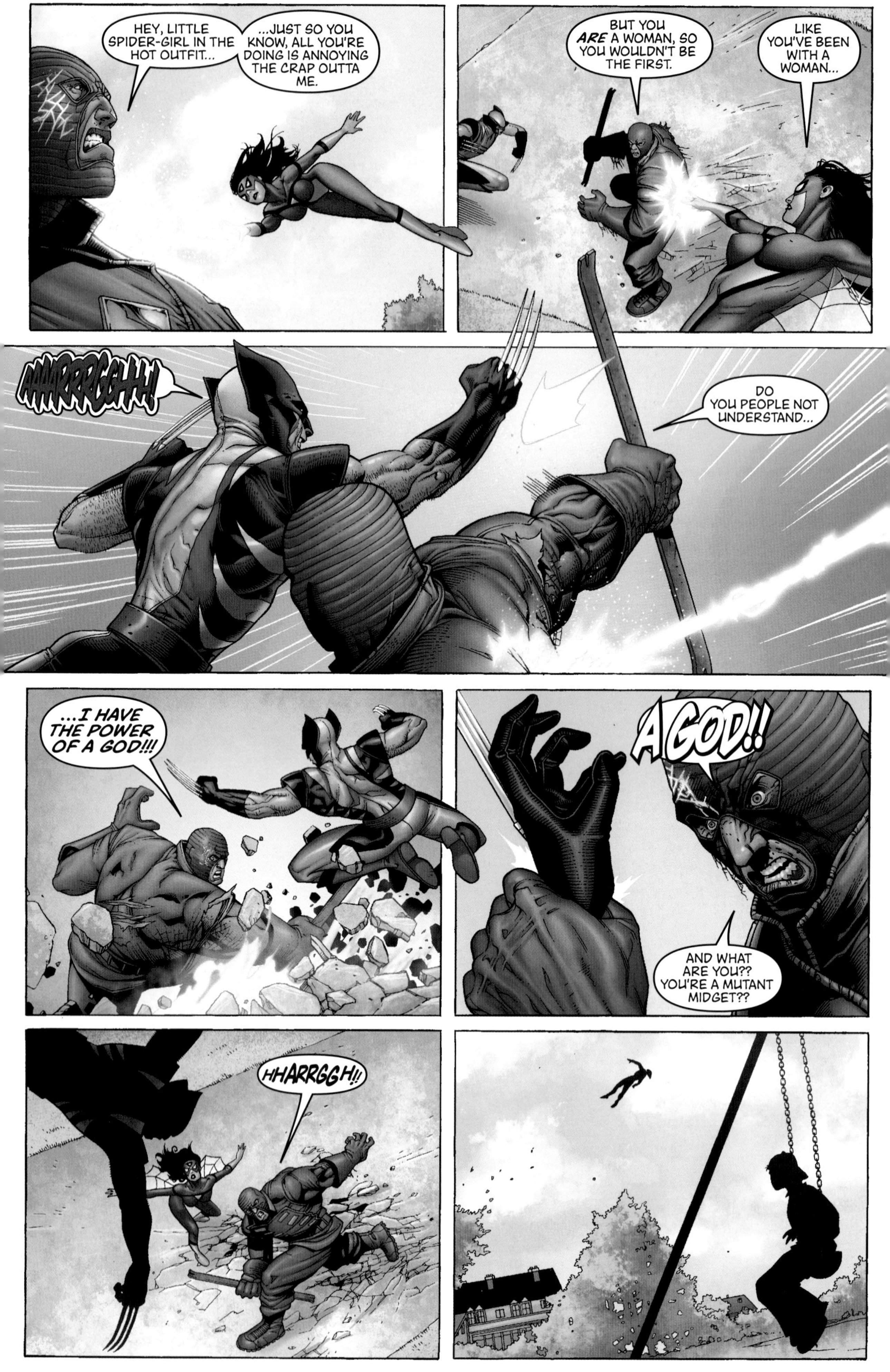
HEY, LITTLE SPIDER-GIRL IN THE HOT OUTFIT...
...JUST SO YOU KNOW, ALL YOU'RE DOING IS ANNOYING THE CRAP OUTTA ME.
LIKE YOU'VE BEEN WITH A WOMAN...
BUT YOU *ARE* A WOMAN, SO YOU WOULDN'T BE THE FIRST.
AAAARRRGGHHH!
DO YOU PEOPLE NOT UNDERSTAND...
...I HAVE THE POWER OF A GOD!!!
A GOD!!
AND WHAT ARE YOU?? YOU'RE A MUTANT MIDGET??
HHARRGGH!!

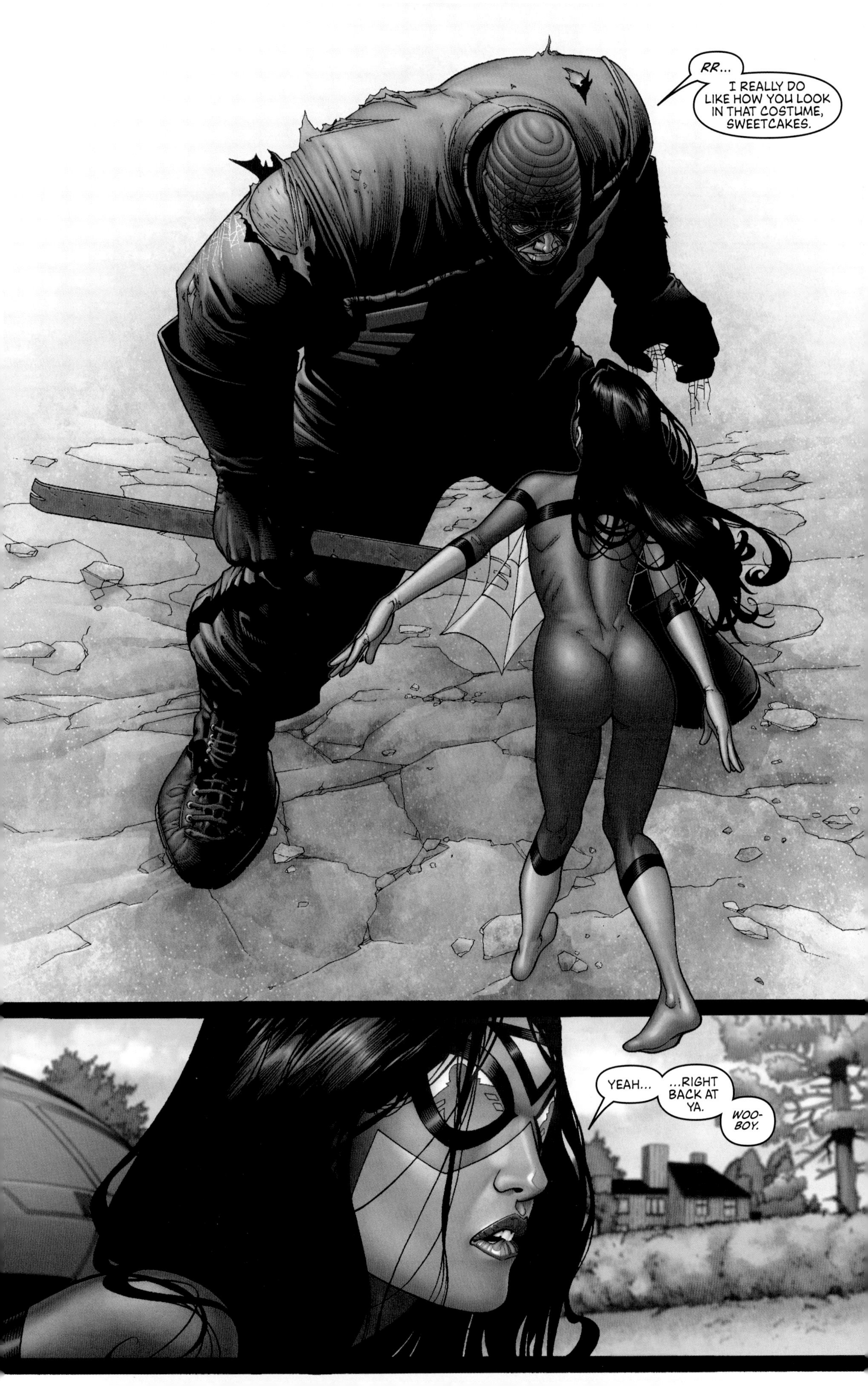
RR... I REALLY DO LIKE HOW YOU LOOK IN THAT COSTUME, SWEETCAKES.
YEAH...
...RIGHT BACK AT YA.
WOO-BOY.

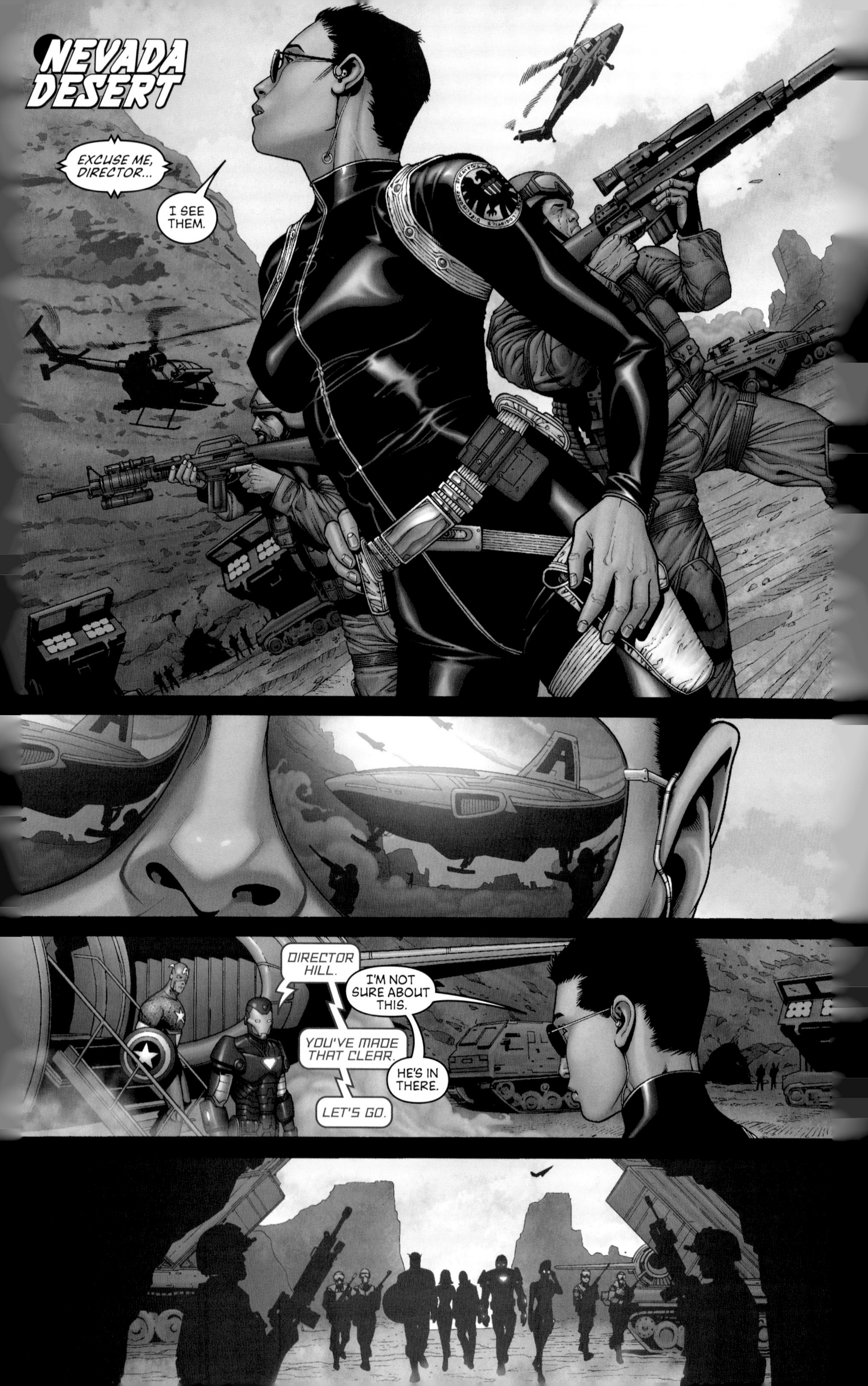
NEVADA DESERT
EXCUSE ME, DIRECTOR...
I SEE THEM.
DIRECTOR HILL.
I'M NOT SURE ABOUT THIS.
YOU'VE MADE THAT CLEAR.
HE'S IN THERE.
LET'S GO.

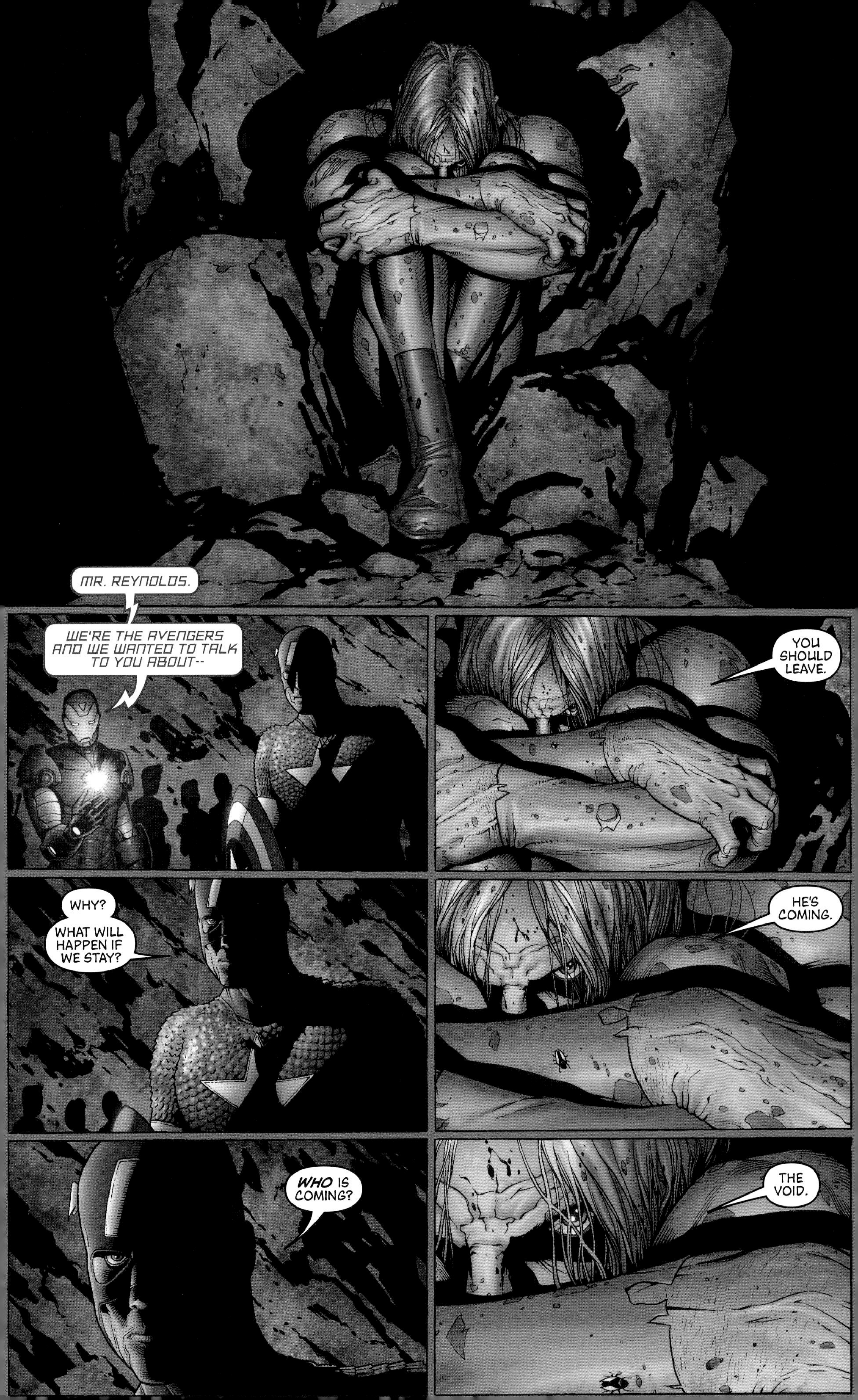
MR. REYNOLDS.
WE'RE THE AVENGERS AND WE WANTED TO TALK TO YOU ABOUT--
YOU SHOULD LEAVE.
WHY?
WHAT WILL HAPPEN IF WE STAY?
HE'S COMING.
WHO IS COMING?
THE VOID.

IS THAT A PERSON OR A CONSTRUCT OR--?

I USED MY POWERS!!!

TO SAVE YOU AND YOUR FRIENDS! I--I--I--I WAS WEAK AND I SAVED YOU AND NOW I WILL PAY THE PRICE.

WE ALL WILL.

I--WE DON'T UNDERSTAND.

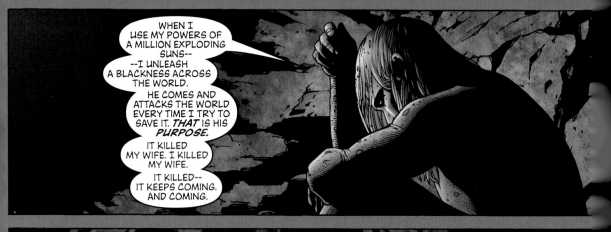

WHEN I USE MY POWERS OF A MILLION EXPLODING SUNS--

--I UNLEASH A BLACKNESS ACROSS THE WORLD.

HE COMES AND ATTACKS THE WORLD EVERY TIME I TRY TO SAVE IT. THAT IS HIS PURPOSE.

IT KILLED MY WIFE. I KILLED MY WIFE.

IT KILLED-- IT KEEPS COMING. AND COMING.

MR. REYNOLDS...

I HAVE--

I BROUGHT SOMEONE HERE TO SEE YOU.

SWEETIE...

I'M NOT--

I'M NOT DEAD.

NDY! NO.

I SAW YOU--I SAW YOU. I--

WHAT'S--BOB, WHAT'S WRONG WITH YOU?

WE'VE BEEN TRYING TO PIECE YOUR STORY TOGETHER ON OUR OWN MR. REYNOLDS.

TRYING TO FIGURE OUT WHAT WE CAN DO TO HELP YOU.

WHO THE SENTRY IS.

SIR, COULD YOU...

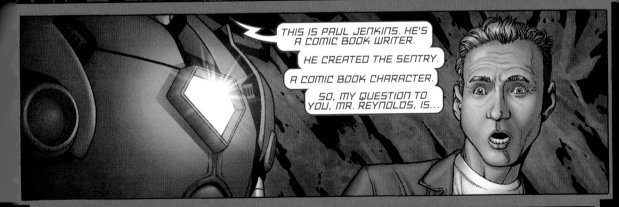

THIS IS PAUL JENKINS. HE'S A COMIC BOOK WRITER.

HE CREATED THE SENTRY.

A COMIC BOOK CHARACTER.

SO, MY QUESTION TO YOU, MR. REYNOLDS, IS...

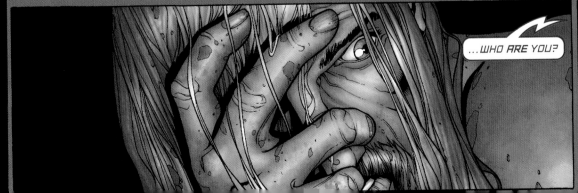

...WHO ARE YOU?

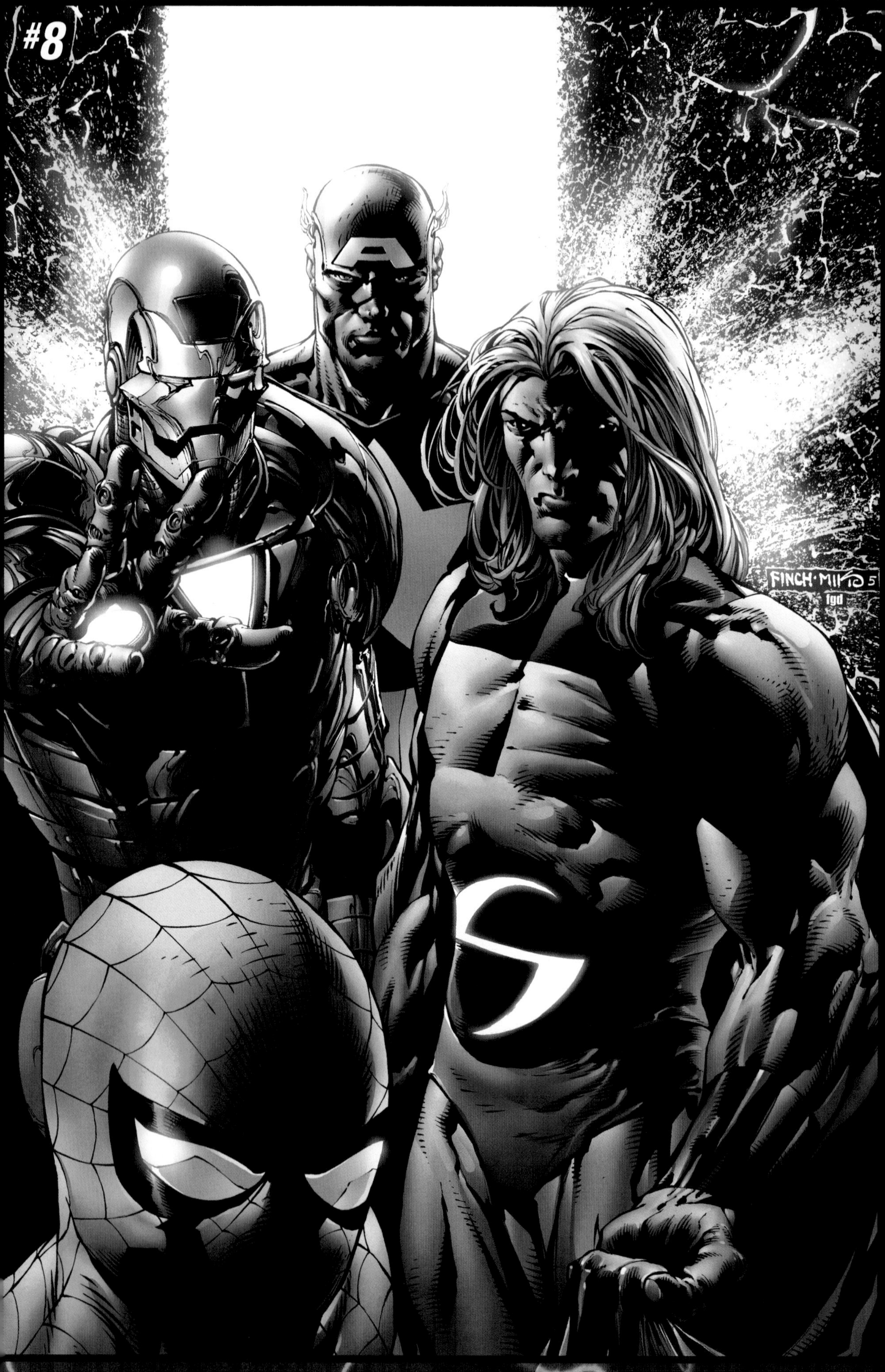
#8

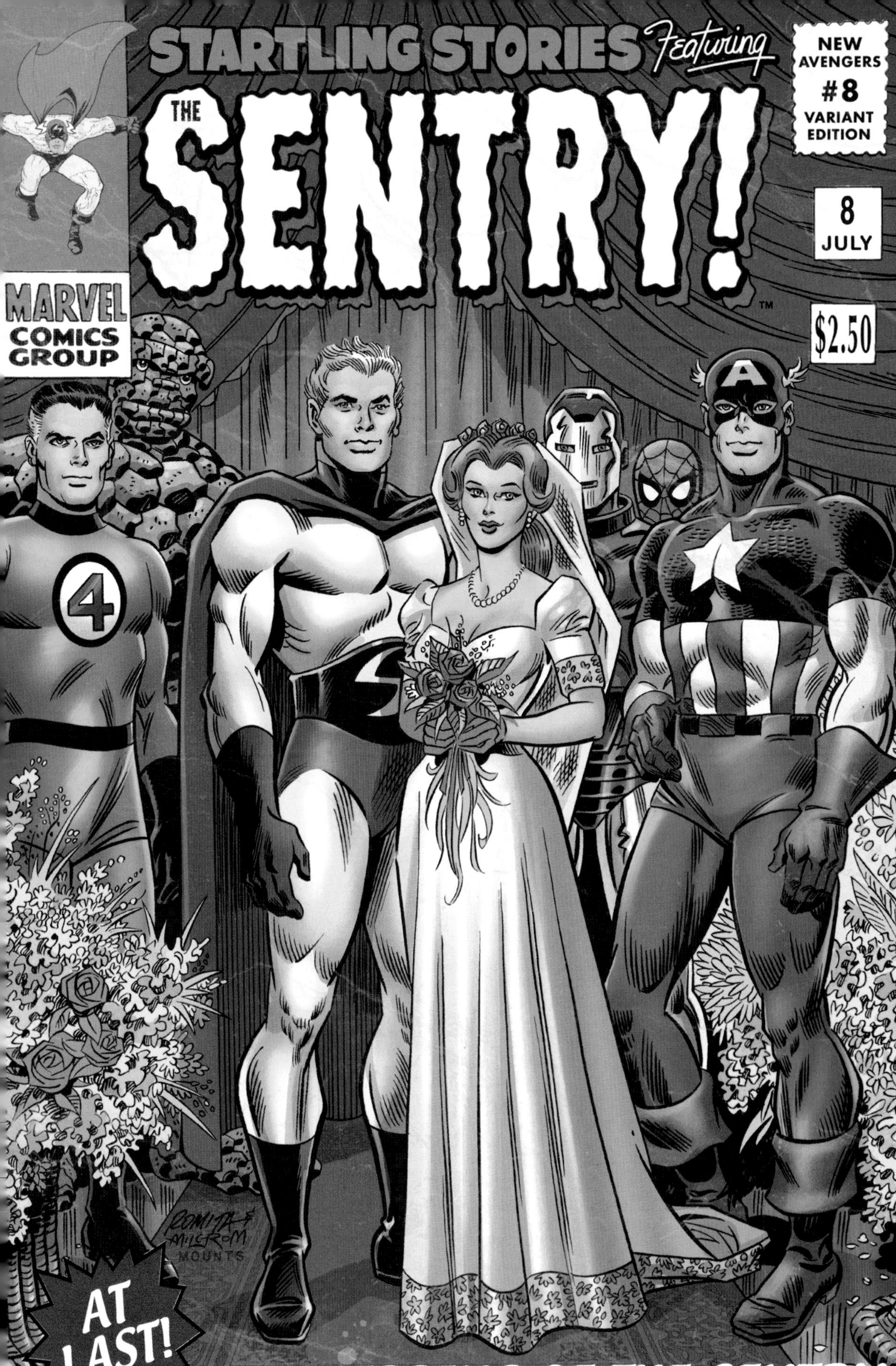
STARTLING STORIES Featuring
THE SENTRY!
NEW AVENGERS #8 VARIANT EDITION
8 JULY
$2.50
MARVEL COMICS GROUP
AT LAST!
THE WEDDING OF THE SENTRY

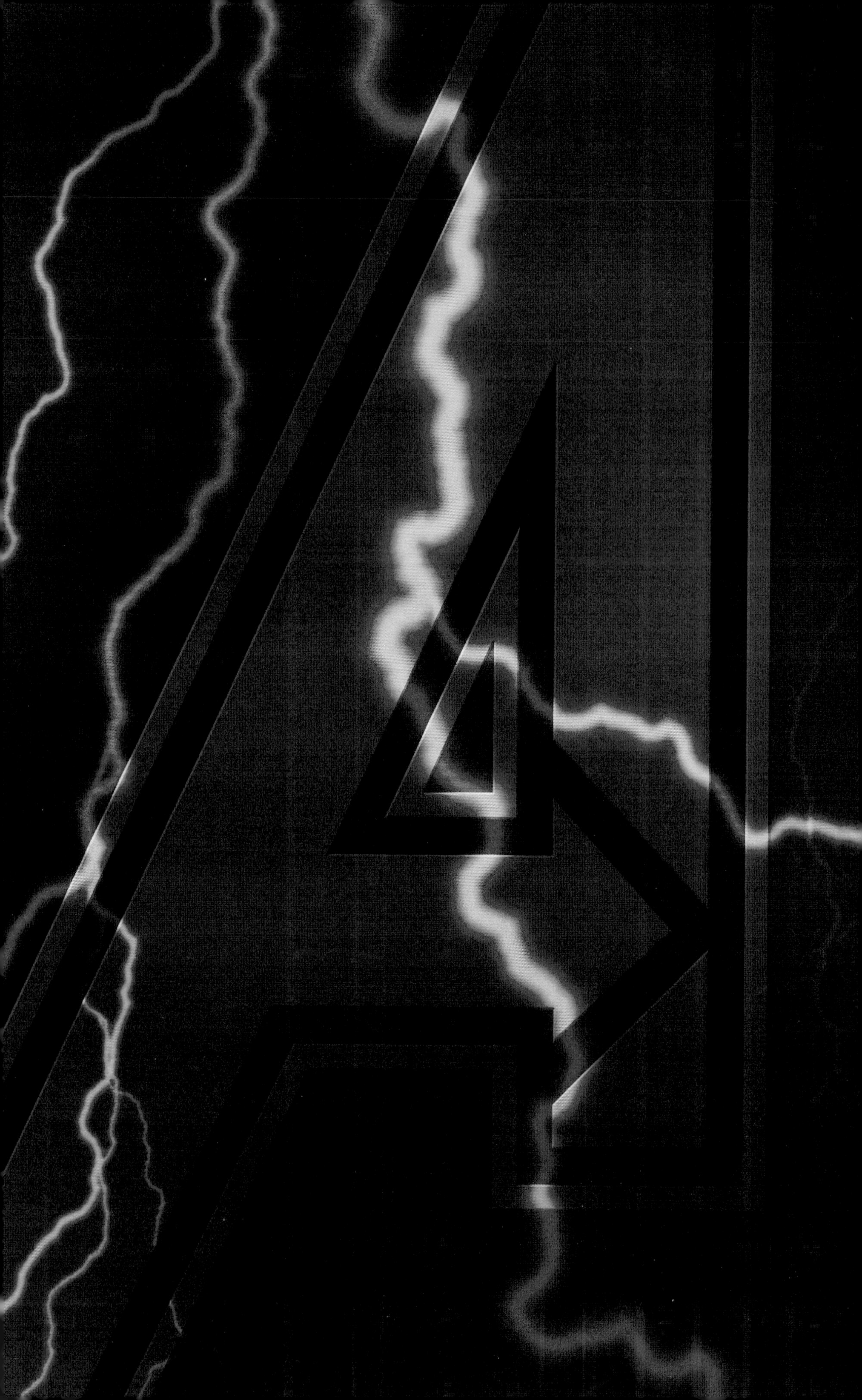

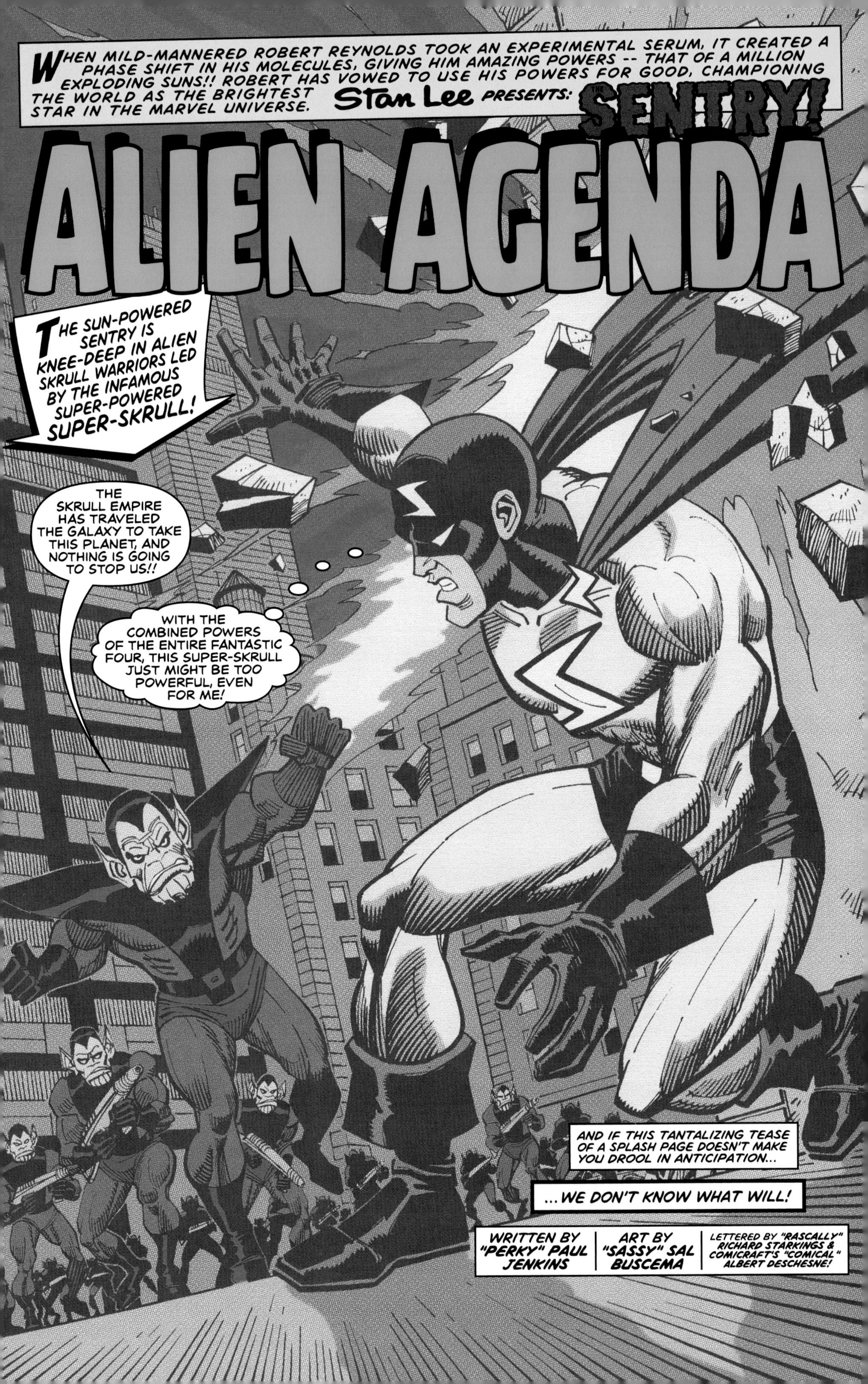
WHEN MILD-MANNERED ROBERT REYNOLDS TOOK AN EXPERIMENTAL SERUM, IT CREATED A PHASE SHIFT IN HIS MOLECULES, GIVING HIM AMAZING POWERS -- THAT OF A MILLION EXPLODING SUNS!! ROBERT HAS VOWED TO USE HIS POWERS FOR GOOD, CHAMPIONING THE WORLD AS THE BRIGHTEST STAR IN THE MARVEL UNIVERSE.
Stan Lee PRESENTS: THE SENTRY!
ALIEN AGENDA
THE SUN-POWERED SENTRY IS KNEE-DEEP IN ALIEN SKRULL WARRIORS LED BY THE INFAMOUS SUPER-POWERED SUPER-SKRULL!
THE SKRULL EMPIRE HAS TRAVELED THE GALAXY TO TAKE THIS PLANET, AND NOTHING IS GOING TO STOP US!!
WITH THE COMBINED POWERS OF THE ENTIRE FANTASTIC FOUR, THIS SUPER-SKRULL JUST MIGHT BE TOO POWERFUL, EVEN FOR ME!
AND IF THIS TANTALIZING TEASE OF A SPLASH PAGE DOESN'T MAKE YOU DROOL IN ANTICIPATION...
...WE DON'T KNOW WHAT WILL!
WRITTEN BY "PERKY" PAUL JENKINS
ART BY "SASSY" SAL BUSCEMA
LETTERED BY "RASCALLY" RICHARD STARKINGS & COMICRAFT'S "COMICAL" ALBERT DESCHESNE!

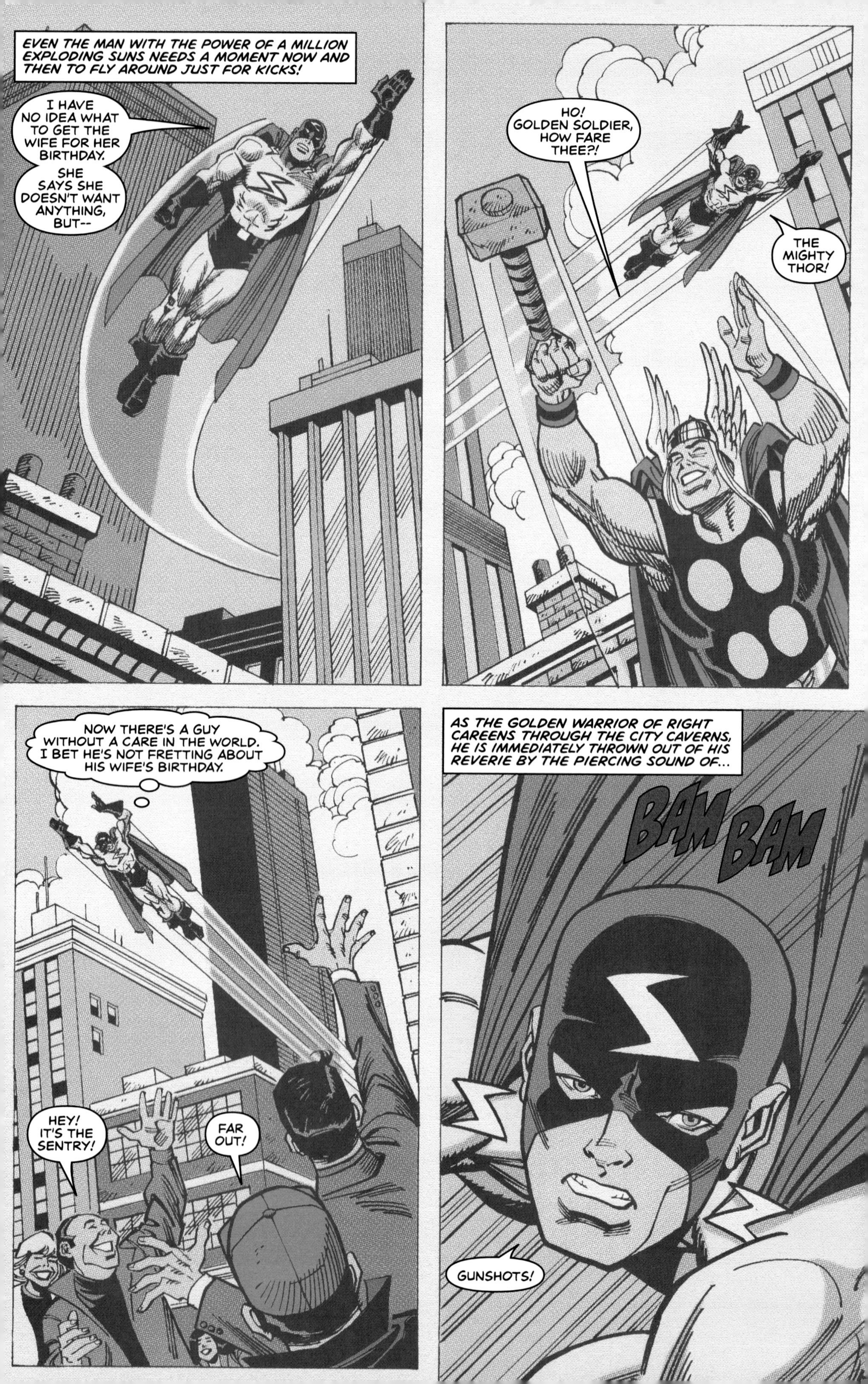
EVEN THE MAN WITH THE POWER OF A MILLION EXPLODING SUNS NEEDS A MOMENT NOW AND THEN TO FLY AROUND JUST FOR KICKS!
I HAVE NO IDEA WHAT TO GET THE WIFE FOR HER BIRTHDAY.
SHE SAYS SHE DOESN'T WANT ANYTHING, BUT--
HO! GOLDEN SOLDIER, HOW FARE THEE?!
THE MIGHTY THOR!
NOW THERE'S A GUY WITHOUT A CARE IN THE WORLD. I BET HE'S NOT FRETTING ABOUT HIS WIFE'S BIRTHDAY.
HEY! IT'S THE SENTRY!
FAR OUT!
AS THE GOLDEN WARRIOR OF RIGHT CAREENS THROUGH THE CITY CAVERNS, HE IS IMMEDIATELY THROWN OUT OF HIS REVERIE BY THE PIERCING SOUND OF...
BAM BAM
GUNSHOTS!

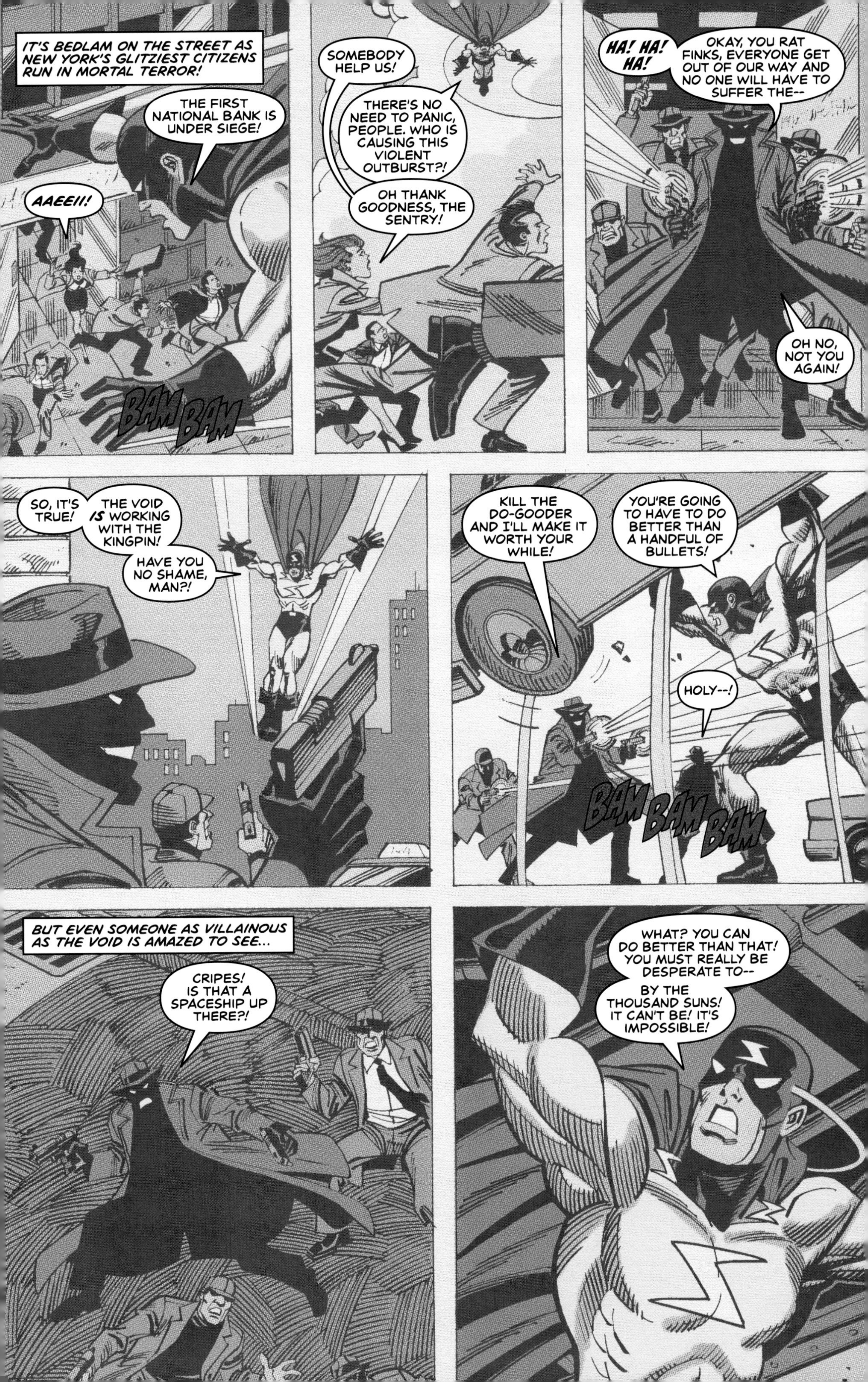
IT'S BEDLAM ON THE STREET AS NEW YORK'S GLITZIEST CITIZENS RUN IN MORTAL TERROR!
THE FIRST NATIONAL BANK IS UNDER SIEGE!
AAEEII!
BAM BAM
SOMEBODY HELP US!
THERE'S NO NEED TO PANIC, PEOPLE. WHO IS CAUSING THIS VIOLENT OUTBURST?!
OH THANK GOODNESS, THE SENTRY!
HA! HA! HA!
OKAY, YOU RAT FINKS, EVERYONE GET OUT OF OUR WAY AND NO ONE WILL HAVE TO SUFFER THE--
OH NO, NOT YOU AGAIN!
SO, IT'S TRUE!
THE VOID IS WORKING WITH THE KINGPIN!
HAVE YOU NO SHAME, MAN?!
KILL THE DO-GOODER AND I'LL MAKE IT WORTH YOUR WHILE!
YOU'RE GOING TO HAVE TO DO BETTER THAN A HANDFUL OF BULLETS!
HOLY--!
BAM BAM BAM
BUT EVEN SOMEONE AS VILLAINOUS AS THE VOID IS AMAZED TO SEE...
CRIPES! IS THAT A SPACESHIP UP THERE?!
WHAT? YOU CAN DO BETTER THAN THAT! YOU MUST REALLY BE DESPERATE TO--
BY THE THOUSAND SUNS! IT CAN'T BE! IT'S IMPOSSIBLE!

MR. REYNOLDS...

...THESE COMIC BOOKS, THEY'RE THE ONLY THING WE COULD FIND IN THE ENTIRE WORLD...THAT EVEN MENTIONS THE SENTRY.

AND THEY'RE JUST COMIC BOOKS. THIS MAN HERE, HE WRITES THEM.

I-I USED TO. YEARS AGO. IT'S NOT--

--THIS IS BLOODY INSANE, IS WHAT THIS IS.

WE ALSO-- WE BROUGHT YOUR WIFE AS WELL.

SEE, WE KNOW WHO BOB REYNOLDS IS.

BUT WE CAN'T FIGURE OUT WHAT OR WHO THE SENTRY IS.

WE'RE VERY CONFUSED AND-- AND WE WANT TO HELP YOU.

CAN YOU HELP US HELP YOU?

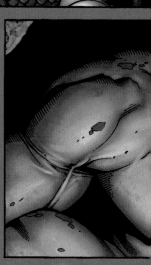

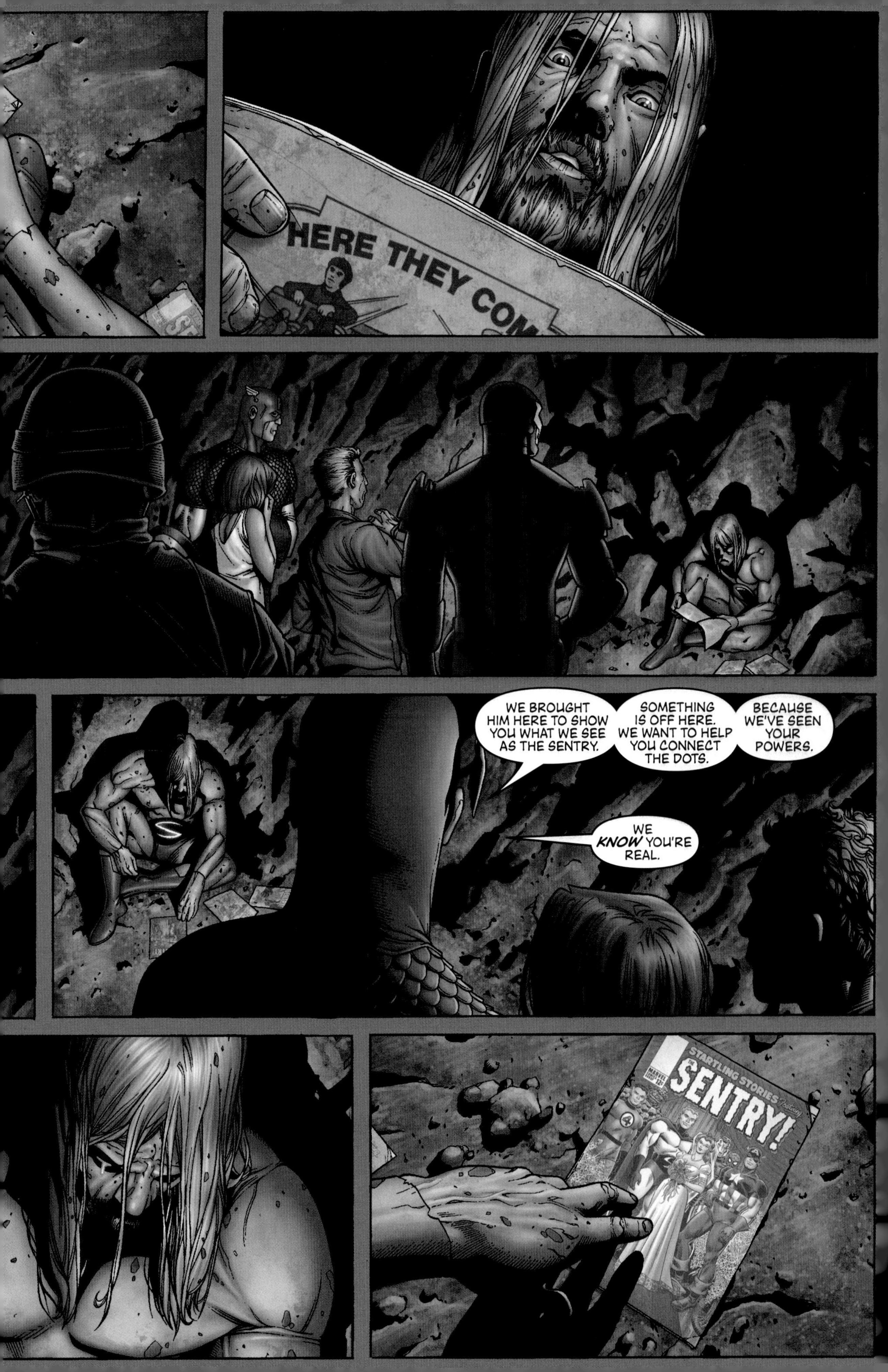

HERE THEY COM
WE BROUGHT HIM HERE TO SHOW YOU WHAT WE SEE AS THE SENTRY.
SOMETHING IS OFF HERE. WE WANT TO HELP YOU CONNECT THE DOTS.
BECAUSE WE'VE SEEN YOUR POWERS.
WE *KNOW* YOU'RE REAL.
STARTLING STORIES
SENTRY!

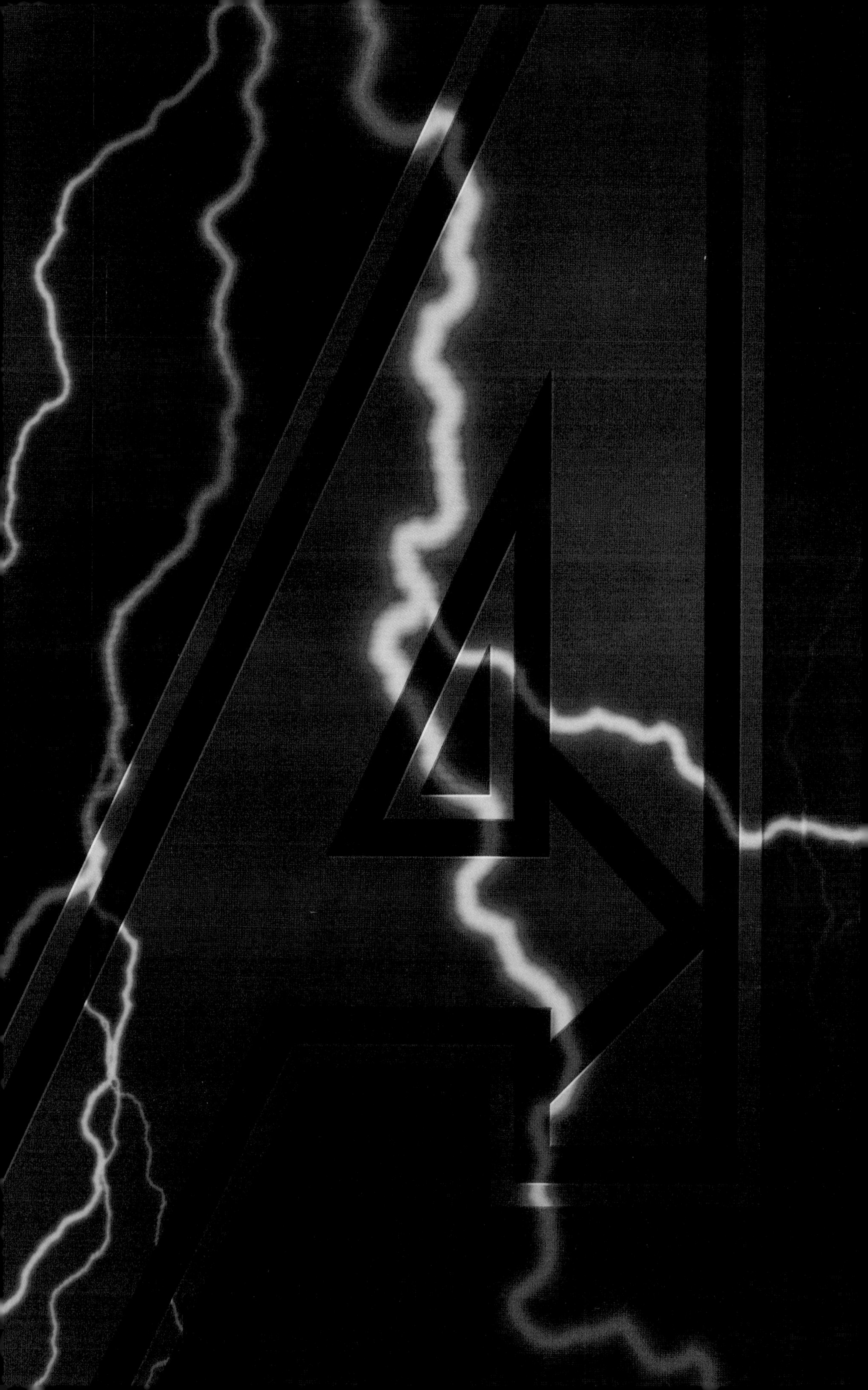

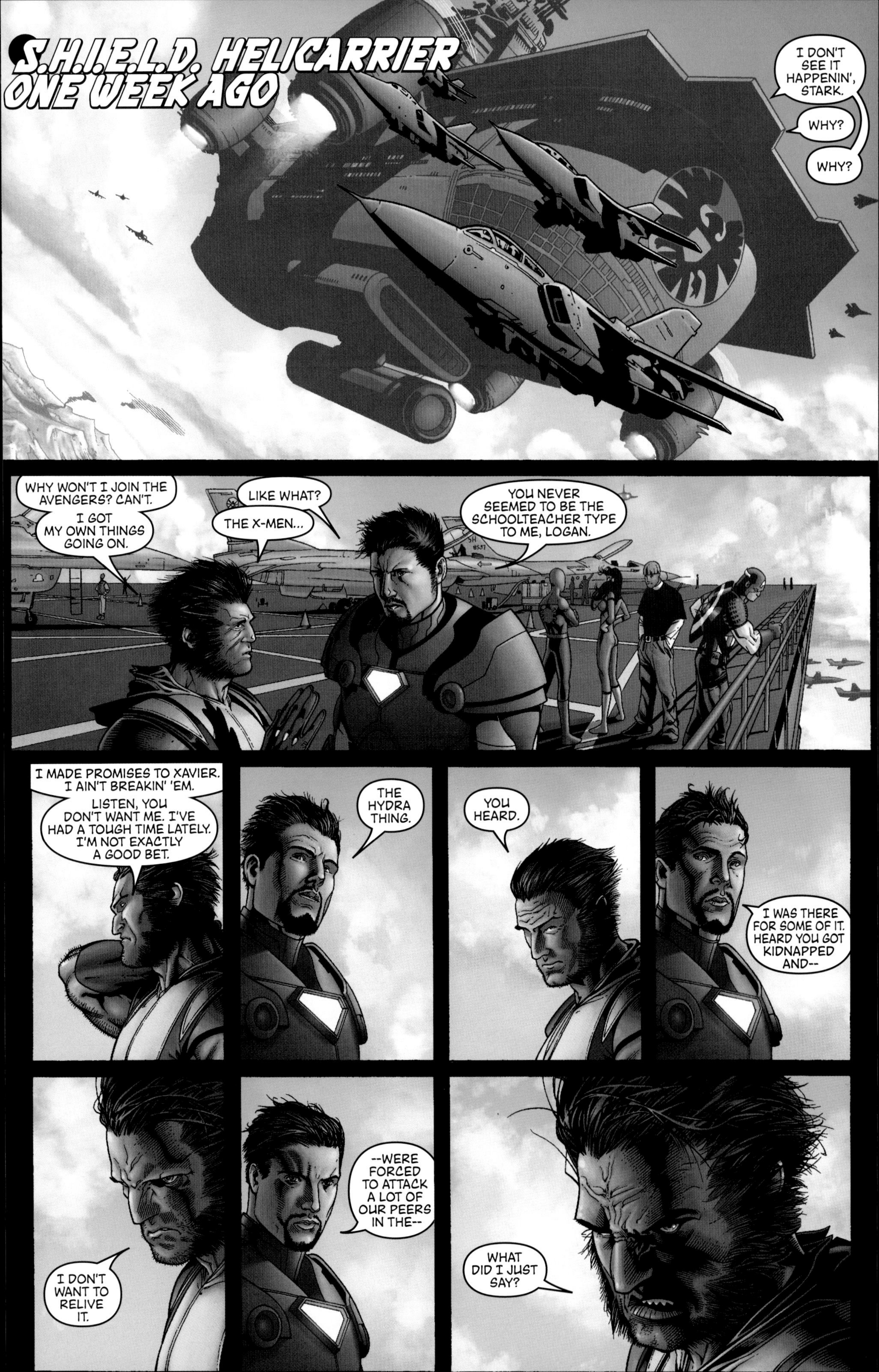
S.H.I.E.L.D. HELICARRIER ONE WEEK AGO
I DON'T SEE IT HAPPENIN', STARK.
WHY?
WHY?
WHY WON'T I JOIN THE AVENGERS? CAN'T.
I GOT MY OWN THINGS GOING ON.
LIKE WHAT?
THE X-MEN...
YOU NEVER SEEMED TO BE THE SCHOOLTEACHER TYPE TO ME, LOGAN.
I MADE PROMISES TO XAVIER. I AIN'T BREAKIN' 'EM.
LISTEN, YOU DON'T WANT ME. I'VE HAD A TOUGH TIME LATELY. I'M NOT EXACTLY A GOOD BET.
THE HYDRA THING.
YOU HEARD.
I WAS THERE FOR SOME OF IT. HEARD YOU GOT KIDNAPPED AND--
I DON'T WANT TO RELIVE IT.
--WERE FORCED TO ATTACK A LOT OF OUR PEERS IN THE--
WHAT DID I JUST SAY?

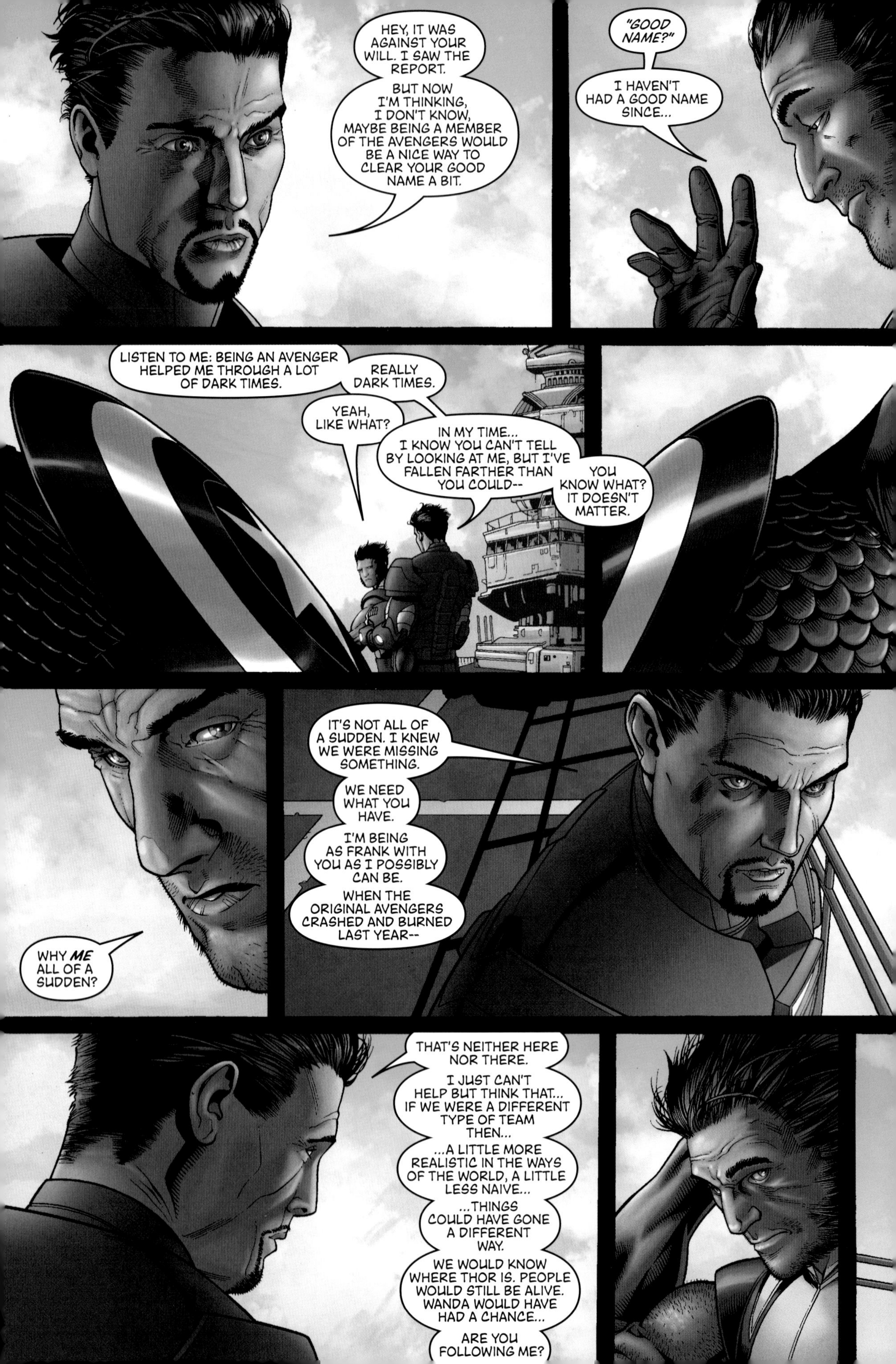
HEY, IT WAS AGAINST YOUR WILL. I SAW THE REPORT.
BUT NOW I'M THINKING, I DON'T KNOW, MAYBE BEING A MEMBER OF THE AVENGERS WOULD BE A NICE WAY TO CLEAR YOUR GOOD NAME A BIT.
"GOOD NAME?"
I HAVEN'T HAD A GOOD NAME SINCE...
LISTEN TO ME: BEING AN AVENGER HELPED ME THROUGH A LOT OF DARK TIMES.
REALLY DARK TIMES.
YEAH, LIKE WHAT?
IN MY TIME... I KNOW YOU CAN'T TELL BY LOOKING AT ME, BUT I'VE FALLEN FARTHER THAN YOU COULD--
YOU KNOW WHAT? IT DOESN'T MATTER.
WHY *ME* ALL OF A SUDDEN?
IT'S NOT ALL OF A SUDDEN. I KNEW WE WERE MISSING SOMETHING.
WE NEED WHAT YOU HAVE.
I'M BEING AS FRANK WITH YOU AS I POSSIBLY CAN BE.
WHEN THE ORIGINAL AVENGERS CRASHED AND BURNED LAST YEAR--
THAT'S NEITHER HERE NOR THERE.
I JUST CAN'T HELP BUT THINK THAT... IF WE WERE A DIFFERENT TYPE OF TEAM THEN...
...A LITTLE MORE REALISTIC IN THE WAYS OF THE WORLD, A LITTLE LESS NAIVE...
...THINGS COULD HAVE GONE A DIFFERENT WAY.
WE WOULD KNOW WHERE THOR IS. PEOPLE WOULD STILL BE ALIVE. WANDA WOULD HAVE HAD A CHANCE...
ARE YOU FOLLOWING ME?

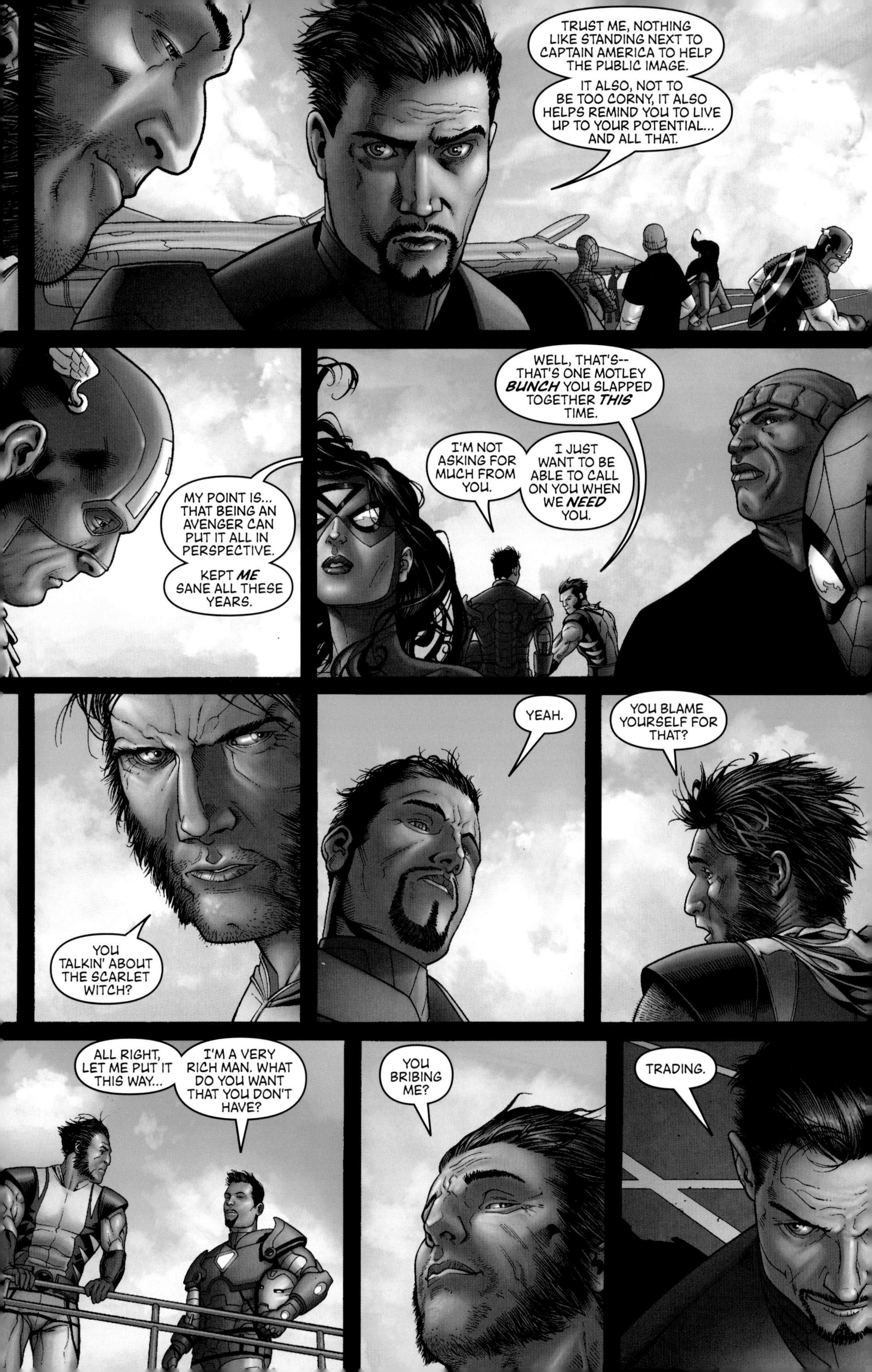
TRUST ME, NOTHING LIKE STANDING NEXT TO CAPTAIN AMERICA TO HELP THE PUBLIC IMAGE.
IT ALSO, NOT TO BE TOO CORNY, IT ALSO HELPS REMIND YOU TO LIVE UP TO YOUR POTENTIAL... AND ALL THAT.
MY POINT IS... THAT BEING AN AVENGER CAN PUT IT ALL IN PERSPECTIVE.
KEPT *ME* SANE ALL THESE YEARS.
WELL, THAT'S-- THAT'S ONE MOTLEY *BUNCH* YOU SLAPPED TOGETHER *THIS* TIME.
I'M NOT ASKING FOR MUCH FROM YOU.
I JUST WANT TO BE ABLE TO CALL ON YOU WHEN WE *NEED* YOU.
YOU TALKIN' ABOUT THE SCARLET WITCH?
YEAH.
YOU BLAME YOURSELF FOR THAT?
ALL RIGHT, LET ME PUT IT THIS WAY...
I'M A VERY RICH MAN. WHAT DO YOU WANT THAT YOU DON'T HAVE?
YOU BRIBING ME?
TRADING.

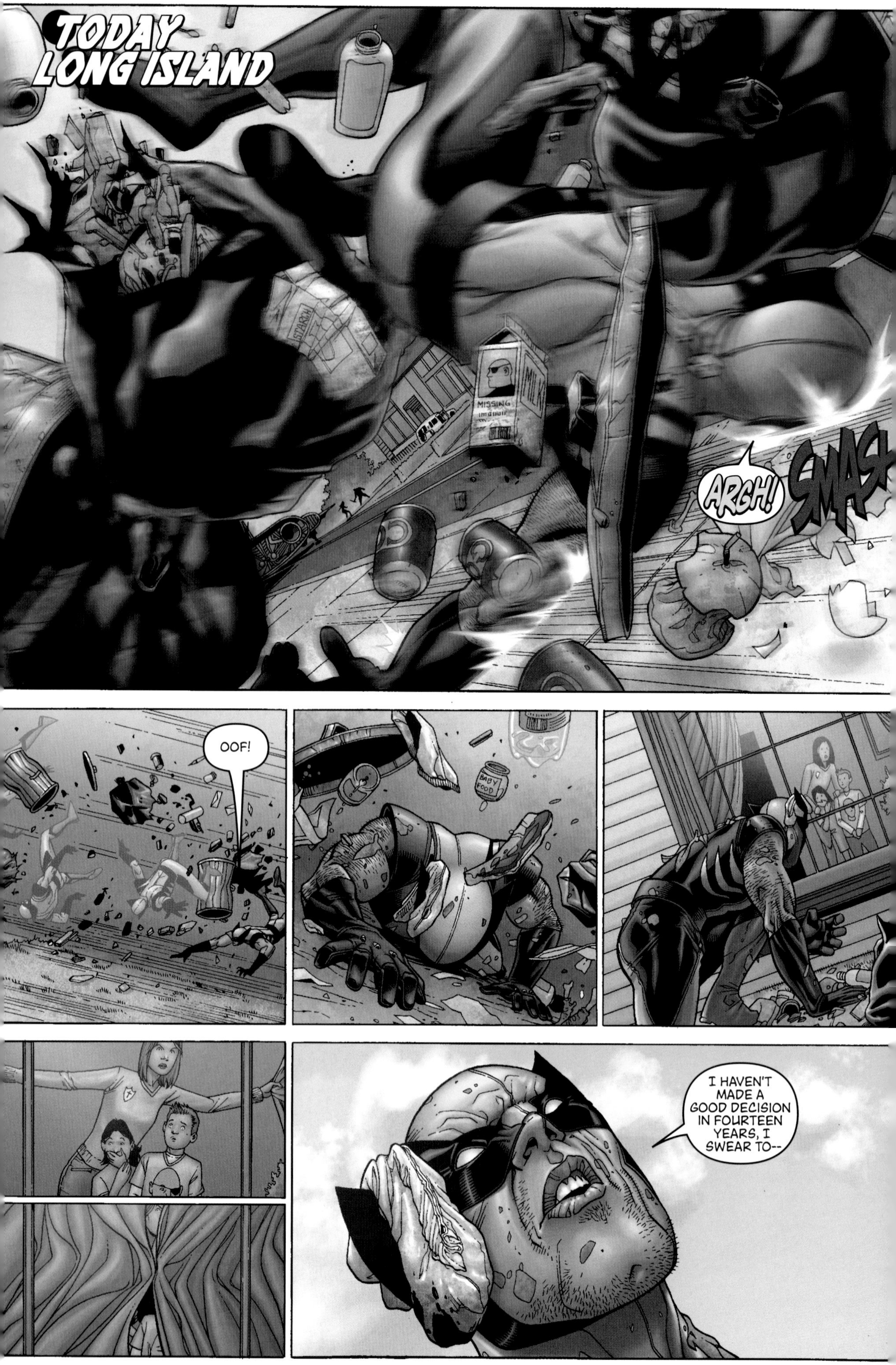
TODAY
LONG ISLAND
STARCH
MISSING
MILK
ARGH!
SMASH
OOF!
BABY FOOD
I HAVEN'T MADE A GOOD DECISION IN FOURTEEN YEARS, I SWEAR TO--

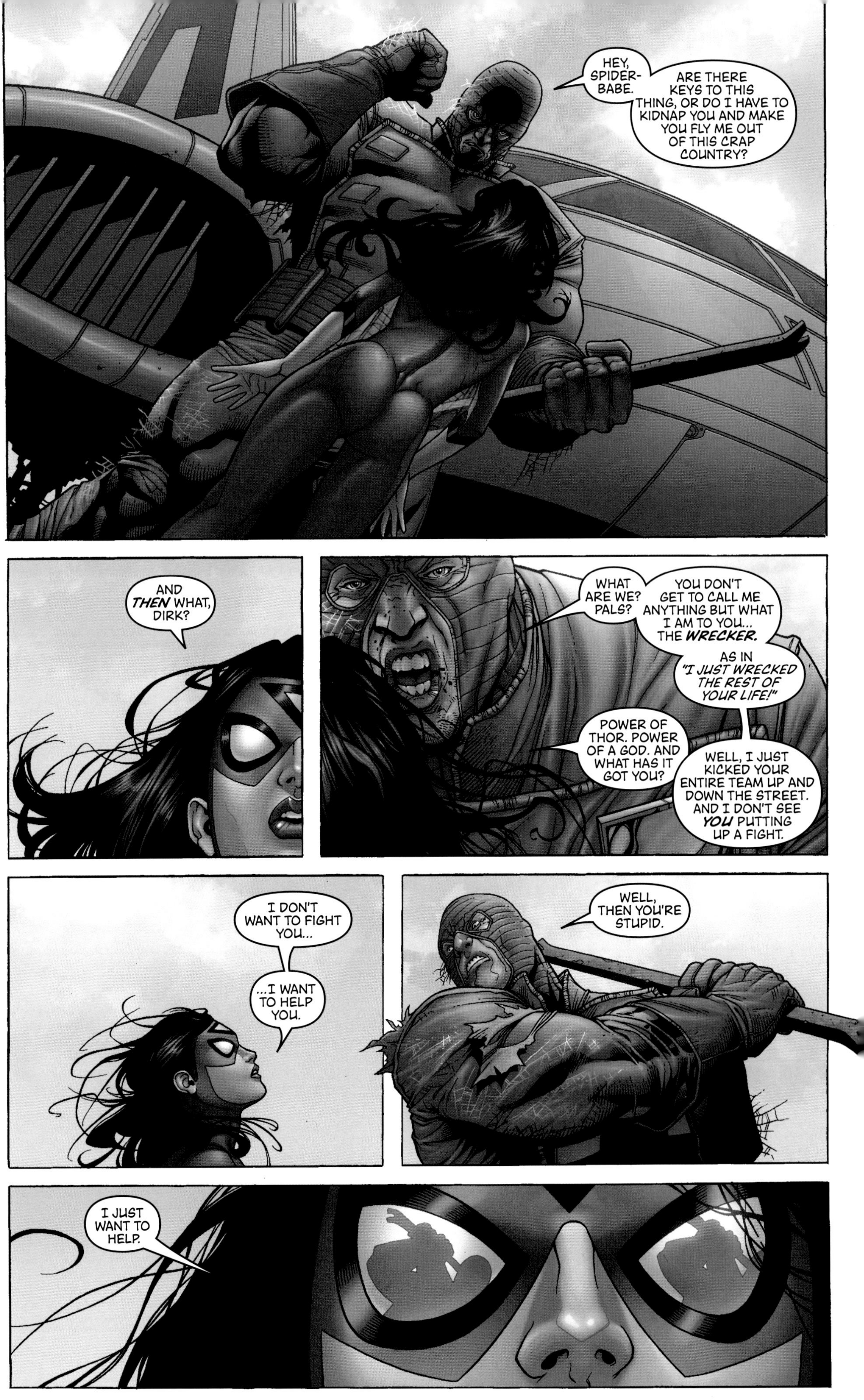

HEY, SPIDER-BABE.
ARE THERE KEYS TO THIS THING, OR DO I HAVE TO KIDNAP YOU AND MAKE YOU FLY ME OUT OF THIS CRAP COUNTRY?
AND *THEN* WHAT, DIRK?
WHAT ARE WE? PALS?
YOU DON'T GET TO CALL ME ANYTHING BUT WHAT I AM TO YOU... THE ***WRECKER.***
AS IN *"I JUST WRECKED THE REST OF YOUR LIFE!"*
POWER OF THOR. POWER OF A GOD. AND WHAT HAS IT GOT YOU?
WELL, I JUST KICKED YOUR ENTIRE TEAM UP AND DOWN THE STREET. AND I DON'T SEE ***YOU*** PUTTING UP A FIGHT.
I DON'T WANT TO FIGHT YOU...
...I WANT TO HELP YOU.
WELL, THEN YOU'RE STUPID.
I JUST WANT TO HELP.

BOB?
BOB, I THOUGHT YOU LEFT ME.

I DIDN'T KNOW WHERE YOU WERE OR WHY YOU LEFT.

I THOUGHT YOU WERE KILLED OR--OR I THOUGHT YOU LEFT ME.

YOU'VE BEEN GONE FOR WEEKS.

DO--DO YOU KNOW WHO I AM? DO YOU RECOGNIZE ME?

DO YOU KNOW I'M YOUR WIFE?

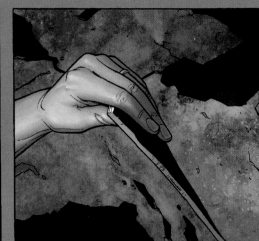

BOB... CAN YOU HEAR ME?

PLEASE?

OF COURSE I KNOW WHO YOU ARE.

WHO AM I?

I SAW YOU DEAD, LINDY.

I SAW IT.

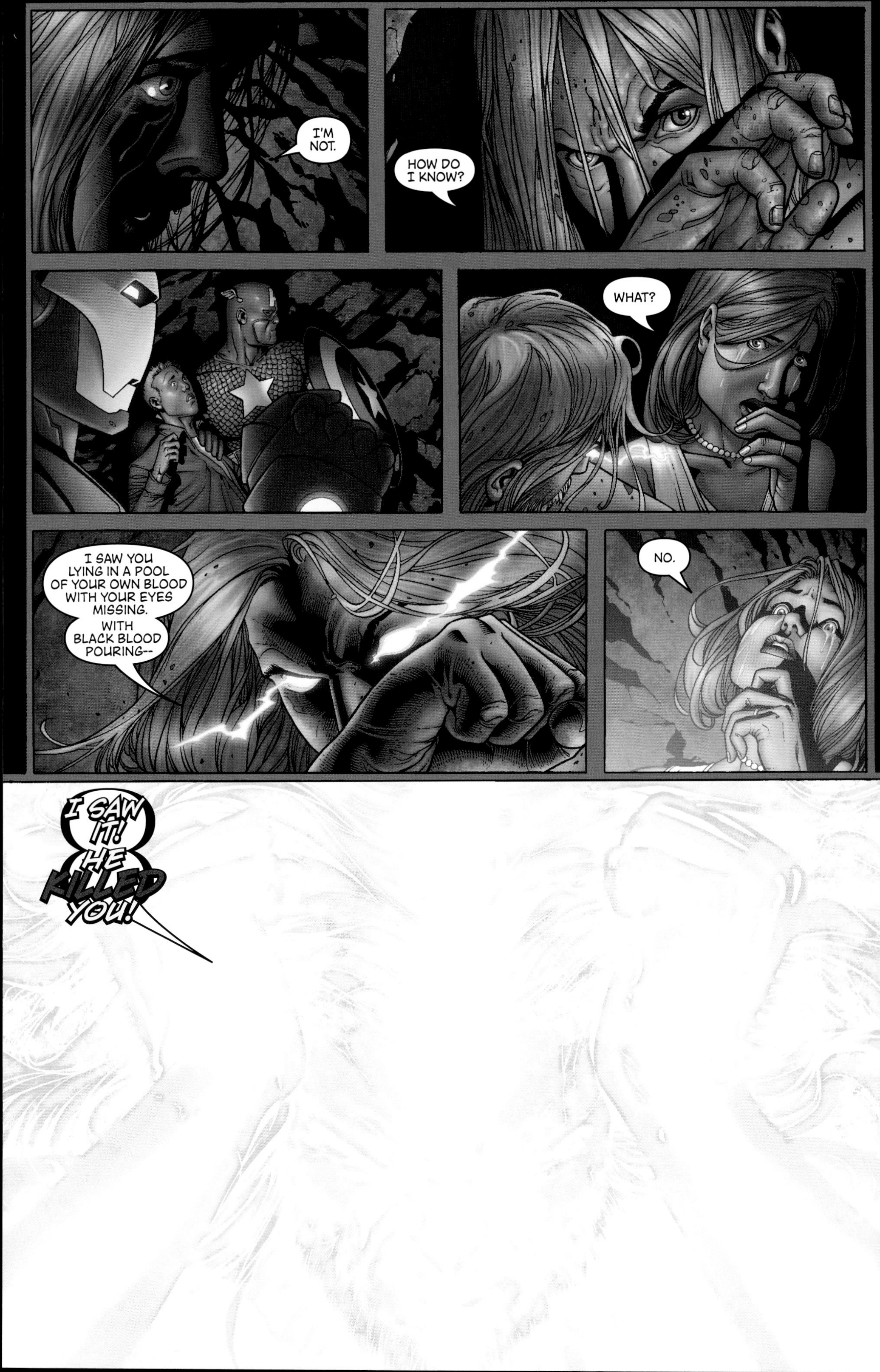
I'M NOT.
HOW DO I KNOW?
WHAT?
I SAW YOU LYING IN A POOL OF YOUR OWN BLOOD WITH YOUR EYES MISSING.
WITH BLACK BLOOD POURING--
NO.
I SAW IT! HE KILLED YOU!

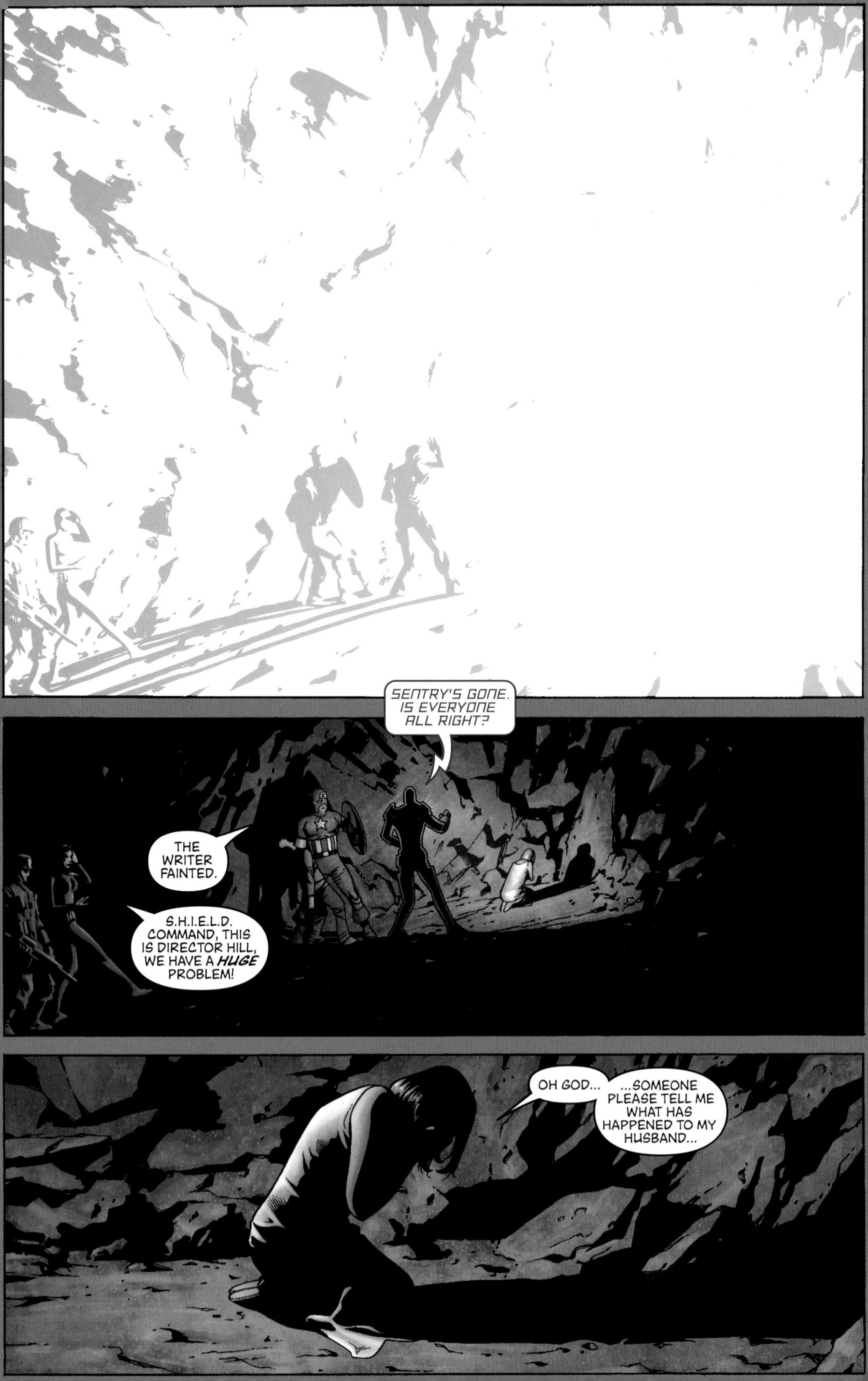
SENTRY'S GONE. IS EVERYONE ALL RIGHT?
THE WRITER FAINTED.
S.H.I.E.L.D. COMMAND, THIS IS DIRECTOR HILL, WE HAVE A *HUGE* PROBLEM!
OH GOD...
...SOMEONE PLEASE TELL ME WHAT HAS HAPPENED TO MY HUSBAND...

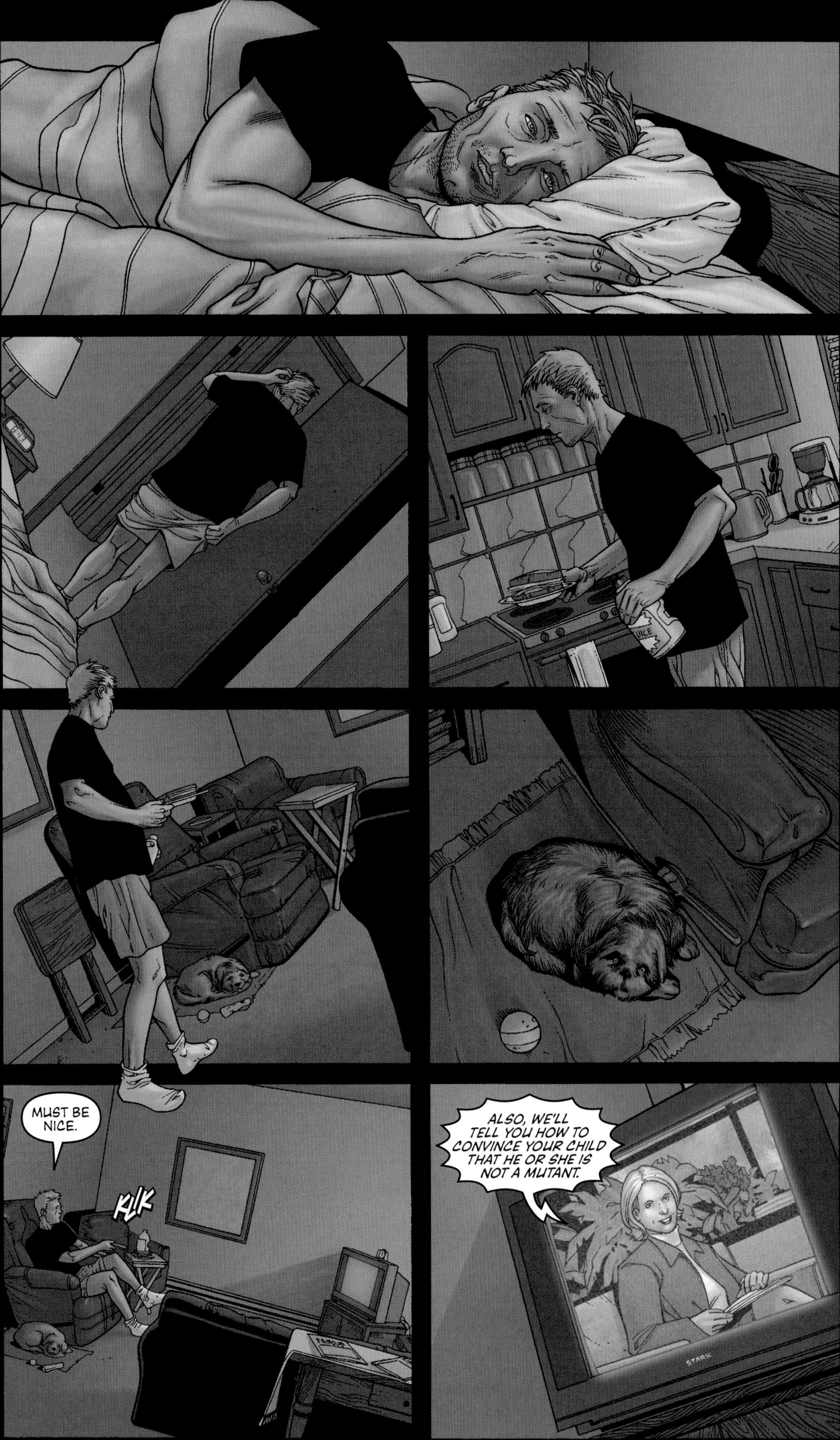
MUST BE NICE.
KLIK
ALSO, WE'LL TELL YOU HOW TO CONVINCE YOUR CHILD THAT HE OR SHE IS NOT A MUTANT.

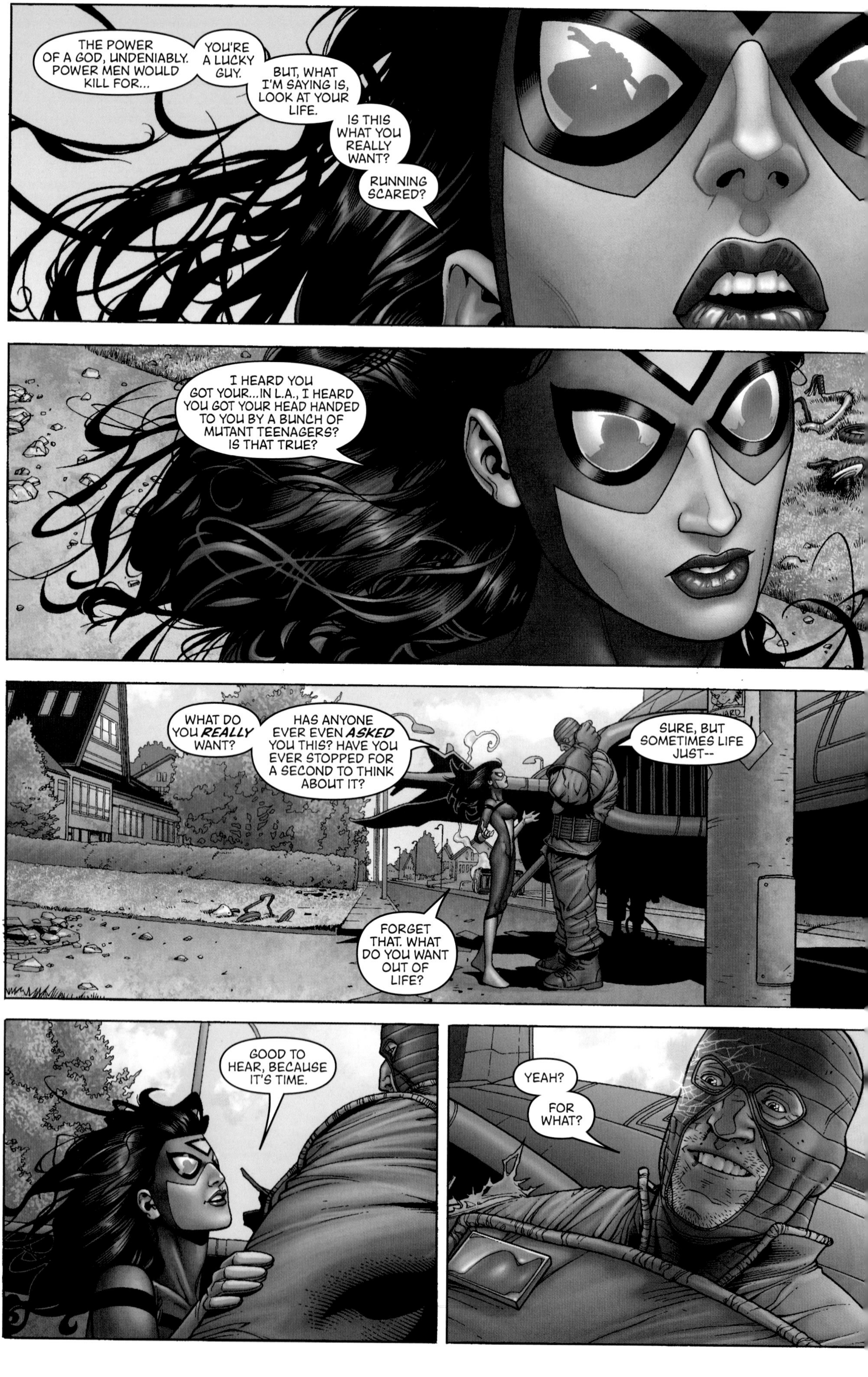
THE POWER OF A GOD, UNDENIABLY. POWER MEN WOULD KILL FOR...
YOU'RE A LUCKY GUY.
BUT, WHAT I'M SAYING IS, LOOK AT YOUR LIFE.
IS THIS WHAT YOU REALLY WANT?
RUNNING SCARED?
I HEARD YOU GOT YOUR...IN L.A., I HEARD YOU GOT YOUR HEAD HANDED TO YOU BY A BUNCH OF MUTANT TEENAGERS? IS THAT TRUE?
WHAT DO YOU **REALLY** WANT?
HAS ANYONE EVER EVEN **ASKED** YOU THIS? HAVE YOU EVER STOPPED FOR A SECOND TO THINK ABOUT IT?
SURE, BUT SOMETIMES LIFE JUST--
FORGET THAT. WHAT DO YOU WANT OUT OF LIFE?
GOOD TO HEAR, BECAUSE IT'S TIME.
YEAH?
FOR WHAT?

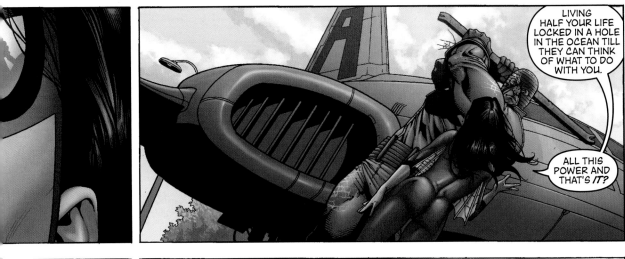

LIVING HALF YOUR LIFE LOCKED IN A HOLE IN THE OCEAN TILL THEY CAN THINK OF WHAT TO DO WITH YOU.

ALL THIS POWER AND THAT'S *IT*?

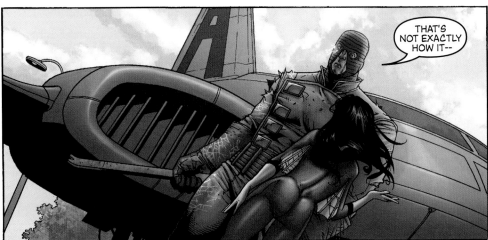

THAT'S NOT EXACTLY HOW IT--

I GOTTA SAY...IT'S--IT'S NICE TO BE ASKED.

THIS.

AND I SINCERELY HOPE IT HURTS, YOU TUBBY $%^#.

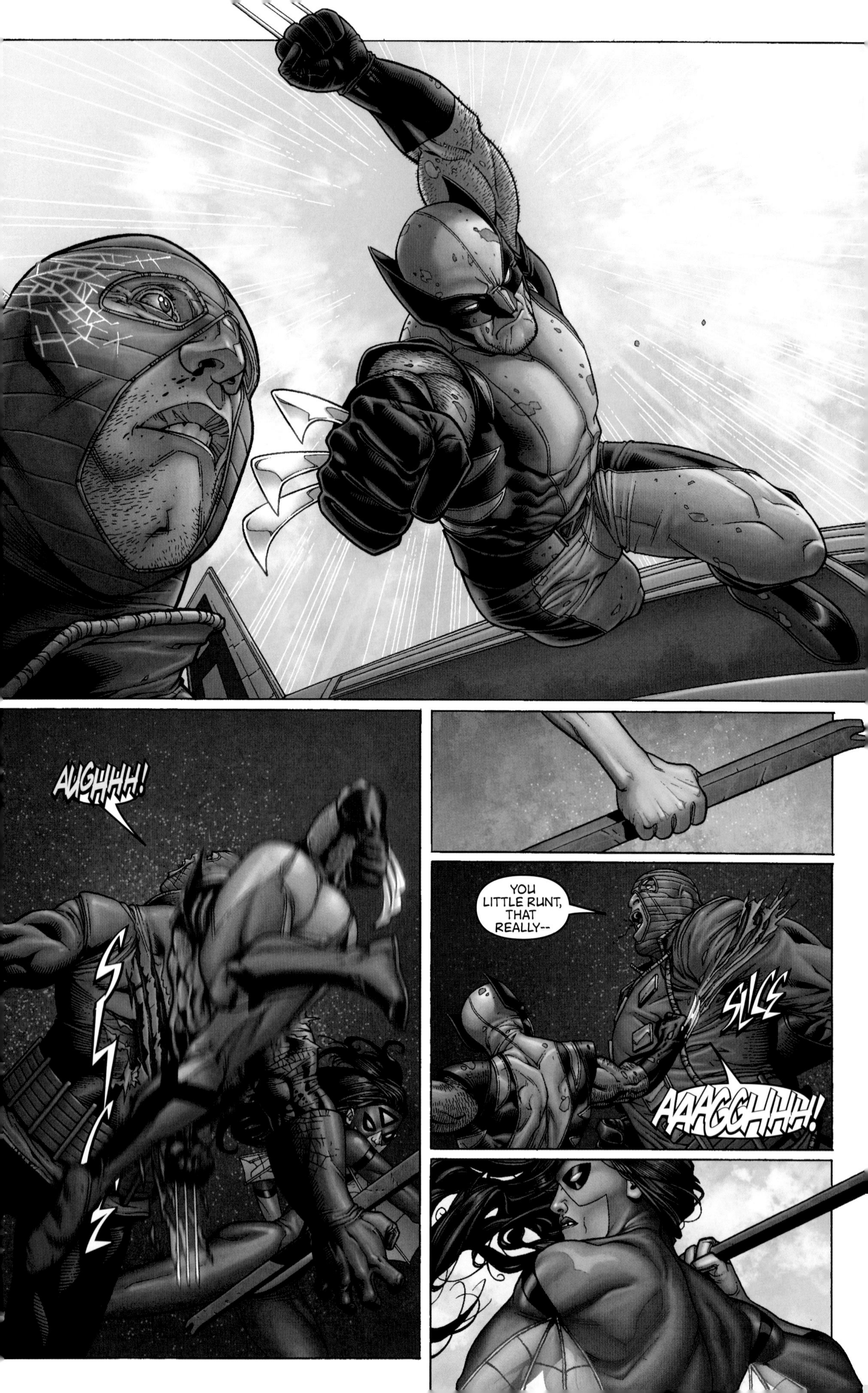
AUGHHH!
YOU LITTLE RUNT, THAT REALLY--
SLICE
AAAGGHHH!

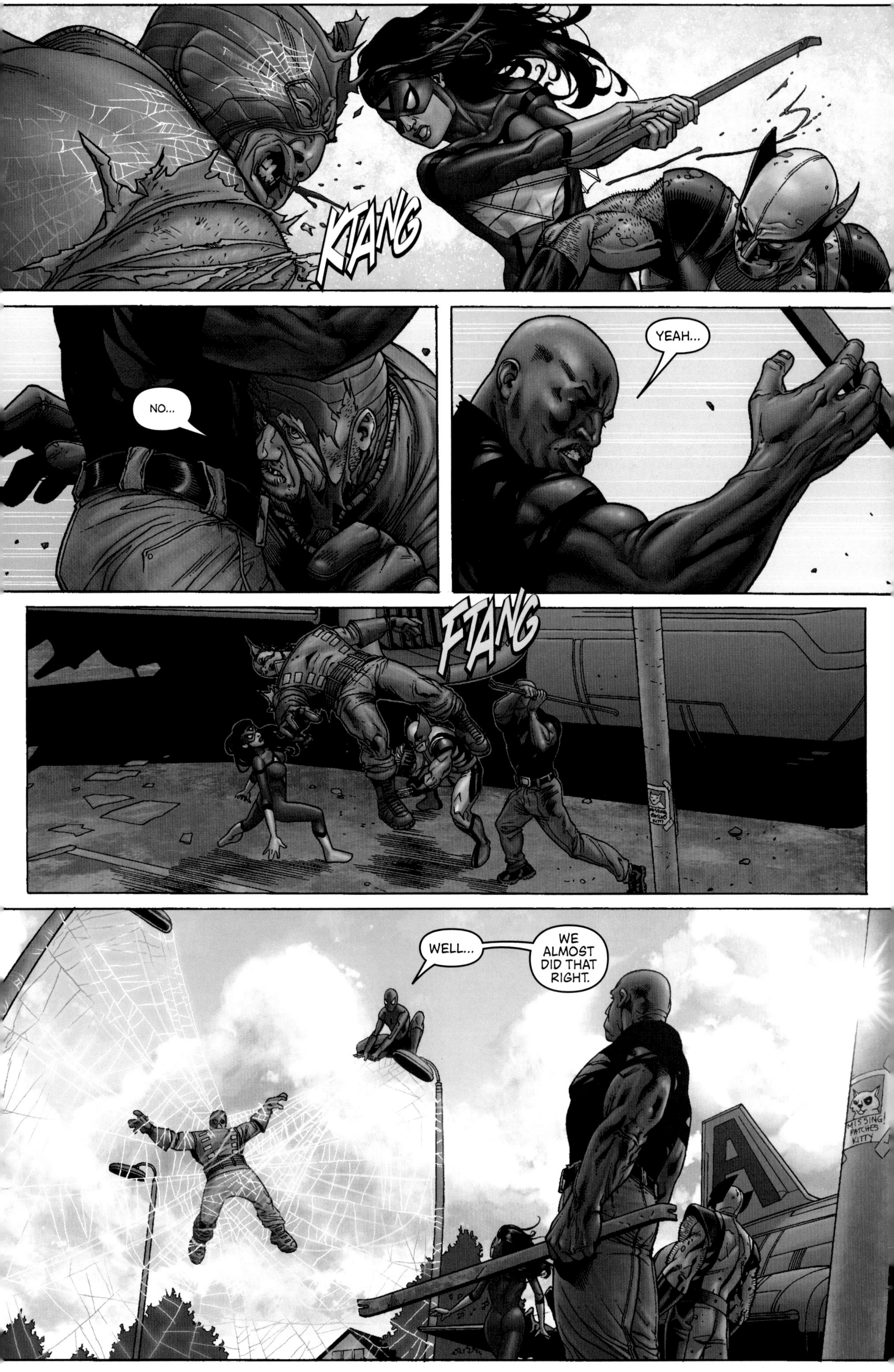
KTANG
NO...
YEAH...
FTANG
WELL...
WE ALMOST DID THAT RIGHT.
MISSING! PATCHES KITTY

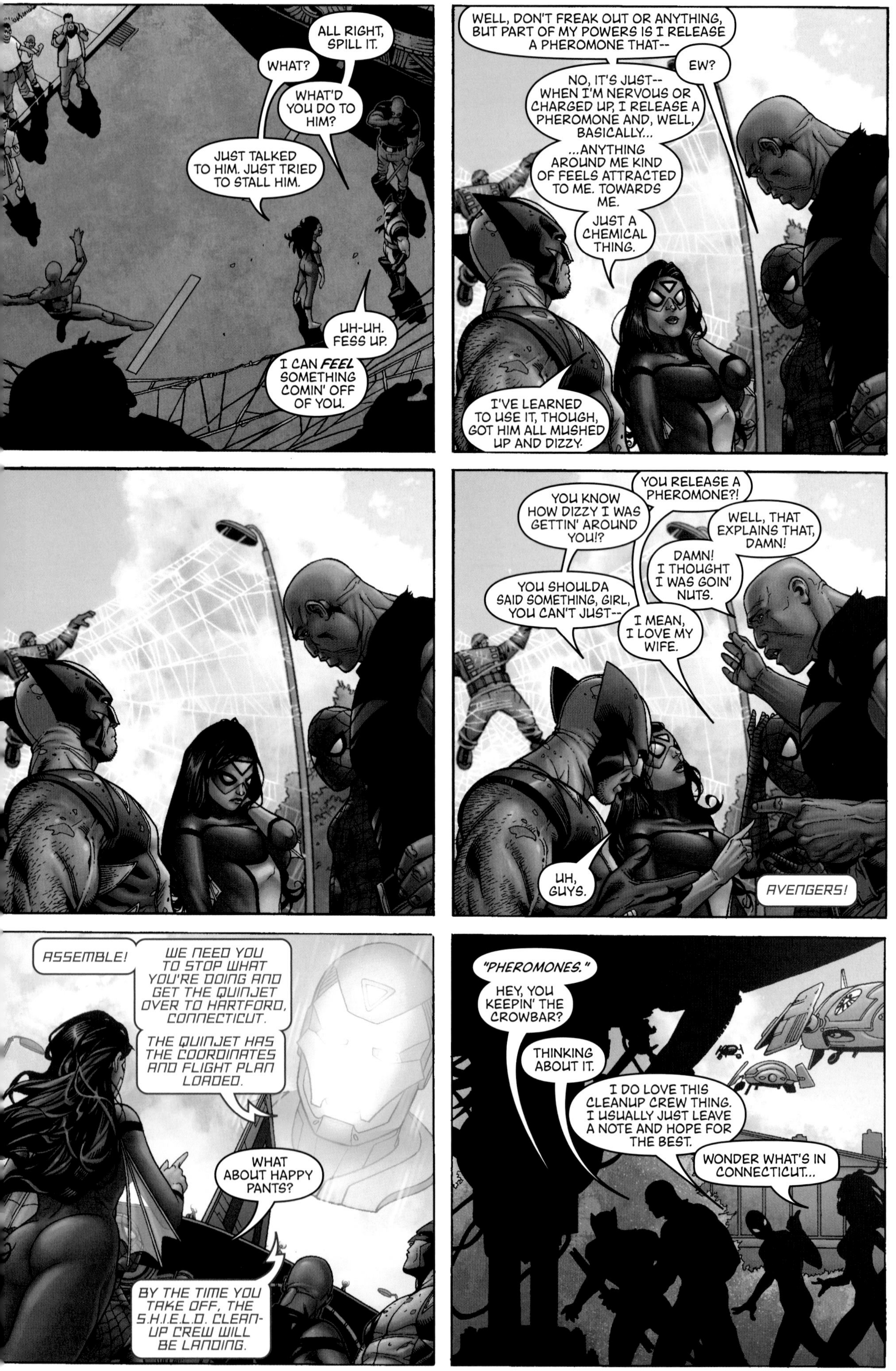
ALL RIGHT, SPILL IT.
WHAT?
WHAT'D YOU DO TO HIM?
JUST TALKED TO HIM. JUST TRIED TO STALL HIM.
UH-UH. FESS UP.
I CAN *FEEL* SOMETHING COMIN' OFF OF YOU.
WELL, DON'T FREAK OUT OR ANYTHING, BUT PART OF MY POWERS IS I RELEASE A PHEROMONE THAT--
EW?
NO, IT'S JUST-- WHEN I'M NERVOUS OR CHARGED UP, I RELEASE A PHEROMONE AND, WELL, BASICALLY...
...ANYTHING AROUND ME KIND OF FEELS ATTRACTED TO ME. TOWARDS ME.
JUST A CHEMICAL THING.
I'VE LEARNED TO USE IT, THOUGH, GOT HIM ALL MUSHED UP AND DIZZY.
YOU RELEASE A PHEROMONE?!
YOU KNOW HOW DIZZY I WAS GETTIN' AROUND YOU!?
WELL, THAT EXPLAINS THAT, DAMN!
DAMN! I THOUGHT I WAS GOIN' NUTS.
YOU SHOULDA SAID SOMETHING, GIRL, YOU CAN'T JUST--
I MEAN, I LOVE MY WIFE.
UH, GUYS.
AVENGERS!
ASSEMBLE!
WE NEED YOU TO STOP WHAT YOU'RE DOING AND GET THE QUINJET OVER TO HARTFORD, CONNECTICUT.
THE QUINJET HAS THE COORDINATES AND FLIGHT PLAN LOADED.
WHAT ABOUT HAPPY PANTS?
BY THE TIME YOU TAKE OFF, THE S.H.I.E.L.D. CLEAN-UP CREW WILL BE LANDING.
"PHEROMONES."
HEY, YOU KEEPIN' THE CROWBAR?
THINKING ABOUT IT.
I DO LOVE THIS CLEANUP CREW THING. I USUALLY JUST LEAVE A NOTE AND HOPE FOR THE BEST.
WONDER WHAT'S IN CONNECTICUT...

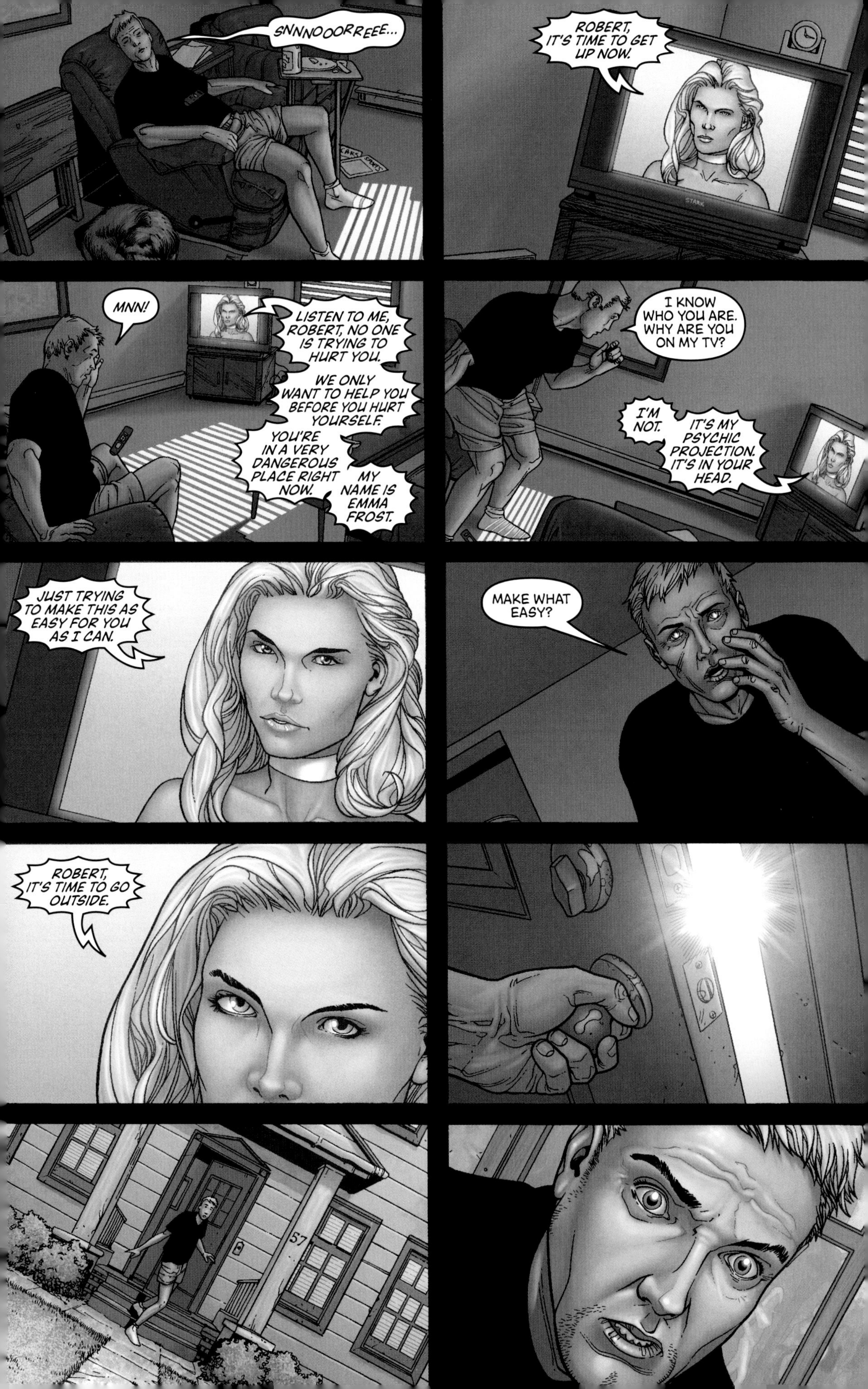
SNNNOOORREEE...
ROBERT, IT'S TIME TO GET UP NOW.
MNN!
LISTEN TO ME, ROBERT, NO ONE IS TRYING TO HURT YOU.
WE ONLY WANT TO HELP YOU BEFORE YOU HURT YOURSELF.
YOU'RE IN A VERY DANGEROUS PLACE RIGHT NOW.
MY NAME IS EMMA FROST.
I KNOW WHO YOU ARE. WHY ARE YOU ON MY TV?
I'M NOT.
IT'S MY PSYCHIC PROJECTION. IT'S IN YOUR HEAD.
JUST TRYING TO MAKE THIS AS EASY FOR YOU AS I CAN.
MAKE WHAT EASY?
ROBERT, IT'S TIME TO GO OUTSIDE.
57

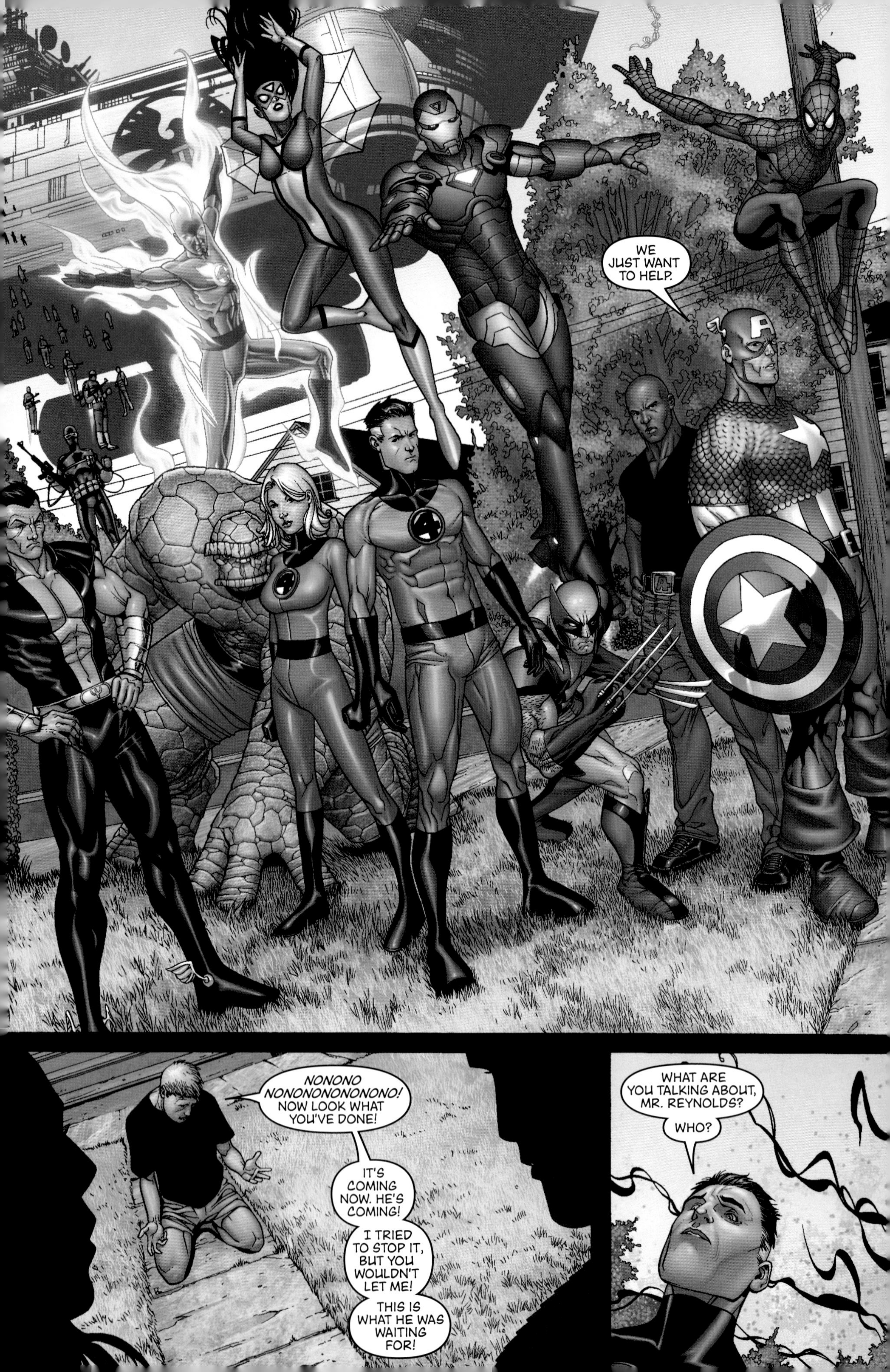
WE JUST WANT TO HELP.
NONONO NONONONONONONO! NOW LOOK WHAT YOU'VE DONE!
IT'S COMING NOW. HE'S COMING!
I TRIED TO STOP IT, BUT YOU WOULDN'T LET ME!
THIS IS WHAT HE WAS WAITING FOR!
WHAT ARE YOU TALKING ABOUT, MR. REYNOLDS?
WHO?

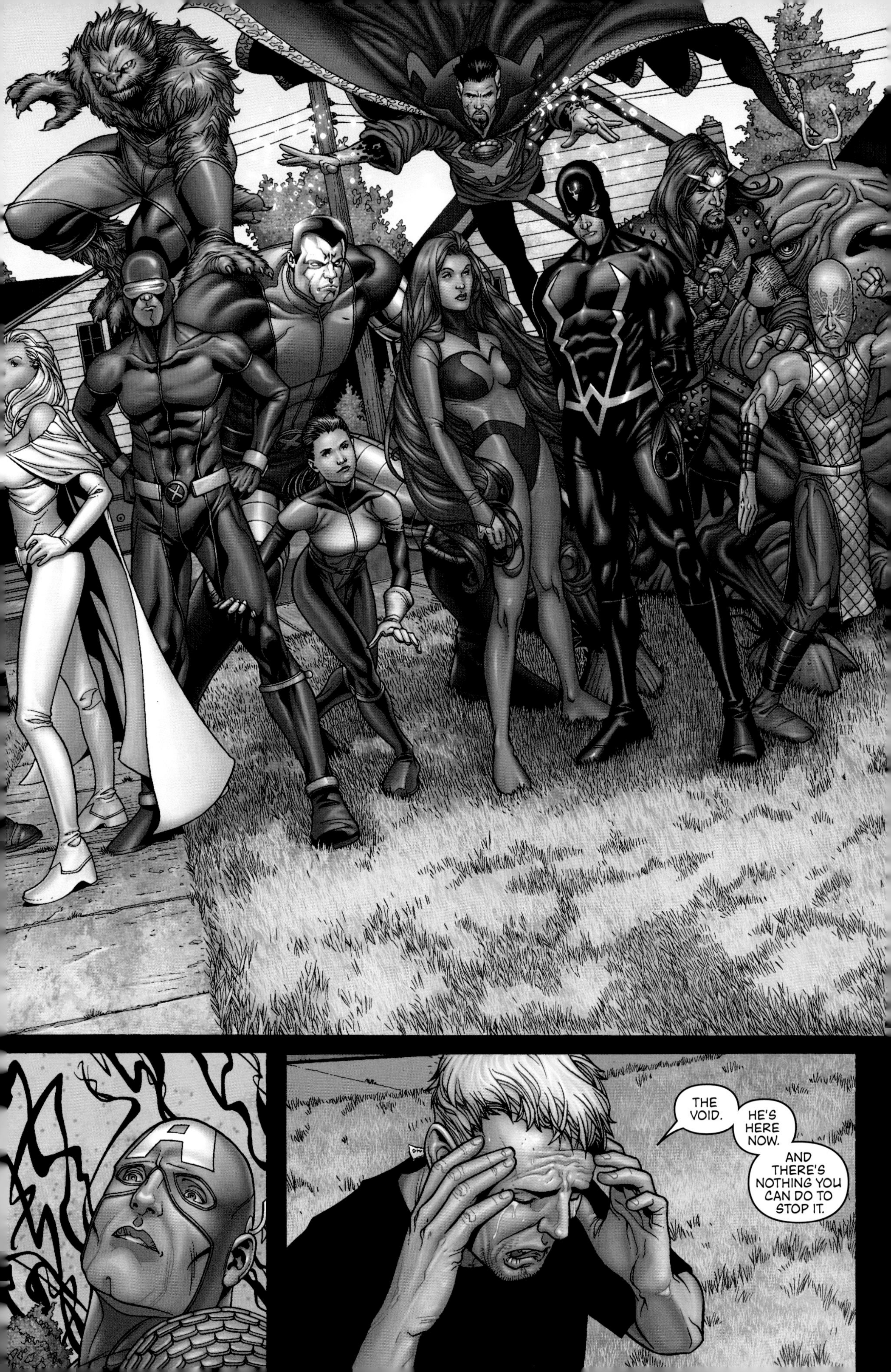
THE VOID.
HE'S HERE NOW.
AND THERE'S NOTHING YOU CAN DO TO STOP IT.

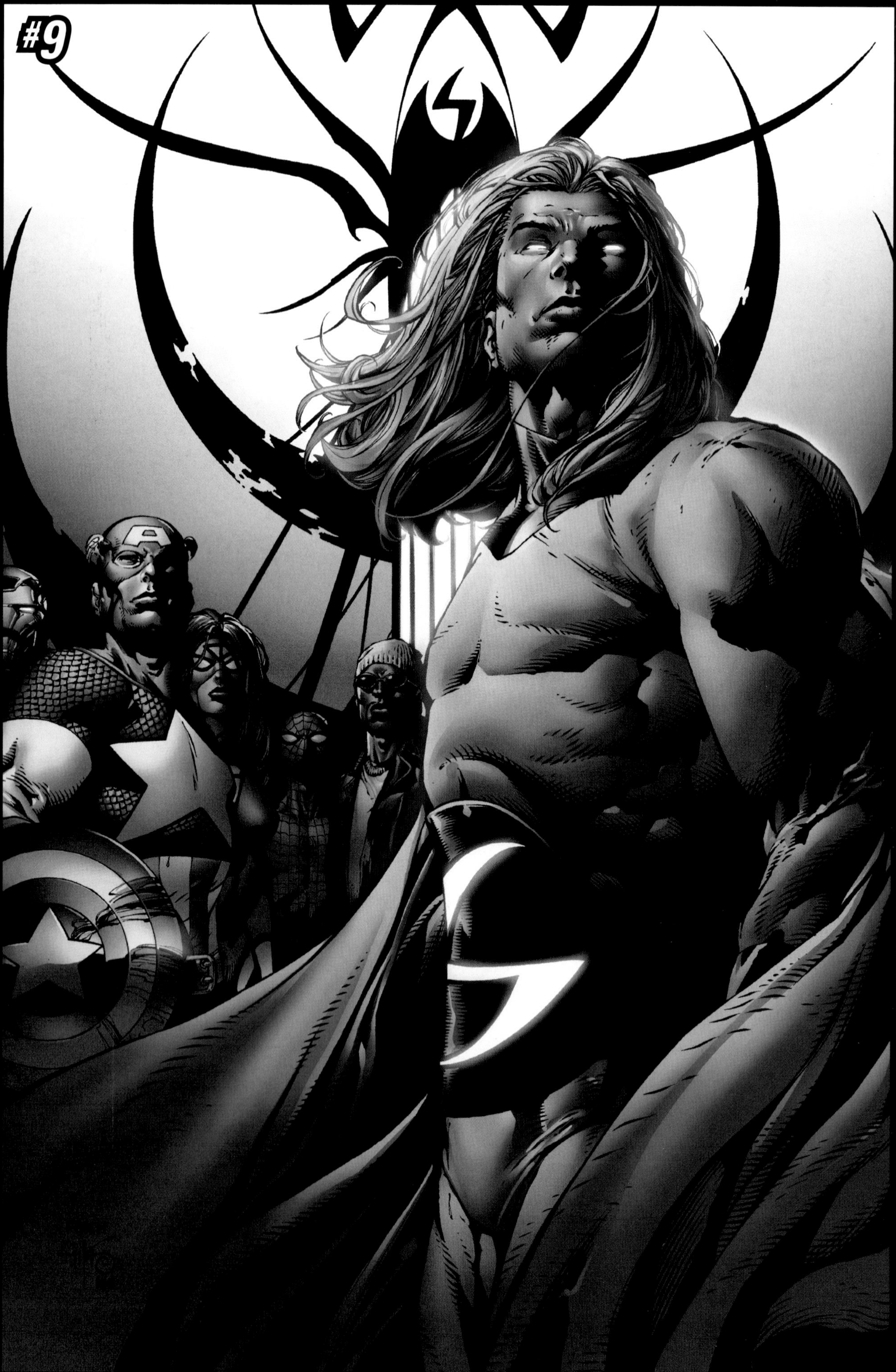
#9

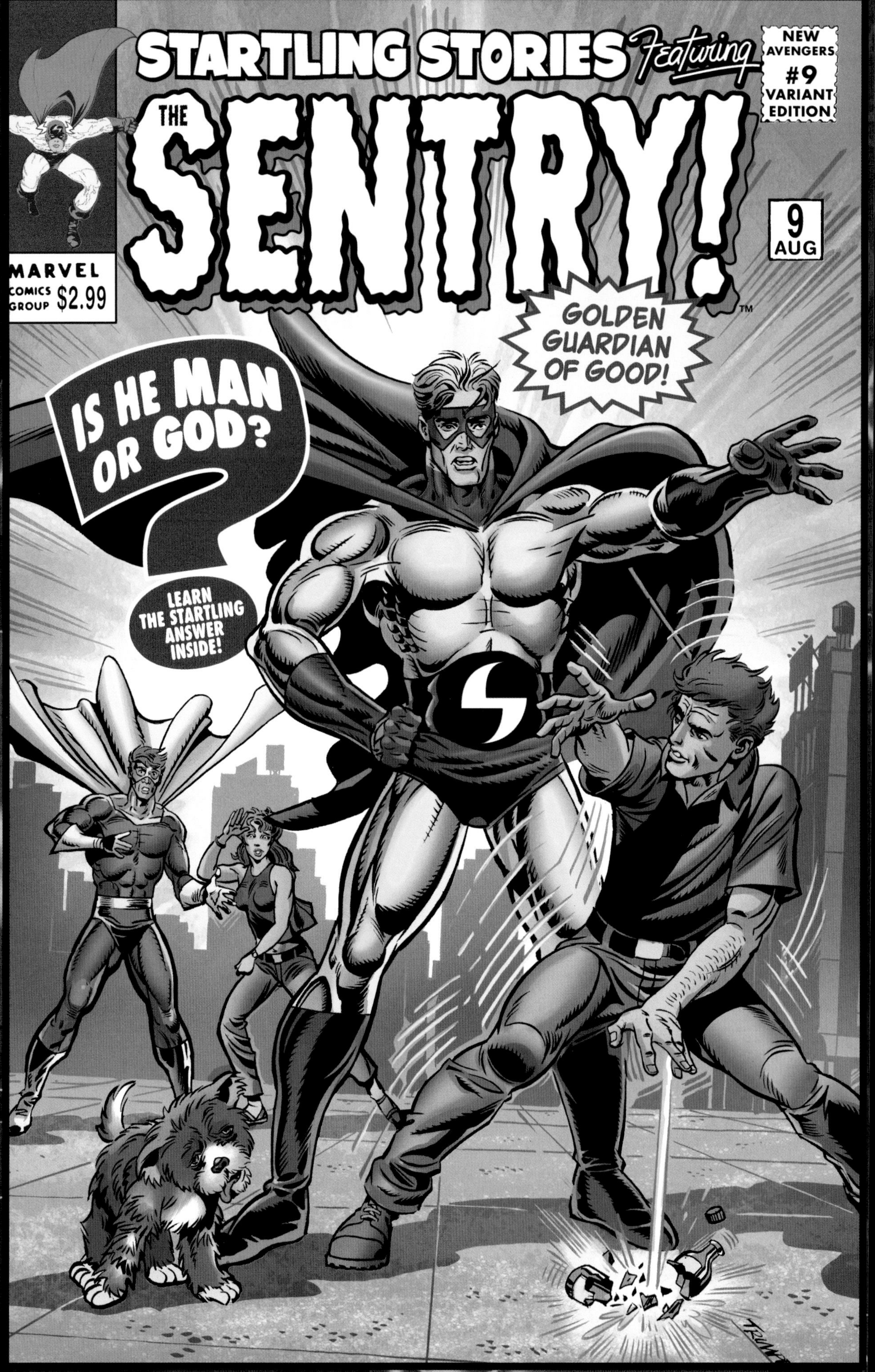
STARTLING STORIES Featuring
THE
SENTRY!
NEW AVENGERS #9 VARIANT EDITION
9
AUG
MARVEL
COMICS GROUP $2.99
GOLDEN GUARDIAN OF GOOD!
IS HE MAN OR GOD?
LEARN THE STARTLING ANSWER INSIDE!

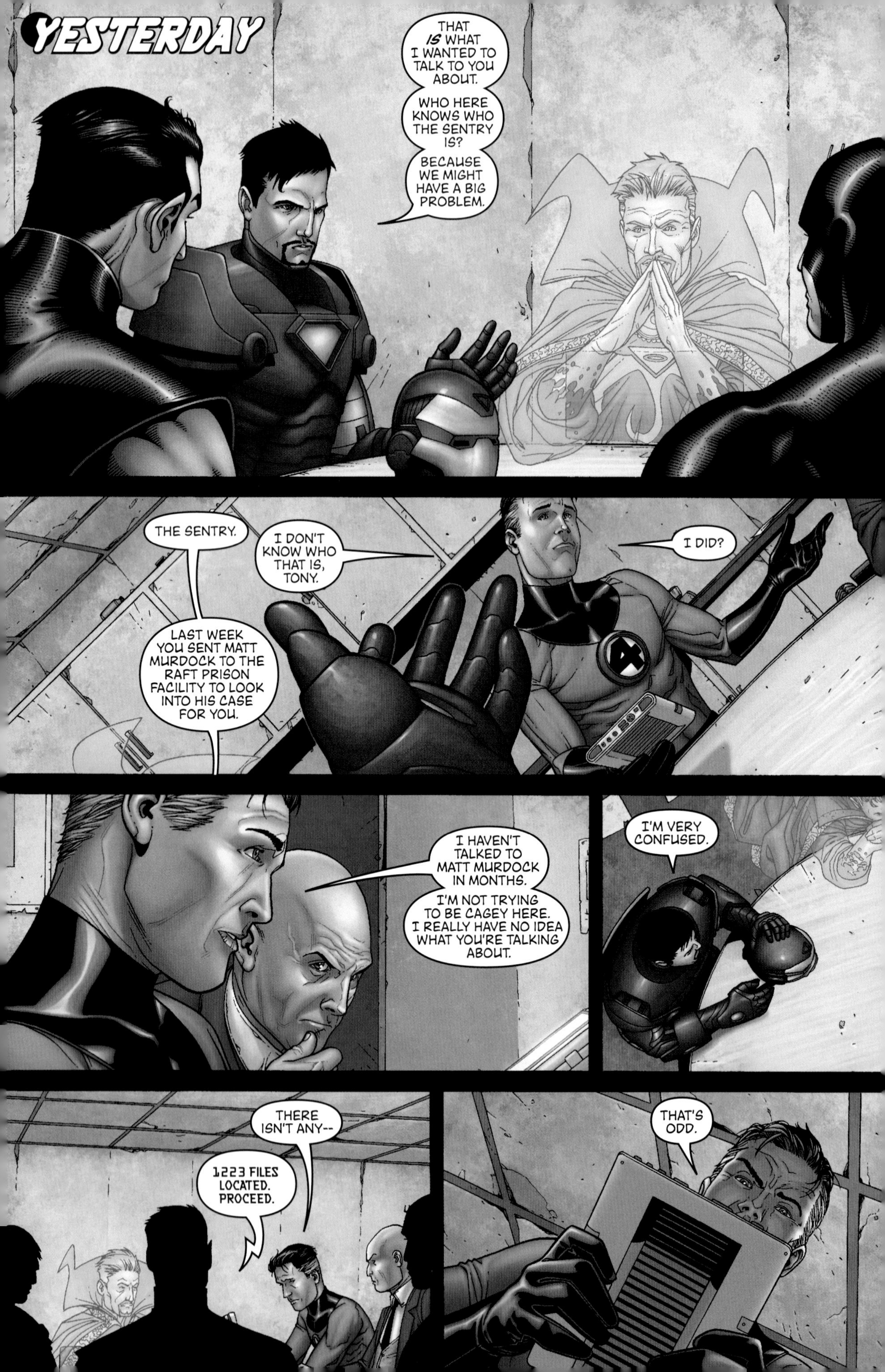
YESTERDAY
THAT *IS* WHAT I WANTED TO TALK TO YOU ABOUT.
WHO HERE KNOWS WHO THE SENTRY IS?
BECAUSE WE MIGHT HAVE A BIG PROBLEM.
THE SENTRY.
I DON'T KNOW WHO THAT IS, TONY.
LAST WEEK YOU SENT MATT MURDOCK TO THE RAFT PRISON FACILITY TO LOOK INTO HIS CASE FOR YOU.
I DID?
I HAVEN'T TALKED TO MATT MURDOCK IN MONTHS.
I'M NOT TRYING TO BE CAGEY HERE. I REALLY HAVE NO IDEA WHAT YOU'RE TALKING ABOUT.
I'M VERY CONFUSED.
THERE ISN'T ANY--
1223 FILES LOCATED. PROCEED.
THAT'S ODD.

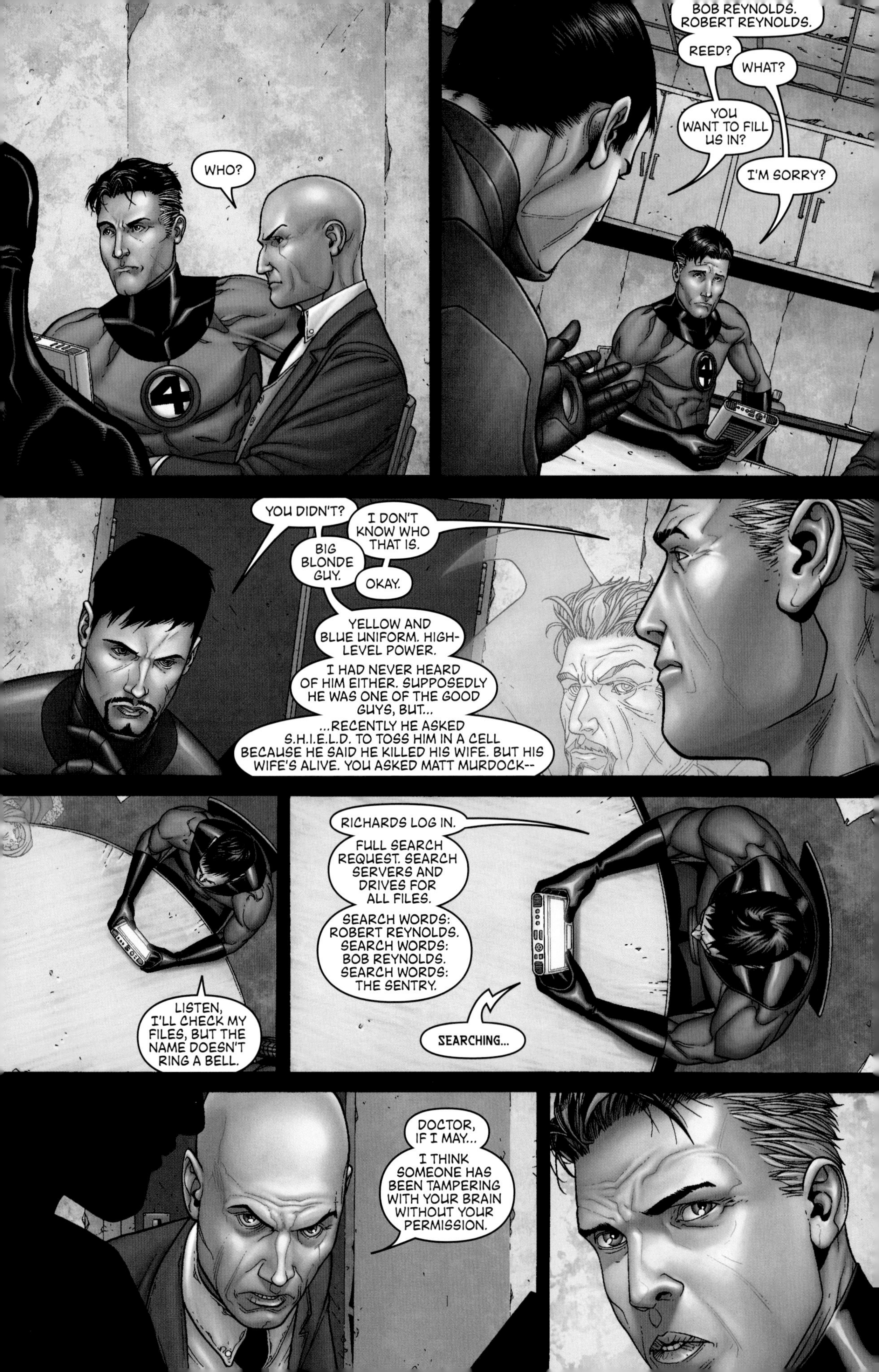
WHO?
BOB REYNOLDS. ROBERT REYNOLDS.
REED?
WHAT?
YOU WANT TO FILL US IN?
I'M SORRY?
YOU DIDN'T?
I DON'T KNOW WHO THAT IS.
BIG BLONDE GUY.
OKAY.
YELLOW AND BLUE UNIFORM. HIGH-LEVEL POWER.
I HAD NEVER HEARD OF HIM EITHER. SUPPOSEDLY HE WAS ONE OF THE GOOD GUYS, BUT...
...RECENTLY HE ASKED S.H.I.E.L.D. TO TOSS HIM IN A CELL BECAUSE HE SAID HE KILLED HIS WIFE. BUT HIS WIFE'S ALIVE. YOU ASKED MATT MURDOCK--
LISTEN, I'LL CHECK MY FILES, BUT THE NAME DOESN'T RING A BELL.
RICHARDS LOG IN.
FULL SEARCH REQUEST. SEARCH SERVERS AND DRIVES FOR ALL FILES.
SEARCH WORDS: ROBERT REYNOLDS. SEARCH WORDS: BOB REYNOLDS. SEARCH WORDS: THE SENTRY.
SEARCHING...
DOCTOR, IF I MAY...
I THINK SOMEONE HAS BEEN TAMPERING WITH YOUR BRAIN WITHOUT YOUR PERMISSION.

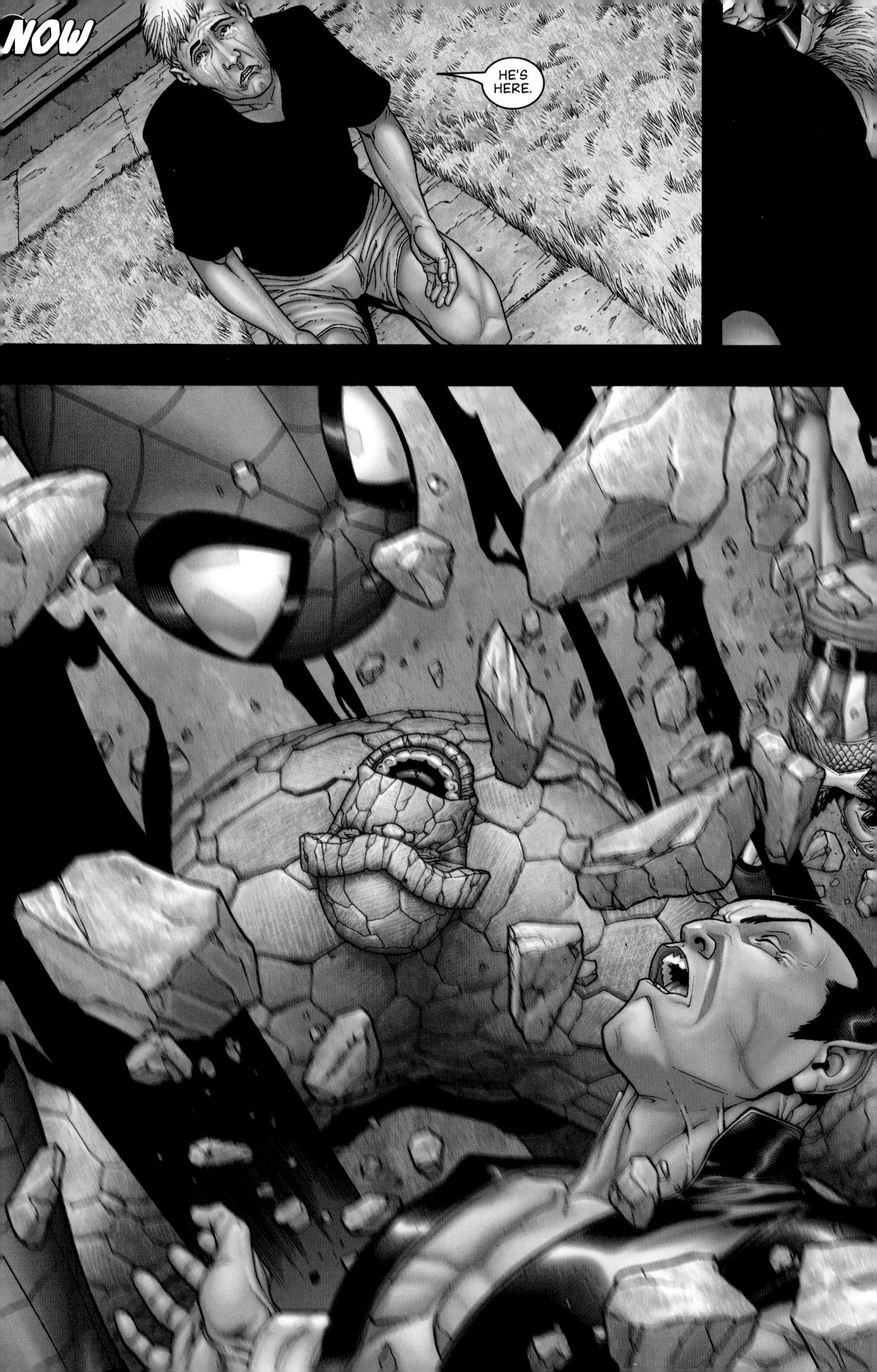
NOW
HE'S HERE.

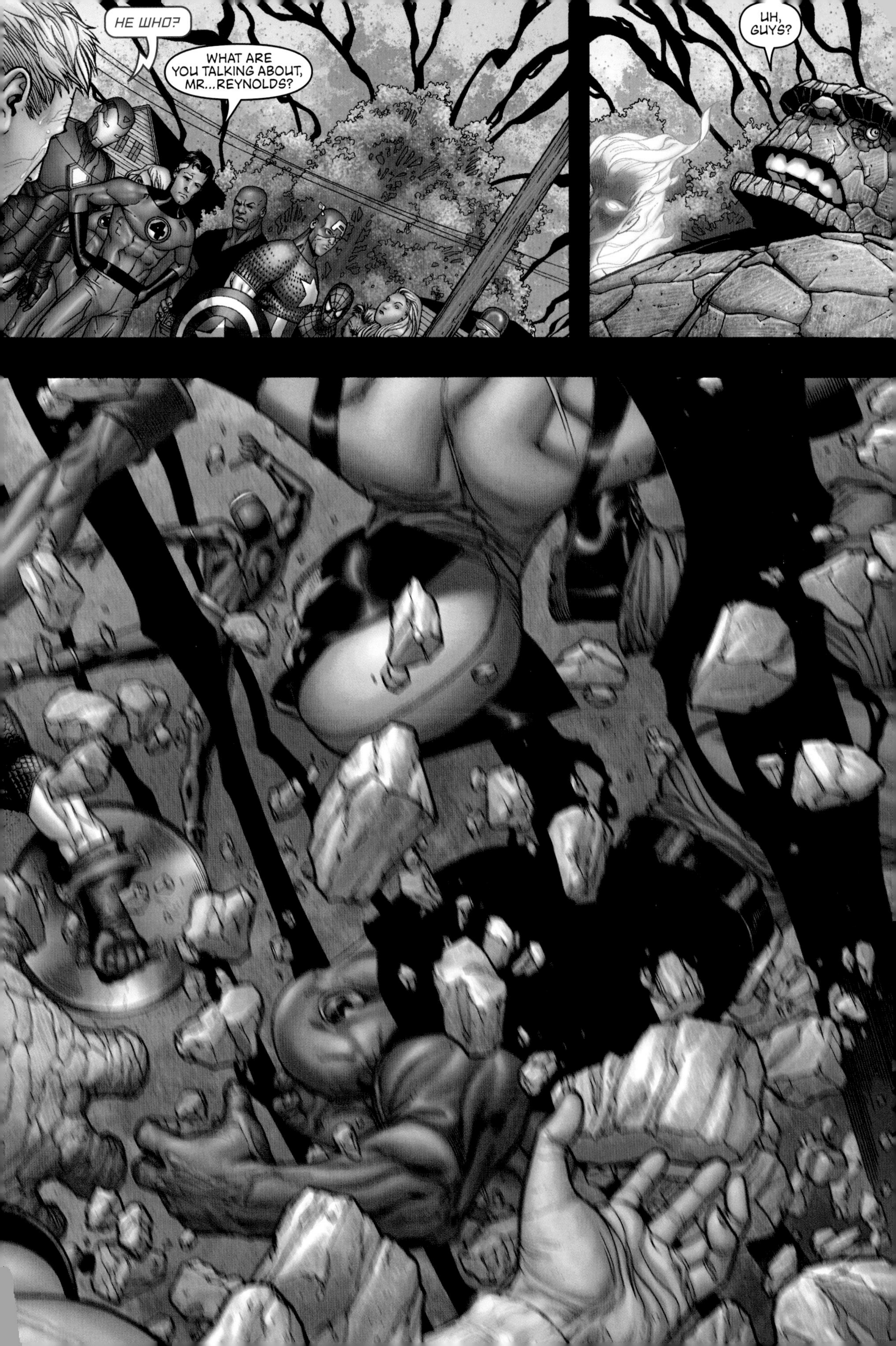
HE WHO?
WHAT ARE YOU TALKING ABOUT, MR...REYNOLDS?
UH, GUYS?

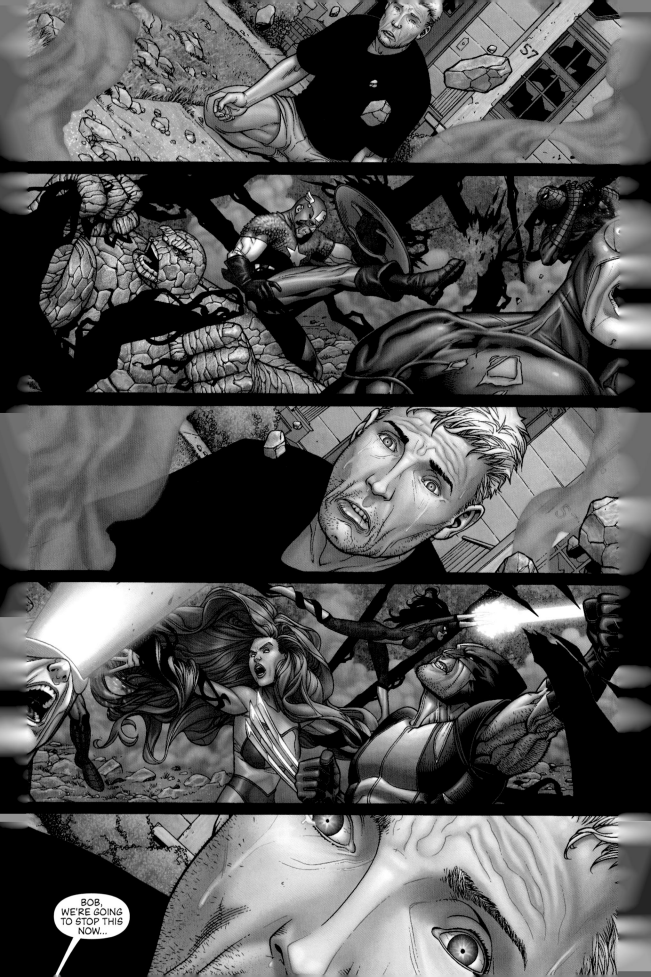

BOB, WE'RE GOING TO STOP THIS NOW...

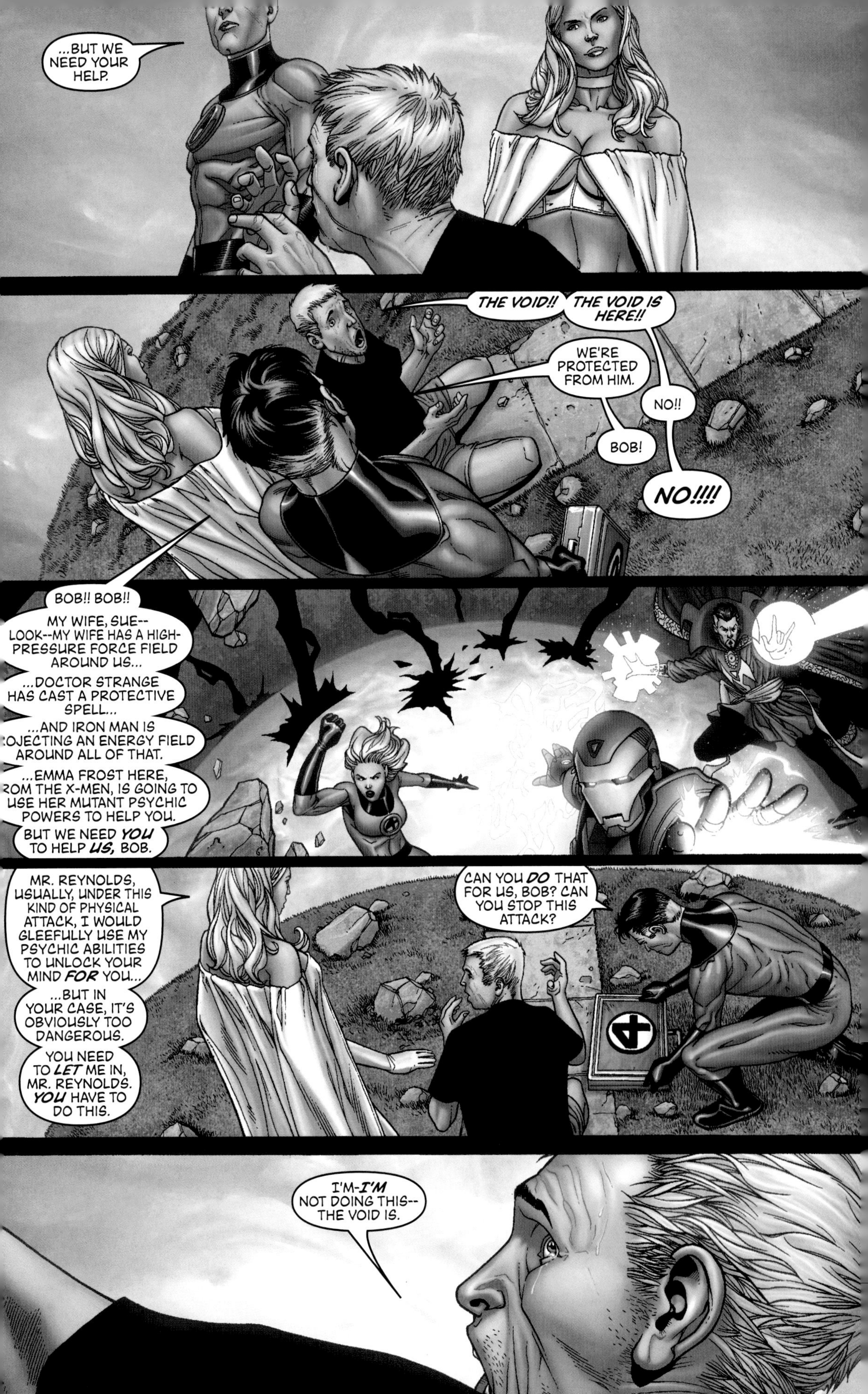
...BUT WE NEED YOUR HELP.
THE VOID!!
THE VOID IS HERE!!
WE'RE PROTECTED FROM HIM.
NO!!
BOB!
NO!!!!
BOB!! BOB!!
MY WIFE, SUE--
LOOK--MY WIFE HAS A HIGH-PRESSURE FORCE FIELD AROUND US...
...DOCTOR STRANGE HAS CAST A PROTECTIVE SPELL...
...AND IRON MAN IS ROJECTING AN ENERGY FIELD AROUND ALL OF THAT.
...EMMA FROST HERE, ROM THE X-MEN, IS GOING TO USE HER MUTANT PSYCHIC POWERS TO HELP YOU.
BUT WE NEED *YOU* TO HELP *US,* BOB.
MR. REYNOLDS, USUALLY, UNDER THIS KIND OF PHYSICAL ATTACK, I WOULD GLEEFULLY USE MY PSYCHIC ABILITIES TO UNLOCK YOUR MIND *FOR* YOU...
...BUT IN YOUR CASE, IT'S OBVIOUSLY TOO DANGEROUS.
YOU NEED TO *LET* ME IN, MR. REYNOLDS. *YOU* HAVE TO DO THIS.
CAN YOU *DO* THAT FOR US, BOB? CAN YOU STOP THIS ATTACK?
I'M-*I'M* NOT DOING THIS-- THE VOID IS.

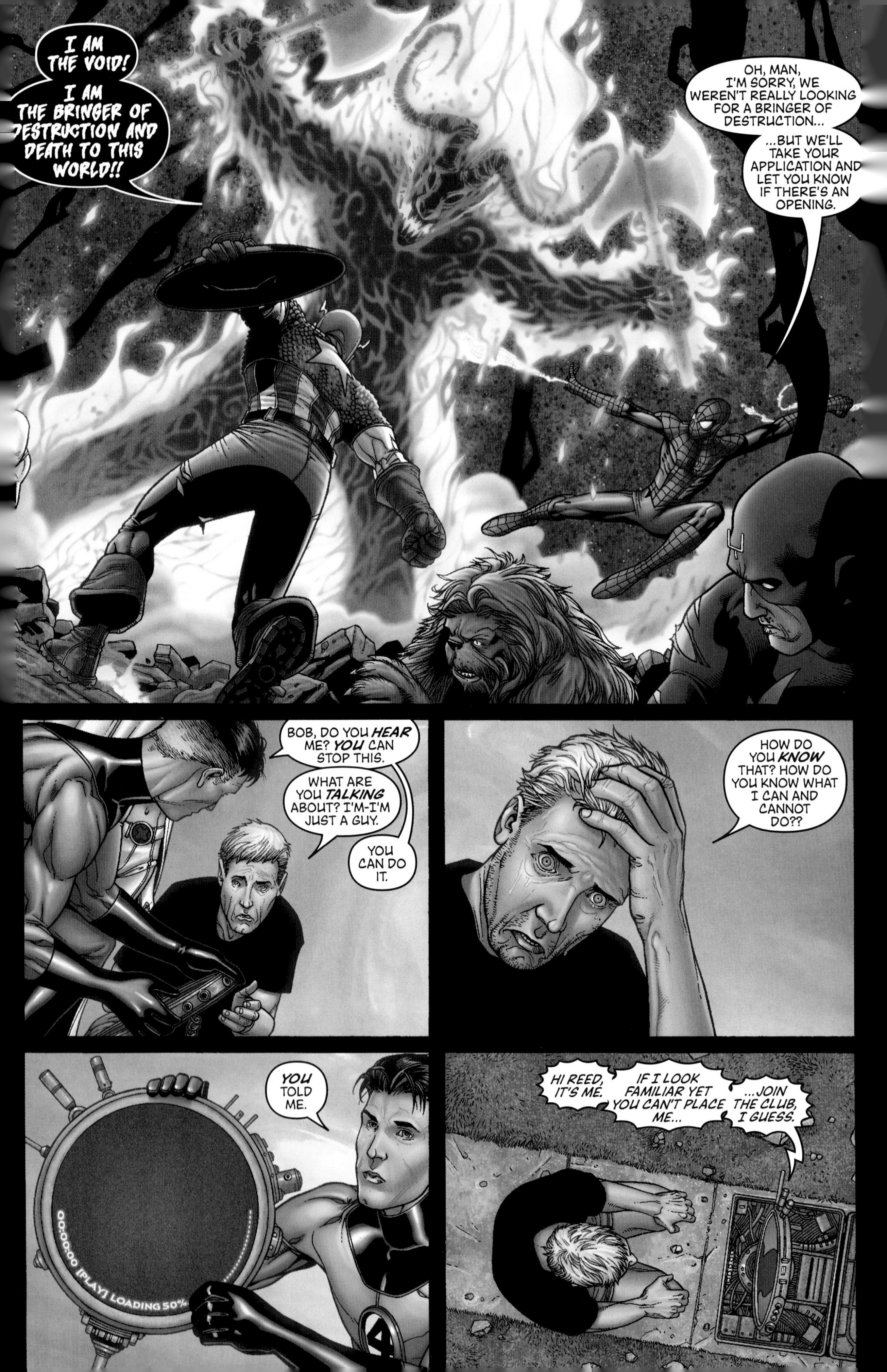
I AM THE VOID!
I AM THE BRINGER OF DESTRUCTION AND DEATH TO THIS WORLD!!
OH, MAN, I'M SORRY, WE WEREN'T REALLY LOOKING FOR A BRINGER OF DESTRUCTION...
...BUT WE'LL TAKE YOUR APPLICATION AND LET YOU KNOW IF THERE'S AN OPENING.
BOB, DO YOU HEAR ME? YOU CAN STOP THIS.
WHAT ARE YOU TALKING ABOUT? I'M-I'M JUST A GUY.
YOU CAN DO IT.
HOW DO YOU KNOW THAT? HOW DO YOU KNOW WHAT I CAN AND CANNOT DO??
YOU TOLD ME.
00:00:00 [PLAY] LOADING 50%
HI REED, IT'S ME.
IF I LOOK FAMILIAR YET YOU CAN'T PLACE ME...
...JOIN THE CLUB, I GUESS.

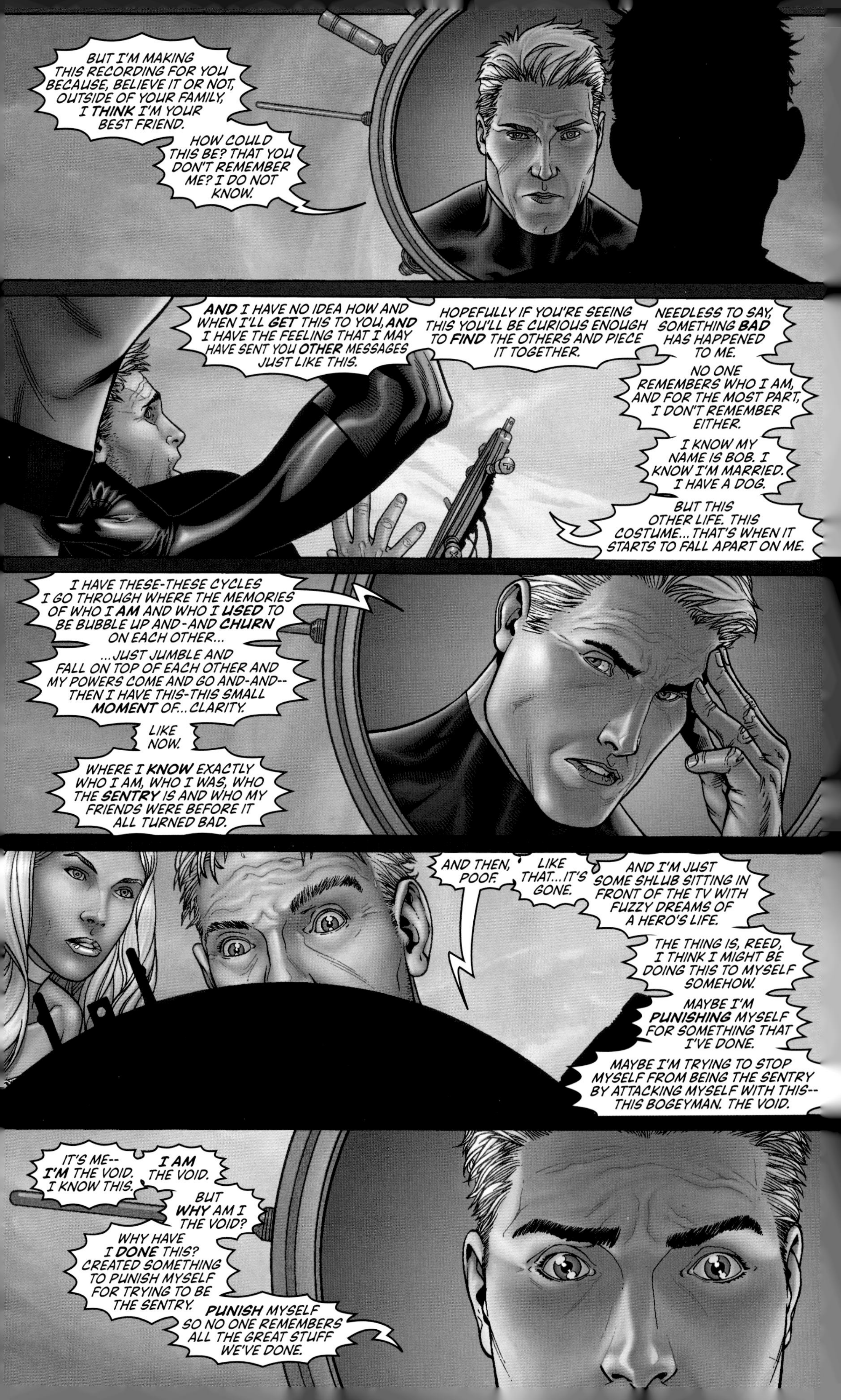
BUT I'M MAKING THIS RECORDING FOR YOU BECAUSE, BELIEVE IT OR NOT, OUTSIDE OF YOUR FAMILY, I **THINK** I'M YOUR BEST FRIEND.
HOW COULD THIS BE? THAT YOU DON'T REMEMBER ME? I DO NOT KNOW.
AND I HAVE NO IDEA HOW AND WHEN I'LL **GET** THIS TO YOU, **AND** I HAVE THE FEELING THAT I MAY HAVE SENT YOU **OTHER** MESSAGES JUST LIKE THIS.
HOPEFULLY IF YOU'RE SEEING THIS YOU'LL BE CURIOUS ENOUGH TO **FIND** THE OTHERS AND PIECE IT TOGETHER.
NEEDLESS TO SAY, SOMETHING **BAD** HAS HAPPENED TO ME.
NO ONE REMEMBERS WHO I AM, AND FOR THE MOST PART, I DON'T REMEMBER EITHER.
I KNOW MY NAME IS BOB. I KNOW I'M MARRIED. I HAVE A DOG.
BUT THIS OTHER LIFE. THIS COSTUME... THAT'S WHEN IT STARTS TO FALL APART ON ME.
I HAVE THESE-THESE CYCLES I GO THROUGH WHERE THE MEMORIES OF WHO I **AM** AND WHO I **USED** TO BE BUBBLE UP AND-AND **CHURN** ON EACH OTHER...
...JUST JUMBLE AND FALL ON TOP OF EACH OTHER AND MY POWERS COME AND GO AND-AND-- THEN I HAVE THIS-THIS SMALL **MOMENT** OF... CLARITY.
LIKE NOW.
WHERE I **KNOW** EXACTLY WHO I AM, WHO I WAS, WHO THE **SENTRY** IS AND WHO MY FRIENDS WERE BEFORE IT ALL TURNED BAD.
AND THEN, POOF.
LIKE THAT... IT'S GONE.
AND I'M JUST SOME SHLUB SITTING IN FRONT OF THE TV WITH FUZZY DREAMS OF A HERO'S LIFE.
THE THING IS, REED, I THINK I MIGHT BE DOING THIS TO MYSELF SOMEHOW.
MAYBE I'M **PUNISHING** MYSELF FOR SOMETHING THAT I'VE DONE.
MAYBE I'M TRYING TO STOP MYSELF FROM BEING THE SENTRY BY ATTACKING MYSELF WITH THIS-- THIS BOGEYMAN. THE VOID.
IT'S ME-- **I'M** THE VOID. I KNOW THIS.
I AM THE VOID.
BUT **WHY** AM I THE VOID?
WHY HAVE I **DONE** THIS? CREATED SOMETHING TO PUNISH MYSELF FOR TRYING TO BE THE SENTRY.
PUNISH MYSELF SO NO ONE REMEMBERS ALL THE GREAT STUFF WE'VE DONE.

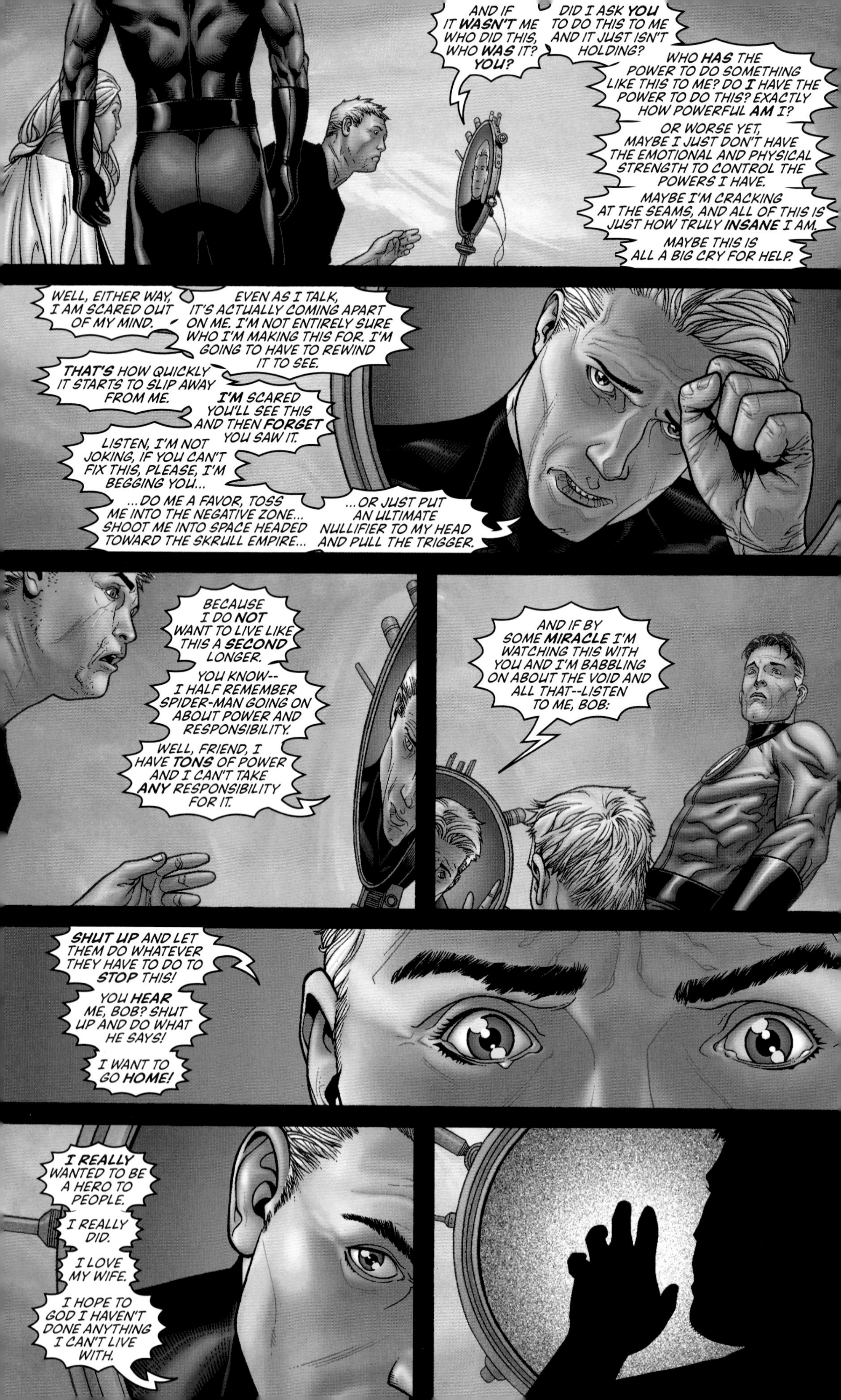
AND IF IT WASN'T ME WHO DID THIS, WHO WAS IT? YOU?
DID I ASK YOU TO DO THIS TO ME AND IT JUST ISN'T HOLDING?
WHO HAS THE POWER TO DO SOMETHING LIKE THIS TO ME? DO I HAVE THE POWER TO DO THIS? EXACTLY HOW POWERFUL AM I?
OR WORSE YET, MAYBE I JUST DON'T HAVE THE EMOTIONAL AND PHYSICAL STRENGTH TO CONTROL THE POWERS I HAVE.
MAYBE I'M CRACKING AT THE SEAMS, AND ALL OF THIS IS JUST HOW TRULY INSANE I AM.
MAYBE THIS IS ALL A BIG CRY FOR HELP.
WELL, EITHER WAY, I AM SCARED OUT OF MY MIND.
EVEN AS I TALK, IT'S ACTUALLY COMING APART ON ME. I'M NOT ENTIRELY SURE WHO I'M MAKING THIS FOR. I'M GOING TO HAVE TO REWIND IT TO SEE.
THAT'S HOW QUICKLY IT STARTS TO SLIP AWAY FROM ME.
I'M SCARED YOU'LL SEE THIS AND THEN FORGET YOU SAW IT.
LISTEN, I'M NOT JOKING, IF YOU CAN'T FIX THIS, PLEASE, I'M BEGGING YOU...
...DO ME A FAVOR, TOSS ME INTO THE NEGATIVE ZONE... SHOOT ME INTO SPACE HEADED TOWARD THE SKRULL EMPIRE...
...OR JUST PUT AN ULTIMATE NULLIFIER TO MY HEAD AND PULL THE TRIGGER.
BECAUSE I DO NOT WANT TO LIVE LIKE THIS A SECOND LONGER.
YOU KNOW-- I HALF REMEMBER SPIDER-MAN GOING ON ABOUT POWER AND RESPONSIBILITY.
WELL, FRIEND, I HAVE TONS OF POWER AND I CAN'T TAKE ANY RESPONSIBILITY FOR IT.
AND IF BY SOME MIRACLE I'M WATCHING THIS WITH YOU AND I'M BABBLING ON ABOUT THE VOID AND ALL THAT--LISTEN TO ME, BOB:
SHUT UP AND LET THEM DO WHATEVER THEY HAVE TO DO TO STOP THIS!
YOU HEAR ME, BOB? SHUT UP AND DO WHAT HE SAYS!
I WANT TO GO HOME!
I REALLY WANTED TO BE A HERO TO PEOPLE.
I REALLY DID.
I LOVE MY WIFE.
I HOPE TO GOD I HAVEN'T DONE ANYTHING I CAN'T LIVE WITH.

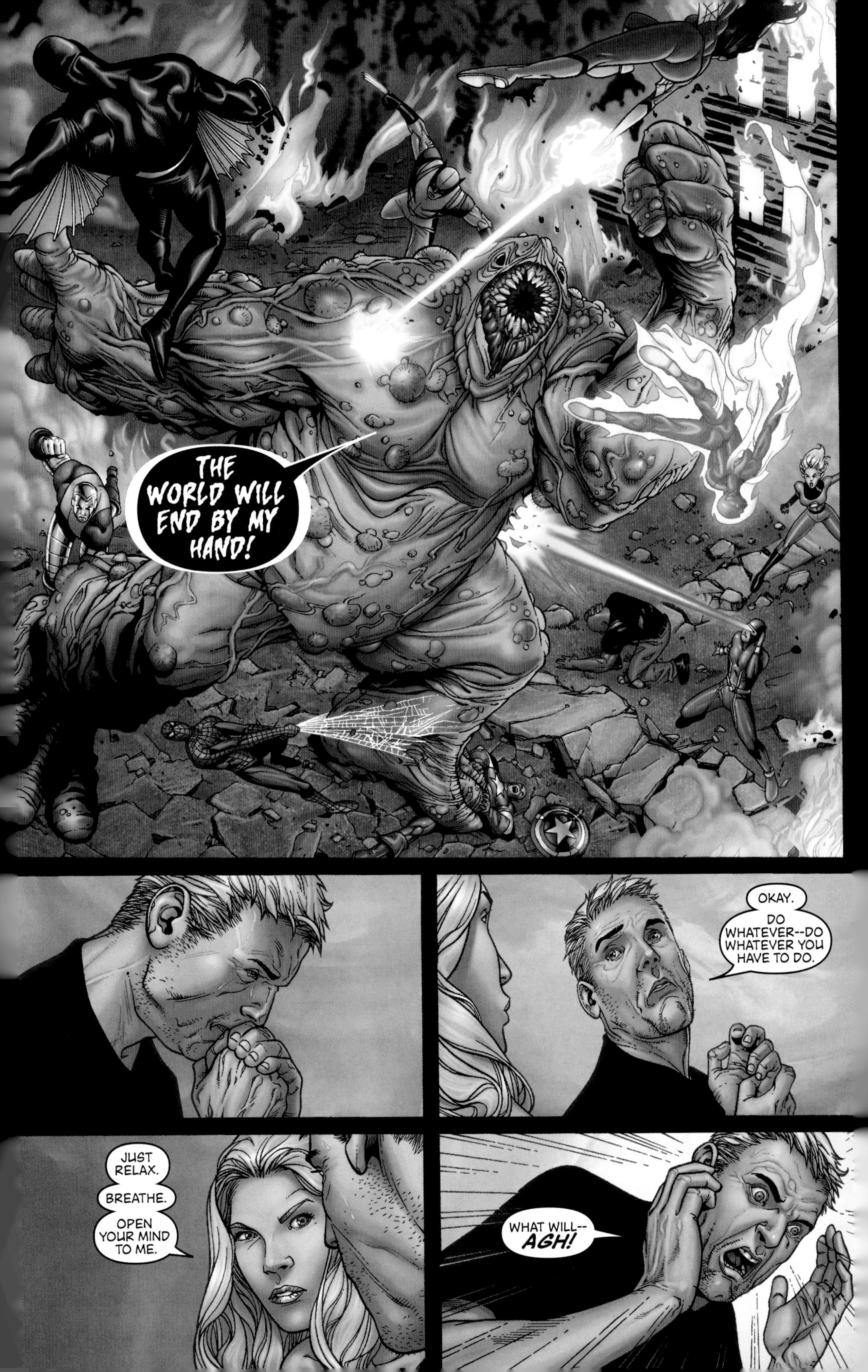
THE WORLD WILL END BY MY HAND!
OKAY.
DO WHATEVER--DO WHATEVER YOU HAVE TO DO.
JUST RELAX.
BREATHE.
OPEN YOUR MIND TO ME.
WHAT WILL-- AGH!

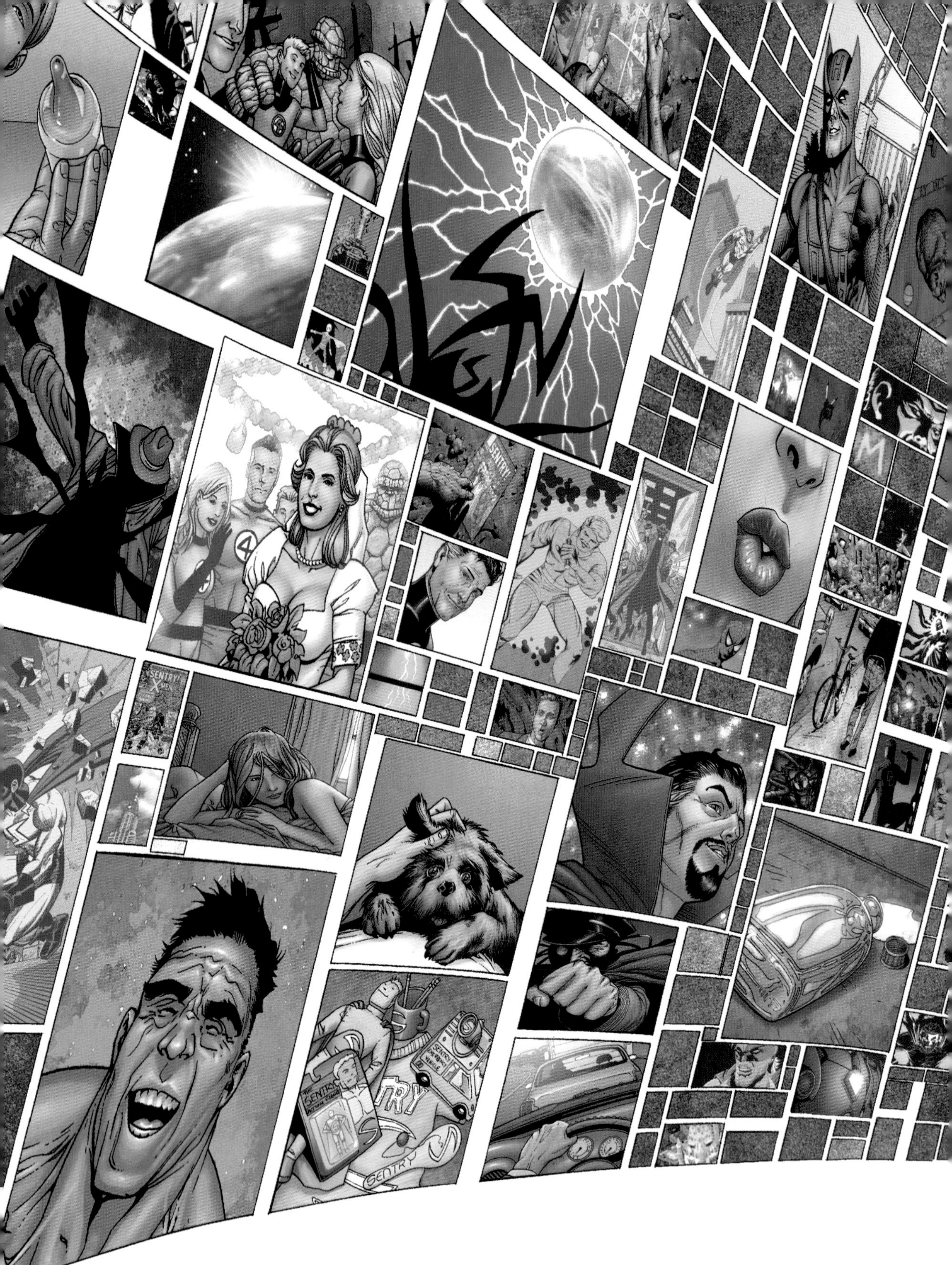
SENTRY!
SENTRY!
X-MEN
THE SENTRY ACTION FIGURE
SENTRY EMERGENCY VEHICLE
TRY
SENTRY

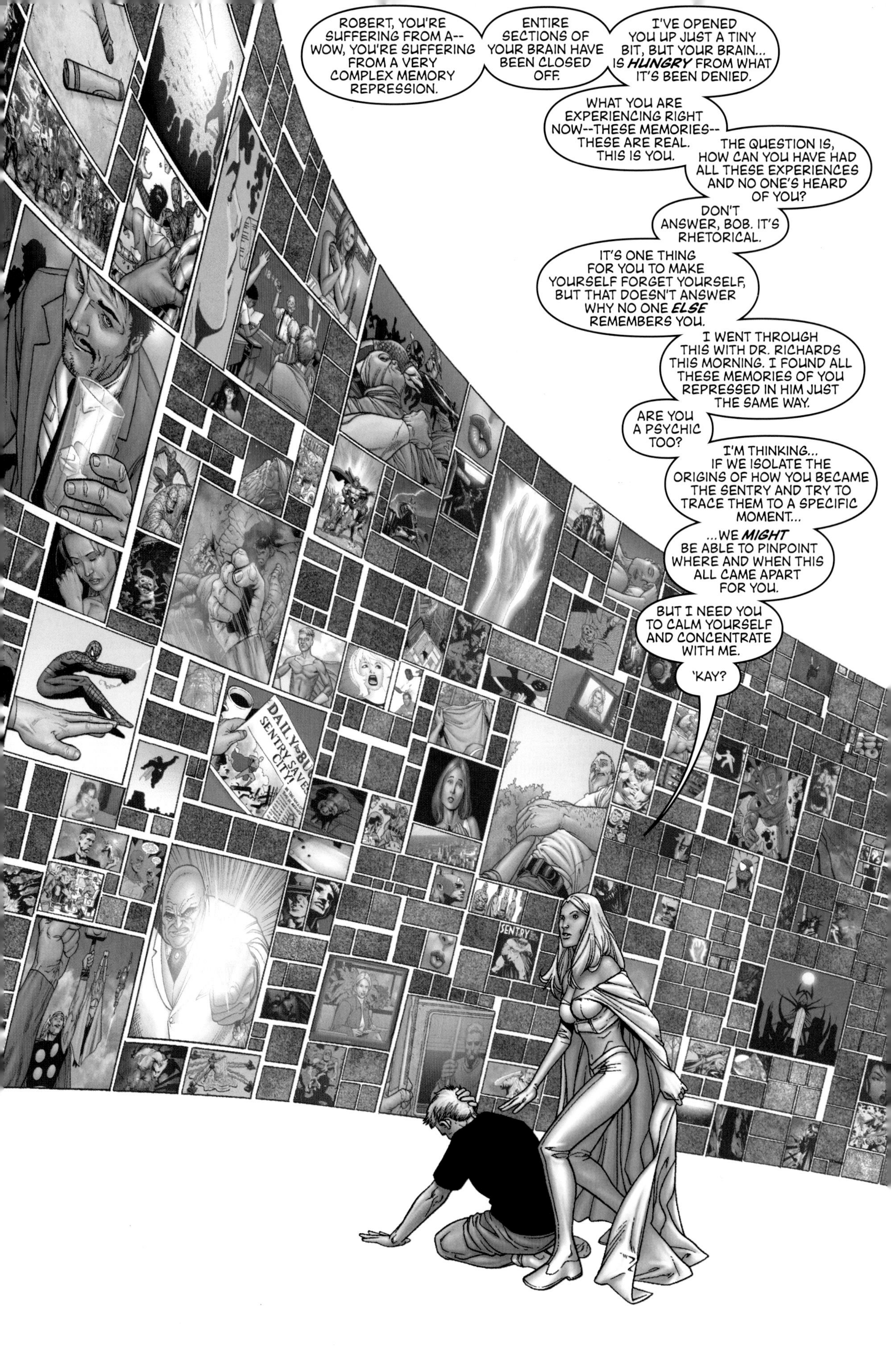
ROBERT, YOU'RE SUFFERING FROM A-- WOW, YOU'RE SUFFERING FROM A VERY COMPLEX MEMORY REPRESSION.
ENTIRE SECTIONS OF YOUR BRAIN HAVE BEEN CLOSED OFF.
I'VE OPENED YOU UP JUST A TINY BIT, BUT YOUR BRAIN... IS *HUNGRY* FROM WHAT IT'S BEEN DENIED.
WHAT YOU ARE EXPERIENCING RIGHT NOW--THESE MEMORIES-- THESE ARE REAL. THIS IS YOU.
THE QUESTION IS, HOW CAN YOU HAVE HAD ALL THESE EXPERIENCES AND NO ONE'S HEARD OF YOU?
DON'T ANSWER, BOB. IT'S RHETORICAL.
IT'S ONE THING FOR YOU TO MAKE YOURSELF FORGET YOURSELF, BUT THAT DOESN'T ANSWER WHY NO ONE *ELSE* REMEMBERS YOU.
I WENT THROUGH THIS WITH DR. RICHARDS THIS MORNING. I FOUND ALL THESE MEMORIES OF YOU REPRESSED IN HIM JUST THE SAME WAY.
ARE YOU A PSYCHIC TOO?
I'M THINKING... IF WE ISOLATE THE ORIGINS OF HOW YOU BECAME THE SENTRY AND TRY TO TRACE THEM TO A SPECIFIC MOMENT...
...WE *MIGHT* BE ABLE TO PINPOINT WHERE AND WHEN THIS ALL CAME APART FOR YOU.
BUT I NEED YOU TO CALM YOURSELF AND CONCENTRATE WITH ME.
'KAY?
SENTRY SAVES CITY!
SENTRY

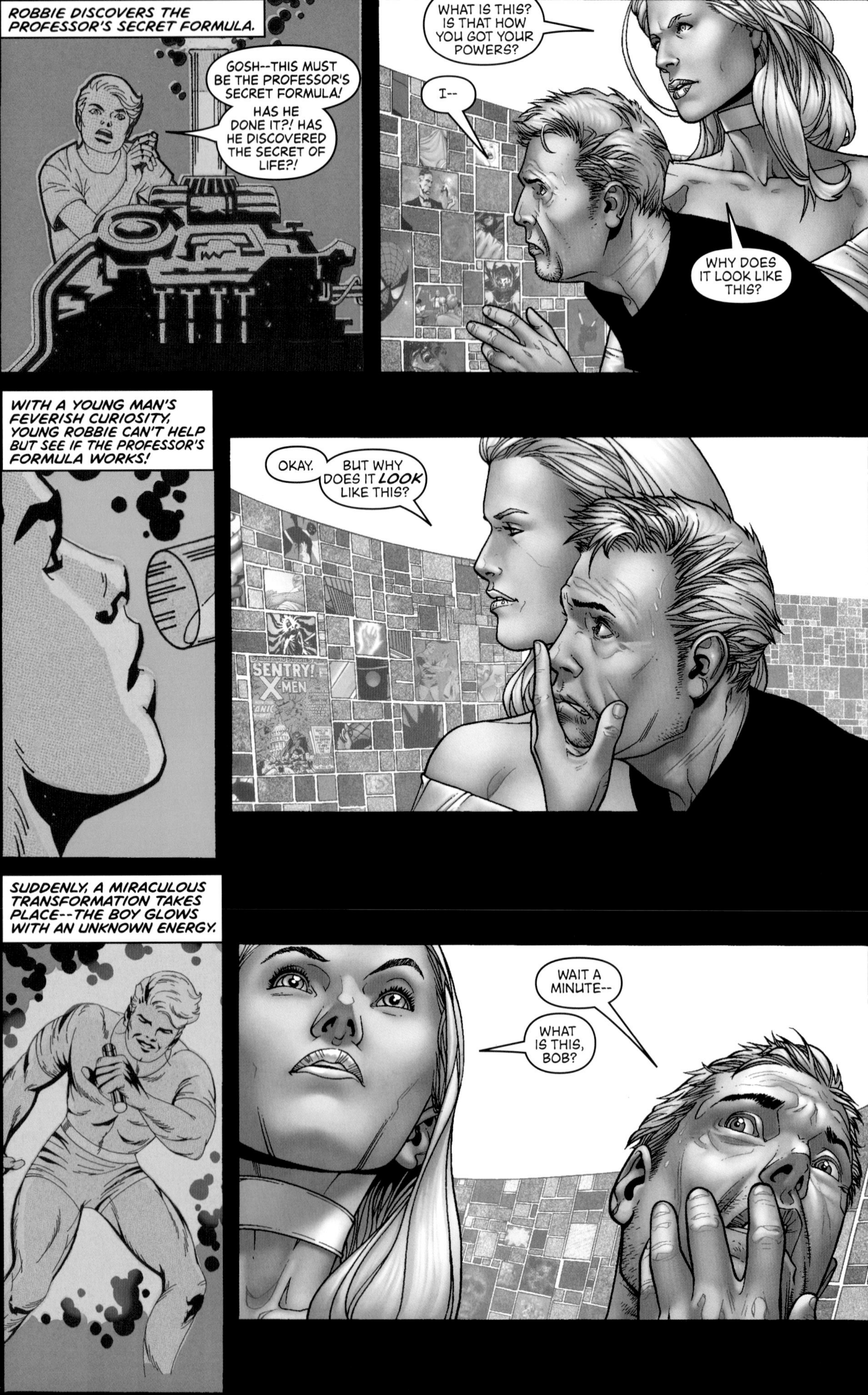
ROBBIE DISCOVERS THE PROFESSOR'S SECRET FORMULA.
GOSH--THIS MUST BE THE PROFESSOR'S SECRET FORMULA!
HAS HE DONE IT?! HAS HE DISCOVERED THE SECRET OF LIFE?!
WHAT IS THIS? IS THAT HOW YOU GOT YOUR POWERS?
I--
WHY DOES IT LOOK LIKE THIS?
WITH A YOUNG MAN'S FEVERISH CURIOSITY, YOUNG ROBBIE CAN'T HELP BUT SEE IF THE PROFESSOR'S FORMULA WORKS!
OKAY.
BUT WHY DOES IT LOOK LIKE THIS?
SENTRY!
X-MEN
SUDDENLY, A MIRACULOUS TRANSFORMATION TAKES PLACE--THE BOY GLOWS WITH AN UNKNOWN ENERGY.
WAIT A MINUTE--
WHAT IS THIS, BOB?

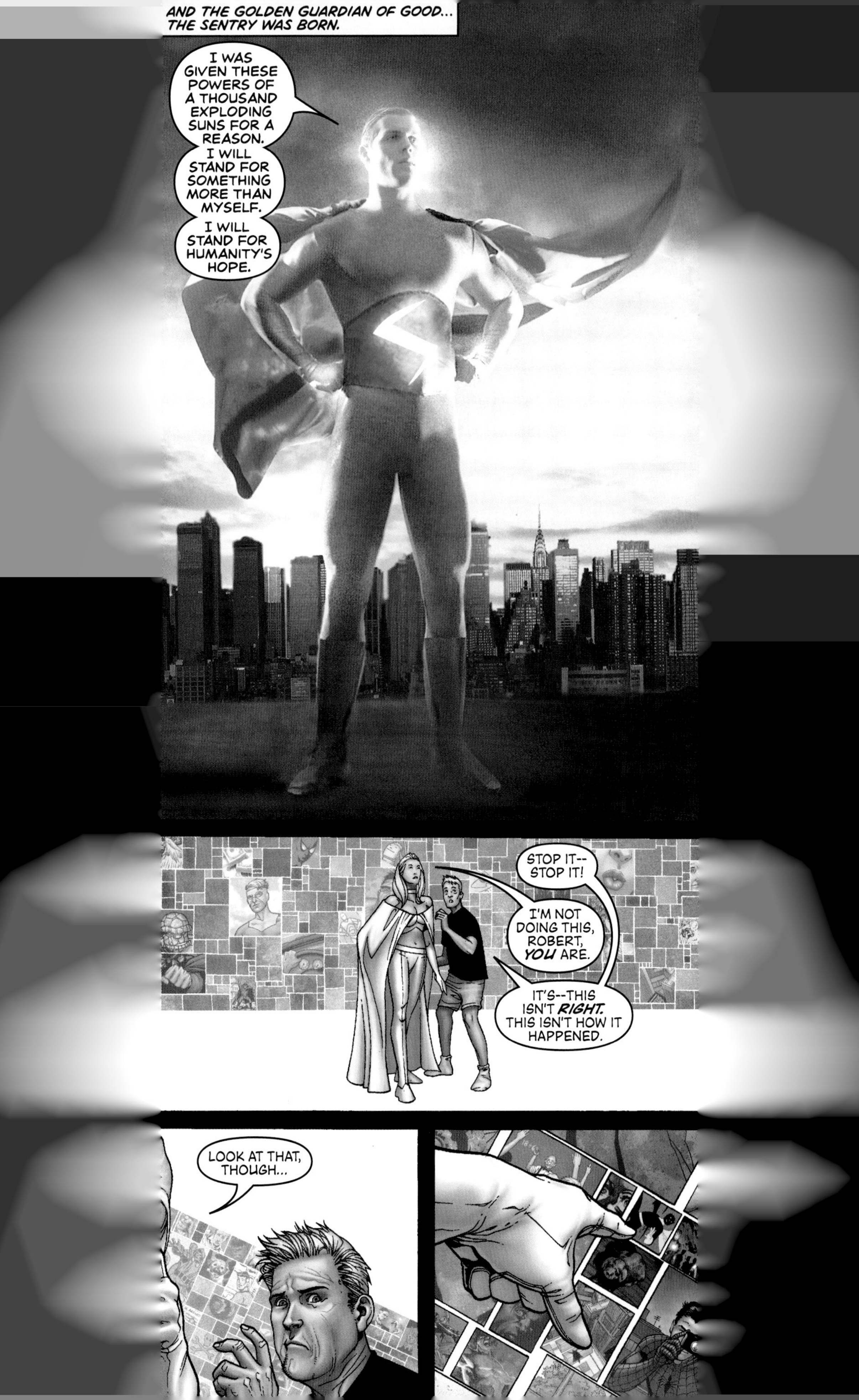
AND THE GOLDEN GUARDIAN OF GOOD... THE SENTRY WAS BORN.
I WAS GIVEN THESE POWERS OF A THOUSAND EXPLODING SUNS FOR A REASON.
I WILL STAND FOR SOMETHING MORE THAN MYSELF.
I WILL STAND FOR HUMANITY'S HOPE.
STOP IT-- STOP IT!
I'M NOT DOING THIS, ROBERT, YOU ARE.
IT'S--THIS ISN'T RIGHT. THIS ISN'T HOW IT HAPPENED.
LOOK AT THAT, THOUGH...

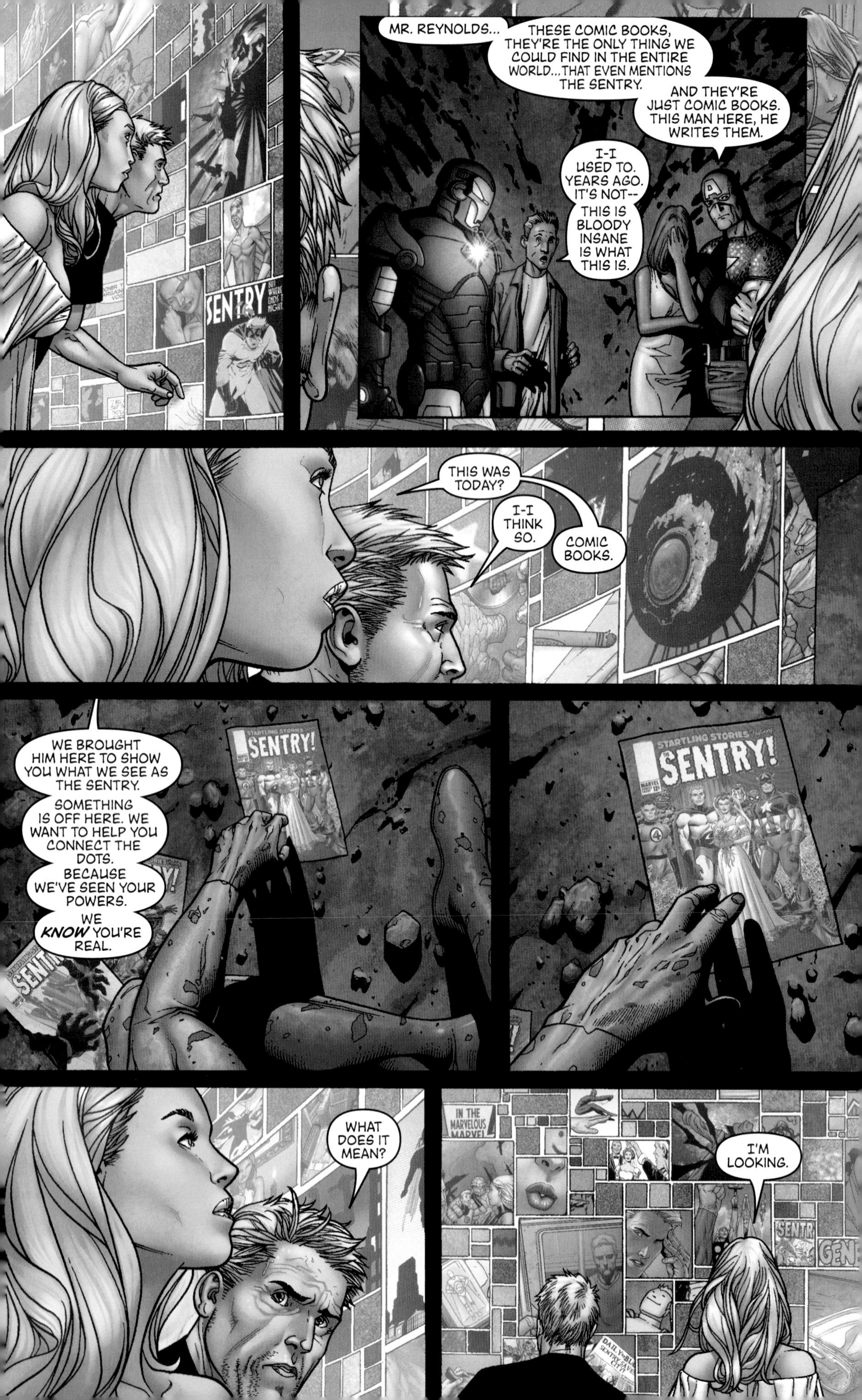
SENTRY
MR. REYNOLDS...
THESE COMIC BOOKS, THEY'RE THE ONLY THING WE COULD FIND IN THE ENTIRE WORLD...THAT EVEN MENTIONS THE SENTRY.
AND THEY'RE JUST COMIC BOOKS. THIS MAN HERE, HE WRITES THEM.
I-I USED TO. YEARS AGO. IT'S NOT--
THIS IS BLOODY INSANE IS WHAT THIS IS.
THIS WAS TODAY?
I-I THINK SO.
COMIC BOOKS.
WE BROUGHT HIM HERE TO SHOW YOU WHAT WE SEE AS THE SENTRY.
SOMETHING IS OFF HERE. WE WANT TO HELP YOU CONNECT THE DOTS.
BECAUSE WE'VE SEEN YOUR POWERS.
WE *KNOW* YOU'RE REAL.
STARTLING STORIES SENTRY!
STARTLING STORIES SENTRY!
WHAT DOES IT MEAN?
IN THE MARVELOUS MARVEL
I'M LOOKING.

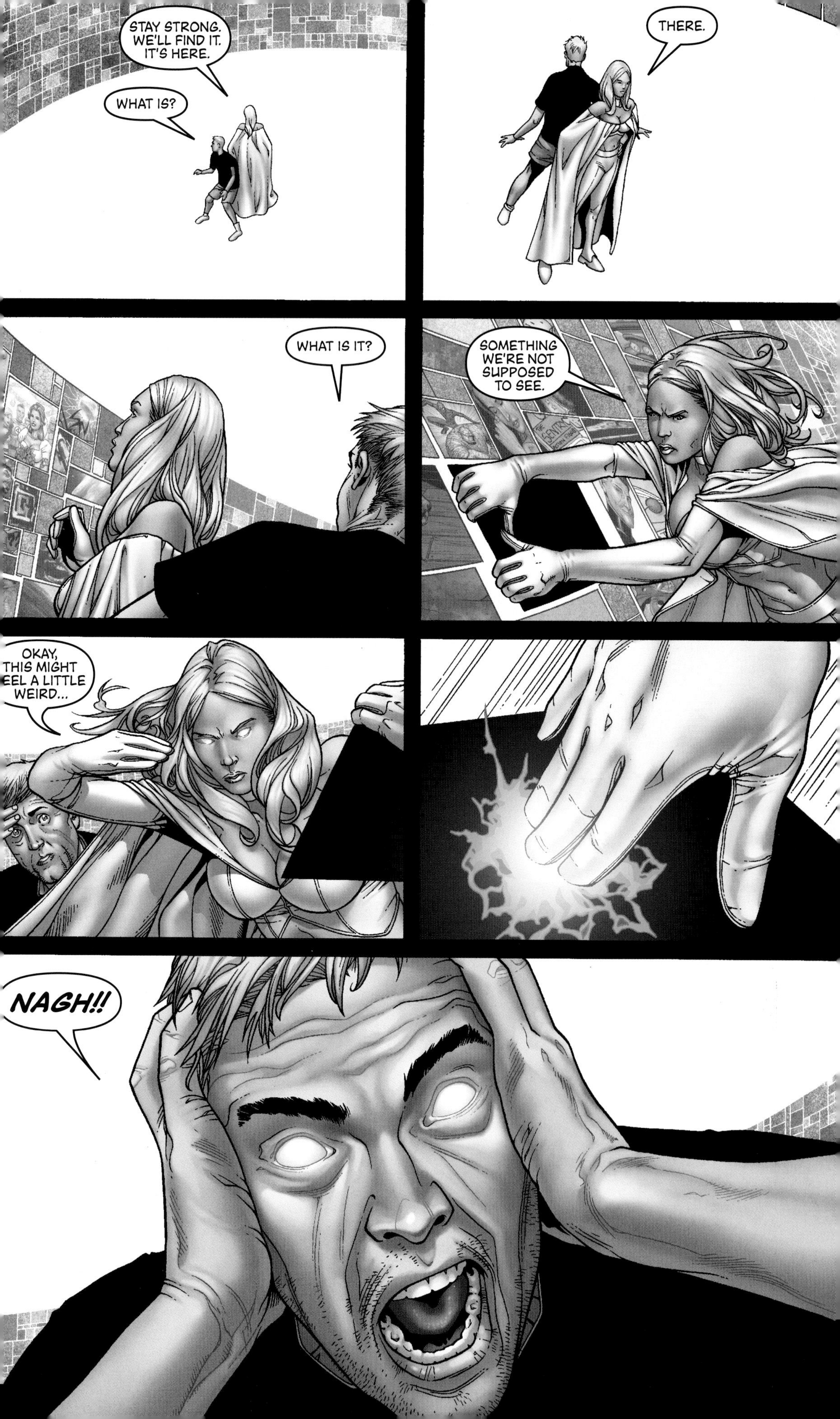
STAY STRONG. WE'LL FIND IT. IT'S HERE.
WHAT IS?
THERE.
WHAT IS IT?
SOMETHING WE'RE NOT SUPPOSED TO SEE.
OKAY, THIS MIGHT FEEL A LITTLE WEIRD...
NAGH!!

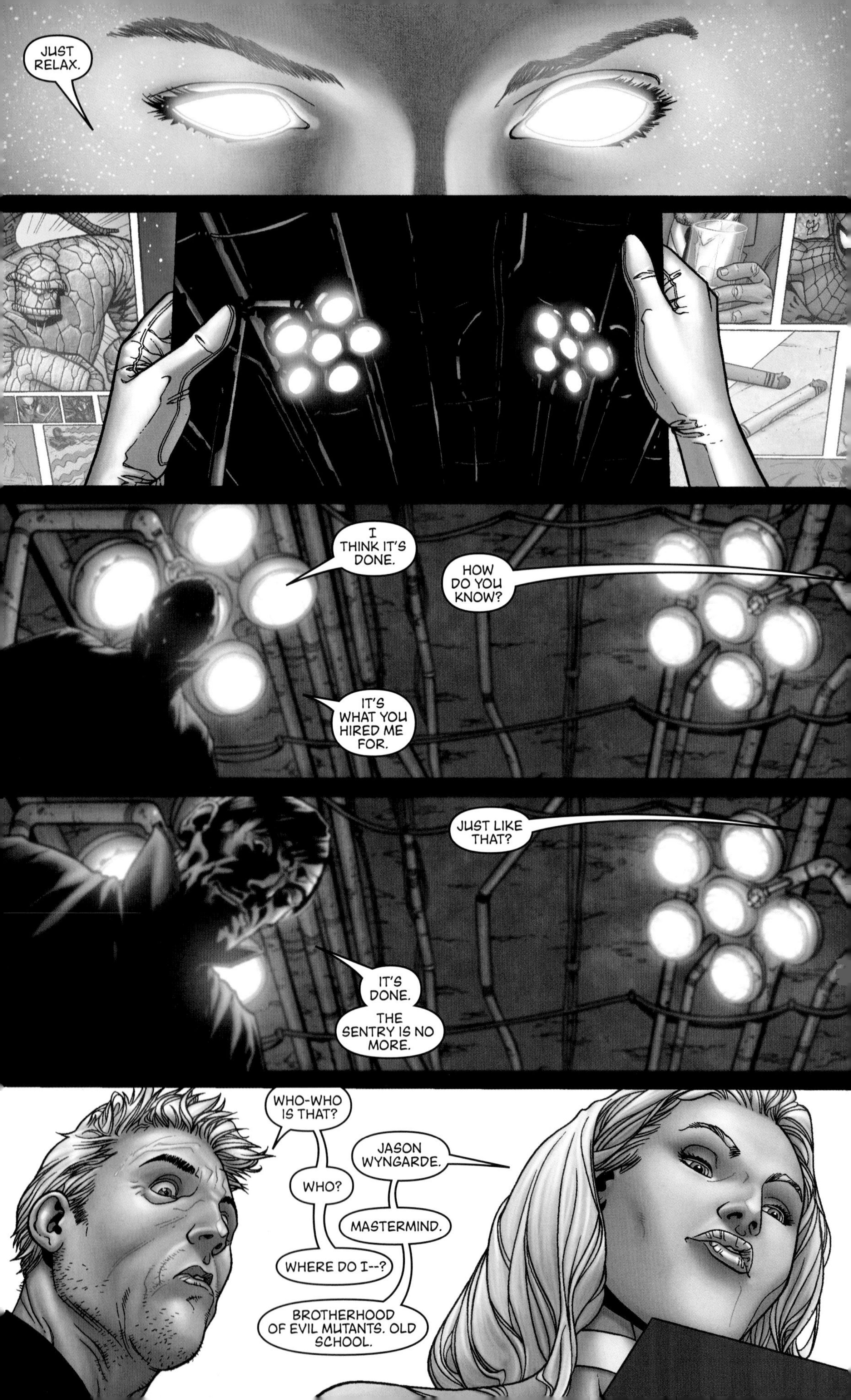
JUST RELAX.
I THINK IT'S DONE.
HOW DO YOU KNOW?
IT'S WHAT YOU HIRED ME FOR.
JUST LIKE THAT?
IT'S DONE.
THE SENTRY IS NO MORE.
WHO-WHO IS THAT?
JASON WYNGARDE.
WHO?
MASTERMIND.
WHERE DO I--?
BROTHERHOOD OF EVIL MUTANTS. OLD SCHOOL.

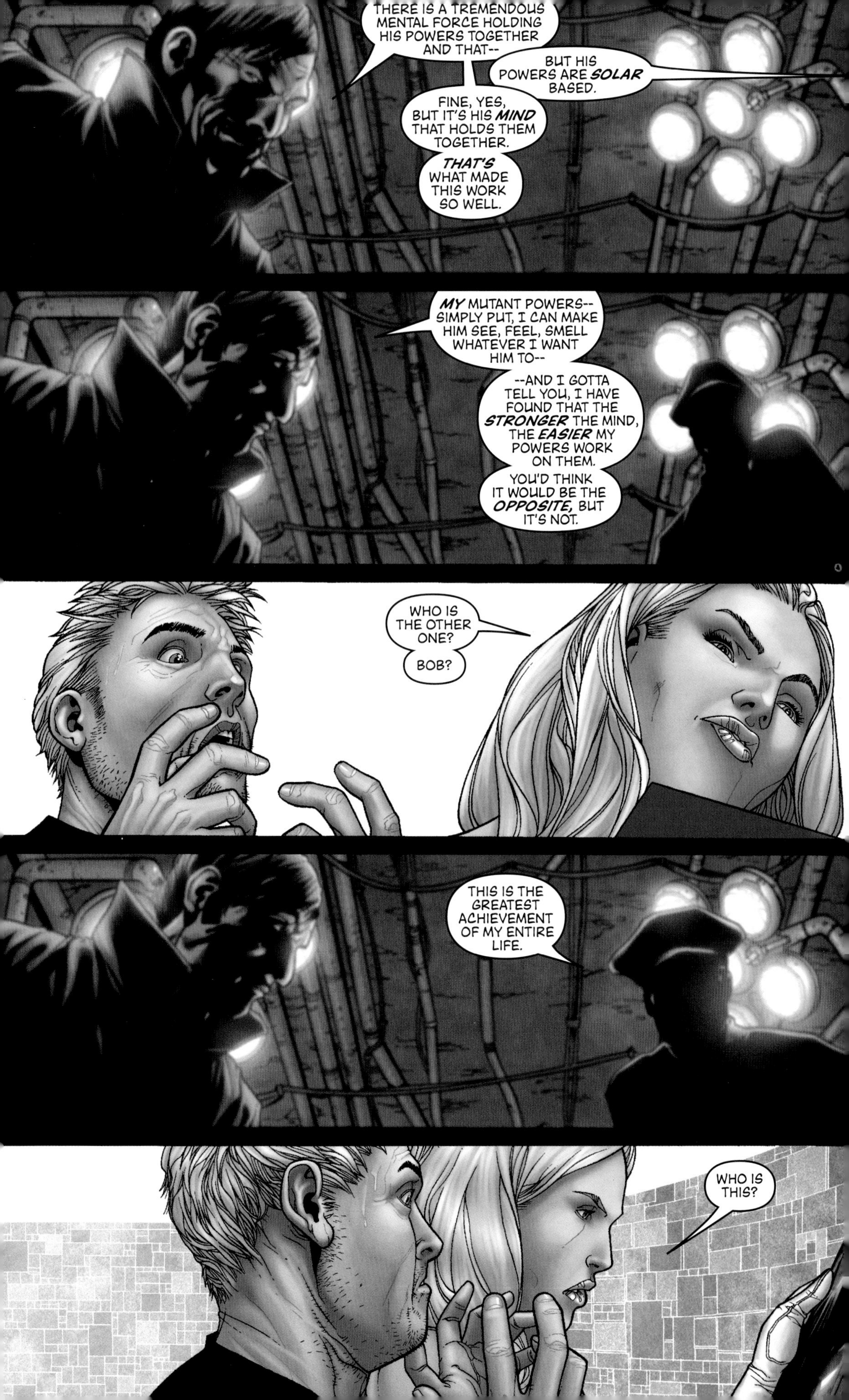
THERE IS A TREMENDOUS MENTAL FORCE HOLDING HIS POWERS TOGETHER AND THAT--
BUT HIS POWERS ARE *SOLAR* BASED.
FINE, YES, BUT IT'S HIS *MIND* THAT HOLDS THEM TOGETHER.
THAT'S WHAT MADE THIS WORK SO WELL.
MY MUTANT POWERS-- SIMPLY PUT, I CAN MAKE HIM SEE, FEEL, SMELL WHATEVER I WANT HIM TO--
--AND I GOTTA TELL YOU, I HAVE FOUND THAT THE *STRONGER* THE MIND, THE *EASIER* MY POWERS WORK ON THEM.
YOU'D THINK IT WOULD BE THE *OPPOSITE,* BUT IT'S NOT.
WHO IS THE OTHER ONE?
BOB?
THIS IS THE GREATEST ACHIEVEMENT OF MY ENTIRE LIFE.
WHO IS THIS?

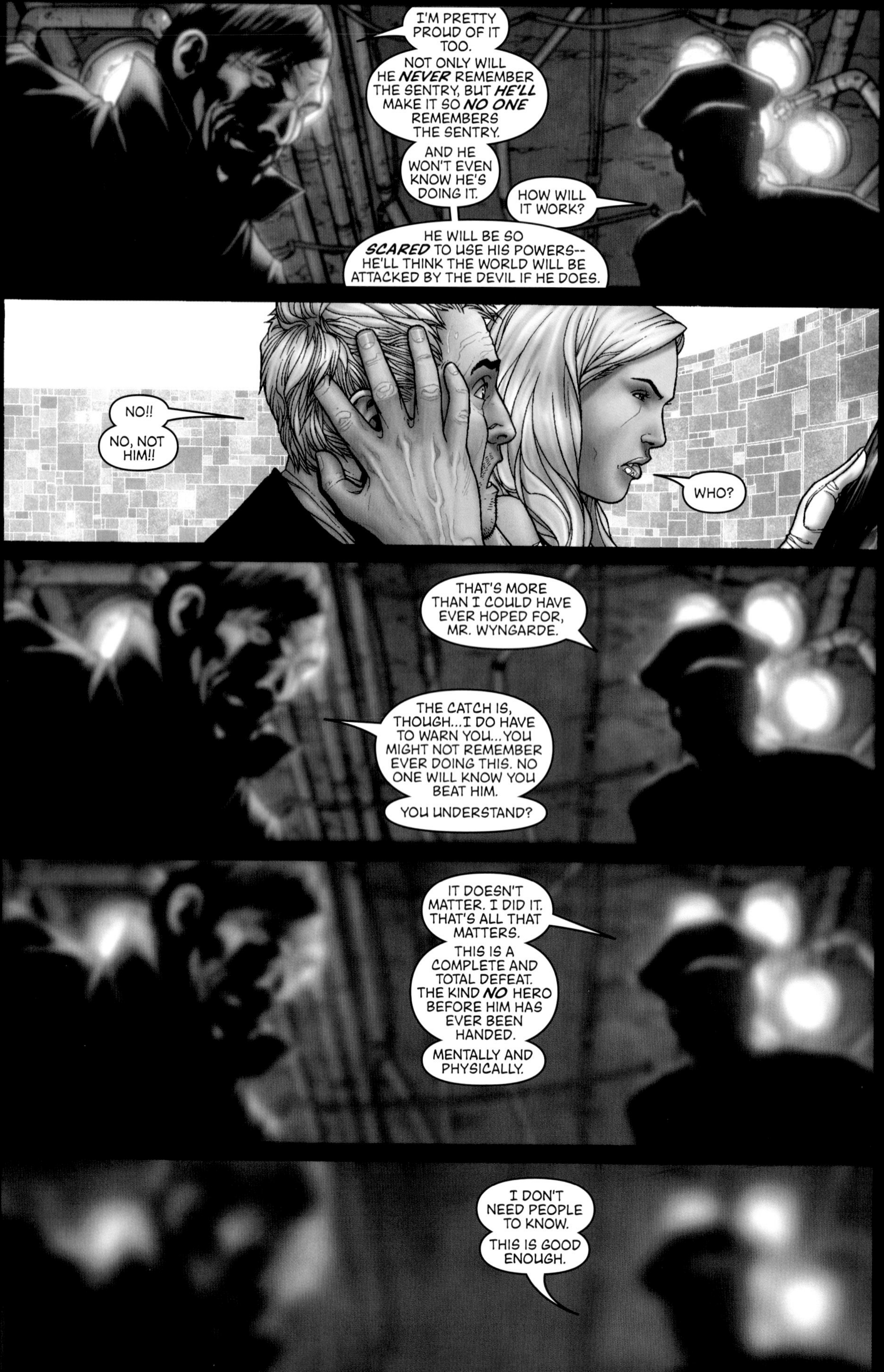
I'M PRETTY PROUD OF IT TOO.
NOT ONLY WILL HE *NEVER* REMEMBER THE SENTRY, BUT *HE'LL* MAKE IT SO *NO ONE* REMEMBERS THE SENTRY.
AND HE WON'T EVEN KNOW HE'S DOING IT.
HOW WILL IT WORK?
HE WILL BE SO *SCARED* TO USE HIS POWERS-- HE'LL THINK THE WORLD WILL BE ATTACKED BY THE DEVIL IF HE DOES.
NO!!
NO, NOT HIM!!
WHO?
THAT'S MORE THAN I COULD HAVE EVER HOPED FOR, MR. WYNGARDE.
THE CATCH IS, THOUGH...I DO HAVE TO WARN YOU...YOU MIGHT NOT REMEMBER EVER DOING THIS. NO ONE WILL KNOW YOU BEAT HIM.
YOU UNDERSTAND?
IT DOESN'T MATTER. I DID IT. THAT'S ALL THAT MATTERS.
THIS IS A COMPLETE AND TOTAL DEFEAT. THE KIND *NO* HERO BEFORE HIM HAS EVER BEEN HANDED.
MENTALLY AND PHYSICALLY.
I DON'T NEED PEOPLE TO KNOW.
THIS IS GOOD ENOUGH.

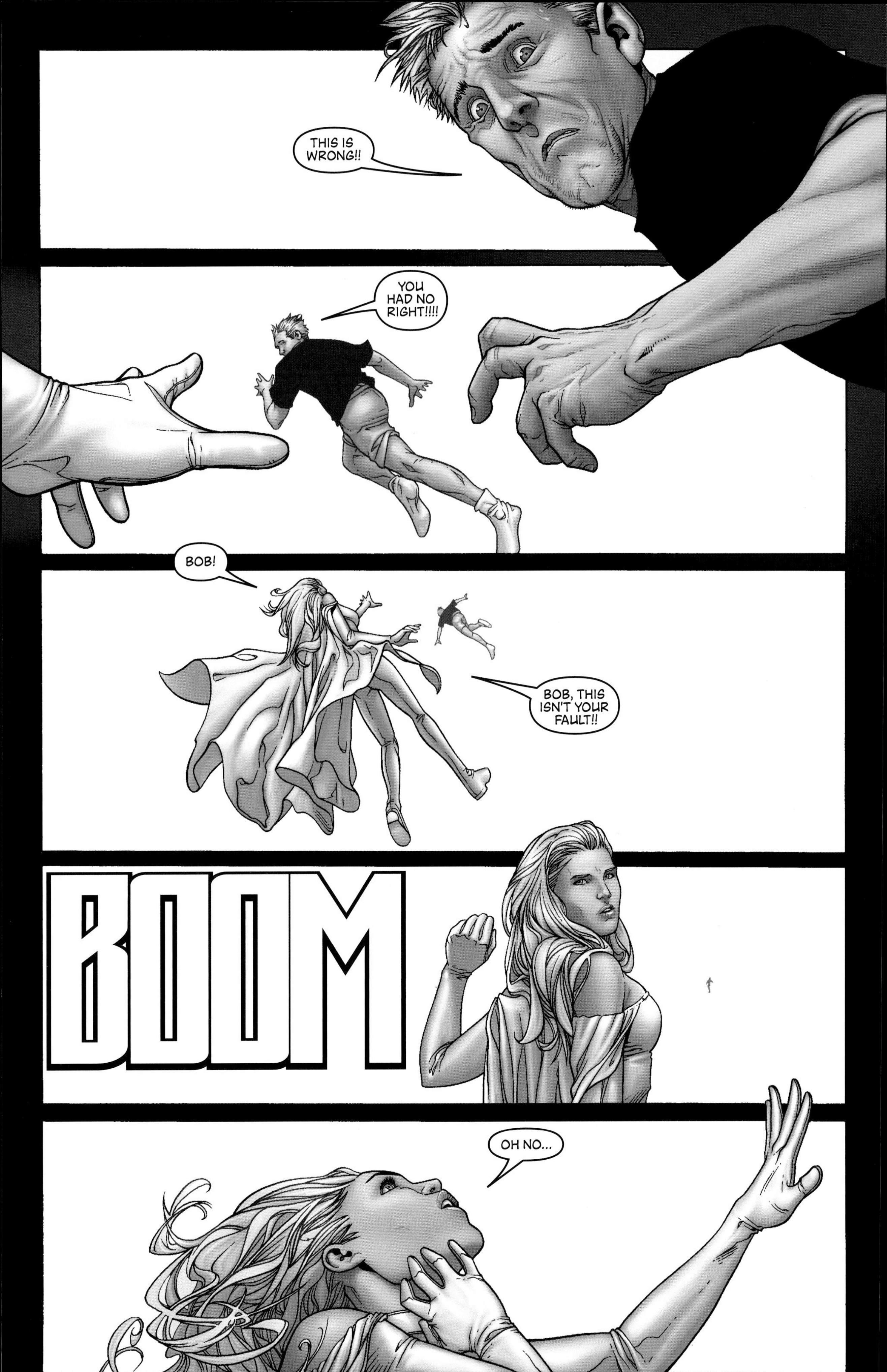
THIS IS WRONG!!
YOU HAD NO RIGHT!!!!
BOB!
BOB, THIS ISN'T YOUR FAULT!!
BOOM
OH NO...

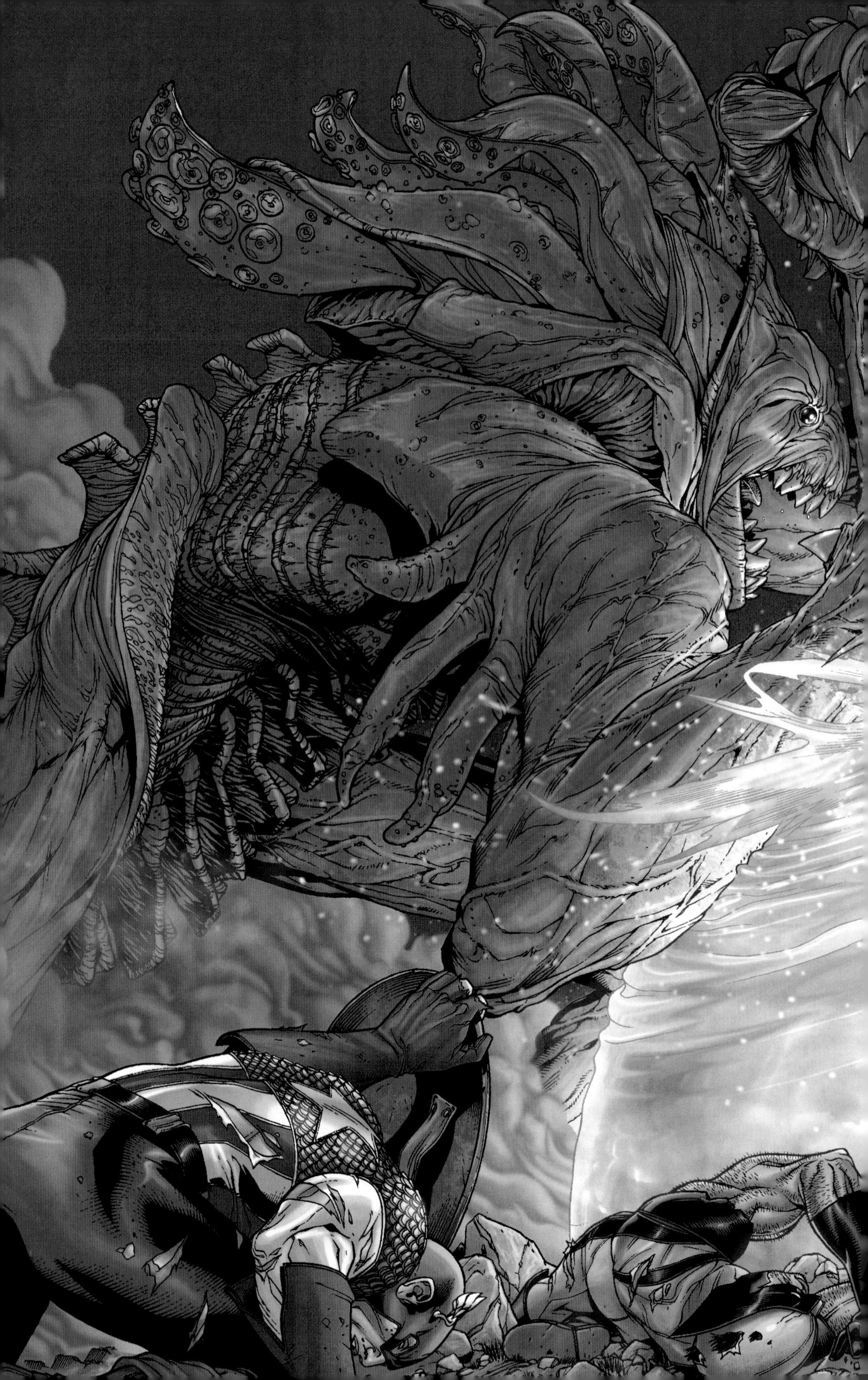

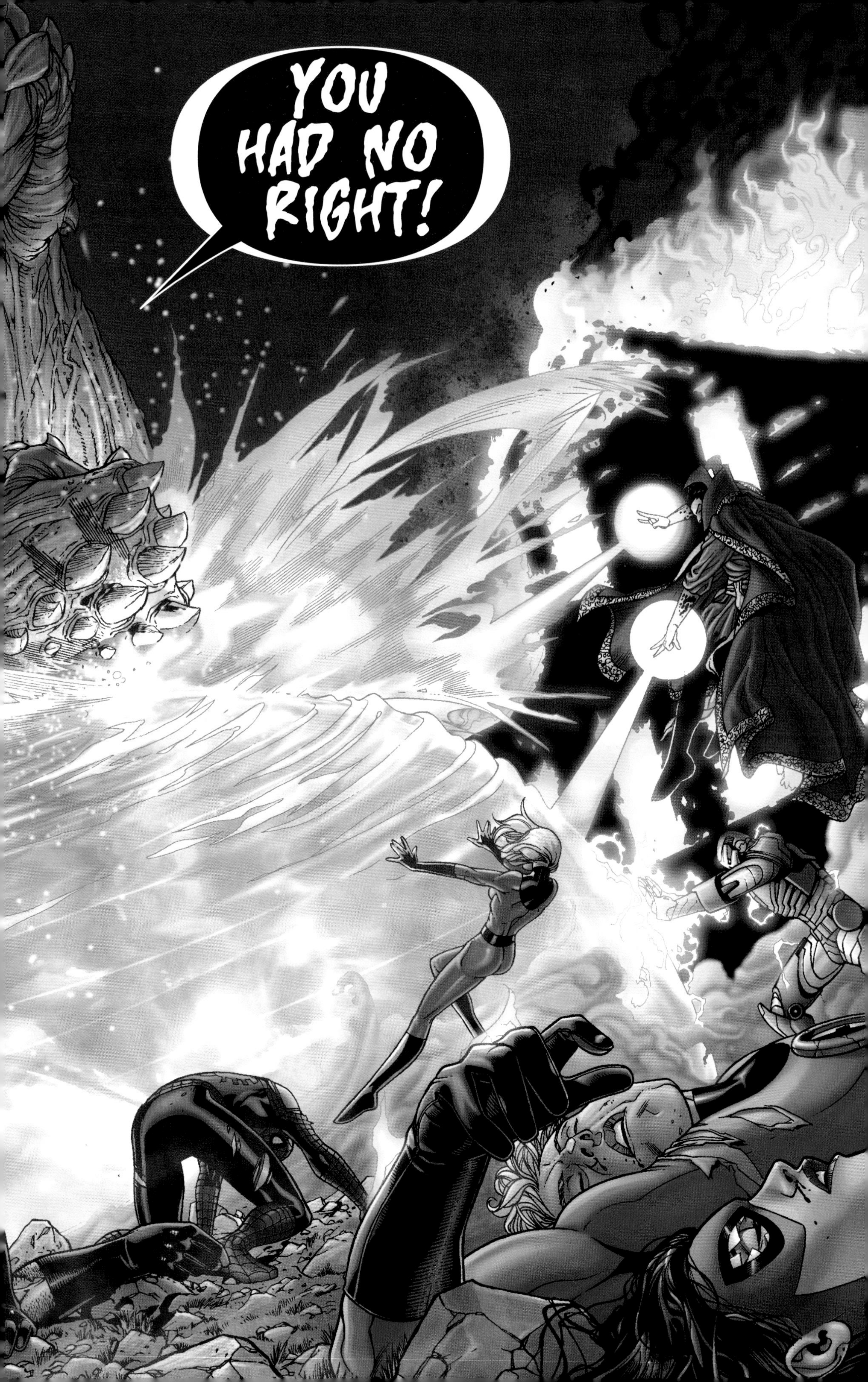
YOU HAD NO RIGHT!

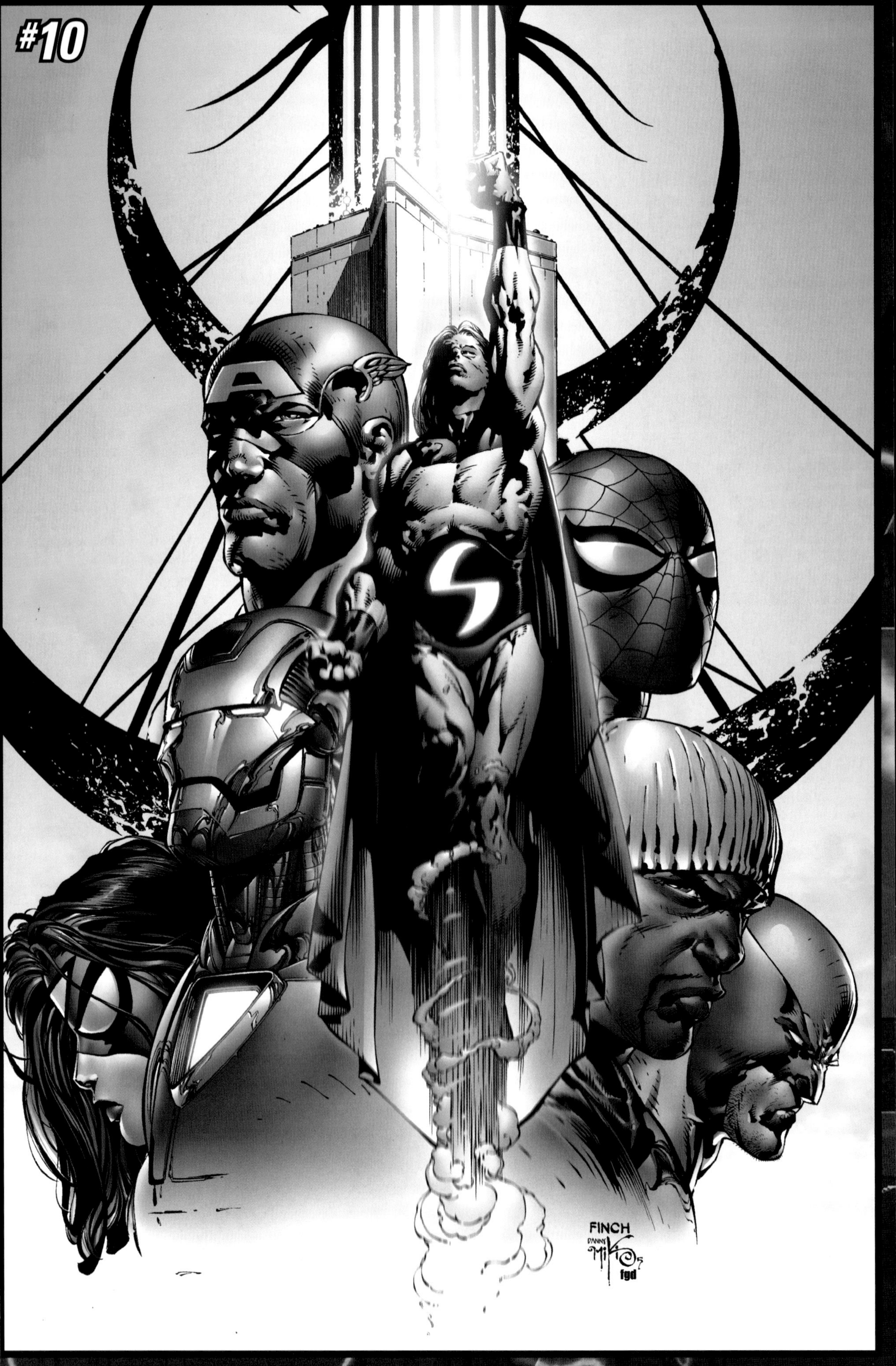
#10
FINCH

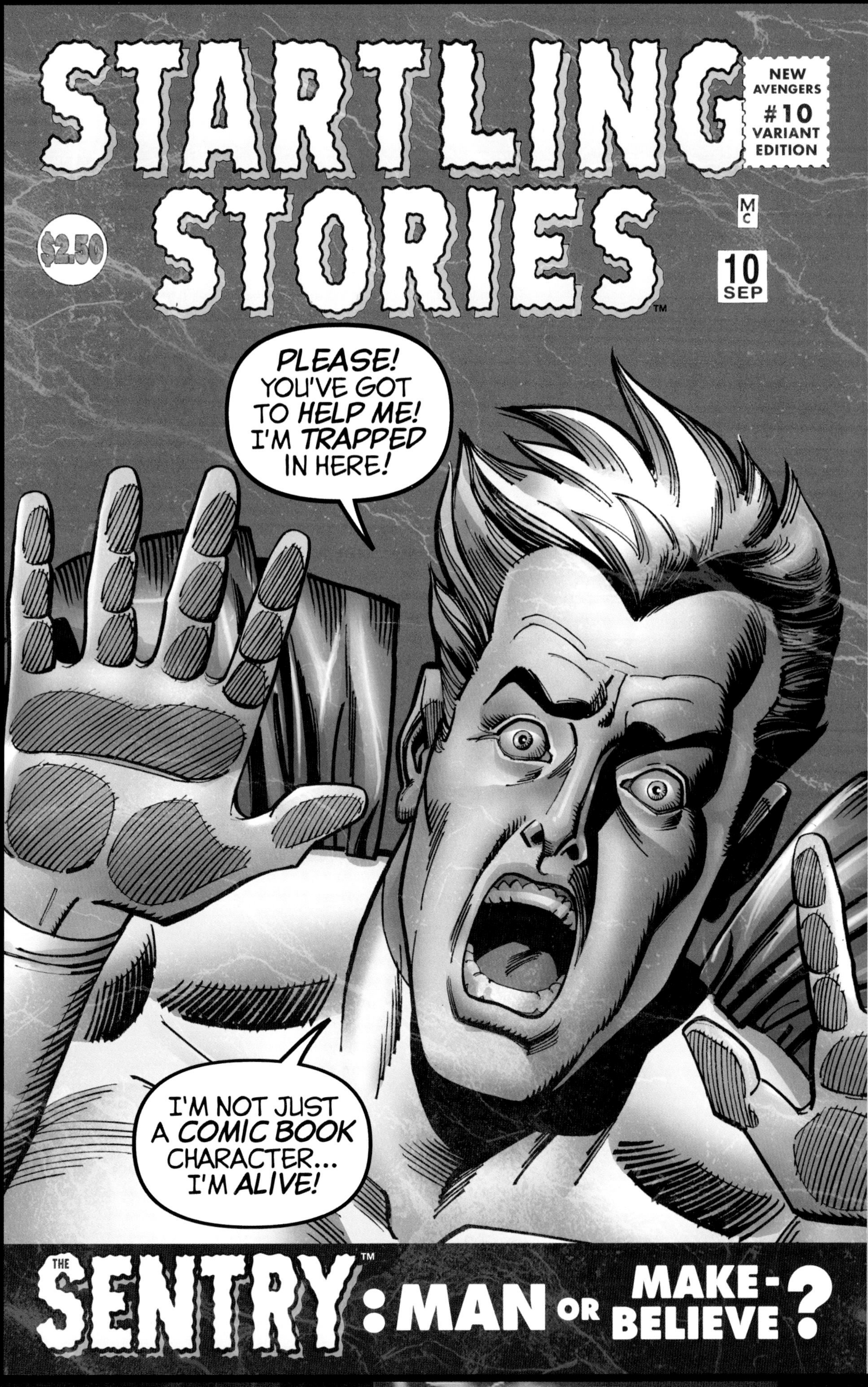
STARTLING STORIES
NEW AVENGERS #10 VARIANT EDITION
MC
$2.50
10 SEP
PLEASE! YOU'VE GOT TO HELP ME! I'M TRAPPED IN HERE!
I'M NOT JUST A COMIC BOOK CHARACTER... I'M ALIVE!
THE SENTRY: MAN OR MAKE-BELIEVE?

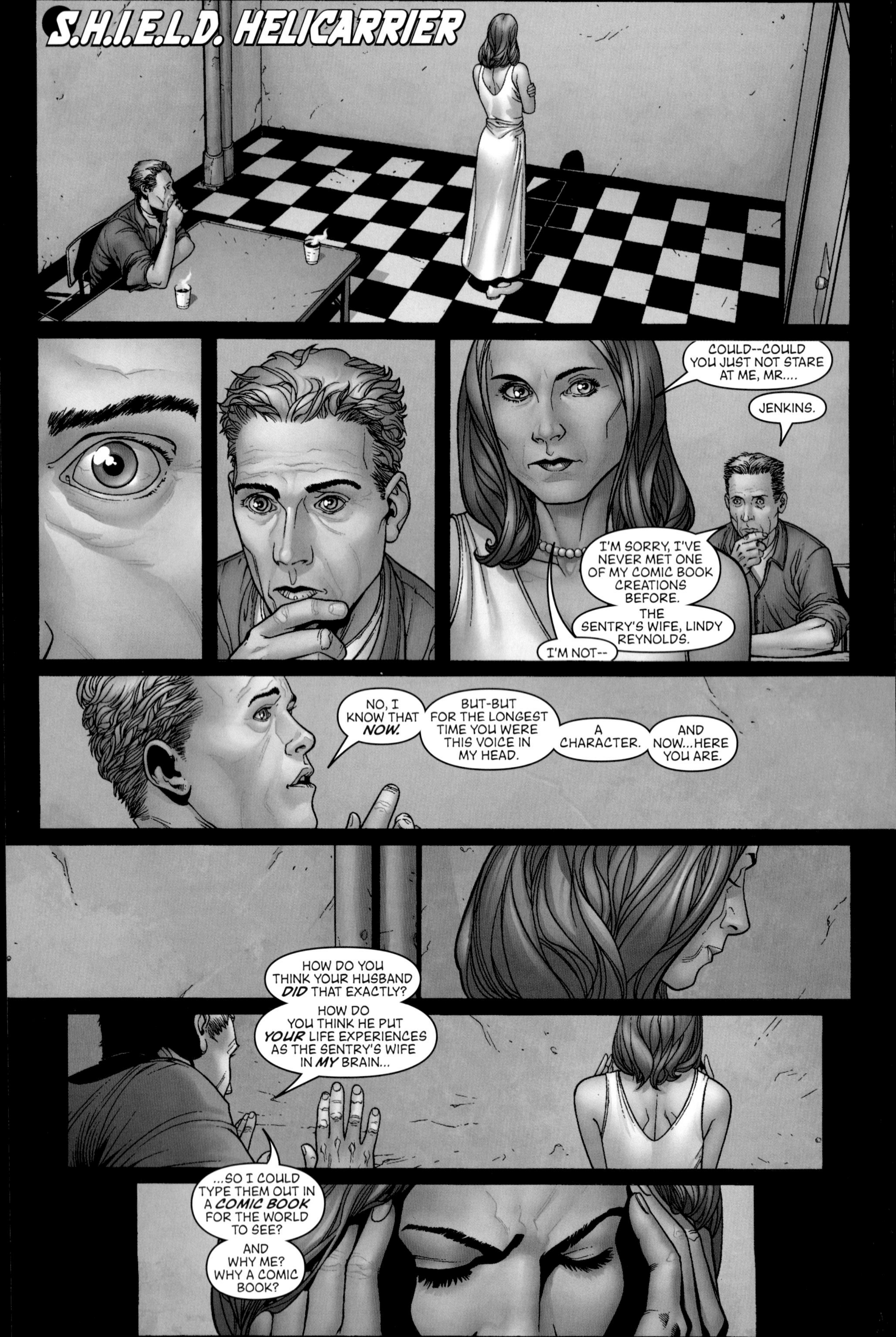
S.H.I.E.L.D. HELICARRIER
COULD--COULD YOU JUST NOT STARE AT ME, MR....
JENKINS.
I'M SORRY, I'VE NEVER MET ONE OF MY COMIC BOOK CREATIONS BEFORE.
THE SENTRY'S WIFE, LINDY REYNOLDS.
I'M NOT--
NO, I KNOW THAT *NOW.*
BUT-BUT FOR THE LONGEST TIME YOU WERE THIS VOICE IN MY HEAD.
A CHARACTER.
AND NOW...HERE YOU ARE.
HOW DO YOU THINK YOUR HUSBAND *DID* THAT EXACTLY?
HOW DO YOU THINK HE PUT *YOUR* LIFE EXPERIENCES AS THE SENTRY'S WIFE IN *MY* BRAIN...
...SO I COULD TYPE THEM OUT IN A *COMIC BOOK* FOR THE WORLD TO SEE?
AND WHY ME? WHY A COMIC BOOK?

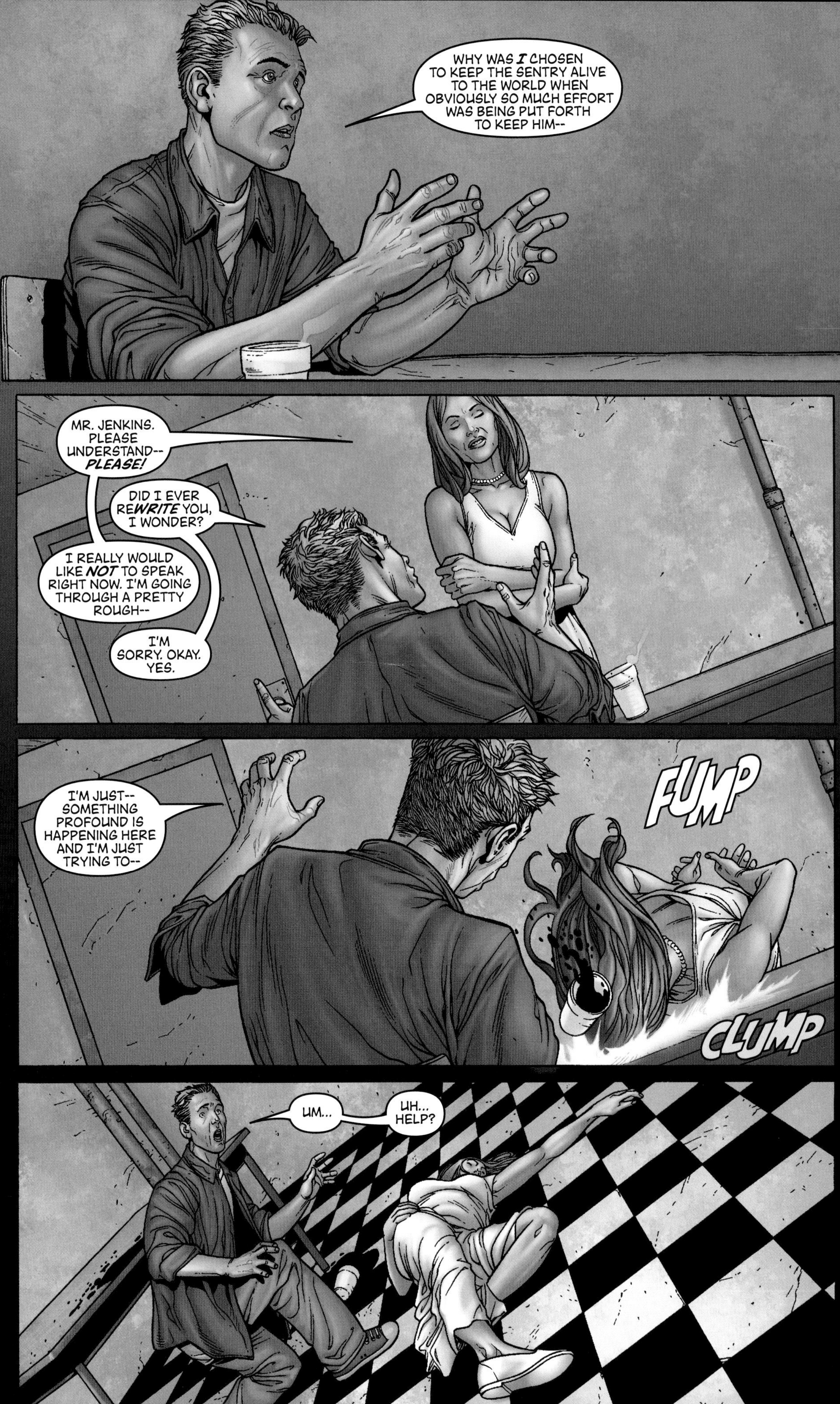
WHY WAS I CHOSEN TO KEEP THE SENTRY ALIVE TO THE WORLD WHEN OBVIOUSLY SO MUCH EFFORT WAS BEING PUT FORTH TO KEEP HIM--
MR. JENKINS. PLEASE UNDERSTAND-- PLEASE!
DID I EVER REWRITE YOU, I WONDER?
I REALLY WOULD LIKE NOT TO SPEAK RIGHT NOW. I'M GOING THROUGH A PRETTY ROUGH--
I'M SORRY. OKAY. YES.
I'M JUST-- SOMETHING PROFOUND IS HAPPENING HERE AND I'M JUST TRYING TO--
FUMP
CLUMP
UM...
UH... HELP?

OH MY GOD... I'M DEAD.

YOU'RE NOT DEAD, LINDY. YOU'RE FINE.

YOU'RE IN--WELL, I'M SORRY TO SAY IT SO *BLUNTLY* BECAUSE I UNDERSTAND THIS IS NOT AN EVERYDAY OCCURRENCE...

...BUT *YOUR* SUBCONSCIOUS HAS BEEN PLACED INSIDE YOUR *HUSBAND'S* SUBCONSCIOUS.

MY NAME IS EMMA FROST. I'M AN X-MAN.

I USED MY MUTANT PSYCHIC ABILITIES TO--

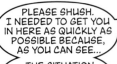

WH-WHAT?

PLEASE SHUSH. I NEEDED TO GET YOU IN HERE AS QUICKLY AS POSSIBLE BECAUSE, AS YOU CAN SEE...

...THE SITUATION WITH YOUR HUSBAND IS *NOT* GOOD.

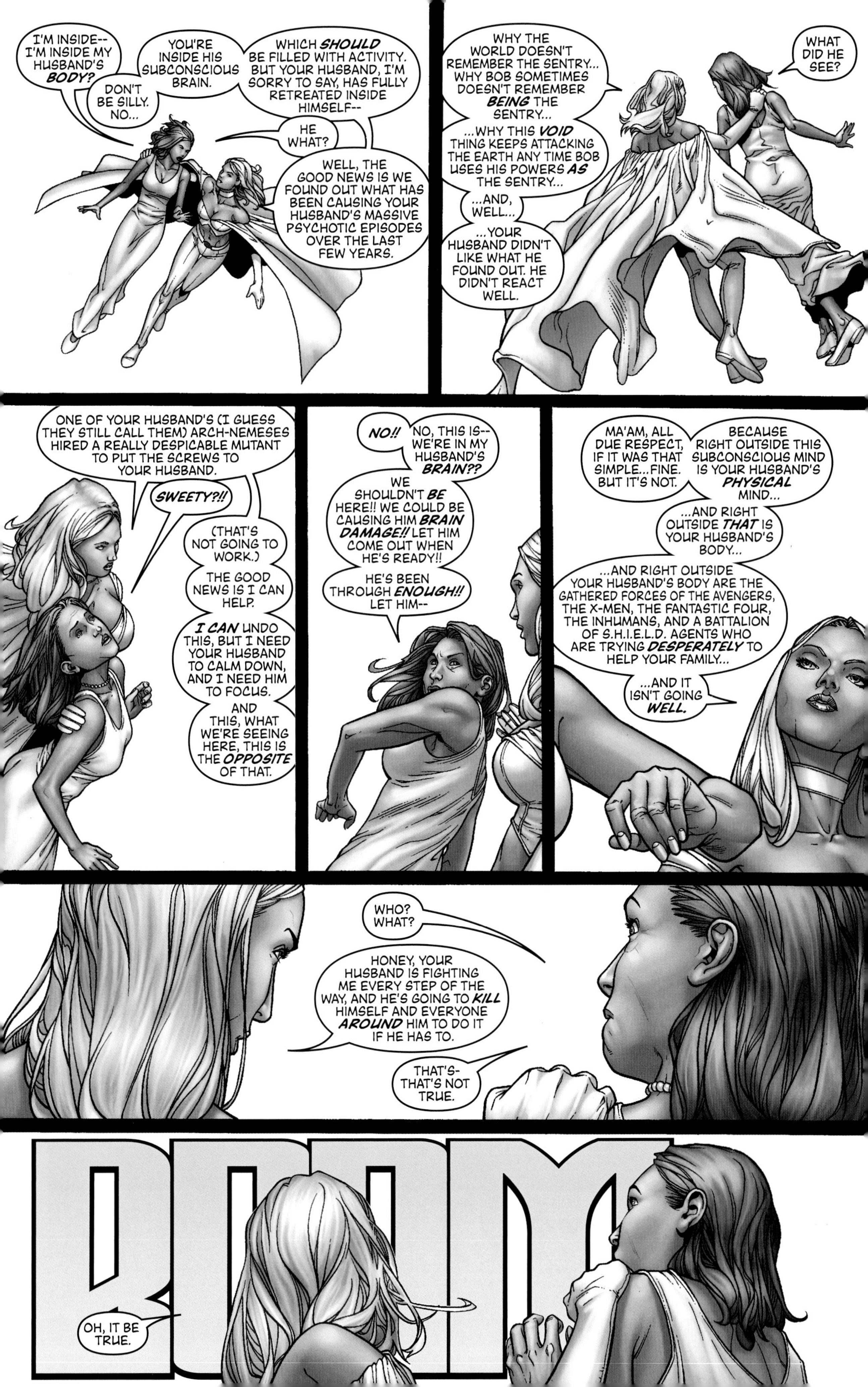

I'M INSIDE-- I'M INSIDE MY HUSBAND'S BODY?
YOU'RE INSIDE HIS SUBCONSCIOUS BRAIN.
DON'T BE SILLY. NO...
WHICH SHOULD BE FILLED WITH ACTIVITY. BUT YOUR HUSBAND, I'M SORRY TO SAY, HAS FULLY RETREATED INSIDE HIMSELF--
HE WHAT?
WELL, THE GOOD NEWS IS WE FOUND OUT WHAT HAS BEEN CAUSING YOUR HUSBAND'S MASSIVE PSYCHOTIC EPISODES OVER THE LAST FEW YEARS.
WHY THE WORLD DOESN'T REMEMBER THE SENTRY... WHY BOB SOMETIMES DOESN'T REMEMBER BEING THE SENTRY...
...WHY THIS VOID THING KEEPS ATTACKING THE EARTH ANY TIME BOB USES HIS POWERS AS THE SENTRY...
...AND, WELL...
...YOUR HUSBAND DIDN'T LIKE WHAT HE FOUND OUT. HE DIDN'T REACT WELL.
WHAT DID HE SEE?
ONE OF YOUR HUSBAND'S (I GUESS THEY STILL CALL THEM) ARCH-NEMESES HIRED A REALLY DESPICABLE MUTANT TO PUT THE SCREWS TO YOUR HUSBAND.
SWEETY?!!
(THAT'S NOT GOING TO WORK.)
THE GOOD NEWS IS I CAN HELP.
I CAN UNDO THIS, BUT I NEED YOUR HUSBAND TO CALM DOWN, AND I NEED HIM TO FOCUS.
AND THIS, WHAT WE'RE SEEING HERE, THIS IS THE OPPOSITE OF THAT.
NO!!
NO, THIS IS-- WE'RE IN MY HUSBAND'S BRAIN??
WE SHOULDN'T BE HERE!! WE COULD BE CAUSING HIM BRAIN DAMAGE!! LET HIM COME OUT WHEN HE'S READY!!
HE'S BEEN THROUGH ENOUGH!! LET HIM--
MA'AM, ALL DUE RESPECT, IF IT WAS THAT SIMPLE...FINE. BUT IT'S NOT.
BECAUSE RIGHT OUTSIDE THIS SUBCONSCIOUS MIND IS YOUR HUSBAND'S PHYSICAL MIND...
...AND RIGHT OUTSIDE THAT IS YOUR HUSBAND'S BODY...
...AND RIGHT OUTSIDE YOUR HUSBAND'S BODY ARE THE GATHERED FORCES OF THE AVENGERS, THE X-MEN, THE FANTASTIC FOUR, THE INHUMANS, AND A BATTALION OF S.H.I.E.L.D. AGENTS WHO ARE TRYING DESPERATELY TO HELP YOUR FAMILY...
...AND IT ISN'T GOING WELL.
WHO? WHAT?
HONEY, YOUR HUSBAND IS FIGHTING ME EVERY STEP OF THE WAY, AND HE'S GOING TO KILL HIMSELF AND EVERYONE AROUND HIM TO DO IT IF HE HAS TO.
THAT'S- THAT'S NOT TRUE.
OH, IT BE TRUE.

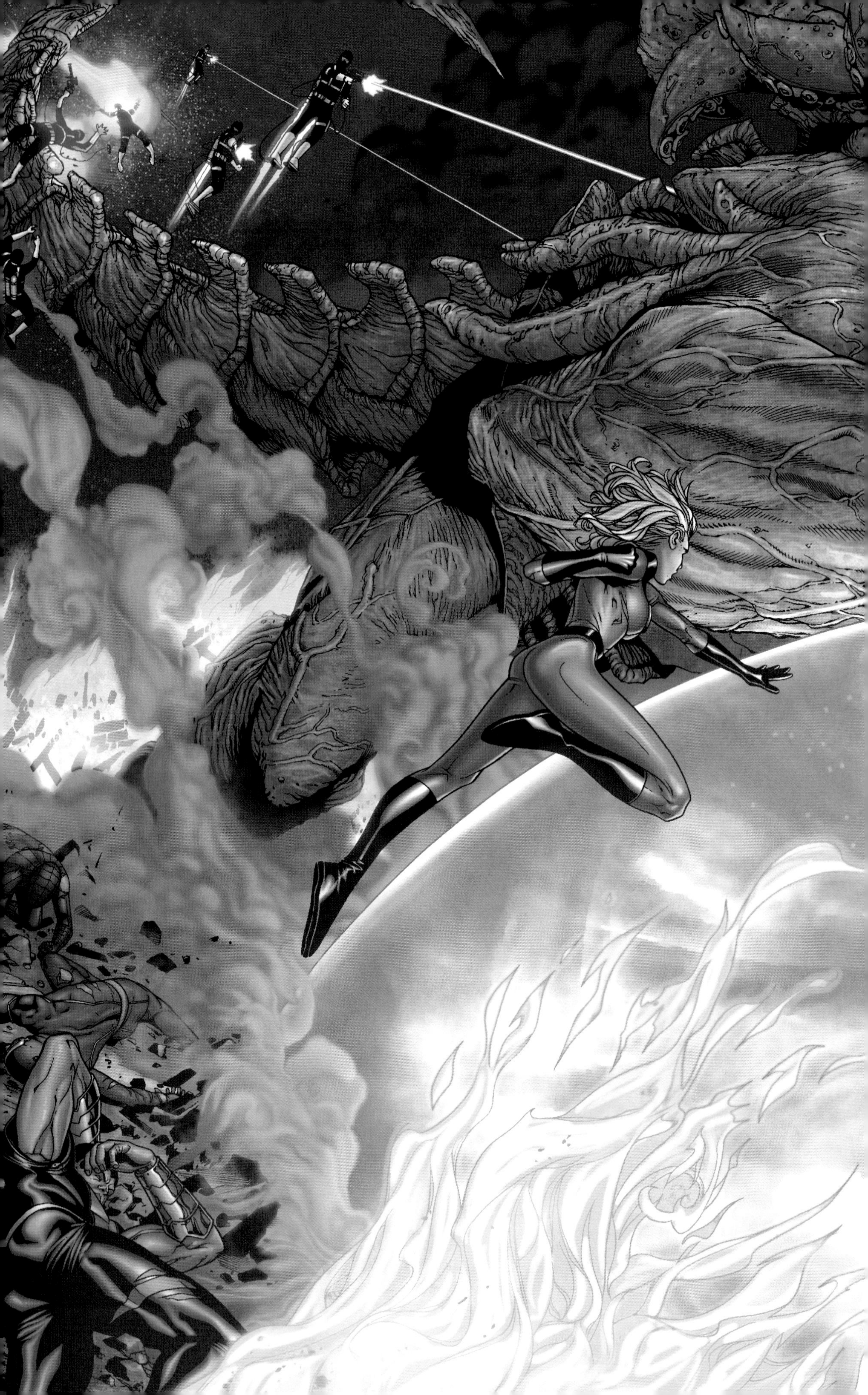

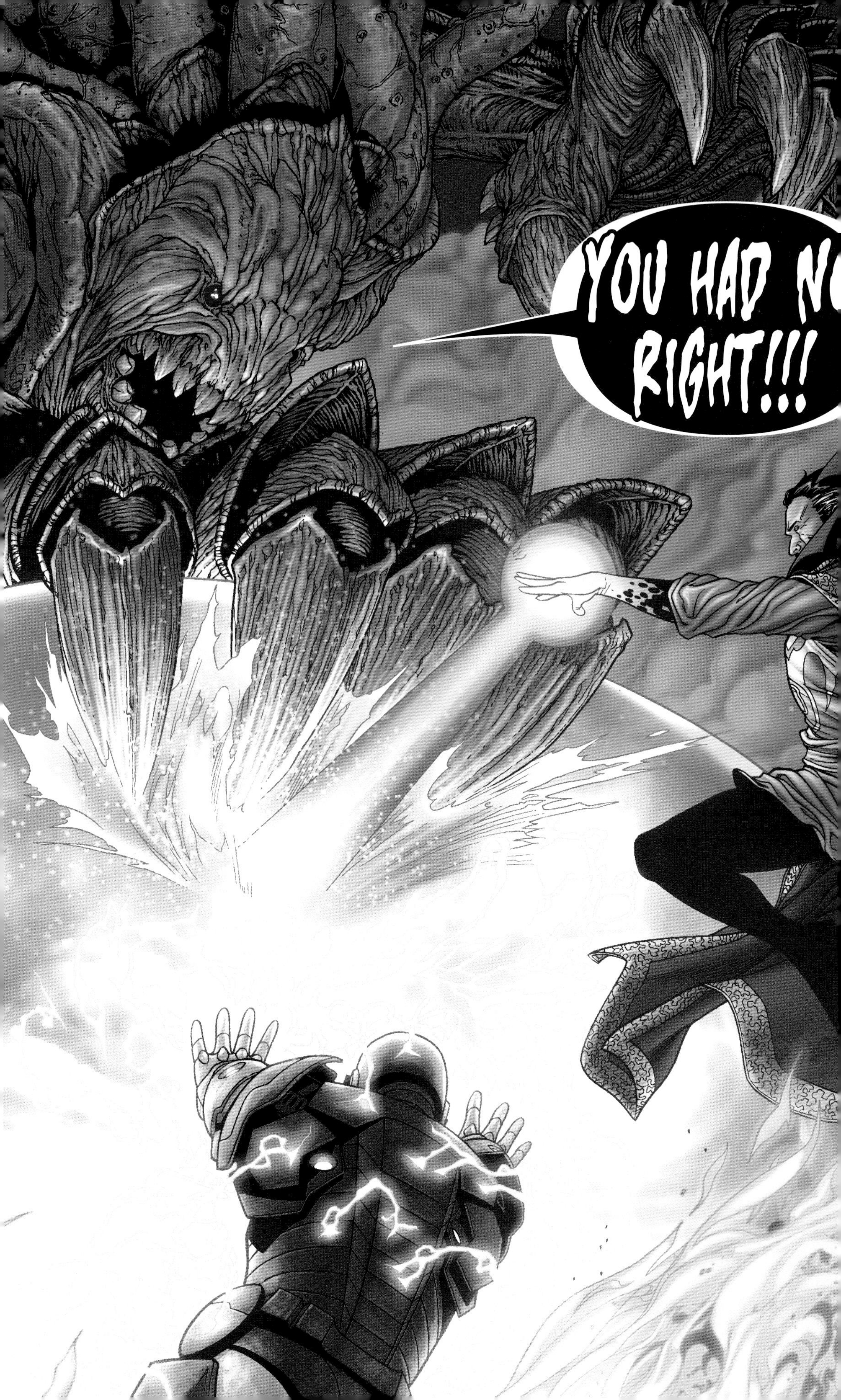
YOU HAD N
RIGHT!!!

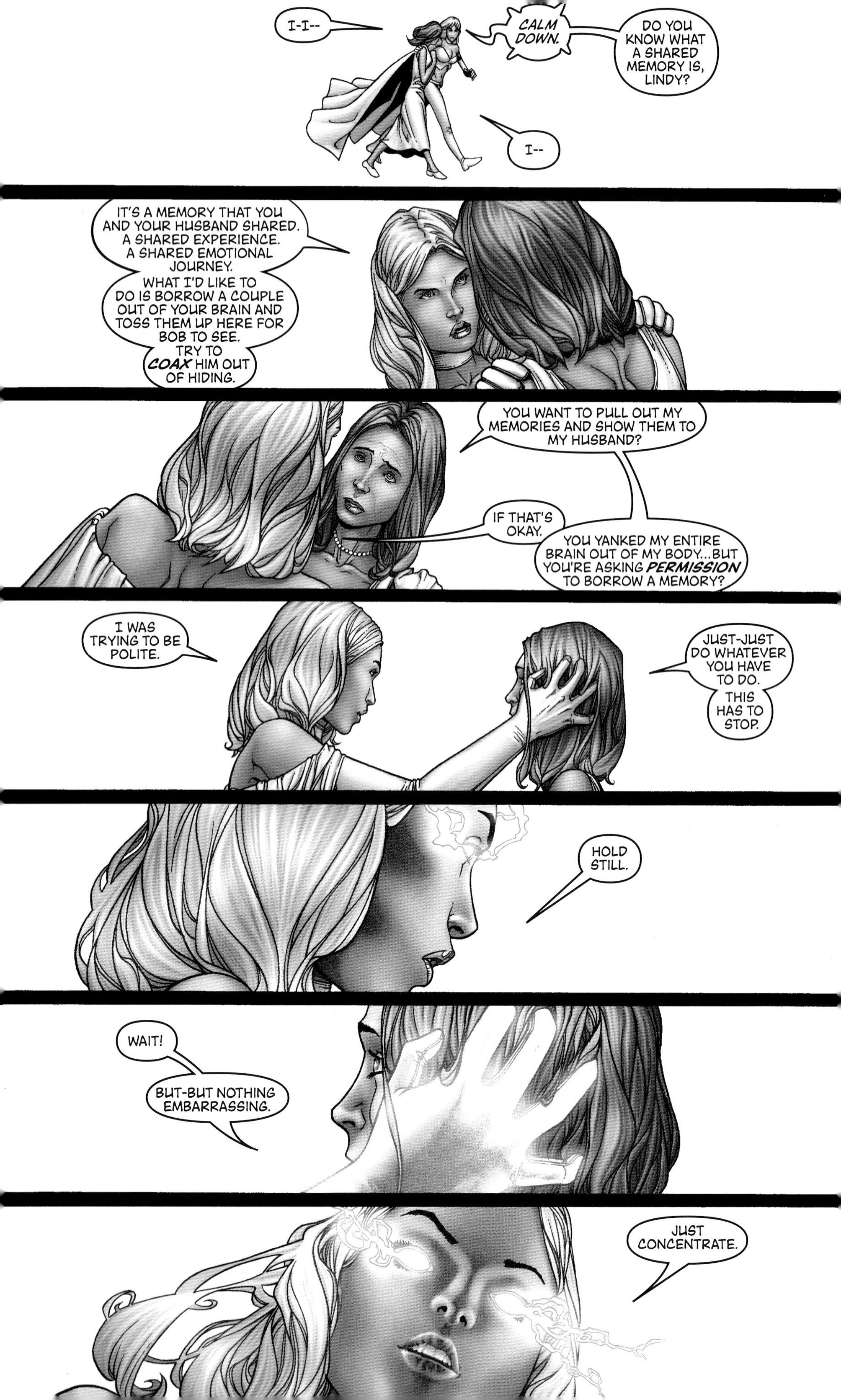
I-I--
CALM DOWN.
DO YOU KNOW WHAT A SHARED MEMORY IS, LINDY?
I--
IT'S A MEMORY THAT YOU AND YOUR HUSBAND SHARED. A SHARED EXPERIENCE. A SHARED EMOTIONAL JOURNEY.
WHAT I'D LIKE TO DO IS BORROW A COUPLE OUT OF YOUR BRAIN AND TOSS THEM UP HERE FOR BOB TO SEE. TRY TO *COAX* HIM OUT OF HIDING.
YOU WANT TO PULL OUT MY MEMORIES AND SHOW THEM TO MY HUSBAND?
IF THAT'S OKAY.
YOU YANKED MY ENTIRE BRAIN OUT OF MY BODY...BUT YOU'RE ASKING *PERMISSION* TO BORROW A MEMORY?
I WAS TRYING TO BE POLITE.
JUST-JUST DO WHATEVER YOU HAVE TO DO.
THIS HAS TO STOP.
HOLD STILL.
WAIT!
BUT-BUT NOTHING EMBARRASSING.
JUST CONCENTRATE.

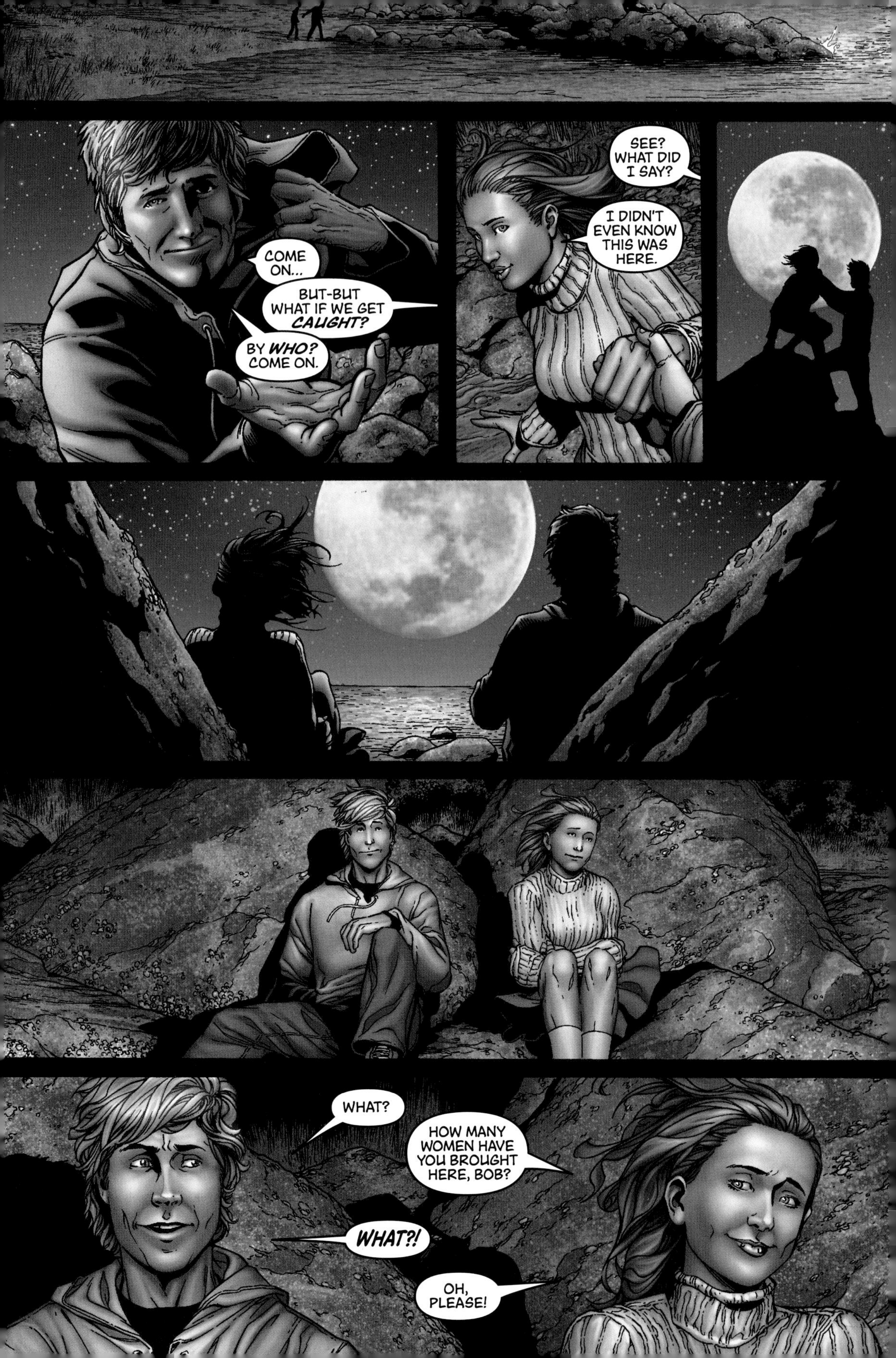
COME ON...
BUT-BUT WHAT IF WE GET *CAUGHT?*
BY *WHO?* COME ON.
SEE? WHAT DID I SAY?
I DIDN'T EVEN KNOW THIS WAS HERE.
WHAT?
HOW MANY WOMEN HAVE YOU BROUGHT HERE, BOB?
WHAT?!
OH, PLEASE!

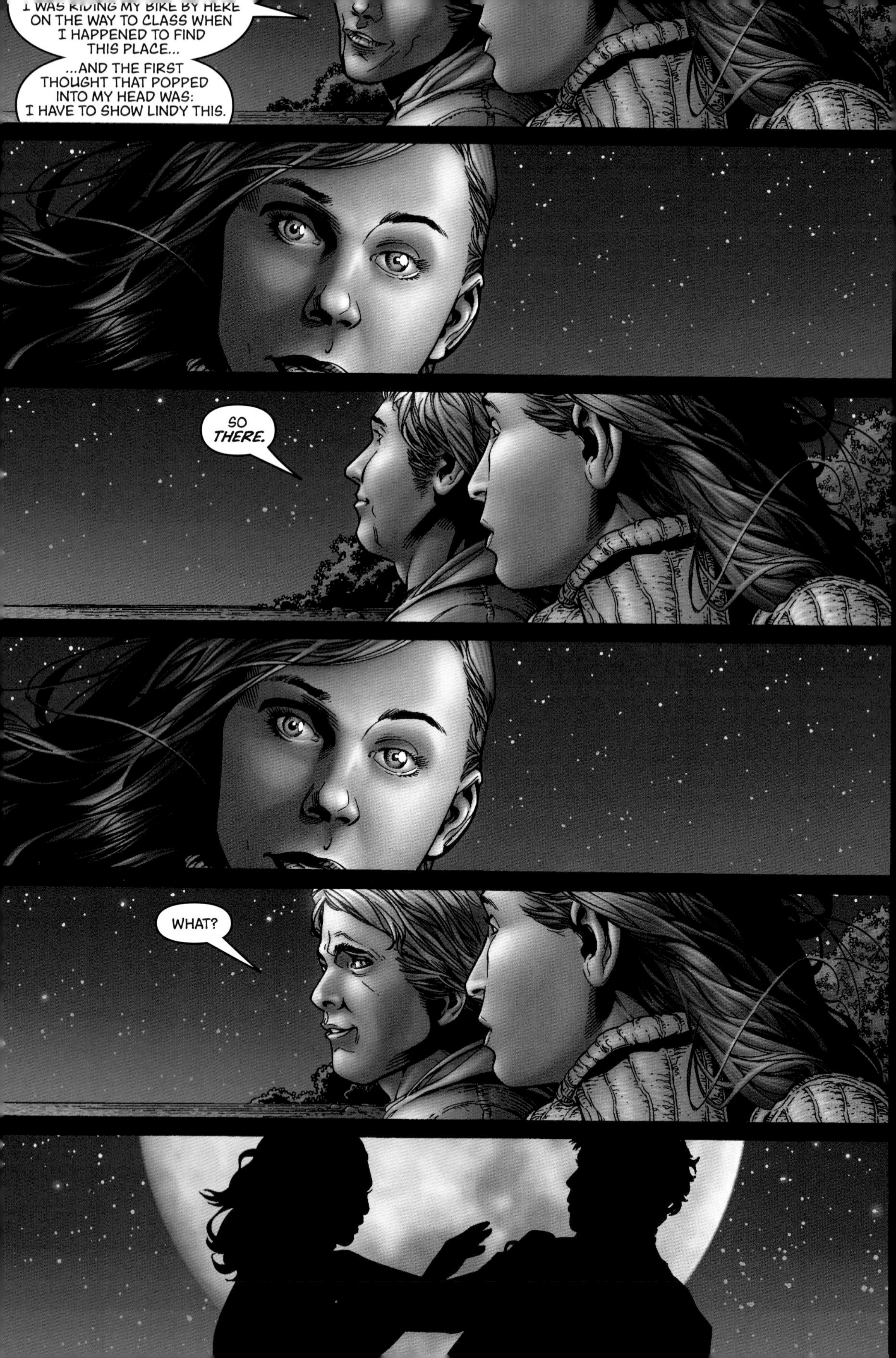
I WAS RIDING MY BIKE BY HERE ON THE WAY TO CLASS WHEN I HAPPENED TO FIND THIS PLACE...
...AND THE FIRST THOUGHT THAT POPPED INTO MY HEAD WAS: I HAVE TO SHOW LINDY THIS.
SO THERE.
WHAT?

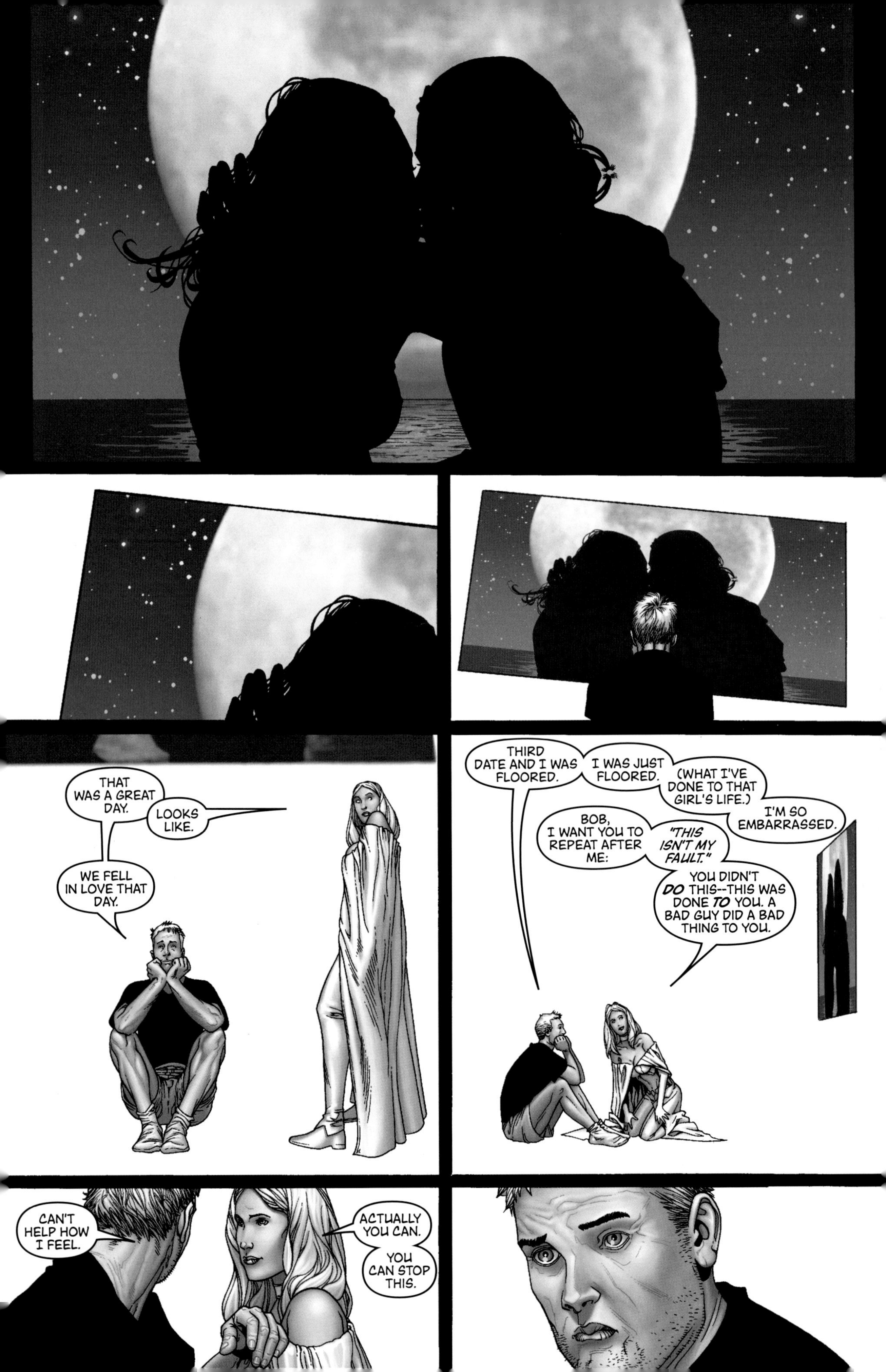

THAT WAS A GREAT DAY.
LOOKS LIKE.
WE FELL IN LOVE THAT DAY.
THIRD DATE AND I WAS FLOORED.
I WAS JUST FLOORED.
(WHAT I'VE DONE TO THAT GIRL'S LIFE.)
I'M SO EMBARRASSED.
BOB, I WANT YOU TO REPEAT AFTER ME:
"THIS ISN'T MY FAULT."
YOU DIDN'T DO THIS--THIS WAS DONE TO YOU. A BAD GUY DID A BAD THING TO YOU.
CAN'T HELP HOW I FEEL.
ACTUALLY YOU CAN.
YOU CAN STOP THIS.

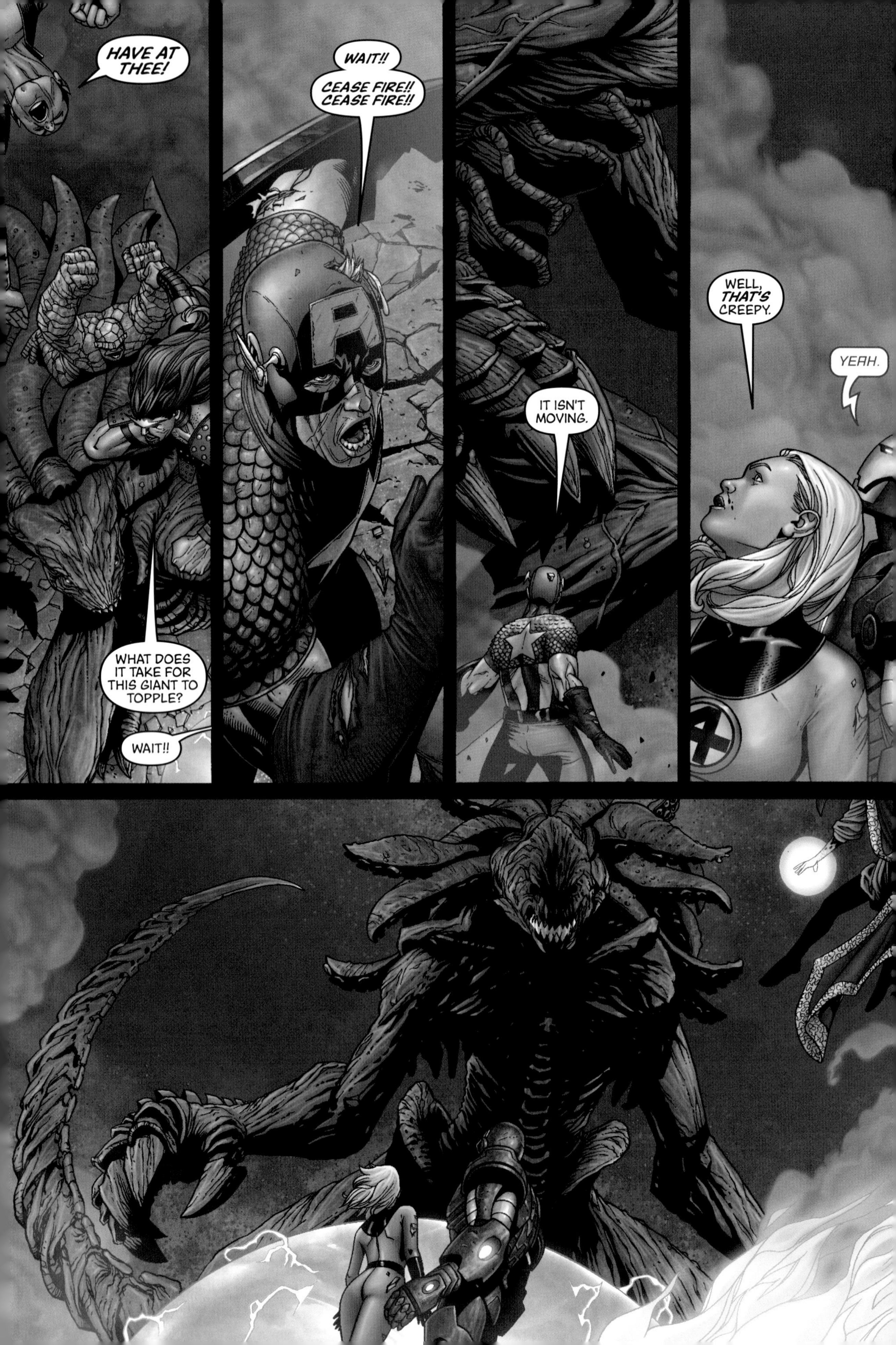
HAVE AT THEE!
WHAT DOES IT TAKE FOR THIS GIANT TO TOPPLE?
WAIT!!
WAIT!!
CEASE FIRE!! CEASE FIRE!!
IT ISN'T MOVING.
WELL, THAT'S CREEPY.
YEAH.

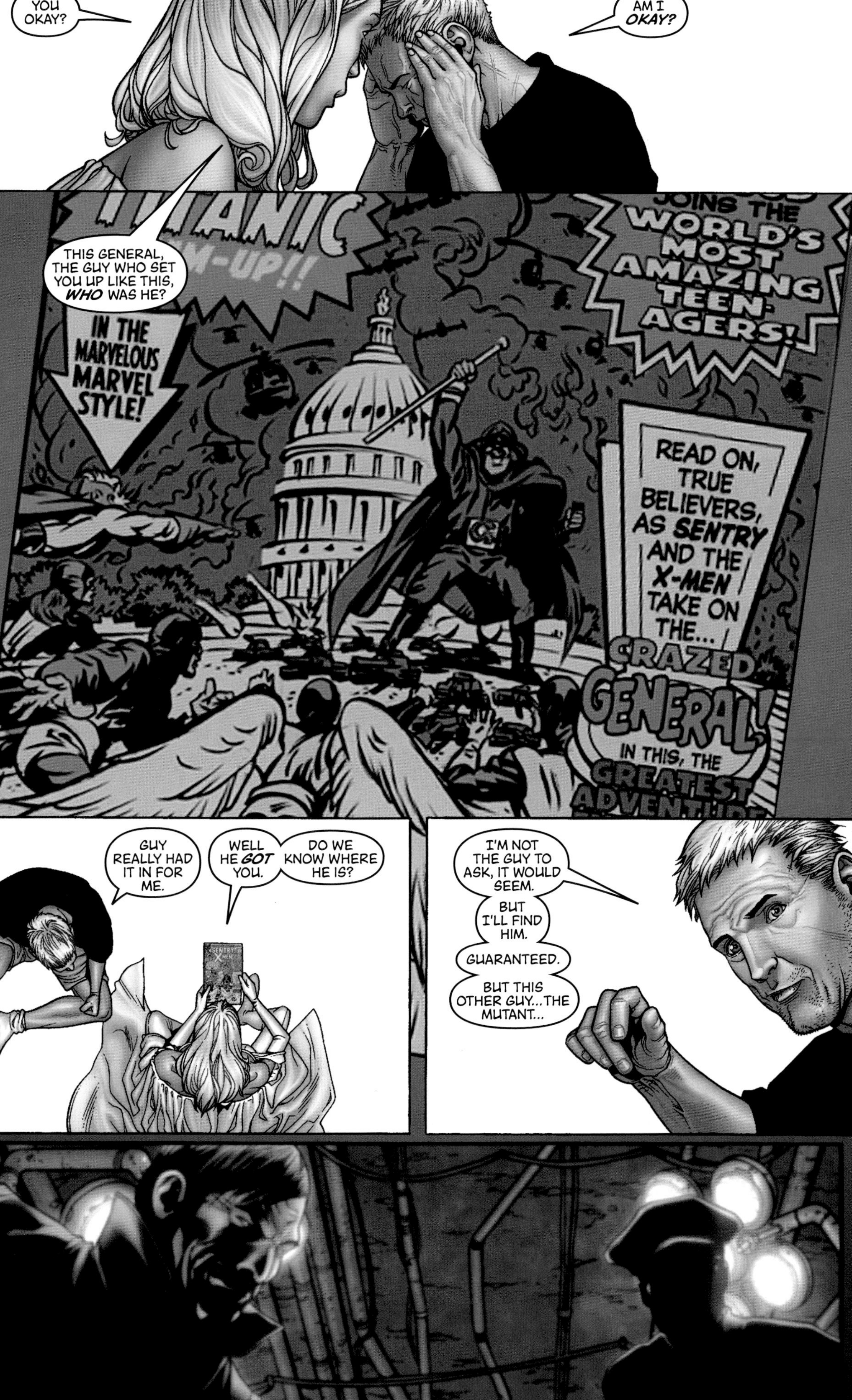
YOU OKAY?
AM I OKAY?
THIS GENERAL, THE GUY WHO SET YOU UP LIKE THIS, WHO WAS HE?
TITANIC
M-UP!!
JOINS THE WORLD'S MOST AMAZING TEEN-AGERS!
IN THE MARVELOUS MARVEL STYLE!
READ ON, TRUE BELIEVERS, AS SENTRY AND THE X-MEN TAKE ON THE... CRAZED GENERAL! IN THIS, THE GREATEST
GUY REALLY HAD IT IN FOR ME.
WELL HE GOT YOU.
DO WE KNOW WHERE HE IS?
I'M NOT THE GUY TO ASK, IT WOULD SEEM.
BUT I'LL FIND HIM.
GUARANTEED.
BUT THIS OTHER GUY... THE MUTANT...

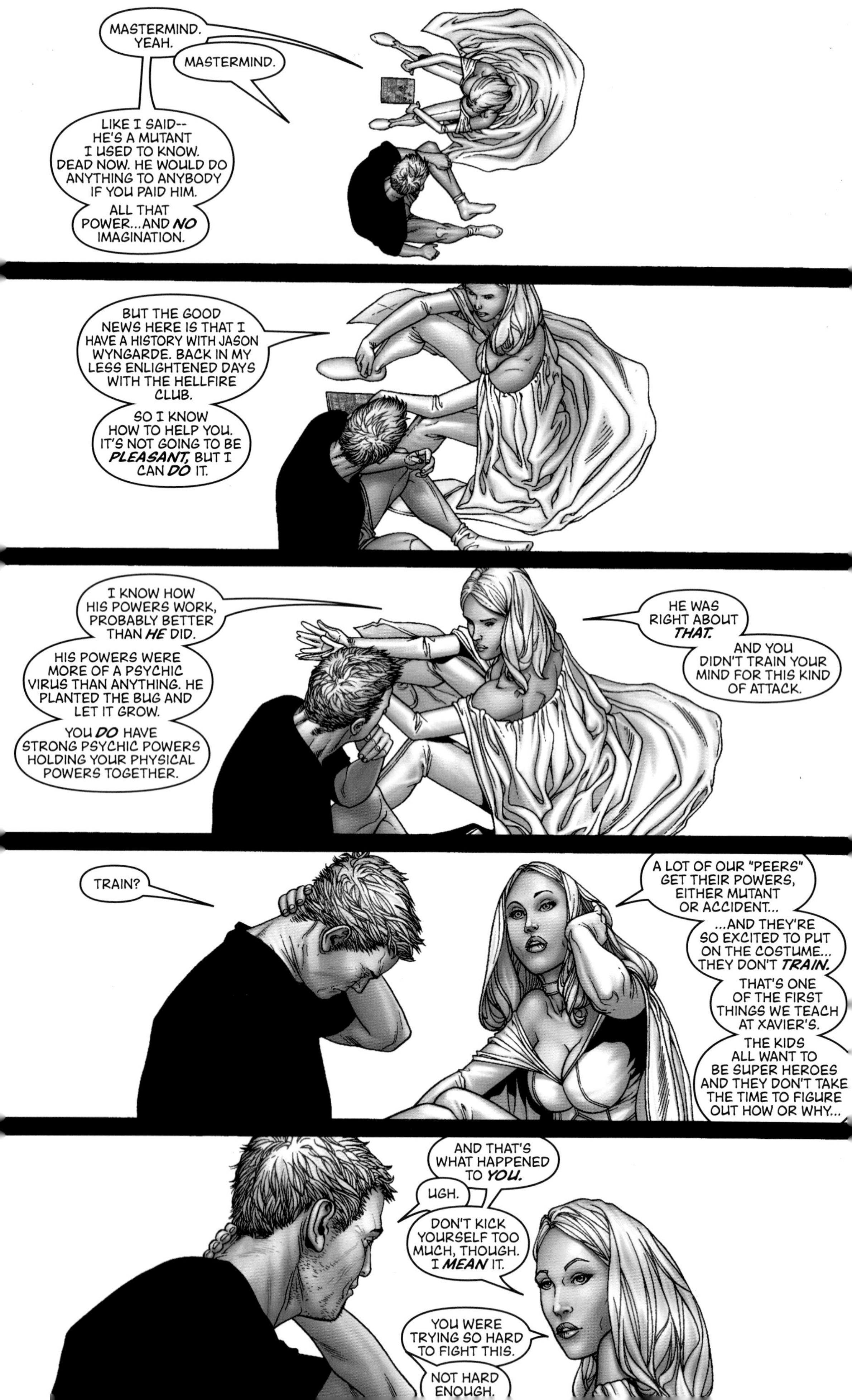

MASTERMIND. YEAH.
MASTERMIND.
LIKE I SAID-- HE'S A MUTANT I USED TO KNOW. DEAD NOW. HE WOULD DO ANYTHING TO ANYBODY IF YOU PAID HIM.
ALL THAT POWER...AND NO IMAGINATION.
BUT THE GOOD NEWS HERE IS THAT I HAVE A HISTORY WITH JASON WYNGARDE. BACK IN MY LESS ENLIGHTENED DAYS WITH THE HELLFIRE CLUB.
SO I KNOW HOW TO HELP YOU. IT'S NOT GOING TO BE PLEASANT, BUT I CAN DO IT.
I KNOW HOW HIS POWERS WORK, PROBABLY BETTER THAN HE DID.
HIS POWERS WERE MORE OF A PSYCHIC VIRUS THAN ANYTHING. HE PLANTED THE BUG AND LET IT GROW.
YOU DO HAVE STRONG PSYCHIC POWERS HOLDING YOUR PHYSICAL POWERS TOGETHER.
HE WAS RIGHT ABOUT THAT.
AND YOU DIDN'T TRAIN YOUR MIND FOR THIS KIND OF ATTACK.
TRAIN?
A LOT OF OUR "PEERS" GET THEIR POWERS, EITHER MUTANT OR ACCIDENT...
...AND THEY'RE SO EXCITED TO PUT ON THE COSTUME... THEY DON'T TRAIN.
THAT'S ONE OF THE FIRST THINGS WE TEACH AT XAVIER'S.
THE KIDS ALL WANT TO BE SUPER HEROES AND THEY DON'T TAKE THE TIME TO FIGURE OUT HOW OR WHY...
AND THAT'S WHAT HAPPENED TO YOU.
UGH.
DON'T KICK YOURSELF TOO MUCH, THOUGH. I MEAN IT.
YOU WERE TRYING SO HARD TO FIGHT THIS.
NOT HARD ENOUGH.

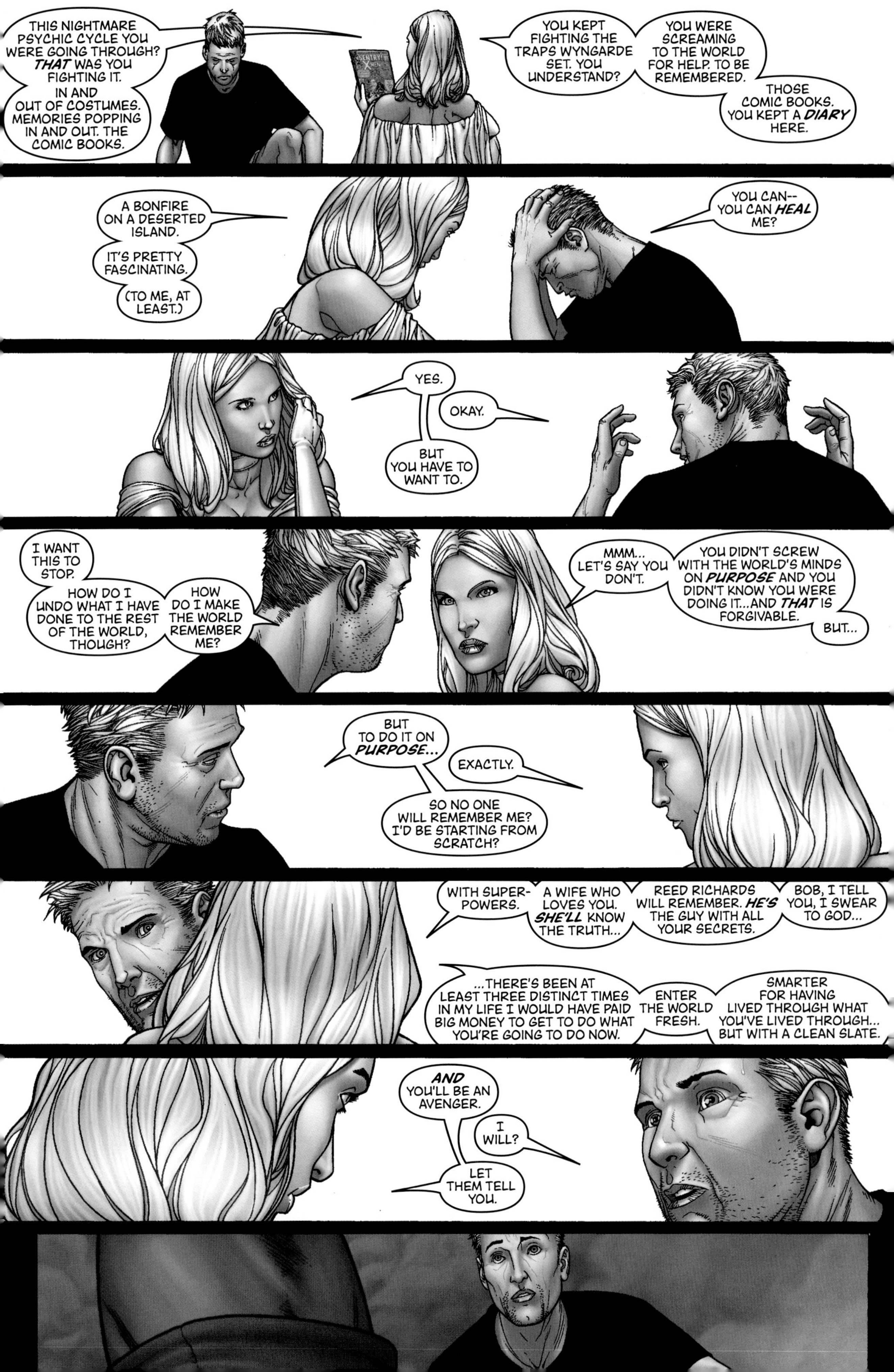
THIS NIGHTMARE PSYCHIC CYCLE YOU WERE GOING THROUGH? *THAT* WAS YOU FIGHTING IT.
IN AND OUT OF COSTUMES. MEMORIES POPPING IN AND OUT. THE COMIC BOOKS.
YOU KEPT FIGHTING THE TRAPS WYNGARDE SET. YOU UNDERSTAND?
YOU WERE SCREAMING TO THE WORLD FOR HELP. TO BE REMEMBERED.
THOSE COMIC BOOKS. YOU KEPT A *DIARY* HERE.
A BONFIRE ON A DESERTED ISLAND.
IT'S PRETTY FASCINATING.
(TO ME, AT LEAST.)
YOU CAN-- YOU CAN *HEAL* ME?
YES.
OKAY.
BUT YOU HAVE TO WANT TO.
I WANT THIS TO STOP.
HOW DO I UNDO WHAT I HAVE DONE TO THE REST OF THE WORLD, THOUGH?
HOW DO I MAKE THE WORLD REMEMBER ME?
MMM... LET'S SAY YOU DON'T.
YOU DIDN'T SCREW WITH THE WORLD'S MINDS ON *PURPOSE* AND YOU DIDN'T KNOW YOU WERE DOING IT...AND *THAT* IS FORGIVABLE.
BUT...
BUT TO DO IT ON *PURPOSE...*
EXACTLY.
SO NO ONE WILL REMEMBER ME? I'D BE STARTING FROM SCRATCH?
WITH SUPER-POWERS.
A WIFE WHO LOVES YOU. *SHE'LL* KNOW THE TRUTH...
REED RICHARDS WILL REMEMBER. *HE'S* THE GUY WITH ALL YOUR SECRETS.
BOB, I TELL YOU, I SWEAR TO GOD...
...THERE'S BEEN AT LEAST THREE DISTINCT TIMES IN MY LIFE I WOULD HAVE PAID BIG MONEY TO GET TO DO WHAT YOU'RE GOING TO DO NOW.
ENTER THE WORLD FRESH.
SMARTER FOR HAVING LIVED THROUGH WHAT YOU'VE LIVED THROUGH... BUT WITH A CLEAN SLATE.
AND YOU'LL BE AN AVENGER.
I WILL?
LET THEM TELL YOU.

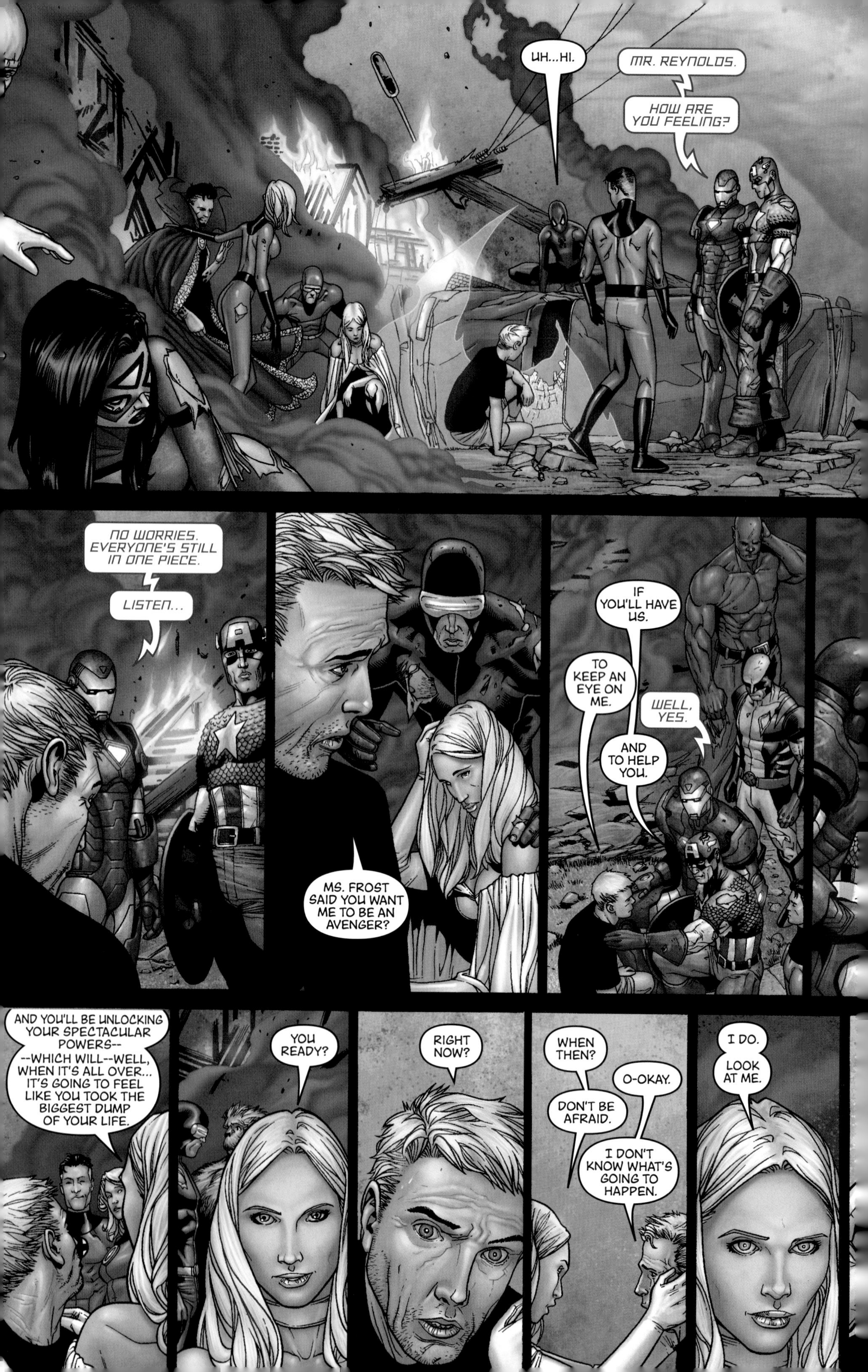
UH...HI.
MR. REYNOLDS.
HOW ARE YOU FEELING?
NO WORRIES. EVERYONE'S STILL IN ONE PIECE.
LISTEN...
MS. FROST SAID YOU WANT ME TO BE AN AVENGER?
IF YOU'LL HAVE US.
TO KEEP AN EYE ON ME.
WELL, YES.
AND TO HELP YOU.
AND YOU'LL BE UNLOCKING YOUR SPECTACULAR POWERS-- --WHICH WILL--WELL, WHEN IT'S ALL OVER... IT'S GOING TO FEEL LIKE YOU TOOK THE BIGGEST DUMP OF YOUR LIFE.
YOU READY?
RIGHT NOW?
WHEN THEN?
O-OKAY.
DON'T BE AFRAID.
I DON'T KNOW WHAT'S GOING TO HAPPEN.
I DO.
LOOK AT ME.

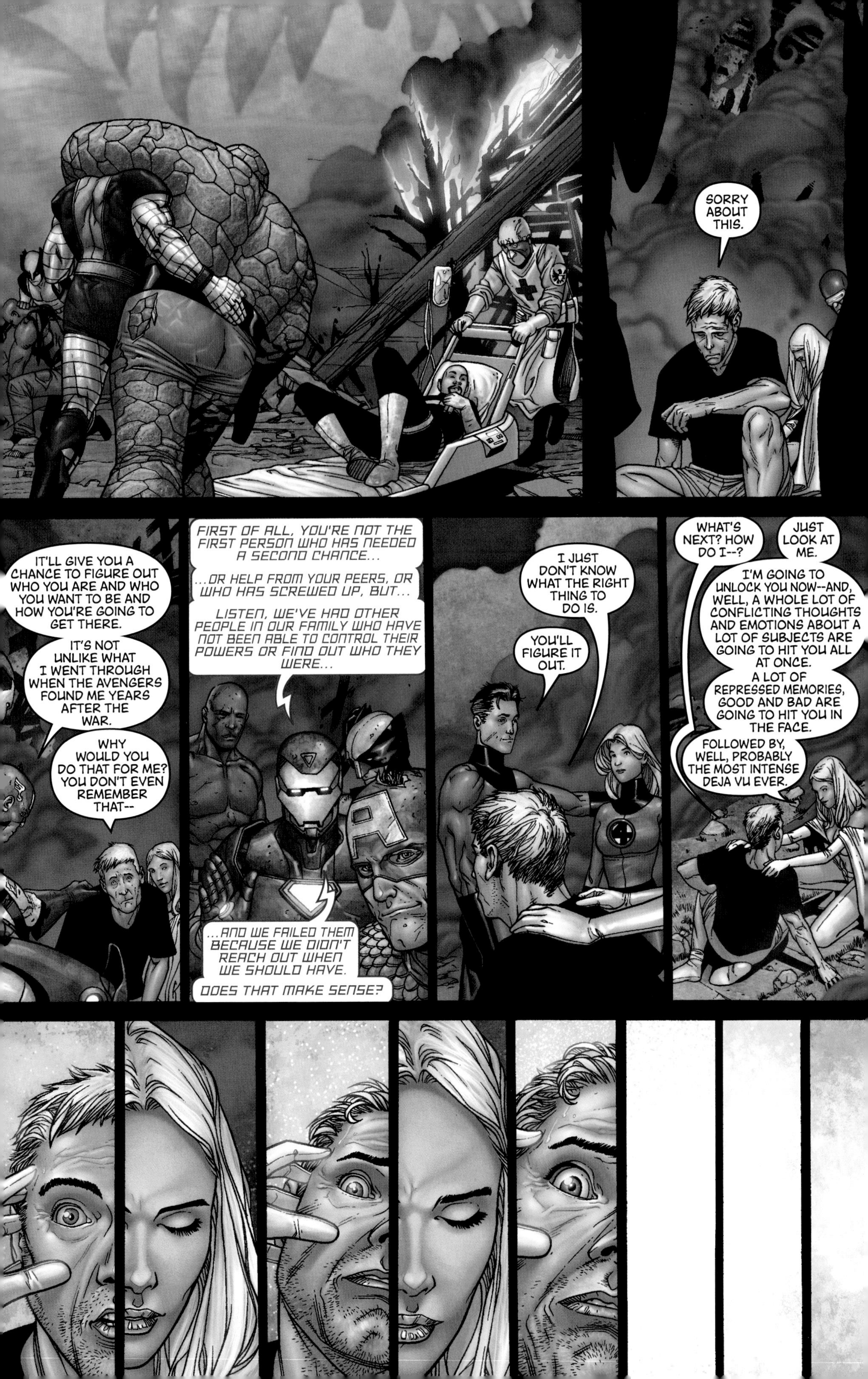
SORRY ABOUT THIS.
IT'LL GIVE YOU A CHANCE TO FIGURE OUT WHO YOU ARE AND WHO YOU WANT TO BE AND HOW YOU'RE GOING TO GET THERE.
IT'S NOT UNLIKE WHAT I WENT THROUGH WHEN THE AVENGERS FOUND ME YEARS AFTER THE WAR.
WHY WOULD YOU DO THAT FOR ME? YOU DON'T EVEN REMEMBER THAT--
FIRST OF ALL, YOU'RE NOT THE FIRST PERSON WHO HAS NEEDED A SECOND CHANCE...
...OR HELP FROM YOUR PEERS, OR WHO HAS SCREWED UP, BUT...
LISTEN, WE'VE HAD OTHER PEOPLE IN OUR FAMILY WHO HAVE NOT BEEN ABLE TO CONTROL THEIR POWERS OR FIND OUT WHO THEY WERE...
...AND WE FAILED THEM BECAUSE WE DIDN'T REACH OUT WHEN WE SHOULD HAVE.
DOES THAT MAKE SENSE?
I JUST DON'T KNOW WHAT THE RIGHT THING TO DO IS.
YOU'LL FIGURE IT OUT.
WHAT'S NEXT? HOW DO I--?
JUST LOOK AT ME.
I'M GOING TO UNLOCK YOU NOW--AND, WELL, A WHOLE LOT OF CONFLICTING THOUGHTS AND EMOTIONS ABOUT A LOT OF SUBJECTS ARE GOING TO HIT YOU ALL AT ONCE.
A LOT OF REPRESSED MEMORIES, GOOD AND BAD ARE GOING TO HIT YOU IN THE FACE.
FOLLOWED BY, WELL, PROBABLY THE MOST INTENSE DEJA VU EVER.

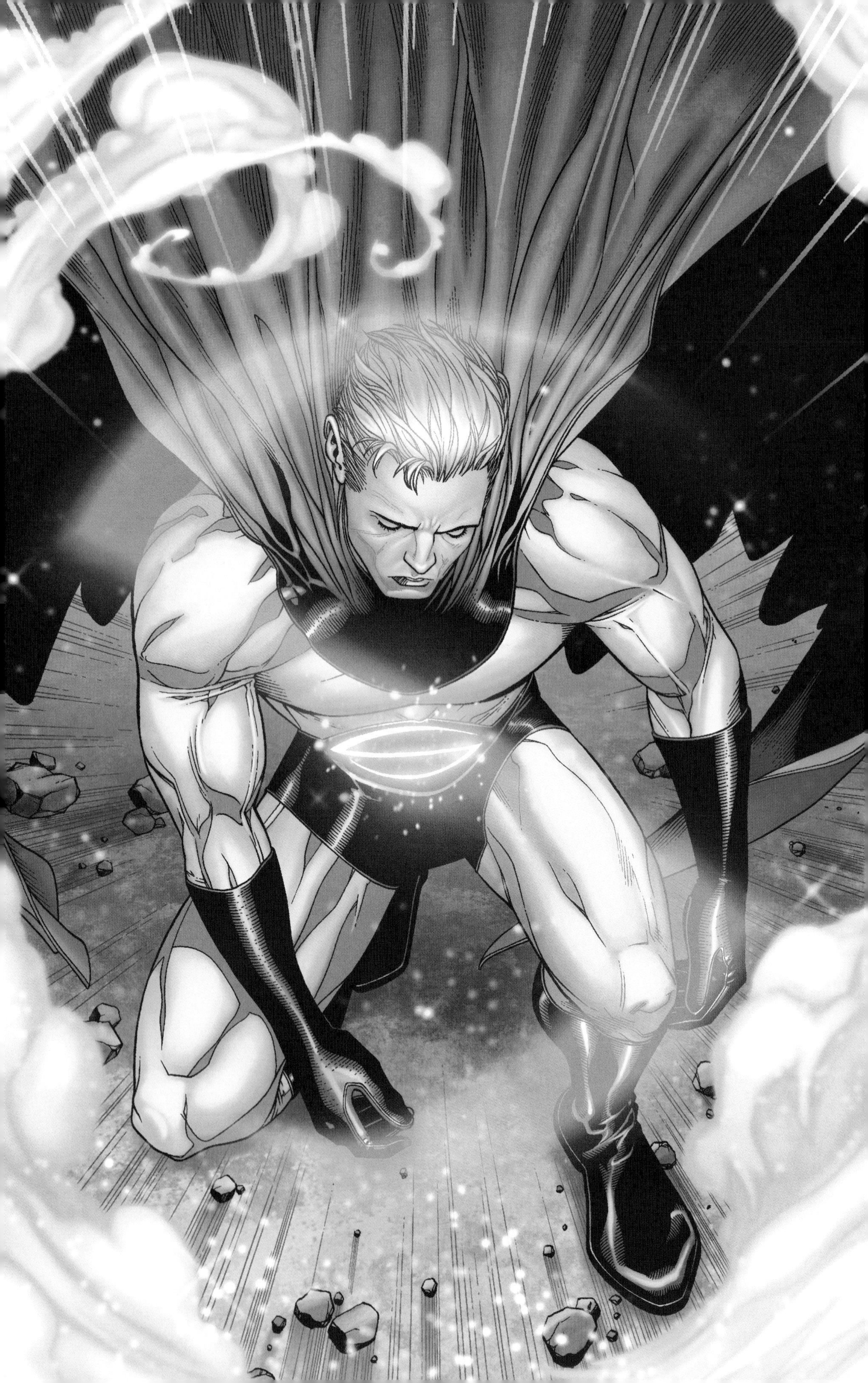

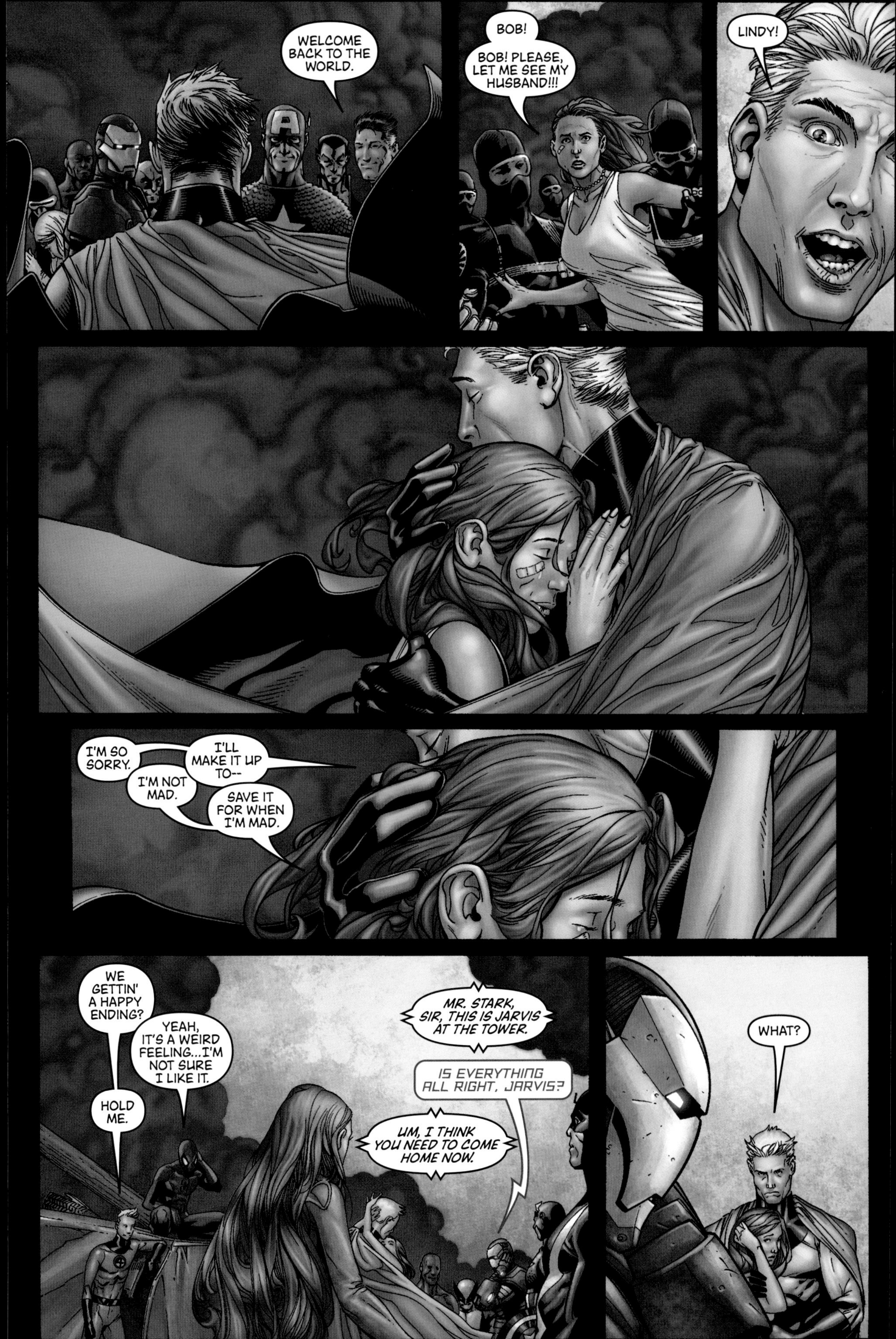

WELCOME BACK TO THE WORLD.
BOB!
BOB! PLEASE, LET ME SEE MY HUSBAND!!!
LINDY!
I'M SO SORRY.
I'LL MAKE IT UP TO--
I'M NOT MAD.
SAVE IT FOR WHEN I'M MAD.
WE GETTIN' A HAPPY ENDING?
YEAH, IT'S A WEIRD FEELING...I'M NOT SURE I LIKE IT.
HOLD ME.
MR. STARK, SIR, THIS IS JARVIS AT THE TOWER.
IS EVERYTHING ALL RIGHT, JARVIS?
UM, I THINK YOU NEED TO COME HOME NOW.
WHAT?

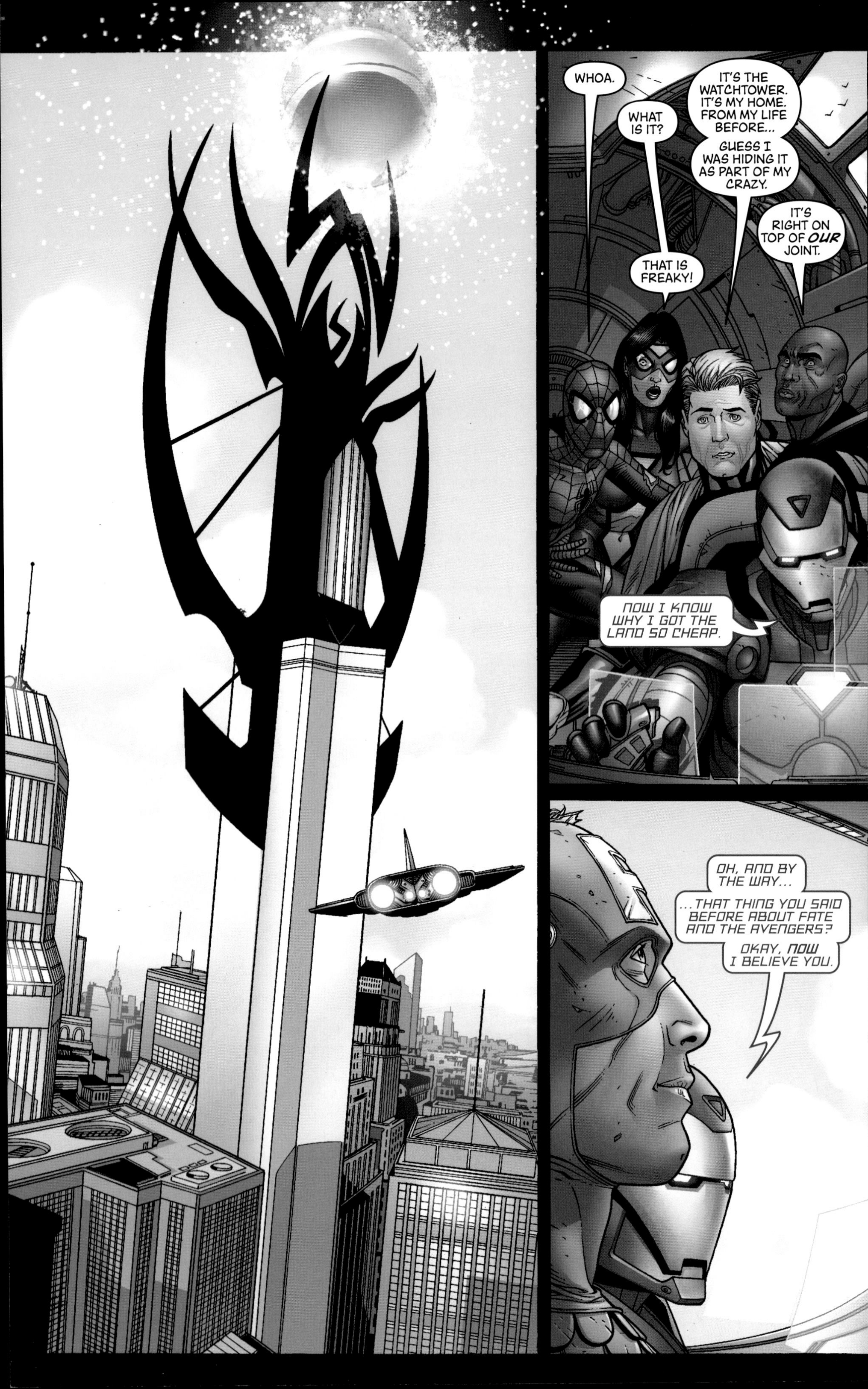
WHOA.
WHAT IS IT?
IT'S THE WATCHTOWER. IT'S MY HOME. FROM MY LIFE BEFORE...
GUESS I WAS HIDING IT AS PART OF MY CRAZY.
THAT IS FREAKY!
IT'S RIGHT ON TOP OF OUR JOINT.
NOW I KNOW WHY I GOT THE LAND SO CHEAP.
OH, AND BY THE WAY...
...THAT THING YOU SAID BEFORE ABOUT FATE AND THE AVENGERS?
OKAY, NOW I BELIEVE YOU.

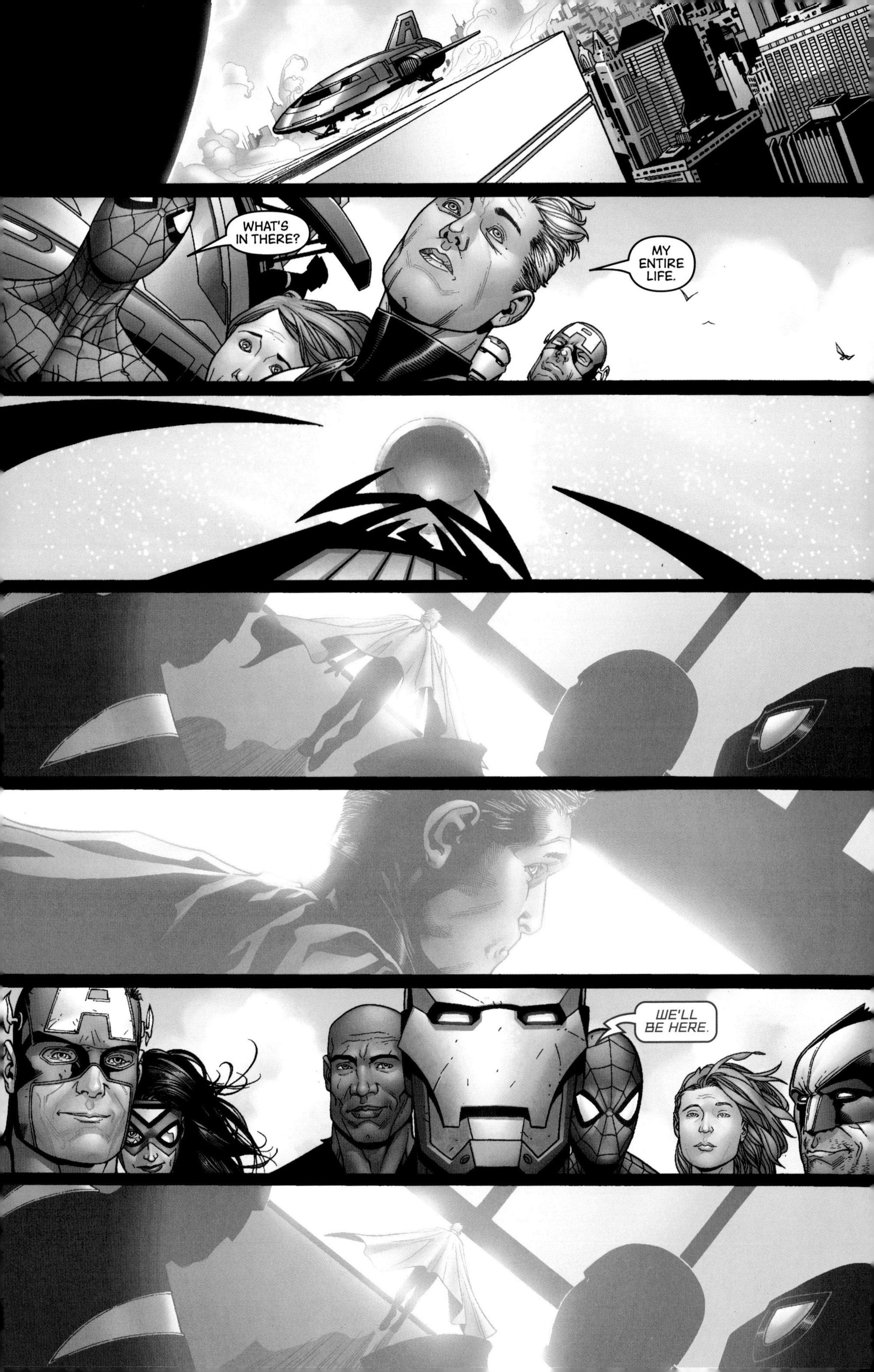
WHAT'S IN THERE?
MY ENTIRE LIFE.
WE'LL BE HERE.

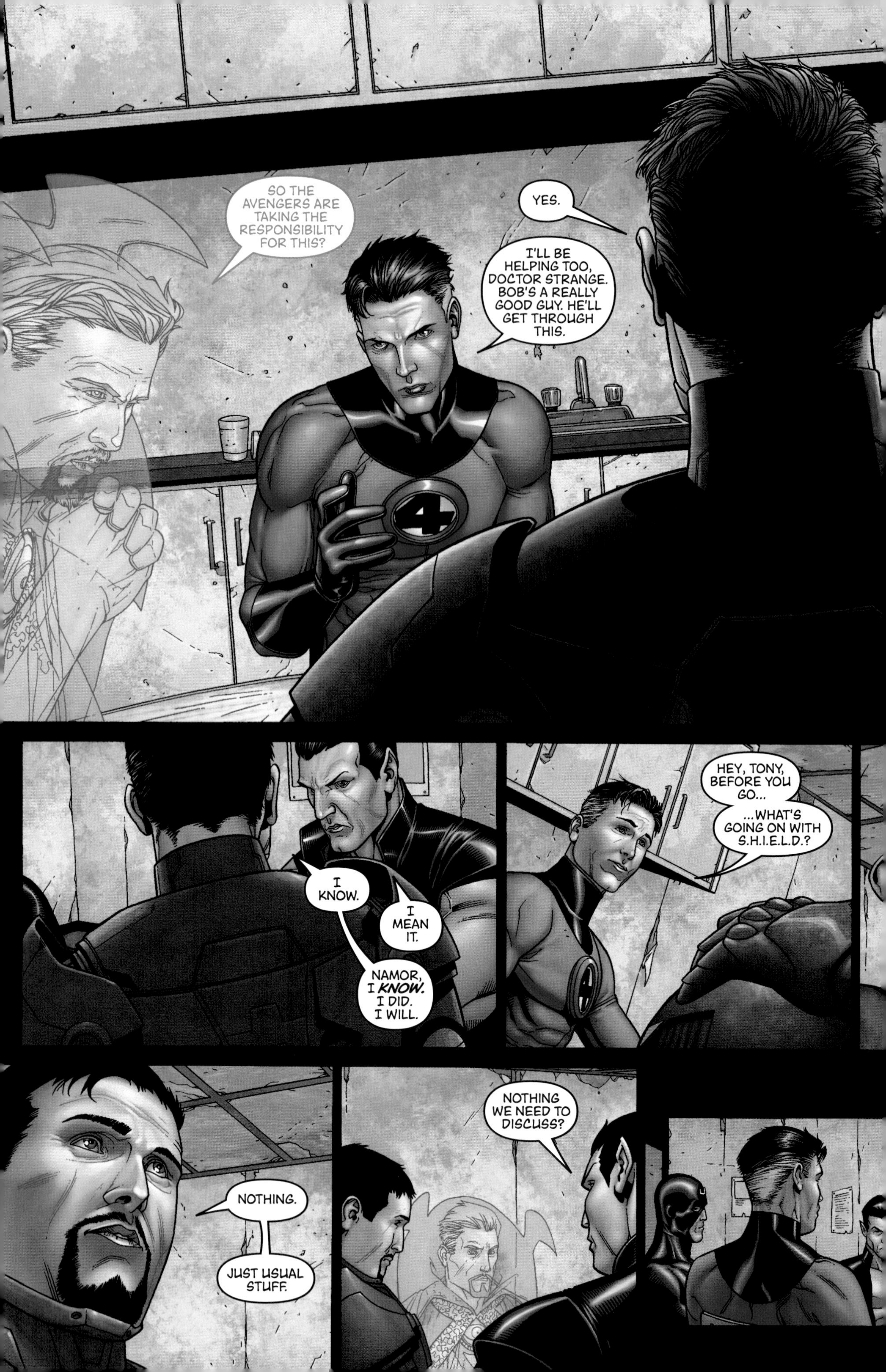

SO THE AVENGERS ARE TAKING THE RESPONSIBILITY FOR THIS?
YES.
I'LL BE HELPING TOO, DOCTOR STRANGE. BOB'S A REALLY GOOD GUY. HE'LL GET THROUGH THIS.
I KNOW.
I MEAN IT.
NAMOR, I *KNOW.* I DID. I WILL.
HEY, TONY, BEFORE YOU GO...
...WHAT'S GOING ON WITH S.H.I.E.L.D.?
NOTHING.
JUST USUAL STUFF.
NOTHING WE NEED TO DISCUSS?

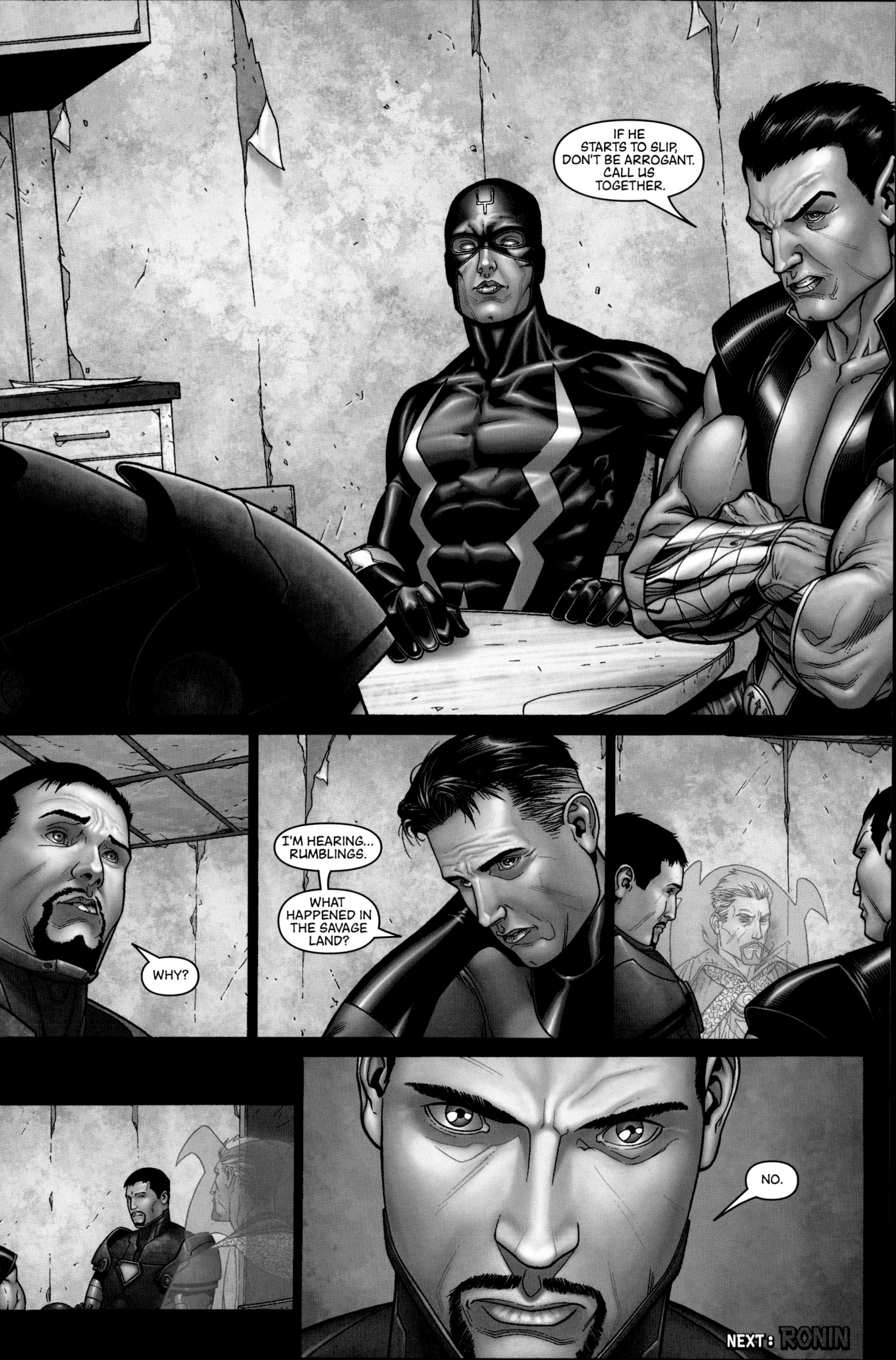
IF HE STARTS TO SLIP, DON'T BE ARROGANT. CALL US TOGETHER.
WHY?
I'M HEARING... RUMBLINGS.
WHAT HAPPENED IN THE SAVAGE LAND?
NO.
NEXT: RONIN

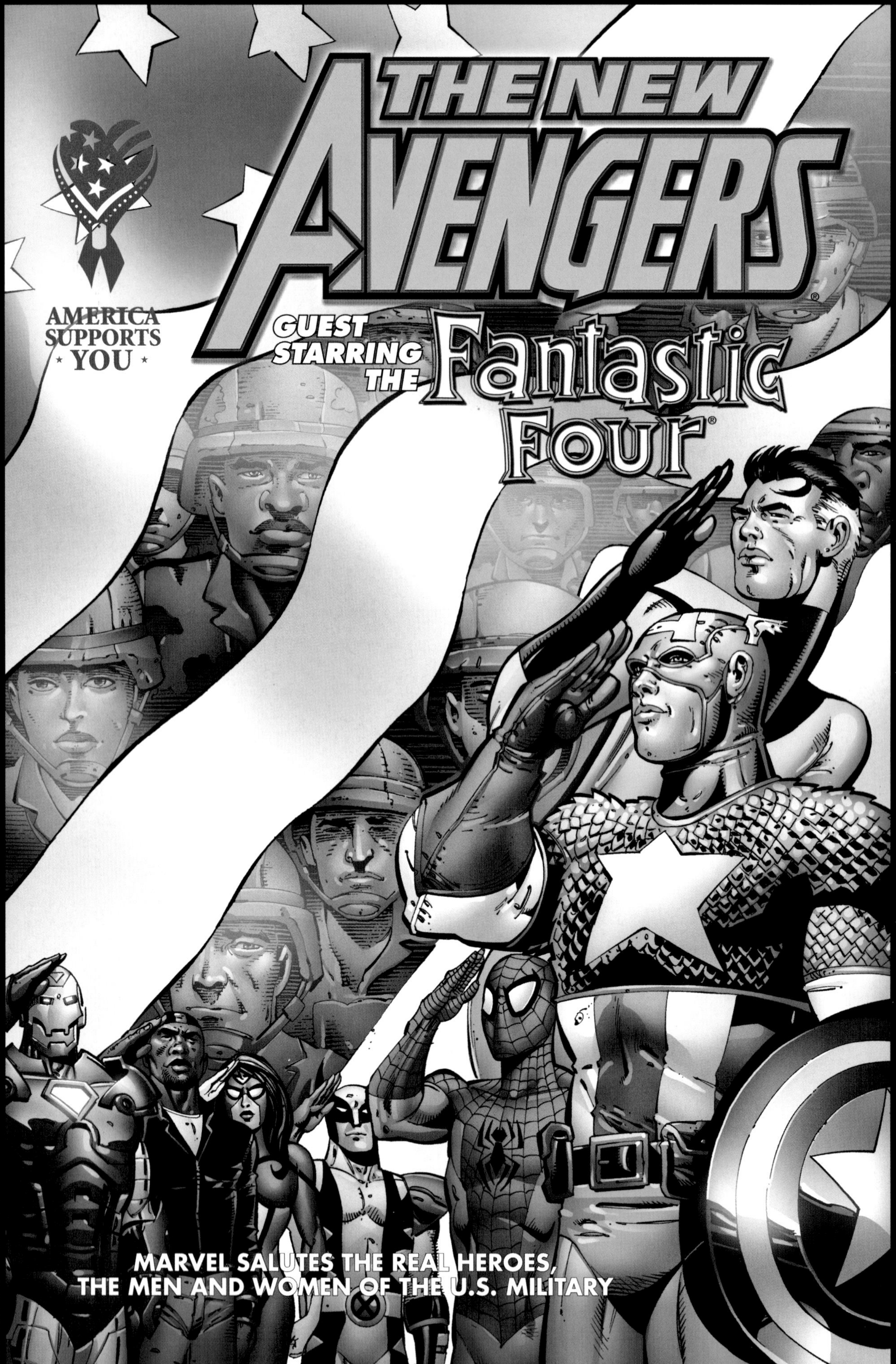
THE NEW AVENGERS
GUEST STARRING THE Fantastic Four
AMERICA SUPPORTS YOU
MARVEL SALUTES THE REAL HEROES,
THE MEN AND WOMEN OF THE U.S. MILITARY

WHEN WE CALLED S.H.I.E.L.D. TO REPORT THE FIND, WE DIDN'T EXPECT ACTUAL SUPER HEROES TO DROP IN.

WELL, THIS *TYPE* OF FINDING--

WE'RE ALL GLAD TO BE ON THIS MISSION WITH YOU, DR. RICHARDS.

AND I DON'T KNOW IF YOU REMEMBER ME, IRON MAN, BUT I WAS AT THE BATTLE OF RED ZONE.

GLAD YOU MADE IT OUT SAFE.

AREN'T YOU HOT IN THAT ARMOR?

AIR-CONDITIONING WAS THE FIRST THING I INSTALLED.

WHO FOUND THIS THING WE'RE GOING TO LOOK AT?

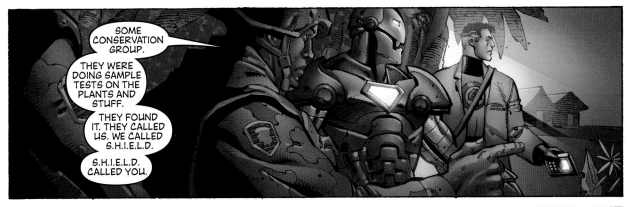

SOME CONSERVATION GROUP.

THEY WERE DOING SAMPLE TESTS ON THE PLANTS AND STUFF.

THEY FOUND IT. THEY CALLED US. WE CALLED S.H.I.E.L.D.

S.H.I.E.L.D. CALLED YOU.

WE DON'T EXACTLY KNOW WHAT IT IS. WE SCANNED IT WITH ALL OUR SENSORS, TRIED TO ANALYZE--

OH.

WHAT?

NOT BLAMING YOU, BUT ACTIVE SENSING CAN PRODUCE FALSE DATA ON SOMETHING LIKE THIS...

SOMETHING LIKE *WHAT?*

THAT'S THE THING. WE--WE DON'T KNOW WHAT IT *IS...*

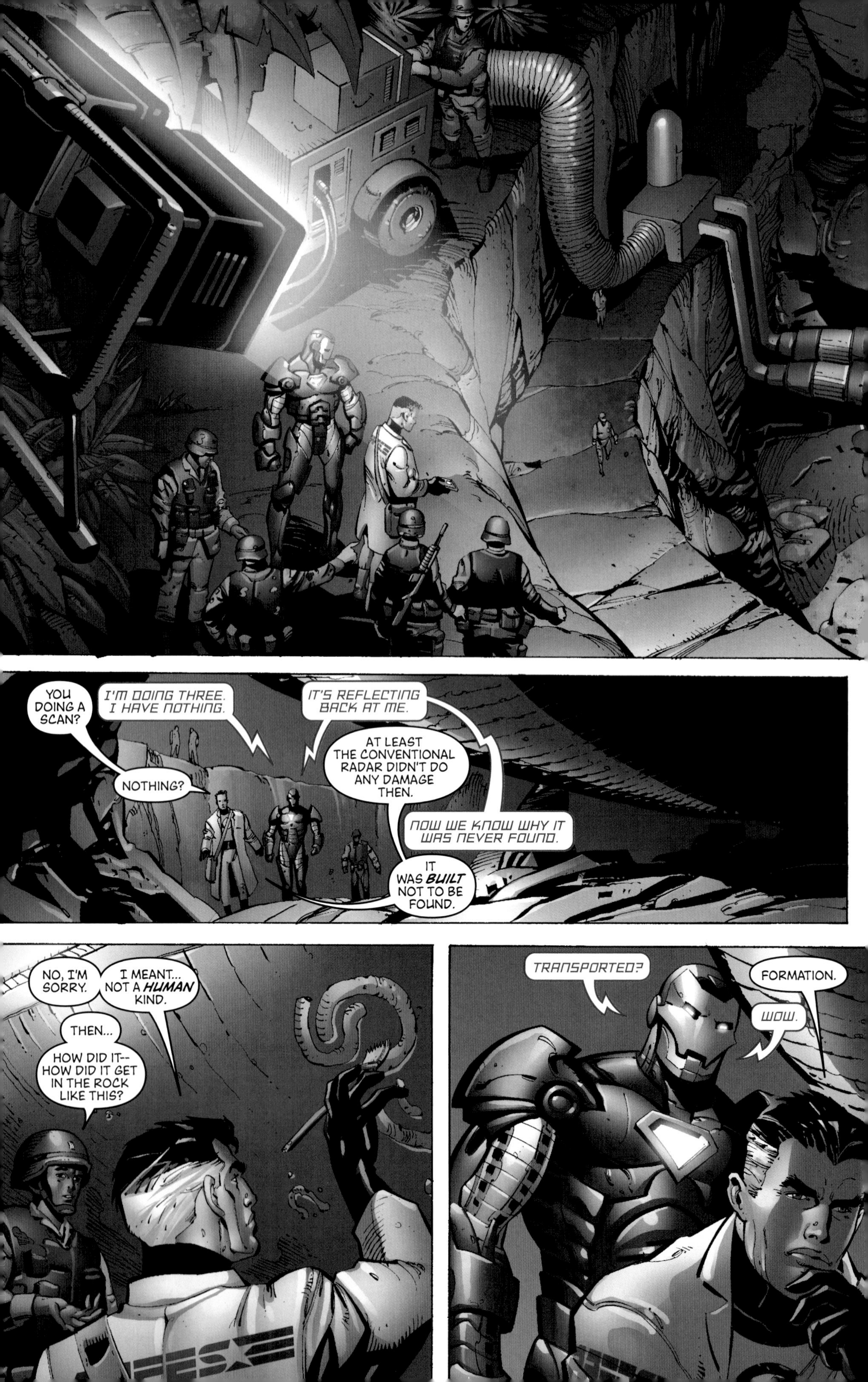
YOU DOING A SCAN?
I'M DOING THREE. I HAVE NOTHING.
NOTHING?
IT'S REFLECTING BACK AT ME.
AT LEAST THE CONVENTIONAL RADAR DIDN'T DO ANY DAMAGE THEN.
NOW WE KNOW WHY IT WAS NEVER FOUND.
IT WAS BUILT NOT TO BE FOUND.
NO, I'M SORRY.
I MEANT... NOT A HUMAN KIND.
THEN...
HOW DID IT-- HOW DID IT GET IN THE ROCK LIKE THIS?
TRANSPORTED?
FORMATION.
WOW.

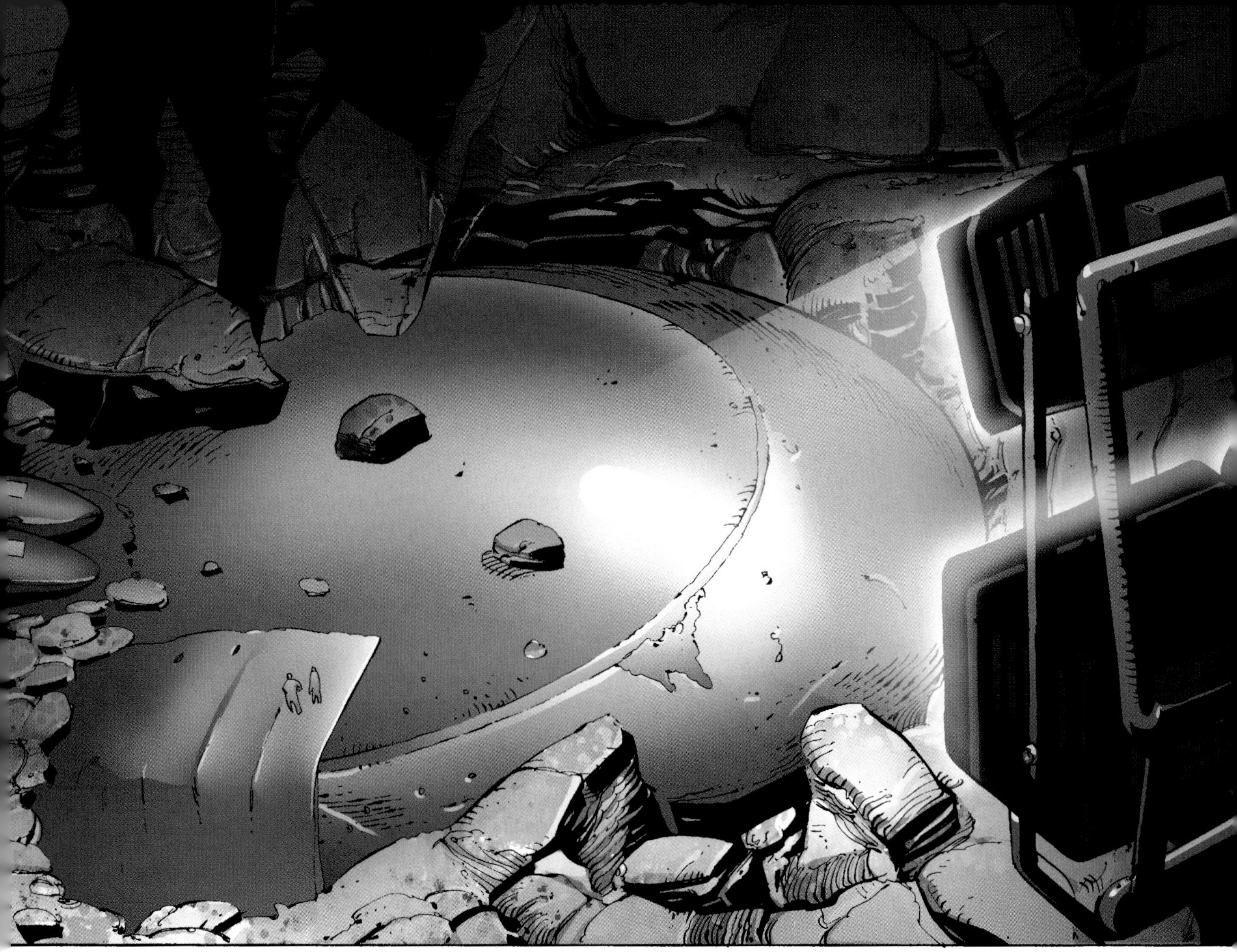

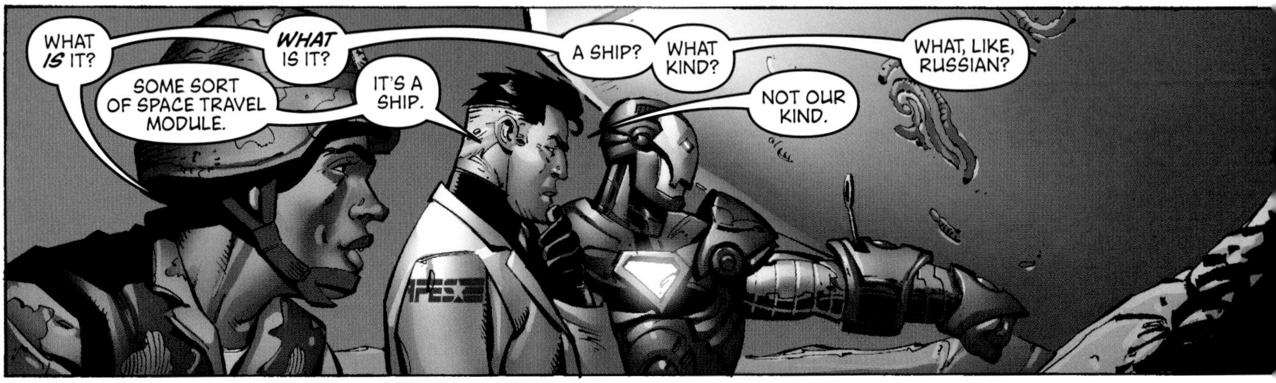
WHAT *IS* IT?
SOME SORT OF SPACE TRAVEL MODULE.
WHAT IS IT?
IT'S A SHIP.
A SHIP?
WHAT KIND?
NOT OUR KIND.
WHAT, LIKE, RUSSIAN?

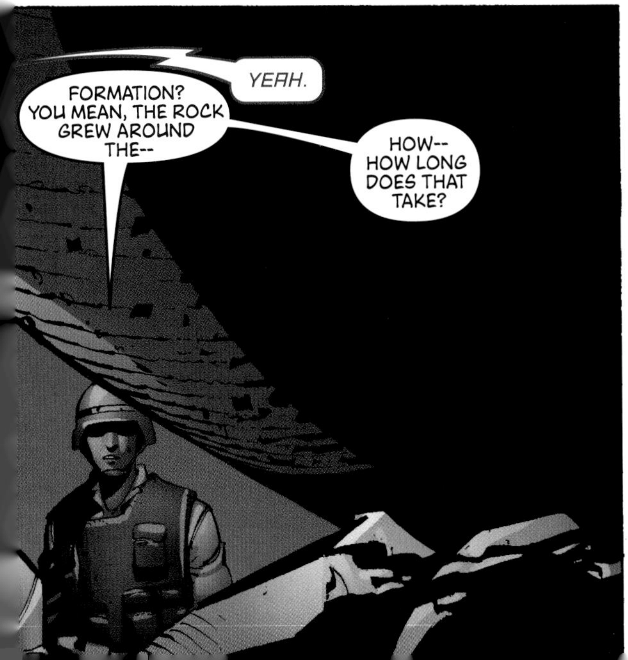
FORMATION? YOU MEAN, THE ROCK GREW AROUND THE--
YEAH.
HOW-- HOW LONG DOES THAT TAKE?

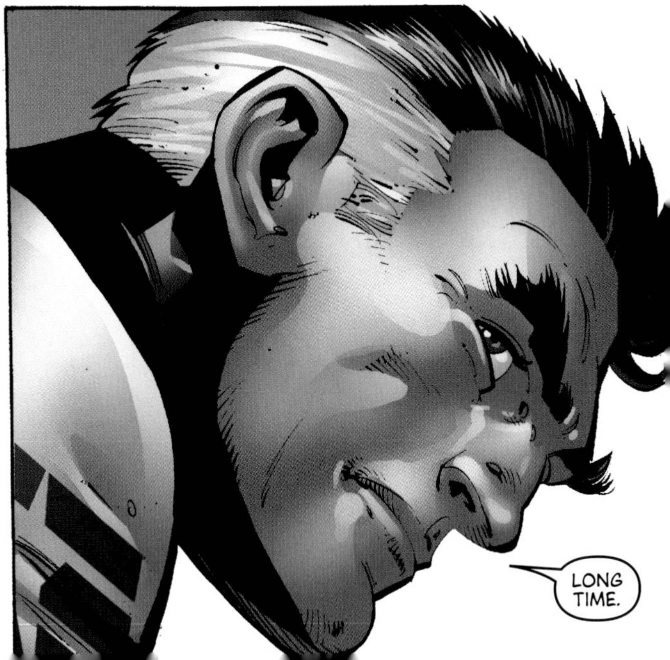
LONG TIME.

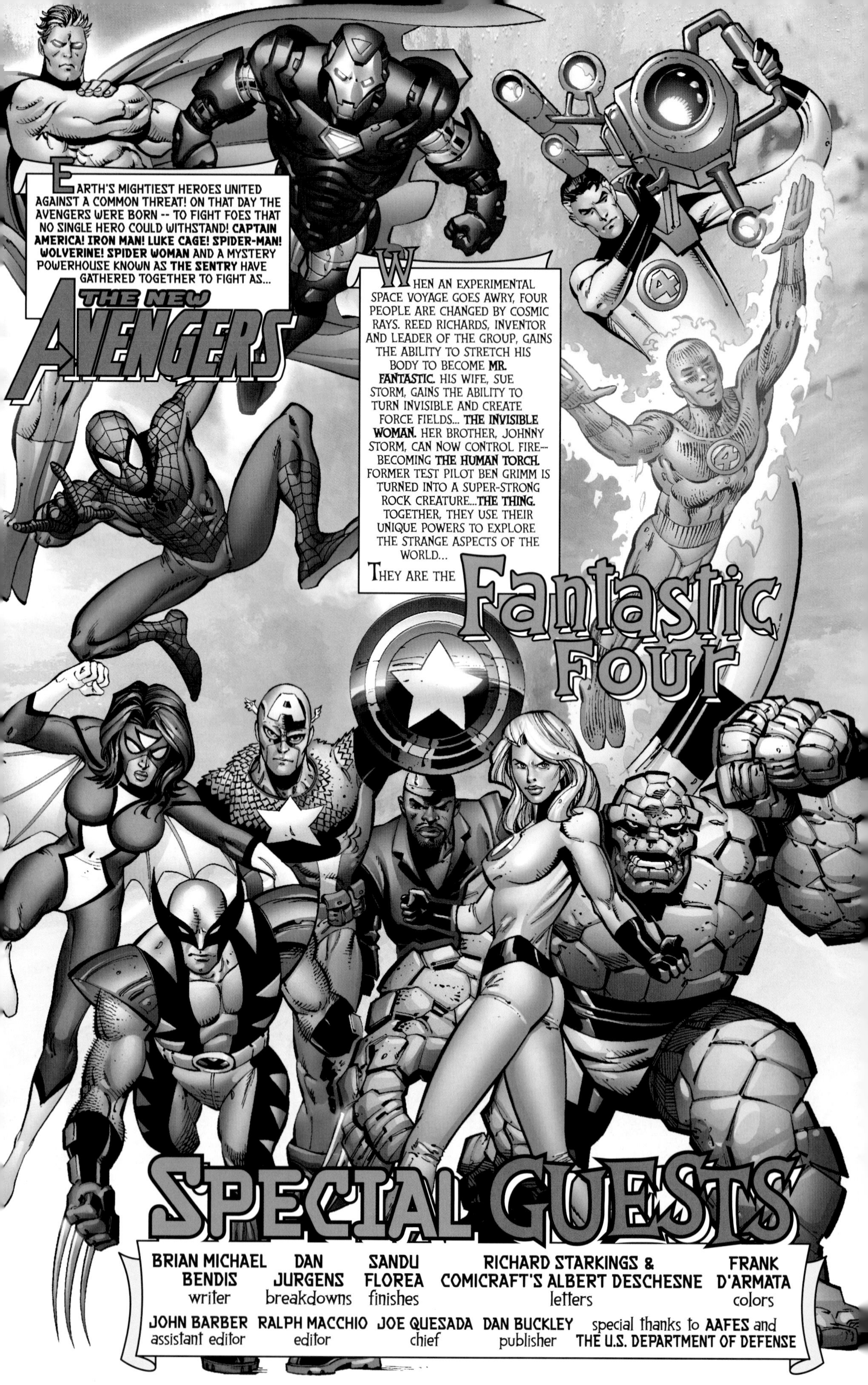
EARTH'S MIGHTIEST HEROES UNITED AGAINST A COMMON THREAT! ON THAT DAY THE AVENGERS WERE BORN -- TO FIGHT FOES THAT NO SINGLE HERO COULD WITHSTAND! CAPTAIN AMERICA! IRON MAN! LUKE CAGE! SPIDER-MAN! WOLVERINE! SPIDER WOMAN AND A MYSTERY POWERHOUSE KNOWN AS THE SENTRY HAVE GATHERED TOGETHER TO FIGHT AS...
THE NEW AVENGERS
WHEN AN EXPERIMENTAL SPACE VOYAGE GOES AWRY, FOUR PEOPLE ARE CHANGED BY COSMIC RAYS. REED RICHARDS, INVENTOR AND LEADER OF THE GROUP, GAINS THE ABILITY TO STRETCH HIS BODY TO BECOME MR. FANTASTIC. HIS WIFE, SUE STORM, GAINS THE ABILITY TO TURN INVISIBLE AND CREATE FORCE FIELDS... THE INVISIBLE WOMAN. HER BROTHER, JOHNNY STORM, CAN NOW CONTROL FIRE-- BECOMING THE HUMAN TORCH. FORMER TEST PILOT BEN GRIMM IS TURNED INTO A SUPER-STRONG ROCK CREATURE...THE THING. TOGETHER, THEY USE THEIR UNIQUE POWERS TO EXPLORE THE STRANGE ASPECTS OF THE WORLD...
THEY ARE THE Fantastic Four
SPECIAL GUESTS
BRIAN MICHAEL BENDIS writer
DAN JURGENS breakdowns
SANDU FLOREA finishes
RICHARD STARKINGS & COMICRAFT'S ALBERT DESCHESNE letters
FRANK D'ARMATA colors
JOHN BARBER assistant editor
RALPH MACCHIO editor
JOE QUESADA chief
DAN BUCKLEY publisher
special thanks to AAFES and THE U.S. DEPARTMENT OF DEFENSE

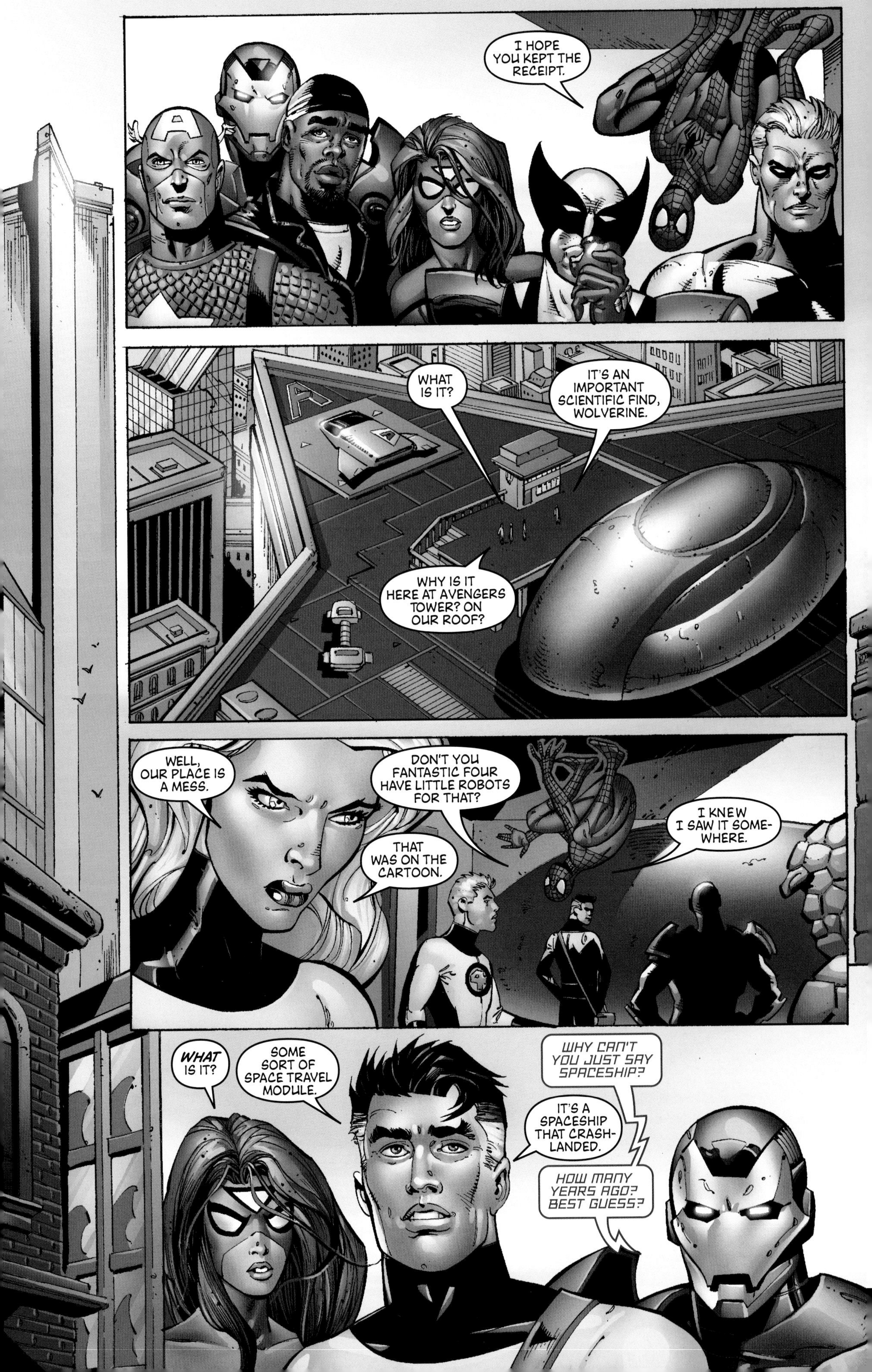
I HOPE YOU KEPT THE RECEIPT.
WHAT IS IT?
IT'S AN IMPORTANT SCIENTIFIC FIND, WOLVERINE.
WHY IS IT HERE AT AVENGERS TOWER? ON OUR ROOF?
WELL, OUR PLACE IS A MESS.
DON'T YOU FANTASTIC FOUR HAVE LITTLE ROBOTS FOR THAT?
THAT WAS ON THE CARTOON.
I KNEW I SAW IT SOME-WHERE.
WHAT IS IT?
SOME SORT OF SPACE TRAVEL MODULE.
WHY CAN'T YOU JUST SAY SPACESHIP?
IT'S A SPACESHIP THAT CRASH-LANDED.
HOW MANY YEARS AGO? BEST GUESS?

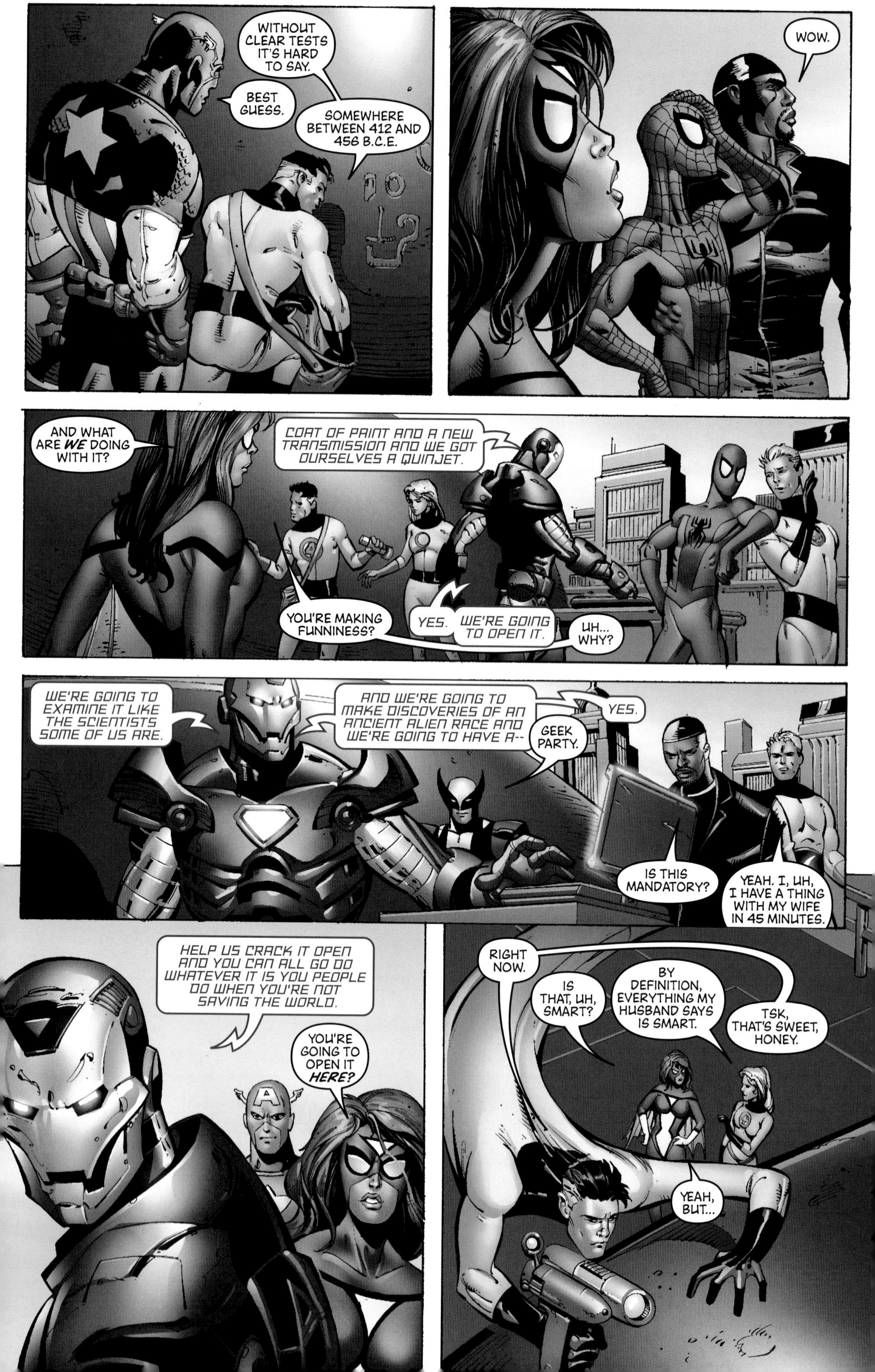
WITHOUT CLEAR TESTS IT'S HARD TO SAY.
BEST GUESS.
SOMEWHERE BETWEEN 412 AND 456 B.C.E.
WOW.
AND WHAT ARE *WE* DOING WITH IT?
COAT OF PAINT AND A NEW TRANSMISSION AND WE GOT OURSELVES A QUINJET.
YOU'RE MAKING FUNNINESS?
YES.
WE'RE GOING TO OPEN IT.
UH... WHY?
WE'RE GOING TO EXAMINE IT LIKE THE SCIENTISTS SOME OF US ARE.
AND WE'RE GOING TO MAKE DISCOVERIES OF AN ANCIENT ALIEN RACE AND WE'RE GOING TO HAVE A--
YES.
GEEK PARTY.
IS THIS MANDATORY?
YEAH. I, UH, I HAVE A THING WITH MY WIFE IN 45 MINUTES.
HELP US CRACK IT OPEN AND YOU CAN ALL GO DO WHATEVER IT IS YOU PEOPLE DO WHEN YOU'RE NOT SAVING THE WORLD.
YOU'RE GOING TO OPEN IT *HERE?*
RIGHT NOW.
IS THAT, UH, SMART?
BY DEFINITION, EVERYTHING MY HUSBAND SAYS IS SMART.
TSK, THAT'S SWEET, HONEY.
YEAH, BUT...

YOU DON'T KNOW WHAT IS *IN* IT AND YOU'RE GOING TO OPEN IT INTO THE AIR?

RIGHT IN THE MIDDLE OF NEW YORK CITY?

WHAT IF IT'S AN ALIEN SPORE?

MAYBE WE SHOULD TAKE IT TO JERSEY AND OPEN IT THERE.

LOOK BEHIND YOU. WE'RE BEING SEALED IN.

COULDN'T MAKE JERSEY WORSE.

YOU'RE DOING JERSEY MATERIAL?

THAT WAS BENEATH ME?

I BELIEVE IT WAS.

THAT GLASS DOME WILL SEAL ANYTHING IN--

WITH US.

WE HAVE THE MOST ADVANCED LAB EQUIPMENT AND COMPUTER SYSTEMS ON THE PLANET EARTH RIGHT HERE.

LOOK. WE DRILLED A TINY HOLE WITH AN ADAMANTIUM NEEDLE BACK IN THE JUNGLE AND DID AN INTERIOR ATMOSPHERE TEST.

THERE'S NO ATMOSPHERE IN THERE AT ALL. NOTHING FOREIGN. NOTHING HARMFUL.

ANYTHING ALIVE?

NOT BY OUR STANDARDS.

WE'VE DONE STUFF LIKE THIS BEFORE.

DIDN'T YOU GET YOUR POWERS BY ACCIDENTLY SCREWING SOMETHING UP IN OUTER SPACE?

YEAH, BUT WE'RE SMARTER NOW.

YEAH, YOU LOOK IT.

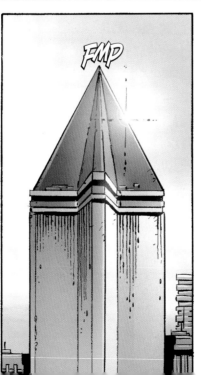

FMP

LOGAN, IF YOU'D STAND HERE.

BOB, IF YOU AND BEN WOULD STAND OVER THERE AND IF YOU, MR. STARK, IF YOU'D POWER UP...

I AM. BUT THE METAL ISN'T MAGNETIC.

I UNDERSTAND. WE MAY NEED YOUR ENHANCED STRENGTH ON TOP OF EVERYONE ELSE'S.

GOTCHA.

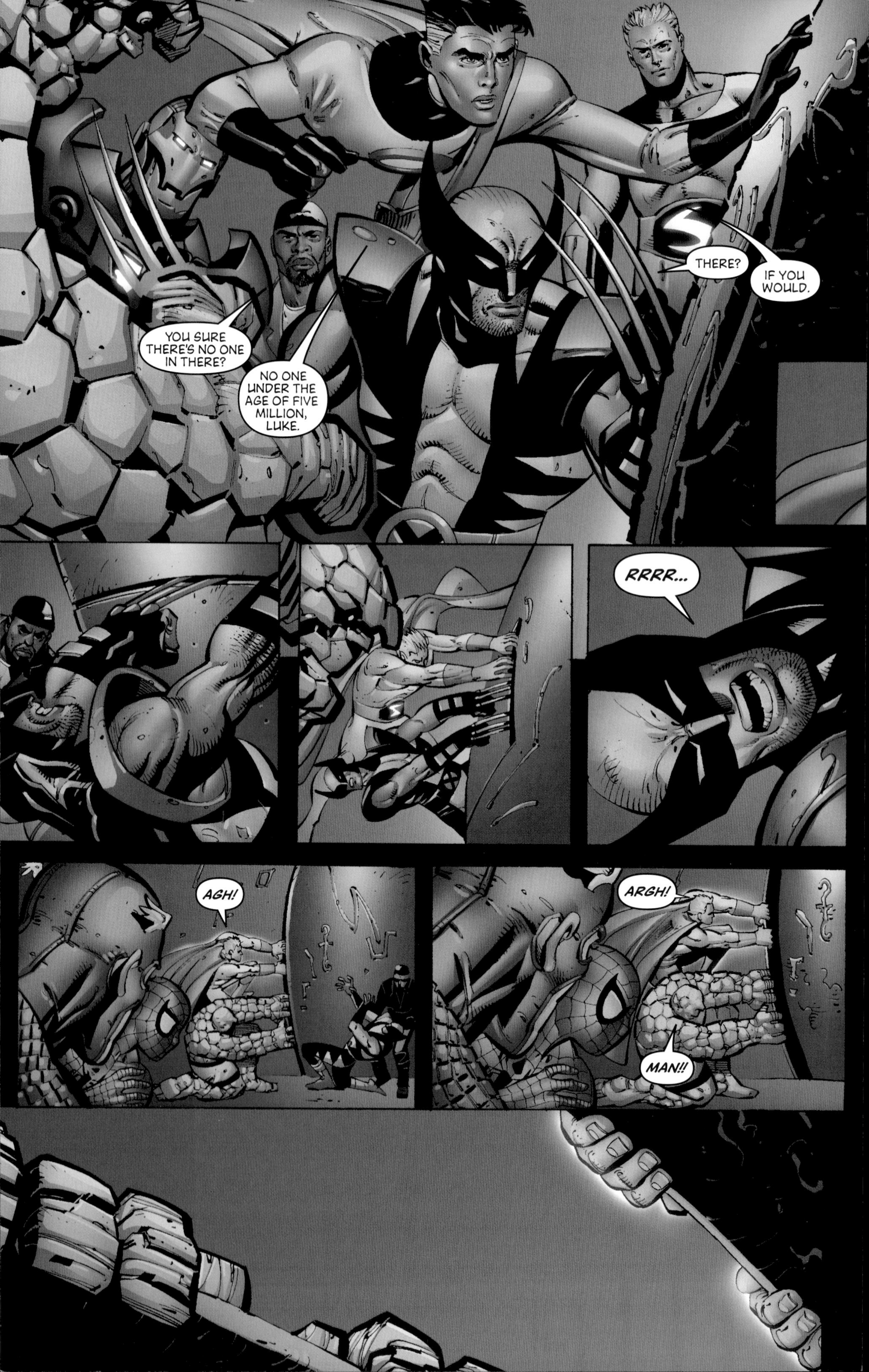
THERE?
IF YOU WOULD.
YOU SURE THERE'S NO ONE IN THERE?
NO ONE UNDER THE AGE OF FIVE MILLION, LUKE.
RRRR...
AGH!
ARGH!
MAN!!

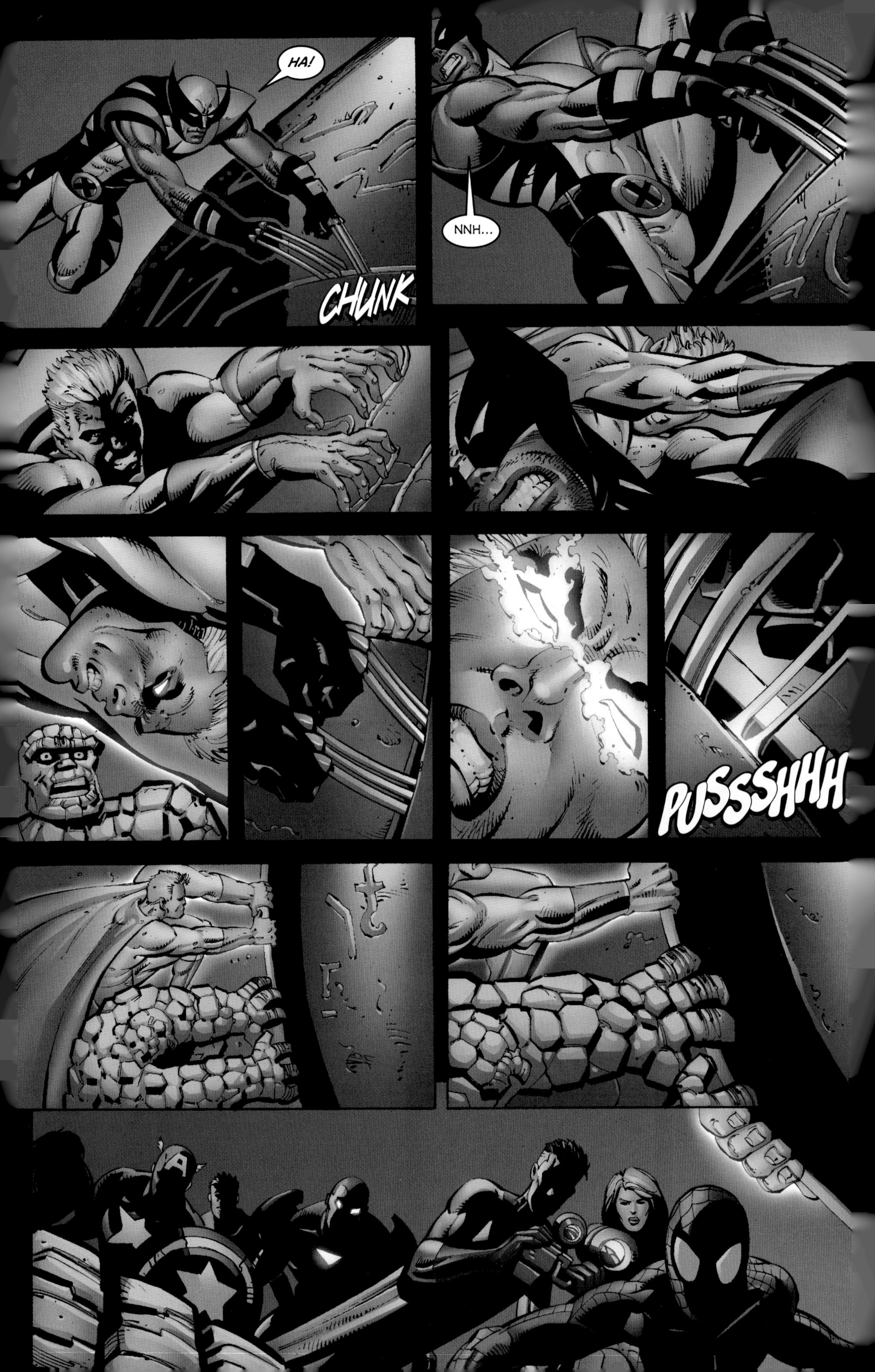
HA!
CHUNK
NNH...
PUSSSHHH

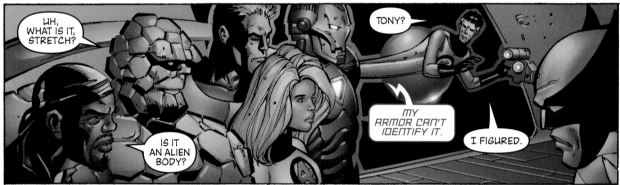

UH, WHAT IS IT, STRETCH?

IS IT AN ALIEN BODY?

TONY?

MY ARMOR CAN'T IDENTIFY IT.

I FIGURED.

CAN YOU AT LEAST TELL WHAT IT'S *MADE* OF?

THERE'S NO REFERENCE FOR OUR INSTRUMENTS TO IDENTIFY IT.

MEANING?

IT'S FROM A SCIENCE OR BIOLOGY THAT WE'VE NEVER SEEN BEFORE.

IT'LL TAKE YEARS JUST TO FIGURE OUT *HOW* TO ANALYZE IT.

MAYBE WE KILLED IT WHEN WE OPENED IT UP?

IT'S BEEN IN THERE FOR CENTURIES.

STILL.

MAYBE IT'S SHY. MAYBE SOMEONE SHOULD SAY HI.

YEAH, IT SPEAKS ENGLISH.

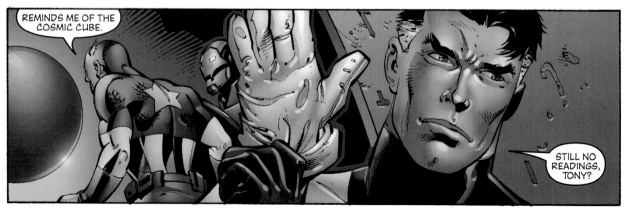

REMINDS ME OF THE COSMIC CUBE.

STILL NO READINGS, TONY?

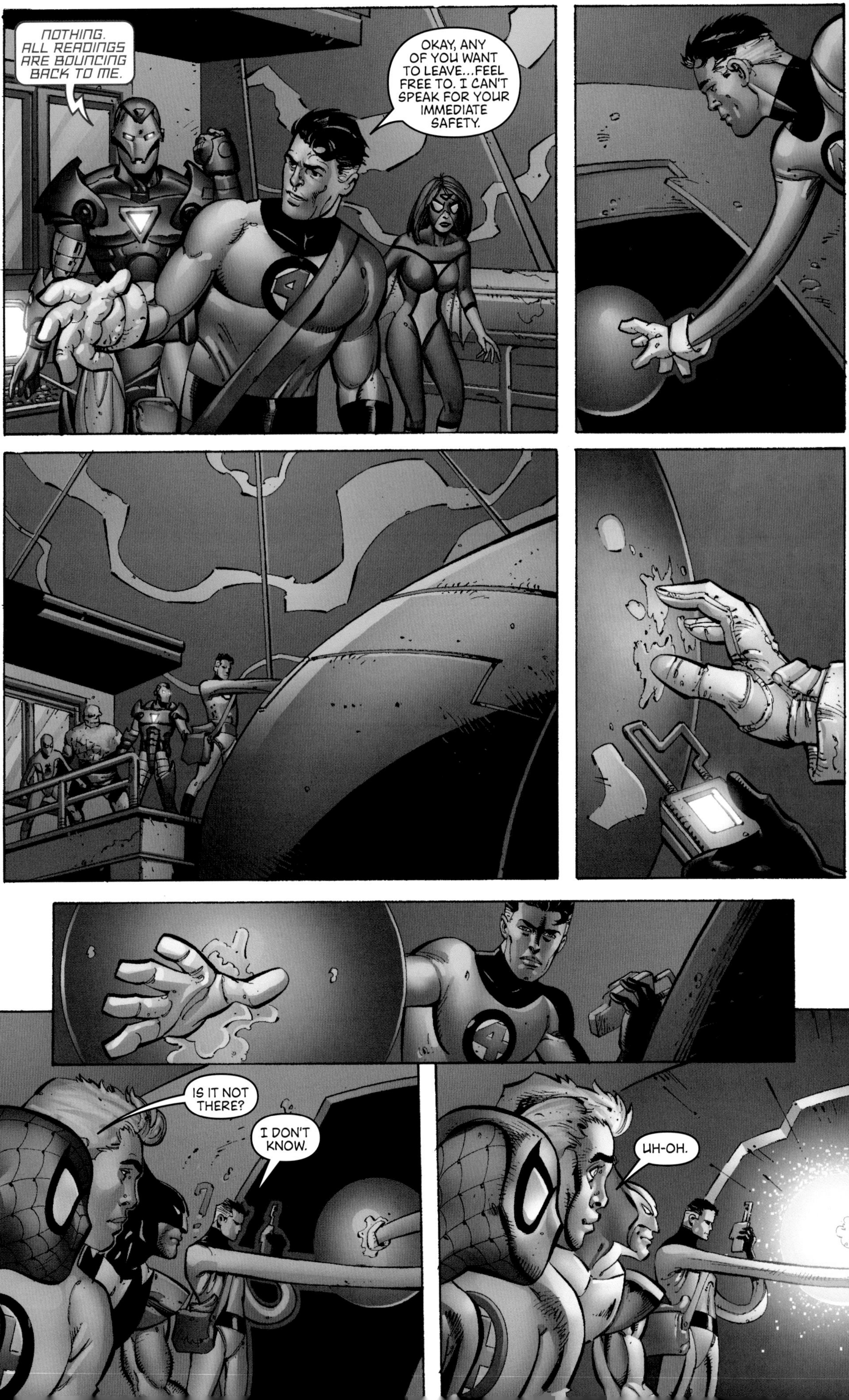
NOTHING. ALL READINGS ARE BOUNCING BACK TO ME.
OKAY, ANY OF YOU WANT TO LEAVE...FEEL FREE TO. I CAN'T SPEAK FOR YOUR IMMEDIATE SAFETY.
IS IT NOT THERE?
I DON'T KNOW.
UH-OH.

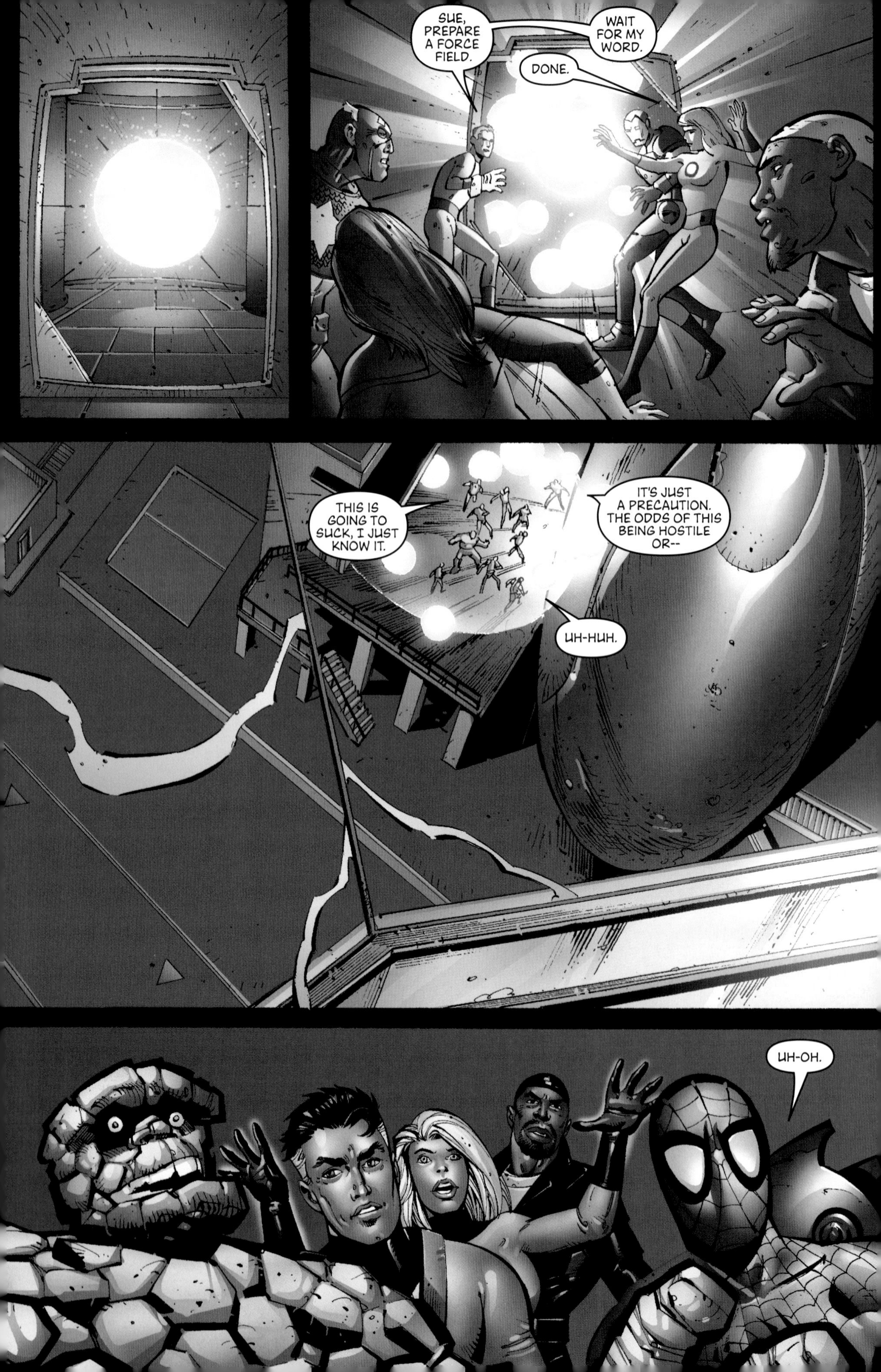
SUE, PREPARE A FORCE FIELD.
WAIT FOR MY WORD.
DONE.
THIS IS GOING TO SUCK, I JUST KNOW IT.
IT'S JUST A PRECAUTION. THE ODDS OF THIS BEING HOSTILE OR--
UH-HUH.
UH-OH.

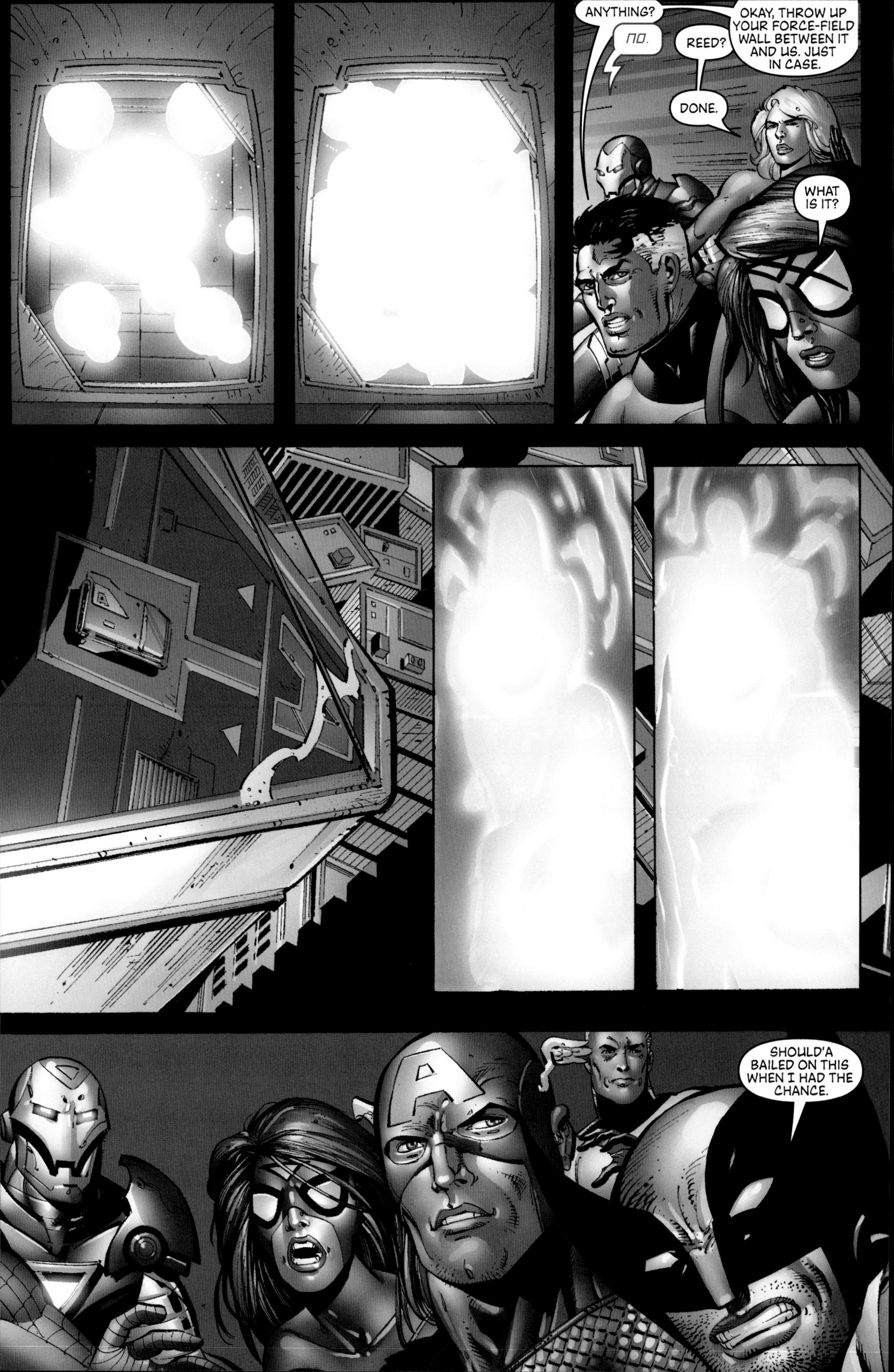
ANYTHING?
no.
REED?
DONE.
OKAY, THROW UP YOUR FORCE-FIELD WALL BETWEEN IT AND US. JUST IN CASE.
WHAT IS IT?
SHOULD'A BAILED ON THIS WHEN I HAD THE CHANCE.

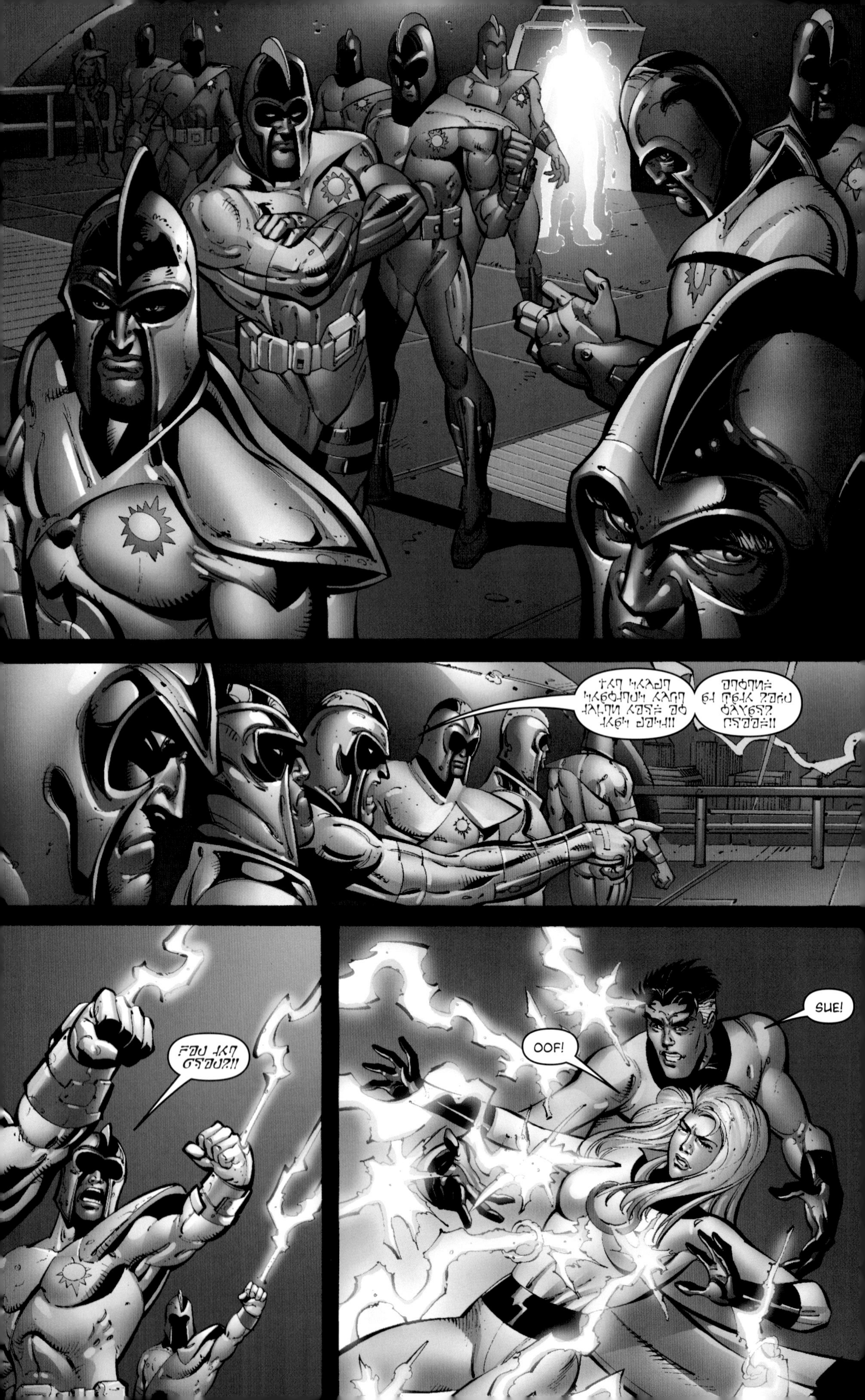
OOF!
SUE!

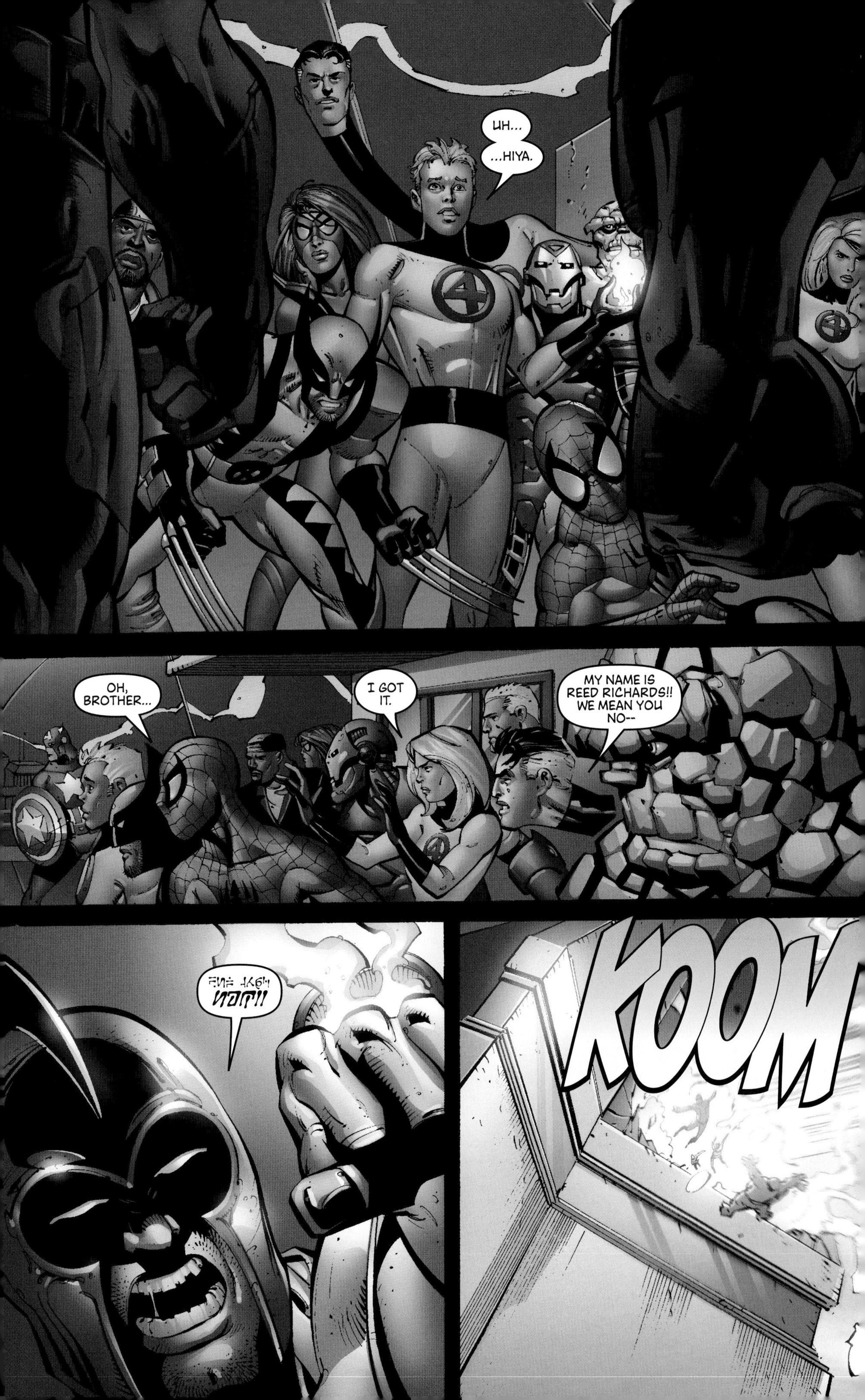
UH...
...HIYA.
OH, BROTHER...
I GOT IT.
MY NAME IS REED RICHARDS!! WE MEAN YOU NO--
KOOM

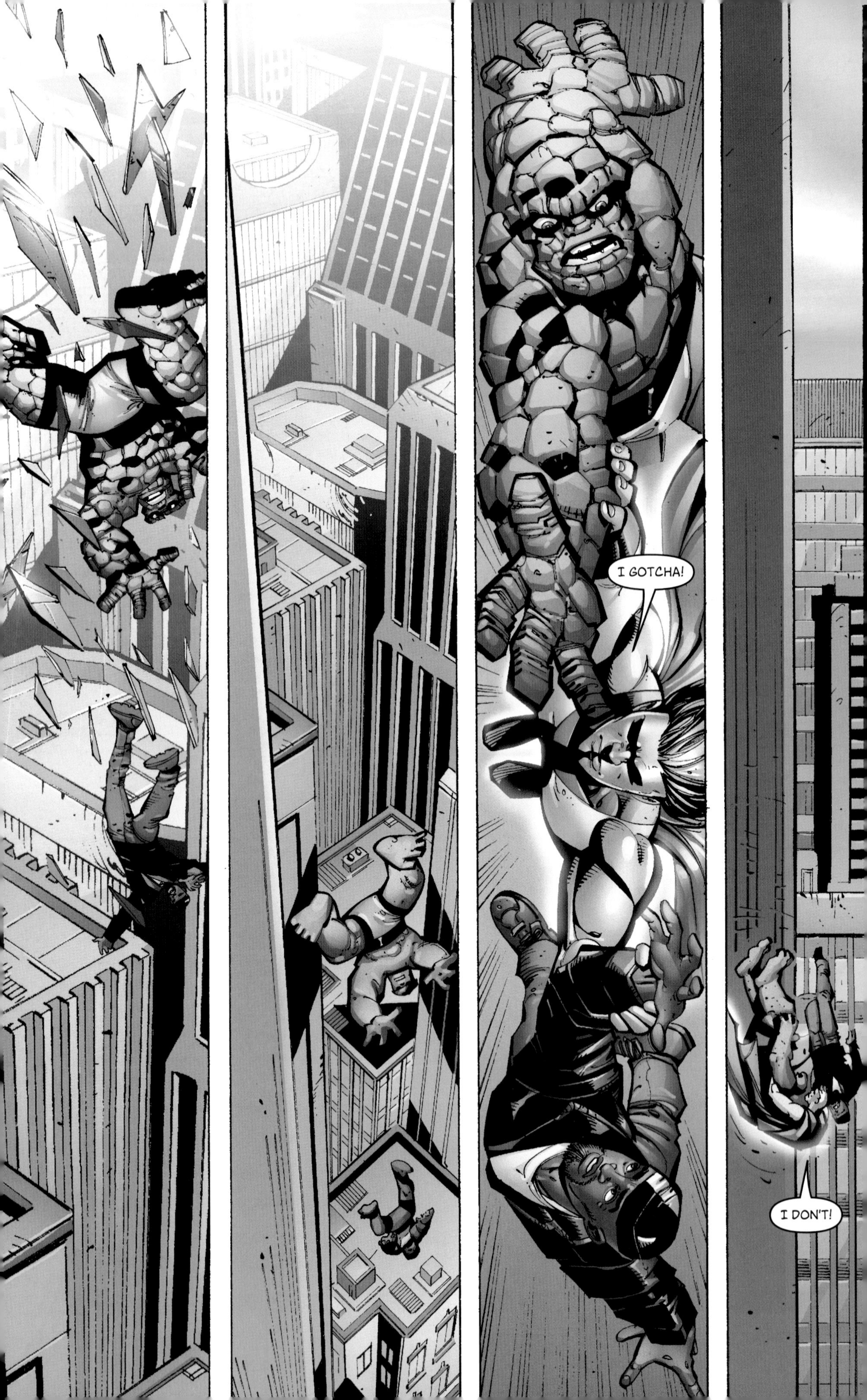
I GOTCHA!
I DON'T!

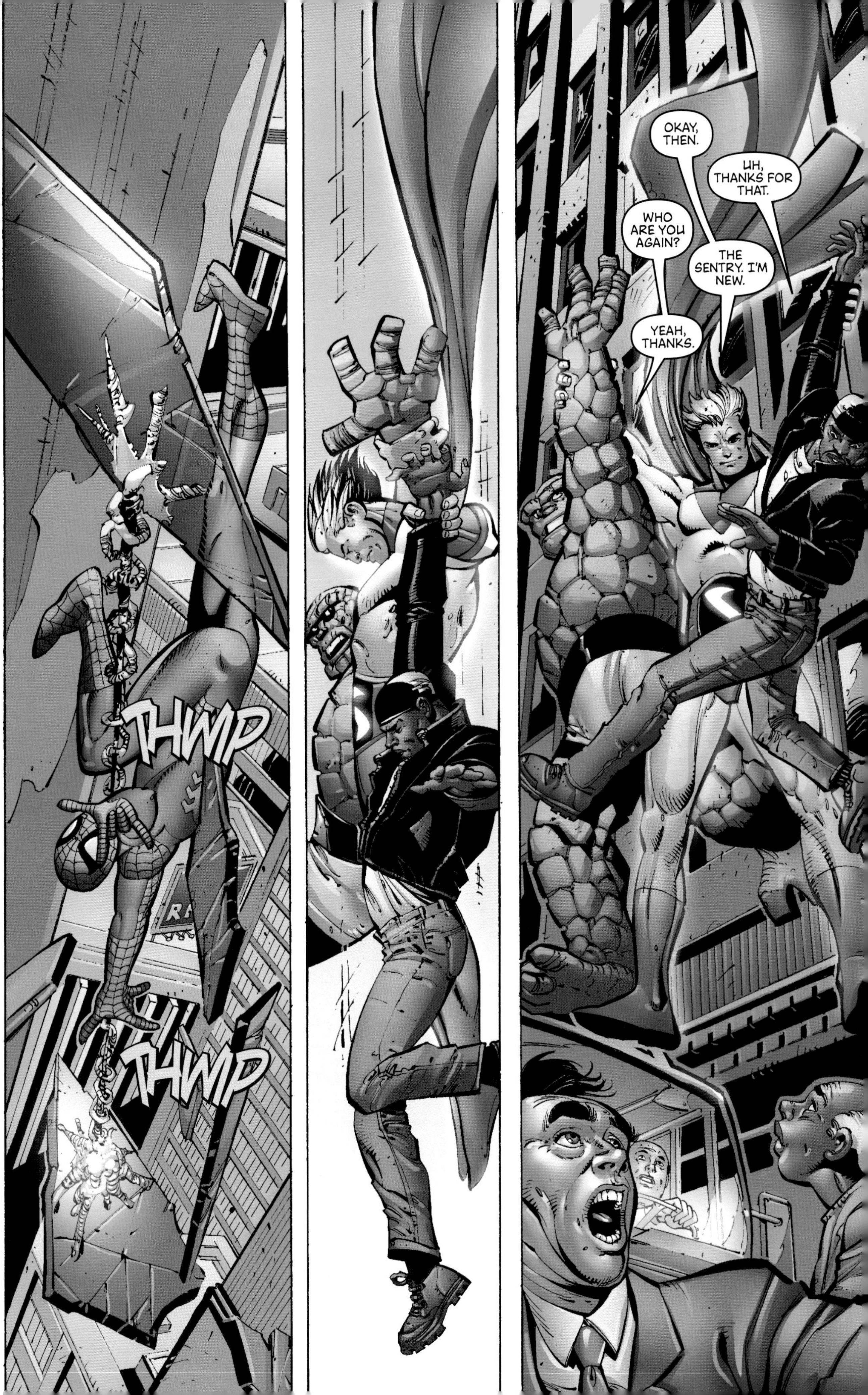
THWIP
THWIP
OKAY, THEN.
UH, THANKS FOR THAT.
WHO ARE YOU AGAIN?
THE SENTRY. I'M NEW.
YEAH, THANKS.

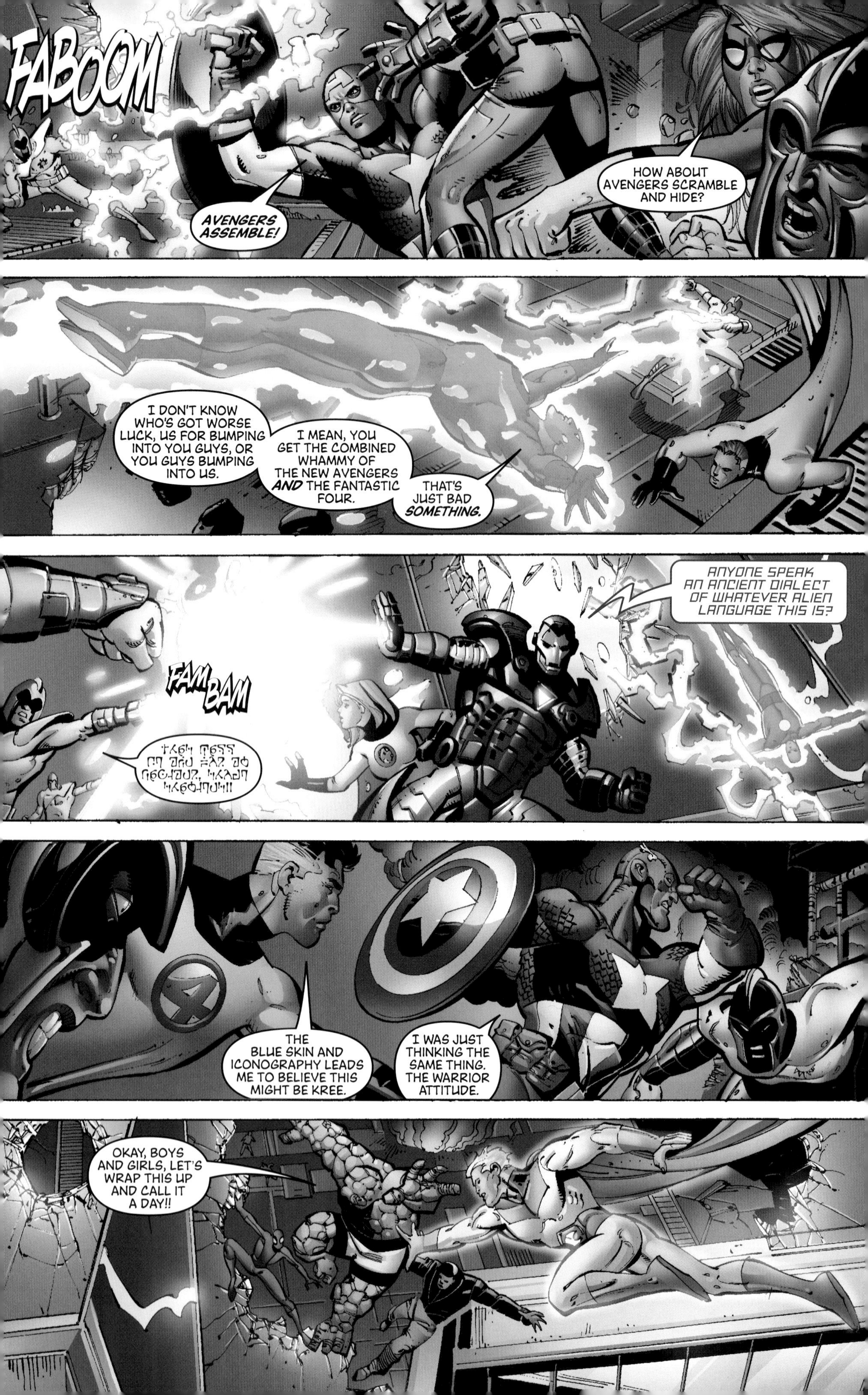
FABOOM
AVENGERS ASSEMBLE!
HOW ABOUT AVENGERS SCRAMBLE AND HIDE?
I DON'T KNOW WHO'S GOT WORSE LUCK, US FOR BUMPING INTO YOU GUYS, OR YOU GUYS BUMPING INTO US.
I MEAN, YOU GET THE COMBINED WHAMMY OF THE NEW AVENGERS AND THE FANTASTIC FOUR.
THAT'S JUST BAD SOMETHING.
ANYONE SPEAK AN ANCIENT DIALECT OF WHATEVER ALIEN LANGUAGE THIS IS?
FAM BAM
THE BLUE SKIN AND ICONOGRAPHY LEADS ME TO BELIEVE THIS MIGHT BE KREE.
I WAS JUST THINKING THE SAME THING. THE WARRIOR ATTITUDE.
OKAY, BOYS AND GIRLS, LET'S WRAP THIS UP AND CALL IT A DAY!!

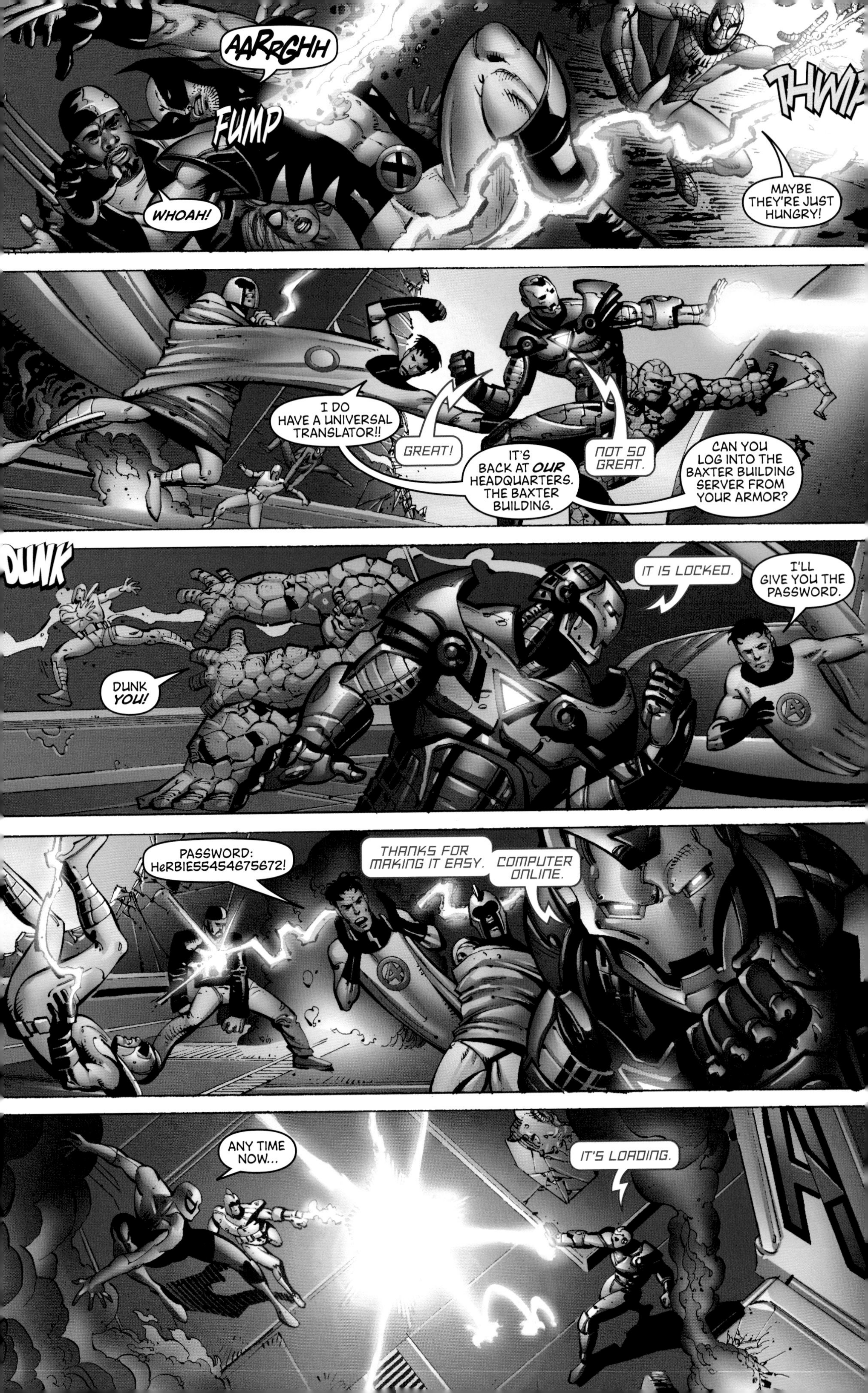
AARRGHH
FUMP
WHOAH!
THWIP
MAYBE THEY'RE JUST HUNGRY!
I DO HAVE A UNIVERSAL TRANSLATOR!!
GREAT!
IT'S BACK AT OUR HEADQUARTERS. THE BAXTER BUILDING.
NOT SO GREAT.
CAN YOU LOG INTO THE BAXTER BUILDING SERVER FROM YOUR ARMOR?
DUNK
DUNK YOU!
IT IS LOCKED.
I'LL GIVE YOU THE PASSWORD.
PASSWORD: HeRBIE55454675672!
THANKS FOR MAKING IT EASY.
COMPUTER ONLINE.
ANY TIME NOW...
IT'S LOADING.

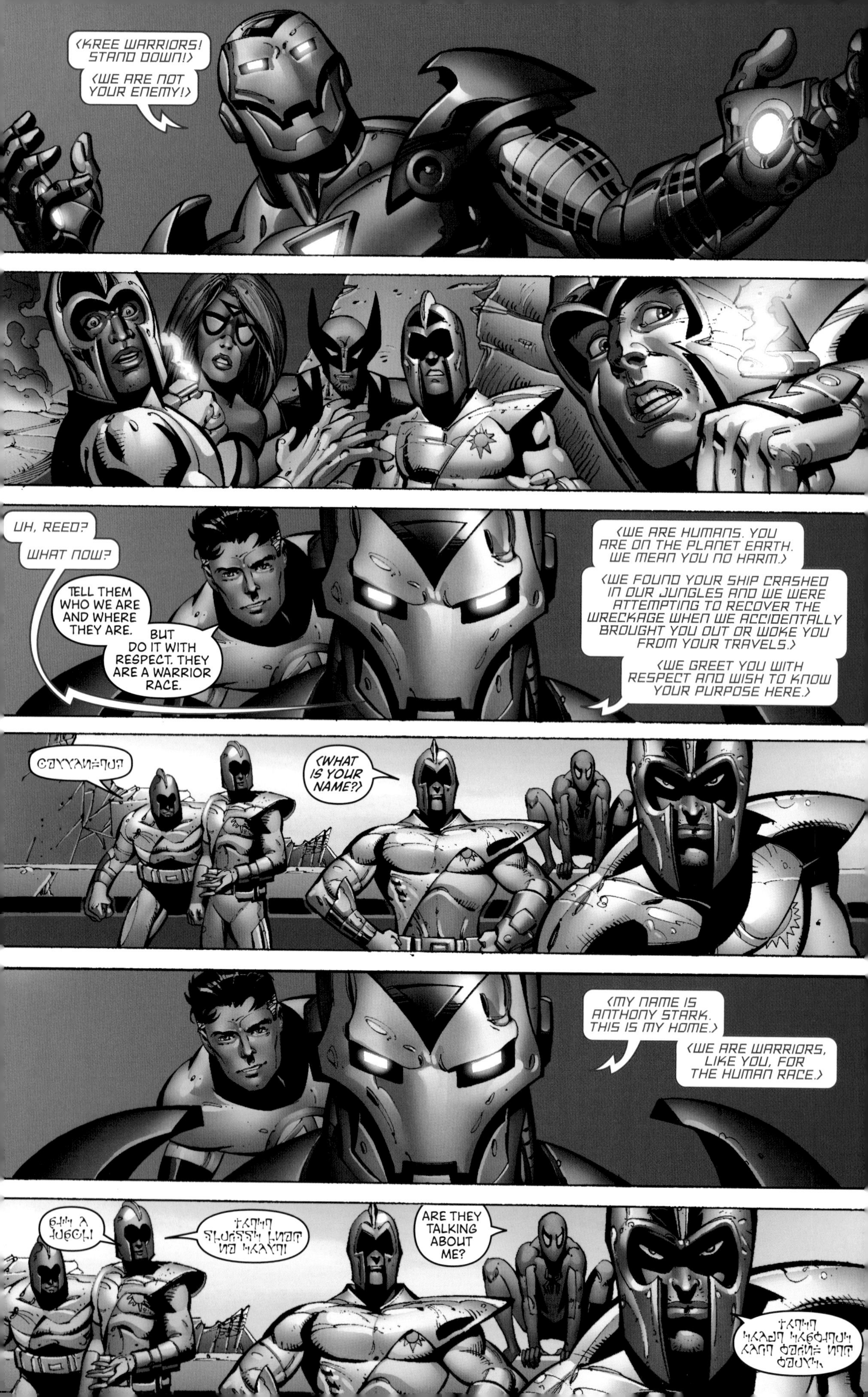

<KREE WARRIORS! STAND DOWN!>
<WE ARE NOT YOUR ENEMY!>
UH, REED?
WHAT NOW?
TELL THEM WHO WE ARE AND WHERE THEY ARE.
BUT DO IT WITH RESPECT. THEY ARE A WARRIOR RACE.
<WE ARE HUMANS. YOU ARE ON THE PLANET EARTH. WE MEAN YOU NO HARM.>
<WE FOUND YOUR SHIP CRASHED IN OUR JUNGLES AND WE WERE ATTEMPTING TO RECOVER THE WRECKAGE WHEN WE ACCIDENTALLY BROUGHT YOU OUT OR WOKE YOU FROM YOUR TRAVELS.>
<WE GREET YOU WITH RESPECT AND WISH TO KNOW YOUR PURPOSE HERE.>
<WHAT IS YOUR NAME?>
<MY NAME IS ANTHONY STARK. THIS IS MY HOME.>
<WE ARE WARRIORS, LIKE YOU, FOR THE HUMAN RACE.>
ARE THEY TALKING ABOUT ME?

THEY THINK WE'RE SKRULLS.

TELL THEM THE WAR BETWEEN THE KREE AND THE SKRULL EMPIRES ENDED YEARS AGO. BACK ON THE KREE HOMEWORLD.

⟨THE KREE/SKRULL WAR ENDED YEARS AGO. BACK ON THE KREE HOMEWORLD. WE WERE THERE.⟩

⟨WHO...WAS VICTORIOUS?⟩

⟨THE KREE EMPIRE.⟩

SOMETHING IN KREE!!

⟨STOP!⟩

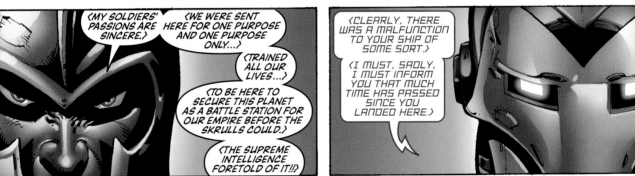

⟨MY SOLDIERS' PASSIONS ARE SINCERE.⟩

⟨WE WERE SENT HERE FOR ONE PURPOSE AND ONE PURPOSE ONLY...⟩

⟨TRAINED ALL OUR LIVES...⟩

⟨TO BE HERE TO SECURE THIS PLANET AS A BATTLE STATION FOR OUR EMPIRE BEFORE THE SKRULLS COULD.⟩

⟨THE SUPREME INTELLIGENCE FORETOLD OF IT!!⟩

⟨CLEARLY, THERE WAS A MALFUNCTION TO YOUR SHIP OF SOME SORT.⟩

⟨I MUST, SADLY, I MUST INFORM YOU THAT MUCH TIME HAS PASSED SINCE YOU LANDED HERE.⟩

⟨HOW MUCH TIME??⟩

⟨WE DO NOT KNOW.⟩

⟨BUT IT IS MANY MILLENNIA, A VERY LONG TIME.⟩

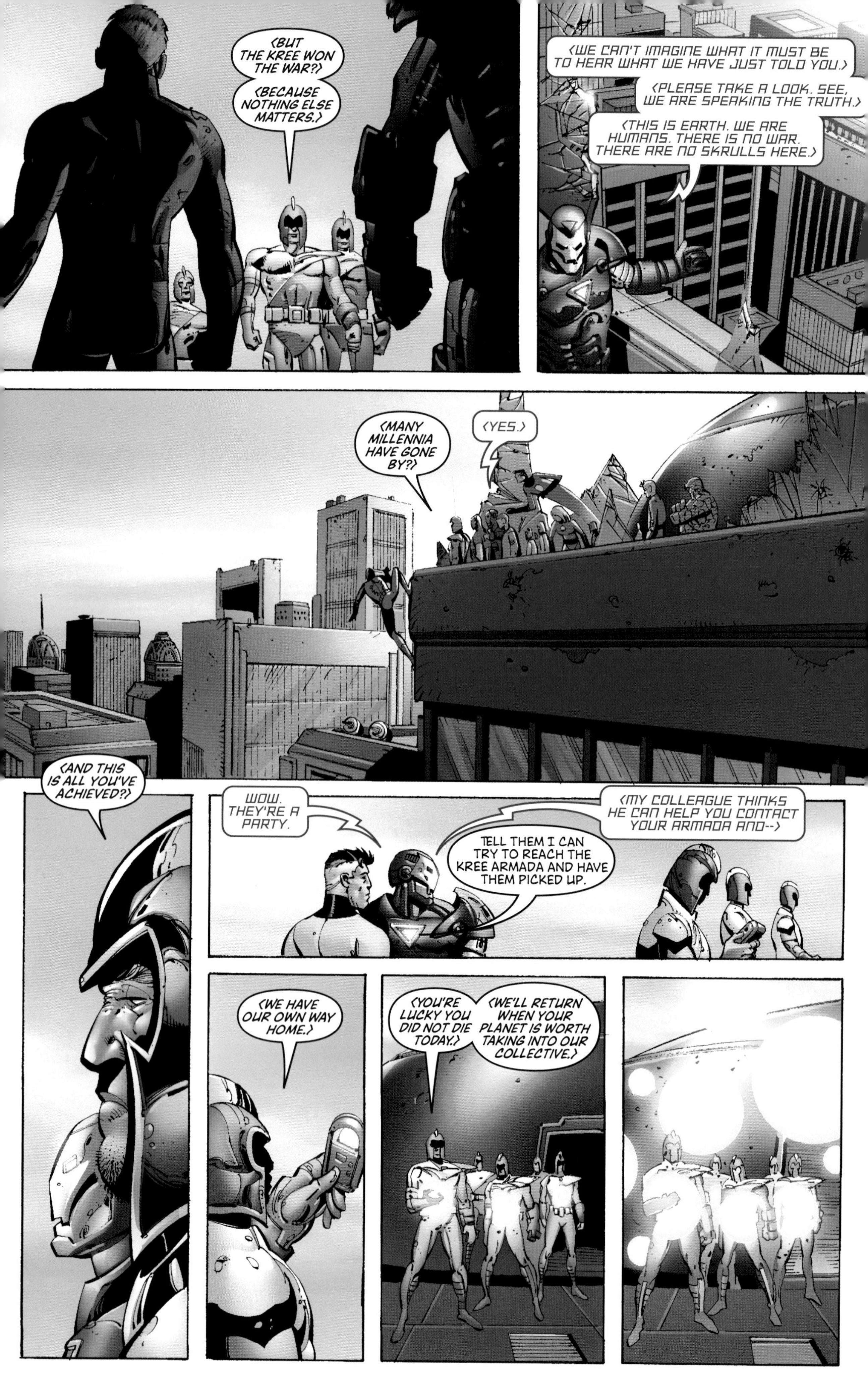

<BUT THE KREE WON THE WAR?>
<BECAUSE NOTHING ELSE MATTERS.>
<WE CAN'T IMAGINE WHAT IT MUST BE TO HEAR WHAT WE HAVE JUST TOLD YOU.>
<PLEASE TAKE A LOOK. SEE, WE ARE SPEAKING THE TRUTH.>
<THIS IS EARTH. WE ARE HUMANS. THERE IS NO WAR. THERE ARE NO SKRULLS HERE.>
<MANY MILLENNIA HAVE GONE BY?>
<YES.>
<AND THIS IS ALL YOU'VE ACHIEVED?>
WOW. THEY'RE A PARTY.
TELL THEM I CAN TRY TO REACH THE KREE ARMADA AND HAVE THEM PICKED UP.
<MY COLLEAGUE THINKS HE CAN HELP YOU CONTACT YOUR ARMADA AND-->
<WE HAVE OUR OWN WAY HOME.>
<YOU'RE LUCKY YOU DID NOT DIE TODAY.>
<WE'LL RETURN WHEN YOUR PLANET IS WORTH TAKING INTO OUR COLLECTIVE.>

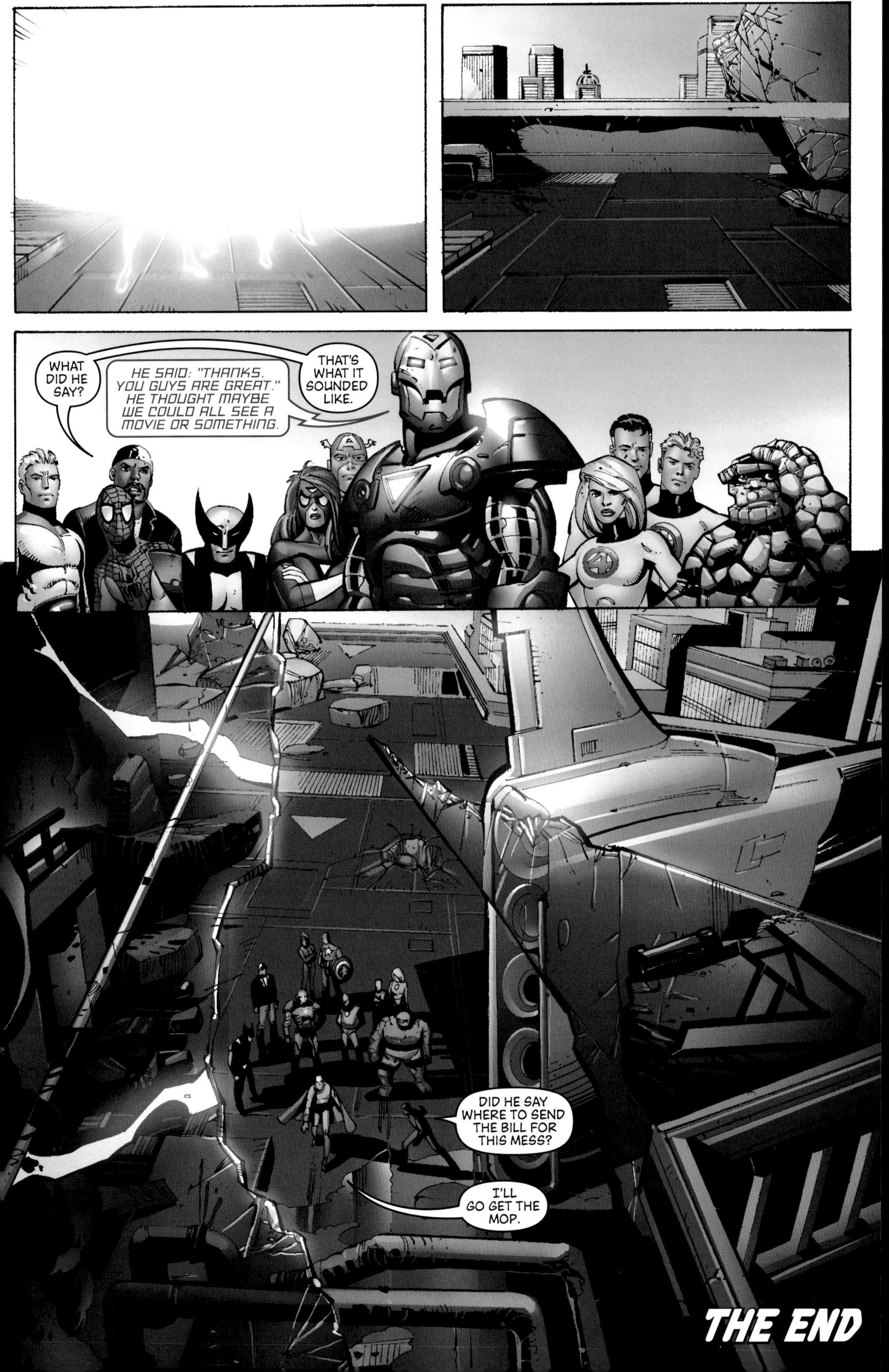
WHAT DID HE SAY?
HE SAID: "THANKS. YOU GUYS ARE GREAT." HE THOUGHT MAYBE WE COULD ALL SEE A MOVIE OR SOMETHING.
THAT'S WHAT IT SOUNDED LIKE.
DID HE SAY WHERE TO SEND THE BILL FOR THIS MESS?
I'LL GO GET THE MOP.
THE END

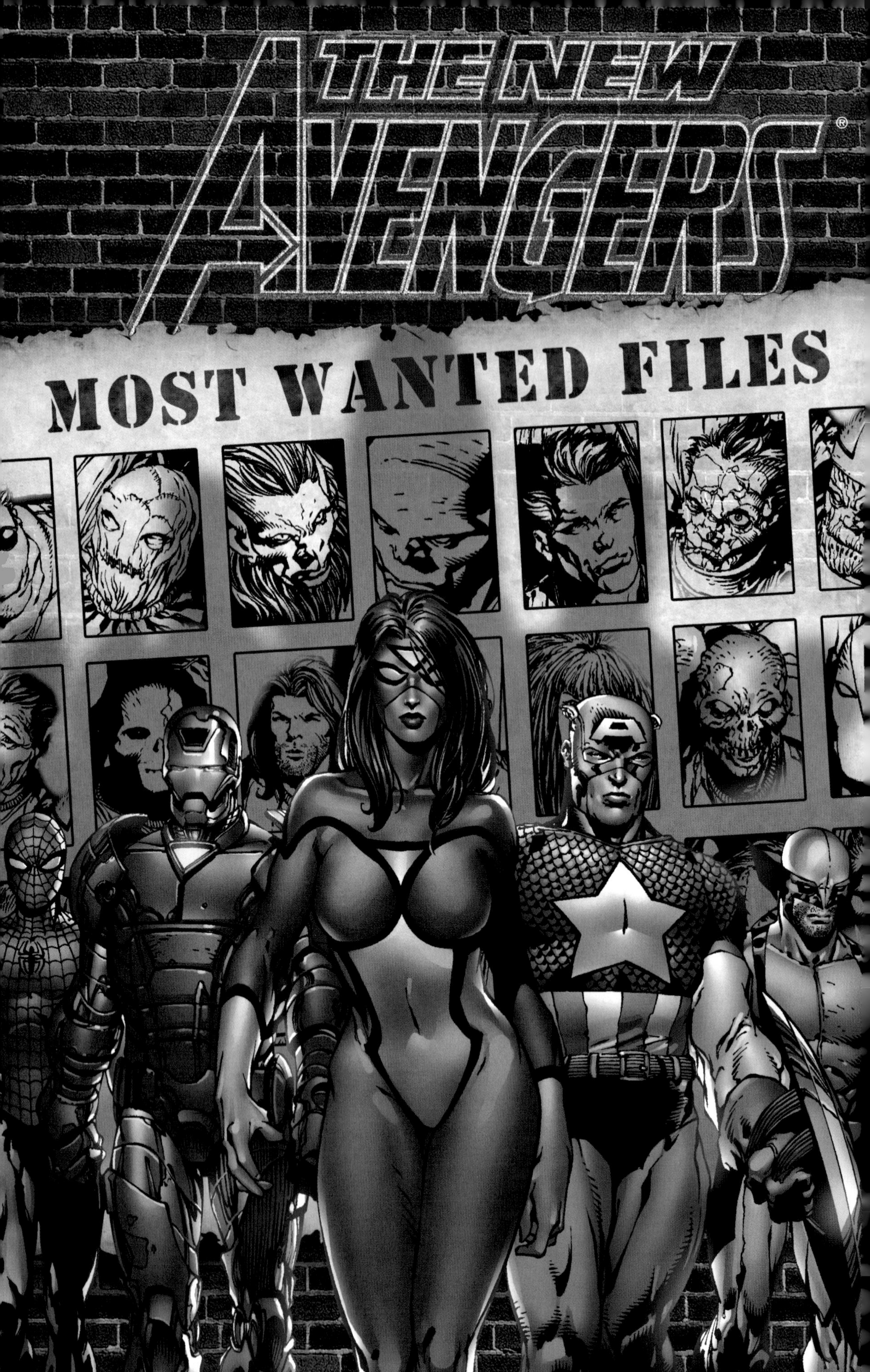
THE NEW AVENGERS®
MOST WANTED FILES

ALCATRAZ
Californian island prison, operational 1859-1963, held superhuman criminals in 1940s. Marvel Mystery Comics #25 (1941)

ALMAGORDO
NM nuclear testing facility, held Armageddon Man and perhaps others in suspended animation. X-Men #12 (1992)

ANVIL
Penal colony on planet Annoval XIV, site of attempted breakout by Nebula. Silver Surfer #74 (1993)

AREA 52
Utah facility containing "mysteries of America," including superhuman-related technology, allegedly replaced Nevada's Area 51. Uncanny X-Men #363 (1999)

AREA 102
Government facility to prepare for and contain superhuman threats, used by "Thunderbolt" Ross as Hulkbuster base. Incredible Hulk #462 (1998)

BIG HOUSE
NY prison, housed superhuman criminals shrunken by Yellowjacket's Pym particles, expanded into Lang Memorial Penitentiary (a.k.a. Ant Farm). She-Hulk #5 (2004)

BLACK HOLE
Research facility, experimented on occult superhumans, directed by Spook. Ghost Rider #62 (1995)

BRAINSTORM WARD
Mental institution, a.k.a. the Mad Dog Ward, secretly funded by Kingpin, created superhuman assassins, exposed by Spider-Man. Web of Spider-Man #33 (1987)

CAGE
Island prison for superhumans, built over French Prison de la Morte, dampened super-powers regardless of source, plagued by corrupt personnel. Wolverine #164 (2001)

CITADEL
Centuries-old French prison, used to hold sorcerers. Fantastic Four Annual 1999 (1999)

COLD IRON
Adirondacks military base, sought scientific basis for supernatural beings, illegally studied corpses of John Blaze's allies. Spirits of Vengeance #20 (1994)

CUBE
Prison for psychopathic superhumans, declared "capital of the new Kree Empire" by Noh-Varr (a.k.a. Marvel Boy). Marvel Boy #6 (2001)

DAMNATION CITY
Intergalactic alien prison, possibly destroyed after invasion by Deadpool to rescue Dirty Wolff. Deadpool #41 (2000)

DESECRATION ANNEX
Celestial space station imprisoning cosmic-powered beings. Captain Marvel #5 (1996)

DORKHAM ASYLUM
Insane asylum in Visigoth, MA, housed several superhumans, many mutated by Jack Serious. Sensational She-Hulk #19 (1990)

FENG-TU
Chinese underground prison for mutants. X-Men Annual 2001 (2001)

FORT CHEER
Federal prison, maximum security, unjustly held espionage operative Susan Jacobson, broken into by Hulk and Pantheon. Incredible Hulk #410 (1993)

FORTRESS
Superhuman research facility, created sleeper agents for U.S. government and others, trained New Genix in simulated future environment. Marvel Comics Presents #112 (1992)

GAMMA BASE (a.k.a. HULKBUSTER BASE)
Originally NM base dedicated to Hulk's capture, held other gamma-powered superhumans, relocated to Nevada, acquired by Operation: Zero Tolerance. Incredible Hulk #145 (1971)

HANGAR 18
Extraterrestrial-oriented research facility, allegedly located at Wright-Patterson Air Force Base, studied Skrulls captured in 1947. Blackwulf #2 (1994)

HOUSE OF CORRECTION
Inhumane prison for rebellious teenagers (mutant and otherwise), site of forced cybernetic transformation by Warden Coffin. Generation X #64 (2000)

ICE BOX
Canadian maximum security prison, held crimelord Ivan the Terrible. Maverick #8 (1998)

IRON ROCK
Facility to hold advanced technology confiscated from super-villains. Sensational Spider-Man #8 (1996)

KYLN
Intergalactic alien prison, supposedly located near universe's edge, holds the universe's deadliest criminals. Thanos #7 (2004)

MONSTER ISLAND
Island in Bermuda Triangle, connected to Subterranea, former Deviant mutate breeding site, ruled by Mole Man, occasionally used as dumping ground for gigantic creatures by U.S. government and possibly by Japanese government as well. Fantastic Four #1 (1961)

MUIR ISLAND
Mutant research facility off Scottish coast, partially sponsored by Professor X, held mutant criminals as needed. X-Men #104 (1977)

NEVERLAND
Weapon X detention facility, supposedly designed to hold mutant terrorists, actually served as mutant concentration camp. Weapon X #5 (2003)

PROJECT: PEGASUS
NY-based government facility, investigated alternate power sources, studied various superhumans (willing or otherwise), served as de facto prison for years. Marvel Two-in-One #42 (1978)

PROVINCE 13
Russian research base and prison, collected and studied mutants. X-Men: Liberators #1 (1998)

RAVENCROFT
Institute for the Criminally Insane Asylum established by Dr. Ashley Kafka to treat insane superhumans, site of several breakouts. Spider-Man Unlimited #1 (1993)

RYKER'S ISLAND
Maximum security prison off NYC coast, included special wing to hold superhuman criminals, subject to many breakouts. Amazing Spider-Man #213 (1981)

RYKING HOSPITAL FOR PARAHUMAN RESEARCH
New Mexico facility, likened to "the Betty Ford clinic for rich super folk," which held Ryking's son Hazard. X-Men #12 (1992)

SALAMANCA
High-security prison for superhuman criminals, patrolled by flying armored guards. Daredevil Vs. Punisher #4 (2005)

SAUERBRATEN MENTAL HEALTH FACILITY
Ohio institution used as front by Doctor Reich, briefly held Howard the Duck and Winda Wester. Howard the Duck #12 (1977)

SEAGATE PRISON
Maximum security prison off Georgia coast, formerly held Luke Cage, later added wing for superhuman criminals. Hero for Hire #1 (1972)

SKRAGGMORE PENITENTIARY
Illinois prison, formerly held the Zaniac. Thor #371 (1986)

SUNSHINE CITY
Government-run site of procedures by Puppet Master to control criminally insane in order to rehabilitate them. Fantastic Four #45 (2001)

VAULT
Immense facility for holding superhuman criminals, located in Colorado Rocky Mountains, contained special wing for extraterrestrial prisoners, rebuilt in Negative Zone by Mister Fantastic. Avengers Annual #15 (1986); Fantastic Four: Foes #5 (2005)

WORMWALL
NY prison, held Doctor Angst for years. Sensational She-Hulk #14 (1990)

HEAD WRITER/COORDINATOR: **JEFF CHRISTIANSEN**

WRITERS: **SEAN McQUAID, MICHAEL HOSKIN, MARK O'ENGLISH, RONALD BYRD, STUART VANDAL, ERIC J. MOREELS, ANTHONY FLAMINI & BARRY REESE**

COVER ARTISTS: **DAVID FINCH, DANNY MIKI & FRANK D'ARMATA**
ART RECONSTRUCTION: **POND SCUM & JERRON QUALITY COLOR**
SELECT COLORING: **CHRIS SOTOMAYOR & JERRON QUALITY COLOR**

EDITOR: **JEFF YOUNGQUIST**
CONSULTING EDITOR: **TOM BREVOORT**
ASSISTANT EDITORS: **JENNIFER GRÜNWALD & MICHAEL SHORT**

DIRECTOR OF SALES: **DAVID GABRIEL**

DESIGNER: **JEOF VITA**
CREATIVE DIRECTOR: **TOM MARVELLI**

EDITOR IN CHIEF: **JOE QUESADA**
PUBLISHER: **DAN BUCKLEY**

SPECIAL THANKS TO THE GUYS AT THE APPENDIX (WWW.MARVUNAPP.COM)
THE OFFICIAL HANDBOOK OF THE MARVEL UNIVERSE FREQUENTLY ASKED QUESTIONS PAGE, INCLUDING ERRATA AND EXPLANATIONS: HTTP://WWW.MARVUNAPP.COM/OHOTMU/OHOTMUFAQ.HTM

encryption sequence: 1001011010000100010010000001000100011101000111110

from: runciter@admin.shield.gov [Agent Gail Runciter]
to: jdrew@superop.shield.gov [Agent Jessica Drew]
cc: arachnophilia@newavengers.stark.net [Spider-Woman]
subject: Getting the bad guys, then, now, and later; tying the Raft together

Aside from early efforts like the Alcatraz annex, Tombs, or Almagordo, a program to imprison superhuman offenders didn't get going until S.H.I.E.L.D. was up and running. You probably know it started with the Ryker's Island Special Wing, but multiple escapes and lawsuits from the families of "normal" criminals ultimately shut that down. Holding them at Project: PEGASUS and "studying" their powers worked for a while but detracted from the facility's research and got too close to human rights violations. We had high hopes for the Vault, which lasted for years but got too expensive. The Black Hole was an intel-run facility that became uncontrollable, while the Cage, an island prison built over a power suppression source, was corrupted from the inside. Ravencroft was underfunded because the suits didn't like "counseling" super-lunatics, and the Cube...I don't even have clearance for what went down at the Cube. The Big House, Hangar 18, the Fortress, Area 52, Area 102, Gamma Base, Cold Iron, Sunshine City, the setups at Muir and Monster Island, abominations like Neverland and the House of Correction, and these are just the ones we're authorized to discuss. All failed as prisons. Until a few months ago, we were back to modifying conventional prisons, and totally renovating Seagate was on the board until we went back to basics and gave Ryker's a twin island: The Raft, the latest stop on a long trip.

Thing is, the Raft was never intended to be a general population prison, only to hold super-powered multiple murderers either too insane to execute or that we can't even figure out how to execute — Carnage, Purple Man, Hyde, Nefaria — and expanded over time. But when word got out, prisons all over the country wanted grade-B super-crooks off their hands, and truth is, the red tape in getting those skells anywhere after the other super-prison fiascos was wrapped too tight to hold for long, so we had to improvise a lot. By the time the Raft was scheduled to hold ten, we had over four dozen on our hands. Resources were already stretched before we got blacked out like a cheap film set.

We've pieced together (correct me if I get anything wrong) that Electro was paid by Brainchild of the Savage Land Mutates (I love a job where you get to type things like this) to break Sauron out of the Raft, and the other escapees were freebies to confuse the issue. Fortunately, you, along with bodyguard Luke Cage, were on site to protect attorneys consulting their client, an inmate called the Sentry, and you initiated containment. Captain America, Spider-Man and Iron Man arrived on the scene to coordinate efforts, and with last-minute pitch-in by the Sentry himself, the Raft was retaken by S.H.I.E.L.D., but not before over forty felons escaped.

Mass breakouts always leave people wondering if it's all just too much for us. They don't realize for every repeat escapee, every Doctor Octopus or Bullseye or whoever, there are plenty (Aryan, Cold War, Flambe, Glowworm, Kogar, Lullaby, Manticore, Printout Man, Psiphon, Razorhead, Serpentino, and Vampiro, to pick a random dozen from the transfer request list) who've been locked up since their sentencing and are staying there. Some are even smart enough to stay in their cells when the escapes go down. Now and then we even get sincere reformations like Mr. Rasputin, Battler, or Equinox. The number of super-villains active at a given time are a fraction of the ones still on ice, and every day we get more villain-holding data from Seagate, the Ant Farm, Fort Cheer, Wormwall, Dorkham, Skraggmore, Iron Rock, Brainstorm Ward, Salamanca, Sauerbraten, and a hundred others that helped fill the gaps, more tips on a better louse-trap. It's not an unwinnable war.

Attached are cheatsheets on the escapees for ready study; real names are added to codenames with multiple users, with the exceptions of highly classified names (Spider-Man (Parker), Iron Man (Stark)) and codenames whose primary users are obvious unless otherwise specified (Captain America (Rogers), Hawkeye (Clint Barton), Hulk (Bruce Banner), Thor (Odinson), Wolverine (Logan), etc.). Input is welcome since we're still looking for what works. Next time you hear about the Raft, it may be completely revised or relocated. Or exactly the same. Or we both might be under orders to deny it ever existed. No matter what, we'll have somewhere to put these losers, so you guys catch as many as you can.

--Gail

fw: allavengers@newavengers.stark.net

Guys, feel free to make any serious comments (that means you, Pete!). I've reviewed Project: PEGASUS' superhuman database and supplied clarifications against characters with the same codenames.

Jess

ANSWER
AARON NICHOLSON

History: Aaron Nicholson worked for Wilson (Kingpin) and Richard (Schemer/Rose/Bloodrose) Fisk when they ran a Las Vegas Hydra division. Their top hit man, he had the angle, or answer, to every problem. He volunteered to be the test subject for the Kingpin's superhuman power project using the late Harlan Stillwell's equipment. Seemingly unchanged, he soon discovered the nature of his new powers as he developed brief super-strength to overpower attackers and then flight to escape an exploding boiler. As the Answer, he served the Kingpin in multiple plots against Spider-Man and the Black Cat; stole the seeming corpse of the cyborg Silvermane for use as a potential assassin; reasoned that the vigilante Dagger's light powers could cure the ill Vanessa Fisk; and even sacrificed his own life force to restore Dagger's power, though she refused to help the Kingpin.

Left a discorporated, unconscious energy-being, the Answer regained awareness during the "implosion of the Multiverse Matrix" caused when Captain Britain (Brian Braddock) destroyed Merlyn's multiversal lighthouse tower. Seeking the answer to his non-corporeal existence, he contacted Dr. Octopus (Otto Octavius) via a computer chip Octopus had used to control his Adamantium arms. Octopus duped a would-be-scientist Guardsman into creating a machine to restore the Answer's form, and Octopus then controlled the Answer via their mental link to force him to complete their agreement to arrange Octopus' release and the restoration of his robot arms. The Answer eventually generated an interference field against Octopus' influence and fought him, but dividing his power thusly resulted in the Answer's defeat and subsequent arrest.

Sent to the Raft, the Answer escaped during the big breakout, despite the efforts of the future New Avengers. With the Kingpin out of action, the Answer attempted to impress the Owl (Leland Owlsley) by robbing banks. He was confronted by new vigilante Toxin (Patrick Mulligan), who offered to let him go if he could help with his current problem: being a former policeman bonded to a dangerous alien symbiote. Not liking the Answer's solution to kill himself, Toxin sent the Answer back to the Raft.

Height: 6'
Weight: 170 lbs.
Eyes: Brown
Hair: Black (sometimes dyed blond)

Abilities: Nicholson's powers are the answer to whatever he needs to resolve any given situation; though he usually only develops 1-2 powers at a time, he has shown superhuman strength, speed and durability, as well as flight, force field formation, enhanced senses, etc. This can be a conscious effort, such as enhancing his hearing to listen to distant activities, or unconscious, as his body responds to stress. Usually his powers respond almost instantly, but he is occasionally taken by surprise before he can adapt. Flight may be a power he possesses continually. His costume is specially designed to be frictionless (except his boot soles and glove palms), preventing adherence of Spider-Man's webs.

Highly intelligent, Nicholson can mentally determine the answer to many problems without using his powers. He can analyze data (scientific, legal, physical, etc.) and rapidly determine solutions. He has proven fiercely loyal (at least to the Kingpin), putting his employer's desires before his own.

USER NOTES:
Spider-Man: I hate fighting this guy, too unpredictable. Still, he's not good with multi-pronged assaults, so I'll gladly take him on with the Avengers at my back.

Project: PEGASUS clarifications: No known connection to the Answer (David Ferrari).

Captain America: I have encountered David Ferrari, a former S.H.I.E.L.D. agent (part of their chemical/biological weapons handling Furnace division) and U.S. soldier. He appeared to die while destroying an AIM base developing the Omega Compound, after which I stopped his and the unidentified Crimson Dynamo's world-conquering plot. He is strength-augmented and has mind-control powers. I also dated David's sister, Connie.

ARMADILLO

ANTONIO RODRIGUEZ

History: Antonio "Tony" Rodriguez was a small-time thug released from prison whose wife, Maria Bonita Rodriguez, was incurably paralyzed. Conventional doctors refused them after Antonio's money ran out, but his underworld contacts brought him to criminal geneticist Dr. Karl Malus. Malus developed Bonita's cure, asking in exchange that Antonio submit to experimental treatments and serve him. Agreeing, Antonio underwent repeated genetic modification and surgeries to become the monstrous Armadillo. Running Malus' errands, he broke into the Avengers' California compound to retrieve the comatose Goliath (Erik Josten), but Captain America stopped him. When Rodriguez told Captain America his story, the Captain allowed Rodriguez to return to Malus, following him there to confront the doctor. Afraid of damaging Bonita's life-maintaining equipment in a fight, Captain America called the police and both men were arrested. The Armadillo was freed when the Avengers didn't press charges, and the cured Bonita convinced Antonio to remain the Armadillo, believing they could make a lot of money with his powers. Rodriguez agreed, and joined Ed Garner's Unlimited Class Wrestling Federation. As the Awesome Armadillo (or "Mr. A"), Antonio moved through the Federation's ranks, and was positioned for a lucrative title fight after beating Doc Sawbones in Madison Square Garden. However, the Armadillo discovered his wife's adulterous affair with her hairdresser and went on a suicidal rampage through New York. When Antonio's manager Lennie J. Feitler intervened, the unthinking Armadillo backhanded Lennie across the block, where only the quick actions of a NYC officer saved him from a potentially fatal fall. Unaware, the Armadillo climbed the Empire State Building, jumping from 82 stories. The injured Armadillo was transported to the Vault for treatment and to serve prison time for damage done to Feitler and the city.

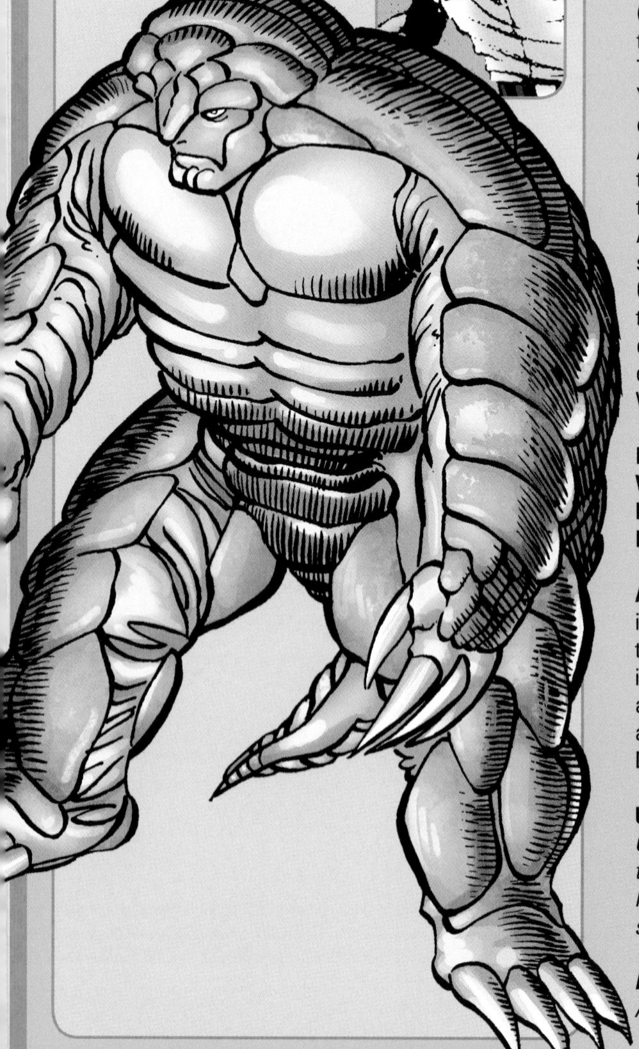

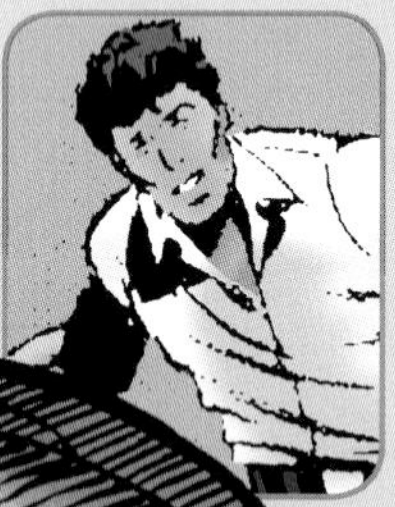

When Iron Man crashed the Vault, the Armadillo attempted escape, but the neophyte heroine Vagabond talked him into voluntarily returning to his cell. He became a model prisoner, but during Loki's engineered mass escape the Armadillo was mind-controlled by Dr. Doom and transported to Washington D.C. where he disrupted Congress' debate on the Super Heroes Registration Act. During a subsequent break-out, Antonio aided the guards in trying to subdue his fellows, attacking Venom. When Baron Zemo engineered still another mass escape to retrieve Moonstone (Karla Sofen) for his new team of Thunderbolts, Armadillo went along with the escapees, but after being recaptured by Atlas (Erik Josten), Antonio claimed he'd again been trying to stop the escape. Completing his term, Armadillo was released. The Armadillo fell back in with criminals, frequenting New York City's "Bar With No Name." Contacted by Coach Cady of Rey Trueno's unsanctioned Ultimate Fighting League, the Armadillo was successful as an in-ring brawler, becoming the New Jersey Regional Champ. When Cady tired of him, the Armadillo was set up to be beaten by the Battler (Daniel Axum) and Antonio found himself homeless, living on the street. Alongside Jack O'Lantern (Steve Levins) and the Constrictor, the Armadillo attempted to rob an armored truck but Hercules intervened, and the threesome was captured. The Armadillo was placed in the Raft, escaping during Electro's breakout, but was recaptured by the New Warriors.

Height: 7'6"
Weight: 540 lbs.
Eyes: Brown
Hair: None

Abilities: The Armadillo's super-durable hide is six inches thick at its thinnest points, has proven resistant to temperature extremes and acids, and can withstand impacts up to anti-tank weaponry. His hand and foot claws are sharp enough to rend steel and enable him to burrow at about 8 feet per minute, and he can lift an estimated 25 tons. Despite his size, he moves with the speed of a normal man.

USER NOTES:
Captain America: *This is one case where I don't think he's truly a bad guy, just lost. If we can get to Antonio before he's too far gone, and find a place for him, I think there's still hope here.*

Iron Man: *She-Hulk reports once battling a time-traveling Armadillo as well.*

BARBARUS

History: Born into the Swamp Men of the Antarctic prehistoric jungle the Savage Land, Barbarus was one of several of his people artificially mutated into superhumans through technological means by Magneto. Dubbing them the Savage Land Mutates, Magneto sent them to battle Ka-Zar and the X-Men, but they were defeated and Magneto's machines destroyed, causing the Mutates to revert briefly to their original states; however, the lasting effects of Magneto's technology ensure the Mutates regain their superhuman abilities should they ever lose them. Renaming themselves the Beast Brood, the restored Mutates captured scientists in hopes of forcing them to mutate other Savage Land natives into superhumans, but were defeated by the Avengers and delivered to legal authorities in Chile.

The Mutates eventually escaped and returned home, where one of the Mutates, Brainchild, became their leader. Under his direction, the Mutates clashed with the Angel (Warren Worthington III) and Spider-Man, who were searching for Karl Lykos, the human alter ego of the pterodactyl-like mutate Sauron. Captured and mutated by Brainchild's transformer device, the heroes were freed by Lykos and Ka-Zar. During the clash, the transformer was destroyed and Lykos transformed into Sauron once more after draining the mutated heroes' energy, restoring them to normal. Assuming control of the Mutates, Sauron pitted them against the X-Men, but they were again defeated and reverted to their original forms. Regaining their powers, the Mutates came under the leadership of Savage Land priestess Zaladane, who led the Mutates in raiding Antarctic research stations, plundering Chilean cities, and kidnapping scientists in an effort to cement her seat of power in the Savage Land. Zaladane then dispatched the Mutates to kidnap the former X-Man Polaris, leading to another defeat by the X-Men. Barbarus later romanced his fellow Mutate Whiteout before the Mutates encountered their former master, Magneto, who easily defeated them and killed Zaladane. Led by Sauron again, the Mutates clashed twice more with the X-Men before Sauron was reduced to a primitive state. Barbarus then briefly took over leadership of the group before Brainchild again assumed authority.

When the X-Men were helping the reptilian Saurids return to the Savage Land, the Mutates opposed them but were again defeated and turned over to the Land's United Tribes. Later, Barbarus and the Mutates became involved in an attempt by the reptilian Hauk'ka to restructure the Earth's biosphere. Joining forces with the United Tribes, Ka-Zar, and the X-Men, the Mutates helped defeat the Hauk'ka, though they attempted to betray the alliance at the last minute and were captured. Barbarus was subsequently incarcerated in the maximum security superhuman prison the Raft, and was among those inmates released by Electro as a cover for Sauron's escape. Returning to the Savage Land, Sauron and the Mutates then worked with a rogue S.H.I.E.L.D. faction illegally stockpiling Vibranium, but were opposed by Wolverine and a new Avengers team.

Height: 6'2"
Weight: 235 lbs.
Eyes: Brown
Hair: Dark brown

Abilities: Barbarus possesses four superhumanly strong arms and can lift at least 30 tons. Barbarus also has enhanced durability, endurance, and a speed that belies his massive frame. Barbarus occasionally employs crude weapons such as spears and knives, but most often relies on brute strength.

USER NOTES:
Spider-Man: *Bar-bar-bar bar-barbarus!*

Captain America: *Peter...*

Spider-Man: *Okay, okay... sorry, Cap. Anyway, this guy's tough, but not big on smarts, so using his strength against him is the way to go. Can be a handful when he's with the other Mutates, especially when they use teamwork — which, thankfully, they don't do all that often.*

Cage: *This guy's in my strength ballpark, decent scrapper too, but low on skill. Plus I am WAY meaner, and that's what counts. I'll take out this guy any day of the week.*

Spider-Man: *But will you buy him flowers and candy first?*

Captain America: *Peter...*

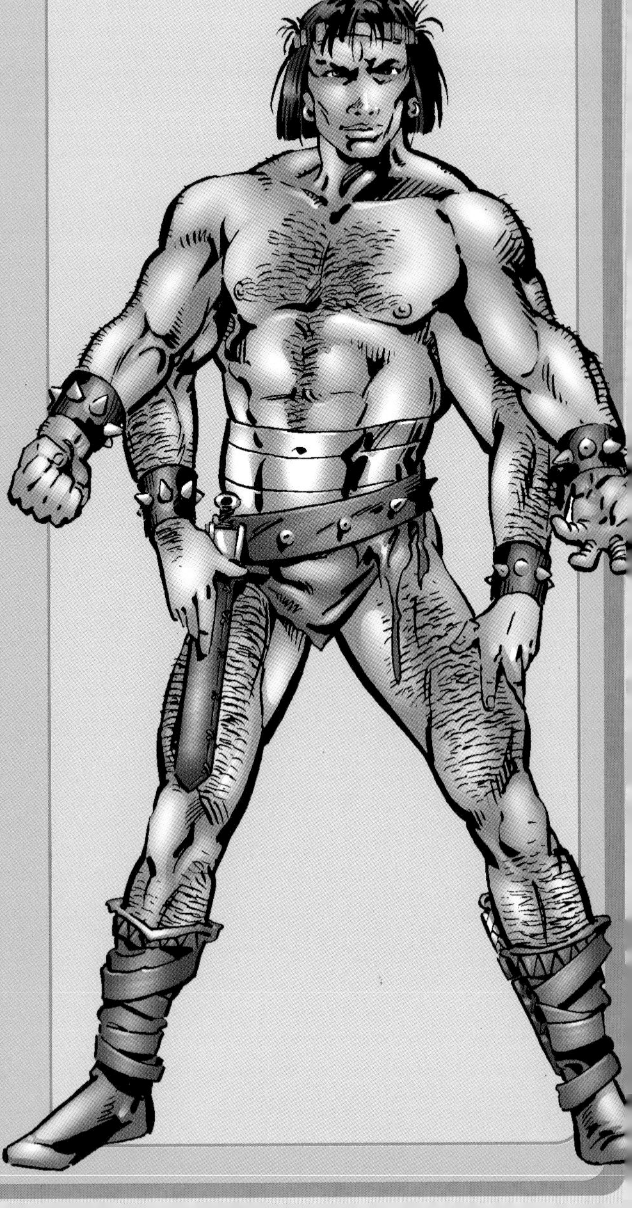

BLACKOUT

History: Descended from the Lilin demon-race, the albino known only as Blackout shunned sunlight, preferring to cloak himself in perpetual darkness. His light-dampening power manifested in his adolescence, driving Blackout even further into the shadowy world of the occult and encouraging him to pattern himself after the vampires that populated his favorite fictions. The adult Blackout did mercenary work, developing a taste for killing in the process. Blackout used his pay to finance a series of painful operations, gaining bionic fangs and allowing him to further mimic the appearance of traditional vampires.

Shortly after becoming an employee of Deathwatch, Blackout was sent to recover a series of stolen biotoxin canisters. This led him to clash with the Ghost Rider (Dan Ketch) in the Cypress Hills Cemetery. During this battle, Blackout attempted to bite the hero but the Hellfire surrounding Ghost Rider's skull left Blackout horribly scarred. Infuriated, Blackout set out to humiliate and destroy Ghost Rider. Learning of the hero's secret identity,

Blackout murdered his sister Barbara and threatened Dan's mother and girlfriend. He also began murdering anyone that Dan came into contact with, including a priest who heard Dan's confession and a street vendor. When a group of Morlocks led by the mutant Pixie began abducting children to protect them from the evil Morlock leader Masque, Ghost Rider mistakenly assumed Blackout to be involved. Blackout followed Ghost Rider to the Morlock lair beneath the cemetery and slew Pixie, but Ghost Rider enabled the other Morlocks to escape and the children to return home. The Ghost Rider later defeated Blackout with the aid of the mercenaries of H.E.A.R.T. (Humans Engaging All Racial Terrorism), and John Blaze, who further scarred Blackout with Hellfire. Arrested and imprisoned, Blackout was freed and employed by the Firm — secretly led by the Soulless Man, Centurious — which desired Ghost Rider's Medallion of Power. Blackout seemingly slew Dan Ketch, but the Ghost Rider survived and sealed Blackout in a mausoleum. Freed by the Firm, Blackout allied himself with the demonqueen Lilith, who revealed his Lilin lineage, augmented his abilities, and restored his former appearance; but Ghost Rider and his Midnight Sons overcame even Lilith, Centurious, and their allies. On his own again and seeking to renew his mercenary career, Blackout attempted to strike a deal with Ghost Rider: if the Spirit of Vengeance ignored Blackout's activities, he would promise not to target Dan Ketch's friends and family. Ghost Rider refused, defeating his old foe in single combat and leaving him tied to the antenna atop the Empire State Building, where Blackout's tender flesh began to burn as the sun rose. Retrieved by the authorities, Blackout was placed in the Raft, where he remained until Electro initiated a massive breakout.

Height: 6'0"
Weight: 165 lbs.
Eyes: Red
Hair: White

Abilities: Blackout can absorb all the light in a given area, leaving it in total darkness. He has superhuman strength (enough to lift two tons), durability, agility and healing abilities. He has razor-sharp fangs and claws, and his skin burns in direct sunlight.

USER NOTES:
Captain America: Reports paint this gentleman as a chilling figure with few (if any) qualms about murder or torture. Handle him with extreme caution.

Wolverine: I hear Blackout's gone back to merc jobs, working for anyone who can meet his price. He ain't usually on the radar of groups like the Avengers, but that don't make him any less dangerous.

Project: PEGASUS clarifications: No known connection to the Darkforce-powered Marcus Daniels, Blackout of the Masters of Evil; or to Landau, Luckman, and Lake's Blackout Troopers.

BLOOD BROTHERS

History: Twin natives of the Roclite race from the planet Rocklon in the Tarl system of the Milky Way, this duo became known as the Blood Brothers and entered the service of the alien despot Thanos. The earliest reports of their activity on Earth come from Iron Man's encounter with them in a base belonging to Thanos. Drax the Destroyer was imprisoned by Thanos, and telepathically contacted Iron Man (Anthony Stark) and directed him to Thanos' hidden underground Arizona base just west of the small town of Devil's Tongue, New Mexico. The Brothers, acting as servants to Thanos, were defeated by Iron Man and Drax and the base seemingly destroyed. When Thanos gained control of the Cosmic Cube, Iron Man returned to that base's remains seeking clues, and again encountered and defeated the Brothers, this time with the help of the Thing (Ben Grimm). Believed destroyed by Thanos for their failure, they were actually transported to a still-hidden deeper portion of the base. Cross-country trucker C.W. Crenshaw met the Blood Brothers when they stopped his truck on Interstate 10 and forced him to transport them to New York City, where they hoped to free the Controller. Exposed near New York by police, they battled both Iron Man and Daredevil, who defeated them when it was learned, to the Blood Brothers' apparent surprise, that they shared a "symbionic link," and their strength depended on how close the Brothers were to each other (presumably this link was created by Thanos, possibly using the Cosmic Cube). With this information in hand, the pair was separated, one brother placed in the ultra-security section of Ryker's Island, the other placed in a similar cell in New Jersey's McGuire Air Force Base.

Years later, the U.S. Air Force discovered that Thanos's Arizona base still existed, extending nearly a mile underground. Scientists there accidentally triggered a long-range molecular transmitter grid, teleporting both Blood Brothers to the base. The Avengers recaptured them, and Starfox (Eros of Titan) adapted a symbio-nullifier from the base's equipment to nullify each Brother's powers. The pair was placed in the Vault, but when Quasar (Wendell Vaughn) proposed removing the pair from Earth, his offer was accepted and the two were left on the surface of Mars. One Blood Brother was subsequently encountered and captured in Arnette, Texas by the USAgent, and his unexplained presence alerted the U.S. government's Superhuman Tactical Activities Response Squad (STARS) to a plot by the Kree/Ruul attempting to declare Earth an intergalactic prison. The uncaptured Blood Brother freed his partner, but the two were almost immediately recaptured by the X-Men's Rogue and a renegade Skrull named Z'Cann.

S.H.I.E.L.D. retained the Blood Brothers for study when the other alien "prisoners" were deported from Earth, isolating the Brothers for individual examination. After one Brother nearly escaped the Raft during Electro's break-in, the Brothers were again transported off-planet, as per "Maximum Security" protocols, although contact with their prison transport ship has since been lost.

Height: 8'
Weight: 800 lbs.
Eyes: Red
Hair: None

Abilities: The Blood Brothers are symbionically linked, such that the nearer they are to each other, the stronger they grow. When in close proximity to each other, they can each lift 50 tons and have been able to fell Iron Man and the Thing. The Blood Brothers' dietary needs include chemicals found in human blood, forcing them to act semi-vampirically while on Earth. The Brothers' lungs are also highly adaptable; each is capable of withstanding extreme and diverse atmospheres so that their need to breathe is almost nonexistent.

USER NOTES:
Iron Man: These guys are brutal. If you see one, look out for the other. By any means you can, get them as far apart as possible. I've found out the hard way that trying to take them on as a pair is a big mistake. Ben Grimm will back me up on this.

Project: PEGASUS clarifications: No known connection to the motorcycle gang encountered by X-51 (Machine Man).

BROTHERS GRIMM
NATHAN DOLLY/ PERCY AND BARTON GRIMES

History: The criminal Brothers Grimm began with curio dealer Nathan Dolly, who wielded an African witch doctor's pain-inducing voodoo doll as the criminal extortionist Mister Doll (also know as Mister Pain in some reports). Defeated by Iron Man (Tony Stark) and stripped of his doll, Nathan later bought two skull-faced dolls carved from the mystical wood of Wundagore Mountain by Django Maximoff. Each doll could be animated by an outside consciousness; but while trying to animate one of them later, Nathan accidentally mind-linked with both dolls and trapped his consciousness inside them. Aided by his wife Priscilla, he later transferred his spirit into a pair of full-size mannequins and committed crimes as the mystically empowered Brothers Grimm (or sometimes as a solitary Brother Grimm). Priscilla crafted civilian identities for the Brothers as her supposed sons Jake and William Dolly. After clashes with Spider-Woman (Jessica Drew) and the Hangman (Harlan Krueger), Nathan tried to usurp the body of Drew's associate Jerry Hunt, but the sorcerer Magnus foiled this plan and Nathan's spirit apparently dispersed.

A broken Priscilla soon died, and her Playhouse Theatre base of operations was bought by realtor siblings Barton and Percy Grimes, who found the inert Brothers Grimm mannequins and discovered that their costuming somehow retained Nathan's conjuring powers. The siblings began leading a super-criminal double life as the new Brothers Grimm, even besting the new Iron Man (Jim Rhodes); however, Tony Stark uncovered incriminating evidence which led to their exposure and arrest. Escaping, the Grimes brothers joined the Night Shift criminal gang. Unknown to the gang, their leader, the Shroud, was really an altruistic vigilante posing as a criminal to infiltrate the underworld, so the Night Shift preyed almost exclusively on other criminals, though they sometimes came into conflict with heroes such as Captain America and the Avengers. Meanwhile, the Brothers continued to freelance as a duo. When Crossfire placed a bounty on the archer Hawkeye's arm, the Brothers were part of a small army of criminals who tried unsuccessfully to collect the reward, defeated by Hawkeye, Mockingbird and Trick Shot. Later, the Brothers were twice manipulated into battling Spider-Man and twice defeated, the second time alongside Goliath (Erik Josten), Graviton, Titania (Mary MacPherran) and Trapster. The Night Shift eventually split with Shroud to follow a genuinely criminal leader, the new Hangman (Jason Roland), who led them against the Avengers and tricked them into serving the demon Satannish, in exchange for fame and enhanced powers; but the Night Shift turned against Hangman and Satannish after learning the bargain would cost their souls. Captured by the Avengers, the Brothers escaped in time to attend the wedding of Absorbing Man and Titania. Recaptured and imprisoned in the Raft, they escaped during the mass breakout sparked by Electro and remain at large.

Height: (both) 5'10"
Weight: (both) 210 lbs.
Eyes: (Barton) green, (Percy) blue
Hair: (Barton) brown, (Percy) black

Abilities: The Brothers Grimm can conjure up a seemingly endless supply of magical tools and weapons disguised as comedic props, children's toys, fairy tale objects and so on, such as specially gimmicked pies (some filled with hostile blackbirds), hurricane-strength whoopee cushions, corrosive-filled eggs, near-unbreakable thread, exploding jacks which produce blinding fireworks, electrified yoyos, masses of sticky dough which can engulf and restrain their foes, paralytic "stardust," and beans that sprout instantly into huge beanstalks suitable for scaling great heights or entangling opponents. The Brothers often ride atop levitating stars or clouds which they conjure to serve as transportation. Their accessories and physical abilities were temporarily augmented while they served Satannish, but those enhancements have long since faded.

Captain America: The Brothers remain a serious threat and should not be underestimated. Their weirdly varied arsenal often affords them the element of surprise, so during battle it's best to take them down as quickly as possible — otherwise, you never know what they might pull out of their bag of tricks next.

Spider-Woman: I've always kind of wondered if those Grimm costumes are possessed by Dolly or something, since they still have his powers. Maybe we could ask Doctor Strange to look into it...

BARTON

PERCY

BUSHWACKER
CARL BURBANK

History: Carl Burbank was a priest, but several traumas, including the deaths of young parishioners from drugs distributed by rising crimelord Nicky Lambert, led him to abandon his vows. He became a C.I.A. assassin, codenamed Bushwacker, with a cybernetic limb concealing various guns, using the thrill of killing to temporarily drown his haunting memories. At some point after marrying Marilyn Rogers, he went freelance. The Marauders paid him to murder mutant creative geniuses, which put Wolverine on his trail. Worried her husband was going insane, Marilyn enlisted Matt Murdock's aid to get him committed, unaware the lawyer was Daredevil. Meanwhile, Bushwacker took a side job to kill reporter Ben Urich and informant Patrick Nidetz, slaying the latter, but sparing Urich upon learning Nicky Lambert was his employer. Urich's story got Lambert arrested, but he was freed due to lack of evidence and later murdered, presumably by Bushwacker. Daredevil and Wolverine simultaneously located Bushwacker, but failed to save his next victim. Cornering Bushwacker, Wolverine doused him in gasoline; Bushwacker opened fire, igniting the fuel. Daredevil pulled him clear, but Bushwacker suffered severe facial scarring. Typhoid later freed him and others to attack Daredevil; he left the vigilante near death for his allies to finish off and returned to killing mutants.

The Kingpin sent Bushwacker after the Punisher (Frank Castle); Bushwacker believed he had successfully slain the Punisher, but Castle survived and tracked Bushwacker to the Burbank home where Marilyn witnessed her husband's work and fled. Bushwacker abandoned the fight to pursue his wife; he was shot by the Punisher and fell from a bridge to his apparent death. Surviving, Bushwacker underwent an upgrade, having much of his body replaced with an unknown substance. He worked for the Kingpin alongside Bullseye to poison Government Plaza's water supply, but was caught afterwards by Daredevil. Later, Bushwacker was one of a number of cyborgs captured by Mechadoom, then freed by Deathlok (Michael Collins). Learning his ex-brother-in-law Troy Donahue had taken his infant niece from her mother, Bushwacker tried to win Marilyn back by retrieving the child. Tracking Troy to Las Vegas, Bushwacker was tricked into taking "Bucky" (Julia Winter), Nomad's adopted daughter, instead. After fighting both Nomad and the Punisher, he fled empty handed. He then encountered both Daredevil and Deathlok again while trying to kill teenage hacker Max E. Mumm. Walter Jenkins subsequently contracted him to kill Daredevil. Pursuing his target into the sewers, he encountered the Mayan Devourer, retired hero the Peacekeeper, and future cyborg the Demolisher (formerly the Luther Manning Deathlok); outmatched and out of ammunition, Bushwacker retreated. He surfaced again trying to assassinate the Architect, battling Boomerang and others; during this fight, Elektra sliced off Bushwacker's prosthetic limb with a razorang. Soon apprehended and imprisoned on the Raft, Bushwacker recently escaped during Electro's mass breakout. The Jackal (Miles Warren) paid him to eliminate the Punisher; they fought, but Bushwacker was ultimately taken down by Daredevil.

Height: 6'0"
Weight: 225 lbs.
Eyes: Blue
Hair: Blond

Abilities: Bushwacker's right arm transforms into a range

of different caliber guns, including automatic weapons, shotguns and pistols; he has to carry regular ammunition to load these weapons. Much of his body is composed of a flesh-like substance which can liquefy to seal wounds, making him resistant to gunfire and able to mask his facial scars when he wants to (though he often chooses not to when confronting Daredevil, whom he blames for these injuries). He has claimed to be a mutant rather than a cyborg, and his left arm has been seen to transform too; however, given that on occasion his right-side mechanical arm has been removed by the authorities, this may be a deception, and his new abilities simply further cybernetic enhancements.

USER NOTES:

Wolverine: *Bushwacker's obsessed with making his kills "aesthetically pleasing," thinkin' of himself as an artist more'n an assassin. It's probably the only reason Castle survived their first battle. Look at Castle's track record, tho', and you can figure that Bushwacker's an enemy not to be underestimated.*

CARNAGE
CLETUS KASADY

History: Cletus Kasady was already one of the world's most notorious serial killers when he merged with an alien symbiote to become Carnage. Kasady had been sentenced to eleven consecutive life terms for his crimes (which may have included murdering his own parents as a child), but the real horror began with his new cellmate: Eddie Brock, host to the Venom symbiote. Kasady was present when Brock's symbiote helped him escape the prison and noticed that a small trace of symbiotic fluid had been left behind. This mass grew into an individual symbiote, one far more vicious and dangerous than Brock's. Together, this alien entity and Kasady formed Carnage, escaping their cell and embarking on a killing spree that ended only when Spider-Man and Venom put aside their differences to stop him.

Carnage was placed in psychiatric custody at the Ravencroft Institute, but all treatments proved ineffective in dealing with Kasady's mental illness. Carnage eventually escaped and formed a makeshift family of fellow lunatics, teaming with Shriek, Carrion, Demogoblin and Doppelganger. Spider-Man was again forced to ally with Venom, along with a host of other heroes, to stop the events that the media dubbed "Maximum Carnage." Returned to Ravencroft, Carnage began a pattern of escapes and defeats at Spider-Man's hands. During this period, the symbiote briefly abandoned Kasady and adopted a series of temporary hosts: John Jameson, Spider-clone Ben Reilly ("Spider-Carnage") and the Silver Surfer ("Carnage Cosmic") among them. Eventually, the symbiote returned to Kasady, but Venom had tired of his spawn's activities and forcibly reabsorbed it. This seemed to end Kasady's threat, but the killer proved to be more resourceful than the authorities gave him credit for. He escaped Ravencroft on his own, following a call that led all the way into the Negative Zone. There he encountered another symbiote, one that bonded with him to form a new version of Carnage. After another losing battle against Spider-Man, Carnage was returned to custody.

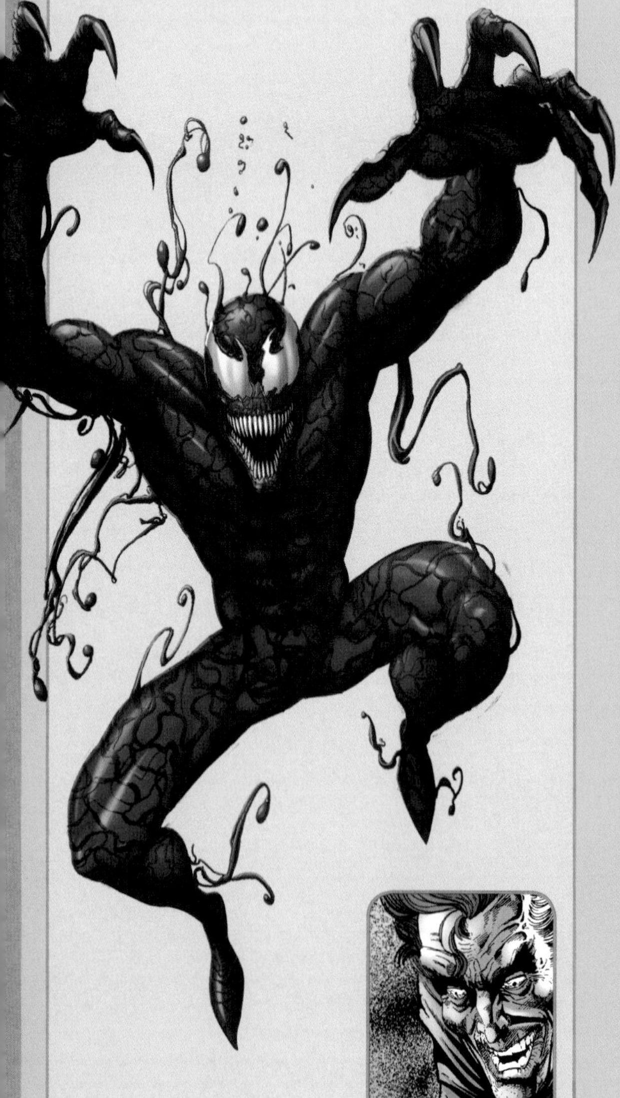

Escaping again, Carnage rampaged through New York City as he suffered through the effects of an asexual pregnancy. His spawn eventually formed the entity known as Toxin, while Carnage was captured once more. After his numerous escapes from Ravencroft, it was decided that Carnage needed higher security than the hospital could provide, and he was placed in the Raft prison.

During Electro's assault on the Raft facility, Carnage clashed with Cage, Spider-Woman and Daredevil before the Sentry seized him and flew him into space. In the upper atmosphere, Carnage was ripped apart and left to die. It remains to be seen whether or not Kasady or the symbiote survived this assault.

Height: 6'1"
Weight: 190 lbs.
Eyes: Green
Hair: Red

Abilities: As Carnage, Kasady can lift 35 tons and produce a variety of snares, weapons and swing lines from his own body. He can also bypass Spider-Man's spider-sense.

USER NOTES:
Spider-Man: *Carnage. I don't even like talking about him to be honest. Kasady on his own is dangerous enough, but you give him the power of an alien symbiote and he goes from being a serial killer to an Avengers-level concern. I hope I never have to face him again.*

Luke Cage: *I was there when this dude went crazy in the Raft... it was like Hannibal Lecter on steroids. The guy's way beyond insane. Personally, I think somebody oughtta give Sentry a medal for icing this guy.*

CENTURIUS
NOAH BLACK

History: Dr. Noah Black attended the 1928 genetics conference in Geneva, where his peers included Wladyslav Shinsky and Arnim Zola, but though he won the Nobel Prize in the 1930s, Black was ridiculed by his colleagues for theorizing that every atom was a sub-miniature solar system. Black shunned humanity, establishing the island fortress of Valhalla off the U.S. Pacific Coast. He constructed his Evolutionizer, maintaining his youth over the decades while producing hundreds of life forms; amongst these were his semi-humanoid servants, the Arms-Men. Centurius eventually began beaming his life forms to his orbiting Automated Rebirth Colonizer (ARC); seeing humanity already hell-bent on its own destruction, he intended to hasten this by assailing Earth with all-consuming radioactive fire, and his ARC would return exactly 100 years later to create a new world bereft of mankind's evils. Centurius' plot was discovered and threatened by S.H.I.E.L.D. agents Nick Fury and Jimmy Woo. Intending to become a superior being, Centurius leapt into his Evolutionizer, which completed his life cycle, turning him into a handful of protoplasmic slime. With Centurius seemingly dead, his ARC fell out of orbit and crashed on Valhalla, destroying it. Eventually re-evolving as intended, Centurius established a new island fortress in the mid-Atlantic and allied himself with the Conspiracy, a group of five beings seeking the extradimensional power of the Bloodgem fragments. Utilizing his Arms-Men and the giant monster Goram, Centurius began abducting a number of the world's greatest minds and draining their energies, as well as accruing Bloodgem fragments. These plots attracted Iron Man (Tony Stark) and Ulysses Bloodstone, who invaded the island base. While they battled Centurius' forces, Centurius was confronted by the alien Ulluxy'l Kwan Tae Syn, who had led incarnations of the Conspiracy for millennia. Despite Syn's power, Centurius used the psychic energies of his captives, channelled through a Bloodgem fragment, to slay him and usurp his position with the Conspiracy. While Centurius abandoned and destroyed his own base, the Conspiracy eventually captured Ulysses, cut off his Bloodgem fragment, and used the combined fragments to summon the gem's sentience, the Exo-Mind. Instead of receiving power, however, the Conspiracy member's souls were pulled into the Bloodgem, which assumed a giant humanoid crystalline form. His body clinging to life, Ulysses managed to temporarily destroy the Exo-Mind, apparently killing the Conspiracy members trapped within it. Centurius, alive and well, was later captured by S.H.I.E.L.D. and imprisoned within the Raft, from which he escaped during the breakout initiated by Electro.

Height: 6'0"
Weight: 225 lbs.
Eyes: Brown
Hair: Bald, formerly black

Abilities: Centurius is an extraordinary genius with exceptionally advanced knowledge of science and technology, especially genetic engineering. His genetically enhanced body resists disease and aging, and retains athletic physical abilities and fighting skills without regular exercise or training. He may retain clone bodies into which he can transfer his mind following physical death. Centurius wears light armor of unknown composition and uses a variety of highly advanced technology for transport (air and space craft, monorail, teleporter, thermalic suppression beam for transporting objects from Earth to space), communication (hologram projectors, long distance T-Viewers), and combat (stun-discs, ray guns). He typically works from an island fortress, and he utilizes his Arms-Men, robot warriors, and giant mutates.

USER NOTES:
Iron Man: *I'm pretty sure that Reed Richards eventually debunked the microscopic universe idea, proving that microverses were just accessed via the energies of shrinking. Not being a geneticist, I'd guess Black actually just mutated and evolved microscopic life forms.*

Captain America: *I saw the corpses of Centurius and the rest of the Conspiracy within their base below Central Park. I wonder about the others.*

Project: PEGASUS clarifications: *No known connection to Centurious, the Soulless Man, who has fought both the Blaze and Ketch Ghost Riders.*

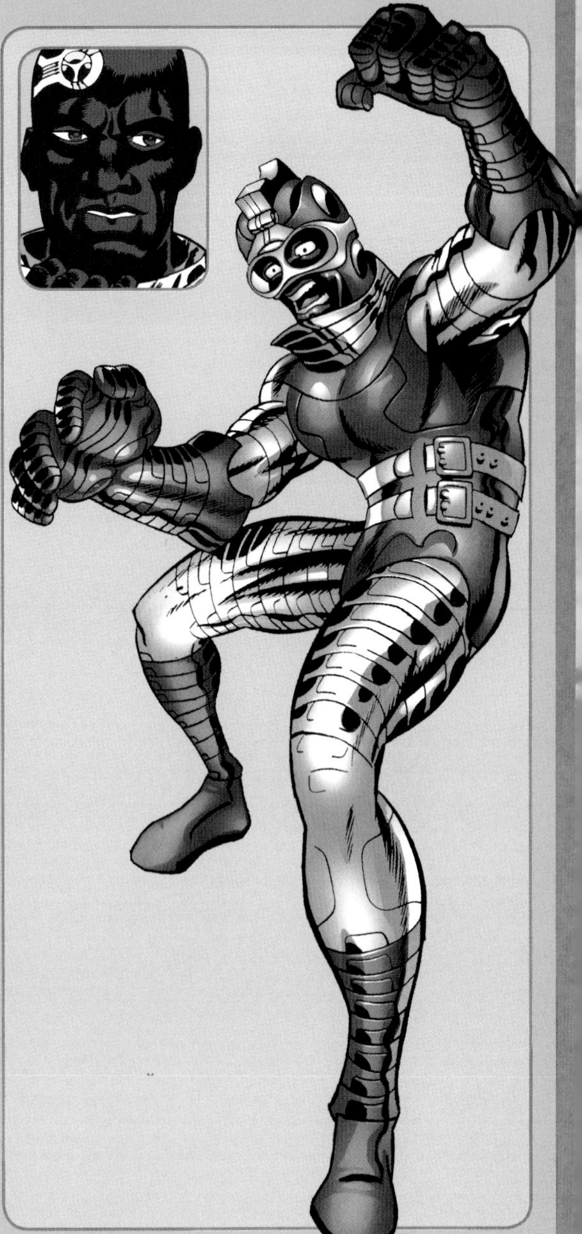

CHEMISTRO
CALVIN CARR

History: Calvin Carr is the brother of Curtis Carr, a research scientist who accidentally discovered a radioactive compound capable of transmuting matter, which he used to power an "alchemy gun." Fired by Horace C. Claymore from Mainstream Motors for refusing to share his discovery, Curtis, as Chemistro, embarked on a revenge campaign and clashed with hero for hire Luke Cage. During one battle, Carr transformed his right foot into steel for protection, only to watch it crumble to dust from his ray's unstable properties. Sentenced to prison, Carr, devastated by the results of his foolhardiness, resolved to go straight.

While in prison, Carr was assaulted by another prisoner, Arch Morton, who forced him to reveal the secret of the alchemy gun. When both men were released, Carr stuck to legal endeavors, but Morton's attempt to recreate the gun ended in an explosion which imbued his hands with transformative power. Hired by up-and-coming crimelord the Baron, Morton, as Chemistro, attacked Cage (then known as Power Man), claiming to have been sent by the

Baron's rival, the cyborg Big Brother. Cage nullified Morton's power with a device created by Carr, then defeated both Big Brother and the Baron, while Carr gained employment with Stark International.

Although Morton remained in prison, the Chemistro identity was revived by Calvin, an ex-con hoping to capitalize on his brother's invention. Hired by the criminal Mingo, the new Chemistro fought Power Man and his partner Iron Fist. Showing signs of mental instability, Calvin was more bloodthirsty than his predecessors, using the alchemy gun to partially or entirely transform those who got in his way, including martial artists Bob Diamond and Colleen Wing. Curtis developed a mixture to render Cage and Iron Fist immune, and they soon defeated Chemistro, who was sentenced to prison but released before the so-called "Acts of Vengeance" crime spree. Hired by the Wizard, who reworked the alchemy gun into wrist-blasters, Chemistro attacked Iron Man, wreaking havoc at Stark Prosthetics, where his brother was now R&D Director. Confronted by Curtis, Calvin contemptuously disintegrated his brother's left foot, but Iron Man destroyed his blasters, prompting a speedy surrender.

Although Curtis Carr, as High-Tech, later stole technology from corrupt corporations, he confessed at the urgings of the cyborg Deathlok and returned to probation. Calvin Carr remained in prison until the recent Raft breakout; his whereabouts are unknown.

Height: 6'1"
Weight: 235 lbs.
Eyes: Brown
Hair: Black

Abilities: Chemistro's "alchemy gun" or wrist-blasters are empowered by a compound capable of transmuting any material, including human tissue, into any other form of matter; the devices are cybernetically linked to the user, enabling Chemistro to work any transformation he can imagine. The gun can also alter the temperature and shape of an object. The transformations are not permanent, and transformed material usually crumbles to dust after some time.

USER NOTES:
Luke Cage: Too bad that fool gun's power made its transformations turn to dust, Curtis could've just gotten rich by turning a building into gold and...nah, I don't want to joke about turning buildings into gold.

Curtis was smart, Morton was powerful, but in a way Calvin was the worst because he was the only guy willing to transform people. The other two were out for money, but Calvin's one of those guys, gets a little power, thinks he's king of the world, has to show off, prove how great he is. But he spooks easy if he thinks he might lose, and if he starts winning he forgets to be careful. Grab his gun or blasters or whatever, he's done.

Without his gadget, Calvin's just a guy, so why was he at the Raft at all? Did he get the power in his hands, like Morton? He'd be a whole different sort of trouble then...

CONSTRICTOR
FRANK PAYNE

History: When Frank Payne was a child, his mother's common-law husband McAvey killed her and Frank's sister Amy, traumatizing Frank for life. Frank grew up to be an agent of S.H.I.E.L.D., and Director Nick Fury assigned him to infiltrate the Corporation, a Chicago-based crime outfit posing as a legitimate business. Payne assumed the cover identity of Frank Schlichting. One night, the Corporation was attacked by a gang while laundering money, and Payne shot back, killing one of the attackers. A shaken Frank went to Fury for advice. Fury told him to return to the mission to deal with his problems, but Payne never returned.

Payne went over to the other side, serving the Corporation faithfully in his new identity of the Constrictor. The Corporation provided him with a pair of Adamantium coils to use as weapons, and he fought the Hulk and Captain America on their behalf. When the Corporation collapsed, he became a mercenary serving employers such as Justin Hammer, the Viper & Dennis Golembuski, and began a partnership with Sabretooth against Power Man (Luke Cage) and Iron Fist. Invited to become a founding member of the Serpent Society, Constrictor rejected their offer and attempted to expose them to Captain America. The Society put him in the hospital, where he was nearly killed by the Scourge of the Underworld. He has also served in the Crimson Cowl's Masters of Evil and the Wizard's Frightful Four.

Despite his reputation as a ruthless assassin, the Constrictor suffered occasional bouts of regret for the life he led, and still cared for his daughter Mia; but he kept his distance from her, preferring her to think he was dead. He even turned on his own employers on occasion, once turning on the Viper when he was shocked by her nihilism. He eventually gave up his Adamantium coils so that they could be used to save Sabretooth's life after Sabretooth's own Adamantium was removed. Justin Hammer then outfitted him with Vibranium coils.

After altering his features to protect his identity, Frank found that his own home security system didn't recognize him, and he wound up moving into Dr. Octopus' house, where he had to take on Deadpool and Titania as roommates. The arrangement came to an end after "Titania" proved to be the shapeshifter Copycat. Later, the Constrictor became the envy of the super-villain community when he won a multi-million dollar lawsuit against Hercules, after the Avenger used excessive force against him.

Fury has shown some interest in rehabilitating the Constrictor, even arranging for him to serve in G.W. Bridge's most recent incarnation of the Six Pack to oppose Cable, as well as sending him against A.I.M., but Payne has returned to the underworld each time. Following his escape from the Raft, the Constrictor was picked up by Spider-Man and Moon Knight, but the charge was thrown out. He has since turned his efforts toward trying to enter high society thanks to the money he got from Hercules.

Height: 5'11"
Weight: 190 lbs.
Eyes: Brown-grey
Hair: Black

Abilities: The Constrictor wears a pair of cybernetically controlled Vibranium coils which elongate from the wrists of his costume. The coils can expand up to 30 feet, enwrap a target, and constrict it, crushing with a force of 115 lbs. per square inch. The coils can also release an electrical charge.

USER NOTES:
Luke Cage: Up until I met his daughter, I didn't think much of the Constrictor — he and Sabretooth gave me and Danny enough trouble back in the day. But now that Mia knows he's alive, she's desperate for him to come home, and even hired me to try and corral him. This guy's messed up, and probably needs a lot of headshrinking to work through his problems, but I'd actually like to see him make good. I know what it means to be an ex-con, and soon I'll be a father too. I hope he makes the right decision, for Mia's sake.

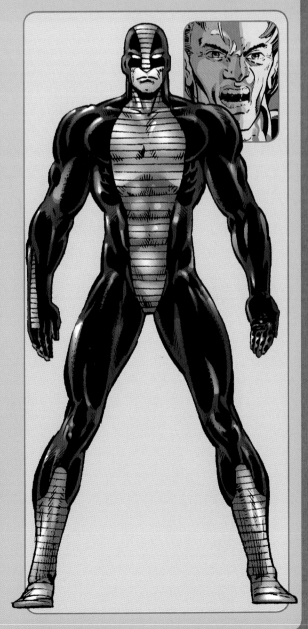

CONTROLLER
BASIL SANDHURST

History: Bedridden by meningitis as a child, Basil Sandhurst's obsession with control became his downfall as a scientist when his refusal to obey ethical restraints had him barred from most research facilities. Disdainful of the supposedly "menial" work he was later assigned at Cordco, Sandhurst was subject to fits of rage, and in the course of calming him, his brother Vincent inadvertently triggered a laboratory explosion, scarring and crippling Basil. When the guilt-ridden Vincent outfitted him with an automated lab, Basil bonded a super-strong exoskeleton to his body, powered by cerebral energies from those around him. As the Controller, he planned to enslave New York, but Iron Man ended his scheme, leaving him comatose.

Institutionalized, the Controller recovered and seized control of hospital staff, only to fall before Iron Man again. Months later, he was released by the ruthless alien Thanos, who upgraded his technology. Promised rulership of Earth, the Controller enslaved dozens of operatives; but his egotistical displays endangered Thanos's security, and when the Controller failed to defeat Thanos's enemy Captain Mar-

vell, the alien left him for dead. Reviving soon afterward, the Controller again fought Iron Man and was again defeated.

The Controller went underground for years, upgrading via stolen Stark technology from Justin Hammer, and eventually enslaved a "cult" of Californians. However, Iron Man vanquished him once more, burning out the exoskeleton's Stark components. Sentenced to the Vault, where he joined Crossfire's crew, the Controller soon escaped, only to be captured by the Red Skull, who controlled the Controller via the mesmerizing Voice. Defeated by Captain America, the Controller escaped and briefly helped form the Inner Circle of the New Enforcers, but his exoskeleton's systems broke down from Iron Man's earlier attack. Undaunted, the Controller lived multiple vicarious lives via both human pawns and mutated cyborgs, but he overreached himself by enslaving telepath Sarah Jessup, whose psionic power overloaded while he fought Iron Man, and he was left comatose once more.

Revived by the world-conquering Master, the Controller became the Master's pawn against the Avengers and Heroes for Hire. Abandoned after a later defeat, the Controller, in an ironic nod to his many hospitalizations, acquired his own clinic, where he influenced the wealthy to do his bidding. However, the Controller could not resist enslaving Tony Stark as well, leading to his latest defeat by Iron Man. Remanded to the Raft, the Controller escaped with dozens of others but was recaptured during a clash with the U-Foes and Avengers.

Height: 6'2"
Weight: 565 lbs.
Eyes: White, formerly black
Hair: Black

Abilities: The Controller wears an exoskeleton that grants him mobility, as well as superhuman strength (lifting 1000 pounds) and endurance. He uses "slave discs" to control others, up to several dozen at a time, draining cerebral energy to magnify his exoskeleton's strength (to lift up to 50 tons and possibly more) and duplicate his victims' abilities. He can psionically control "weak-willed" subjects even without his discs. He flies via boot-jets and has employed image inducers, stun mists, and other technology as needed.

USER NOTES:
Iron Man: A classic case of genius undermining itself, Sandhurst was a borderline sociopath before his accident. Now he sees others as no more than tools, batteries, badges of his supposed greatness. I'm genuinely amazed that he retains enough social skills to be a member of a team. But the Controller's greatest weakness is what controls him: ego. No matter how much power he has, it's never enough, he overreaches himself every time. He can't just win, he has to win gloriously. And, so far, there's always been someone there to catch him at that moment of weakness between wanting and having. So far...

Project: PEGASUS clarifications: No known connection to Control 7, the mercenary espionage unit.

CORRUPTOR
JACKSON DAY

History: A law-abiding pharmaceutical factory worker, Jackson Day was exposed to psychoactive chemicals during a fire; although rescued from the flames by Thor, Day had already mutated in both form and mind, becoming a blue-skinned madman whose touch sent the thunder god on a rampage. While then-novice hero Nova (Richard Rider) calmed Thor, Day's transformation fluctuated, varying between the horrified Day and the ranting Controller. Defeated before he could do much damage, Day was transferred to Avengers Mansion for treatment but escaped, abandoning his wife, Doris, and becoming the head of the criminal Inner Circle, using his power to amass wealth and extort people in financial need to commit crimes on his behalf. But his megalomania kicked in, and when his impractical plan to overrun New York with a "mindless legion" of corruptees was foiled by Nova, the Corruptor abandoned the Circle.

The Corruptor next directed the mysterious Night Flyer to fight the Hulk, who was distracted long enough for the Corruptor to gain control of him, and he forced the Hulk's companion Rick Jones to summon the Avengers, hoping to corrupt them as well. However, the Corruptor's own high-tech base slowed the transmission, only summoning super-heroes in the immediate vicinity: Red Wolf (Will Talltrees), Firebird (Bonita Juarez), Phantom Rider (Hamilton Slade), Texas Twister and Shooting Star, who formed the sporadically active Rangers super-team as of this adventure. During the battle, Day overplayed his hand and lost control of the Hulk, who teamed with the Rangers to defeat and capture the Corruptor. Escaping months later, Day relocated to Japan but was quickly immobilized by Sunfire.

The Corruptor served his remaining time in the Vault, where he befriended Crossfire and other criminals. Upon release, he gained control of the Hope Foundation, where he subtly (and unprovenly) manipulated others, including Nova, to his own ends. However, his time as corporate mastermind ended when Imus Champion forced him to infiltrate Project: PEGASUS as staff member Andrew, controlling the extradimensional Squadron Supreme to distract the Avengers. Exposed and sentenced to the Raft, he escaped during Electro's mass breakout. During his group's feud with the U-Foes, Day was the only member of Crossfire's crew to evade the Avengers, and he remains at large.

Height: 6'1"
Weight: 225 lbs.
Eyes: Red, formerly blue
Hair: White, formerly reddish-blond

Abilities: The Corruptor's sweat glands exude psychoactive drugs which enable him to, by touch, subvert the will of any individual; his touch releases his victim's inhibitions, so that, if not given specific instructions, the victim will revert to uncontrollable behavior. Early in his career, the Corruptor demonstrated such powers as super-strength, eye-beams, and teleportation, none of which he seems to possess today. He has used various forms of highly advanced computer technology, its origins unrevealed.

USER NOTES:
Captain America: Mind control. I didn't like it when the Red Skull, the Artist, and the rest used it in the forties, I don't like it now. More often than not, you end up fighting remote-controlled innocents while the man behind the curtain gets away. And if he gets hold of you, next thing you know, you're fighting your teammates or making public declarations against everything you stand for. I hate it when that happens. Like most mind controllers, Day prefers to let his pawns do his fighting; get past them, avoid being controlled yourself, and he's finished. His "untouchable" corporate act protected him from the law for a while, but he seems too much the grandstander to settle for that. The only wild card would be the extra powers he had at the beginning. He hasn't used them in years, so they might be gone, but I know better than to count on that. From Thor's report, Day's transformation was partial at first, the decent man at war with his monstrous power; his subconscious even hatched some scenario where he was "all the evil of the ages combined." Since giving himself over to his dark (blue) side, Day's been more sensible, but also subtler and therefore more dangerous. So the first person Day ever corrupted was...himself. But I suppose that's true of any criminal.

Project: PEGASUS clarifications: *No known connection to the Corrupt, the townspeople of Christ's Crown mutated by Blackheart.*

COUNT NEFARIA
LUCHINO NEFARIA

History: Count Luchino Nefaria was born into wealthy Italian nobility and secretly became a high-tech criminal mastermind within the international Maggia crime cartel. When the Avengers opposed Maggia operations, Nefaria tried to frame them for treason, but they defeated him and exposed him as a criminal. Regrouping, Nefaria recruited his long-lost adult daughter Whitney Frost (raised in America to protect her from her father's enemies), and she reluctantly became his Maggia second-in-command. Trying unsuccessfully to destroy Iron Man (secretly Avengers financier Tony Stark) using an illusion-casting "nightmare machine," Nefaria also conspired with Stark's cousin Morgan Stark to ruin Tony's reputation, but this scheme failed. Nefaria later held the entire city of Washington for ransom, but he and his super-criminal accomplices were defeated by the original X-Men, and his daughter (later known as Madame Masque) took over their Maggia crime family. Becoming an independent criminal operator, Nefaria seized the North American Air Defense Command at Valhalla Mountain in Colorado with the aid of the Ani-Men and threatened to launch America's nuclear arsenal unless

he was paid an enormous ransom. He was defeated by the new X-Men, including Thunderbird (John Proudstar), who died trying in vain to prevent Nefaria's escape.

Nefaria next assembled Living Laser, Power Man (Erik Josten) and Whirlwind as a new Lethal Legion, had their powers boosted by scientist Kenneth Sturdy, then stole their powers for himself, magnified a hundredfold. Defeated by the Avengers despite his newly god-like power, Nefaria began aging rapidly as a result of his new mutations. Becoming an aged invalid, Nefaria escaped custody with the aid of the Ani-Men and his daughter, now Tony Stark's lover. When Stark (as Iron Man) tried to take Nefaria back into custody, the Count was seemingly slain during the struggle. Traumatized, Whitney went into hiding for years, operating mostly through surrogates such as her rebellious "bio-duplicate" Masque, a one-time Avengers associate. Reviving thanks to his ionic-powered physiology, Nefaria found that he needed to drain ionic energy from others to survive. He stalked various ionic-powered beings, killing some and imprisoning others, but was eventually exposed by Iron Man. Later, Nefaria experimented on the Savage Land's inhabitants, trying to create an ionic race to feed his needs, but Captain America and Sharon Carter defeated him. Discovering he could mentally control fellow ionics, Nefaria enslaved ionic-powered heroes Atlas and Wonder Man, sought to consolidate the Maggia crime families under his leadership and tried to force Whitney to rejoin him, all as part of a larger scheme to mutate all of humanity with ionic radiation and enslave the entire world. His plot was thwarted by Whitney, the Avengers and the Thunderbolts, though not before Nefaria murdered the heroic bio-duplicate Masque, thinking she was Whitney. In the end, Nefaria appeared to have been blown to atoms, but instead survived and was jailed in the Raft super-prison, where he recently escaped during a prison break sparked by Electro.

Height: 6'2"
Weight: 230 lbs.
Eyes: Blue
Hair: Black

Abilities: Fully charged, Nefaria has nearly immeasurable superhuman strength and durability, superhuman speed, the power of flight, and the ability to fire powerful laser beams from his eyes. More recently, he has also proven capable of forming and manipulating crude ionic energy constructs, such as an energy lasso. Nefaria must periodically absorb ionic energy from outside sources or his powers fade and he ages rapidly. Nefaria apparently shares the regenerative powers typical of ionic beings, enabling him to heal himself from a seemingly deceased state or even reintegrate his bodily matter after exploding. Nefaria is a charismatic natural leader and a capable criminal strategist, well-versed in the use of various exotic technologies

USER NOTES:
Iron Man: In a way, Nefaria is everything Tony Stark has tried to avoid becoming — intellect, wealth and power twisted to selfish, destructive ends. Throw in vast ionic might and you've got someone who really shouldn't be running around loose if we can help it. When we track him down, here's hoping Whitney doesn't get caught in the crossfire...

Project: PEGASUS clarifications: Nefarius (Lloyd Bloch, a.k.a. Moonstone) was also empowered by Sturdy's method. He was later seemingly slain by Count Nefaria.

CROSSBONES
BROCK RUMLOW

History: Young Brock Rumlow led the Savage Crims gang on New York's lower east side. After he brutalized fifteen year old Rachel Leighton, two of her brothers assaulted Brock; the eldest brother was killed. Rumlow fled, entering the Taskmaster's school for criminals, and within three years became an instructor there under the name Bingo Brock. As a mercenary, he enlisted with the communist Red Skull in Algeria, serving him as "Frag" until he was sent to invade Arnim Zola's Switzerland chateau. Ultimately the only team member to survive the assault, Rumlow there met and impressed the Nazi Red Skull; this Skull accepted Brock's services, code-naming him "Crossbones."

Sent to retrieve the five Bloodstone fragments, Crossbones shadowed Helmut Zemo's search for them. While Zemo battled Captain America, Crossbones knocked out Cpt. America's pilot, John Jameson, and stole two fragments; when he got near the other three, the five combined to re-animate Heinrich Zemo's corpse under control of the alien Hellfire Helix. Unobserved, Crossbones destroyed the Helix (worn on the corpse's forehead) with a crossbow bolt. Brock then kidnapped Diamondback (whom he recognized as Rachel Leighton), using her as bait to trap Captain America; but when the Skull learned of Crossbones' involvement with the Captain, he ordered Crossbones to flee. Crossbones recruited the Controller and Voice of Doom to serve the Skull, led the Skeleton Crew against the Hellfire Club's Selene, and, using psychic Tristam Micawber, located the Skull after Magneto kidnapped him. He attempted assassinating the Kingpin, was stopped by Typhoid Mary, and battled Bullseye when the Kingpin retaliated. He led the Skeleton Crew when they were captured by the Schutz-Heiliggruppe (Blitzkrieger, Hauptmann Deutschland, Zeitgeist); after Arnim Zola rescued them, the Skull faked the assassination of himself, Mother Night, and Crossbones. The Red Skull finally fired Crossbones for questioning the Skull's decision to ally with Viper.

Crossbones headed east, working briefly in Chicago for druglord Marco Sanzionare against SuperPro. In New York, Crossbones kidnapped and brainwashed Diamondback by abusing her repeatedly and forcing her through a rigid combat training routine. Forcing Diamondback to steal Captain America's super-soldier treated blood from Avengers Mansion, Crossbones returned to the Skull. When the Skeleton Crew's new leader, Cutthroat, plotted Crossbones' murder, Mother Night warned Brock, who slit Cutthroat's jugular. Diamondback escaped, summoning Captain America and the Falcon to capture the Skull's operatives; Crossbones was imprisoned, but eventually convinced officials he was rehabilitating, partly by defeating the terrorist cell "Fortress" when they invaded a Denver hospital. Exploiting his jailors' gullibility, Crossbones escaped, and was hired by Hydra to bomb New York's embassy row alongside the Absorbing Man, but the pair was stopped by Captain America. Betrayed by Hydra, Crossbones fled, wreaking vengeance on his bosses. He was hired by New Son to assassinate Gambit, but despite allying with Batroc and Zaran, was defeated by the combined efforts of New Orleans' assassins' and thieves' guilds; Crossbones was imprisoned in the Raft until Electro's break-in freed him. The Skull promptly rehired him, and he was aiding in repowering a Cosmic Cube when Aleksander Lukin's Winter Soldier assassinated the Red Skull and stole the Cube. Lukin anonymously accused Captain America for the Skull's death, but Crossbones soon realized the truth and pointed Captain America toward Lukin.

Height: 6'4"
Weight: 290 lbs.
Eyes: Brown
Hair: Black

Abilities: Crossbones is a world-class hand-to-hand fighter. He is an expert pilot and a marksman with crossbows, guns and throwing knives. His weaponry includes firearms, a collapsible crossbow, a wrist spike, wrist-mounted spring-loaded stilettos, various explosives and poisoned knives.

USER NOTES:
Captain America: Crossbones' face was hideously scarred, so badly that he was allowed to wear his mask in prison. This is no longer the case. Regardless, Crossbones is one of my deadliest opponents, hands down. Do not take him lightly.

CROSSFIRE
WILLIAM CROSS

History: CIA interrogation expert William Cross was already building his own rogue covert operations when he romanced federal corrections officer Rozalyn Backus, with whom he developed ultrasonic brainwashing technology. Backus was unaware of Cross's illicit activities, and they were engaged to be married until Cross stole the technology and disappeared, faking his own murder and framing Backus for the crime. Surviving an attempt on his life which cost him an eye and an ear, Cross replaced them with cybernetic implants and became a prosperous high-tech freelance subversive as Crossfire. Plotting to make the growing superhero community exterminate each other via ultrasonic mind control, Crossfire abducted the Thing (Ben Grimm) to test his technology, but Moon Knight (secretly Cross's ex-CIA colleague Marc Spector) interfered and Crossfire was defeated. Crossfire secretly rebuilt his operations at Cross Technological Enterprises (CTE), founded by his cousin, Darren Cross. When Hawkeye and Mockingbird investigated, Crossfire first tried to eliminate them using the assassins Bombshell, Oddball and Silencer, then decided Hawkeye would make an ideal test subject

for his superhero mind control plot — prominent enough for his death to attract the superhero community en masse, but weak enough to be an easy target. Hawkeye thwarted the brainwashing, captured the criminals and rescued Mockingbird, whom he soon married. A vengeful Crossfire subsequently stalked the newlyweds at the estate of silent film star Moira Brandon, who was declared an honorary Avenger after she helped the heroes recapture Cross. The criminal mercenary jugglers known as the Death-Throws freed Cross from police custody, but when he proved unable to pay them, they held Cross for ransom until Captain America, Hawkeye and Mockingbird captured the whole gang. Crossfire later escaped and placed a bounty on Hawkeye's arm, hoping to destroy the hero's archery skills and break his spirit, but Cross and his small army of super-criminal bounty hunters were defeated and captured by Hawkeye, Mockingbird and Trick Shot.

At some point, Cross had befriended U-Foes leader Vector, whose secret power nullification technology Crossfire hoped to exploit. Recaptured following an encounter with S.H.I.E.L.D., Cross was imprisoned in the Vault, where Roz Backus (long since exonerated) joined the Vault's Guardsman force. Seemingly aiding and then foiling an escape plotted by the U-Foes and Crossfire, Backus turned the criminals against each other, faked her own death, and stole a fortune in cash and goods from the criminals, including Vector's power nullification chamber (which Backus later claimed she secretly destroyed since she felt it was too dangerous to preserve). The criminals were later transferred to the new Raft super-prison, and all escaped during Electro's mass breakout, with Crossfire leading a gang of fellow mind-manipulators: Controller, Corruptor, Mandrill and Mister Fear (Alan Fagan). Pursuing Backus, the chamber and their grudges against each other, the U-Foes and Crossfire's crew fought a super-powered gang war in New York until the Avengers broke it up. Crossfire and his gang were recaptured and Backus surrendered.

Height: 6'0"
Weight: 190 lbs.
Eyes: Blue
Hair: White, formerly brown

Abilities: An expert spy, marksman and strategist, Crossfire is a master brainwasher who uses mind-influencing ultrasonic devices. His cybernetic infrared eye can see in the dark, and his left "ear" is an adjustable, super-acute audio sensor. His bulletproof Kevlar costuming conceals miniaturized accessories such as firearms, surveillance devices, ultrasonics and an oxygen supply. The same explosion that claimed his left eye and ear left him with 85% hearing loss in his right ear.

USER NOTES:
Captain America: Crossfire is a formidable master planner, albeit seldom much of a physical threat. Never much cared for these mind-control types like Doctor Faustus — they're not exactly big on fair fights. Crossfire has an obsessive grudge against Hawkeye, but Clint always proved more than a match for Cross.

Spider-Woman: Crossfire's full S.H.I.E.L.D. file is massive, most of it highly classified — and that's just the stuff we know about. He had his fingers in so many pies for so many years that law-enforcement's probably gonna be dealing with fallout from his operations long after he's dead.

CRUSADER
ARTHUR CHARLES BLACKWOOD

History: Arthur Charles Blackwood studied the Crusades from childhood; obsessed with his ancestry, which could be traced back to the 12th century, Arthur became an expert swordsman as a teen. Arthur's great-grandfather had founded Chicago's Blackwood Seminary; that family money got him admitted as a divinity student, but Arthur's unforgiving, eye-for-an-eye vision of Christianity got him expelled after assaulting one Father William. Visiting the family crypt in Mundelin Cemetery, he experienced a vision of his ancestors commanding him to take up arms against non-believers. The cemetery groundskeeper, Stanislaus Polowski, became caught up in it, as Blackwood named him Peleus and demanded he become Blackwood's squire; Polowski reported the Crusader's sword, shield, and armor all appeared in a flash that night. As the Crusader, Blackwood attacked Thor in Chicago and ultimately ran Thor through with his sword, at which point Thor's then-girlfriend Sif rescued him. Returning the following morning, fully healed and his faith restored by Odin, Thor shattered the Crusader's sword and defeated him. Blackwood fled, and the Chicago police eventually dropped the case. Apparently putting his religious life behind him, Blackwood married Eleanor Blackwood, adopting her daughter, Jenny. Over time, though, Blackwood again became obsessed with the Crusader, attempting to reforge his shattered sword. When Ghulistan's Emir announced a visit to the United States, Blackwood readopted the Crusader's identity and came to Washington D.C. to kill the man. On the night before the Emir's arrival, the Crusader killed two petty thugs who were robbing a church. The following day, the Crusader attacked the Emir (calling him the "Saracen"), but the Black Knight (Dane Whitman) intervened. The Crusader had the upper hand until his step-daughter Jenny intervened, shocking Blackwood to his senses. He shattered his own sword and shield, and voluntarily surrendered.

Imprisonment apparently damaged Blackwood's fragile psyche, and he escaped confinement to reappear in Chicago's Canindelein Cemetery, where he slew three vandals. Seemingly more unbalanced than ever, the unshaven Crusader rode a motorcycle into downtown Chicago, violently attempting to force a local newspaper, the Chicago Spectator, to promote his brand of faith. He was opposed by Luke Cage, who once again shattered the Crusader's sword. Captured again, Blackwood escaped and retreated to an Irish monastery where he lived in seclusion, trying to avoid all modern life. Seeing a newspaper article billing mutant faith healer Nate Grey (X-Man) as "the second coming," Blackwood became the Crusader again. He confronted Grey in downtown London, nearly killing him until Grey saved a bystander who reminded Blackwood of his stepdaughter Jenny; Arthur came to his senses and surrendered. While the monks Blackwood had stayed with requested custody, Blackwood was instead turned over to S.H.I.E.L.D. Imprisoned in the Raft, Crusader escaped during Electro's mass breakout, attacking Spider-Man on his way out; however, Blackwood's subsequent assault on "pagan" sorcerer Doctor Strange saw the Crusader swiftly defeated and recaptured.

Height: 6'2"
Weight: 225 lbs.
Eyes: Blue
Hair: Brown

Abilities: The Crusader's strength and durability, as well as the power of his sword and shield, are directly related to his will and belief; while he is confident, they appear practically unlimited (sufficient to go toe-to-toe with Thor), but crises of faith weaken him or revert him to normal. While he has instantly summoned his armor and weaponry, this does not seem to be under Blackwood's conscious control.

USER NOTES:
Luke Cage: Don't worry about this faith mumbo-jumbo: once I broke this loony's sword, he folded on the spot. It looks like pretty much every time he was done, the sword broke. Shatter the damn sword!

Project: PEGASUS clarifications: Other unrelated Crusaders include Robert Grayson (Marvel Boy); the 12th century el Alemain; Perseus Ablemarle of Earth-238; Sarah Rogers of Earth-9811; the 14th century warrior of Earth-93060; and the World War II era Crusaders (Captain Wings, Dyna-Mite, Ghost Girl, Spirit of '76, Thunderfist and Tommy Lightning).

CUTTHROAT
DANIEL LEIGHTON

History: Daniel "Danny" Leighton was second child in a family of four. His father brought the family to New York City from Texas, and after he left them the family fell on hard times, living off the mother's small wages and the disability income of the older brother, William (who had lost use of his legs in military action). Danny and his younger brother Ricky fell in with a local gang, the Savage Crims, led by Brock Rumlow (later Crossbones); but when their youngest sibling, fifteen-year-old Rachel, was raped and beaten by Rumlow, William and Ricky went after Brock with a gun. William was killed, Brock fled, and Danny left the family in shame. Traveling to Europe, Danny grew skilled with knives, became a small-time criminal and then a mercenary, and decided to become a super-villain. As Cutthroat, he accepted a contract to assassinate Spider-Man in a publicity stunt to promote Amos Jardine's circus. Danny purchased an expensive experimental rifle-sized rocket gun for the attempt, but the mutant Nightcrawler intervened, and Cutthroat was defeated when the weapon exploded. Left lightly bound in webbing for the police,

Cutthroat temporarily sacrificed his armor to escape, and returned to Europe for further training.

When the Red Skull advertised for a new leader for his Skeleton Crew after firing the old leader, Crossbones, Cutthroat decided this was his shot at the big leagues and applied. At the Skull's Colorado mountain headquarters, Cutthroat was the last man standing after one-on-one-on-one combat with the other two candidates, Mangler (Lucius O'Neil) and Deathstroke, and was accepted to lead the Skeleton Crew. In the following weeks, he was trained extensively by the Taskmaster. On an early mission, Cutthroat and Mother Night rescued new Skeleton Crew recruits Blackwing (Joseph Manfredi) and Jack O'Lantern (Steve Levins) from Captain America and Thunderstrike, though Night was captured in the process. Bailing herself out, Mother Night was physically abused by the Skull for her failure. Leighton, feeling both sorry for and attracted to Mother Night, told her she deserved better and began a romantic relationship with her behind the Red Skull's back.

Crossbones soon returned to reclaim his position, bringing along an unwilling Diamondback, whom he wrongly believed he had brainwashed. Cutthroat recognized Diamondback as his sister Rachel and briefly embraced her in secret, revealing his identity and asking forgiveness for abandoning the family ten years previously. Realizing Crossbones threatened his position, Cutthroat planned to assassinate Crossbones while he slept (though Danny remained unaware of Crossbones' identity as the man who had killed his brother and brutalized his sister). However, he informed Mother Night of his plans, and she, hoping to stop the pair from fighting, secretly told Crossbones of Danny's intentions. When Cutthroat entered Crossbones' chamber, Crossbones first broke Danny's wrist and then slit his throat; on the Red Skull's orders, Blackwing disposed of the body. Captain America and the Falcon, accompanied by Avengers' pilot Zach Moonhunter, invaded the facility to find Diamondback, capturing Crossbones, Jack O'Lantern, Blackwing and Mother Night. Transferred into S.H.I.E.L.D. custody, Blackwing confessed the location of Leighton's body, and it was covertly retrieved for treatment.

Cutthroat was incarcerated in the Raft at the time of Electro's break-out, and took part in the mass assault on Spider-Man. He was recaptured during the ensuing melee, and is being temporarily transferred to a secondary facility while repairs are effected.

Height: 6'2"
Weight: 200 lbs.
Eyes: Blue-green
Hair: Brown, balding (bleached blonde as a youth)

Abilities: Cutthroat is highly skilled with daggers and knives, both thrown and in hand-to-hand combat. He's an above average fighter, and a moderately skilled marksman with guns. His costume is a light protective armor, and he carries a variety of specialty daggers, most adamantium-edged.

USER NOTES:
Captain America: I was sure he was dead. Does Rachel know this?

History: Deathwatch's true origins are shrouded in mystery, though he is known to be part of an extradimensional race called the Translords. In one of his earliest recorded criminal schemes, he sought three stolen canisters containing enough biotoxin to kill the entire Tri-State population, hoping to feed off the resultant death energies; this would have given him enough strength to replace New York City's Kingpin of Crime (Wilson Fisk). Deathwatch had built up a large criminal empire by this time, utilizing underlings to do his dirty work. He sent the pseudo-vampire Blackout to acquire the biotoxin, which had fallen into the hands of the teenage Cypress Hills Jokers. Blackout's actions led to the wounding of young Barbara Ketch and the subsequent transformation of her brother Daniel into the Spirit of Vengeance, Ghost Rider. Ghost Rider foiled Deathwatch's scheme to unleash the biotoxin, starting a long feud between the two men. Deathwatch later used his pawns Snowblind, Hag and Troll in various failed attempts to destroy Ghost Rider. He also used agents in the news media, such as Linda Wei, to smear Ghost Rider's name, turning the authorities against him. Deathwatch eventually collapsed an entire building on the hero, killing hundreds of innocent people, but Ghost Rider survived and continued to hound Deathwatch. Shortly thereafter, the Spirit of Vengeance cornered Deathwatch and pierced his heart with a dagger forged of the hero's mystic chain.

Not truly slain, Deathwatch entered a state of "non-death" in which he existed as a comatose being, unable to interact with the world around him. His former pawns Hag and Troll protected him during this period, hoping that he would reward them upon his resurrection. Hag and Troll took him to the Deathspawn, a group of followers who had given their life essence to empower Deathwatch in the past, but the Deathspawn's attempt to revive him was foiled by Ghost Rider, John Blaze, Venom (Edward Brock) and Spider-Man.

Centurious the Soulless Man eventually restored Deathwatch to something akin to normality, though Deathwatch was temporarily bound to the will of Centurious. Deathwatch attempted to gain control of the magical Medallion of Power that the Ghost Rider possessed, planning to turn it over to Centurious, but he was once again defeated. Incarcerated in the Raft, Deathwatch escaped during Electro's assault on the prison.

Height: 6'1"
Weight: 200 lbs.
Eyes: Red
Hair: Red

Abilities: Deathwatch gains strength and vitality through the absorption of death energies. Deathwatch frequently utilizes a violent form of telepathy to link with his victims, deriving sustenance from their dying moments. This telepathy also allows him to induce extreme pain in his enemies, useful for interrogations.

USER NOTES:
Spider-Man: Though Deathwatch was inert when I encountered him, I understand this guy is one apple short of a bushel. If I had to face him alone, I might be a little worried, but there's no way he could stand toe-to-toe with the Avengers.

Spider-Woman: S.H.I.E.L.D.'s got a folder a mile thick on Deathwatch, full of all sorts of nasty business. He's been quiet lately but he retains several dangerous qualities, most notably his willingness to sacrifice innocent lives to gain power. He has used the alias Stephen Lords in the past.

Wolverine: This guy is one nasty piece o' work. I faced him an' his ninjas once with Ghost Rider an' Brass (Sean Watanabe), and wouldn't mind a chance ta finish what we started that day. Which reminds me - never did hook up with Brass ta go after the Mandarin...

Project: PEGASUS clarifications: No known connection to the Deathwatcher (Samson Scythe).

DR. DEMONICUS

DOUGLAS BIRELY

History: Obsessed with atomic mutation, genetics researcher Dr. Douglas Birely was fired after he deliberately exposed himself to radiation in a misguided attempt to gain super-powers, developing skin cancer and going mad. Birely later tracked down the Lifestone, a massive radioactive meteorite, in the Aleutian islands. Inspired by the mutated dinosaur Godzilla, Birely used the Lifestone to mutate various creatures into the giant monsters Batragon, Centipor, Ghilaron and Lepirax. As the costumed criminal Doctor Demonicus, Birely recruited a private army (his "Demon-Soldiers") who helped him occupy the Lifestone site and enslave the local Inuit populace. Since his monsters needed periodic Lifestone exposure to survive, Demonicus had his slaves start constructing a transport composed of Lifestone ore, intending to loot and terrorize the entire world once his monsters were more mobile. After Batragon ran afoul of Godzilla while raiding a Liberian oil tanker, a three-way battle ensued between the Demonicus forces, Godzilla, and S.H.I.E.L.D. troops then hunting Godzilla. The Inuit helped S.H.I.E.L.D. subdue the Demon-Soldiers, Godzilla apparently slew the Demonicus monsters, and S.H.I.E.L.D. agent Gabe Jones captured Demonicus himself. S.H.I.E.L.D. destroyed the Lifestone, not knowing that Demonicus had hidden fragments elsewhere. Demonicus escaped with the aid of Maur-Kon, a chaos-fomenting scientist-sorcerer of the extraterrestrial Myndai race. Maur-Kon supplied Demonicus with a satellite headquarters hidden behind the dark side of Earth's moon, where he used genetics and Myndai robotics technology to create his new giant servants: Cerberus, the Hand of Five and Starchild. Plotting to conquer Earth by bombarding it with redirected asteroids, Demonicus targeted the Shogun Warriors, giant robots created by the Myndai's ancestral enemies and piloted by human adventurers Richard Carson, Genji Odashu and Ilongo Savage. Demonicus hoped to add the robots to his arsenal; but in the end, the Shoguns destroyed his creations and his satellite and delivered him into S.H.I.E.L.D. custody. He escaped again, establishing a new undersea South Pacific base, forming a new army and enslaving a further-mutated Godzilla; but his forces were defeated by the Avengers, and Demonicus himself was recaptured during a retaliatory attack on Iron Man.

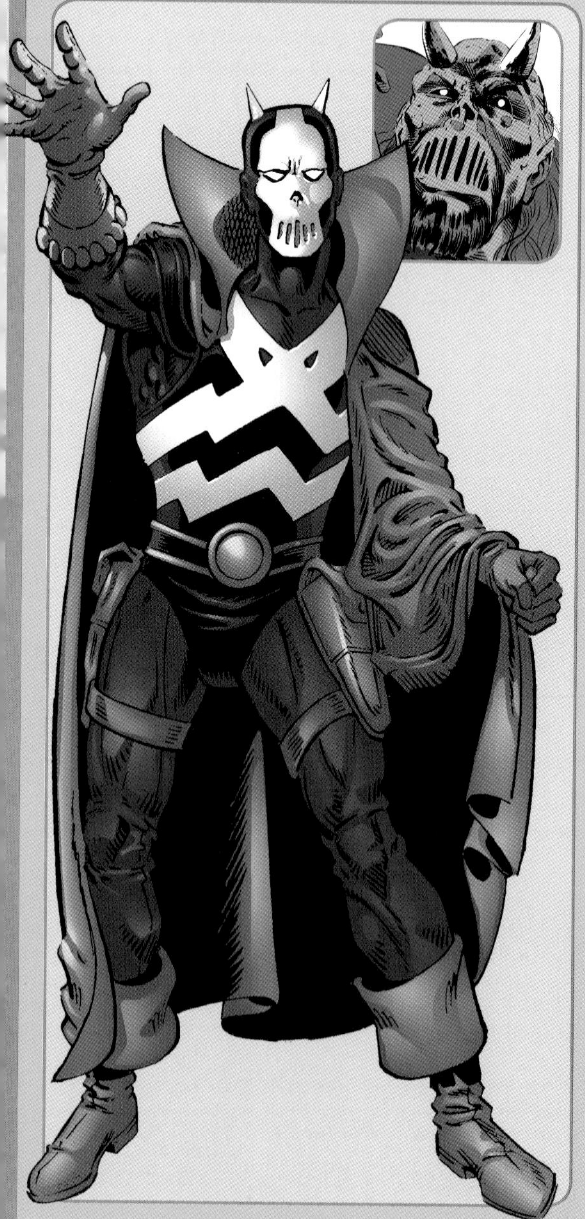

Disfigured by cancer, Demonicus escaped and formed a new super-criminal gang, the Pacific Overlords, most of whom he empowered via Lifestone mutations. Despite the interference of the Avengers, the Overlords successfully raised a new mineral-rich island from the Pacific Ocean's floor and convinced the United Nations to recognize it as the sovereign nation Demonica, ruled by Doctor Demonicus; however, Demonicus soon began acting under the influence of the demon Raksasa, declaring Demonica a theocracy dedicated to the demon's worship, secretly plotting to help Raksasa destroy the world, mind-controlling his reluctant Overlords, recruiting super-agents Zvezda Dennista and Ulysses Klaw, and alienating the international community with extreme measures such as declaring a huge no-fly zone around his island. Alerted to the crisis early on by the Overlords' Kuroko (Demonicus's most loyal and ardent follower), the Avengers soon intervened; but during the ensuing battle, Klaw undermined the island's foundation and Demonica crumbled into the ocean, taking Demonicus and most of his Overlords with it. Birely, however, secretly survived the disaster and was recaptured. Incarcerated at the Raft, he and many other inmates escaped during Electro's mass breakout.

Height: 5'11"
Weight: 170 lbs.
Eyes: Grey
Hair: Brown
Other Distinguishing Features: Mottled skin, horn-like forehead features and skull-like facial disfigurement shaped by the contours of his mask over time

Abilities: Birely is a genetics genius specializing in super-powerful mutations of both human and non-human life, particularly the creation of giant monsters. He sometimes wields high-tech weapons such as concussion ray guns and mind-controlling "menta-probes." His lightweight armored costume inhibits the progress of his skin cancer.

USER NOTES:
Project: PEGASUS clarifications: *No known connection to Demonicus, a.k.a. The Demon, a mystical minion of Baron Mordo. No definitive word yet on whether Birely's "Lifestone" was related to the alien "Lifestone" whose fragments empowered Bloodstone, Blue Diamond, Doctor Spectrum, Man-Wolf, Moonstone and others.*

FOOLKILLER
KURT GERHARDT

History: Kurt Gerhardt was a loan officer at New York's Silver Eagle Bank when his father, William R. Gerhardt, was killed by muggers irate that he only had six dollars on him. Gerhardt lost his job in a downsizing three months later, and he sank further into depression after months of failed job-seeking. After his wife, Eleanor, divorced him, taking everything but his clothes and computer, Gerhardt took a job at Burger Clown. After being beaten up while trying to stop some thieves, Gerhardt had an epiphany upon seeing Greg Salinger on the Runyan Moody show. Salinger had been the Foolkiller, a vigilante who used his Purification Gun to slay those who — as he saw it — lacked poetry in their souls. Salinger had slain Blockbuster (Bart Dietzel, formerly Man-Brute), and encountered Omega the Unknown, the Defenders, and Spider-Man, the latter of whom had captured him. Sent to Central Indiana Mental Institution, Salinger had stabilized sufficiently to be allowed this public appearance as part of his therapy. Inspired by Salinger, Gerhardt began writing to him and even discretely communicating via posting to an internet bulletin board, with Gerhardt as "Miles Fish" and Salinger as "Ian Byrd." After describing his own predecessor, Ross G. Everbest (who had slain the morally bankrupt before dying in battle with the Man-Thing), Salinger instructed Gerhardt how to find his associate, Merle Singer, who gave him copies of the Foolkiller costume and gun.

Gerhardt became the next Foolkiller, using the gun against drug-dealers, muggers and rapists. When he went after larger prey, the criminal enforcer Backhand, he was overpowered and almost killed by his bodyguard, Warren. Narrowly escaping, Gerhardt began a rigorous exercise program, after which he created a new costume, as well as cards to leave behind on his victims to warn others. As his skills improved, so did his personal life: he obtained a job in data services at the TRX Corporation and began dating Linda, his former Burger Clown co-worker. Still communicating with Salinger, Gerhardt refined his definition of fools and he sent a message to the local newspaper: "The sane must inherit the Earth: From this moment forward, the penalty for senseless violence, for unthinking greed, for wanton ambition, for reckless destruction in the pursuit of momentary gratification or profit will be death."

After amassing a large death count, Gerhardt targeted Darren Waite, a millionaire involved with rain forest stripping, as well as drug dealing and evicting paying renters so he could build high society apartments. Waite employed Emilio Mendosa, through whom he directed Backhand and other street criminals. After killing Waite, the Foolkiller went from tacitly approved vigilante to public enemy number one. Gerhardt slew Backhand and Warren, as well as Runyan Moody, then framed Mendosa as the Foolkiller, whom the police slew. Scarring his face with acid, Gerhardt established a false identity as Gregory Ross Curtis, relocated to Albuquerque, New Mexico, and sought a reconstructive specialist. Gerhardt was eventually located and sent to the Raft, from which he escaped during the breakout initiated by Electro. Written on Gerhardt's wall, hundreds of times each, were two phrases: "When the world begets too many fools, nature always provides a Foolkiller" and "Actions Have Consequences."

Height: 5'10"
Weight: 180 lbs.
Eyes: Brown
Hair: Green

Abilities: The Foolkiller's Purification Gun is a potent laser able to disintegrate a person on contact (assuming a central body part is hit). Gerhardt is self-trained in combat, achieving above average strength, fighting skills, and marksmanship, as well as a high tolerance for pain.

USER NOTES:
Spider-Man: A fanatic with a disintegrator weapon is NEVER a good thing. Gerhardt is delusional, imagining him and me as arch-foes when we just had a near-miss encounter. I also heard that Salinger was briefly released from prison and sent out on another spree by rogue government agent Mike Clemson in a plot to frame that Ghost Rider-wannabe, Vengeance.

Project: PEGASUS clarifications: An army of Foolkillers — presumably inspired by Ross, Salinger, etc. — existed on Earth-928, circa 2094 A.D. They trained the Foolkiller who assaulted the X-Men and the Lawless circa 2099 A.D.

GRAVITON

FRANKLIN HALL

History: Canadian physicist Franklin Hall was trying to develop teleportation technology when a lab accident infused his body with subatomic graviton particles. Discovering he could control gravity, a power-mad Hall dubbed himself Graviton and turned the research center into his own private floating kingdom, demanding that world leaders declare him ruler of Earth or he would destroy their greatest cities. Meanwhile, he tried to intimidate his colleague Judy Parks into becoming his consort. When the Avengers intervened, Hall overpowered them, but he went berserk after Parks seemingly jumped to her death rather than remain with him (she was actually rescued by Avengers butler Edwin Jarvis). His power raging out of control, Graviton and his base collapsed in upon themselves like a black hole, compressing into a super-compact mass while the Avengers and the hostages escaped. Graviton survived to clash with the Thing and Black Bolt, then kidnapped an entire department store in search of a new consort, but Thor defeated him and exiled him to an interdimensional void. Accidentally restored to Earth by novice super-criminal the Blank, Graviton became a Los Angeles crimelord with Blank as his lieutenant until Hall wearied of Blank's weakness and hurled him out to sea. Despite his vast power, Graviton was soundly defeated and captured by the new western Avengers roster. Escaping custody, Graviton teamed with Quantum, Halflife and Zzzax against the Avengers and sought Tigra as a consort, but the Avengers foiled him. After mostly unsuccessful battles with the Fantastic Four, Spider-Man and the Avengers, Graviton was trapped in another dimension, where the native P'Tah race treated him like a god.

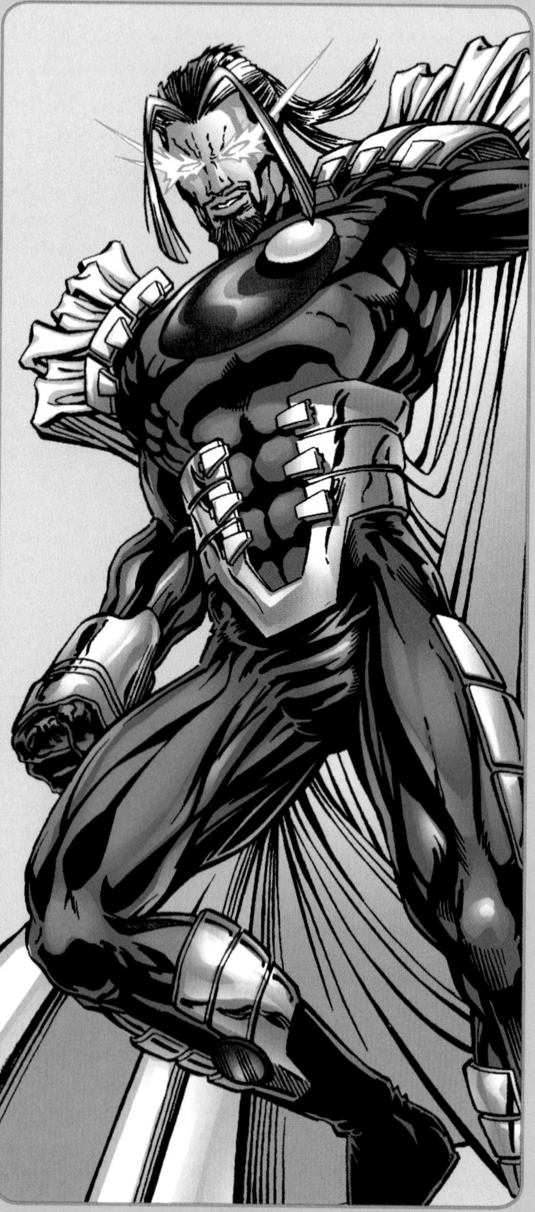

Returning to Earth, Graviton battled the Thunderbolts (plus their hapless imitators the Lightning Rods) but withdrew after Moonstone (Karla Sofen) forced him to realize he lacked purpose. He later founded his own floating nation Sky Island, populated by largely criminal "Sky Raiders" who swore allegiance to Graviton in exchange for the power of flight. Battling the Thunderbolts again, Graviton propositioned Moonstone but she mockingly spurned him, and the team defeated Graviton with the aid of Archangel and Machine Man. Still infatuated with and intimidated by Sofen, Graviton later hired Moonstone as his personal advisor after the Thunderbolts disbanded. Honing his powers and building his confidence under Sofen's guidance, Graviton launched his latest world conquest scheme by slaughtering the Redeemers, a new government super-team which had replaced the Thunderbolts. Suspending most of the world's remaining superheroes and Earth's great cities in mid-air, Graviton began reshaping the planet in his image, literally, but he was opposed by the reunited Thunderbolts, and was shocked to learn that his P'Tah allies had been tapping his power to stage their own invasion of Earth. Prodded by Moonstone, a wounded, seemingly dying Graviton freed his captives, restored the Earth and helped thwart the P'Tah invasion, disappearing in an implosion. Secretly surviving, he was eventually taken into SHIELD custody and held at the Raft until he escaped during the mass breakout staged by Electro.

Height: 6'1"
Weight: 200 lbs.
Eyes: Blue-grey
Hair: Black, white at temples

Abilities: Hall can mentally manipulate gravitational force, augmenting it or negating it or redirecting it at will. He can manipulate these forces on a planetary scale if need be, or control masses as small as pebbles; he can even use gravity to warp and redirect various forms of energy, such as light or radio waves, by affecting the particles or waves of same. Able to perceive the entire planet via bent light or through its gravitational field, he can manipulate gravity anywhere in the world even if he is not physically present at that location. He can focus redirected gravity into powerful force blasts or near-impenetrable force fields. Hall has remarkable physical stamina, perhaps somehow augmented by his powers.

USER NOTES:
Captain America: *Physically speaking, Graviton is literally a force of nature, seemingly unbeatable. Psychologically speaking, Hawkeye's one-time associate Moonstone may have said it best in the Thunderbolts records: "He's a frightened little man whose vanity and insecurity doom him to perpetual failure."*

GREY GARGOYLE
PAUL PIERRE DUVAL

History: French chemist Paul Pierre Duval was working as a lab assistant when he accidentally spilled a random chemical mixture on his hand, transforming it into a stone-like substance. He soon discovered that this hand's touch could turn people and objects to stone, and that he could become a being of living, mobile stone by applying this power to himself. Turning to crime, Duval accumulated a fortune but soon wearied of his new wealth and set a new goal: immortality. Duval terrorized New York as the Grey Gargoyle and sought to steal Thor's hammer, mistakenly assuming it was the source of Thor's longevity. He was twice defeated by Thor and once by the time-displaced Thor Corps. After Iron Man (Tony Stark) and S.H.I.E.L.D. agent Jasper Sitwell foiled Duval's attempted theft of Tony Stark's new cobalt super-weapon, Duval sought the dangerous compound "Element X" but was shot into space through the combined efforts of Captain America (Steve Rogers), Falcon (Sam Wilson) and S.H.I.E.L.D. director Nick Fury. Returning with the aid of new partners AIM (Advanced Idea Mechanics), Duval plotted world conquest; but a battle with Captain America and Spider-Man accidentally hurled Duval into space again.

Rescued by the alien starship Bird of Prey, Duval soon rose to command the vessel but later turned against its crew alongside Thor, Sif, the Warriors Three and other captives in hopes of returning to Earth. Seemingly slain, Gargoyle survived and made his way home, where he fought Daredevil and the Avengers. Recaptured, he fought Iron Man during an abortive breakout at Ryker's Island, and was later freed and recruited by Baron (Helmut) Zemo's Masters of Evil. Teamed with Screaming Mimi, Duval freed the new Yellowjacket (Rita DeMara) from prison to join the Masters; but during this mission, Duval and Mimi were themselves captured by Wasp, Paladin and the Black Knight (Dane Whitman). Escaping again, Duval resurfaced as "artist" Paul St. Pierre, selling statues that were secretly petrified human victims sealed in a special polymer which preserved their transformation; but he was exposed by Iron Man and fled. Attacking the Hulk (Bruce Banner) on behalf of Doctor Doom, Duval was painfully defeated. Incarcerated at the Vault super-prison, Duval participated in a mass breakout foiled by the Avengers and Freedom Force. Later, he was part of the "Doom's Brigade" hired to protect Doctor Doom, though Captain America and Spider-Man penetrated their defenses. After attending an AIM weapons expo, Duval and Killer Shrike were unwittingly duped into helping the alien dragon-slayer Surge hoax the She-Hulk. Recaptured repeatedly by the likes of Fantastic Force, Daredevil and Black Widow (Natasha Romanoff), Duval was hired by the Gideon Trust to attack the Thing, but the Fantastic Four defeated him and the Thing regained his ability to resume human form as a side-effect of the attack. Influenced by the death of childhood friend Gary Lesgetti, Duval resumed his quest for immortality, savagely attacking female Thor equivalent Tarene ("Thor Girl") and stealing her mystical hammer, but a confrontation with the god-slayer Desak and a sound beating by Thor quashed Duval's delusions of godhood. Miniaturized and held in the Big House micro-prison (where a mass escape was foiled by She-Hulk), Duval was transferred to the Raft and escaped during its Electro-led breakout, only to be recaptured and incarcerated in the Fantastic Four's new Vault prison.

Height: 5'11"
Weight: (human) 175 lbs., (stone) 750 lbs.
Eyes: (human) blue, (stone) white with no visible pupils
Hair: (human) brown, (stone) grey

Abilities: The touch of Duval's right palm can transform anyone or anything into immobile, granite-like stone. The transformation often lasts about one hour. By applying his palm to himself, Duval can transform into living stone, fully mobile, unlike his victims. His stone form is superhumanly strong and durable.

USER NOTES:

Captain America: The trick with the Grey Gargoyle is to attack from a distance and keep moving — otherwise, that stone touch of his can end a battle quickly. Without it, he's little more than another generic powerhouse.

GRIFFIN
JOHN HORTON

History: After New Orleans gang member John "Johnny" Horton caught the attention of a Chicago Secret Empire member, a Secret Empire doctor injected Horton with a bioadaptive genetic serum and grafted mutated animal parts to Johnny's flesh, turning him into a humanoid griffin. Horton was sent to attack the Queens Brand facility, a move which brought him into conflict with the Angel (Warren Worthington III) and the Beast. Quickly defeated, the Griffin was sentenced and jailed. While in prison, Horton mutated, growing stronger and developing a tail. Horton escaped from the physicians examining him and located the doctor who had "created" him. With the doctor unable to help him find the now-dismantled Secret Empire, Griffin killed him. Despite developing the power to control gulls, Horton was defeated by Spider-Man and the Beast and returned to prison. He was soon freed by the Titanium Man (Boris Bullski), and was well-paid to aid Bullski, Darkstar, and a new Crimson Dynamo (Yuri Petrovitch) in freeing Rampage (Stuart Clarke) from the Champions, who had recently defeated Clarke. Their alliance collapsed when the Dynamo proved unstable and Darkstar betrayed them, and the Griffin

was sent back to prison.

Eventually escaping, the Griffin attacked Avengers Mansion seeking vengeance against the Beast and battled Spider-Man and Wonder Man. Evolving repeatedly in response to stress during the fight, the Griffin had become purely animalistic in body and mind by the time he was buried under a flaming Quinjet. The Griffin burrowed away and lived as a wild animal in the Adirondacks. Found by Headlok, the Griffin was mind-controlled into attacking the Avengers; but while the Thing defeated Headlok, Tigra's animal side connected with the Griffin, pacifying it. The Griffin was locked in the Vault to finish Horton's sentence. It was involved in several subsequent escape attempts, once recaptured by D-Man and the Falcon, later by Captain America and Henry Pym. Successfully escaping, the Griffin was acquired by corporate raider Desmond Marrs, who sent it to attack Namor MacKenzie's Oracle, Inc. Namor defeated the Griffin and exerted dominance over the beast, making it recognize him as its master. Wrongly associating the Griffin's early appearances at Brand with Brand's later corporate owner, the Roxxon Energy Corporation, Namor released the Griffin into a boardroom at One Roxxon Plaza and warned them against attacking him. Capturing the Griffin, Roxxon transported it towards their Bolivian research facility, but the Griffin was freed in an accident and returned to seek out Namor, tracking him to Connecticut. Namor used the Griffin as a steed and transported him to the Savage Land, where he, Namorita, Shanna, and the Griffin disrupted a plot by the Super-Skrull (masquerading as Daniel Rand) to destroy the Earth. Namor abandoned the Griffin in the Savage Land; S.H.I.E.L.D. agents there encountered the creature, which was captured for further research into the genetic serum which had created it. The Griffin was stored in the Raft until Electro's break-in, when it escaped.

Height: 6'9" (18' wingspan)
Weight: 250 lbs.
Eyes: Yellow
Hair: Yellow

Abilities: The Griffin's genetic structure actively evolves, responding to stress by adapting the creature to better deal with its opponents. With the dissolution of Horton's mind, the Griffin experiences less stress, and thus its form has been relatively stable in recent years. While Horton's mind was still active, he displayed the ability to control certain avians; however, this ability has apparently not survived later changes. The Griffin has proven able to track people/ places across continents.

USER NOTES:
Spider-Man: Big, big difference between fighting Griffy alongside Beast and alongside Wonder Man; he definitely changed over the course of the fights. I almost wonder if poor Johnny's still alive in there somewhere — if the Griffin needed to evolve an intelligence, would Johnny re-emerge?

Project: PEGASUS clarifications: No known relation to the mythological beast (spawn of Medusa the Gorgon); the guardian at the Babylonian Temple of Marduk; the robot by Gregson Gilbert; the demons summoned by Apocalypse of Demon's Fire; Lord Griffen of Gallifrey; Lincoln Griffin of Earth-148611 ("New Universe"); Mys-Tech's Bronwen Gryffn; Operation: Zero Tolerance's Gryphon.

HYDRO-MAN
MORRIS BENCH

History: Morris Bench was a crewman aboard the S.S. Bulldog cargo ship during the testing of a powerful new experimental underwater generator. Accidentally knocked overboard during a battle between Spider-Man and Namor, Bench was mutated by the interaction of the generator's energies with undersea volcanic gases; within hours, he began to transform into living water. Calling himself Hydro-Man, Bench attacked Spider-Man, but he evaporated after Spider-Man scattered his liquid across the city's sun-baked rooftops. Soon reintegrating, Bench became a super-criminal. When he and similarly-powered rival criminal Sandman (William Baker) competed for the affections of barfly Sadie Frickett, the two foes accidentally merged into a monstrous "mud-thing" that the police were ultimately forced to dehydrate into seemingly inert rubble. Hydro-Man and Sandman eventually managed to separate back into their original forms, but both were traumatized by the experience. Hydro-Man did most of his criminal work in groups from that point on, perhaps seeking safety in numbers. Battling Spider-Man, Sandman, Silver Sable and others as a founder of the mercenary Sinister Syndicate, Bench also fought the Fantastic Four as a member of the Wizard's Frightful Four, and battled the Avengers as part of the short-lived Assembly of Evil during the Acts of Vengeance conspiracy.

Working with various partners, employers and teammates, Bench was defeated repeatedly by heroes such as Spider-Man, the Fantastic Four, Captain America, the New Warriors, Thunderstrike, Gambit, Sandman, Black Panther and the Thunderbolts. After in-fighting broke up the Sinister Syndicate for good, several members (including Bench) served briefly as Maggia agents. Hydro-Man was also one of many super-criminals employed by corrupt billionaire Justin Hammer for a time, and later served in the Masters of Evil assembled by Hammer's daughter Justine, alias the Crimson Cowl. The Thunderbolts hindered both enterprises, and after Justine's arrest and Justin's apparent demise, Hammer Industries phased out its criminal enterprises and Bench was laid off. Hydro-Man teamed with his occasional partner and fellow Hammer castoff the Shocker (Herman Schultz) for one more big theft to set them up for retirement, but Bench's inability to resist seeking vengeance on Spider-Man botched the job and got them both captured. Trying to go straight, Bench took a job at a water park but soon blundered into yet another battle with Spider-Man and the Human Torch (Johnny Storm). He was rescued by the Wizard, who altered Bench's powers and recruited him back into the Frightful Four. Escaping after another defeat by the Fantastic Four, Hydro-Man briefly joined other Spider-Man foes in Norman Osborn's Sinister Twelve, but was subsequently taken into S.H.I.E.L.D. custody and imprisoned at the Raft, where he escaped during Electro's mass breakout. Hydro-Man was one of many Fantastic Four foes captured by the FF and imprisoned in the new Vault.

Height: 6'2"
Weight: 265 lbs.
Eyes: Brown
Hair: Light Brown

Abilities: Hydro-Man can transform himself wholly or partially into a water equivalent which he mentally animates and manipulates — for instance, producing high-pressure water blasts or engulfing foes in a massive wave. Bench controls every drop of his bodily liquid, and his watery form gradually reintegrates if it is vaporized or dispersed. He can merge with or absorb ordinary water, thereby increasing in size. His strength is slightly enhanced by his abnormal physiology. Recent alterations of Bench's powers by the Wizard have enabled Bench to manipulate water sources separate from his own body, and have given Bench a finer degree of control over his own fluid form; however, the Wizard also intentionally weakened Bench's molecular cohesion, and developed a device enabling him to reduce Bench to an inert mass of liquid if necessary, ensuring Hydro-Man's loyalty.

USER NOTES:
Spider-Man: Someone has to say it: Bench is all wet. A guy with this much power should be a major threat, but since poor Morrie's dumb as a post, he's strictly hench-thug material. Dangerous but dim.

Project: PEGASUS clarifications: No known connection to the Hydro-Men , a.k.a. the Amphibians of Hydro-Base, who were humans mutated by a Terrigen Mist variant.

JIGSAW
WILLIAM RUSSO

History: A mob assassin for the Costa family of the Maggia, William "Billy the Beaut" Russo was known for his stunning good looks. Sent to kill Frank Castle and others associated with the execution of Forrest Hunt and the subsequent chaos, Russo slew reporter Mike McTeer and then planted a bomb in Castle's house. Alerted by a trampled flowerbed, Castle escaped the explosion, then donned a confronted Russo as the Punisher, kicking him face first through a plate glass window. Recovering, Russo took the name Jigsaw from his scarred face and became leader of a small gang, seeking to lure the Punisher to investigate. The Punisher was joined by Nightcrawler (Kurt Wagner) and Spider-Man, and Jigsaw was defeated and left for the police. Shortly thereafter, Jigsaw led his men in crimes designed to avoid superhuman involvement, and when Spider-Man confronted him, he surrendered without a fight.

Regaining his confidence in Ryker's Island prison, Jigsaw joined with Don Cervello in an escape attempt which was foiled by the Punisher, who had been briefly remanded

there. Jigsaw was then brainwashed by the militant vigilante group known as the Trust, who outfitted him in Punisher-like fashion as one of their Punishment Squad. Despite regaining his wits after seeing the real Punisher, Jigsaw was defeated again. Jigsaw later teamed with the Rev (the Reverend Sammy Smith) in a plot to amass a sterilization drug from the Piña flower. The Rev used his powers to heal Jigsaw's scars, but the Punisher defeated them both and severely lacerated Jigsaw's face on a yucca plant. Back at Ryker's, Jigsaw became a leader alongside the Nubian Nation's Gregario. When Castle was again sent to Ryker's, Jigsaw slashed his face repeatedly, though Castle escaped. Freed soon after, Jigsaw refused to help set a trap for the Punisher, warning the others that Castle would find a way to turn the tables on them, which he did.

After the Punisher had seemingly been legally executed in prison for a false charge of killing an innocent, Jigsaw had his own appearance altered to more closely resemble Castle's (though he retained his scars), and donned a version of Castle's costume. As the Jigsaw Punisher, he began executing those who had allegedly killed the Punisher, because he had wanted to do this himself. This quest led him into conflict with Daredevil, as well as the Punisher, who had survived the execution. Jigsaw was pleased to have the chance to kill Castle, but Castle took him down in a fist fight and left him for the police. Free again, Jigsaw teamed with Firefox, Hachiman and Tombstone in an assault on the mansion of the Punisher's then-allies, the Geraci family. Jigsaw used a rocket launcher to collapse the building on the Punisher, but Castle survived and came after him. Jigsaw tossed Leslie Geraci off a building so he could shoot Castle while he tried to save her, but Leslie made herself fall to prevent this, and Castle shot a glancing blow to Jigsaw's head, causing him to fall to the streets below.

His standard appearance restored, Jigsaw was sent to the Raft, but soon escaped and started a gunrunning operation on the North Shore pier. Taken down by Daredevil and the Black Widow (Natasha Romanoff), Jigsaw was allegedly released on bail and attempted to kill Matt Murdock (who had been publicly outed as Daredevil in the Daily Globe), but Natasha dropped Jigsaw and the police sent him back to the Raft. He escaped again during the breakout initiated by Electro.

Height: 6'2"
Weight: 250 lbs.
Eyes: Blue
Hair: Black, formerly dyed brown

Abilities: Jigsaw is an experienced streetfighter, specializing in the use of various knives and firearms. He frequently employs small armies of criminals, and formerly wore a strength-enhancing exoskeleton.

USER NOTES:
Spider-Man: Everyone else, the Punisher kills. Not this guy...Jigsaw's like his only recurring foe. Castle — when he wasn't shooting at me — once told me that Jigsaw now believes that he killed Castle's family.

Project: PEGASUS clarifications: No known connection to Jigsaw of Earth-928 (a.k.a. Multi-Fractor) circa 2099 A.D.

KING COBRA
KLAUS VOORHEES

History: Dutch ex-convict Klaus Voorhees helped humanitarian Ezekiel Shecktor develop a universal snake venom anti-toxin and then stole it, faking an accident by letting a cobra bite both Shecktor and himself, but only anti-venoming himself. Unknown to Voorhees, Shecktor had irradiated that cobra; Voorhees developed superhuman powers, calling himself the Cobra (briefly the Human Cobra). Adapting Shecktor's toxins, Voorhees outfitted himself with venom darts and bombs and hijacked a jet to New York. Intending to create an army of Cobras and rule the world, he fought Thor but soon fled. Cobra teamed with Mr. Hyde to seek revenge on Thor, but they were defeated twice, despite Loki's increasing their powers on the latter attempt. They also were beaten by Daredevil twice, once teamed with the Jester (Jonathan Powers). Tiring of Hyde's disdain, Cobra designed weaponry for the Eel (Leopold Stryke) and Viper (Jordan Dixon), and the trio, as the Serpent Squad, attacked Captain America in Virginia. Cobra later joined Viper (Madame Hydra)'s Serpent Squad; ultimately, she shot him and he was rescued by Captain America (then Nomad). Cobra re-teamed with Mr. Hyde at least twice, actually defeating Daredevil while under the Purple Man's control, but their partnership deteriorated; the Cobra finally bluntly abandoned Hyde during an escape from Ryker's. Excepting a brief encounter with Spider-Man, Cobra lived a low-key life until an angry Hyde escaped and hunted him. Hyde would continue haunting Cobra even in prison.

Voorhees joined Sidewinder's Serpent Society. When Viper infiltrated the Serpent Society, Cobra sided with her but ultimately betrayed and defeated her, surrendering her to Captain America; the remaining serpents chose Cobra to lead them. After seeing his team defeated by the X-Men, Cobra sought out, attacked, and defeated Mr. Hyde; his self-confidence briefly restored, Klaus renamed himself King Cobra. He had Diamondback captured, fearing she'd revealed Society secrets; this led to an insurrection, and the arrest of most of the Society. Sidewinder freed Voorhees from the Vault, but Klaus returned to prison rather than appear to have run out on his Society. When the team finally escaped, King Cobra moved them to Sandhaven, Arizona, taking only low-risk jobs. Considering retiring, Voorhees briefly outfitted the vigilante Jack Flag in his Cobra suit, but Flag betrayed them and most of the Society was captured. Cobra's defeat of Hyde let Hyde see Cobra as an equal, and they teamed together again effectively. Despite being arrested by Captain America and then by Spider-Man and Alyosha Kravinoff during this period, Cobra raised enough money to finance the creation of new Sidewinders, enabling him to free his Serpent Society. Again hunting Diamondback, the team was defeated by Captain America; Voorhees escaped and briefly allied himself with Lucia von Bardas before he was recaptured and placed in the Raft. Escaping during Electro's break-in, Cobra was recaptured by Toxin.

Height: 5'10"
Weight: 160 lbs.
Eyes: Blue
Hair: Bald

Abilities: Voorhees' entire body is resilient and flexible, allowing Cobra to squeeze through holes as small as four inches in diameter, or wrap his arms and torso around opponents in a nearly unbreakable "Cobra grip". Voorhees' suit is chemically treated for extreme slipperiness; he utilizes venom darts (shot from wrist shooters), smoke and gas bombs (carried in his belt and other compartments), and an entangling "Cobra coil" mounted in his suit's chest. He employs the Serpent Society's "Serpent Saucers" and the teleportational services of the newest Sidewinder.

USER NOTES:

Captain America: A potential threat if he pulls himself together mentally, he's built for stealth and guile but acts like a bruiser, notably in using the Serpent Society as a brute force team acting for personal aggrandizement instead of profit. Play on his fears and insecurities.

Project: PEGASUS clarifications: No known connection to the 1940s Cobras who fought Namor and the Human Torch; King Cobra, who fought Miss America; James Lardner, mutated by Operation: Cobra; or the New Men's Cobrah/Kobrah.

MANDRILL
JEROME BEECHMAN

History: Jerome Beechman was born a dark-skinned, strangely hairy mutant to Caucasian parents, probably due to an accidental radiation leak at the Los Alamos Atomic Proving Grounds where Jerome's father, Frederic, worked as a research scientist. Alienated from his peers and even his parents by his freakish appearance, Jerome was abandoned by his father in the desert at the age of ten, swearing he would exact revenge. While there, Jerome met and befriended young albino mutant Nekra Sinclair, a runaway whose own unique appearance was also tied to the Los Alamos accident (Nekra's African-American mother Gemma Sinclair had worked there). Jerome found a kindred spirit in Nekra, who had been similarly ill-treated by her family and her community. The two mutant youths spent years wandering the Southwest together, shunning ordinary humanity and stealing whatever they needed to survive and to educate themselves. Attacked in New Mexico by a fearful, hate-filled mob, the outcast duo discovered their mutant powers while defending themselves, killing some of their tormentors and driving off the rest. Beechman realized that his pheromones compelled women to do his bidding,

and his superhuman, increasingly monkey-like physique prompted him to adopt the alias Mandrill.

The Mandrill launched a political scheme to take over several small African nations, employing Nekra as the high priestess of his cult of personality; but their plot was thwarted by Shanna the She-Devil. Mandrill and Nekra next organized Black Spectre, a group of African American women dedicated to the overthrow of the U.S. government, but this enterprise was broken up by Shanna, Daredevil, the Black Widow (Natasha Romanoff) and the Thing (Ben Grimm). Mandrill escaped, and a captured Nekra swore revenge on him for abandoning her. Assembling the Fem-Force (another all-female army) and recruiting the super-criminal Mutant Force, Mandrill sought world conquest; but he was thwarted repeatedly by the Defenders, who captured his Mutant Force, foiled his assault on Las Animus Airbase, and put an end to his smuggling of exotic Wakandan technology. Mandrill ultimately targeted the Arrowshaft Nuclear Plant because his parents now worked there, but the Defenders prevented a nuclear disaster and Mandrill was shot by his own mother, Margaret. Eventually recovering, Mandrill learned of Nekra's murder by the zombie Grim Reaper and attacked the Reaper seeking vengeance, but the zombie impaled Mandrill and siphoned away his life force, reducing him to a skeletal husk. Somehow surviving, Mandrill attended an illicit auction crashed by Spider-Man and Alpha Flight. Incarcerated in the Vault, Mandrill nearly escaped during a mass breakout foiled by the Thunderbolts. Transferred to the "Big House" miniaturized prison, Mandrill was a key player in a mass breakout foiled by She-Hulk. Transferred again to the Raft, Mandrill escaped during the Electro breakout and joined a gang of mind-controlling criminals led by Crossfire, but their violent feud with the U-Foes led to the gang's capture by the Avengers.

Height: 6'0"
Weight: 270 lbs.
Eyes: Brown
Hair: Brown
Other Distinguishing Features: Beechman physically resembles an actual mandrill.

Abilities: Beechman constantly generates pheromones which chemically enslave the minds of women in his general vicinity (though some exceptionally strong-willed women can resist him). His control can be disrupted by electrical shock. Males are generally immune to his power, though he has used technological aids to affect the minds of male opponents. Beechman's strength and agility are enhanced well beyond human norms, as are his speed, stamina, durability and reflexes to some extent. Beechman is a capable leader, organizer and strategist.

USER NOTES:
Spider-Woman: I've tangled with Mandrill's old partner Nekra (nasty piece of work), but never the monkey-man himself. I'd be curious to see how his pheromone powers stack up against mine. I'm also curious about how he survived being skewered and sucked dry by the Reaper — of course, these animalistic mutant types often come complete with healing factors, so maybe that explains it.

Wolverine: First wise guy who suggests that me and monkey boy might be related gets a sample of what I do best — and what I do best isn't very nice...

MENTALLO
MARVIN FLUMM

History: Marvin Flumm is a mutant telepath who was recruited by Niles Nordstrom, director of S.H.I.E.L.D.'s then-new ESP division. When Nordstrom discovered Flumm was secretly plotting to take over S.H.I.E.L.D., Flumm fled and became the costumed subversive Mentallo. Partnered with inventive genius the Fixer (Paul Norbert Ebersol), Mentallo invaded S.H.I.E.L.D.'s Manhattan headquarters, but the duo was ultimately captured. Escaping, they joined a new faction of the terrorist group Hydra led by Silvermane, and Mentallo served as head of its reconnaissance division. After Silvermane's Hydra splintered apart, the Fixer-Mentallo duo tried to assassinate the U.S. President using a mind-controlled Deathlok (Luther Manning), but Nick Fury and the Fantastic Four foiled this scheme. Rejoining Hydra, the pair debugged Hydra's data-stealing computer system Computrex until it was wrecked by the Micronauts, who rendered Flumm comatose. Professor Anthony Power and the Fixer later tried to force the telepathic Professor Xavier to revive Mentallo so he could in turn revive Power's traumatized son; however, Xavier defeated Flumm on the psychic plane while Spider-Man bested the Fixer. Mentallo eventually revived, but suffered further mental trauma when he ran afoul of the Super-Adaptoid while it was posing as the Fixer, though he was rescued by the Avengers.

Serving briefly with the mutant terrorist group Resistants under the code name Think-Tank, Flumm was defeated by the government's new Captain America (John Walker). Incarcerated in the Vault, Mentallo facilitated a mass escape attempt led by Venom (Eddie Brock) until the Avengers and Freedom Force foiled the breakout, partly by turning Flumm's powers against his fellow inmates. Escaping to lead a fruitless mass assault on the Thing and the Hulk, Mentallo attended an AIM weapons expo before he joined the secret "Inner Circle" of the short-lived new Enforcers criminal gang. After facing Hulk on behalf of the Red Skull (Johann Shmidt) and attending the wedding of Absorbing Man and Titania (Mary MacPherran), Mentallo worked with AIM to create a global telepathic "web" accessing virtually every mind on Earth, but Iron Man (Tony Stark) defeated Flumm and destroyed the web, leaving Mentallo comatose. Stored in stasis in the superhuman cell block of Seagate, Mentallo was remotely awakened by criminal entrepreneur Justin Hammer, who used Flumm's telepathy to communicate covertly with various prisoners. Mentallo helped plan a breakout which was thwarted by Abe Jenkins. Later, after Hammer's apparent demise, Mentallo offered to protect then-incarcerated Avengers veteran Hawkeye (Clint Barton) in exchange for Barton helping him escape, ignorant that Barton had been recruited by S.H.I.E.L.D. to spy on Hammer-related dealings. Mentallo arranged the escape of Barton and several other prisoners (including Headlok, who was psychically possessed by Mentallo), then enlisted them in the search for the late Hammer's ultimate weapon, which is what S.H.I.E.L.D. had hoped to find through Barton in the first place. In the end, Hawkeye betrayed Mentallo to the authorities before finally finding and neutralizing Hammer's weapon with the aid of his new team of Thunderbolts. Transferred from Seagate to the Raft, Mentallo escaped during Electro's mass breakout.

Height: 5'10"
Weight: 175 lbs.
Eyes: Brown
Hair: Brown

Abilities: Flumm can read minds; remotely link with another person's mind, experiencing that person's sensory input,

or vice versa; scan for minds by tracking specific mental patterns; mentally inhabit and control the body of another person; exert more rudimentary control over many minds simultaneously (forcing an angry mob to stop fighting, for instance); project his thoughts; enable the minds of others to communicate via telepathic links; cast illusions; and remotely analyze the basic physical characteristics of unseen objects by probing them with psionic energy and reading the psychic feedback. All these powers are effective in his immediate vicinity or, to a lesser extent, over great distances — even many miles away. Often unusually vulnerable to the powers of other telepaths, he has worn a special "ESP-proof" helmet (stolen from S.H.I.E.L.D.) to protect him from telepathic assaults and psychic feedback.

USER NOTES:
Project: PEGASUS clarifications: *No known connection to Destiny (Paul Destine), a.k.a. Mentallo.*

MR. FEAR
ALAN FAGAN

History: As a teenager, Alan Fagan rejected his girlfriend, Cora Tremmore, after their daughter Ariel's birth. After his father's death, he squandered wealth and scholarships; but when his uncle, Larry Cranston, faked his own death, Cranston's Mister Fear paraphernalia, used by earlier Fears — Zoltan Drago and Samuel "Starr" Saxon (now Machinesmith) — was deeded to Fagan. Fancying himself a mastermind, the new Fear stole a dangerous isotope from Cross Technological Enterprises guarded by Hawkeye. Temporarily unnerved by Fagan's chemicals, Hawkeye regained his senses and, accompanied by Spider-Man, tracked and defeated Fagan.

Fagan later hired an unidentified chemist to expand his repertoire with pheromones that attracted women. After a chance meeting with the Daily Bugle's Betty Brant, he manipulated her into luring Spider-Man into a trap, but both Spider-Man and Brant overcame his influence while Fagan fell towards seeming death.

Fagan resurfaced in the "Inner Circle" of the New Enforcers, a criminal unit employed by the Foreigner and possibly Hydra that fought Spider-Man. Imprisoned, Fagan was attacked, and his face skinned, by inmates bribed by his abandoned daughter Ariel Tremmore, now a teenager. Using Fagan's skin, Tremmore mutated herself to dispatch fear pheromones directly. As Shock, she committed robberies to finance treatment for her ailing mother but was soon defeated by Daredevil. Meanwhile, Fagan recovered from the attack, leaving him with vows of vengeance and a skull-like face with which to mutter them. Fagan was sent to the Vault and fell in with Crossfire's crew. During this time Cranston resurfaced and resumed the Mister Fear identity, plotting vengeance against Daredevil. Escaping, Fagan was given armor by the Tinkerer and used as a pawn against the heroes involved with Nick Fury's Secret War. Sent to the Raft, he and other inmates escaped during Electro's break-in. Although Cranston had reclaimed the Fear identity, Fagan stayed with Crossfire's crew in a grudge against the U-Foes. However, when an altercation was interrupted by Spider-Man, Fagan was quickly defeated, disabled by his own gas pellets. Abandoned, he testified against his teammates and remains in custody.

Height: 5'11"
Weight: 165 lbs.
Eyes: Hazel
Hair: Brown (sometimes dyed silver)

Abilities: Mister Fear's gun shoots pellets containing a pheromone-based compound, inducing fear in whoever inhales it; the effect lasts anywhere from five to fifteen minutes and can also be absorbed through the skin at a slower rate. Fear once used a hypodermic ring to inject the compound and occasionally carried other weapons, such as an energy-discharge gun; he has access to pheromone variations, including one which renders him appealing to women. Although Fear's skin is saturated with fear pheromones, he has demonstrated no superhuman power.

USER NOTES:
Spider-Man: *Hawkeye's dead and this guy's alive, who's running the universe, anyway?*

Legacy villains give me a pain, and I've fought enough Jack O'Lanterns, Mysterios, Doctor Octopuseseses, Goblins, and more to know what I'm talking about. He's building on the loser status of a predecessor who's back now anyway; it's pointless on so many levels. And that's before I read his file. He had money, education, and a kid, and he threw it away for his uncle's leftovers? How can anyone treat their kid that way? And then his daughter puts on his face to steal the money he wouldn't ante up? Most people would say that's the most screwed-up thing they ever heard, and even I'd put it somewhere in the top ten.

Anyway, his fright-gas is pretty bad, but his motif's to scare and run. If you know what you're dealing with, you can overcome it pretty easy before he gets far. Focus on the job, and Fear's nothing.

Project: PEGASUS clarifications: *No known connection to World War II villains Doctor Fear or Professor Fear.*

MR. HYDE
CALVIN ZABO

History: A brilliant but unscrupulous medical scientist, Dr. Calvin Zabo was obsessed with the story of Doctor Jekyll and Mister Hyde and sought a means of artificially augmenting a person's evil nature. He probably experimented on himself for many years — which might explain why his daughter, Daisy Johnson (fathered with Jennifer Johnson and adopted by the Sutton family), was born with mutant earthquake-triggering powers which she later used as a super-agent of S.H.I.E.L.D.. Moving from job to job over time and robbing his employers to fund his experiments, Zabo eventually applied to work with Dr. Don Blake, who rejected Zabo because of his shady work history. Despite this setback, Zabo finally perfected his evil-augmentation formula and used it on himself, transforming into the superhumanly powerful and savagely evil Mister Hyde. The change so distorted his features, even his fingerprints, that he felt he could operate as a criminal without fear of his activities ever being traced back to Zabo. Seeking revenge on Blake, Hyde was repeatedly defeated by Thor, even after forming a partnership with fellow Thor foe the Cobra. Hyde and Cobra also repeatedly battled Daredevil, sometimes in concert with criminals such as Jester (Jonathan Powers) and Gladiator (Melvin Potter), but were consistently defeated by him as well. In addition, Hyde briefly, unsuccessfully teamed with the Scorpion (Mac Gargan) against Captain America and the Falcon. Hyde scorned Cobra as a weakling and a coward, routinely mocking and sometimes betraying his partner; but when the Cobra abandoned him during an escape from Ryker's Island prison, a furious Hyde swore revenge. Reluctantly aided by the mercenary Batroc, Hyde blackmailed Manhattan with the threat of detonating a stolen oil supertanker, secretly planning to blow up the supertanker regardless of the outcome since he hoped Cobra would be killed along with much of the rest of the city; but Captain America and Batroc joined forces to stop Hyde. Zabo continued to stalk the Cobra thereafter, sometimes coming into conflict with heroes such as Spider-Man and the Black Cat.

Seeking to avenge his defeats by Thor and Captain America, Mister Hyde joined Baron (Helmut) Zemo's Masters of Evil in their invasion and occupation of Avengers Mansion, personally torturing Avengers butler Jarvis and helping other Masters beat Hercules nearly to death; but in the end, the Masters were defeated and Hyde was captured. Imprisoned in the Vault (where he shared a fleeting prison romance with Nekra), Hyde participated in attempted mass escapes foiled by the Avengers, Freedom Force, Iron Man and the Captain (Steve Rogers), then successfully broke out during the Acts of Vengeance conspiracy. Hyde abandoned his long vendetta against the Cobra after his ex-partner finally defeated him in single combat. Since then, Hyde has clashed with adventurers such as Hulk, Ghost Rider (Dan Ketch), Alpha Flight, Captain America, Spider-Man, the Avengers, Daredevil and others. Incarcerated in the Raft super-prison, Hyde participated in Electro's mass breakout and was recaptured by the group of heroes who became the new Avengers; but he soon escaped, becoming a manufacturer and distributor of the illegal drug MGH (Mutant Growth Hormone), using it to augment his own powers. Defeated by the Thunderbolts, Hyde remained at large until the Young Avengers subdued him with a forced overdose of MGH and sent him back to prison.

Height: (Zabo) 5'11", (Hyde) 6'5"
Weight: (Zabo) 185 lbs., (Hyde) 420 lbs.

Eyes: Brown
Hair: (Zabo) grey, (Hyde) brown

Abilities: In his Hyde form, Zabo has tremendous superhuman strength, durability and recuperative powers, and an inhuman tolerance for pain. He must periodically ingest his Hyde formula in order to sustain or regain his Hyde physique. In either identity, he is a gifted biochemist. As Hyde, his personality is exceptionally savage and bestial in nature, though still intelligent.

USER NOTES:
Captain America: Hyde is truly a monster, and not just in the obvious classical sense — he's infinitely ruthless and cruel, and derives sadistic pleasure from the pain and suffering of others.

Project: PEGASUS clarifications: Not to be confused with the Mr. Hyde robot used by extratemporal robot Mr. Kline against Daredevil.

MOLECULE MAN
OWEN REECE

History: Owen Reece was a weak-willed Acme Atomics employee when a particle generator accident bombarded him with other-dimensional energy. Reece's face was given unusual scars, and he found that he could control molecules through a wand he wielded. Seemingly limited only by an inability to manipulate organic matter, Reece became the Molecule Man and lashed out against the world until the Fantastic Four intervened; he was taken into custody by Uatu the Watcher, who imprisoned him in an alien dimension.

Reece created a son for himself in his dimension of exile, and upon his death, transferred his powers and the wand to him. The new Molecule Man eventually returned to Earth and fought the Thing and Man-Thing, but his life-force was bonded to the wand, and he died when he was separated from it. The wand went on to possess others, acting as a host for the Molecule Man's consciousness, until it finally recreated Reece's original body. Reece's experiences had left him emotionally vulnerable, and during a confrontation

with the Avengers he befriended Tigra, who convinced him that he wasn't evil, just confused, and that he should seek psychiatric help.

However, the Molecule Man wound up being summoned to "Battleworld" by the Beyonder to serve in an army of villains led by Dr. Doom. Doom immediately saw that Reece was his most powerful ally despite his self-imposed limits, and helped inspire him to use his powers against their foes. Reece gradually became more confident, realizing that he could affect organic matter but had held back because he thought himself incapable. He also fell in love with Volcana (Marsha Rosenberg), another of Doom's lieutenants. When Doom claimed the Beyonder's power for himself, Reece departed Battleworld with the other villains, levitating a segment of a Denver suburb and transporting it through space with an artificial atmosphere within.

Owen lived in peace with Marsha for awhile, but the Beyonder eventually came to Earth in the form of a mortal, seeking to understand humankind. Owen helped the heroes of Earth oppose the Beyonder, who attempted to be "reborn" into an infant's body until Owen wrecked the Beyonder's machines, seemingly killing him. Owen then undid the Beyonder's damage with his powers, but pretended to lose his own powers in the process so that the heroes wouldn't think him a threat.

Eventually, the Beyonder returned, and he and Owen finally learned that the energies which had empowered Owen came from the dimension of the Beyonders, and that their combined power would form a Cosmic Cube. The two joined together to complete the Cube, and it eventually took on the form of Kosmos. Owen was dispatched from the Cube, powerless, but had left a portion of his power in Volcana, and she was able to restore his powers to him. However, Volcana was no longer certain about their relationship, and wanted some time apart from him. Hurt, Owen complied. Since then, Owen has been fixated on Volcana, seeking ways to win back her approval, even consulting Doc Samson for advice, and was told by him people should be drawn together like molecules. Owen has created statues in Volcana's image —even turning one of the heads on Mount Rushmore into hers — but has yet to win her back.

The Molecule Man was finally imprisoned at the Raft during a period when his mental state had fluctuated enough to make his power level manageable; but since the breakout, his current power level and goals are unknown.

Height: 5'7"
Weight: 140 lbs.
Eyes: Brown
Hair: Brown

Abilities: The Molecule Man can reshape all forms of matter and energy, limited only by his belief in his abilities.

USER NOTES:
Project: PEGASUS clarifications: *Not to be confused with the Molecule Man of Earth-9732, a 1950s era radiation-powered "commie-smasher" type.*

NITRO
ROBERT HUNTER

History: Robert Hunter was a ham radio operator who came into contact with the Lunatic Legion, a band of renegade extraterrestrial Kree who recruited him to serve as their agent on Earth. They genetically modified Hunter into a human bomb and sent him to obtain a nerve gas called Compound 13. As he was escaping with the gas, Nitro was opposed by Captain Mar-Vell, and the tank of gas accidentally opened during their clash. When Nitro detonated himself against Mar-Vell, Mar-Vell used his own ability to exchange atoms with Rick Jones to disperse Nitro's body.

Nitro finally regained his physical form and sought vengeance upon Mar-Vell, but he mistakenly targeted Omega the Unknown, who encased him in a steel cylinder and shot him into orbit. When he finally found Mar-Vell, Nitro was soundly beaten again, and imprisoned in a container which kept him from resuming his physical form. Nitro was initially imprisoned at Project: PEGASUS, but after his daughter Virginia arranged his release, he went on a rampage. Again determined to confront Mar-Vell, he set out to rob banks to prepare for his mission, but he was stopped by Spider-Man and sent back to the Project. When he was finally brought up for a hearing, he was enlisted in an escape attempt by the Vulture, and wound up battling Rusty Collins and Skids of the New Mutants. Skids used her force field to dissipate Nitro once more.

Nitro regained his form, joined Tombstone's Untouchables and was sent by Hardcore to capture Dakota North, but his own teammate Kickback was so concerned about Nitro's insanity that he ultimately abandoned him to distract North's ally Luke Cage. Following this, Nitro teamed with Rhino, the Super-Skrull, Titanium Man and Geatar to retrieve the Oracle of Ancient Knowledge for Thanos, but Thanos abandoned them on the planet H'aarg after getting what he wanted. Nitro was saved from the natives by the Silver Surfer and Legacy (Genis-Vell, later Photon), and set off to find his old Kree allies.

In the years since their first battle, Mar-Vell had died of cancer from exposure to Compound 13, making Nitro partially responsible for his death. Legacy was the cloned son of Mar-Vell, and was shocked to learn that he had let the man implicated in his father's demise slip through his fingers. He tracked down Nitro on the Kree homeworld of Hala, and was tempted to kill him in order to avenge his father, but brought him to Titan to be imprisoned instead.

Eventually returning to Earth, Nitro assumed various mercenary jobs. He was hired by unknown parties to assault railroad lines in New York, but was defeated by the Heroes for Hire. He later tried unsuccessfully to kill Norman Osborn. He was also hired by Count Nefaria to kill Tony Stark, but was beaten by Iron Man, who learned how to cybernetically force Nitro to explode and reform so many times that he was too weak to fight back. Nitro was one of several criminals who attempted to claim Sammy Silke's bounty on Matt Murdock, but was beaten by Daredevil. He was finally imprisoned in the Raft, but escaped during Electro's mass breakout and remains at large.

Height: 6'3"
Weight: 235 lbs.
Eyes: Blue
Hair: White

Abilities: Nitro can explode with a force equivalent to that of 250 lbs. of TNT, and can then reconstitute his body. He can control the explosions so that either all or part of his body explodes.

USER NOTES
Iron Man: Nitro's insanity is the only thing holding him back from being one of the most dangerous super-villains on Earth. When you consider that even in his most unbalanced state, he inflicted the attack that ultimately took the life of Captain Mar-Vell, you have to fear what he might accomplish at full mental capacity.

PURPLE MAN
ZEBEDIAH KILLGRAVE

History: Zebediah Killgrave was a Yugoslavian spy assigned by communists to steal an experimental U.S. military nerve gas. Captured while infiltrating an American army base, Killgrave was accidentally exposed to the nerve gas, which turned his entire body purple; it also gave him a superhuman power of suggestion, which he realized after a soldier accepted his absurdly flimsy explanation for being there and set him free. Killgrave quietly indulged himself for years, even mind-controlling a woman named Melanie into marrying him. Hoping she might love him without his power, Killgrave eventually freed her mind. She promptly left him and secretly gave birth to their daughter, Kara, who grew up to be the Canadian superhero Purple Girl (later Persuasion). Tiring of anonymity, Killgrave committed more public crimes and was soon captured by Daredevil, who could resist his power to some extent. Later, Purple Man teamed with Electro for a scheme foiled by Daredevil and the Black Widow (Natasha Romanoff). Escaping, Killgrave established a Southwestern headquarters which was destroyed by Hawkeye (Clint Barton) and the Two-Gun Kid.

Manipulating industrialist Maxwell Glenn and ultimately driving him to suicide, Killgrave pitted Cobra, Mister Hyde, Jester (Jonathan Powers) and Gladiator (Melvin Potter) against Daredevil, who prevailed with the aid of the super-mercenary Paladin.

Mentally enslaving novice heroine Jewel (Jessica Jones), Killgrave demeaned and tortured her for months before dispatching her to attack the Avengers in a fit of temper, sparking a battle that left Jones temporarily comatose and lastingly traumatized. Forced to serve the Kingpin, Purple Man fought Spider-Man, Daredevil, Power Man (Luke Cage), Iron Fist and Moon Knight, the latter of whom defeated Killgrave by using earplugs to ignore his commands. Killgrave was later enslaved by Doctor Doom, who used his power to rule the world; but Doom wearied of so easy a conquest and allowed the Avengers to mount a successful rebellion, during which Namor seemingly slew Killgrave. Mystically revived in an undead state by the Dream Queen, Killgrave attacked his daughter and was seemingly destroyed. Later fully recovered, Killgrave manipulated and was soon defeated by the vastly powerful mutant X-Man (Nate Grey). Captured by the Defenders and incarcerated in the Raft super-prison, Killgrave escaped and went after his old pawn Jessica Jones, but she resisted him using a psychic defense trigger supplied by Phoenix (Jean Grey) and beat Killgrave senseless. Sent back to the Raft, Killgrave tried to escape during Electro's mass breakout, but his powers were inhibited by drugs and Jones's new boyfriend Luke Cage pummeled him into submission. Somehow escaping yet again, the Purple Man made the Thunderbolts his pet project, manipulating the reformed ex-villains in various damaging ways and grooming a new Swordsman to infiltrate the group and betray them; but when Killgrave took over all of Manhattan, it was the Thunderbolts who defeated him and sent him back to prison, his mind shattered by a taste of cosmic awareness forced upon him by Photon (Genis-Vell).

Height: 5'11"
Weight: 165 lbs.
Eyes: Purple
Hair: Purple

Abilities: Killgrave's body emits will-sapping psychoactive pheromones that render most people in his general vicinity extremely suggestible, such that he can make almost anyone do almost anything simply by issuing verbal commands. Only a few exceptionally strong-willed or physiologically unique individuals can resist his power. Killgrave's mutated body apparently has potent (albeit slow-acting) regenerative properties enabling him to recover from most injuries, even seemingly fatal ones. Killgrave and his pawns sometimes employ chemicals derived from his pheromones to subjugate people in his absence, or to spread his control over wider areas (for instance, spiking a city's water supply).

USER NOTES:
Luke Cage: Just so the rest of you know, anytime this sucker's dumb enough to cross our path again, he's mine. After the stuff he's done to Jess and all those other people, after the stuff he threatened to do to my woman and my kid, he better hope he stays in prison. Believe it.

RAMPAGE
STUART CLARKE

History: Stuart Clarke was the scientifically brilliant but economically naïve founder of Clarke Futuristics, a struggling Los Angeles high-tech design and manufacturing firm. Clarke's lawyer and financial manager Crawley urged Stuart to sell his company to a larger corporation, which could have made Clarke very wealthy; but the idealistic Clarke refused to "sell his soul" to big business and held onto his company, which sank deep into debt during a subsequent economic recession. Ultimately forced to declare bankruptcy, an enraged Clarke fired Crawley. Blaming the government for his troubles due to their mismanagement of the economy, Clarke decided he would seek profit at the government's expense.

Clarke had previously designed a super-powerful armored exoskeleton, but Stark International had launched a similar project and got all the related government contracts. Taking his unsold exoskeleton prototype out of storage, Clarke planned to use it to steal the money he needed from FDIC (Federal Deposit Insurance Corporation)-protected banks, believing that no regular people would suffer since these banks' losses would be covered by the government. During Clarke's first attempted bank robbery, he was opposed by the city's then-new Champions super-team, who foiled his theft, though not before he seriously injured their ally Ivan Petrovich. Fearful he had killed Petrovich, Clarke (dubbed "Rampage" by the police and the media) was shocked back to his senses and fled, deciding to abandon his criminal plans and dismantle the armor; but Crawley had recognized Clarke's armor in news reports and tipped off the police, who quickly surrounded Clarke. After a losing battle with the Champions, a despairing Clarke tried to blow himself up, though instant ice shielding from Iceman saved his life. Clarke was hospitalized and the sympathetic Champions offered him legal counsel, but he refused and soon escaped with the aid of a Russian-backed team of super-criminals led by Yuri Petrovich, who were targeting the Champions for reasons of their own. Quickly deciding that Clarke was an expendable liability, the criminals tricked him into blowing himself up inside Champions headquarters. Clarke survived, albeit crippled and badly burned, and he later mind-controlled Iceman into attacking Champions founder Angel (Warren Worthington III) and Spider-Man, who freed Iceman from Clarke's power.

Eventually recovering, Clarke returned to crime as Rampage with a gang of similarly-outfitted accomplices, his Recession Raiders, but he was captured by Wonder Man and the Beast. Bailed out and employed by wealthy crime boss Lotus Newmark, Clarke outfitted her Armed Response team, an armored security force for hire who were secretly protection racketeers. When Wonder Man and the Crazy Eight amateur super-team interfered in Newmark's plans, Lotus dispatched various agents against them, including Rampage; but her agents were all defeated and Armed Response was exposed as a protection scam. Later, Clarke worked with mercenary Parnell Jacobs, providing tech support and modifying Parnell's salvaged model of Stark's original "War Machine" armor; but their employer, criminal industrialist Sunset Bain, fired them both after Jacobs' old army buddy Jim Rhodes convinced him to end their Bain-mandated attack on Iron Man. Eventually recaptured by authorities and incarcerated in the Raft super-prison, Clarke escaped during Electro's mass breakout and remains at large.

Height: 5'10"
Weight: (unarmored) 185 lbs., (armored) 210 lbs.

Eyes: Blue
Hair: Black

Abilities: Clarke is a gifted mechanical engineer and inventor. His "Rampage" armored exoskeleton is composed of lightweight flexible alloys reinforced by magnetic fields and powered by miniature generators. The armor greatly augments the wearer's strength and durability, and its boot jets enable flight (though Clarke has also used an ionic-powered jet pack). Clarke has used a limited force field generator and hypnotic gas in the past, though these items are not usually part of his arsenal.

USER NOTES:

Captain America: Reports paint Clarke as a poor man's Iron Man — an impressive inventor and armor designer, but nowhere near in the same class as Tony; however, his access to Stark technology during his collaboration with the new War Machine may result in more formidable Clarke designs in the future.

RAZOR-FIST
DOUGLAS SCOTT

History: Three individuals are known to have assumed the identity of the blade-handed Razor-Fist. The first, William Young, was an employee of the druglord Carlton Velcro, and had two steel blades in place of his hands. Razor-Fist served Velcro faithfully against Shang-Chi, but Velcro lost faith in him and ordered his men to open fire on him and Shang-Chi. Although Shang-Chi evaded the gunfire, Razor-Fist was killed. Velcro later employed two brothers (Douglas and William Scott) to assume the guise of Razor-Fist. Each brother had one hand replaced with a steel blade, leaving them with the use of one hand. The two brothers also fought Shang-Chi, and when William heard how their predecessor had died because of Velcro, Velcro panicked and accidentally shot William dead.

Douglas Scott eventually had his other hand replaced with a steel blade, replicating the appearance of the original Razor-Fist. He continued on as a mercenary, even finding work from S.H.I.E.L.D. when the organization was infiltrated by the Deltites. He accepted assignments from the Architect, Crossfire and the Madripoor crimelord Roche, fighting the likes of the Avengers, Wolverine, Shen Kuei (the Cat), Elektra and Spider-Man.

Razor-Fist took up residence in a place known only as "the House of Razor." Pampered by luxurious women who helped him eat and bathe, he relaxed there in-between jobs. At one point, he was outfitted with a pair of cybernetic hands with blades attached to their wrists, but he only used them on one assignment before abandoning them, preferring his regular blades.

Razor-Fist was finally imprisoned in the Raft, but escaped during the recent breakout. Unable to return to the House of Razor, he sought a new home among the homeless of New York. Razor-Fist began collecting followers, attracting many young people who had a fetish for cutting themselves. He imparted knowledge to these people like a grand sage, teaching them to learn control through inflicting pain, while recruiting their services to help feed and clean him. These followers included Perkins, a police officer, and a band of twisted children called "the Piranha Tots."

Spider-Man asked his symbiote-bonded ally Toxin (Patrick Mulligan) to bring Razor-fist in. Toxin found Razor-Fist with the aid of one of his followers, a young man named Anton, but the symbiote's poor cooperation led to Razor-Fist's escape. Realizing that Toxin could track him, Razor-Fist masked his scent by having his followers douse him in perfume. After killing 28 people in an Italian restaurant, Razor-Fist sent a videotape to the local news station, demanding that the people of New York donate money to his bank account or he and his followers would cause a "slasherday" of mayhem and violence. Fearing that Toxin was the one person who could stop him, Razor-Fist learned from Perkins that police officer Eddie Meadows was affiliated with Toxin. After torturing Meadows, Razor-First learned Toxin's true identity and killed Toxin's father, Jim Mulligan. With "slasherday" on the horizon, Toxin tracked down Razor-Fist and beat him, removing his steel blades. Razor-Fist was outfitted with prothestic hands and returned to Ryker's Island, but many of his followers are still at large, including the Piranha Tots.

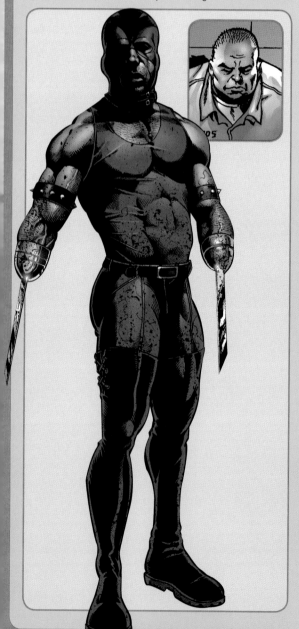

Height: 6'3"
Weight: 260 lbs.
Eyes: Blue
Hair: Bald

Abilities: Razor-Fist is a master of unarmed combat, and wears a pair of razor-sharp steel blades in place of his hands. He wields these blades so precisely that he can slice through flesh without making it bleed, and grasp some instruments without the need for hands.

USER NOTES:
Project: PEGASUS clarifications: *No known connection to Razorfist, who fought Thor alongside a woman named Spiral (not Mojo's agent). Dr. Doom also used a pair of robot duplicates of the William Young version.*

SAURON
KARL LYKOS

History: While on an expedition to Tierra del Fuego with his father, young Karl Lykos was bitten by a mutated pterodactyl from the prehistoric Savage Land which infected him with a genetic virus, forcing him to drain the life energy of others to survive. Eventually becoming a hypnotherapist, Lykos constructed a device to help drain his patients' energies. After absorbing the mutant Havok's energy, Lykos transformed for the first time into the pterodactyl-like Sauron, named after the arch-villain of Tolkien's The Lord of the Rings novels. He battled the X-Men, but soon began reverting back to Lykos and fled. Later, as Sauron, he attempted to kill his own lover Tanya Andersson, but was again opposed by the X-Men. As Lykos, he became despondent over his behavior, and after Tanya and the X-Men found him in South America he ran over a precipice and was believed dead.

Lykos survived and journeyed to the Savage Land, where he once again fought the X-Men as Sauron. For a time, as Lykos, he proved an ally to both the X-Men and Ka-Zar. Ultimately reverting to his Sauron form, he usurped the leadership of the Savage Land Mutates and fought Ka-Zar, Spider-Man, and the X-Men. Defeated, he reverted to human form again and was reunited with Tanya. Later, he and Tanya were captured by the Toad, who was seeking recruits for a new Brotherhood of Evil Mutants. Forced to absorb Tanya's energy (possibly fatally), Lykos was transformed into Sauron again and joined the Brotherhood in battling first X-Force and then X-Factor. After the Brotherhood disbanded, Sauron returned to the Savage Land and fought various X-Men with the Mutates. Capturing Cyclops and Havok, Sauron drained their energies and mutated further. Jean Grey engaged Sauron telepathically, helping Lykos' personality force his alter ego's psyche to make a suicide leap into the abyss of his own mind, thus reducing Sauron to the state of a mindless pterodactyl.

Sauron's suppressed persona eventually returned, but the X-Men defeated him. He was subsequently recruited into the new Weapon X Project as a field agent, but internal feuding tore apart the Project and he was incarcerated in the maximum security superhuman prison the Raft. The Mutates engineered a breakout of the Raft's other inmates as a cover for Sauron's escape, and he returned to the Savage Land where he and the Mutates became involved with a rogue S.H.I.E.L.D. faction illegally stockpiling Vibranium. Opposed by Wolverine and a new Avengers team, Lykos was attacked by Wolverine, allowing him to use the mutant's energy to transform into Sauron. The fight was interrupted by S.H.I.E.L.D. troopers led by the Black Widow (Belova), who shot Sauron in the head. The stress caused Sauron's powers to mutate further, allowing him to access the healing factor from the energy he absorbed from Wolverine, thus surviving the fatal shot. Ultimately, Sauron was defeated and remanded into S.H.I.E.L.D. custody, who in turn handed him back to Weapon X.

Height: (Lykos) 5'9", (Sauron) 7'
Weight: (Lykos) 170 lbs., (Sauron) 200 lbs.
Eyes: (Lykos) Brown, (Sauron) Red
Hair: (Lykos) Brown, (Sauron) None

Abilities: As Sauron, Lykos has a toothed beak, a 12-foot wingspan, razor-sharp claws, superhuman strength and a hypnotic gaze. Genetic enhancement by the Weapon X Program granted Sauron the ability to expel the energy he absorbs as blasts of concussive energy from his hands. Recently, Sauron's powers mutated further, allowing him to utilize the powers of any mutant whose energy he absorbs as though they were his own, as well as breathe fire.

USER NOTES:
Spider-Man: *I really hate this guy. Flight, strength, claws, hypnosis, and now fire? Yeesh! Best to take him down as Lykos before he can do his energy-drain thing and turn into Pterodactyl-Man...*

Wolverine: *Too bad about Lykos getting mixed up with Weapon X, but after all the crappy things he's done, he deserves to be taken down permanently. Parker's right about taking him down as Lykos, but don't let a mutant do it, 'coz Sauron can be a right royal pain in the #@$.*

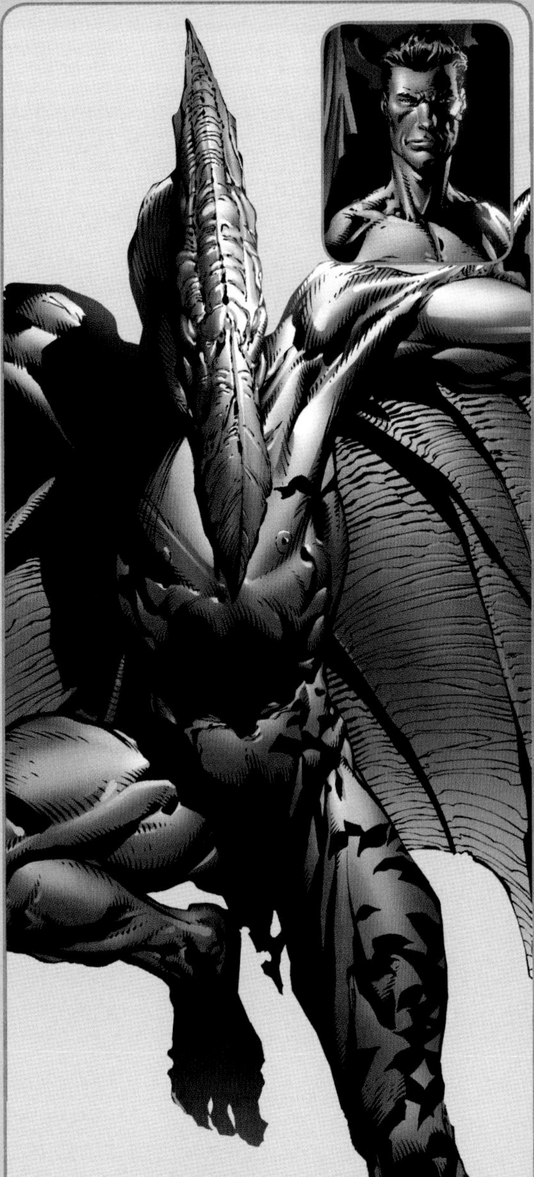

SCARECROW
EBENEZER LAUGHTON

History: Ebenezer Laughton's alcoholic mother would beat him severely when he misbehaved, then give him presents to ease her feelings of guilt. This dysfunctional discipline convinced Ebenezer that rewards always followed punishment, and his behavior grew worse as he sought beatings and the gifts that came with them. Socially backward, young Ebenezer found a sense of purpose after he saw a "rubber man" performing at a traveling carnival. Obsessed with mastering this unique skill, the slender, double-jointed Laughton trained for years, becoming a gifted contortionist, escape artist and acrobat. As an adult, he successfully auditioned for a spot in a live variety show, where he performed as "Umberto the Uncanny"; however, he found a new calling after Iron Man (Tony Stark) chased a thief into the theatre. Using his acrobatics to capture the lawbreaker in hopes of good publicity, "Umberto" realized that his skills could make him a formidable burglar. Stealing a scarecrow outfit from a costume shop and a flock of trained crows from fellow stage performer Thornton, Laughton retrained the birds (who were already familiar with him) to serve as his accomplices. Thus outfitted as the Scarecrow, Laughton burglarized the apartment of wealthy industrialist Tony Stark, narrowly escaping after scuffles with Stark's chauffeur Happy Hogan and Iron Man. Finding some top-secret defense plans among his burglary loot, Laughton began trying to sell them, but Iron Man took them back and the Scarecrow fled to Cuba.

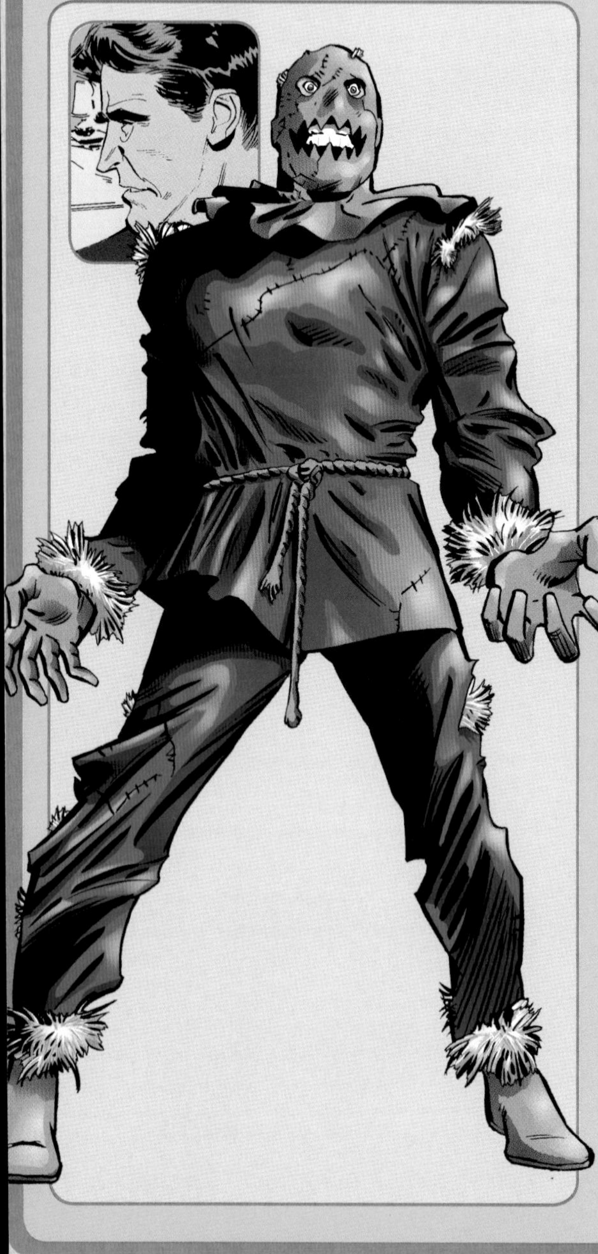

Returning to America, Scarecrow was defeated by Spider-Man, then joined the Maggia as one of Count Nefaria's super-agents alongside Eel (Leopold Stryke), Plantman, Porcupine and Unicorn (Milos Masaryk), battling the X-Men when Nefaria unsuccessfully held Washington, D.C. for ransom. Nefaria's super-agents (with Jordan Dixon, alias Viper, in place of Unicorn) next helped the Cowled Commander (corrupt NYPD sergeant Brian Muldoon) stage a crime wave designed to terrorize New Yorkers into bolstering their police force, but they were defeated and exposed by Captain America (Steve Rogers) and the Falcon (Sam Wilson). Later, placed in solitary confinement for nearly a year after another defeat by Captain America, Laughton snapped. Escaping, he went on a killing spree until Captain America recaptured him. Imprisoned in the Vault, Scarecrow was present for two mass breakouts; but the first was foiled completely by the Avengers and Freedom Force, and during the second, Hawkeye and Iron Man recaptured Scarecrow. Escaping and resuming his serial slayings, Scarecrow was impaled and left for dead following a battle with Ghost Rider (Dan Ketch), but the shadowy organization the Firm surgically restored him — complete with new fear-based powers — to serve as their agent. Defeated by Ghost Rider and Captain America, then killed in yet another battle with Ghost Rider, Scarecrow was resurrected by the demon Blackheart as a bodiless spirit who possessed the corpse of Ghost Rider's late sister, Barbara Ketch. Defeated and cast into Hell, Scarecrow somehow returned to physical life and menaced some children until he was recaptured by the Falcon. Incarcerated in the Raft super-prison, Scarecrow escaped during Electro's mass breakout.

Height: 6'0"
Weight: 165 lbs.
Eyes: Brown
Hair: Brown

Abilities: Scarecrow's pheromones trigger panic attacks in those around him, and this fear enhances his strength, agility and recuperative powers to superhuman levels. Scarecrow is an expert contortionist, escape artist and bird trainer. His crows are trained to attack his enemies and perform other simple tasks, responding to his hand gestures, verbal commands and other predetermined cues. Scarecrow's favorite weapon is a pitchfork.

USER NOTES:
Iron Man: *Hard to believe this maniac's the same glorified acrobat I chased out of the country years ago — sometimes it seems like all these supercrooks are just getting scarier with the passage of time. And none of them stay dead, either, which is getting really old...*

Project: PEGASUS clarifications: *No known connection to the supernatural "Fear Lord" the Straw Man, a.k.a the Scarecrow; the giant monster Scarecrow, an actual scarecrow temporarily transformed into a living giant by atomic radiation; or several other scarecrows brought to life.*

SHOCKWAVE
LANCASTER SNEED

History: Lancaster Sneed grew up a lonely boarding school boy in Great Britain, his boredom relieved only occasionally by visits from his uncle, veteran intelligence agent Sir Denis Nayland Smith. Fascinated by Smith's spy stories yet resentful of his uncle's long absences, Sneed grew up to become an MI-6 agent like his uncle. Caught in an explosion during his first field mission, Sneed was surgically rebuilt and reinforced with metal plating; but his injuries left him badly scarred and mentally unstable, and MI-6 fired him. After studying martial arts in Asia, Sneed became a carnival performer as "Shockwave," wearing an armored costume that enabled him to conduct electricity through his body's metal plating. The embittered Sneed eventually became an agent of his uncle's longtime foe, the criminal mastermind Fu Manchu. Shockwave battled and nearly defeated Fu Manchu's renegade son, the altruistic adventurer Shang-Chi, before MI-6 head Black Jack Tarr forced Shockwave to flee. Defeated and captured during a subsequent battle with Shang-Chi, Shockwave was framed for the shooting of Sir Denis by old family friend Dr. James Petrie, who had fallen under Manchu's control. While in custody, Shockwave was brainwashed into serving MI-6 by MI-6 ally Ward Sarsfield, who suspected Shang-Chi and his associates were withholding information regarding Fu Manchu. As Sarsfield's agent, Sneed savagely beat Sir Denis, attacked secretary Melissa Greville and injured former MI-6 agent Clive Reston, but Shang-Chi and agent Leiko Wu drove him off. Partnered with the robot Brynocki and assigned to interrogate Black Jack Tarr on Mordillo Island, Shockwave fought Leiko Wu and Shang-Chi but was forced into an alliance with his enemies after Brynocki turned on him. As they fought their way off the island, his new allies learned of Shockwave's background and saw his scarred face; sympathetic, they offered to seek a means of undoing his brainwashing and planned to bring down Sarsfield using Sneed's information.

As a freelance mercenary, Shockwave teamed with Razor-Fist (Douglas Scott) and Maximillian Zaran to attack the Avengers on behalf of the Deltite conspirators who had then infiltrated S.H.I.E.L.D., but the trio was defeated and forced to flee. Later, Shockwave attended the AIM Weapons Expo and skirmished unsuccessfully with Captain America. Shockwave re-teamed with Razor-Fist to kidnap the son of the Cat (Shen Kuei) on behalf of parties unknown, but the Cat and Spider-Man defeated them and rescued the child. Sneed next teamed with Whiplash, Orka and Killer Shrike to seize the aircraft carrier Intrepid as part of an extortion scheme, but they were defeated by Heroes for Hire. The Crimson Cowl (Justine Hammer) later recruited Shockwave into her Masters of Evil, and he participated in her global weather control blackmail scheme; but the Thunderbolts defeated them, capturing Shockwave and most of the other Masters. A power-mad, other-dimensional cosmic scholar then enlisted Shockwave and dozens of other criminals to guard his fortress, but they were defeated through the combined efforts of the Avengers and a league of heroes from a divergent cosmos. Incarcerated at the Raft superprison, Shockwave escaped during the mass breakout engineered by Electro and remains at large.

Height: 5'11"
Weight: (unarmored) 170 lbs., (armored) 182 lbs.

Eyes: Green
Hair: Black, formerly red-brown

Abilities: Sneed wears an armored exoskeleton which can deliver a powerful electrical charge on contact; it also slightly enhances his strength and durability, which is further augmented by his body's metal plating. An experienced martial artist and intelligence agent, Sneed is also trained in demolitions.

USER NOTES:

Iron Man: Sneed was on the short list of crooks who may have stolen elements of my Iron Man technology a while back — I keep meaning to check him out. Put up a good fight that one time we skirmished, but nothing I couldn't handle.

Project: PEGASUS clarifications: No known connection to Shockwave (Kathy Ling) of Earth-148611 ("New Universe"). A Shockwave robot was also used by Dr. Doom.

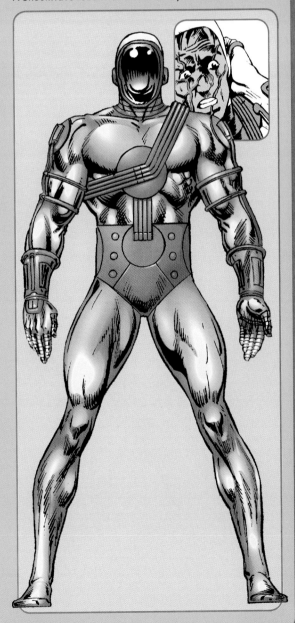

SILVER SAMURAI
KENUICHIO HARADA

History: Kenuichio Harada is the son of Shingen Harada, one-time head of Japan's Clan Yashida. Although Kenuichio honed his mutant abilities to become a powerful samurai warrior, his father virtually disowned him, refusing to acknowledge his place in the family. Kenuichio became a mercenary assassin as the Silver Samurai.

After serving fellow mutants Nekra and Mandrill, Kenuichio began a long association with the Viper, and was devoted to her to the point of infatuation. After losing one of the Viper's teleportation rings in an encounter with Spider-Man and the Black Widow (Natasha Romanoff), he raided the stages of the television program Saturday Night Live to recover it. Kenuichio then helped Viper try to crash the S.H.I.E.L.D. Helicarrier into the U.S. Capitol, but was beaten by the combined forces of Spider-Man, Nick Fury, Shang-Chi and the Black Widow. He also aided the Viper in attempting to capture Michael Kramer, "the Judas Man," battling Spider-Woman (Jessica Drew) in the process. He confronted the students of Charles Xavier when he and the Viper attempted

to steal the Cavorite crystal and the New Mutants opposed them. While fleeing their base, Kenuichio set it to explode, and seemingly slew Karma (Xi'an Coy Manh) as a result. His duties alongside the Viper finally set him against his own family in Japan. Although Shingen had died battling Wolverine, it was Kenuichio's half-sister Mariko who now led the clan, and intended to marry Wolverine. Kenuichio and the Viper tried to force Mariko to transfer leadership from her to him, but the X-Men defended her, and Kenuichio was soundly beaten by Wolverine; however, Mariko ultimately rejected Wolverine as her husband due to the influence of Mastermind (Jason Wyngarde), and she chose Kenuichio as her heir. Having obtained everything he had wanted, Kenuichio gave up crime and tended to the duties of his family. He once sought the "Black Blade," a cursed muramasa sword, and proved immune to its powers once he obtained it. Deciding it was karma that he possess the blade, he kept it.

After Mariko was slain by the Hand, Kenuichio assumed leadership of the clan. The clan's interests sometimes set him against the X-Men, such as when he defended Lord Nyoirin, who was implicated in the transformation of the assassin Kwannon into Psylocke, and he once confronted Wolverine and Cecilia Reyes over the custody of Inazo Uehara, a suspected spy. He eventually became a defender of his country and served as field-commander of the national super-hero team Big Hero 6, working alongside his cousin Shiro Yoshida (Sunfire) against the Everwraith and the thing called X. Eventually departing their ranks, Kenuichio was replaced with the Ebon Samurai.

Under the influence of the mutant Blindspot, Kenuichio was regressed back to his ambitious ways, and he allied himself with Lady Deathstrike in an attempt to conquer the Yakuza of Japan and install himself as the "Silver Shogun." He also helped expose the earlier criminal dealings of Sunfire in hopes of driving Sunfire to commit ritual seppuku, but Sunfire and Rogue defeated him. Imprisoned at the Raft, he escaped during Electro's breakout and returned to Japan where he became involved with the Viper once more.

Height: 6'6"
Weight: 250 lbs.
Eyes: Brown
Hair: Black

Abilities: A master swordsman and warrior, the Silver Samurai can surround his sword with a tachyon field which cuts through virtually any substance. While serving with the Viper he wore a ring which could teleport him to any location on the globe.

USER NOTES:
Wolverine: I got no love for Kenuichio. He might've been interested in going straight once, but thanks to Blindspot, it' ain't gonna take. He and I will meet again.

SLUG

ULYSSES X. LUGMAN

History: Miami-born Ulysses X. Lugman formed a small southern Florida gang which eventually expanded into a coalition of Florida's non-Maggia criminal organizations, stretching from Pensacola to Miami. Investing his illegal Latin American drug trade profits in legitimate businesses, Lugman soon built a vast, diversified business empire. As the Slug, he conducted his drug trade from his massive private luxury yacht, the "Nowhere Fast," anchored outside U.S. territorial waters to avoid legal jurisdiction. A grease fire set by Nomad (Jack Munroe), who was working undercover as one of Slug's enforcers, sank the yacht, but Slug simply floated away. Slug faced another major setback when the High Evolutionary attempted to eradicate the Central American drug trade as part of his misguided plan to evolve humanity. The resulting drug shortage forced Slug into a joint venture with New York's Kingpin (Wilson Fisk), but their brief alliance proved unprofitable due to the interference of Spider-Man, Man-Thing, and Poison (Cecilia Cardinale), a Miami-based vigilante who gained super-powers after merging with the other-dimensional entity Ylandris. Afterwards, the Slug rebuilt his empire just as he had created it.

As First South Coast Bank's biggest depositor, the Slug arranged the firing of Joe Trinity, the bank's newly appointed vice-president of investment counseling, who refused to handle Slug's illegal accounts. Trinity's replacement, Dallas Kerr, dated Trinity's wife and laundered Slug's capital from detectable cash stores into securities, choosing profitable investments so that Slug acquired several new legitimate firms. As a favor to Kerr, Slug agreed to have Trinity killed; but unbeknownst to all, Trinity merged with Mrinhä, an entity from the same dimension as Ylandris, and was transformed into the super-powered "Mop-Man." Poison and Trinity dispatched several of Slug's best assassins, before confronting the Slug himself.

After Daredevil and Hydra toppled the Kingpin from power, the Slug attended the Las Vegas meeting to divide up the Kingpin's former empire, leaving in disgust when the criminal delegates were unable to reach an agreement. The Slug was next nearly killed by Nomad, who had been brainwashed by the criminal psychologist Dr. Faustus into thinking he was a Nazi and sent to assassinate the narco-trafficker; but Lugman was saved by Captain America, who brought Nomad back to his senses.

When an armada of Platoon war-suits attacked the Brooklyn Bridge, Slug watched the event on live television and considered placing an order with Alternative Resource Munitions Supply (A.R.M.S.), the war-suits' manufacturer, but ended negotiations when Spider-Man and Iron Fist defeated the armada. Slug later traveled to Manhattan and formed a temporary union with several other crimelords aimed at killing Fortunato, who had taken over much of the Kingpin's former territory in New York, and then dividing the city amongst themselves. However, Fortunato had allied himself with Hydra, who forced the Slug and his allies to pledge loyalty to Fortunato, but they were rescued by Spider-Man, Daredevil, and Jimmy-6, Fortunato's own son. The Slug was finally convicted for his crimes and sent to the Raft, escaping during the breakout initiated by Electro.

Height: 6'8"
Weight: 1,068 lbs.
Eyes: Blue
Hair: White

Abilities: The Slug is so obese that he can asphyxiate a person in the folds of his flesh. The Slug's legs are no longer able to support his body mass for any length of time, thus requiring him to use a hi-tech wheelchair for locomotion.

USER NOTES:
Captain America: *The Slug may be the Kingpin's Miami counterpart, but he's certainly not Wilson Fisk's physical equal. Too overweight to defend himself, Slug surrounds himself with a legion of armed enforcers to ensure his safety.*

Spider-Man: *Either prison or Atkins helped this guy shed more than half his weight, or he had a body double in the Raft. Regardless, I'm betting he's back to old habits and up to his former size in a couple months.*

Project: PEGASUS clarifications: *No known connection to the princess of the Microverse; the alien associated with Century and the Broker; and the agent of Australian slave-trader Sultan.*

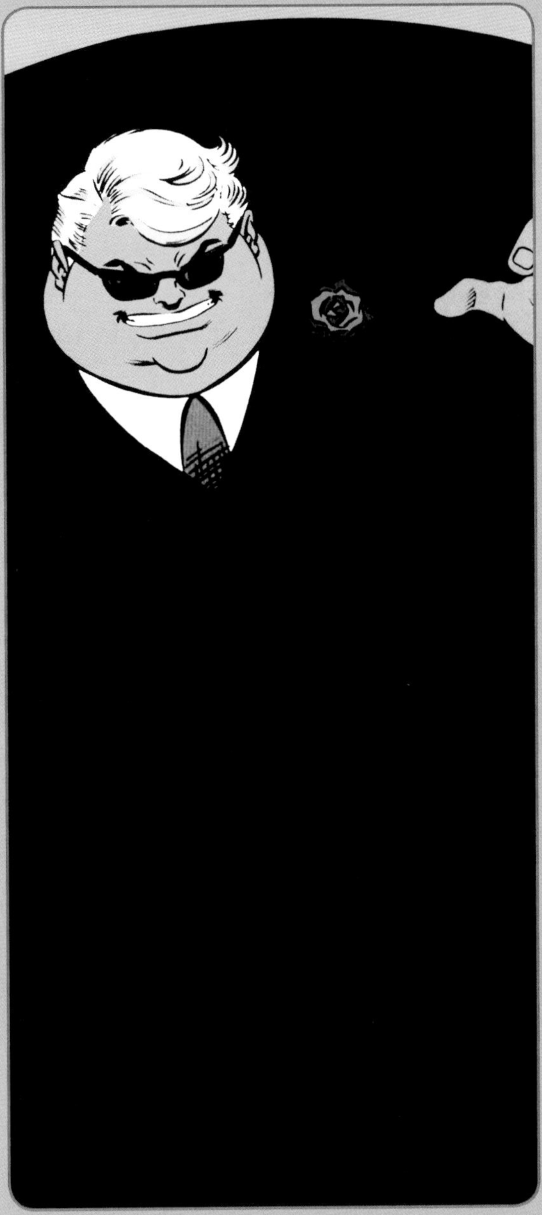

TIGER SHARK
TODD ARLISS

History: Todd Arliss was an Olympic champion swimmer until he seriously injured his back and legs while rescuing a man who had fallen overboard during a sea cruise. Desperate, Arliss hired criminal scientist Doctor Lemuel Dorcas, who promised to restore his abilities. Despite the objections of Todd's sister Diane, Dorcas subjected Todd to a series of regenerative radiation procedures culminating in his treatment with the gene-imprinting "morphotron" device. Dorcas had planned to imprint Arliss with the genetic code of sharks; but having captured the super-amphibian Namor the Sub-Mariner by chance, Dorcas imprinted Arliss with a combination of genetic coding from both the sharks and Namor. The process transformed Todd into a power-mad super-amphibian who renounced his humanity, calling himself Tiger Shark. Besting a weakened Namor in combat, Tiger Shark forced Namor's betrothed, Dorma, to accompany him back to Namor's undersea kingdom Atlantis, where Arliss defeated the warlord Seth and briefly seized the throne until Namor returned and defeated him.

In the years ahead, Tiger Shark repeatedly battled Namor and other foes such as Human Torch (Johnny Storm), Spider-Man, Hulk, Namorita, Ms. Marvel (Carol Danvers), Doctor Doom and aquatic adventurer Stingray (Walter Newell), who would later marry Diane Arliss. Tiger Shark also allied himself with various other seafaring criminals, such as Dr. Dorcas, Llyra, Lymondo and the barbarian warlord Attuma. During one battle with Namor and Stingray, Tiger Shark even murdered Namor's long-lost father, Leonard McKenzie, and Tiger Shark's ally Dr. Dorcas was killed during a subsequent battle with Namor. Serving with two incarnations of the Masters of Evil under Egghead and Baron (Helmut) Zemo, Tiger Shark battled the Avengers and was later captured by Hellcat and Tigra. Imprisoned in the Vault, Arliss escaped by feigning illness and taking his sister Diane hostage; but when she was trapped in an undersea cave-in during his subsequent battle with Stingray, Tiger Shark actually helped dig her out, seemingly sacrificing himself in an ensuing explosion while the Newells escaped. Surviving, Arliss battled La Bandera and Wolverine in Tierra Verde. He was later captured for experimental purposes by Dr. Barnabas Cross, but a sympathetic Namor rescued him.

Arliss found peace with an isolated clan of nomadic Atlanteans as Arlys Tigershark, marrying a woman named Mara who became pregnant with his child; but the clan, including Mara, was wiped out by the Faceless Ones, whom the Old Ones had dispatched to attack Atlantis. His bloodlust reawakened, Tiger Shark joined the Atlantean war against the Old Ones and their king, Suma-Ket, whom Namor ultimately slew. During the war, Tiger Shark befriended aquatic alien Tamara Rahn, who became his lover. The duo became occasional allies of Atlantis, aiding Namor, the Fantastic Four and others against foes such as Llyra, Llyron and the Starblasters; however, Arliss mutated into a more bestial state and, leaving Tamara, was recruited by the Crimson Cowl (Justine Hammer) for her Masters of Evil until he and most of her other Masters were captured by the Thunderbolts. Escaping, he helped Attuma and others seize the Atlantean throne until the Defenders overthrew them. Imprisoned in the experimental "Big House" miniaturized prison, Tiger Shark participated in a mass breakout foiled by She-Hulk before he was transferred to the Raft, where he escaped during Electro's mass breakout, but he was recaptured by the New Warriors.

Height: 6'0"
Weight: 165 lbs.
Eyes: Red
Hair: White

Abilities: Arliss can survive in air or water, but weakens rapidly away from water. At his peak, Arliss has tremendous superhuman strength, stamina and durability, as well as enhanced speed (superhuman while swimming), agility and reflexes. His costume is lined with an internal water circulation system which keeps him constantly moist. His mutated physiology has fluctuated repeatedly over the years, alternately enhancing or impairing his powers and mental faculties.

USER NOTES:
Captain America: Given his mental and physical instability, Arliss might not be entirely responsible for his actions, similar to Namor's own history of chemical imbalance. It may be worth investigating that angle during his future incarcerations, with an eye towards treatment.

TYPHOID MARY
MARY MEZINIS

History: Born with dissociative identity disorder, Mary Mezinis grew up under study in psychiatric institutions. Her more aggressive persona, dubbed Typhoid for its continual fever, was hardened in her youth by sexual assaults from both doctors and male relatives. Mary allegedly had psychic surgery and served as a field operative for a covert group — possibly the Project under Dr. Sidney Joern, though evidence is lacking. She eventually escaped and emerged as Mary, becoming a noted stage actress before vanishing again. As Lyla, she worked as a prostitute in New York City until being nearly killed by neophyte hero Daredevil. Suppressing this last memory, she became Typhoid again, acting as a master thief and blackmailer in Chicago. On a months-long sojourn to Belize, she romanced the mercenary T-Ray before parting harshly. Returning to New York, she was hired by an impressed Kingpin (Wilson Fisk). While innocent Mary seduced Matt Murdock, Typhoid assaulted Daredevil. Romancing the Kingpin as well, Typhoid ultimately dispatched agents Ammo, Bullet, Bushwacker and Wildboys Jet and Spit against Daredevil. They nearly killed Daredevil, but Mary brought Murdock to a hospital. While Daredevil recovered, Typhoid became the Kingpin's chief assassin, encountering the monstrous Lifeform and assisting in a power struggle against the Red Skull (Johann Shmidt).

Daredevil returned and seduced Typhoid, driving her into her Mary persona and leaving her in psychiatric care. Mary escaped and sought out the Project to cure her identity disorder, but Wolverine saved her from sabotage at their hands. Mary subsequently joined the Woman's Action Movement, befriended Dan Ketch, and aided the Ghost Rider against the madness demon Dusk. She helped Wolverine, Vengeance (Michael Badalino) and Steel Raven free young metamorph/empath Jessie from the Fortress (formerly the Project), but the Fortress captured and mind-raked Typhoid in an effort to control her, only to unleash a third persona, Bloody Mary. With Jessie's help, she developed a fourth persona, Mary Walker, an amalgam of the others. Using all four personalities, Mary targeted misogynists, but encountered Spider-Man and admitted herself to Ravencroft. Released to a halfway house, Mary worked as a private detective, discovering those behind the West Side Ripper. She regained her suppressed memories in battle with Deadpool, then assaulted both Daredevil and Deadpool. The innocent Mary persona eventually regained control via hypnotherapy and she returned to her acting career, but a violent confrontation with the Kingpin restored Typhoid's ascendance. Fisk sent Typhoid to kill Daredevil, but she was defeated with the aid of Cage and Jessica Jones and sent to the Raft, though she escaped during the recent breakout.

Height: 5'10"
Weight: 140 lbs.
Eyes: Brown
Hair: Brown

Abilities: Mary's various personae alter her physical form sufficiently to fool even the likes of Daredevil. As Typhoid and Bloody Mary she has low-level telekinesis, pyrokinesis and mental suggestion powers. She also disrupts Daredevil's radar sense. She is a master armed and unarmed combatant, using various blades, as well as nearby objects, as weapons. She has exceptional, though not superhuman, physical abilities (strength, speed, agility, stamina, reflexes). Her shifting personae are both a strength and a weakness, as innocent Mary is powerless.

USER NOTES:

Wolverine: Here's the lowdown: Mary's yer friend, Typhoid seduces you intending to kill you, and Bloody Mary just hates all guys. Don't let yer guard down around her for a second, 'coz one o' her nastier selves could pop out and you could find yerself missin' a body part or two you'd have rather kept. She fools my senses, too.

Spider-Woman: I may be the only one of us who hasn't tangled with her, but I think you'd better let me handle this one, because it seems like she can wrap you men around her little finger.

U-FOES

History: Former U.S. Representative and industrialist Simon Utrecht (soon to become Vector) decided that economic and political power was insufficient, and sought super-powers. Scientist Michael Steel (later Ironclad) identified a window where the conditions which created the Fantastic Four could be duplicated, so Utrecht hired him to design, build and fly a spaceship. Accompanied by life support specialist Ann Darnell (later Vapor) and her brother, propulsion engineer James "Jimmy" Darnell (later X-Ray), the foursome rocketed into the cosmic rays and were changed. Physicist Bruce Banner (Hulk) found their New Mexico launch facility and aborted the flight; believing Banner had prevented them from gaining greater powers, the foursome (naming themselves the U-Foes after Utrecht) attacked Banner, but their unfamiliarity with their powers let the Hulk defeat them. Fearing their lack of control could prove fatal, Utrecht funded research into technology to further this control. This technology proved capable of "curing" certain powers, which later intrigued Utrecht's friend and associate, rogue CIA agent William Cross (Crossfire). Seeking recognition and revenge, the U-Foes attempted the Hulk's execution on live television, but the Hulk defeated them with help from the alien Bereet.

The four accidentally exiled themselves to the Crossroads of Reality when Vector's escape efforts repelled the U-Foes' home dimension from them. There, they again met the Hulk, who briefly trapped them in four separate dimensions with the aid of the Puffball Collective, an alien life form. Regrouping, they were returned to Earth by the mutant Portal (Charles Little Sky) but immediately defeated by the Avengers. Ironclad, Vapor, and X-Ray were placed in the Vault, but escaped during the so-called "Acts of Vengeance." Led by Loki to believe that the Avengers had slain Utrecht, the threesome attacked the Avengers Compound before learning the truth and fleeing. Vapor briefly joined Superia's female army, but the foursome reunited to seek Portal's aid in recovering some extra-dimensional artifacts. Interrupted

by Captain America, Daredevil and Darkhawk, the four were returned to prison before being freed by the Leader, for whom they broke into the Pantheon's Mount. Vector was later sighted at the Brass Bishop's energy auction of the corpses of Silver and Auric, and the four were shortly thereafter recaptured. Imprisoned in the Vault, they allied with Crossfire to attempt escape, but project director Rozalyn Backus stole much of Utrecht's wealth (including his power nullification technology) and tricked Utrecht into believing Crossfire had betrayed them, sparking conflicts between the U-Foes and Crossfire's mind-controlling clique. The Thunderbolts foiled another escape attempt before the Master freed the U-Foes, using them to contact the evolved White Tiger and then to break into the Vault for him. At the Master's behest they captured the Hulk and several U.N. scientists, using the Controller's discs to drain information from them. The nascent Heroes for Hire team stopped them, but they escaped and captured Luke Cage for the Master before being betrayed and left comatose by their employer.

Imprisoned in the miniaturized "Big House," they were part of that facility's mass escape, but She-Hulk, Southpaw, and Henry Pym recaptured them and they were moved to the Raft. Escaping, they fought a running battle with Crossfire's gang while both groups sought the Vault's corrupt former administrator Rozalyn Backus and Vector's lost technology. She claimed to have destroyed Utrecht's power-removing technology, destroying the U-Foes' ability to regain their humanity, so Vector vengefully destroyed Backus' charitable projects. The U-Foes later battled the Thunderbolts.

Ironclad / Vapor / Vector / X-Ray
Height: 6'7" / 5'6" / 6' / 5'9"
Weight: 650 lbs. / 0 lbs. / 195 lbs. / 0 lbs.
Eyes: White / White / White / White
Hair: None / Auburn / None / None

Abilities: Ironclad can lift 60 tons, and possesses a harder-than-steel body. Vapor can transform her body into any form of gas. Vector can repel anything from him at will, including physical, energy, magical, interdimensional, and psionic objects. X-Ray exists in energy form, and is capable of flying and projecting any form of radiation.

UTRECHT

STEEL

J. DARNELL

A. DARNELL

VERMIN
EDWARD WHELAN

History: Sexually abused as a child by his father, a prominent judge, Edward Whelan developed dissociative identity disorder to deal with the trauma. Whelan repressed these painful memories and grew up to be a research scientist in genetics. At age 31, Whelan traveled to Mexico in search of the notorious geneticist Arnim Zola. Instead, Whelan found Baron (Helmut) Zemo and Primus (an artificial humanoid created by Zola), who used Zola's research to mutate Whelan into the cannibalistic man-rat Vermin after Whelan objected to Zemo's experiments on human subjects. Zemo sent Vermin to Manhattan to attack Captain America, but Whelan was defeated and taken into S.H.I.E.L.D. custody. Vermin soon escaped in a breakout orchestrated by Zemo and Primus, but was imprisoned alongside Captain America because Zemo no longer had use for him. The trapped rat-man savagely lashed out, killing Michael (partner of Captain America's friend Arnie Roth), whose mind was transferred into a mutate body. Vermin escaped and attacked Zemo aboard his retreating aircraft.

Vermin later resurfaced in New York and was brutally beaten by Kraven the Hunter (Sergei Kravinoff), who had incapacitated and assumed the identity of Spider-Man. Landing in the care of Reed Richards, Vermin was placed under the treatment of Dr. Ashley Kafka at New York University. Vermin escaped from NYU and returned to his childhood home in Scarsdale, New York to confront his parents about the abuse he sustained as a child, but was drawn into a fight between Spider-Man and Green Goblin (Harry Osborn) after discovering he was incapable of killing his father. Vermin was returned to NYU where his psychological treatment continued under Dr. Kafka, allowing Whelan's persona to slowly reemerge; but his treatments were interrupted when he was kidnapped by Zemo's other mutates, who had also rebelled against Zemo and wanted to make Vermin their leader. Vermin accepted and led his fellow mutates on a crime spree in New York. But after Zemo resurfaced and attempted to reassert control of the mutates, Whelan was able to restrain himself from killing his former master, seemingly ridding himself of the Vermin persona permanently and reverting to human form. Represented by Matt Murdock, Whelan was acquitted of his crimes as Vermin and began working as Kafka's assistant at NYU. When Kafka was hired as Director of the Ravencroft Institute, an asylum for insane superhumans, Whelan was also brought on board to specialize in mutate research.

Unfortunately, Whelan eventually reverted to his Vermin persona at the touch of the vampire-like Bloodscream, who sought to recruit the man-rat into the service of the cannibalistic necromancer Mauvais. Under Mauvais' influence, Vermin was defeated by Wolverine. Returning to New York, Vermin helped the Punisher track down Daredevil and was soon imprisoned in the Raft, escaping during Electro's attack upon the superhuman prison. Since this most recent escape, Vermin has fallen under the influence of the demon Hive and attacked Nightcrawler on behalf of his new master.

Height: 6'
Weight: 220 lbs.
Eyes: Brown (as Whelan), Red (as Vermin)
Hair: Hair: Black (as Whelan), Brown (as Vermin)

Abilities: Vermin possesses superhuman strength, speed and agility as well as an enhanced sense of smell. His nails and teeth are razor sharp and able to rend wood and soft metals. Vermin can communicate with and command all rats and dogs within a 2-mile radius, but it is unknown whether this ability is hypersonic or telepathic in nature.

USER NOTES:

Spider-Man: This one's a real tragedy. Dr. Kafka's therapy came so close to finally straightening him out, but his Vermin persona won in the end. Sometimes I wonder if Edward Whelan still exists behind those creepy red eyes . . .

Project: PEGASUS clarifications: No known connection to Rodent, a.k.a. Vermin.

Captain America: The childlike Vermin is far less predictable than Rodent, who is obsessed with protecting his beloved rats. Cloak & Dagger told me about the Rodent, who possesses similar powers and began holding human children hostage in retaliation for the city's fumigation of the sewer system.

WRECKING CREW

History: Dirk Garthwaite was the son of Burt Garthwaite, a loutish construction worker and abusive father. Dirk grew up to become a burglar, wielding a crowbar as his chief weapon to remind himself of the crowbar his father used. Dirk once broke into a hotel room and overpowered its occupant, the Asgardian god Loki, who had just requested mystical enhancements from Karnilla the Norn Queen to oppose Thor. Karnilla accidentally cast the spell upon Dirk instead. Becoming the Wrecker, Dirk went on a rampage, battling Thor, but was finally beaten by the magical Destroyer construct, animated by the spirit of Sif.

During a subsequent battle with Thor, the Wrecker struck the third rail of a subway track and the magic powering him was driven from his body into the crowbar. Without the crowbar, he was sent to Ryker's Island. There, he befriended fellow convicts Dr. Eliot Franklin, Brian Philip Calusky and Henry Camp, and arranged to spring them when he made his escape to retrieve the crowbar. Obtaining the crowbar, the Wrecker had his three friends grasp it with him in an electrical storm, and the storm transferred the power amongst the four of them. Franklin became Thunderball; Calusky became Piledriver; and Camp became Bulldozer. Together, they became known as the Wrecking Crew.

Thunderball had previously built a Gamma Bomb for Richmond Enterprises, but executive J.C. Pennysworth had stolen it and Franklin had been sent to prison while trying to steal it back. He convinced his allies that they should capture the bomb and use it to ransom New York. They began to tear apart buildings owned by Richmond Enterprises to find the bomb, attracting the attention of the Defenders, including Nighthawk (Kyle Richmond himself). The Crew was defeated by the Defenders and dispersed to different prisons.

After regaining his crowbar, the Wrecker freed his allies and they decided to publicly defeat Thor in order to salvage their reputations. When they encountered Iron Fist and threatened his girlfriend Misty Knight, Iron Fist offered to gain them access to Avengers Mansion in order to save her. The Wrecking Crew invaded the mansion, finding only Captain America present; but he and Iron Fist managed to outfight the Wrecking Crew, and they were all sent back to prison. From his cell at Ryker's, the Wrecker concentrated upon his crowbar's power and used it to compel a guard to release him. He and the Wrecking Crew finally had their first shot at Thor as a team, but Thor bested them all, and only Thunderball escaped. Thunderball acted on his own for a while, battling Iron Man (James Rhodes), and later recovering the crowbar for himself and battling Spider-Man, but he was ultimately sent back to Ryker's.

The Wrecking Crew were freed by the Beyonder and transported to "Battleworld" to serve in Dr. Doom's army of super-villains against the heroes gathered there. They proved to be useful thugs for Doom's purposes, but they finally abandoned him after he gained the Beyonder's power, returning to Earth with the aid of the Molecule Man. The entire Wrecking Crew then joined Helmut Zemo's Masters of Evil and helped provide intelligence on Hercules, uncovering the Avenger's drinking problem. The Wrecking Crew joined with Goliath (Erik Josten) and Mr. Hyde in a savage assault on Hercules at Avengers Mansion that left him comatose. When Thor came to avenge his comrade, he used the power of his hammer to transfer all of the Wrecking Crew's

PILEDRIVER   THUNDERBALL   WRECKER   BULLDOZER

energies into the crowbar, and the Wrecker himself was beaten in combat by Captain America.

The Wrecker soon escaped prison and freed the Crew, and they continued to use Zemo's remaining resources while they prepared to regain their powers. Thunderball began rebuilding the Gamma Bomb in the hopes of another blackmail attempt, but his one-time use of the crowbar had left him craving its power, and he ultimately turned on the Wrecker, wanting all the power for himself. Faced with the combined powers of Spider-Man and Spider-Woman (Julia Carpenter), the divided Wrecking Crew fell. Some of the Wrecking Crew participated in the so-called "Acts of Vengeance" as Thunderball fought the Fantastic Four, the Wrecker fought Iron Man, and the entire Crew fought Damage Control, who were secretly aided by Thunderball (who was friends with Damage Control's John Porter). The Wrecker continued to resent Thunderball's attempts at claiming his power and mantle of leadership, and began to hunt the now-powerless Franklin. The Wrecker tracked Franklin to his Yancy Street safehouse, but encountered the Thing there and was beaten. The entire Crew were imprisoned at the Vault for a time, participating in an uprising when Venom staged a breakout. Thunderball opposed even Venom's leadership, and led a splinter team of escapees against the Avengers when they tried to lockdown the facility, but he finally sided with the Avengers to help stop a core breach in the Vault.

Finally escaping the Vault, the Wrecker and Thunderball were forced to establish a working relationship, but could never entirely trust one another again. The Crew faced Hercules again, and battling them helped Hercules overcome the fear of combat he had suffered since his beating at their hands. They fought the NYPD's special task force Code: Blue while holding a hostage, and lost their hostage to the police squad. Ultimately, Loki decided that he wanted the power of the Wrecker for himself, since it had been meant for him, and while the Crew were battling Thor and the Ghost Rider (Daniel Ketch), he had the Enchantress and Ulik bring down each member of the Crew, until only the Wrecker remained. Loki proceeded to torture the Wrecker, and finally cast him into another dimension.

Deprived of the Wrecker's power, Thunderball worked with the Secret Empire, and was outfitted with armor which mimicked some of his magical abilities. They attempted to harness the powers of Nova, but were opposed by the combined forces of Spider-Man, Moon Knight, Darkhawk, Night Thrasher and the Punisher, and ultimately surrendered to them. The Wrecker finally returned to Earth and was reunited with the Crew, but their powers began fading when many of Asgard's links to Earth were separated after Odin attempted to evade Ragnarok, and they were defeated by Code: Blue. They were then hired by Arnim Zola to battle the Thunderbolts (unaware that the Thunderbolts included many of their former allies in the Masters of Evil), receiving an artificial power boost from him, but the Thunderbolts defeated the Crew.

Defeated again by Spider-Man, the Sub-Mariner and the Thing, the Crew were next hired by the Doomsday Man to locate Warbird (Carol Danvers), and they decided to start robbing banks to bring her out. They wound up battling the Avengers, and were accidentally sent to Polemachus by the Scarlet Witch. In Polemachus, they set out to defeat Arkon and Thundra so that they could rule that dimension and claim its energies to repower themselves, but the Avengers followed them there and defeated them. The Crew battled Thor and the Warriors Three next, and Thunderball nearly killed Hogun the Grim. Thor caught up to the Crew and beat them all. After this, the Crew were shuffled to several prisons, including the Cage, Seagate and the Big House, making escapes along the way to battle the Fantastic Four. They were also made pawns by the sorceress Morgan Le Fay, who replaced Thunderball with her magical agent the Knight in disguise, all as part of her plan to claim the enchanted arrows of Hawkeye; but the Crew were defeated by the Avengers and Kelsey Leigh, who was resurrected as the new Captain Britain after the Knight slew her.

Piledriver decided that the Wrecking Crew should be preparing for their later years by training a new generation into the Crew, and brought his teenage son Ricky onboard as Excavator. Learning that the Pride, one-time criminal masterminds of Los Angeles had apparently been slain, the Crew decided to hit banks there now that the Pride were no longer in control, and because of the smaller super-hero population. However, Excavator's presence had drawn the attention of the Pride's children, who came to return him to his grandparents. They beat the entire 5-man Wrecking Crew in battle, and left them for the police.

The Wrecking Crew were sent to the Raft, but escaped during the mass breakout. The Wrecker and Piledriver set out to find the Wrecker's "spare" crowbar which he had hidden in the Museum of Modern Art, and to steal from the paintings there. However, they were defeated by Toxin. The Wrecker managed to get away again, but was recaptured by the new team of Avengers which had formed in the aftermath of the Raft breakout. The other members of the Wrecking Crew are still at large.

Bulldozer / Excavator / Piledriver / Thunderball / Wrecker
Height: 6'4" / 5'4" / 6'4" / 6'6" / 6'3"
Weight: 325 lbs. / 180 lbs. / 310 lbs. / 350 lbs. / 320 lbs.
Eyes: Brown / Blue / Blue / Brown / Blue
Hair: Black / Blond / Blond / Black / Brown

Abilities: Each member of the Wrecking Crew possesses superhuman strength (lifting from 10-40 tons), stamina and durability, portioned out roughly evenly between them. The Wrecker (or whoever wields his crowbar) possesses greater powers when not sharing with the others. The crowbar also allows the wielder to teleport, fire energy blasts, and create an energy shield. Thunderball also wields an enchanted wrecking ball, and Excavator uses an enchanted shovel.

USER NOTES:
Spider-Man: Lately it seems a week doesn't go by where at least one of us doesn't tangle with the Crew. They must be racking up the "Frequent Fighter Mileage" on their credit cards...

ZZZAX

History: Zzzax was created when terrorists attacking a Consolidated Edison nuclear power plant caused an explosion, sparking an atomic chain reaction that formed a mass of sentient electrical energy. Incinerating the nearest humans and absorbing their brains' electrical fields, the newborn electrical entity dubbed itself "Zzzax" as an onomatopoeic echo of its body's own crackling energies. Zzzax's destructive killing spree was opposed by the Hulk (Bruce Banner) and Hawkeye (Clint Barton), who managed to dissipate Zzzax by firing a conductive cable through the creature into the East River. Months later, Soul Star Research scientists Alexandria Knox, Stan Landers and Mark Revel accidentally re-created Zzzax, who absorbed Landers. Influenced by Stan's affection for Alexandria, Zzzax abducted Knox and fought the Hulk again until Revel dispersed Zzzax using a copper wire and a lightning storm. Rematerializing during a meltdown in a new Illinois Edison breeder reactor, Zzzax abducted Knox again, preparing a molecular transformer in hopes of converting her into an electrical being like itself. Knox's recent acquaintance Power Man (Luke Cage) opposed this, and their battle blew up the transformer, dissipating Zzzax again. Reintegrating its energies in a Soul Star Research power generator sold to Bruce Banner's Northwind Obsveratory, Zzzax fought a then-intelligent Hulk, who transmitted Zzzax into outer space. Returning with the aid of the super-criminal Graviton, Zzzax fought the Avengers alongside Graviton's other new allies, Half-Life and Quantum; but Hawkeye and Wonder Man used a busted water main and yet another conductive cable to ground Zzzax, disrupting its energies.

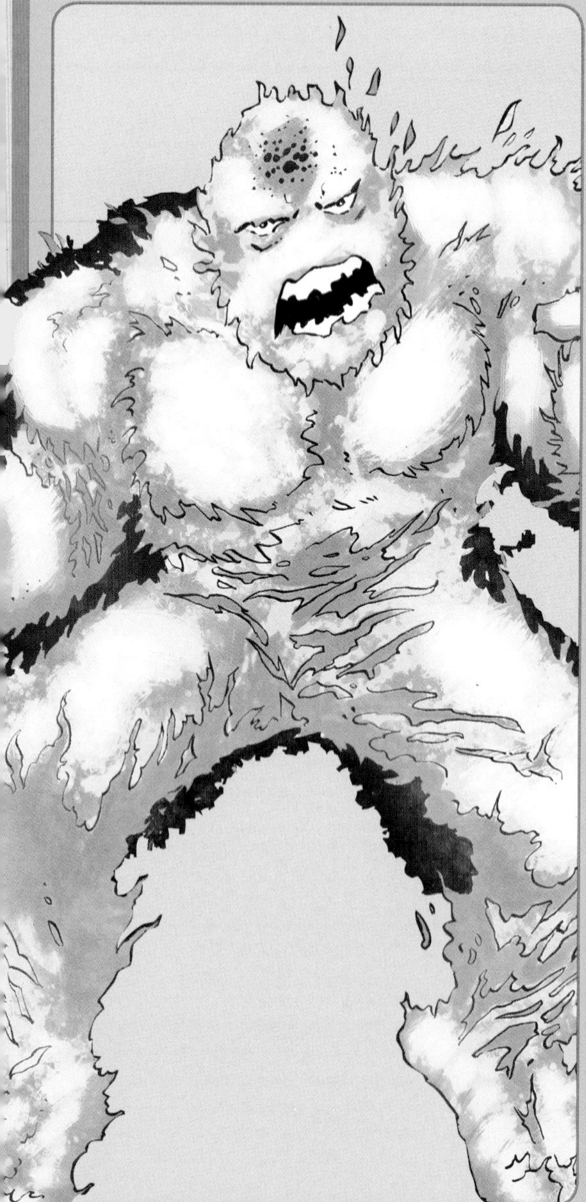

Trapped by S.H.I.E.L.D. in an insulated vacuum tube, Zzzax was subjected to an experiment which tried to replicate its powers in a voluntary human test subject, the Hulk's longtime foe General Ross; but the experiment went awry and Zzzax absorbed Ross's mind. Ross's human body fell comatose, but Ross's consciousness actually took full control of Zzzax, battling both the Hulk and Rick Jones (who had briefly assumed a Hulk-like form). When the Hulk forced Ross to see he had become the same sort of monster he always hated, Ross returned to his human body, which retained limited electrical powers for a time. Ross seemingly sacrificed his life using these powers to stop the mutant menace Nevermind, but would later be revived by the Leader (Samuel Sterns) and Soul Man. Free of Ross, Zzzax next emerged from an experimental static electricity power collector invented by Tony Stark, but Stark short-circuited Zzzax as Iron Man. Deliberately restored by the electrical mutant criminal Paralyzer (Randall Darby), Zzzax found itself under combined attack by Spider-Man; many of the Midnight Sons; and freakish, mystically transformed vigilante Spider-Man imitator Spider-X. Zzzax was overloaded and dispersed during the battle, Spider-X was killed, and Paralyzer was captured. S.H.I.E.L.D. later reactivated Zzzax to use against the mutant soldier Cable, whose psionic powers were uniquely vulnerable to the creature, but Cable shorted out Zzzax using a water main. Placed back in containment by S.H.I.E.L.D., Zzzax was stored at the Raft super-prison but escaped during Electro's mass breakout.

Height: 40' (maximum)
Weight: Negligible
Eyes: Variable
Hair: None

Abilities: Zzzax is a sentient electrical field possessed of superhuman strength and durability and rudimentary intelligence (sometimes temporarily enhanced or altered by absorbing the electrical impulses of human brains, though a sufficiently powerful human consciousness can influence or even dominate Zzzax's actions after absorption). Zzzax sustains itself by feeding on or outright absorbing other electrical fields. Zzzax can hover or fly at will, fire electrical blasts, and generate hundreds of thousands of volts of electricity.

USER NOTES:
Spider-Man: *Monsters like Zzzax make me glad I grew up a science nerd — as long as you've got the materials at hand to short-circuit him or ground him or whatever, he goes down pretty easy. Of course, he can do plenty of damage in the meantime...*

Luke Cage: *Come to snap-crackle-poppa! I'd half-convinced myself I imagined this ugly mother (kind of like Mister Fish, only the smell he left on my costume convinced me I didn't dream that one up, either).*

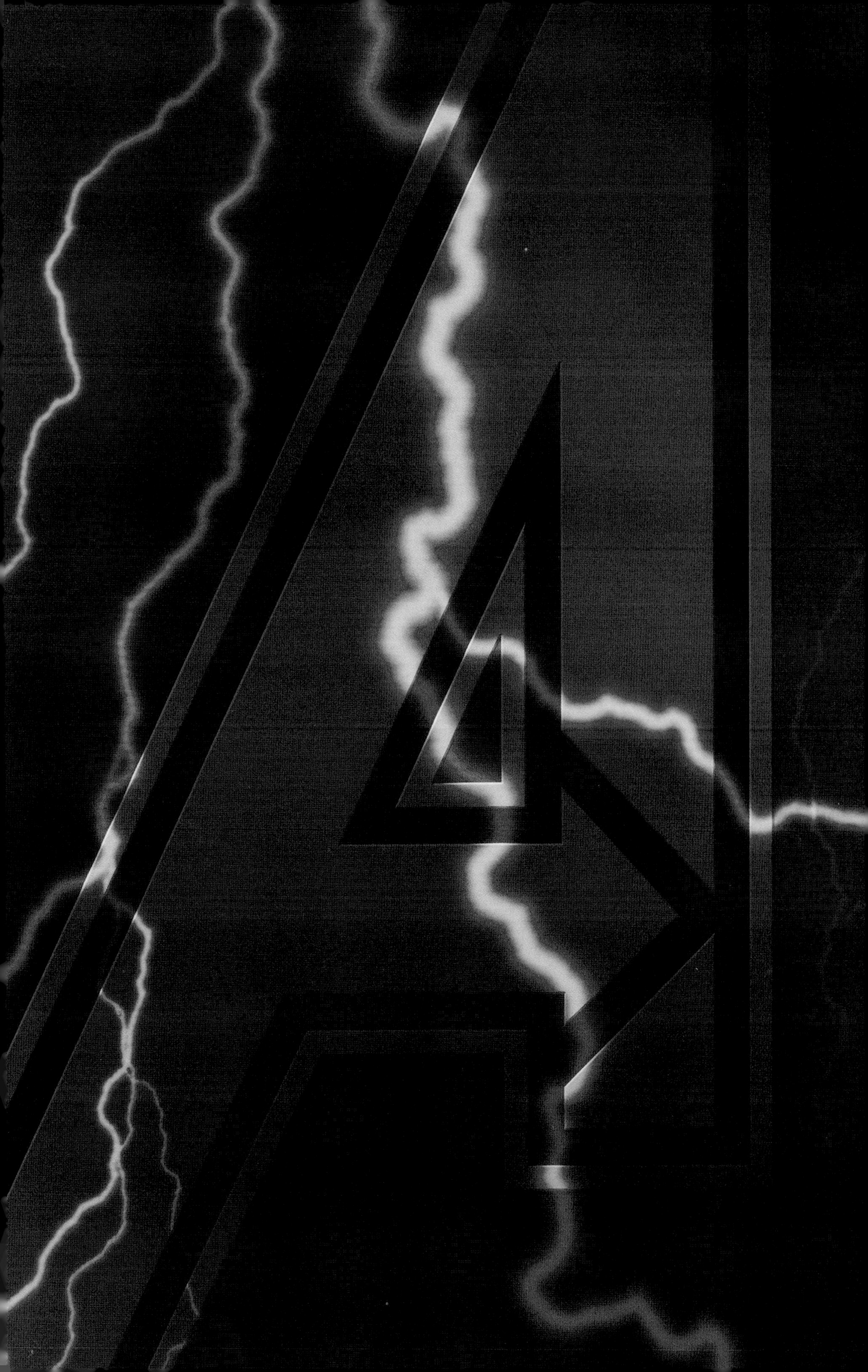

NEW AVENGERS
ISSUE #1 SCRIPT

BY BRIAN MICHAEL BENDIS
PENCILS BY DAVID FINCH

PAGE 1-

1- Int. Backroom- night

Electro sits at a table, lit by a single lamp from above, shadow everywhere. We imagine he is sitting in the back office of some factory somewhere. Hidden away, private.

The table is small, round, and we can't see what is on it.

Electro is talking to a stranger sitting across from him. The stranger, even though he sits at the table, is totally immersed in shadows.

Electro has his costume on under a leather jacket and his mask is on the table, but not in view. We can't see his costume clearly yet, just hints of it.

He is nervous and desperate, but trying not to show it. The lighting, ironically, isn't helping. We imagine he needs this gig badly. It's a lot of money and he doesn't want to blow it.

VOICE:

The deal is acceptable?

ELECTRO:

It's still kind of vague.

VOICE:

But the money-

ELECTRO:

I'm talking about the plan. The plan is vague to me.

2- From over Electro's shoulder, looking mid wide into this dark back room. We see that we cannot see who Electro is talking to.

There is a high, barred window in the distance showing the hazy sun outside, but that's all.

VOICE:

The plan is up to you.

We don't care how you do it.

You're a talented man and we wouldn't be so arrogant as to tell you how to do what you do.

But you'll need to create a distraction so complete-

That the authorities won't even know what has actually happened until it is long past.

3- Tight on Electro. He is looking at the plans down on the table. We can't see what he sees.

VOICE:

We need the trail cold... before they even figure out where the trail is.

ELECTRO:

It's more than I've ever tried. And the target-

VOICE:

We have faith.

ELECTRO:

And if I %@#&* it up, you don't have to pay me the other half.

4- Same as 2.

VOICE:

There's that too.

ELECTRO:

When would you like this done?

VOICE:

Our intelligence says that the Fantastic Four are out of the country and the X-Men are preoccupied.

The Avengers called it quits.

We believe the time is now.

5- Electro's head sparks a little on his head. He is powering up. Just a little- for show. He is deciding to do it. He cocks an eyebrow. He is ready.

ELECTRO:

Costume or no costume?

VOICE:

That is completely up to you.

wider shot of Electro. Table and torso up of Electro. He powers up. A sincere, confident look on his face.

It's Electro!! Electro is back, baby!! in costume. The same one used in MK Spider-Man. It's a damn nice design.

He is just about to pick his mask off the table. The papers and file on the table describing a target and plan that we still can't see.

ELECTRO:

Costume.

PAGE 3-

RECAP AND CREDIT PAGE.

Earth's Mightiest Heroes united against a common threat! On that day The Avengers were born - to fight foes that no single hero could withstand!

PREVIOUSLY IN THE AVENGERS...

It is the worst day in Avengers' history. The Scarlet Witch had a total nervous breakdown after losing control of her reality-altering powers.

In the chaos created around the breakdown beloved Avengers Hawkeye, Ant-Man, The Vision lost their lives.

Many of the other Avengers were hurt, emotionally or physically. Without funding to keep going, the rest of the team quietly disbanded.

That was six months ago.

PAGE 4-

- Ext. Ryker's Island- day

A helicopter's p.o.v. A dreary establishing shot of this famous jail. The Rock of the Marvel Universe.

See Daredevil 38 for a nice establishing shot reference of it. It's a grey day. The sky is blood red at dusk. The sun setting.

Caption: Ryker's Island Maximum Security Penitentiary

2- Same, but shifting to the right, revealing THE RAFT, a smaller man-made island a mile out. It's another more high-tech prison.

The Raft. It's a small island a mile off of Ryker's Island. And the location for the first two issues so give it all you got.

Caption: The Raft, Ryker's maximum, maximum security installation.

- Same but tighter. A military helicopter flying into the shot from the left, going right for The Raft island.

4- Int. Ryker's Island's the raft- day

The helicopter lands on a typical, albeit highly guarded, heliport.

A dozen armed S.H.I.E.L.D. agents and guards, guns out and aimed at the landing copter, ready for the order to shoot.

The guards surround a calm and cool Jessica Drew. Her back to us as she is watching the helicopter land.

Manhattan miles away in the hazy red distance.

5- Jessica Drew, think exactly actress Jennifer Connelly, is standing here. Cool and calm. She is backed up by three armed guards.

She has an electronic Blackberry-type file in her hand- a high-tech mobile web handheld.

Her hair is blowing in helicopter wind, her sunglasses and black turtleneck and mod jacket. She looks amazing, healthy. In her prime.

She has five security laminates around her neck. One is her

Hair whipping around. Matt is in his usual dapper suit and stylish red sunglasses- blind man's cane.

Luke has his headphones on. He is not the hip hop Cage, but the Alias/ Pulse Cage. A proud black man.

But overall, Cage doesn't like being on a prison one damn bit. He used to be in prison as a prisoner, so this is giving him the lip snarls.

PAGE 5-

1- Mid wide of the landing platform. Matt Murdock shakes Jessica Drew's hand. A friendly meeting. Actually Jessica is taking his hand because he's blind, and shaking it.

Luke seems to be the only one skeeved to be at multiple gunpoint.

Dave- important story note. Jessica Drew aka Spider-Woman has, among her other odd powers, the ability to release a pheromone that makes any person near her attracted to her.

So everyone in the group finds themselves oddly attracted to her, but no one speaks or acts on it. It's just there.

But the one person who is very attracted to her is Matt Murdock. Matt has the super senses and he is very affected by Jessica's pheromones.

And eventually they will become a couple. This is the next big Marvel romance.

JESSICA DREW:

Matthew Murdock, I'm Jessica Drew, it's a great honor to meet you.

MATT MURDOCK:

Spider-Woman.

JESSICA DREW:

The first and best.

MATT MURDOCK:

Thank you for helping arrange this.

JESSICA DREW:

I didn't, you did.

You have some powerful friends. They don't let civilians on this facility anymore.

MATT MURDOCK:

Jessica, I'd like you to meet my associate, Luke Cage.

2- Jessica shakes Luke's hand and pats his arm in a friendly way.

She likes Luke- they have had adventures together. Luke is sneering at the guards and guns pointed at him from every direction.

JESSICA DREW:

We've met. You look great.

LUKE CAGE:

They gonna point those things at us all day?

JESSICA DREW:

S.H.I.E.L.D. Policy. You're just going to have to suck

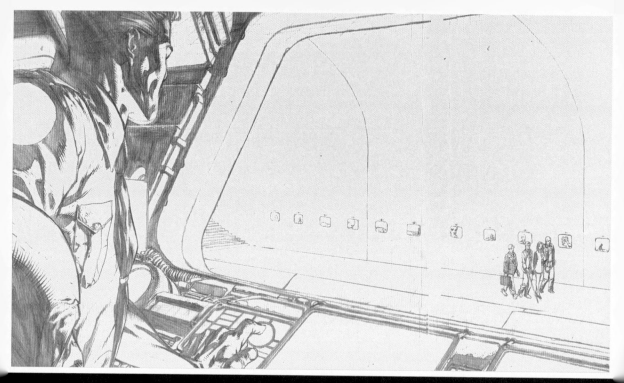

MATT MURDOCK:

And I'd like you to meet my law partner, Foggy Nel... son...

3- Wide of the platform. Matt, Jessica and Luke look around. Where is he? Foggy isn't there.

4- Inside the copter looking out. Matt, Jessica and Luke poke their heads back in to see...

5- Foggy is still in the helicopter, holding on for dear life. A pathological fear of flying.

He is having a full anxiety attack and he doesn't care who sees it.

6- Similar to 4. Matt smirks and holds out his hand to help his longtime friend.

MATT MURDOCK:

Foggy, we landed.

JESSICA DREW:

Let me take you through security and ID check and then we'll go down to meet him.

PAGE 6- 7

Double page spread

1- Int. The Raft- Same.

Big panel. Across both pages.

Establishing shot of the most high-tech and serious prison installation in the country. All white, all sterile.

See Alias 26 for reference. But you can build on it. Give it everything.

High ceilings. No doors. Just huge video monitors where windows would be. We're looking at huge images of the villains being broadcast live.

On each monitor we see the sleeping or bored face of the out of costume super-villain that Jessica mentions. There is a guard station at the end of every corner of this huge hallway like corridor.

Tiny figures of Jessica, Matt, Foggy, and Luke walking down a small set of stairs into the sterile corridor. Five security laminates around

Jessica is reading from her digital files and waving to a nearby S.H.I.E.L.D. Agent.

Behind them we see the security guards are staying in their station but keep their eyes on these visitors. They don't get many visitors.

MATT MURDOCK:

How <u>many</u> are down here?

JESSICA DREW:

Eight levels of them.

FOGGY NELSON:

Jeez!

JESSICA DREW:

Let's see... they got Bushwacker, Carnage, Crossbones, Jigsaw-

FOGGY NELSON:

Great!

JESSICA DREW:

Tiger Shark, Vermin, Scarecrow, Mister Hyde, Purple Man, The whole damn Wrecking Crew...

2- Luke stops her with a shoulder tap. She stops reading and looks up to him. They have stopped right in the middle of this all-white jail.

JESSICA DREW:

The U-foes, whoever they-

LUKE CAGE:

Purple Man is here?

JESSICA DREW:

Right over there. You know him?

er Luke's shoulder, Luke looks at the monitor, the purple man there glazed. His purple skin in direct contrast to his orange n jumpsuit.

ke squints, this man has done a lot of damage in he and Jessica s' life. Jessica, Matt and Foggy look at each other, not sure what ing on.

KE CAGE:

Can he see us?

SSICA DREW:

Yeah.

ke glares at him/ us with fiery hate. Luke and Jessica Jones a deep dark history with him.

e Purple Man stares back with glazed over eyes, head hanging n. His eyes glassy straight ahead. Is he even looking at us?

AGE 8- 9

le page spread

e four walk away from us and towards the round, extremely -tech, well guarded, elevator banks.

is simmering. Jessica and Matt talking casual. Foggy is hugging riefcase and is looking back over his shoulder at all the crazy s on the monitors.

y is acting like he's in a haunted house even though all is calm white and soothing.

SSICA DREW:

He's drugged out of his gourd though.

OGGY NELSON:

And you've got all of these criminals locked up in one place?

You get what I'm saying? All in the same place?

SSICA DREW:

Well, that is what a prison is for.

OGGY NELSON:

I know but-

SSICA DREW:

I'm not exactly thrilled to be hanging out here either.

But no civilian visitor without a superpowered S.H.I.E.L.D. Agent chaperone... and I'm your superpowered S.H.I.E.L.D. Agent chaperone.

he four are at the high-tech elevator. The S.H.I.E.L.D. Guards h Jessica put her palm into the jellypad to read her handprint.

ica is shrugging. This is a pretty boring job really. Foggy is not y. Matt tries to change the subject calmly.

SSICA DREW:

Even super-powered civilians get a super-powered chaperone.

And, I just want to say, Mr.. Murdock, I think it absolutely sucks what the press did to you-

-outting you as Daredevil like that was just-

MATT MURDOCK:

Yes, considering it isn't true.

3- Same. They are waiting for the elevator. Everyone lets Matt be stubborn. His denials are so obviously bull it's almost funny.

4- Same, Foggy pushes past Matt's arrogance and continues his jittery panic attack.

FOGGY NELSON:

What are the- the precautions here? How thick is that glass they got them behind?

JESSICA DREW:

I'm not an expert or anything, but It's not glass, Mr. Nelson. Those were monitors.

Live broadcast of their cells, which is behind a thick steel metal, adamantium-lined cell.

5- Int. Elevator- Same

They all squeeze into a round elevator. Luke barely fits. Jessica being all calm and nice to Foggy's total breakdown.

JESSICA DREW:

I don't know what else they can do to keep all these creeps under wraps.

We're underwater...

An army of highly trained, fully armed S.H.I.E.L.D. Agents...

All of them have been cut off from any and all human contact...

Their powers have been neutralized...

6- Same but tighter, Jessica shrugs at the suggestion, Foggy is looking up at the ceiling as they descend.

LUKE CAGE:

You could take them all out back and shoot them in the head...

JESSICA DREW:

This is America... Everyone has rights.

Even homicidal genetic freaks who hear voices telling them to do whatever it is little voices tell you to do.

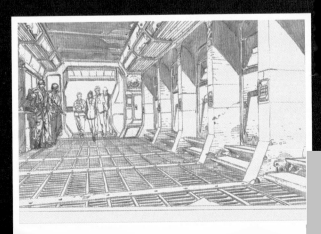

FOGGY NELSON:

I have a little voice that is telling me to run screaming from here.

7- Big panel that makes up all of the background. All the other panels laid on top of it.

The elevator goes down in perspective and away from us. Sliding down to the bottom right on a slant. The elevator is surrounded by black. The entire spread background is black.

Plus, the elevator is sliced in half to show us the four figures riding down, down, down the elevator.

JESSICA DREW:

Come on, you think about it...

This is <u>probably</u> the safest place in New York City.

PAGE 10-

Widescreen panel.

1- Int. The Raft/ lower level- Same

Jessica, Matt, Luke and Foggy get off the elevator. They are on a much danker, dirtier floor.

A bunker, an underwater bunker. This is where they keep the real troublemakers. This is the floor with Carnage, Venom, and all the real trouble.

The light sources are yellow industrial lights lining either side of the long dark hallway. Barely lighting it enough to be a David Fincher film. Heavy shadows down here.

A couple of armed S.H.I.E.L.D. Agents guard the elevator.

LUKE CAGE:

Whend'jou join S.H.I.E.L.D., Jess?

JESSICA DREW:

Couple of years ago. Need the paycheck. Needed some goals.

FOGGY NELSON:

Oh, this isn't <u>too</u> creepy.

JESSICA DREW:

Mr. Nelson, seriously, even if all the billions of dollars of technology all of a sudden malfunctioned...

If all sixty-seven highly trained S.H.I.E.L.D agents, armed agents, fortifying the premises <u>disappeared</u>...

You, sir, <u>still</u> have, not one, but <u>three</u> big-time super heroes standing right next to you.

MATT MURDOCK:

You understand I'm <u>not</u> Dare-

2- Same. Black. The lights go out.

3- Same. Black.

JESSICA DREW:

Oh my god.

FOGGY NELSON:

Is this- are you doing a little shtick here?

4- Same. Black.

FOGGY NELSON:

Wh- what's that noise?

MATT MURDOCK:

It's the generators.

FOGGY NELSON:

What- what are they doing?

MATT MURDOCK:

They're powering down-

5- Same. Black.

JESSICA DREW:

Uh-oh.

PAGE 11-

All widescreen panels.

1- Ext. New York City- dusk

A gorgeous establishing shot of New York at sunset. All the lights are on. The sky pouring from purple to red.

2- Same, but a portion of New York goes dark.

3- Same, but another area of New York goes dark.

4- Same, but another area of New York goes dark. All dark. The power of all of Manhattan has been sucked out.

PAGE 12-

Full page spread

Ext. The Raft- Same

The far corner of the Raft explodes in wild blue Electro electricity. One corner of it is a concentrated spiral of barely contained electrical power.

Electro is breaking into The Raft and using all the power of Manhattan and The Raft to do it.

It is an amazing spectacle that only later will the audience get a complete sense of.

PAGE 13-

1- Int. Parker apartment/ living room- dusk

Peter and MJ are in their living room and they are having a fight. Peter is trying to put his foot down and MJ is shocked by his stubbornness.

They are kind of joking, but we can't tell in the first panel.

Both are in sweat pants and casual—home alone clothes. Of course, MJ, being a super model, looks hotter like this than she does all dolled up. Like Jessica Simpson on Newlyweds.

The Spidey costume lying on the side of a chair in the background or foreground. Just tossed over there.

PETER PARKER:

No!!

MARY JANE WATSON PARKER:

Peter Parker!

PETER PARKER:

MJ, No!

I'm putting my foot down, woman! That is it!! No! And no means no!

2- MJ looks like she doesn't even know how she married this man. Peter shrugs and plops on the couch. He is pouting, that bravado before was just kidding around.

MARY JANE WATSON PARKER:

But I-

PETER PARKER:

We have almost <u>no</u> free time together, MJ... you <u>really</u> want to spend it watching a Hugh Grant movie?

3- MJ slides up on the couch, curling up next to him like a frisky cat. He is wincing at his own weakness. He has lost the fight already... and he knows she knows it.

MARY JANE WATSON PARKER:

It's romantic.

PETER PARKER:

I am so weak.

MARY JANE WATSON PARKER:

Tee hee...

PETER PARKER:

You did not just 'tee hee' me.

MARY JANE WATSON PARKER:

It worked.

4- Same panel, but blackout. Only the dim light from the window lights the room. Both MJ and Peter look up and around.

5- From behind Peter, Mary looks past Peter and out the off panel window. She sees it first. Something is wrong. Her face lit by...

PETER PARKER:

Tsk, that's a shame.

MARY JANE WATSON PARKER:

You did that on...

6- From over Peter and MJ's head and shoulders, they have gotten off the couch and look out their apartment window.

Between the awkward view of all the New York buildings is the water and a mile past that is the electrical ejaculation that is going on at The Raft.

Even from miles away you can see it, albeit it looks like a sparkler from this distance, but we can also see that all the other buildings are dark too.

The power is out and the ocean is being electrocuted.

MARY JANE WATSON PARKER:

...purpose.

7- MJ turns to say...

MARY JANE WATSON PARKER:

Honey, you better-

PAGE 14-

1- ext. Manhattan- dusk

Big panel. Sunset. Manhattan. Spider-Man!!! swings away from his apartment building. MJ is at the window a block back.

Spider-man flings his body towards us. A man with a destination. He is more than just swinging- he is throwing his body into the air.

2- ext. New York pier- dusk

Spidey hops onto a pier rooftop. The huge cityscape in blackout behind him as night approaches.

SPIDER-MAN:

OK, got the costume on, webs are up and working and ready to go...

Now how the hell am I supposed to get <u>out</u> there?

4- over Spidey's head and shoulder. From this vantage point Spidey can see the growing electrical fiesta going on at The Raft miles away.

It's just a teeny, tiny sparkle show distance.

SPIDER-MAN:

The webs only work if there's something to web <u>to</u>...

And there be nothing to-

5- Same, a big black helicopter buzzes right over Spidey's head and is aiming right for The Raft miles away.

This isn't a typical helicopter. This is a super slick, high-tech, S.H.I.E.L.D. Helicopter.

SPX: fupfupfupfupfupfupfupfupfup

6- Spidey thrusts a web line up and off panel. He is getting ready to go.

SPIDER-MAN:

Alright...

SPX: thwip

PAGE 15-

1- Ext. Ocean- Same

High looking down. The black ops S.H.I.E.L.D. Helicopter is swooping down and around towards The Raft, which is clearly under some sort of electrical attack.

Spider-Man is swinging from the bottom of the helicopter from a long web strand- coming right at us.. and he isn't doing it very well.

All of Manhattan behind him. a tilted panel clearly this is a daring stunt that looked good on paper.

SPIDER-MAN:

HaAAAAAAAAAAzzahoozy!!

2- Int. Helicopter- Same

Small panel. From inside 'helicopter one' looking out. On the far left we are tight in on the barking mouth of a person we will reveal to be Captain America.

Past him we can see the nervous pilot/S.H.I.E.L.D. Agent turning his copter hard and giving us a view of The Raft out the front window. The Raft which is still alive with electrical energy and coming up soon.

Cap is yelling into his headset. He is ready to go.

S.H.I.E.L.D. AGENT:

Captain, these readings...

CAPTAIN AMERICA:

Don't fly too close, soldier. Just swing in low and I'll hop out.

S.H.I.E.L.D. AGENT:

But sir...

3- ext. Sky- Same

Very wide of skyline, Spider-Man swinging out of control.

The helicopter has taken an abrupt swoop, dodging a stray electric bolt. Sending Spidey swinging out wide.

SPIDER-MAN:

Yikes!!

S.H.I.E.L.D. AGENT:

Captain!!

SPX: krakoom

4- The copter gets hit by an electric bolt and is enveloped by a web of electricity. The blades and all the mechanisms are overloaded and exploding.

SPX: shababoom

5- Int. Helicopter- Same

Small panel. The copter is on fire from the side, instruments exploding and the copter is out of control. Red. Panicked.

S.H.I.E.L.D. AGENT:

Aaggh!

CAPTAIN AMERICA:

Not your fault, soldier!!

Let's go!!

6- Ext. Sky- Same

Spidey lets go of the web before he is electrocuted. He is flying out to the open sea.

Behind him the copter is spinning out of control. Fire is burning. It's going to crash right into the raft.

PAGE 16-

1- Big panel. The copter explodes in mid air as one silhouette figure carrying another leaps from the fireball and towards us.

We still can't see who it is but we got a good idea.

SPX: fraboom

2- Int. Ocean- Same

Spidey plops right into the raging dark waters of the Atlantic Ocean.

3- Ext. The Raft- Same

Big panel. The S.H.I.E.L.D. helicopter crashes right into The Raft. The black copter crashing into the copter that brought Matt Murdock and company.

S.H.I.E.L.D. Agents are running and diving. The electricity is still tickling the other side of The Raft in the background.

SPX: skaboom

4- Ext. Ocean- Same

Spidey's head pops out of the water. He is flailing and gasping and freezing.

SPIDER-MAN:

Glah!

5- Wide of the ocean. Spidey swims through the dark cold water. Flaming bits of helicopter are in the foreground. He is swimming towards The Raft off panel.

SPIDER-MAN:

And here's me, swimming <u>towards</u> the disaster.

Actually, I only c-c-can <u>imagine</u> that's what I'm doing.

B-b-b-because I lost the feeling in my f-f-feet as soon as I hit the ice cold water of the ice c-c-cold Atlantic Ocean.

6- Ext. Raft- Same

Profile, a freezing Spidey climbs the side of The Raft complex as only Spidey can. He is climbing barnacle covered steel and stone.

SPIDER-MAN:

And assuming, of course, I <u>survive</u> whatever goofball cosmic fiesta I'm diving head first into here...

...<u>now</u> I don't have a <u>ride home.</u>

7- Spidey's head pops over the top. Trying to get a look at what is there for him.

SPIDER-MAN:

Oh man...

My spider-sense is buzzing so loud I can barely hear myself talk to myse...

PAGE 17-

1- Huge panel. Low looking up, Big panel. It's Captain America!!

Cap, backlit, sweaty, cheek cut. Shield on. Holds out his other arm to give Spidey a help up.

Three S.H.I.E.L.D. Agents, also backlit, have their guns firmly pointing at us/Spidey.

Fire behind Cap from the two-copter explosion. The electrical storm on the other side is still visible.

2- Wide of the burning platform. Agents are running. Cap and Spidey are up on the platform. The fires burn. The power is out. The agents run.

SPIDER-MAN:

Whoof! Captain America! Thank goodness.

You didn't happen to bring a spare costume, mine is soaking.

CAPTAIN AMERICA:

What's happening here?

SPIDER-MAN:

I give up, what's happening here?

3- Cap is frustrated with Spidey because he thinks Spidey started this. Spidey half holds up his hands in surrender.

Cap barks at Spidey even though he moves in front of him to use his shield for both of them.

CAPTAIN AMERICA:

We don't have time for smartass, this is-

SPIDER-MAN:

<u>Hey!</u> I just got here.

CAPTAIN AMERICA:

Stay behind me.

SPIDER-MAN:

What <u>is</u> this place?

PAGE 18- 19

Double page spread

1- Int. Raft- main prison hall- Same

This is the exact same place Jessica, Matt, Luke and Foggy walked through. But the power is off.

The guards are dead, gone, or stunned. A couple of stunned guards picking themselves up.

The monitor screens are dead. It's all so quiet.

S.H.I.E.L.D. AGENT:

This is Agent Melvey On level B. We have a real situation here.

2- Same. An electrical outburst explodes right in the center of the hall. Electro is transporting into The Raft.

It's like Star Trek transporting but more spectacular.

His electricity is killing the two guards that were left, lifting them off the ground in electronic spasm. Electro is wielding a stunning amount of power.

S.H.I.E.L.D. AGENT:

ANyyaaagghh!!

3- Same. Electro is forming. A perfect entrance.

He took The Raft all by himself. He is the light source of the room. His form is wildly charged up. This is the most amazing thing he has ever done.

4- Electro holds out his hands and turns the electricity on in the hall. Everything lights up. He is like an orchestra conductor.

5- The security station on this floor explodes. Tickled with cascading electricity.

The dead guard lays on the controls and broken monitors and smokes.

SPX: cricklcrazzkkleeboom!

6- The elevator bank explodes in cascading electricity.

SPX: crakoom

7- Wide of the hall. The thick doors all open. Doors we couldn't even see were there because they were all sealed tight without a doorknob or handle.

As Electro pushes and pulls energy back and forth.

8- A thick metal cell door slides open. The door a foot thick. Layered with different metals.

SPX: boom

9- Another thick metal cell door slides open.

SPX: boom

10- Another thick metal cell door slides open.

SPX: boom

11- Another thick metal cell door slides open.

SPX: foom

12- Another thick metal cell door slides open.

SPX: foom

13- Int. Cell- Same

Electro, still the light source of the scene, looks inside a dark cell.

ELECTRO:

Sir, if you're ready to go...

14- Int. Hallway- Same

In the foreground, some silhouette figures have sauntered into the hall.

Electro, still at the door to the cell he needs, stands back up and yells out to the now occupied hallway.

The doors to all the cells are open.

ELECTRO:

And the rest of you, listen up!!

My name is Max Dillon, some of you know me, some of you don't-

But I broke you losers out!!

Have fun, enjoy your lives... but from here on in, now and forever...

You guys owe me huge!!

PAGE 20- 21

Double page spread

All the big-time Marvel villains are out.

All the villains can include the others mentioned, plus...

Deathwatch, Blackout, The Wrecking Crew (Wrecker, Piledriver. Bulldozer and Thunderball), The U-Foes (Vector, Vapor, X-Ray and Ironclad), Razor-Fist, Dr. Demonicus, The Controller, The Corrupter, Crossfire, The Living Laser, Chemistro, Mister Fear, Foolkiller, Cutthroat, Mentallo, The Answer, The Crusader, The Griffin, Mandrill, Molecule Man, Shockwave, Rampage, Count Nefaria, The Armadillo, Barbarus, The Blood Brothers, The Brothers Grimm, Centurius, Typhoid Mary, Slug, Graviton, ZZZAX, The Constrictor, Grey Gargoyle, Nitro, Bushwacker, Crossbones, Jigsaw, Tiger Shark, Vermin, Sca recrow, Mister Hyde, Purple Man.

Purple Man is front and center in the crowd.

Keep Carnage, Mister Hyde, and a couple of the other toughest villains for another scene next issue.

But remember, no costumes or techware, or villain paraphernalia. The ones that can power up, power up. The ones that can't do not. But they fill the hallway and they are all ready to kill someone.

This is the biggest 'oh $#!%' moment in modern comics!!

ELECTRO:

All of you.

PAGE 22-

1- Ext. Lower level- Same

The elevator explodes and the lights explode from what Electro is doing upstairs. All the doors are opening.

Jessica, Matt, Luke, and Foggy knocked to their feet by the explosions above and below.

The S.H.I.E.L.D. Agents scamper.

SPX: boom!

FOGGY NELSON:

Oh my god!

What is going on?

2- All four are on their knees, on the floor, Matt manhandles Foggy to put him behind Luke. Jessica is checking her cell phone, but it is smoking, it's useless.

MATT MURDOCK:

Stay behind Luke, Foggy.

FOGGY NELSON:

You stay behind him, I'm getting the hell out of-

MATT MURDOCK:

He has unbreakable skin, you stay behind him. That's why we hired him.

JESSICA DREW:

Let's find the stairs.

3- Matt grabs Jessica and frantically asks her.

MATT MURDOCK:

No, we don't know what's happening up there.

Jessica, where is he?

JESSICA DREW:

Who?

MATT MURDOCK:

The man we came to see.

4- From behind Matt, Jessica points to a solitary confinement prison down the dank, dark hallway. The heavy metal door is cracked open. The entire room in shadow.

5- From inside the cell looking out, a backlit Matt has taken off his jacket and opens the thick stone door. It takes a lot to pry the door open even a little.

MATT MURDOCK:

Mr. Reynolds, my name is Matthew Murdock.

I was coming here to see you as a favor to Reed Richards.

But it seems that we are in need of your immediate help.

PAGE 23-

1- Int. Cell- Same

Huge panel. Wide of the solitary cell. Just a dirt cell, concrete and dirt. The only light is the dim light from the hall.

Sitting in the corner, in his dirty costume with no mask or cape, sitting in the corner with his legs folded is... THE SENTRY!!

His face half in shadow. He is living in his own hell. He doesn't respond to Matt at all.

2- Matt, Jessica and Luke, backlit, look in the cell. Matt continues to address him with more respect than it would appear he deserves.

JESSICA DREW:

Who is he?

MATT MURDOCK:

That's Robert Reynolds.

He went by the name of The Sentry.

He's, maybe, according to Reed Richards, the most powerful super hero on the planet Earth.

JESSICA DREW:

What- what's he doing here?

3- Same as one, but tighter. Tighter on The Sentry. Head and shoulders.

His face, turned away from us, half dipped in shadow. He is a defeated man. He doesn't look at them or us.

MATT MURDOCK:

He killed his wife.

To be continued...

#1 Cover Pencils by David Finch

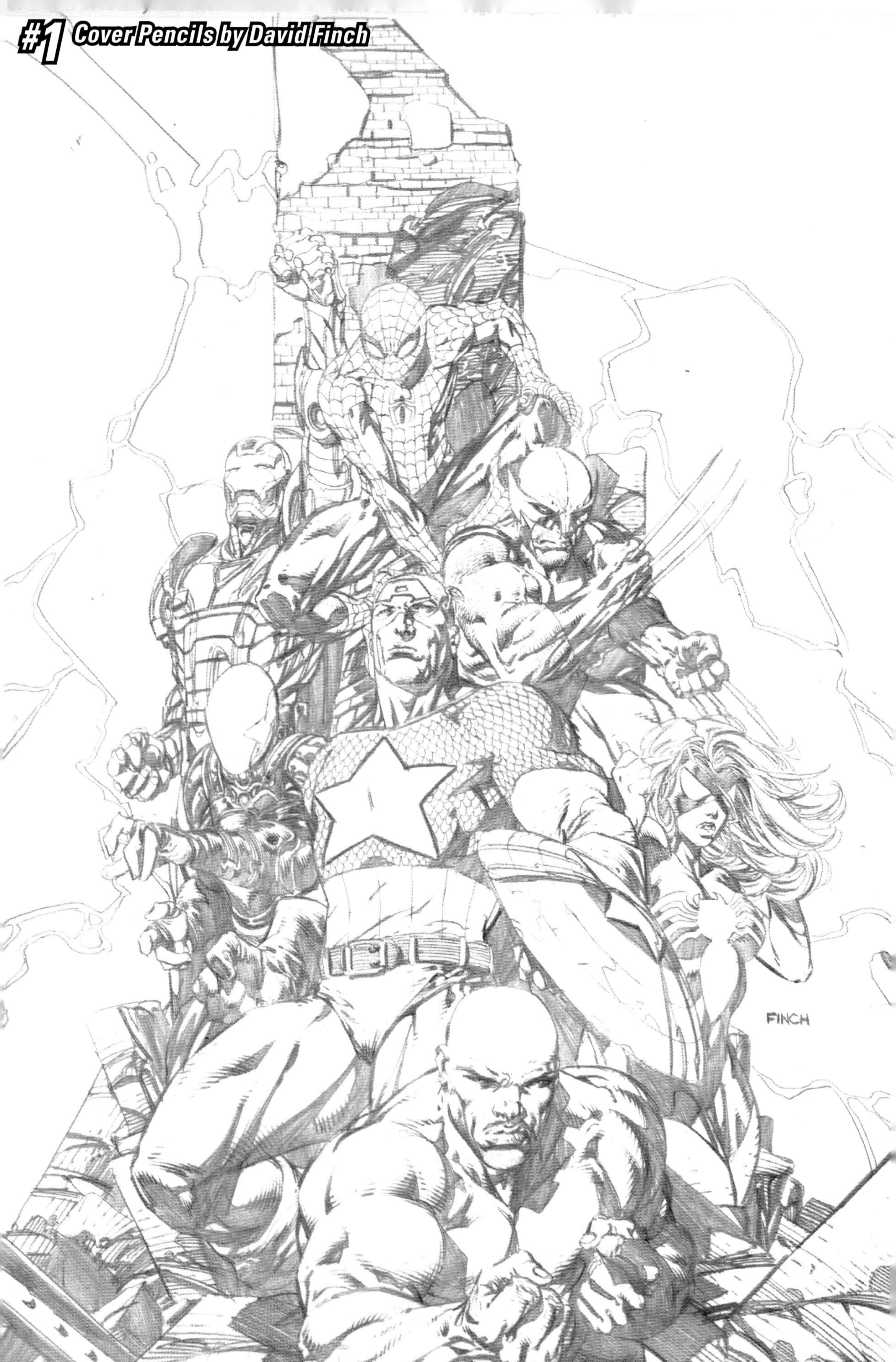
FINCH

#2, Page 18 Pencils by David Finch

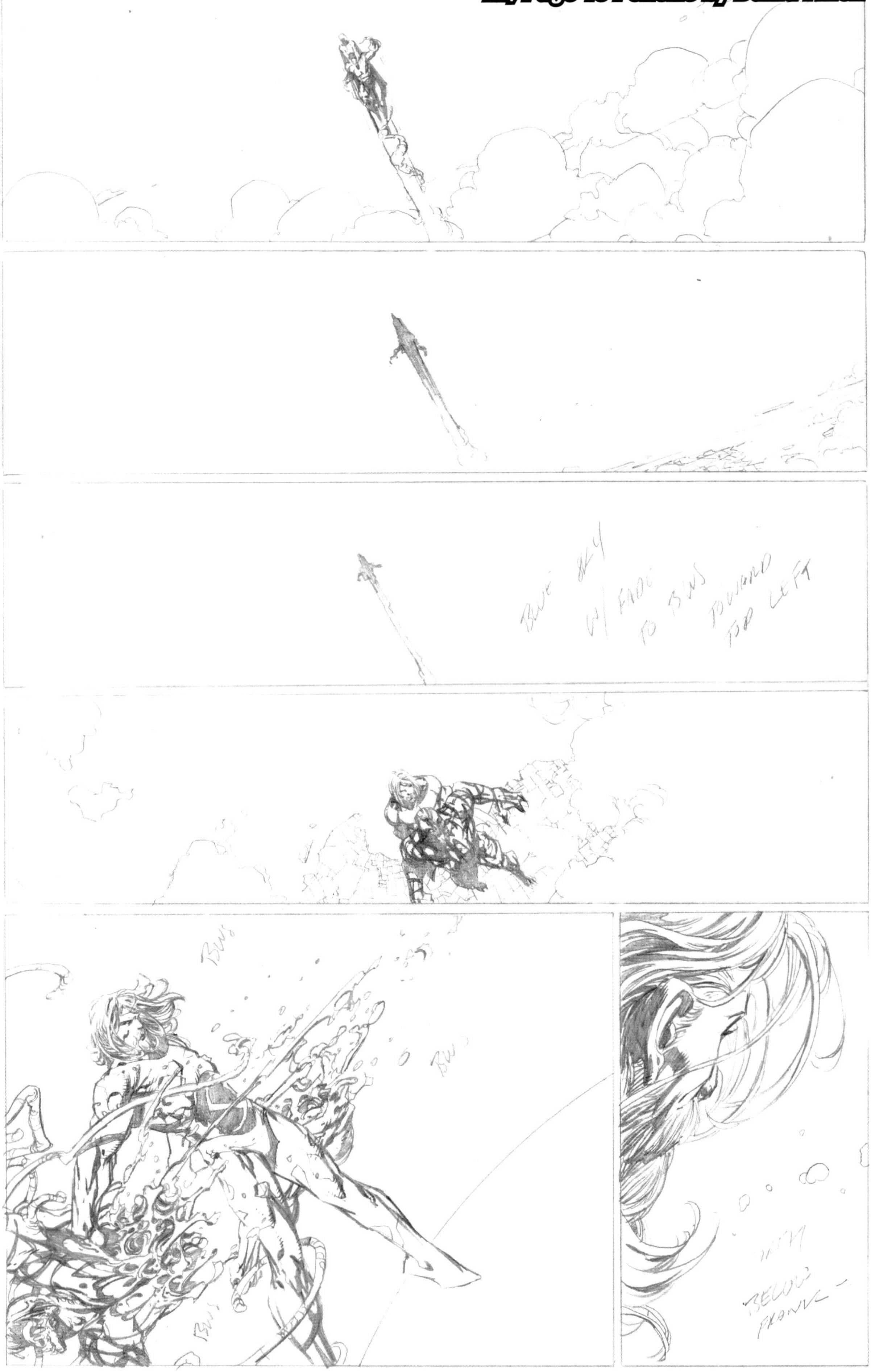

#3, Page 6 Pencils by David Finch

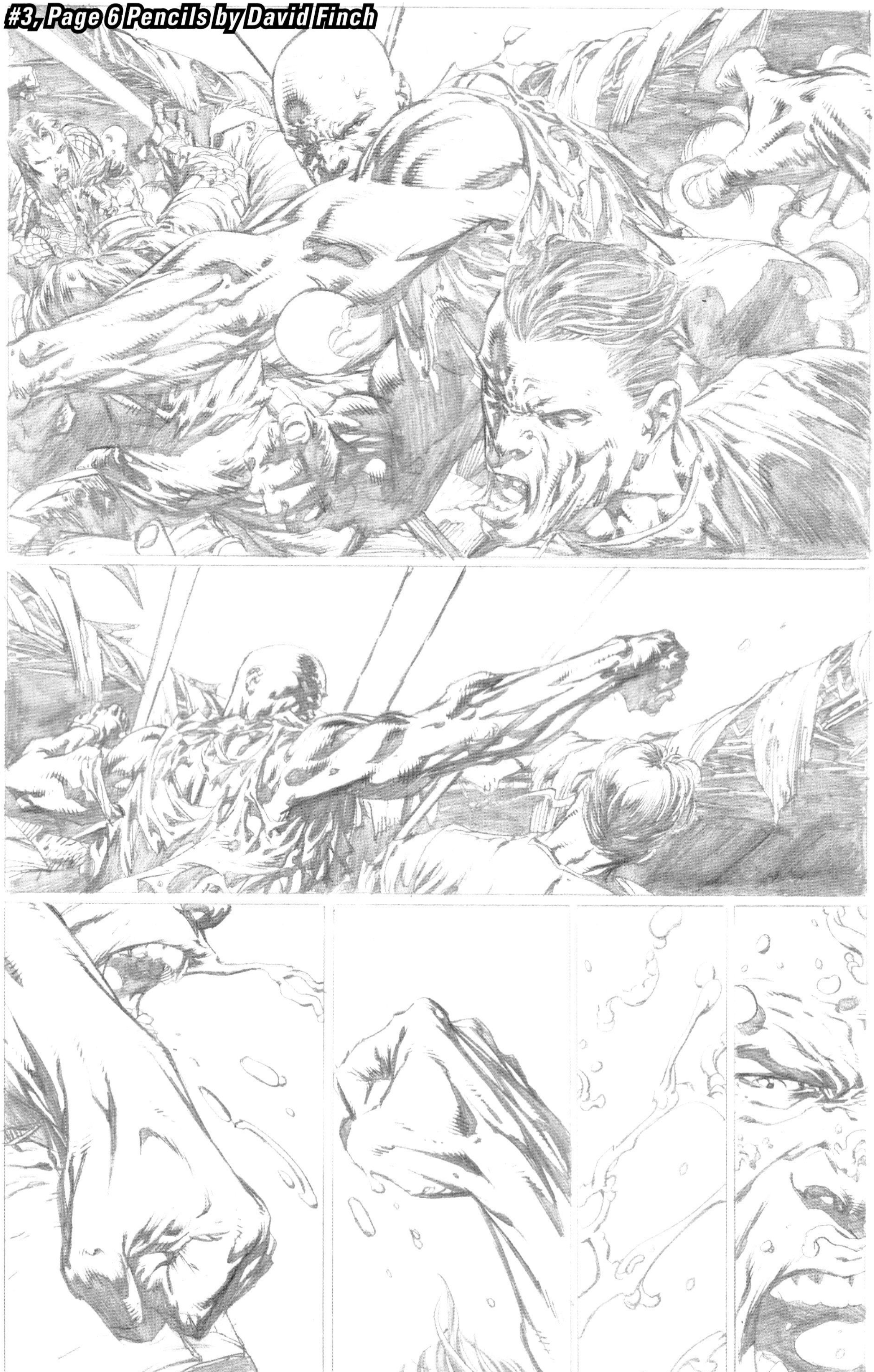

#3, Page 8 Pencils by David Finch

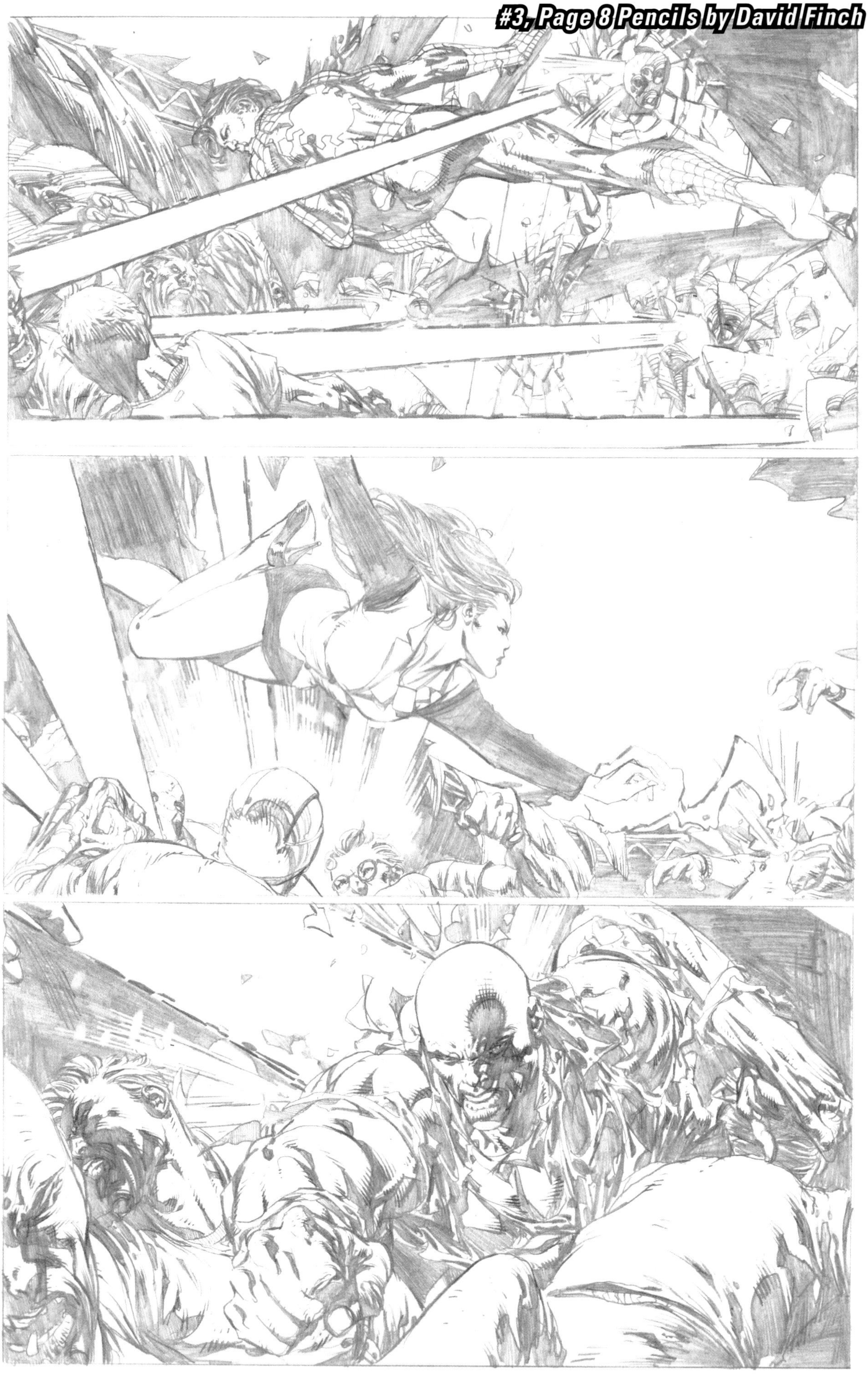

#3, Page 20 Pencils by David Finch

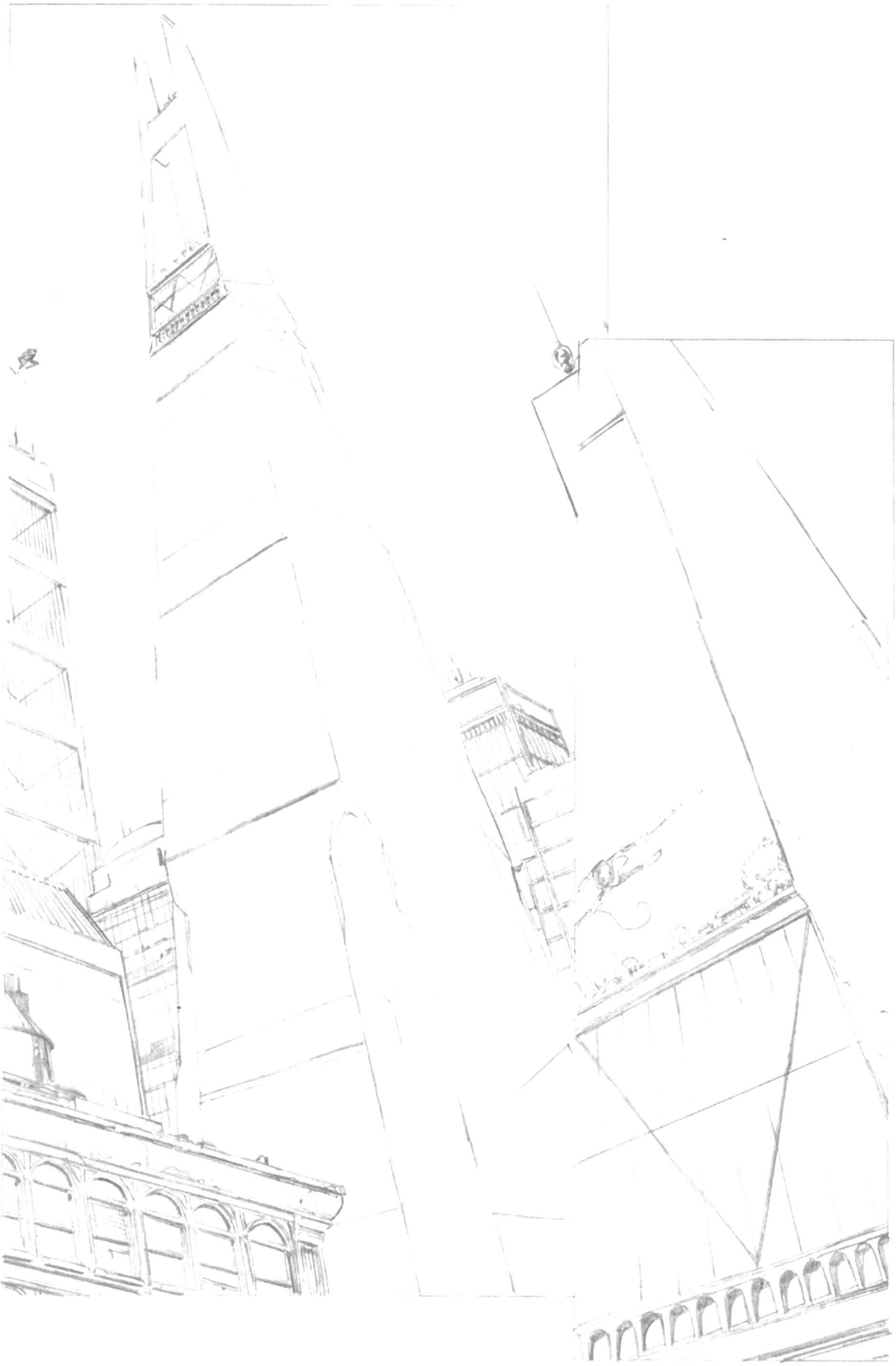

#3, Page 23 Pencils by David Finch

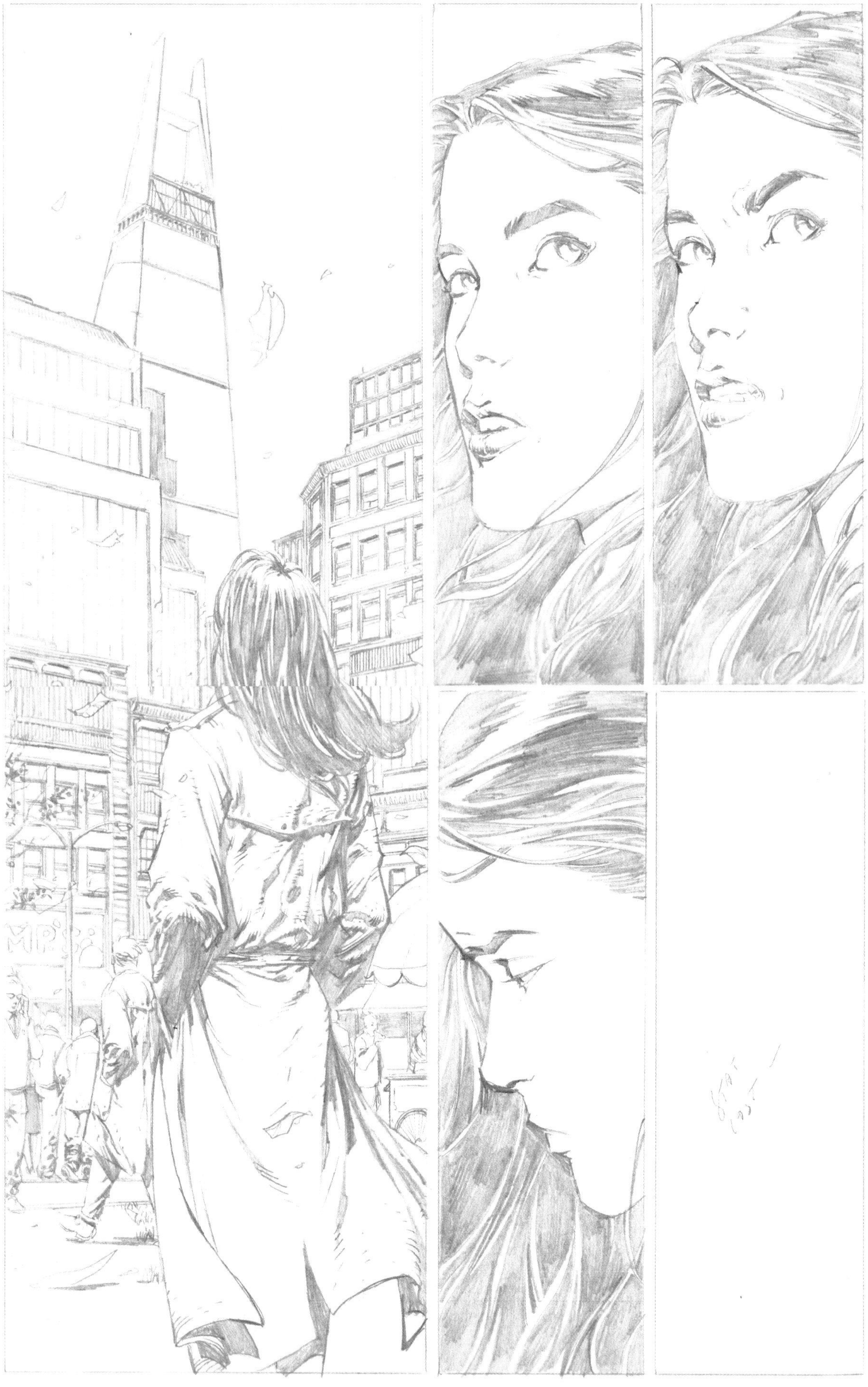

#7, Page 3, Panels 1 & 5 layouts by Steve McNiven

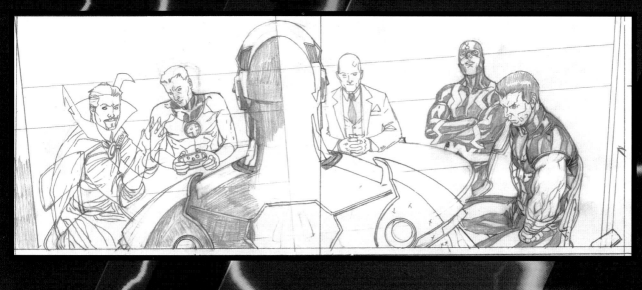

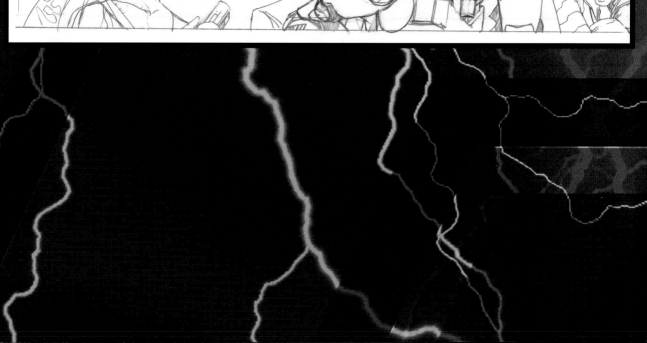

#7, Page 5 , Panel 3 layout by Steve McNiven

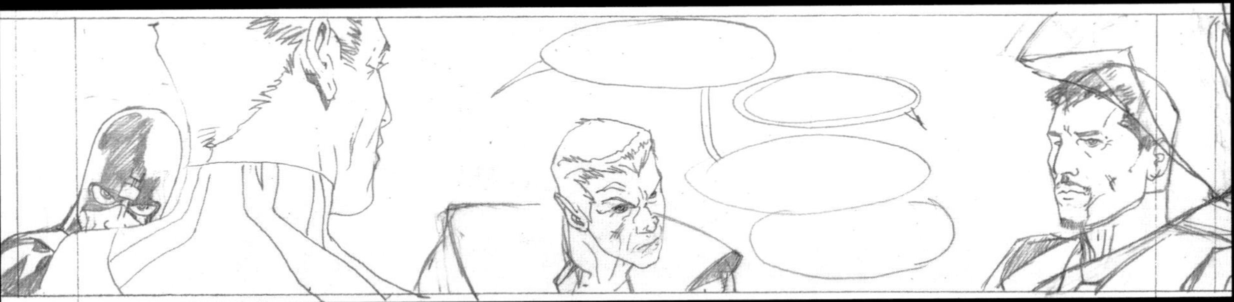

#7, Page 7 , Panel 2 layout by Steve McNiven

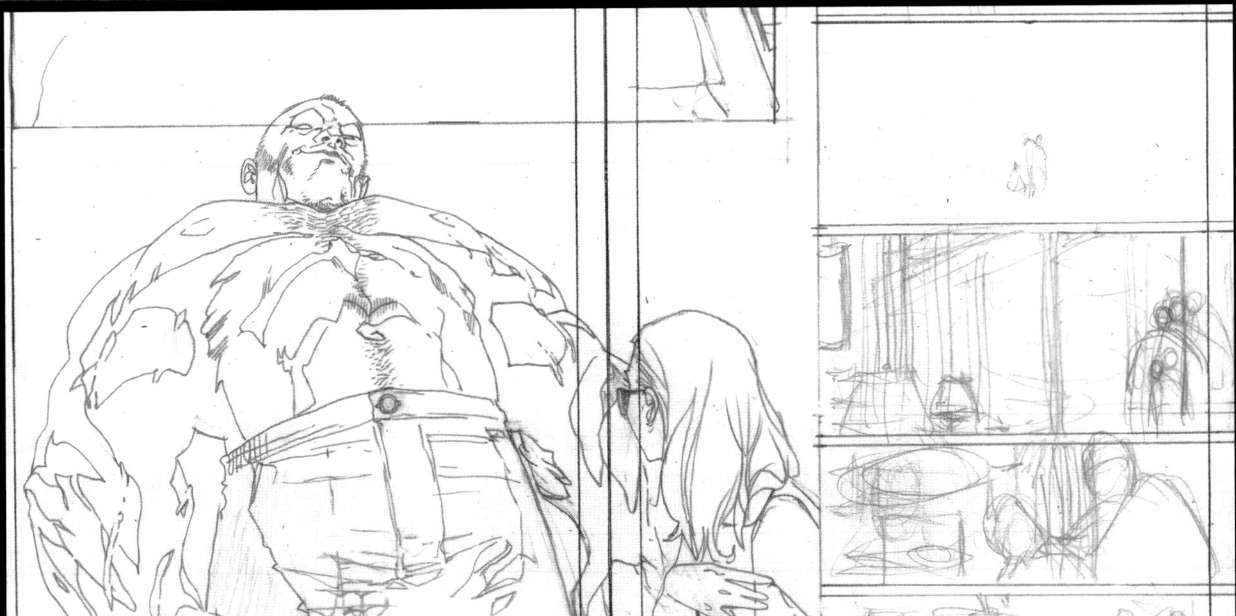

#7, Page 12 , Panel 1 layout by Steve McNiven

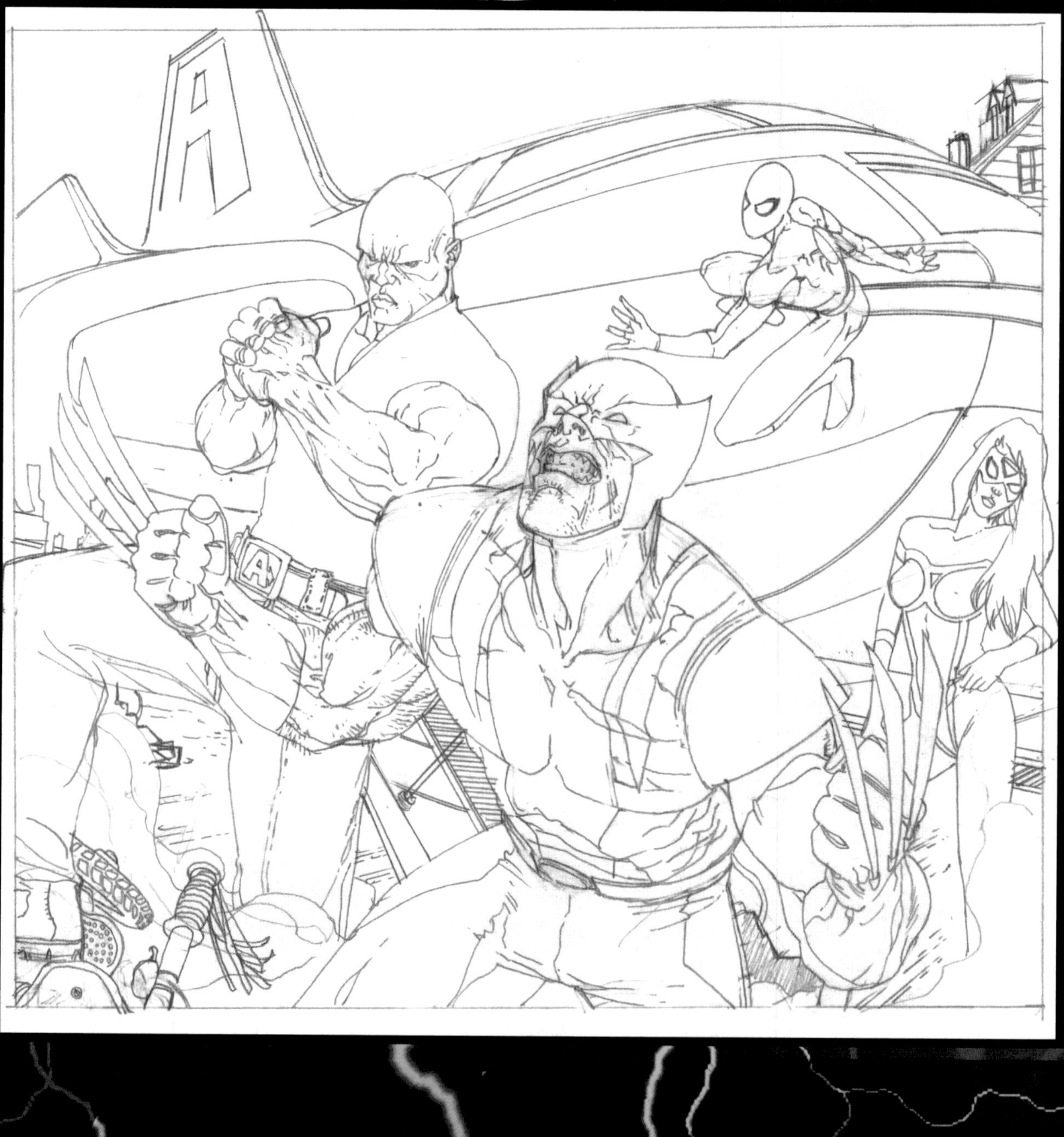

#7, Pages 13-14, Panels 2 & 3 layouts by Steve McNiven

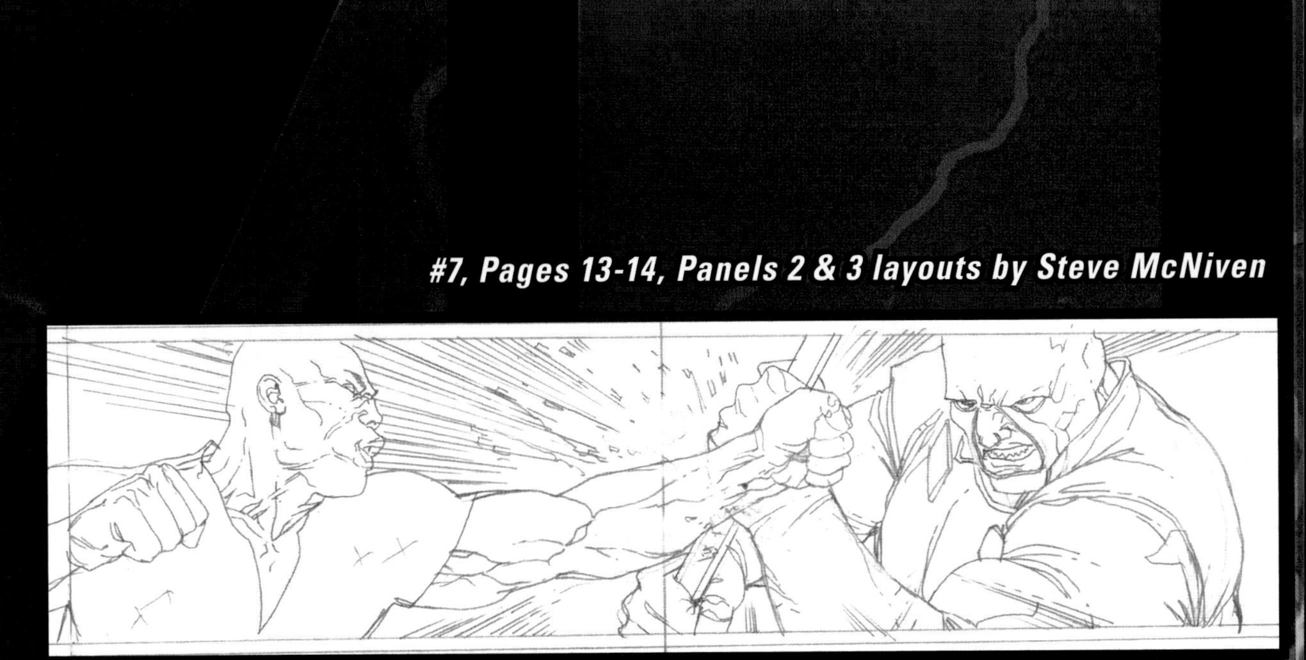

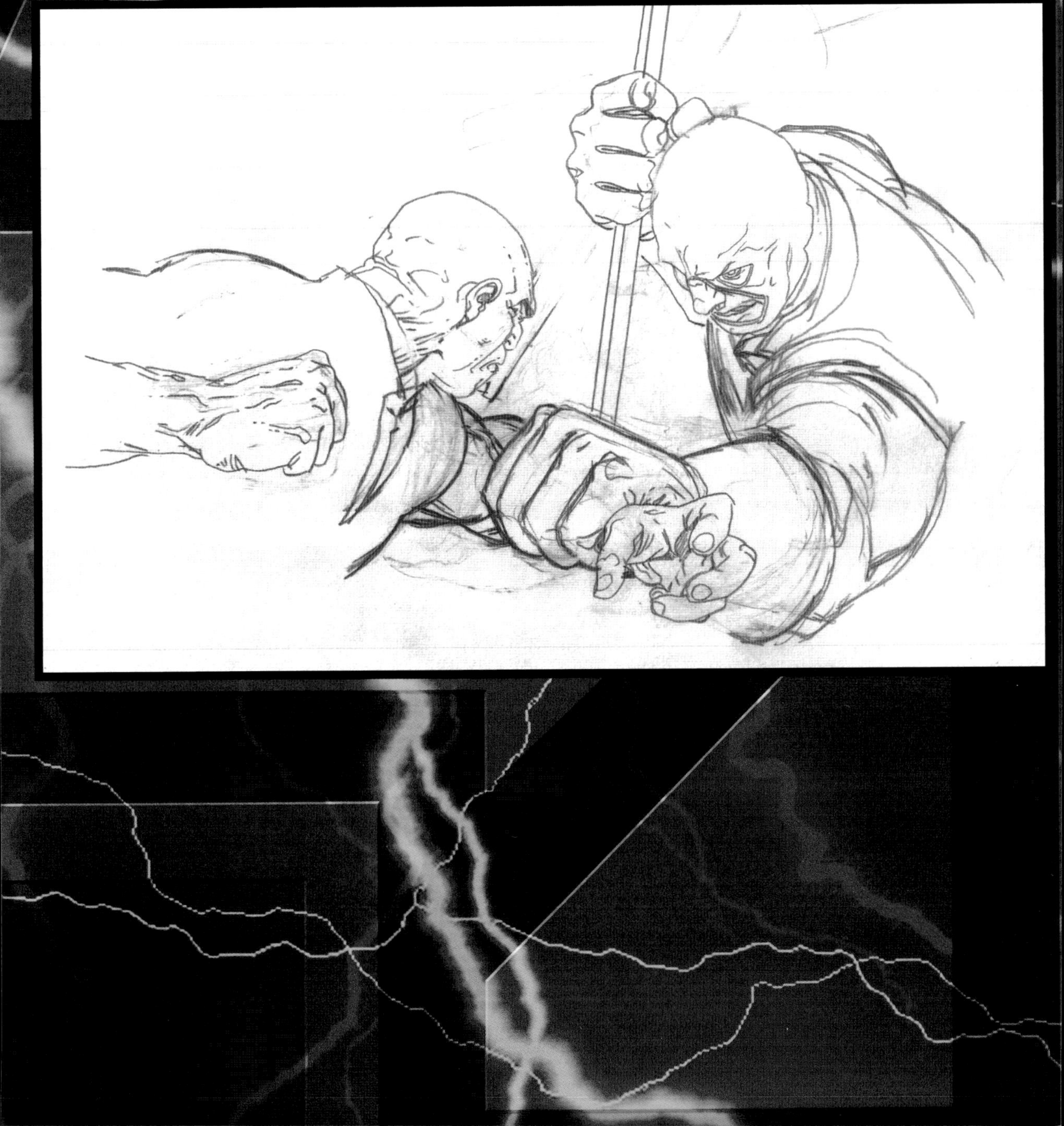

#7, Pages 15, Panel 3 layout by Steve McNiven

#8, Page 6, Panel 2 layout by Steve McNiven

#8, Page 17, Panel 1 layout by Steve McNiven

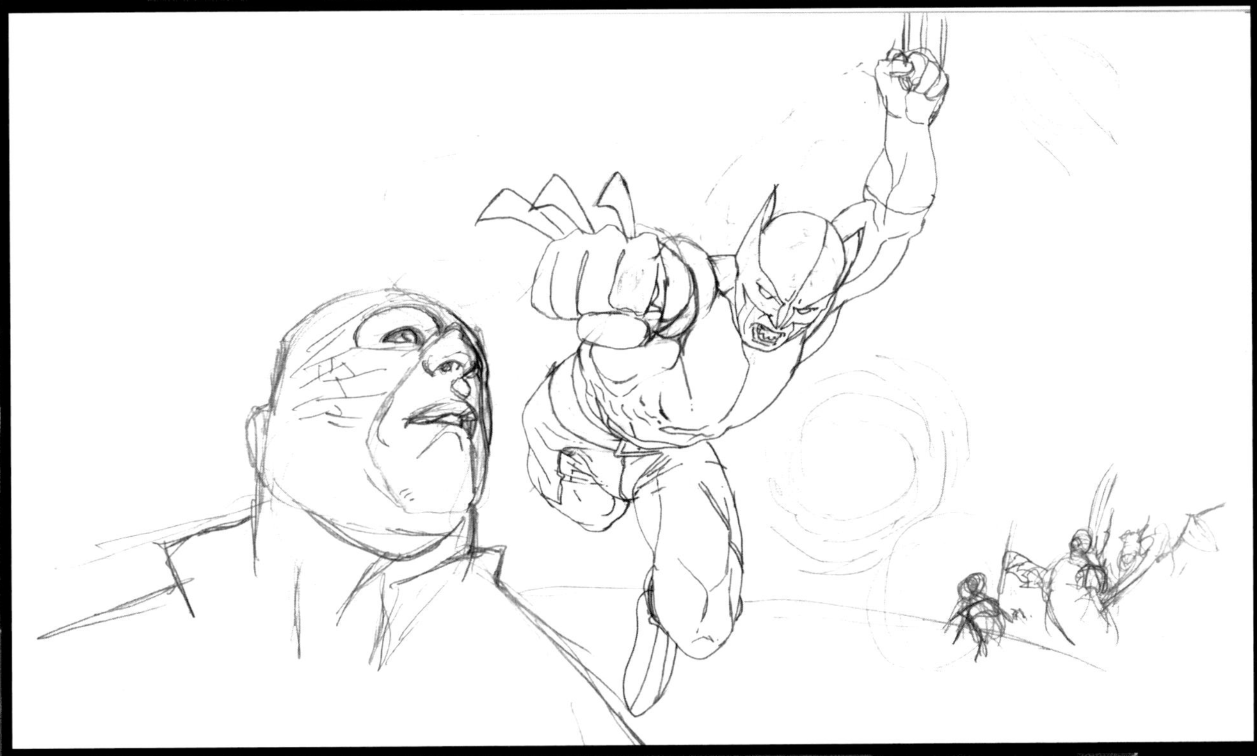

#8, Page 17, Panels 3 & 4 layouts by Steve McNiven

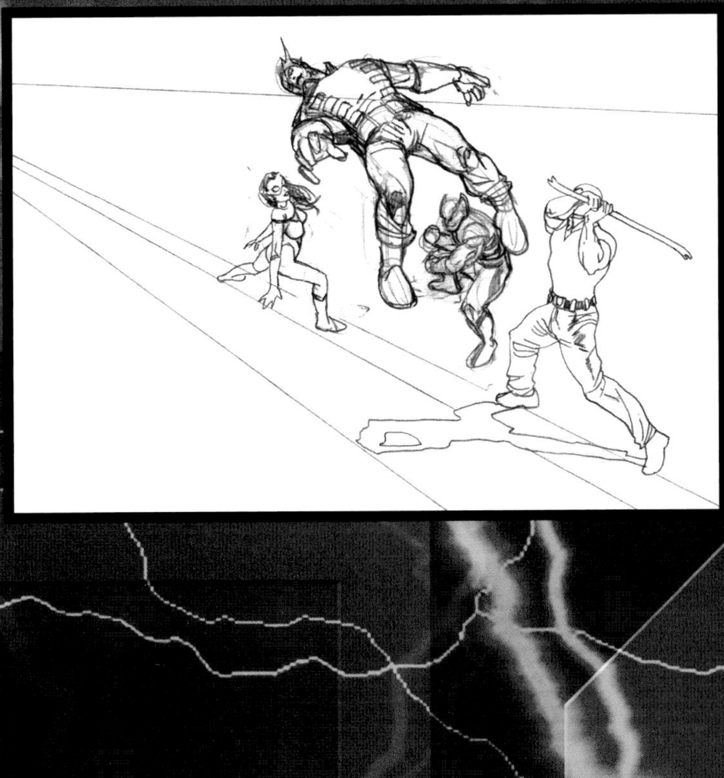

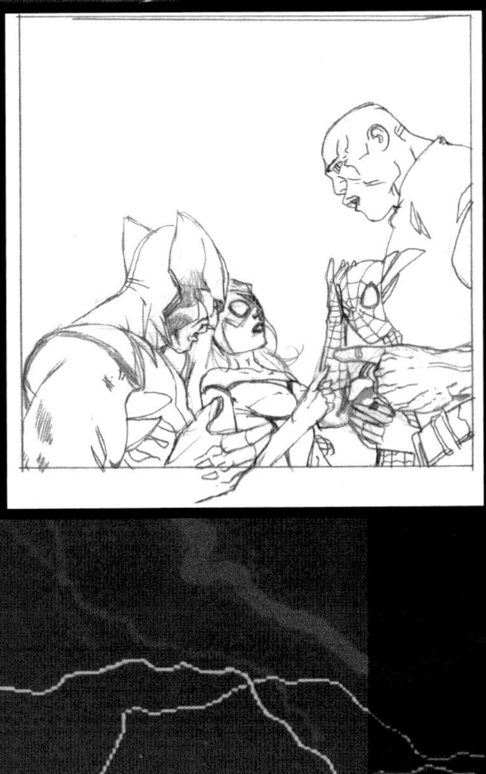

#9, Pages 1-2, Panel 5 layout by Steve McNiven

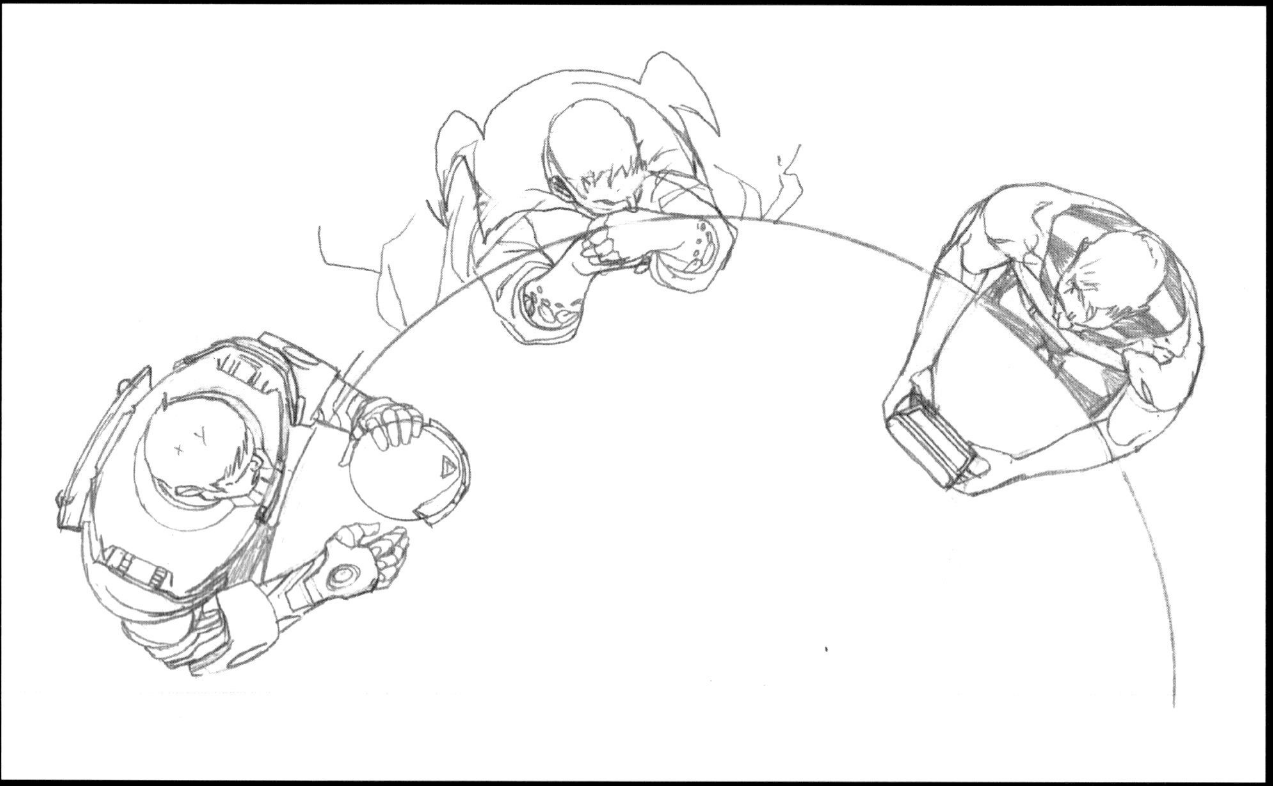

#9, Pages 3-4, Panel 4 layout by Steve McNiven

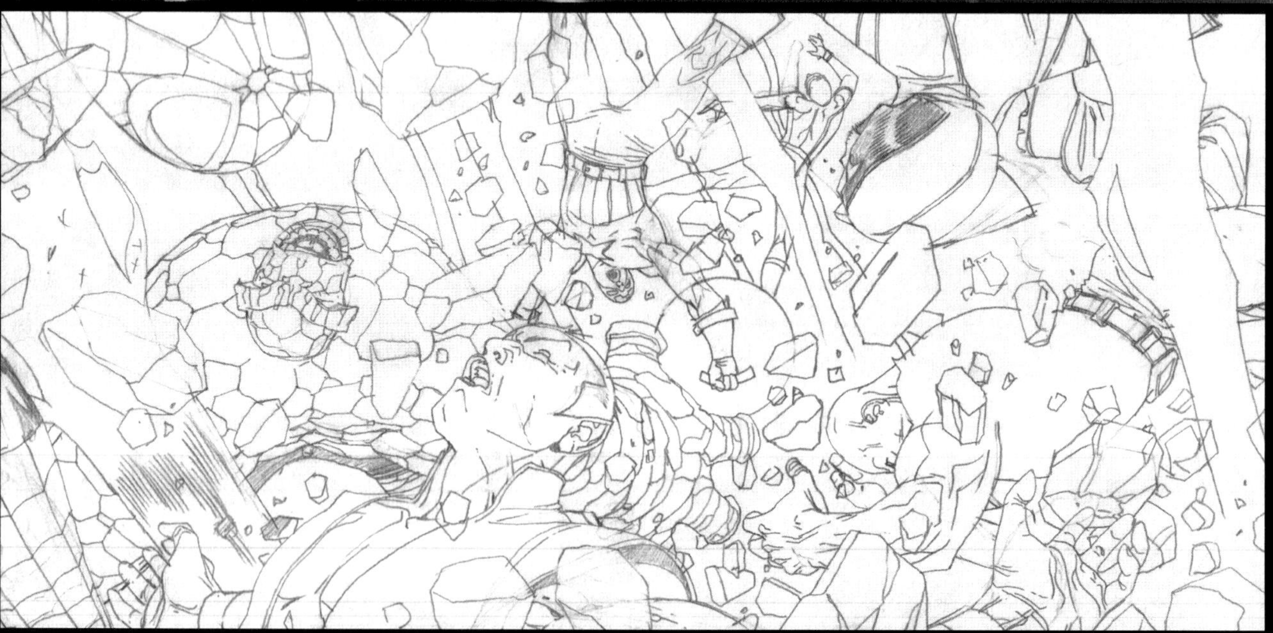

#9, Page 10, Panel 1 layout by Steve McNiven

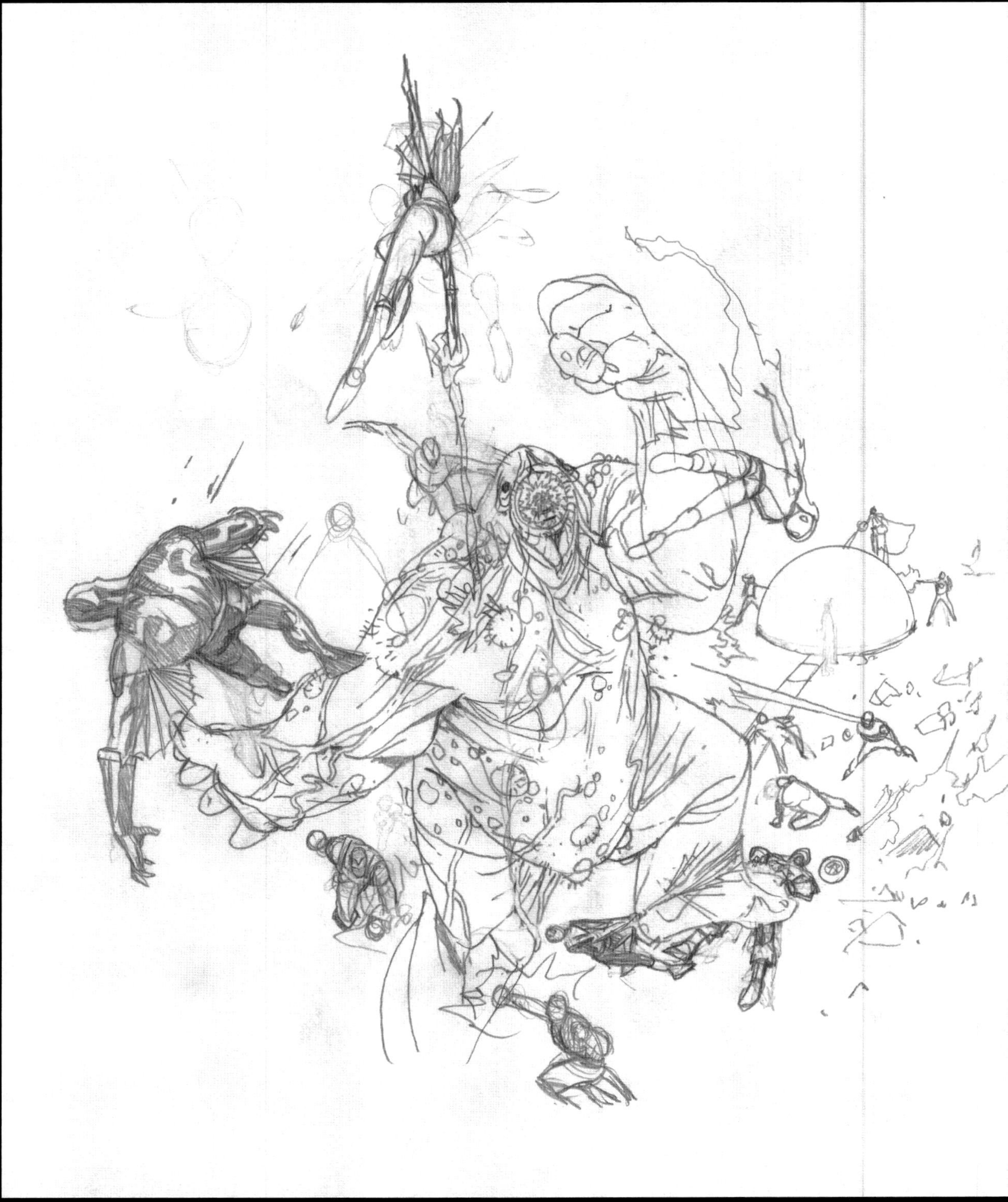

#9, Pages 21-22, layout by Steve McNiven

#10, Pages 5-6, layout by Steve McNiven

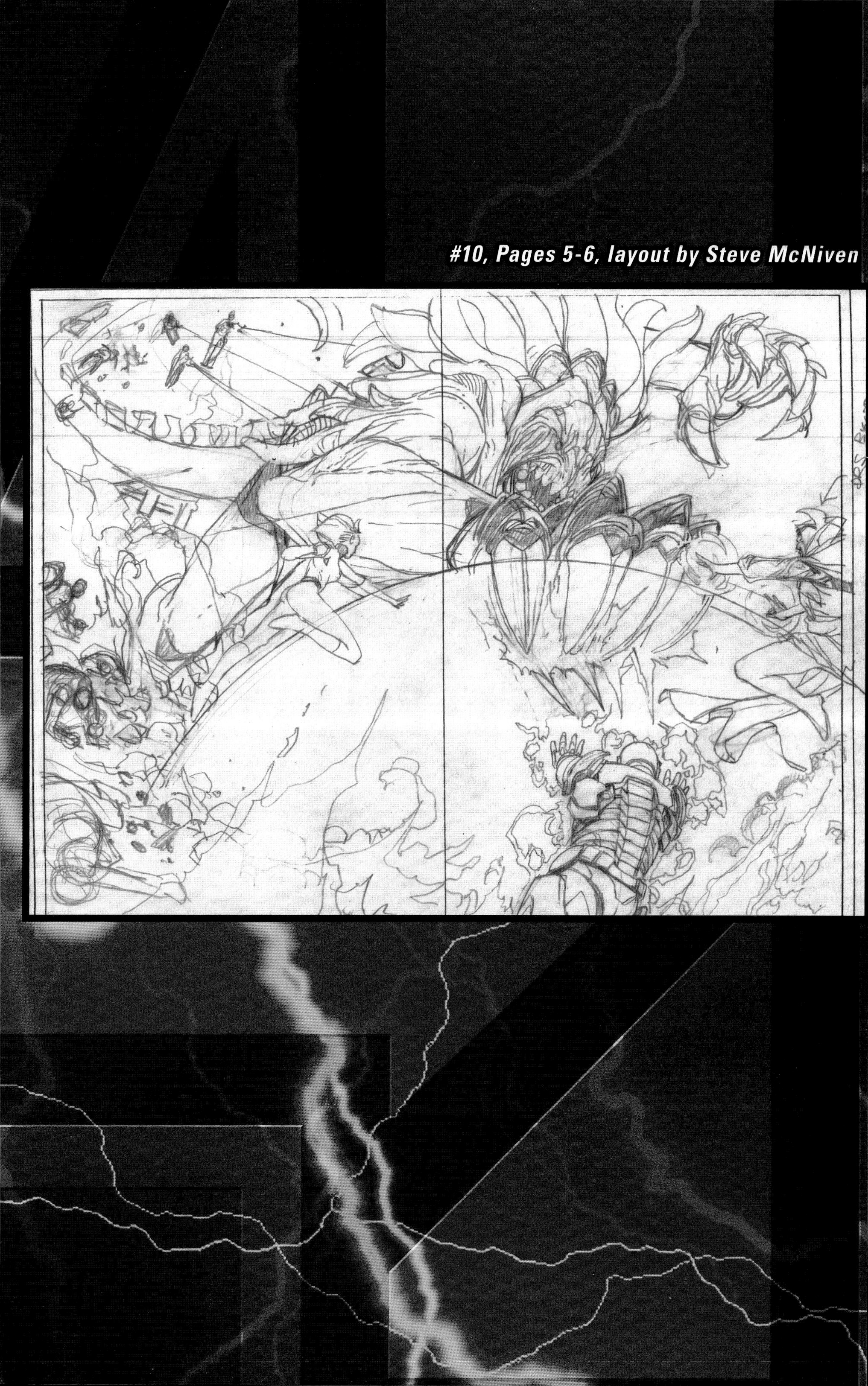

New Avengers Vol. 2: Sentry Premiere HC Cover by Steve McNiven

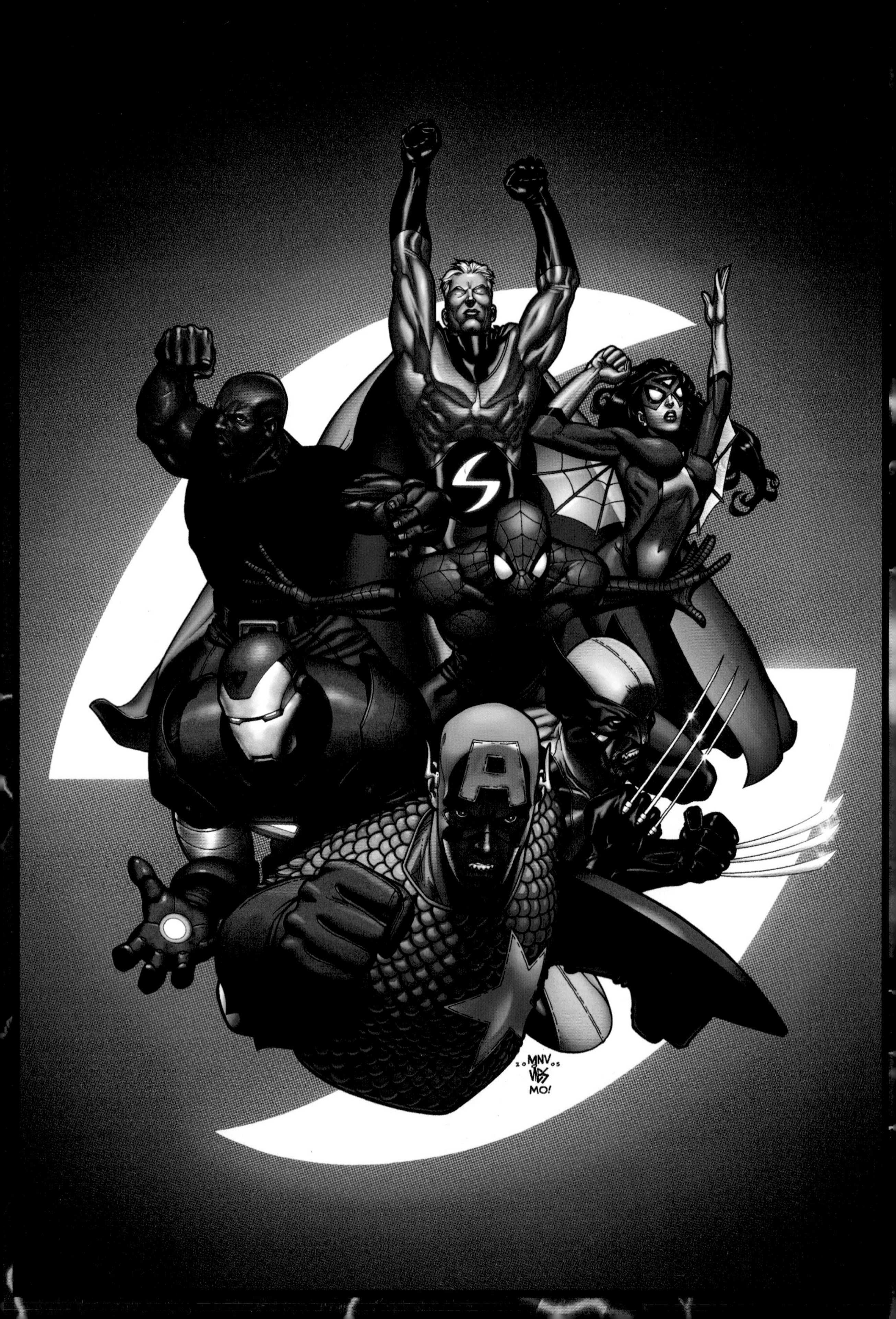

Wizard #161 Cover by Greg Horn

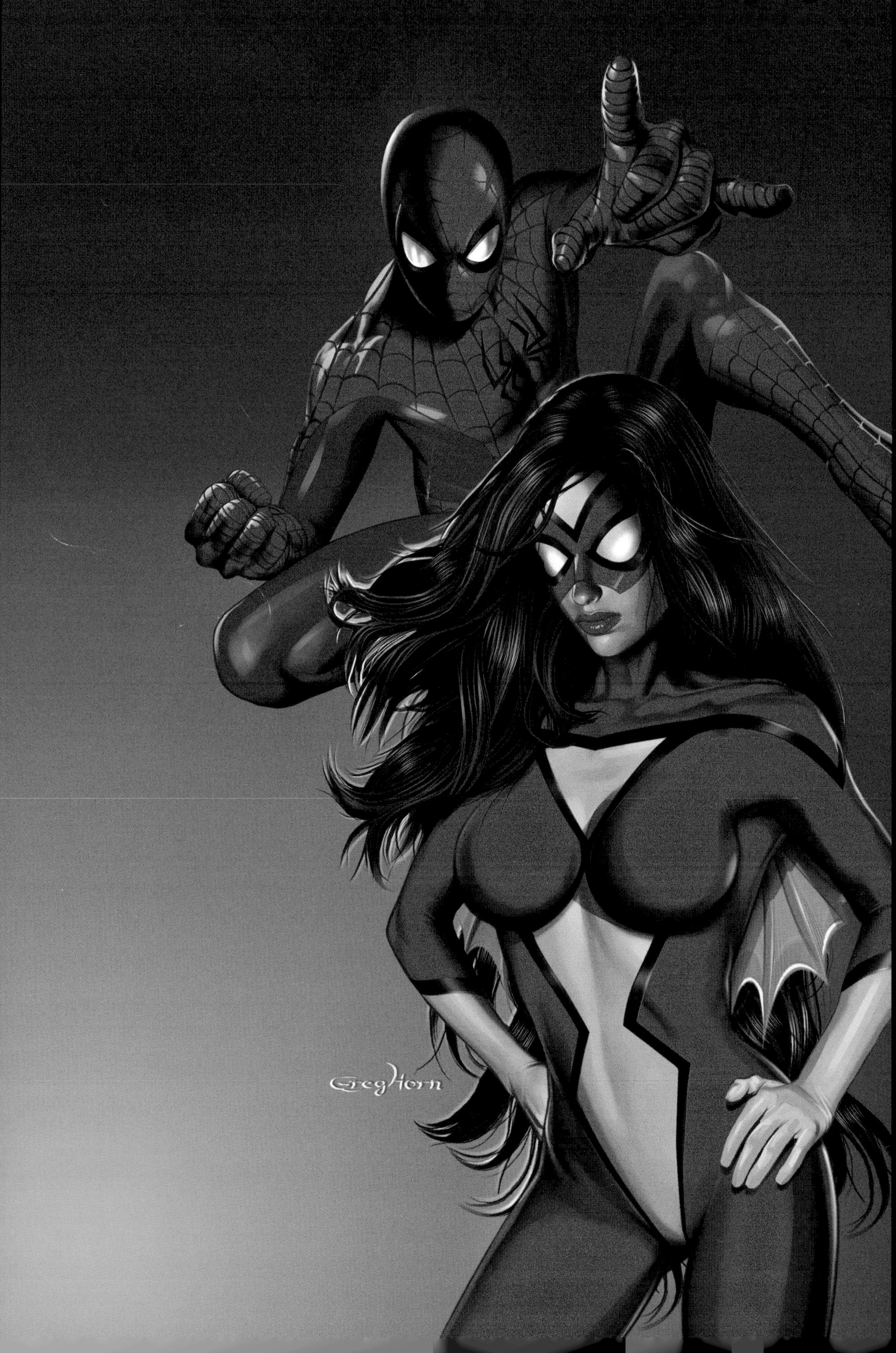
Greg Horn

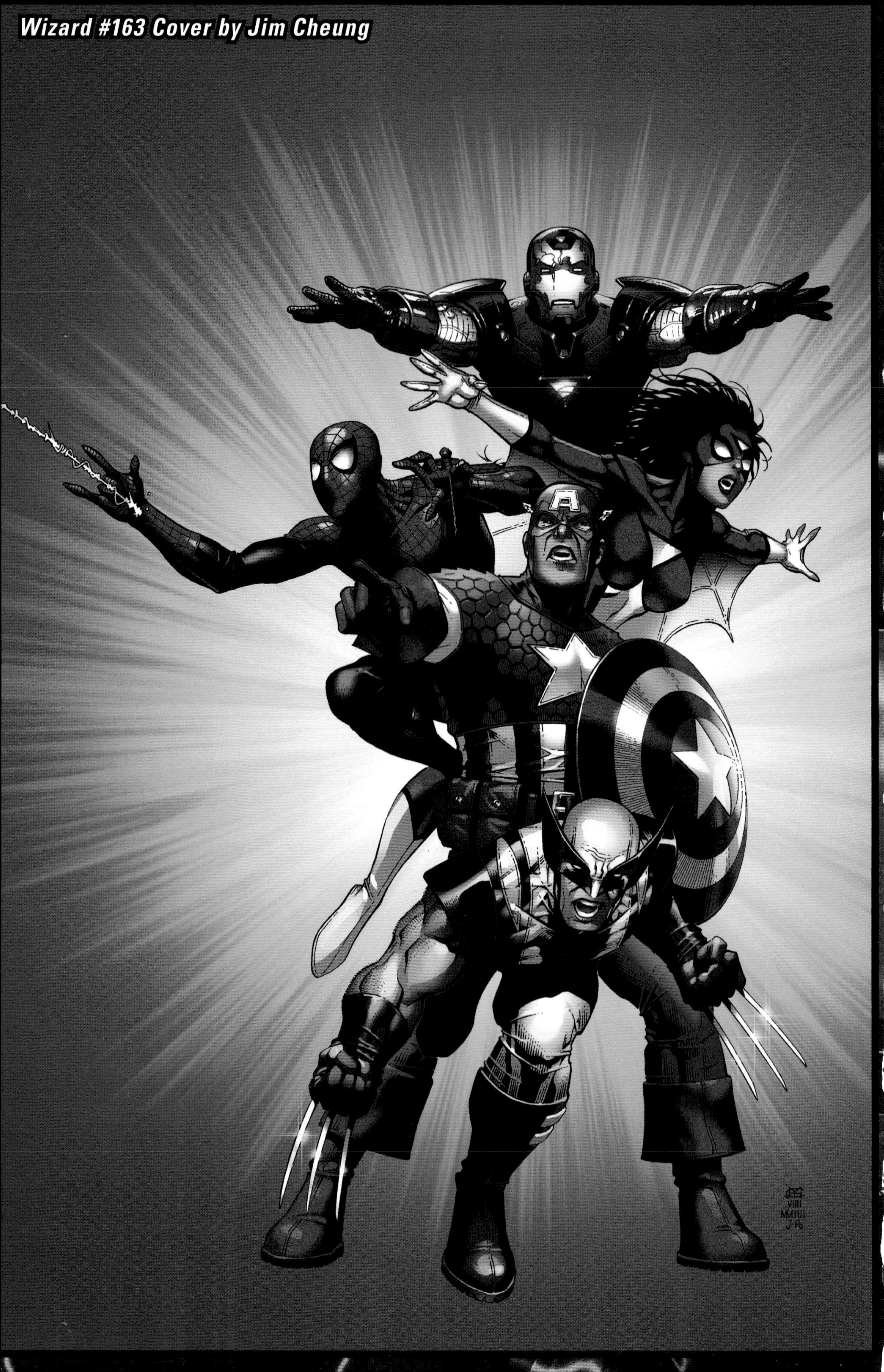

Wizard #163 Cover by Jim Cheung